THE EU'S ROLE IN GLOBAL GOVERNANCE

The EU's Role in Global Governance

The Legal Dimension

Edited by
BART VAN VOOREN
STEVEN BLOCKMANS
and
JAN WOUTERS

OXFORD
UNIVERSITY PRESS

OXFORD
UNIVERSITY PRESS

Great Clarendon Street, Oxford, OX2 6DP,
United Kingdom

Oxford University Press is a department of the University of Oxford.
It furthers the University's objective of excellence in research, scholarship,
and education by publishing worldwide. Oxford is a registered trade mark of
Oxford University Press in the UK and in certain other countries

First Edition published in 2013

Impression: 1

British Library Cataloguing in Publication Data
Data available

ISBN 978-0-19-965965-4

Printed and bound in Great Britain by
CPI Group (UK) Ltd, Croydon, CR0 4YY

Table of Contents

PART V THE EU AND GLOBAL FINANCIAL GOVERNANCE

PART VI THE EU AND GLOBAL SOCIAL GOVERNANCE

CLOSING PART

List of Contributors

- Fabian Amtenbrink is Professor of European Union Law of the Erasmus School of Law, Erasmus University Rotterdam, The Netherlands. He is also Visiting Professor at the College of Europe (Bruges) and member of the governing board of the Centre for the Law of EU External Relations (CLEER).
- Steven Blockmans is Senior Research Fellow and Head of the EU Foreign Policy Unit at the Centre for European Policy Studies (CEPS), Professor of EU External Relations Law and Governance at the Faculty of Law of the University of Amsterdam, Special Visiting Professor at the University of Leuven and member of the governing board of the Centre for the Law of EU External Relations (CLEER).
- Marise Cremona is Professor of European Law at the European University Institute, Florence.
- Geert De Baere is Assistant Professor of International Law and EU Law at the Faculty of Law and Senior Member at the Leuven Centre for Global Governance Studies, University of Leuven.
- Gráinne de Búrca is Florence Ellinwood Allen Professor of Law, NYU Law School.
- Bruno De Witte is Professor of European Union Law at Maastricht University and part-time professor at the Robert Schuman Centre of the European University Institute in Florence.
- Frank Hoffmeister (Dr iur) is Professor (part-time) at the Free University of Brussels and Deputy Head of Cabinet to the EU Commissioner for Trade, Karel De Gucht.
- Jeff Kenner is Professor of European Law at the University of Nottingham.
- Panos Koutrakos is Professor of European Union Law and Jean Monnet Professor of European Law at the University of Bristol and Professor of Law at the University of Antwerp.
- Joris Larik is Researcher/PhD candidate at the European University Institute.
- Gracia Marín Durán is Lecturer in International Economic Law and Director of the LLM Programme in International Economic Law at the University of Edinburgh School of Law.
- Hans-W. Micklitz is Professor of Law, Chair for Economic Law, European University Institute Florence, Jean Monnet Chair for Private, Business and Economic Law, University of Bamberg Germany (on leave).
- Elisa Morgera (LLM, PhD) is Lecturer in European Environmental Law, School of Law, University of Edinburgh, UK.
- Jed Odermatt is PhD candidate and Research Fellow at the Leuven Centre for Global Governance Studies and Institute for International Law, University of Leuven.
- Dennis Patterson is Professor of Law and Chair in Legal Philosophy and Legal Theory, European University Institute, Florence; Board of Governors Professor of Law and Philosophy, Rutgers University, New Jersey, USA; Professor of Law and Chair in International Trade and Legal Philosophy, Swansea University, Wales, UK.
- Lavanya Rajamani is Professor at the Centre for Policy Research in New Delhi.

- Aurel Sari is Lecturer in Law, Exeter Law School, UK.
- Joanne Scott is Professor of European Law at University College London.
- Anne Thies is Lecturer in EU and International Law at the University of Reading.
- Daniel Thym (Prof Dr LLM) holds the chair of Public, European and International Law and is Co-Director of the Research Centre Immigration and Asylum Law at the University of Konstanz, Germany.
- Sven Van Kerckhoven is a PhD candidate and Research Fellow at the Leuven Centre for Global Governance Studies, University of Leuven.
- Bart Van Vooren is Assistant Professor of European Union Law and Integration at the University of Copenhagen and Associate Fellow at the Leuven Centre for Global Governance Studies, University of Leuven.
- Ramses A Wessel is Professor of the Law of the European Union and other International Organizations at the Centre for European Studies, School of Management and Governance, University of Twente, The Netherlands.
- Jan Wouters is Jean Monnet Chair *ad personam* EU and Global Governance, Full Professor of International Law and International Organizations, Director of the Leuven Centre for Global Governance Studies and Institute for International Law at the University of Leuven, and Visiting Professor at the College of Europe and at SciencesPo.
- Chien-Huei Wu is Assistant Research Fellow, Institute of European and American Studies, Academia Sinica, Taipei. PhD in Law (EUI).

List of Abbreviations

ACP	African Caribbean and Pacific countries
ACTA	Anti-Counterfeiting Trade Agreement
ADICMA	Association of Industrial Producers of Leather, Leather Manufactures and Related Products
AFSJ	Area of Freedom, Security and Justice
AG	Advocate General
AMM	Aceh Monitoring Mission
ASEAN	Association of South-East Asian Nations
AU	African Union
BIT	Bilateral Investment Treaty
BRIC	Brazil, Russia, India, China
BRICS	Brazil, Russia, India, China, South Africa
CARICOM	Caribbean Community
CARIFORUM	Caribbean Forum
CBD	Convention on Biological Diversity
CBDRRC	Common but Differentiated Responsibilities and Respective Capabilities
CCP	Common Commercial Policy
CDM	Clean Development Mechanism
CERs	Certified Emissions Reductions
CESL	Common European Sales Law
CFSP	Common Foreign and Security Policy
CJEU	Court of Justice of the EU
CLS	Core Labour Standards
COP	Conference of the Parties
COREPER	Committee of Permanent Representatives
CPA	Comprehensive Peace Agreement
CPA	Cotonou Partnership Agreement
CRA	Credit Rating Agency
CRD	Central Registration Depository
CSCE	Commission on Security and Cooperation in Europe
CSDP	Common Security and Defence Policy
CSME	Caribbean Single Market and Economy
CTE	Committee on Trade and Environment
DARIO	Draft Articles on the Responsibility of International Organizations
DDA	Doha Development Agenda
DEVCO	Development Cooperation
DG	Directorate General of the European Commission
DSU	Dispute Settlement Understanding
DWA	Decent Work Agenda
EBA	European Banking Authority
EC	European Community

ECB	European Central Bank
ECFIN	Economic and Financial Affairs
ECJ	European Court of Justice
ECOSOC	European Economic and Social Committee
ECOWAS	Economic Community of West African States
ECR	European Court Reports
ECSC	European Coal and Steel Community
ECtHR	European Court of Human Rights
EEAS	European External Action Service
EEC	European Economic Community
EIDHR	European Instrument for Democracy and Human Rights
EIOPA	European Insurance and Occupational Pensions Authority
EMU	European Monetary Union
ENP	European Neighbourhood Policy
ENPI	European Neighbourhood and Partnership Instrument
EPA	Economic Partnership Agreement
EPC	European Political Cooperation
ESA	European Supervisory Authority
ESDP	European Security and Defence Policy
ESFS	European System of Financial Supervision
ESMA	European Securities and Markets Authority
ESRB	European Systemic Risk Board
ESS	European Security Strategy
ETS	Emissions Trading Scheme
EU	European Union
EUFOR	European Union Force
EUPM	European Union Police Mission
EUSR	European Union Special Representative
EUTM	European Union Training Mission
FAO	Food and Agriculture Organization
FDI	Foreign Direct Investment
FLEGT	Forest Law Enforcement, Governance and Trade Regulation
FRONTEX	European Agency for the Management of Operational Cooperation at the External Borders of the Member States of the European Union
FRY	Federal Republic of Yugoslavia
FSB	Financial Stability Board
FTA	Free Trade Agreement
FTT	Financial Transaction Tax
G20	Group of Twenty
GAM	Free Aceh Movement
GATS	General Agreement on Trade in Services
GATT	General Agreement on Tariffs and Trade
GDP	Gross Domestic Product
GPA	Government Procurement Agreement
GSP	Generalized System of Preferences

HR/VP	High Representative of the Union for Foreign Affairs and Security Policy/ Vice-President of the European Commission
ICAO	International Civil Aviation Organization
ICC	International Criminal Court
ICISS	International Commission on Intervention and State Sovereignty
ICJ	International Court of Justice
ICTY	International Criminal Tribunal for the former Yugoslavia
IEC	International Electrotechnical Commission
ILC	International Law Commission
ILO	International Labour Organization
IMF	International Monetary Fund
IO	international organization
IOSCO	International Organization of Securities Commissions
IPCC	Intergovernmental Panel on Climate Change Guidelines
IPR	intellectual property rights
IR	international relations
ISO	International Organization for Standardization
LDC	Least Developed Country
MDB	Multilateral Development Bank
MDG	Millennium Development Goal
MEA	Multilateral Environmental Agreement
MERCOSUR	Mercado Común del Sur
MFN	Most Favoured Nation
NAMA	non-agricultural market access
NATO	North Atlantic Treaty Organization
NGO	non-governmental organization
OAS	Organization of American States
OCHA	United Nations Office for the Coordination of Humanitarian Affairs
OECD	Organization for Economic Cooperation and Development
OJ	Official Journal
OSA	Open Sky Agreement
OSCE	Organization for Security and Cooperation in Europe
OTC	over the counter
PCIJ	Permanent Court of International Justice
PSD	Peaceful Settlement of Disputes
R2P	Responsibility to Protect
REDD	Reducing Emissions from Deforestation and Forest Degradation
REIO	regional economic integration organization
RMI	Raw Materials Initiative
RTA	Regional Trade Agreement

SEA	Single European Act
SIFI	systemically important financial institution
SPS	Agreement on Sanitary and Phytosanitary Measures
SAA	Stabilization and Association Agreement
SAARC	South Asian Association for Regional Cooperation
SADC	South African Development Community
SADR	Sahari Arab Democratic Republic
SFRY	Socialist Federal Republic of Yugoslavia
SIA	Sustainability Impact Assessment
STO	specific trade obligation
TACIS	Technical Aid to the Commonwealth of Independent States
TBT	Agreement on Technical Barriers to Trade
TEU	Treaty on European Union
TFEU	Treaty on the Functioning of the European Union
TRIPS	Agreement on Trade Related Aspects of Intellectual Property Rights
TSIA	Trade Sustainability Impact Assessment
UN	United Nations
UNC	United Nations Charter
UNCTAD	United Nations Conference on Trade and Development
UNEF	United Nations Emergency Force
UNESCO	United Nations Educational, Scientific and Cultural Organization
UNFCCC	United Nations Framework Convention on Climate Change
UNGC	United Nations Global Compact
UNHCR	United Nations High Commissioner for Refugees
UNSC	United Nations Security Council
UNSCR	United Nations Security Council Resolution
UNSG	United Nations Secretary General
VAT	Value-Added Tax
VPA	Voluntary Partnership Agreement
WCSDG	World Commission on the Social Dimension of Globalization
WEU	Western European Union
WHO	World Health Organization
WIPO	World Intellectual Property Organization
WTO	World Trade Organization

The Legal Dimension of Global Governance: What Role for the European Union? An Introduction

The Editors

1. The EU's Mission Statement in Global Governance

1.1. Rule-of-law based multilateralism in EU international relations...

The European Union (EU) as an international actor takes on a diversity of roles.[1] Its project of attaining an internal market has rendered it a formidable economic player, generating a large body of laws to govern this zone of integrated (economic) activity across its Member States, thereby possibly serving as a model for integration beyond the European continent. As European integration progressed from an economic to a political project, competences in a variety of areas were latched on, from migration to energy policy, from security to environmental policy. In pursuing these activities in a global context, the Union has been assigned, and has happily adopted, the image of a value-based international actor. The 2001 Laeken Declaration on the Future of the European Union strongly re-asserted this self-perception by asking the rhetorical question: 'Does Europe not, now that it is finally unified, have a leading role to play in a new world order, that of a power able both to play a stabilising role worldwide and to point the way ahead for many countries and peoples?'.[2] This role for the Union whereby it 'stabilizes' the world and 'points the way ahead' is not merely a moral imperative proclaimed by its political leaders, but has found its way into EU primary law as a legally binding obligation. Indeed, the Lisbon Treaty sought to increase the effectiveness, coherence and visibility of the EU as an international actor, giving it the constitutional tools to act in pursuit of that global mission. The EU's mission statement can be found in Articles 3(5) and 21 of the Treaty on European Union (TEU). These two provisions form the starting point of this edited volume, and deserve to be recalled in full.

Article 3(5) TEU:

> 'In its relations with the wider world, the Union shall uphold and promote its values and interests and contribute to the protection of its citizens. It shall contribute to peace, security, the sustainable development of the Earth, solidarity and mutual respect among peoples, free and fair trade, eradication of poverty and the protection of human rights, in particular the rights of the child, as well as to the strict observance and the development of international law, including respect for the principles of the United Nations Charter.'

Article 21 TEU:

> '1. The Union's action on the international scene shall be guided by the principles which have inspired its own creation, development and enlargement, and which it seeks to advance in the wider world: democracy, the rule of law, the universality and indivisibility of human rights and fundamental freedoms, respect for human dignity, the principles of equality and solidarity, and respect for the principles of the United Nations Charter and international law.

[1] M Cremona, 'The Union as a Global Actor: Roles, Models and Identity' (2004) 42 *CML Rev* 553–573.
[2] Laeken Declaration, European Council, 14–15 December 2001, subheading 'Expectations of Europe's citizens'.

The Union shall seek to develop relations and build partnerships with third countries, and international, regional or global organizations which share the principles referred to in the first subparagraph. It shall promote multilateral solutions to common problems, in particular in the framework of the United Nations.

2. The Union shall define and pursue common policies and actions, and shall work for a high degree of cooperation in all fields of international relations, in order to:

(a) safeguard its values, fundamental interests, security, independence and integrity;
(b) consolidate and support democracy, the rule of law, human rights and the principles of international law;
(c) preserve peace, prevent conflicts and strengthen international security, in accordance with the purposes and principles of the United Nations Charter, with the principles of the Helsinki Final Act and with the aims of the Charter of Paris, including those relating to external borders;
(d) foster the sustainable economic, social and environmental development of developing countries, with the primary aim of eradicating poverty;
(e) encourage the integration of all countries into the world economy, including through the progressive abolition of restrictions on international trade;
(f) help develop international measures to preserve and improve the quality of the environment and the sustainable management of global natural resources, in order to ensure sustainable development;
(g) assist populations, countries and regions confronting natural or man-made disasters; and
(h) promote an international system based on stronger multilateral cooperation and good global Governance.'

The EU is morally, politically and legally held to pursue equality amongst wealthy and poorer nations, to support their development and ensure 'fairness' between them, to pursue the sustainable management of global natural resources, and so on. In terms of methodology, the EU is to be guided by the principles which inspired its own creation and which it seeks to advance in the world: progressive development of multilateralism based on the rule of law as the preferred approach to conducting international relations. These provisions are the 'external projection' of an internal reality, namely that European integration itself has been progressively constructed through a variety of law-making processes. Indeed, the EU's institutions, its single market and the progression of European integration as a means of responding to (geo)political and socio-economic challenges are all inextricably linked to legal rules and principles knitting together Nation States that had not long ago gone to war. As a consequence, in the context of the Union's relations with the wider world too, this idea plays a crucial role: strong multilateral cooperation based on legal rules spanning the globe. This is the first premise from which the research question of this book sprouts, the real (or perceived) importance of rule-of-law based multilateralism in EU international relations.[3]

1.2. . . . confronted with tectonic shifts in global governance

Global governance is an elusive notion, and definitions burgeoned in the 1990s as scholarship was coming to grips with the novelty of globalization.[4] For the purpose of the present volume, we use the following working definition: 'the complex of formal and informal

[3] In a Communication of 2003, the Commission argued that this 'means more than rhetorical professions of faith. It means taking global rules seriously, whether they concern the preservation of peace or the limitation of carbon emissions; it means helping other countries to implement and abide by these rules; it means engaging actively in multilateral forums, and promoting a forward-looking agenda that is not limited to a narrow defence of national interests'. See 'Communication of the Commission to the Council and the European Parliament on the European Union and the United Nations: The Choice of Multilateralism', COM (2003) 526 final, 10 September 2003, 3.

[4] See inter alia the overview of definitions in H Mürle, *Global Governance. Literaturbericht und Forschungsfragen*, INEF Report 32 (Gerhard-Mercator-Universität, Gesamthochschule Duisburg, 1998); K Dingwerth and Ph Pattberg, 'Global Governance as a Perspective on World Politics' (2006) 12 *Global Governance* 185–203;

institutions, mechanisms, relationships, and processes between and among states, markets, citizens and organizations... through which collective interests on the global planet are articulated, rights and obligations are established, and differences are mediated'.[5] In this context then, the European Union's focus on rule-of-law based multilateralism is to be confronted with the reality of international relations. In the Conclusions of the European Council of 16 September 2010, the Council sought to give new momentum to the Union's external relations in order to take 'full advantage' of the opportunities provided by the Lisbon Treaty. It set out how the changing world posed a challenge for the EU:

> 'Europe is facing many challenges in a rapidly changing world, which all require a concerted international response. The recent economic and financial crisis has dramatically shown the extent to which the well-being, security and quality of life of Europeans depend on external developments. The emergence of new players with their own world views and interests is also an important new feature in the international environment.
>
> The European Union must be an effective global actor, ready to share in the responsibility for global security and to take the lead in the definition of joint responses to common challenges. A strong economy and internal cohesion will strengthen the Union's ability to project its influence in the world. The Union can draw on its firmly-rooted belief in effective multilateralism, especially the role of the UN, universal values, an open world economy and on its unique range of instruments.'[6]

The second premise of this edited volume is thus to connect the Treaty-based mission statement to the changing features of the international environment. Indeed, as a result of globalization, peoples of all continents face social, economic and political challenges of transnational scope and complexity. Solutions lie beyond the grasp of any single state, regional grouping or international organization. At the same time, new actors are claiming a stronger voice on the international scene in an increasingly multi-polar world order. 'The Legal Dimension of Global Governance', the phrase in the title of this volume, refers to the legal principles, processes, modes and institutions through which these global challenges are dealt with.

2. The Research Question and Structure of the Volume

Bringing together these two premises, the guiding question of the book is this:

> 'How, and to which extent can the European Union shape the ongoing reorientation of the legal structures and substance of global governance in a multi-polar world in line with its rule of law based mission statement?'

One should note that in this research question we do not query why the professed rule-of-law based approach of the EU ought to be the preferred option. We rather take Articles 3(5) and 21 TEU at face value as a policy and constitutional choice which has been endorsed by all EU Member States, and seek to explore their concrete effect on the EU's position in engaging global governance.

H Overbeek, K Dingwerth and Ph Pattberg, 'Forum: Global Governance: Decline or Maturation of an Academic Concept?' (2010) 12 *International Studies Review* 696–719.

[5] R Thakur and L Van Langenhove, 'Enhancing Global Governance through Regional Integration' in AF Cooper, CW Hughes and P De Lombaerde (eds), *Regionalisation and Global Governance: The Taming of Globalisation*? (Routledge/Warwick Studies in Globalisation, Routledge, 2008), 17, at 20. See also Weiss and Thakur's definition of global governance: 'Global governance is the sum of laws, norms, policies, and institutions that define, constitute, and mediate relations among citizens, society, markets, and the state in the international arena—the wielders and objects of international public power' in TG Weiss and R Thakur, *Global Governance and the UN: An Unfinished Journey* (Indiana University Press, 2010), 6.

[6] Conclusions, European Council, Brussels, 16 September 2010, 1.

The response to this research question has been clustered together around six themes, each dealt with in a separate part composed of between two and four separate contributions. The volume sets out with a conceptual part exploring the rule-of-law based global mission of the EU itself and what that might mean; followed by five parts covering what we perceive as the most contentious policy areas in which the EU is active and present in a diversity of ways: security, trade, finance, environment, and the human dimension of global governance. The choice of these topics is explained by three key factors: first, the role of the EU as an international actor in the chosen policy field, above and beyond its 27, soon to be 28 Member States. Second, the policy fields covered by the book should be sufficiently diverse so as to allow the drawing of over-arching conclusions and formulation of a response to the research question. Third, the areas covered should be those where most legal change is expected or ongoing.

All authors have been asked to pay particular attention to the sub-elements we consider integral to our approach to the subject at hand:

(1) What makes the EU's role in shaping the legal-substantive and legal-institutional aspects of global governance a success or a failure?
(2) Why might that be the case? Offer suggestions as to how to remedy the Union's existing shortcomings.
(3) Conversely, if the findings were positive, what is the potential for the EU to emulate its successes in other areas?

It is our belief that by imposing upon the book contributors a rather rigorous conceptual structure focused on a central research question, this book presents a sufficiently coherent work advancing legal scholarship in the field of global governance research. Rather than provide brief summaries of the authors' individual responses to the questions raised, we therefore opt to let the contributions speak for themselves and provide a more in-depth concluding chapter at the end of this volume. In that chapter, we draw together the different threads of the nineteen contributions in an empirically well-documented response to the research questions of this book.

Last but not least, we owe a debt of gratitude to a number of persons and funding organizations, as without them this work would not have been possible. The contributors to this volume convened at a conference held at the Faculty of Law, University of Copenhagen in October 2011, so as to exchange views on draft contributions in the present volume. This event was organized by the Centre for European Constitutionalization and Security (CECS) at the Copenhagen Law Faculty, in cooperation with the Leuven Centre for Global Governance Studies, and with the support of the Centre for the Law of EU External Relations (CLEER). Structural funding was provided by the EURECO (European Research in Copenhagen) initiative, as well as the Dreyers Fund. Last but not least, we are grateful to Nathalie Ivanoff and Nanna Louise Jensen for their valuable assistance in editing this volume.

PART I

THE EU AS A LEGAL POWER IN GLOBAL GOVERNANCE?

1

Entrenching Global Governance: The EU's Constitutional Objectives Caught Between a Sanguine World View and a Daunting Reality

Joris Larik

1. Introduction

The international role of the EU and its contribution to global governance have become formidable topics in international relations (IR) scholarship. However, evaluations of both differ widely. One can find learned assessments concluding that the EU is indeed a superpower,[1] a 'freakishly oversized "middle power"',[2] or merely a small power.[3] While some argue that Europe will 'run the 21st century' equipped with its model of integration,[4] others contend that it may be already 'past its peak',[5] facing decline and ultimately irrelevance.[6] With particular regard to global governance, there is agreement, within the liberal current of IR studies, that the EU has made an important contribution by virtue of its mere existence as a form of regional governance,[7] while others, from the realist current, point to its weaknesses and dependence on external power structures.[8]

At the very least it can be argued that the future of the EU and its influence in the world hang in the balance.[9] Either it maintains the status of 'a driving force in shaping the new rules of global governance, or risk[s] being left behind'.[10] Accordingly, a multi-polar world is gradually taking shape, which might well have the effect of undoing the EU's previous successes and rise to international relevance. Events such as the sidelining of the EU at the 2009 Copenhagen Summit on climate change, the inability to find a common position on the recognition of Kosovo and Palestine or within the United Nations Security Council concerning the Libyan civil war, as well as the current debt crisis that has befallen the Eurozone, paint a rather daunting picture of things to come.

At the same time, the Lisbon Treaty, in force since 1 December 2009, has codified a range of objectives with a clear global governance dimension into the EU's primary law. Among

[1] J McCormick, *The European Superpower* (Palgrave Macmillan, 2007).

[2] A Hyde-Price, 'A neurotic "centaur"—The limitations of the EU as a strategic actor' in K Engelbrekt and J Hallenberg (eds), *The European Union and Strategy* (Routledge, 2008) 162.

[3] A Toje, *The European Union as a Small Power: After the Post-Cold War* (Palgrave Macmillan, 2010).

[4] M Leonard, *Why Europe Will Run the 21st Century* (Fourth Estate, 2005).

[5] C Bretherton and J Vogler, 'Past Its Peak? The European Union as a Global Actor 10 Years After' in F Laursen (ed), *The EU as a Foreign and Security Policy Actor* (Republic of Letters, 2009).

[6] R Youngs, *Europe's Decline and Fall: The Struggle Against Global Irrelevance* (Profile Books, 2010).

[7] See eg M Telò, 'Introduction: The EU as a model, a global actor and an unprecedented power' in M Telò (ed), *The European Union and Global Governance* (Routledge, 2009) 15. See also R Cooper, *The Post-Modern State and the World Order* (Demos, 2000); I Manners, 'Normative Power Europe: A Contradiction in Terms?' (2002) 40 *Journal of Common Market Studies* 235, 252.

[8] H Bull, 'Civilian Power Europe: A Contradiction in Terms' (1982) 22 *Journal of Common Market Studies* 149, 151; R Kagan, *Of Paradise and Power: America and Europe in the New World Order* (Knopf, 2003); Hyde-Price, n 2, 156–157.

[9] European Union Institute for Security Studies and the National Intelligence Council, *Global Governance 2025: At a Critical Juncture* (2010) 11 (*Global Governance 2025*).

[10] *Project Europe 2030: Challenges and Opportunities*, A report to the European Council by the Reflection Group on the Future of the EU 2030 (May 2010) 35 (*Project Europe 2030*).

many other things, the Treaties now mandate the Union to expressly 'promote an international system based on stronger multilateral cooperation and good global governance'.[11] These objectives can be said to present the Union's constitutionally stipulated 'world view',[12] ie the kind of world the Treaties envision and to which they mandate the Union to contribute. This introduces a manifest, but thus far rather understudied, legal dimension of global governance.

As we can see from the widely divergent assessments of the EU's role in global governance and the international system in general, which appear to 'depend quite substantially on one's views on the nature of the international system',[13] there is a great need for dependable and justifiable benchmarks in this regard. It is argued here that constitutional foreign policy objectives represent an important—if not *the* most important—source for such benchmarks. This is so, for conceptual, empirical and normative reasons. Conceptually speaking, global governance, as commonly defined in the literature, is an inherently rule-oriented as well as goal-oriented concept. Empirically, such substantive global governance goals can be found today in many constitutions, including those of the rising powers of the emerging multi-polar world. EU primary law post-Lisbon is part of this trend, but also goes further. Next to an extensive collection of substantive objectives, it also puts a distinctive emphasis on law as an essential ingredient of its foreign policy and consequently of its vision for global governance. From a normative point of view, the peculiar features pertaining to constitutional law as a source for global governance guidance, as opposed to policy documents or other law, appear at first sight as problematic. In particular for the EU, facing the challenge of 'relative decline'[14] in a multi-polar world, entrenching such an ambitious agenda in its highest laws may appear as audacious wishful thinking. On closer inspection, however, these particular features reveal the true value of the constitutional codification of a global governance agenda.

2. Global Governance as a Subject of Constitutional Law

As a first step, it will be demonstrated that global governance has become a prominent theme in constitutional documents, above all in the constitutional law of the EU. Let us begin this enquiry by examining the commonly advanced definitions of global governance, which reveal that the concept is based inherently on both rules and goals.

These definitions construe global governance as rule-setting on a global scale through processes which are not in the hands of an overarching authority (as opposed to the idealized domestic setting, ie the state and its *government*), taking place in a multi-level environment involving a multitude of actors.[15] The dynamic character of governance is already present in the term 'governance' itself, which derives from the ancient Greek word meaning 'to steer' (κυβϵρνάν).[16] According to Rosenau, as the trailblazer on this subject, governance 'refers to mechanisms for steering social systems toward their goals'.[17] Most

[11] Art 21(2)(h) TEU.

[12] See H Kelsen, *Essays in Legal and Moral Philosophy* (O Weinberger ed, P Heath tr, D Reidel, 1973), ch 5 on a state's world view (*Weltbild*) linking its internal set-up and foreign policy. See more recently P Häberle, *Verfassungslehre als Kulturwissenschaft* (2nd edn, Duncker & Humblot, 1998) 1132ff.

[13] K Smith, *European Union Foreign Policy in a Changing World* (2nd edn, Polity, 2008) 13.

[14] *Project Europe 2030*, n 10, 11–12.

[15] See the definition used by Telò, n 7, 36: 'both institutionalized and non-institutionalized, formal and informal, public and private modes of regulation and rule-setting at various levels of the globalized world'. Similarly, *Global Governance 2025*, n 9, 17.

[16] See J Rosenau, 'Governance in the 21st Century' (1995) 1 *Global Governance* 13, 14.

[17] J Rosenau, 'Toward an Ontology for Global Governance' in M Hewson and T Sinclair (eds), *Approaches to Global Governance Theory* (State University of New York Press, 1999) 296. See also earlier J Rosenau, 'Governance, order and change in world politics' in J Rosenau and E-O Czempiel, *Governance without government: order and change in world politics* (CUP, 1992) 4.

telling, however, is the definition adopted by Ortega for assessing the EU's contribution to global governance, ie 'the management of global problems and the pursuit of global objectives through concerted efforts of states and other international actors'.[18] The crucial element here is the notion of 'global objectives'. These, according to Ortega, are the latest stage of a historical development, starting from objectives defined by each political community individually (ie the 'national interest') to the emergence of common global objectives during the course of the last century. After the end of the Cold War in particular, these have been 'growing steadily' to include such matters as the prevention of grave human rights violations, crisis and conflict management, peacekeeping, non-proliferation, and protection of the planetary environment.[19]

The notion of these global objectives dovetails with that of so-called 'milieu goals', defined as aims for shaping of a polity's environment, as opposed to 'possession goals', which are based on a more narrow idea of the national interest.[20] Global objectives in the sense of global governance thus represent 'milieu goals' of a worldwide scope.[21] Also in assessing the EU's contribution to global governance, the importance of milieu goals is acknowledged in the need 'to champion an international environment that will enable the EU to promote its agenda'.[22]

Such global goals, on which the idea of global governance is premised, have become a popular topic in constitutional documents, including EU primary law. Given the inclusiveness of the definition of global governance, such goals 'may or may not derive from legal and formally prescribed responsibilities'.[23] However, the fact that documents codifying the highest laws of a given polity increasingly deal with such global objectives is a remarkable development and highlights a significant legal dimension to global governance which goes beyond the realm of international law.[24] Mindful also of the rule-setting focus of global governance, we can distinguish two phenomena, one limited to the respective constitutional order and one transcending legal orders. The first refers to constitutionally entrenched substantive objectives relevant for global governance, such as promoting human rights, environmental protection or non-aggression. While aiming to shape the international order along certain normative lines, they leave the means to do so a priori open. The legal dimension of these thus remains contained within the respective constitutional order. The second one, on the contrary, transcends legal orders by harnessing the use of law in foreign policy. Examples for this would be promoting the rule of law internationally *tout court*, or more specific references to international adjudication and institutionalized international cooperation. These objectives aim to transform the international order into an increasingly rules-based system, thus linking the constitutional and the international legal orders. Where both phenomena are present, the latter also frames the pursuit of substantive goals,

[18] M Ortega, 'Building the future: The EU's contribution to global governance', EUISS Chaillot Paper No 100, April 2007, 46 (italics omitted).

[19] Ibid 47.

[20] See Smith, n 13, 8–9. She refers to the concepts as devised by A Wolfers, *Discord and Collaboration: Essays on International Politics* (Johns Hopkins University Press, 1962). See further on the pursuit of both possession and milieu goals by the EU the contribution by de Búrca to this volume.

[21] To a certain extent, the shaping of a regional milieu can also serve as a contribution to global governance. In the case of the EU, the Schuman Declaration and the founding Treaties already recognized preventing war among its Member States as also being a contribution to 'world peace'. Today, the Union has set itself the goal of establishing 'an area of prosperity and good neighbourliness' with the countries around it: Art 8(1) TEU. See further S Blockmans, 'Friend or foe? Reviewing EU relations with its neighbours post-Lisbon' in P Koutrakos (ed), *The European Union's external relations a year after Lisbon*, CLEER Working Paper 2011/03: <http://www.asser.nl/upload/documents/772011_51358CLEER%20WP%202011-3%20-%20KOUTRAKOS.pdf> accessed 18 March 2012.

[22] *Project Europe 2030*, n 10, 35.

[23] Rosenau, *Governance, order and change in world politics*, n 17, 4.

[24] Ortega points to international law sources such as Arts 1 and 2 of the United Nations Charter: Ortega, n 18, 57–58.

mandating a polity to gearing global governance towards an order that is both more rules-based and value-based.[25] Before entering into the critical assessment of constitutional entrenchment, which will be conducted in the latter half of this chapter, an overview of the content in terms of global governance present in the EU Treaties and comparative constitutional law more generally will be provided.

2.1. Global governance objectives in EU constitutional law

In today's EU primary law, numerous objectives related to global governance can be found. Those include both expressions of substantive goals as well as an emphasis on law in the pursuit of these goals.

First, however, a preliminary matter needs to be addressed given the peculiar nature of the EU. The objectives codified in the original Treaties were rather the hallmark of a functional international organization. Under international law, international organizations are considered derivative legal subjects whose existence is 'entirely instrumental, directly related to the performance of certain functions'.[26] Hence, at the outset European integration was better understood as an instrument of global governance among other international institutions and regimes specifically set up to pursue the goals shared by its members. However, as is widely accepted among scholars of European law, through the deepening of European integration, including the widening of the objectives, competences and fields of activity of the Union (and sustained by the progressive case-law of the European Court of Justice), EU law has acquired a quality that fits uneasily with classic international institutional law. Consequently, today the Union's primary law is predominantly considered as being of a constitutional nature, more akin to the legal order of a state than of an international organization.[27] Hence, from a legal point of view it seems unwarranted to depict the EU as a mere tool of its Member States.[28] Even though the Union remains an actor with only conferred powers, in view of the advanced stage European integration has reached, also in the external sphere, it is no longer a mere functional association, but rather a value-based community with an autonomous legal order.[29]

The Lisbon Treaty has both expanded and streamlined the Union's global objectives. The EU Treaties include now a set of general objectives of the Union, including their external dimension,[30] an article containing general principles and goals of EU external action,[31] and in some cases objectives specific to certain external policies.[32] These principles and objectives are to be respected not only in the explicitly external Union policies, but also with regard to 'the external aspects of its other policies',[33] such as environmental protection.

[25] Ultimately, this would result in the 'constitutionalization' of the international legal order. No constitutional document, however, goes so far as to mandate this specifically.

[26] H Schermers and N Blokker, *International Institutional Law* (4th edn, Martinus Nijhoff, 2003) 11. See also *Advisory Opinion of 8 July 1996 (Legality of the Use of Nuclear Weapons)*, (1996) ICJ Reps 78, para 25, in which the International Court of Justice ruled that international organizations 'are invested by the states which create them with powers, the limits of which are a function of the common interests whose promotion those states entrust to them'.

[27] See E Stein, 'Lawyers, Judges, and the Making of a Transnational Constitution' (1981) 75 AJIL 1; more recently P Craig, 'Constitutions, Constitutionalism, and the European Union' (2001) 7 ELJ 125, 128–130.

[28] This is of course notwithstanding the criticisms of realists and liberal intergovernmentalists pointing to political realities which might suggest otherwise.

[29] The values are also codified: Art 2 TEU. See further A von Bogdandy, 'Founding Principles of EU Law: A Theoretical and Doctrinal Sketch' (2009) 16 ELJ 95; F Reimer, 'Ziele und Zuständigkeiten: Die Funktionen der Unionszielbestimmungen' [2003] *Europarecht* 992, 992–993.

[30] Art 3(5) TEU.

[31] Art 21 TEU.

[32] Arts 206 and 207 Treaty on the Functioning of the European Union (TFEU) for the Common Commercial Policy; Art 208 TFEU for development cooperation; Art 214 TFEU on humanitarian aid.

[33] Art 21(3), first subpar, TEU.

While being careful to refer also to the pursuit of 'interests',[34] thus keeping the door open for the pursuit of 'possession goals', the Treaties contain a wealth of substantive objectives that squarely fall into the category of milieu goals. These include contributions to 'peace, security, the sustainable development of the Earth, solidarity and mutual respect among peoples, free and fair trade, eradication of poverty and the protection of human rights, in particular the rights of the child'.[35] The Treaties also make clear that this is largely an extrapolation of the Union's internal values to the outside world.[36] Nevertheless, these goals are not all autonomously defined by the Union, but are indeed open to input from external sources by drawing on internationally defined concepts such as sustainable development, universal human rights or internationally agreed goals for development cooperation.[37]

In addition, we find a strong emphasis on rule-of-law based goals. The various references to human rights,[38] as *rights*, can also be seen as a matter of law. More straightforwardly, the Treaties oblige the Union to contribute 'to the strict observance and the development of international law'[39] and to spread and consolidate the rule of law in the world at large.[40] They furthermore identify the United Nations as the forum of choice to 'promote multilateral solutions to common problems',[41] which suggests abiding by and utilizing the procedures and means provided under its Charter. Indeed, according to the Treaties, 'stronger multilateral cooperation and good global governance'[42] go hand in hand.

Furthermore, we also find a number of instances where the pursuit of substantive objectives is explicitly framed by law. For instance, both the Union's humanitarian aid policy and its common security and defence policy are to be carried out in accordance with the relevant international law.[43] The best example for connecting and intertwining the Union and international legal orders is the obligation for the Union to accede to the European Convention for the Protection of Human Rights and Fundamental Freedoms (the Human Rights Convention) and its adjudicatory mechanism.[44] In doing so the Union would not only add an additional layer to its own human rights protection, but also become a member of the international institutional framework and contribute to its further development.[45]

In sum, we see that the EU Treaties codify a range of global objectives both in terms of substance but also specifically harnessing law. The many substantive goals for EU external action are indeed an indication that at least constitutionally the EU is 'more inclined to try to shape its surrounding environment than to protect particular interests'.[46] In addition, the Treaties also highlight the importance of law as the 'weapon of choice'[47] for shaping this

[34] Art 3(5) TEU, which also refers to the protection of Union citizens as an objective; also Art 21(2)(a) TEU, referring to the Union's 'fundamental interests'.

[35] Art 3(5) TEU. This is reiterated and elaborated upon in Art 21 TEU and the sector-specific objectives.

[36] Note in particular Art 21(1) TEU: 'The Union's action on the international scene shall be guided by the principles which have inspired its own creation, development and enlargement . . .'.

[37] See in particular Art 208(2) TFEU. See also M Cremona, 'Values in EU Foreign Policy' in M Evans and P Koutrakos (eds), *Beyond the Established Legal Orders: Policy Interconnections Between the EU and the Rest of the World* (Hart Publishing, 2011), who presents value formation as an iterative process between the internal and external spheres.

[38] Arts 3(5); 21(1), first subpara; 21(2)(b) TEU.

[39] Art 3(5) TEU.

[40] Arts 3(5) and 21(2)(b) TEU. See further L Pech, 'Rule of law as a guiding principle of the European Union's external action', CLEER Working Paper 2012/03: <http://www.asser.nl/upload/documents/2102012 _33322cleer2012-3web.pdf> accessed 16 March 2012.

[41] Art 21(1), second subpara, TEU. See also Art 220(1) TFEU on relations of the EU with international organizations.

[42] Art 21(2)(h) TEU.

[43] Art 214(2) TFEU; Art 42(1) TEU.

[44] Art 6(2) TEU.

[45] See further J P Jacqué, 'The Accession of the European Union to the European Convention on Human Rights and Fundamental Freedoms' (2011) 48 *CML Rev* 995, 1008–1011.

[46] Smith, n 13, 9.

[47] Leonard, n 4, 36.

environment accordingly. Together, these elements coincide with the idea of the Union as a 'transformative power', changing not only fundamentally the relations among its members but also of the world around it.[48] As Manners famously put it, the EU aims at 'redefining what can be "normal" international relations'.[49] The *norms* contained in the EU Treaties constitutionally entrench not only a vision of global governance based on certain values, but also based on legal rules and institutions.

2.2. Global governance and the global 'dynamization of constitutional law'

One can observe a general trend in modern comparative constitutional law to introduce internationally oriented objectives to guide a country's foreign policy.[50] In view of the content of these objectives, it cannot be denied that global governance has become a theme of contemporary constitutional law. Due to space constraints, here only a few examples from national constitutions will be provided,[51] distinguishing again between substantive constitutional objectives and those relying specifically on law. Next to examples of constitutions of EU Member States, which are rather extensive in this regard, the constitutions of the four BRIC countries (Brazil, Russia, India, China) will be considered.[52] This seems warranted given the attention devoted to these rising actors and the prospect of a multi-polar world in the IR literature, which is presented as one of the major challenges for the EU.[53]

Among the EU Member States, the cases of Ireland and Portugal stand out. The Irish constitution includes an article on the international relations of the country. In terms of substance, it refers to Ireland's 'devotion to the ideal of peace and friendly co-operation amongst nations founded on international justice and morality'.[54] The international legal dimension becomes apparent in 'its adherence to the principle of the pacific settlement of international disputes by international arbitration or judicial determination',[55] as well as in its acceptance of international law 'as its rule of conduct in its relations with other States'.[56]

A similar but more verbose statement can be found among the seven paragraphs of a long article in the constitution of Portugal. In terms of substance, it states that Portugal's international relations are to be governed by 'the peaceful settlement of international disputes, the non-interference in the internal affairs of other states and cooperation with all other peoples for the emancipation and progress of humanity'.[57] In terms of law as a

[48] Ibid 5.

[49] Manners, n 7, 253.

[50] J Larik, 'Shaping the International Order as a Union Objective and the Dynamic Internationalization of Constitutional Law', CLEER Working Paper 2011/05: <http://www.asser.nl/upload/documents/11222011_91506CLEER%20WP%202011-5-LARIK.pdf> accessed 16 March 2012.

[51] The references to national constitutions in their English language translations draw on the Oceana Law® database 'Constitutions of Countries of the World': <www.oceanalaw.com> accessed 19 March 2012.

[52] The constitution of the most powerful country in the world, the USA, does not contain any objectives relevant for global governance, which may be explained by its age and the few amendments it has undergone. Nevertheless, American foreign policy has long been recognized as 'exceptional' and reflecting its internal values and institutional preferences. See A Bradford and E Posner, 'Universal Exceptionalism in International Law' (2011) 52 Harv ILJ 3, 35–44, who argue that this applies to most other great powers as well.

[53] See eg *Project Europe 2030*, n 10, 12; *Global Governance 2025*, n 9, 25–30. See in detail S Keukeleire and H Bruyninckx, 'The European Union, the BRICs and the Emerging New World Order' in C Hill and M Smith (eds), *International Relations and the European Union* (2nd edn, OUP, 2011).

[54] Art 29(1) Irish constitution. See further G Hogan and G Whyte, *J.M. Kelly: The Irish Constitution* (4th edn, LexisNexis, 2003) 491–506.

[55] Art 29(2) Irish constitution.

[56] Art 29(3) Irish constitution. Note also the constitutional authorization to ratify the Rome Statute of the International Criminal Court (ICC) in Art 29(9).

[57] Art 7(1) Portuguese constitution. See also Art 7(2) for more historically rooted goals (eg 'dissolution of the political-military blocs'). Note furthermore the mandate for privileged cooperation with Portuguese-speaking countries in Art 7(4). See further P J Canelas de Castro, 'Portugal's World Outlook in the Constitution of 1976' (1995) 71 *Boletim da Faculdade de Dereito da Universidade de Coimbra* 489.

foreign policy tool, it has less to offer. Still this dimension is present in its references to certain 'rights', which next to human rights and 'the rights of peoples'[58] include 'the right of peoples to self-determination, independence and development, as well as the right of insurrection against all forms of oppression'.[59] Similarly, the specific provision allowing the country to join the International Criminal Court (ICC) Statute is premised on 'achieving an international justice that promotes respect for the rights of the human person and of peoples'.[60]

The trend of including a global governance agenda into constitutional documents is by no means confined to Europe. As we shall see, three of the four BRIC countries also devote constitutional language to how their countries will contribute to global governance. The Russian constitution, apart from asserting consciousness 'that we are part of the world community',[61] does not contain normative guidance in terms of foreign policy. The case is different with Brazil, China and India. However, while all three contain objectives relevant for global governance in terms of substance, only the Indian constitution puts a comparable emphasis on law.

The constitution of Brazil contains a title on 'fundamental principles'[62] according to which Brazil's international relations are governed, among other things, by the principles of 'prevalence of human rights',[63] 'non-intervention',[64] 'pacific solution of conflicts'[65] and 'repudiation of terrorism and racism'.[66] The legal dimension is less explicit. Next to the reference to human rights, it could be gleaned from the reference to the 'self-determination of peoples',[67] albeit not framed as a right under international law. Moreover, the sole paragraph of this article makes regional integration in Latin America a constitutional objective,[68] which might also imply a stronger rules-based regional community.

The most verbose among the BRIC countries, at least in terms of substance, is the constitution of the People's Republic of China.[69] In its preamble, it is stressed that the 'future of China is closely linked with that of the whole world'.[70] Moreover, in terms of what guides China's global role, the preamble evokes:

> 'the five principles of mutual respect for sovereignty and territorial integrity, mutual non-aggression, non-interference in each other's internal affairs, equality and mutual benefit, and peaceful coexistence in developing diplomatic relations and economic and cultural exchanges with other countries'.[71]

In addition, it contains what can be seen as a clear example of a possession goal, ie 'the great task of reunifying the motherland' with Taiwan.[72] Even though construed as a domestic

[58] Art 7(1) Portuguese constitution.

[59] Art 7(3) Portuguese constitution.

[60] Art 7(7) Portuguese constitution.

[61] Preamble, Russian constitution.

[62] See M Gonçalves Ferreira Filho, 'Fundamental Aspects of the 1988 Constitution' in J Dolinger and K Rosenn, *A Panorama of Brazilian Law* (North–South Center and Editora Esplanada, 1992) 13–15.

[63] Art 4(II) Brazilian constitution.

[64] Art 4(IV) Brazilian constitution.

[65] Art 4(VII) Brazilian constitution.

[66] Art 4(VIII) Brazilian constitution.

[67] Art 4(III) Brazilian constitution.

[68] Art 4 Brazilian constitution.

[69] The lack of judicial review and 'constitutionalism' in general in the People's Republic, however, qualify the importance of the text of its constitution. See Q Zhang, 'A constitution without constitutionalism? The paths of constitutional development in China' (2010) 8 ICON 950.

[70] Preamble, Chinese constitution.

[71] Preamble, Chinese constitution, which furthermore refers to opposition to 'imperialism, hegemonism and colonialism' and support for developing countries. The 'five principles' were first listed in an international agreement between China and India in 1954 and have since been an essential part of Chinese foreign policy. See Bradford and Posner, n 52, 26.

[72] Preamble, Chinese constitution. It should be noted that 'reunification' is also a topic, for instance, in the Irish constitution. The latter, however, expressly states 'that a united Ireland shall be brought about only by peaceful

issue, its international ramifications are undeniable. The Chinese constitution does not address law as a defining factor of its foreign policy. At most, one could see the five principles as a reflection of a traditional Westphalian view of international law.

The picture is different with the Indian constitution and its list of 'directive principles of state policy'.[73] While the constitution states that these principles are non-enforceable in court, they are 'nevertheless fundamental in the governance of the country'.[74] It contains four principles concerning India's foreign policy. The first two are of a substantive character, obliging the state to endeavour to 'promote international peace and security'[75] and to 'maintain just and honourable relations between nations'.[76] The latter two put the emphasis on law, much like the Irish constitution.[77] They mandate the state to 'foster respect for international law and treaty obligations in the dealings of organized peoples with one another'[78] and to 'encourage settlement of international disputes by arbitration.[79]

In sum, we see that global governance is a common theme in contemporary constitutions, including those of the rising powers, which are regularly portrayed as a threat to global governance, bringing 'with them their own vision of the world, which can differ considerably from that of the established ones'.[80] Looking at their highest laws, however, paints a less threatening picture. Evidentially, the preamble of the Chinese constitution with its emphasis on non-interference and sovereignty conveys a more traditional, static image of the international order. This leaves less scope for wide-ranging and ambitious international regulation and powerful institutions.[81] Nevertheless, these objectives all represent milieu rather than possession goals. Leaving China aside, the fact that substantive norms such as human rights are constitutionally entrenched as guiding principles for foreign policy is remarkable. Compared to the comprehensive objectives provided in the EU Treaties, however, the national constitutions examined here give rather sporadic guidance.Concerning the role of law within global governance, we also see a number of national constitutional pronouncements, but markedly fewer. The explicit emphasis and many linkages made between law and the pursuit of substantive objectives in the EU Treaties is not matched in these national constitutions. From the vantage point of constitutional law, we find thus that EU foreign policy represents not only 'a reflection of the global *zeitgeist*',[82] but goes further given both the comprehensiveness in terms of substance and the special emphasis placed on law for the shaping of global governance.

3. Entrenched Global Governance: A Blessing in Disguise

Global governance, by definition heavily reliant on both rules and goals, is addressed in contemporary constitutional documents, above all those of the EU. But why should we, when studying global governance and the EU, pay special attention to objectives found in its constitutional law as opposed to foreign policy documents such as the European Security

means with the consent of a majority of the people, democratically expressed, in both jurisdictions in the island', Art 3(1) Irish constitution.

[73] See O Chinnappa Reddy, *The Court and the Constitution of India: Summits and Shallows* (OUP, 2008), ch 9.

[74] Art 37 Indian constitution.

[75] Art 51(a) Indian constitution.

[76] Art 51(b) Indian constitution.

[77] The Indian 'directive principles' have in fact drawn inspiration from the Irish constitution. See J Usman, 'Non-Justiciable Directive Principles: A Constitutional Design Effect' (2007) 15 Mich St JIL 643, 650–651.

[78] Art 51(c) Indian constitution.

[79] Art 51(d) Indian constitution.

[80] *The New Global Puzzle: What World for the EU in 2025* (EUISS, 2006) 195 (*The New Global Puzzle*).

[81] Even though not constitutionally stated, the same could be said about US foreign policy, but for the different reason of alleged aversion to deferring to 'political and bureaucratic elites' both domestically and internationally. Bradford and Posner, n 52, 42.

[82] Smith, n 13, 231 (italics in the original).

Strategy?[83] Recalling Rosenau's definition, global governance goals must not necessarily be legal in nature, and 'include systems of rules at all levels of human activity—from the family to the international organization'.[84] This notwithstanding, the constitution stands out among these sources as the supreme legally entrenched document organizing a political community into a normative order endowed with institutions to uphold that order and pursue collective goals.[85] Hence, constitutions cover and consolidate a considerable part of 'rules at all levels of human activity' to an extent that hardly any other document could offer.

Consequently, constitutional objectives also distinguish themselves from goals of day-to-day foreign policy. Unlike policy goals, they have been adopted through a legislative procedure. As legal norms, they are in principle justiciable.[86] They are part of a 'stable framework' meant to 'preserve stability and continuity in the legal and political structure, and the basic principles that guide its institutions'.[87] Once adopted, they are entrenched, ie more difficult to alter than ordinary legislation,[88] or *a fortiori* government policy. In the case of the EU, amendments are particularly challenging, as the failure of the Constitutional Treaty and the delayed ratification of the Lisbon Treaty have shown.

Entrenchment poses three main challenges: First, constitutionally codifying a particular vision of global governance may lead to an excessive 'judicialization of politics'; secondly, such objectives are prone to raising unrealistic expectations; and thirdly, it may be undemocratic to lock in place the global governance agenda of a given political community in a fast-changing world. It will be argued here that these challenges ultimately reveal the true merit of the constitutional objectives of the EU and other major powers as a source of guidance for global governance.

3.1. Judicialization of foreign policy—or readjusting the institutional balance

Since these objectives concern foreign policy, the first question that arises is the extent to which constitutional codification constitutes an excessive legalization of foreign policy, especially when this is done in a rather detailed and rule-of-law based fashion, such as in the EU. This in turn also suggests a stronger involvement of the judiciary and especially constitutional courts mandated to interpret the constitution and detect instances where it has been violated.[89] In national settings, constitutional objectives have been criticized for potentially restricting the discretion of the political branches, which would be subject to the

[83] European Council, *A Secure Europe in a Better World, European Security Strategy* (12 December 2003).

[84] Rosenau, 'Governance in the Twenty-first Century', n 16, 13.

[85] This draws on J Raz's concept of a 'thick constitution'. J Raz, 'On the Authority and Interpretation of Constitutions: Some Preliminaries' in L Alexander (ed), *Constitutionalism: Philosophical Foundations* (CUP, 1998) 153. See also with regard to the EU, Craig, n 27, 126–127. As we have seen in the case of the EU, it is not only states that can have constitutions. Even though constitutionalism on a global scale is 'thinner' than at the state or EU level, it is more a question of degree than one of a categorical kind. See M Kumm, 'The Cosmopolitan Turn in Constitutionalism: On the Relationship Between National Constitutional Law and Constitutionalism beyond the State' in J Dunoff and J Trachtman (eds), *Ruling the World? Constitutionalism, International Law, and Global Governance* (CUP, 2009).

[86] Specifically on EU objectives, Reimer, n 29, 1000; C Calliess, 'Kollektive Ziele und Prinzipien im Verfassungsrecht der EU—Bestandsaufnahme, Wirkungen und Perspektiven' in C Hiebaum and P Koller (eds), *Politische Ziele und juristische Argumentation* (Franz Steiner, 2003) 90–93.

[87] Raz, n 85, 153.

[88] Ibid.

[89] In addition, a foreign policy relying heavily on international legal commitments raises the question of the domestic status of international law. Once introduced into the domestic legal order, even though usually at sub-constitutional level, the courts are also called upon to interpret and apply it. See on this perennial question in the EU context, for instance, the various contributions in E Cannizzaro, P Palchetti and R Wessel (eds), *International Law as Law of the European Union* (Martinus Nijhoff, 2012).

ultimate say of a 'government of judges' (*gouvernement des juges*),[90] turning the former into mere 'executors of state objectives' (*Staatsziel Vollstrecker*).[91]

This would appear to apply *a fortiori* to foreign affairs. The traditional view is that in this domain the executive has to act strongly and promptly, leaving only a very limited or non-existent role for the judiciary,[92] a view that is 'premised on the existence of dangers in the wider world that have long been banished at home'.[93] This resonates with the criticisms launched by realist scholars of the alleged successes of the 'post-modern'[94] isle of the blessed created through European integration, the success of which was only possible due to favourable power structures.[95] Whether Europe's model can thus be exported externally, or can at least be preserved in the multi-polar world, is highly questionable from this point of view. This in turn creates tension between the uncertainties pertaining to foreign affairs, which require a free rein for the executive, and the interpretation and application of the constitution, including its ambitious foreign policy objectives, which is incumbent upon the judiciary.

However, this criticism is unwarranted when the wording and particular legal features of constitutional objectives in general, and foreign policy objectives in particular, are taken into account. Although they are in principle justiciable, the scope of their obligation extends to their active pursuit, allowing for various courses of action.[96] Only manifest disregard of an objective would qualify as a constitutional infringement. Consequently, courts usually accord great discretion to the government in pursuing foreign policy.[97] An illustration for this is the *Racke* case before the Court of Justice of the EU (CJEU), in which the Court limited itself to assessing whether the Council had committed 'manifest errors of assessment', of which it found none.[98] The Council's reliance on the *rebus sic stantibus* principle was debatable, not least in view of what the Treaty on European Union (TEU) now calls the 'strict compliance with international law', but hinged on granting the political branches the appropriate leeway, also in view of other objectives such as international peace and security. Moreover, the EU Treaties offer a distinction in terms of legal scrutiny, largely excluding the CJEU's jurisdiction from the Common Foreign and Security Policy (CFSP) but not from other policies.[99] The Treaties thus recognize that in certain cases the rule of law may have to take a back seat, but also circumscribe the scope of this reduced scrutiny lest it spill over into other areas where it would not be necessary.[100]

Moreover, constitutional objectives can only be pursued within the bounds of what is feasible.[101] In this sense, the objectives of the EU, too, are rather defined as superior

[90] P De Montalivet, *Les objectifs de valeur constitutionnelle* (Dalloz, 2006) 64, referring to the French legal discourse, but rejecting this criticism.

[91] From the German point of view, D Merten, 'Über Staatsziele' [1993] *Die Öffentliche Verwaltung* 368, 376; J Isensee, 'Staatsaufgaben' in J Isensee and P Kirchhof (eds), *Handbuch des Staatsrechts der Bundesrepublik Deutschland*, vol 4 (3rd edn, CF Mülller, 2010) 144.

[92] T Franck, *Political Questions/Judicial Answers: Does the rule of law apply to foreign affairs?* (Princeton University Press, 1992) 14. See also D Thym, 'Foreign Affairs' in A von Bogdandy and J Bast (eds), *Principles of European Constitutional Law* (2nd edn, Hart Publishing/CH Beck, 2011) 311–314 on the particularity of foreign policy in the EU legal order.

[93] A-M Slaughter Burley, 'Are Foreign Affairs Different?' (1993) 106 Harv L Rev 1980, 1981.

[94] The term was coined by Cooper, n 7.

[95] See eg Bull, n 8, 151; Hyde-Price, n 2, 156–157; Kagan, n 8.

[96] On the intricacies of choosing between addressing a problem first through an internal or external law-making venue, see the contribution by De Witte and Thies to this volume.

[97] Larik, n 50.

[98] Case C-162/96 *Racke* [1998] ECR I-03655, paras 52–60. See also Case 112/80 *Dürbeck* [1981] ECR 01095, para 44.

[99] Art 24(1), second subpara, TEU and Art 275 TFEU. See also Thym, n 92, 326–330.

[100] Art 40 TEU. The CJEU has exercised its jurisdiction to patrol this dividing line. See B Van Vooren, 'The Small Arms Judgment in an Age of Constitutional Turmoil' (2009) 14 *EFA Rev* 231.

[101] See K-P Sommermann, *Staatsziele und Staatszielbestimmungen* (Mohr Siebeck, 1997) 224, arguing principally from the German perspective.

mandates for action, which, instead of being entirely achieved, can only be approximated.[102] In external affairs, this approximation becomes a crucial qualification, as it requires the consideration of not just the internal political and material constraints, but also those beyond one's own borders. A more practical function of foreign policy objectives hence resides in the interpretation of other constitutional norms in their light, rather than their strict enforcement through courts.[103]

Hence, the actual 'judicialization', ie the extent to which the political branches responsible for the conduct of foreign policy will be held accountable by the courts, is fairly limited. Nevertheless, there is merit in the fact that the judiciary is not entirely excluded. If nothing else, courts serve as the last instance to ensure that the codified goals relevant for global governance are not completely disregarded and factor into the overall interpretation of the constitution. In this way, instead of being distorted, the institutional balance, which is a fundamental principle of EU law,[104] is restored and the rule of law extended further into the area of external relations. This would seem particularly important for the EU as a 'Community based on the rule of law'[105] and whose external action is to 'be guided by the principles which have inspired its own creation',[106] which include this very rule of law.[107] For the sake of credibility these principles should not cease to apply 'at the water's edge'[108] before its own courts. Also from a global governance perspective, in which an entirely 'free hand' of the executive in foreign policy seems increasingly misplaced and other branches of government (as well as non-governmental actors) need to be included in the process, this would only seem appropriate.

3.2. Raising unrealistic expectations—or fostering multilateral solutions

Beyond the involvement of the judiciary, another major criticism to which constitutional foreign policy objectives are prone to be subjected is that of raising unrealistic expectations that will be virtually impossible to satisfy in view of the immense challenges that global governance faces.

Constitutional objectives in national law and EU law have already been castigated for being unrealistic in general. Instead of dependable legal guarantees that can be invoked in court, codified objectives would serve merely to draw up 'political utopias'[109] or represent not more than 'a dustbin of sentiment'.[110] This concerns also so-called 'social rights' such as the right to housing or work. At worst, these objectives might eventually question the very 'effectiveness of constitutional law' (*Leistungsfähigkeit des Verfassungsrechts*).[111] Similar criticisms have been voiced with regard to the EU and its manifold codified objectives, which have been called, for example, a 'Christmas tree'[112] and a

[102] See M Kotzur, 'Die Ziele der Union: Verfassungsidentität und Gemeinschaftsidee' [2005] *Die Öffentliche Verwaltung* 313, 315.

[103] Reimer, n 29, 1000–1005; Calliess, n 86, 92.

[104] See eg K Lenaerts and P Van Nuffel, *European Union Law* (3rd edn, Sweet & Maxwell, 2011) 635–636.

[105] Case 294/83 *Les Verts* [1986] ECR 01339, para 23.

[106] Art 21(1), first subpara, TEU.

[107] The rule of law also appears among the values of the Union, Art 2 TEU. See also Art 21(2)(b) TEU, which states the external consolidation of the rule of law as an explicit objective.

[108] P Eeckhout, *Does Europe's Constitution Stop at the Water's Edge? Law and Policy in the EU's External Relations* (Europa Law, 2005).

[109] Isensee, n 91, 144, on German constitutional objectives. See also Merten, n 91, 373.

[110] This quote stems from T T Krishnamachari, who used it to describe the Indian 'directive principles', cited in Usman, n 77, 651.

[111] P Badura, 'Arten der Verfassungsrechtssätze' in J Isensee and P Kirchhof (eds), *Handbuch des Staatsrechts der Bundesrepublik Deutschland*, vol 8 (1st edn, CF Müller, 1992) 41.

[112] F-X Priollaud and D Siritzky, *Le Traité de Lisbonne: Texte et commentaire article par article des nouveaux traités Européens* (TUE-TFUE) (La Documentation Française, 2008) 35–36, attributing this image to the British delegation at the 2002–2003 Convention on the Future of Europe.

'hodgepodge'.[113] This criticism would apply *a fortiori* to the domain of external relations of the EU and other countries that have included ambitious external objectives in their constitutions. This is already reflected in such commentaries describing them as 'redolent of motherhood and apple pie'[114] or as a 'wish list for a better world' (*Wunschzettel für eine bessere Welt*).[115]

Consequently, the codification of such a 'wish list' in a place as prominent as the constitutional charter would likely serve to widen further the Union's infamous 'capabilities–expectations gap'.[116] The contrast between ambition and reality is bound to become even sharper over the next decades, at least according to the more dire forecasts on the future of global governance and the international role of the EU. What is generally observed is the 'relative decline' of European power and influence in a changing world,[117] for instance through a diminishing share in global wealth[118] and population.[119] At the same time, global problems such as climate change, increased energy consumption and proliferation of weapons of mass destruction, among other things, loom large,[120] making the world of tomorrow 'a far less hospitable place'.[121]

Against this backdrop, the EU can be seen as 'flirting rather dangerously with failure and irrelevance',[122] while its constitution stipulates, among many other things, to do nothing less than to help *eradicate* poverty in the world,[123] integrate all countries into the world economy,[124] and 'develop international measures to preserve and improve the quality of the environment and the sustainable management of global natural resources'.[125] The combination of ambitious goals and limiting capacities may well provide 'a recipe for disappointment'.[126] This is especially true when such ambitions are entrenched in a constitutional document.

However, not all accounts of the future are equally bleak. Despite relative decline and mounting challenges, it is asserted that in '2025, the EU is likely to be still one of the richest and safest parts of the world',[127] retaining its status as the world's second superpower 'for a generation or more'.[128] Therefore, these objectives, even though ambitious, are not entirely unrealistic. Given that the EU will still have considerable capabilities and assets at its disposal, it will be able to continue to actively pursue these goals.

Crucially, the main challenges of global governance are typically beyond the powers of any single state or regional bloc such as the EU. This is most obvious in cases where so-called 'global public goods' are at stake, such as international security and or a healthy global environment. These problems will be solved only by a concerted effort on a global scale

[113] A von Bogdandy, 'The European constitution and the European identity: Text and subtext of the Treaty establishing a Constitution for Europe' (2005) 3 ICON 295, 315, commenting on the failed Constitutional Treaty.

[114] A Dashwood and others, *Wyatt and Dashwood's European Union Law* (6th edn, Hart Publishing, 2011) 903.

[115] W Drescher, 'Ziele und Zuständigkeiten' in A Marchetti and C Demesmay (eds), *Der Vertrag von Lissabon: Analyse und Bewertung* (Nomos, 2010) 68.

[116] C Hill, 'The Capability–Expectations Gap, or Conceptualising Europe's International Role' (1993) 31 *Journal of Common Market Studies* 305.

[117] *Project Europe 2030*, n 10, 11–12.

[118] Youngs, n 6, 7.

[119] Telò, n 7, 15.

[120] *Project Europe 2030*, n 10, 12; Ortega, n 18, 35–40.

[121] *The New Global Puzzle*, n 80, 199. See also Telò, n 7, 20, who speaks of an emerging 'globalization malaise'.

[122] Smith, n 13, 240.

[123] This goal is codified three times in the Treaties: Art 3(5) TEU; Art 21(2)(d) TEU; and Art 208(1), second subpara, TFEU.

[124] Art 21(2)(h) TEU; also Art 208(1), second subpara, TFEU.

[125] Art 21(2)(f) TEU.

[126] *Project Europe 2030*, n 10, 5.

[127] *The New Global Puzzle*, n 80, 203.

[128] A Moracvcsik, 'Why the "Second Superpower" Needs a New Discourse', EUI RSCAS Policy Paper 2011/01, 43: <http://cadmus.eui.eu/bitstream/handle/1814/16356/RSCAS_PP_2011_01.rev.pdf?sequence=4> accessed 18 March 2012. See also Leonard, n 4, 8, who even speaks of a 'New European Century'.

involving a plurality of actors. Therefore, the stress the EU Treaties put on the 'governance mode of foreign policy',[129] ie 'multilateral solutions to common problems'[130] and the furthering of 'an international system based on stronger multilateral cooperation and good global governance'[131] is of crucial significance. Combined with the fact that, albeit to a lesser degree, multilateral cooperation based on certain common principles is also reflected in the constitutions of other major powers, it bolsters the claim that the EU 'would thus act not only by defending the interest of its near 500 million citizens, but also the interests of its 500 million neighbors and even the 6.5 billion inhabitants of the planet'.[132] Since international cooperation is enshrined in many constitutions today, one may even go as far as to speak of a global 'duty of sincere cooperation',[133] with its basis in national or supranational constitutional law. This does not mean that multilateral solutions including legally binding commitments have to be pursued all the time and at all cost.[134] Nevertheless, as we have seen, rules-based solutions within the 'governance mode' doubtlessly enjoy a preference in the EU Treaties. Contrary to any false expectations to single-handedly solving the Herculean tasks facing international society, it is the EU's own experience as a multilateral arrangement based on the rule of law which makes it pre-destined to play a role in co-leadership of multilateral efforts.[135]

3.3. Undemocratic—or the people's call for global governance

The third major criticism that could be launched against constitutional foreign policy objectives, in particular those of the EU, would be that they are undemocratic or counter-majoritarian. Through constitutional entrenchment, certain matters are 'taken off the agenda of normal politics'.[136] This would also apply to entrenching into the constitution a particular vision of global governance that the polity is obliged to pursue, unless and until it is changed through a burdensome amendment procedure. Consequently, the kind of global governance to which the EU will contribute is to a certain extent pre-determined and cannot be changed easily.[137] The EU already suffers from a 'democracy deficit',[138] which would be extended to the external sphere. In terms of a two-level game,[139] this means the possible overlap with other parties and stakeholders of agreeable solutions at the international level is structurally constrained.

But as we have seen, these objectives are neither excessively constraining nor entirely unrealistic, even though EU constitutional law goes further than that of most countries. This means that in the pursuit of these objectives, the political branches possess an ample measure of discretion. Whereas the basic parameters are fixed, whoever is in power in the EU can exercise their competence in external relations as long as constitutional objectives are not manifestly disregarded. Furthermore, as the Lisbon Treaty has expanded the powers

129 To use the term devised by de Búrca in her contribution to this volume.

130 Art 21(1), second subpara, TEU.

131 Art 21(2)(h) TEU.

132 Telò, n 7, 26.

133 Akin to the duty existent already within the EU, Art 4(3) TEU.

134 As the respective contributions by Marín Durán, Morgera, and Scott and Rajamani to this volume show, the same substantive environmental objectives can be pursued through various means, ranging from multilateral treaties to unilateral measures.

135 Telò, n 7, 26.

136 Craig, n 27, 126.

137 This may lead the way to the 'dead hand of the past' criticism of constitutional law in general, which questions the constitutional authority that over time becomes detached from its original authors, Raz, n 85, 164–169. See also Usman, n 77, who sees Indian 'directive principles' as problematic principally for this reason.

138 See eg Lenaerts and Van Nuffel, n 104, 741–742.

139 See R Putnam, 'Diplomacy and Domestic Politics: The Logic of Two-Level Games' (1988) 42 *International Organization* 427. Of course, this can sometimes be used as a bargaining device.

of the European Parliament in the area of external relations,[140] the democratic deficit is somewhat lessened by introducing another institution that can rely on Treaty objectives in scrutinizing the performance of the Council and Commission. In addition, it can give its own—democratically legitimized—interpretations of the objectives in a 'heterarchical' setting involving all constitutional branches.[141]

Apart from that, it can be argued that contents codified and entrenched into a constitutional document enjoy a considerable amount of inherent legitimacy.[142] This actually represents the most important merit of constitutional objectives relevant for global governance. It becomes evident when we consider the '"global governance dilemma", whereby the more global regulation is needed and implemented, the more demands are necessarily going to rise from the bottom up for democratic legitimacy and accountability of decision-makers'.[143] One could thus speak of a global 'democracy deficit' caused by expanding global governance needs.

Constitutional documents would be able to provide such legitimacy. Instead of referring to mere policy documents, decision-makers can point to the democratically established highest laws of their respective political communities to justify their actions with a global governance dimension. This relates, to draw again on Raz's concept of thick constitutionalism, to the aspect of a constitution as 'common ideology', ie principles

> that are generally held to express the common beliefs of the population about the way their society should be governed. It serves, you may say, not only as a lawyers' law, but as the people's law. Its main provisions are generally known, command general consent, are held to be the (or part of the) common ideology that governs public life in that country.[144]

Through the insertion of foreign policy objectives, this 'common ideology' has now acquired an external dimension. It is no longer merely the expression of the people as to how 'their society' within the confines of its borders is to be governed, it also expresses the core principles of how this community is to shape the international order. Otherwise put, it lays down the people's preferences, in their capacity as constitutional legislator or *pouvoir constituant*, for a particular vision of global governance itself.

Being able to point to this factor is not to be underestimated in terms of legitimacy as 'the hard currency of future international relations'[145] and 'a central component of power, or the ability to achieve appointed goals'.[146] Also here, the EU finds itself in the vanguard. Having established the first transnational democratic system,[147] its constitution can be seen as the expression not simply of one people but of the numerous peoples united within the Union. The fact that the EU Treaties have not been voted upon in a direct referendum does not change this.[148] After all, the democratically chosen representatives in the 27 EU Member

[140] Notably, the European Parliament's consent is now required for a wide range of international agreements, including in the area of trade, which was previously not the case, Art 218(6)(a) TFEU; Art 207 TFEU. See further R Passos, 'The European Union's external relations a year after Lisbon: a first evaluation from the European Parliament' in Koutrakos, n 21.

[141] See D Halberstam, 'Constitutional Heterarchy: The Centrality of Conflict in the United States and Europe' in Dunoff and Trachtman (eds), n 85, who argues that all three branches have a role in constitutional interpretation based on their expertise, capacity to represent the people and ability to protect individual rights.

[142] This applies of course to constitutions that have been adopted democratically or have come to be accepted and applied in a democratic system and not those situated in a very 'thin' constitutional context.

[143] Telò, n 7, 19.

[144] Raz, n 85, 153–154.

[145] *The New Global Puzzle*, n 80, 198.

[146] Ibid. See also Telò, n 7, 34.

[147] J Hoeksma, 'The EU as a democratic polity in international law', CLEER Working Paper 2011/2: <http://www.asser.nl/upload/documents/672011_23350CLEER%20WP%202011-2-%20HOEKSMA.pdf> accessed 18 March 2012.

[148] P-C Müller-Graff, 'Verfassungsziele der EG/EU' in M Dauses (ed), *Handbuch des EU-Wirtschaftsrechts* (loose-leaf, 27th edition, updated October 2010, CH Beck, 2010), para 84, who stresses that neither the US nor the German constitutions were ever submitted to a plebiscite.

States have approved the EU Treaties, including the external objectives contained therein. This is nothing less than the expression of a European will to contribute to global governance along the lines provided therein, ie to contribute actively to providing various global public goods such as security or environmentally sustainable prosperity, as well as a global bolstering of the rule of law.

Furthermore, as we have seen, the EU is not alone in this, but is indeed part of a global trend in which democratic constitutions express similar goals for international cooperation, the respect of international law, peaceful resolution of disputes and the spread of human rights. According to Rosenau, 'hierarchy is certainly not a necessary prerequisite to the framing of goals'.[149] Therefore, rather than looking for a top-down imposition of global principles on the international level, or a single list of goals drawn up by adherents of one or the other IR theory, constitutional documents around the world, as the bottom-up crystallization of stable popular preferences, arguably represent a preferable source. From the selection of documents here, the common denominator for a global 'common ideology' (at least among the democratic polities) to guide global governance can already be seen to emerge. However, a strong emphasis on law as part of such an ideology is still a rather unique feature of EU constitutional law.

4. Conclusion

At the outset of this chapter, it was observed that in view of the diverse assessments of the EU's contributions to global governance, there is a great need for stable and justifiable benchmarks. It has been argued that constitutional law can provide exactly that.

Within this constitutional dimension of global governance, a concept inherently based on goals and rules, one can distinguish between the entrenchment of substantive objectives relevant for global governance and constitutional provisions which specifically harness law to frame the pursuit of these goals. We have seen that modern constitutions, including those of the rising powers of a future multi-polar world, are ample providers of substantive objectives. Stressing the importance of law in this context, however, is far from ubiquitous. On the contrary, the post-Lisbon EU Treaties provide both an extensive and sophisticated account of substantive goals as well as a particularly strong emphasis on law in this regard.

Beyond the empirical, it was argued that the particular features pertaining to constitutional law make it a formidable source for framing global governance. Only on the surface did these features appear as problematic. First, instead of overly judicializing the area of foreign affairs, constitutionally entrenching a global governance agenda readjusts the institutional balance and fosters the rule of law internally. It rejects the 'classic' idea of the executive branch acting alone and largely *legibus solutus* in foreign policy. Where constitutions encourage the development of international law and participation in international organizations, as is the case in the EU, a constitutional foundation for extending the rule of law globally is established. This emphasizes the conception of global governance as both *multi*-level and *multi*-actor *rule-setting.*

Secondly, even though codifying foreign policy objectives into a polity's constitution doubtlessly raises expectations as to the performance of that actor, these cannot be considered as entirely unrealistic and unhelpful. Crucially, many of these objectives concern global public goods, which can be provided only through multilateral cooperation. In view of the many constitutional emphases on the need for international cooperation, a global duty to cooperate towards milieu goals based on constitutional law can be discerned. Here, the Union's experience as a community with common goals based on the rule of law can

[149] Rosenau, Governance in the 21st Century, n 16, 14.

serve as inspiration to foster a global framework regulating effectively and equitably the provision of such goods.

Thirdly, constitutional entrenchment can serve as an important source of legitimacy, of which global governance is in dire need. Where a constitution is the highest law within a democratic community, its codified vision for global governance also forms part of the 'common ideology' of that community. Moreover, given the broad substantive similarities in the democratic constitutions reviewed in this regard, a global basic consensus calling for more active contributions to global governance along these broad lines can be seen to emerge. However, the worldwide promotion of the rule of law, while an important part of the constitutional 'common ideology' of the EU, is not generally shared.

Of course, constitutionally entrenching a particular vision for global governance does not automatically bring this vision to life. Indeed, the challenges facing the EU and the international community as a whole are enormous and make the more ambitious constitutional objectives frequently appear overly audacious. But as was shown, this entrenchment serves to establish democratically legitimated, stable expectations, which also feed into the overall interpretation of a political community's highest laws. It mandates the competent constitutional organs to work and cooperate with others towards these goals. This in itself represents a success. In all these respects, the EU and its primary law stand out. The level of comprehensiveness of the substantive objectives present in the EU Treaties surpasses that of any national constitution. At least as important though is their clear preference for multilateralism, as well as their embrace of law as an essential ingredient of global governance. For the time being, it is in the EU Treaties that the legal dimension of global governance finds its strongest and most vigorous constitutional expression.

2

Why Choose Europe? The Place of the European Union in the Architecture of International Legal Cooperation

Bruno De Witte and Anne Thies

1. Introduction: The Choice of the Law-Making Venue

Some twenty years ago, Ludwig Krämer, a leading Commission official, offered the following justification for European Community action in the field of environmental protection—but his words could be repeated identically by one of his colleagues today:

> 'There are transnational environmental problems. Pollution of the Atlantic Ocean, the North, the Baltic or the Mediterranean Seas, air pollution, the disappearance of fauna and flora species, and other environmental problems cannot be resolved by national or regional activity alone. International conventions are not fully enforced; they lack the necessary authority on the one hand and effective enforcement procedures on the other.'[1]

In this extract, the author provides two separate but complementary justifications: one for preferring European Union (EU) action over separate action by its Member States or their regions; and another for preferring EU action over the adoption of international conventions. In the first case, the argument is essentially one of *scale*: the nature of the problem of pollution or environmental degradation requires action at a wider than the national level. In the second case, the argument is founded on the allegedly superior *normative quality* of Union law compared to 'ordinary' international treaties. The *combination* of both factors, namely the scale at which EU law operates combined with that legal order's particular qualities, may help to explain the important place that EU law has come to occupy in the European legal landscape. Indeed, action at the EU level is often less efficient and less enforceable than action at the national level, but this disadvantage can be outweighed by the transnational scale of a problem that calls for common solutions. Conversely, action at the EU level may be less suitable than multilateral action for dealing with worldwide problems, but the superior quality of European law may outweigh that limited geographical scope. It is, therefore, the peculiar mixture of a relatively large-scale scope of activity and a relatively efficient system for 'producing' legal rules which has made the European Union an attractive forum for law-making and, more generally, for helping its Member States to manage globalization.

The fact that Commission officials, such as Mr Krämer, favour action by the EU rather than action in other international fora should not come as a surprise. But it is less clear whether and why EU Member State governments would be inclined to make this 'choice for Europe'.[2] Indeed, for many transnational issues, there is a broad range of available international fora that could deal with them, and this multiplicity creates the possibility for the

[1] L Krämer, 'Community Environmental Law—Towards a Systematic Approach' (1991) 11 *Yearbook of European Law* 151, 151.

[2] We refer, here, to the title of A Moravcsik's, *The Choice for Europe* (UCL Press, 1998), although Moravcsik's book primarily deals with the 'grand bargains' struck on the occasion of European Treaty revisions, rather than with the more mundane policy choices made when launching new pieces of European Union legislation.

main actors (namely states, international organizations (IOs) and non-governmental organizations (NGOs)) to decide which institutional context is most appropriate to negotiate new policy outcomes. The governments of the Member States of the EU often have a choice between either addressing a given transnational policy problem within the context of the European Union, or acting within the context of another (regional or global) international organization, or even acting by means of a series of bilateral negotiations with individual countries or by means of informal trans-governmental networks. This *choice of law-making venue* is sometimes denied, namely when the EU has acquired exclusive competence on a given subject matter; and even when a choice exists, it can be influenced by the activity of EU institutions, in particular by the Commission, that can propose a new piece of EU legislation in order to prevent the Member States from moving to another forum, or may, on the contrary, admit that another international venue is more appropriate and encourage the Member States to act within that other venue.

In this paper, attention will be paid to the factors explaining why, in a given case, a particular venue is chosen. Examples will be given from a variety of policy areas, including migration, labour standards, environmental protection, private international law, transfrontier television, and others, although the nature of this paper precludes the elaboration of any of these examples. The purpose of the paper is, indeed, a fairly general one rather than a policy-specific one, namely to argue that venue choice is an important element of legal agenda-setting in Europe today.

Our analysis is limited to *law-making* taken in a broad sense, ie including executive standard setting, but excluding operational actions, strategies, declarations, statements and other acts resulting from foreign policy activity. The analysis is, furthermore, limited to the choices made by *governmental institutions* (both national and European), although it is clear that non-governmental organizations face similar choices as to which policy-making forum to privilege in their action.[3] Finally, our paper does not address the prior question of how a given subject matter is being defined as a social problem requiring a legal response, that is, how it is decided that the problem is of such a nature that 'there ought to be a law against it'. We also do not address the question how that social problem is categorized as a transnational problem, for which adequate legal solutions cannot be found exclusively at the national level. The latter move is not necessarily, and not exclusively, determined by the 'objective' nature of the problem, but may also be dictated by the will of governments to introduce domestic legal change 'through the back door', namely to use the route of EU or international law-making for dealing with problems which are not inherently international, but for which domestic politics does not offer a solution. Finally, governments may well disagree amongst each other on whether a given problem calls for transnational rather than domestic regulation. On all those questions, we must refer to the rich literature of public policy and international relations studies. There is not much that legal scholarship can contribute to those questions, since there are very few *legal* constraints on categorizing problems as being in need of transnational law-making. There are no international law limits, and hardly any constitutional law limits, on the kinds of issues that states can regulate by means of treaties; and there are few strict limits on the European Union's law-making competences.

In the next section (section 2) of this chapter, we will start by sketching the *historical background* for the current situation of venue choice, by drawing the contours of the fragmented international institutional landscape which the European states have helped to create and in which they now operate. In section 3, we will discuss the main *factors*, most of which are not primarily of a legal nature, that determine the choice for one or other legal

[3] On the factors determining venue choice by domestic interest organizations, see eg J Beyers and B Kerremans, 'Domestic Embeddedness and the Dynamics of Multilevel Venue Shopping in Four EU Member States' (2012) 25 (2) Governance 263.

venue in a given subject area. In section 4, we will complement that discussion by considering the *political and legal constraints* that define the scope of EU Member States' venue choice, possibly prevent them from using rival law-making fora, or determine the way in which they contribute to international law-making. The final section 5 completes the venue-choice panorama by examining the factors that may push the *European Union* itself to participate in broader international law-making processes rather than focusing on internal EU legislation for a given subject matter, highlighting the fact that venue choices are often not exclusive, but *complementary* in that they involve the combined use of various law-making venues in a given time sequence.

2. Historical Evolution

The question of which state parties should be invited to join the negotiations of a law-making treaty, and the question of which among several organizations with overlapping mandates should develop new rules on a given subject matter, are traditional questions of the politics of international law. After the Second World War, the proliferation of new international organizations and the increased recognition of the need for transnational law-making multiplied the occasions for venue choice, and nowhere more so than in (Western) Europe, where new organizations with ambitious mandates were set up.[4]

Within Western Europe, the Council of Europe was created in the 1950s with a broad mandate to develop uniform legal rules for its Member States. The instrument selected for this purpose was not the adoption of unilateral decisions by the Council of Europe. Rather, the law-making instrument of the Council of Europe was, and remains until today, the adoption of conventions, ie international treaties. Their adoption is facilitated by the institutional machinery of the Council of Europe, but their ratification is left to the free choice of each Member State.[5] In the course of time, the Council of Europe has thus developed a large programme of harmonization of the laws of its Member States by means of conventions. There were 211 such instruments altogether at the latest count, but this includes some 75 Protocols modifying earlier conventions, and among the conventions quite a few are 'limping',[6] in that they have not entered into force for lack of a sufficient number of ratifications. It has been suggested that about one-third of Council of Europe conventions are currently the 'common property' of the EU Member States, in the sense that they have all ratified those conventions.[7]

As the legislative competences of the European Union expand with each of its Treaty revisions, there are ever fewer subjects dealt with by Council of Europe conventions that could not also be dealt with by means of EU directives or regulations, and the Council of Europe finds it increasingly difficult to obtain or maintain control of particular issue areas as against the EU's legal interference.[8] Still, there remain a number of important law-making instruments of the Council of Europe for which no EU-based rival instruments have come into existence or are being envisaged, such as the European Convention on Nationality, the Framework Convention for the Protection of National Minorities and its cousin the

[4] See the contributions to N Blokker and H Schermers (eds), *Proliferation of International Organizations: Legal Issues* (Kluwer Law International, 2001).

[5] See F Benoît-Rohmer and H Klebes, *Council of Europe Law: Towards a Pan-European Legal Area* (Council of Europe Publishing, 2005).

[6] A Aust, 'Limping Treaties: Lessons from Multilateral Treaty-making' (2003) 50(3) *Netherlands International Law Review* 243.

[7] Martyn Bond, 'The EU and the Council of Europe: Difference, Duplication or Delegation?', in DJ Galbreath and C Gebhard (eds), *Cooperation or Conflict? Problematizing Organizational Overlap in Europe* (Ashgate, 2010) 11, 13.

[8] For views on the evolution of the institutional ties between the Council of Europe and the European Union, see M Bond (ibid), and T Joris and J Vandenberghe, 'The Council of Europe and the European Union: Natural Partners or Uneasy Bedfellows?' (2008–09) 15(1) *Columbia Journal of European Law* 1.

European Charter for Regional or Minority Languages, and the European Landscape Convention.[9]

When the EEC Treaty was concluded, back in 1957, it was clear to all that the new Community institutions would not provide the exclusive framework for the relations between the six Member States. Apart from the Council of Europe, the Community countries were involved in other institutional cooperation frameworks, and wished to preserve their option of adding new ones. In fact, the EEC Treaty terminated none of the existing bilateral or multilateral treaties between Community Member States. During the negotiation of the EEC Treaty, and in the period immediately afterwards, several such 'partial agreements' were concluded, also on matters related to those covered by the EEC Treaty. A prominent example was the Treaty establishing the Benelux Economic Union that was concluded on 3 February 1958, that is, only one month after the entry into force of the EEC Treaty. In anticipation of this, Article 233 EC (now Article 306 of the Treaty on the Functioning of the European Union (TFEU)) stated—and still states today—that the EEC Treaty does not preclude 'the existence or completion of regional unions between Belgium and Luxembourg, or between Belgium, Luxembourg and the Netherlands . . . '. Soon after, in 1960, eight European states, including five of the six European Community countries, created Eurocontrol, an international organization charged with common air traffic management tasks.[10] Although the European Community gradually developed its own aviation regulations, Eurocontrol has maintained its existence as a separate international organization with a complex legal relation to the European Union.[11] Benelux and Eurocontrol were not the only forms of international cooperation between groups of Member States; for many years, the hegemonic position of the EC was not well established, and the history of relationships between European countries was also one 'of often vigorous regional groupings and intense special partnerships between neighbours'.[12]

In addition to using those 'rival' organizations of European cooperation, the European countries have also continued to conclude numerous specific treaties among each other in areas such as tax law, environmental protection, defence, culture and education which were not (or not immediately) of interest for the Community. The most prominent example of a partial agreement, concluded between some Member States only, was the Schengen cooperation regime, composed of a first Agreement signed in 1985, and an implementing Convention adopted in 1990. Schengen cooperation was started at a time when a general Community-wide consensus on abolishing the controls on persons at the intra-Community borders could not be reached. The Schengen instruments were expressly presented as an interim arrangement in anticipation of a final regime at the level of the European Community, rather than as a separate and rival cooperation regime. The same reasons that justified the rule of Article 233 EEC Treaty, whereby the Benelux countries could adopt more advanced measures of integration, could be applied to Schengen.

In current practice, partial agreements between EU Member States are principally used for more mundane matters. They deal with subjects that are not yet absorbed within the scope of activities of the EU, either because they are of concern only to two or three countries and not to the European Union as a whole (this is typically the case for agreements dealing with the protection of rivers or mountain ranges), or because their subject matter lies

[9] For the complete list of the Council of Europe's treaties see: <http://conventions.coe.int/Treaty/Commun/ListeTraites.asp?CM=8&CL=ENG>.

[10] 'International Convention Relating to Co-operation for the Safety of Air Navigation' (1960) 523 *United Nations Treaty Series* 117. The convention has been amended several times since, and membership has grown to include almost all European countries.

[11] See P Mendes de Leon, 'The Relationship between Eurocontrol and the EC: Living Apart Together' (2007) 4 *International Organizations Law Review* 305.

[12] H Wallace, 'Flexibility: A Tool for Integration or a Restraint on Disintegration?', in K Neunreither and A Wiener (eds), *European Integration After Amsterdam: Institutional Dynamics and Prospects for Democracy* (OUP, 2000) 175, 176.

outside EU law-making competence, as is the case with culture and education,[13] and (more controversially) with bilateral tax treaties. These agreements are still rather numerous but they usually do not deal with vital matters of foreign policy. However, they always remain present in the toolbox of the EU states' foreign policy, as was illustrated by the recent conclusion of the Treaty setting up a European Stability Mechanism, signed by the 17 euro area states on 2 February 2012,[14] and of the Treaty on Stability, Coordination and Governance in the European Union, signed by 25 EU Member States on 2 March 2012.[15]

The fact that the EU Member States may, in principle, continue to conclude treaties between themselves does not mean that they are entirely free to do so as and how they wish.[16] *Inter se* international agreements between two or more Member States of the EU are allowed, but only within the limits set by EU law obligations. The practical importance of the principle of primacy of EU law over partial agreements between Member States was illustrated by a judgment of the European Court of Justice in 2006 that found the application of a Schengen Convention rule to be incompatible with the rights of free movement which third country nationals who are family members of EU citizens derive from EU law.[17] The court's finding was facilitated by the fact that Article 134 of the Schengen Convention contained an express conflict rule giving priority to Community law, but the Court of Justice of the EU would no doubt have come to the same conclusion with regard to a partial agreement that does not contain such an express primacy rule. The legal situation is different, of course, for conflicts between treaties concluded between EU states and third countries. Although the Court of Justice seeks to affirm the prevalence of EU law also in those cases, the rights of those third countries will need to be preserved.[18]

Finally, the various European sites of law-making mentioned above are competing with institutionalized sites of global law-making, some of which pre-dated the European organizations, such as the International Labour Organization and the Hague Conference on Private International Law, whereas others were developed in the post-war period as part of the broad UN family, such as the World Intellectual Property Organization (WIPO), the WHO, the United Nations Economic Commission for Europe, the Codex Alimentarius Commission, etc. Both inside and outside the UN, transcontinental multilateral treaties and organizations were set up to deal with matters that came to be seen as of global concern, such as the protection of human rights, the regulation of the oceans' fishery and other resources, and global environmental problems.[19]

3. Policy Considerations: Factors Influencing Venue Choice

A first factor that may determine the choice of a particular law-making venue is *path dependence*.[20] The existence of a treaty on a given subject matter means that later reforms

[13] According to Art 6 TFEU, the EU is only competent to carry out actions to support, coordinate or supplement Member States' actions in these areas.

[14] <http://www.european-council.europa.eu/media/582311/05-tesm2.en12.pdf>.

[15] <http://european-council.europa.eu/eurozone-governance/treaty-on-stability>.

[16] For a legal analysis of when such agreements are permitted under EU law, see B De Witte, 'Old-fashioned Flexibility: International Agreements between Member States of the European Union', in G de Búrca and J Scott (eds), *Constitutional Change in the EU—From Uniformity to Flexibility?* (Hart Publishing, 2000) 31. See also the study by LS Rossi, *Le convenzioni fra gli Stati membri dell'Unione europea* (Giuffrè, 2000).

[17] Case C-503/03 *Commission v Spain* [2006] ECR I-01097, particularly recitals 33–35.

[18] We will not discuss further, in this chapter, the question of conflicts between EU law and norms contained in treaties between its Member States and third countries. See, for a detailed analysis of this question, J Klabbers, *Treaty Conflict and the European Union* (CUP, 2009).

[19] On the processes and instruments of international law-making, see generally Alan Boyle and C Chinkin, *The Making of International Law* (OUP, 2007). Specifically on law-making by international organizations, see J E Alvarez, *International Organizations as Law-Makers* (OUP, 2005).

[20] This concept is mostly used in the political science literature. See P Pierson, *Politics in Time: History, Institutions, and Social Analysis* (Princeton University Press, 2004), ch 1.

will usually be adopted in the form of protocols or modifications to that treaty, rather than the adoption of legal instruments in another forum. More structurally, organizations that traditionally deal with a given subject area will often seek to protect their 'legal territory' against rival organizations. An interesting example of path dependence, and of its limits, is offered by the venerable Hague Conference, the organization that has promoted the adoption of a long list of conventions in the field of private international law.[21] The existence of this law-making venue with a century-old tradition and a specialized set of officials and country experts did not prevent the European Union from gradually 'occupying' this legal field since the mid-1990s.[22] The fact that a subject matter is traditionally put on some other organization's agenda, or is even the sole reason of existence of that organization (as with the Hague Conference) is obviously not a sufficient reason for the EU to keep clear of it. Conversely, the European Union may be drawn into a new field of regulation as a consequence of earlier, seemingly unrelated, developments in EU law itself. The recent EU legislation on the rights of third-country migrants and asylum-seekers originates from the perceived need of the EU Member States to accompany the opening of the internal frontiers of the EU with a whole range of so-called 'flanking measures', in relation to the access (or non-access) to that borderless territory and, by further extension, to a limited degree of harmonization of the rights of third-country nationals once they are admitted on EU territory. The recognition, by most EU governments,[23] that this is an area requiring common action at the European Union level contrasts with their generally very reluctant attitude towards international law-making initiatives in this area. Here we see that the existence of legal pathways at the multilateral level (both in the UN and in the Council of Europe regime) was not sufficient to convince EU member countries to fully engage with them,[24] whereas they did accept later on to enact EU-level harmonization, once the Union had acquired legislative competences in this area.

A second important factor in deciding whether to 'use' an instrument of secondary EU law or an international treaty with third states is the *geographical nature of the subject matter*. The territorial scope of the problem may define which states need to be involved in its solution, and hence may also determine the law-making venue. Thus, navigation on the river Rhine or protection of the environmental quality of the Rhine water cannot be effectively regulated on the basis of internal EU acts alone; they rather require agreements with Switzerland, due to the upstream location of that country.[25] Similarly, protection of the environment of the Alps requires the participation of as many Alpine countries as possible, but no others, so that the choice of an international agreement with nine contracting parties

[21] For a list of the 'Hague Conventions' see: <http://www.hcch.net/index_en.php?act=conventions.listing>.

[22] For EU legislation in this area see: <http://ec.europa.eu/justice/civil/law/index_en.htm>. On the partial 'displacement' of the Hague Conference by the EU, see, among others: Andrea Schulz, 'The Accession of the European Community to the Hague Conference on Private International Law' (2007) 56 *International and Comparative Law Quarterly* 939; K Boele-Woelki, 'For Better or for Worse: The Europeanization of International Divorce Law' (2010) 12 *Yearbook of Private International Law* 1; J Asmus Bischoff, *Die Europäische Gemeinschaft und die Konventionen des einheitlichen Privatrechts* (Mohr Siebeck, 2010).

[23] As is well known, the UK, Ireland and Denmark have a broad 'opt-out' in this area of EU law. See Consolidated Version of the TEU and TFEU [2008] OJ C115/01, Protocol (No 21) on the position of the United Kingdom and Ireland in respect of the Area, Freedom, Security and Justice, Protocol (No 22) on the position of Denmark, and Protocol (No 19) on the Schengen Acquis Integrated into the Framework of the European Union.

[24] The UN International Convention on the Protection of the Rights of All Migrant Workers and Members of their Families entered into force on 1 July 2003 and currently has 45 state parties, but this number does not include a single EU country. On the reasons for their reluctance, see E MacDonald and R Cholewinski, 'The ICRMW and the European Union' in R Cholewinski, P de Guchteneire and A Pécoud (eds), *Migration and Human Rights. The United Nations Convention on Migrant Workers' Rights* (CUP, 2009) 360. Similarly, the Council of Europe Convention on the Legal Status of Migrant Workers (CETS No 93) entered into force in 1983 but has acquired, 30 years later, only 11 ratifications, including six EU Member States. More generally on the difficult struggle to develop an international legal regime of migration governance, see the chapter by Thym in this volume.

[25] See, on the international legal regime of the Rhine: K Tiroch, 'Rhine River' in *Max Planck Encyclopedia of Public International Law* (OUP, online edition, last updated February 2011).

(including the EU)[26] could seem more appropriate than the adoption of an EU directive whose geographical scope would anyway have been limited to part of the EU territory.

The territorial scale of the problem plays, in fact, a general and ubiquitous role in determining whether internal EU law-making makes sense. For instance, if European countries decide, for a variety of reasons, that the poor labour conditions in developing and emerging countries are a source of concern, this does not make EU legislation a very effective response to that concern. Rather, the European countries (and the EU itself) must give their backing to efforts at global regulation developed, principally, within the context of the International Labour Organization (ILO).[27] Another example is the security of energy supply. Although internal EU measures may go some way to avoiding disruption of energy supply in the individual countries, it was vitally important for EU countries to involve the energy producing non-EU countries in such a regime, hence their interest in concluding the Energy Charter Treaty with major energy supplying countries.[28] In contrast with this example, many other social problems are located both within and outside the EU, so that a 'partial' regulation of that problem in the form of EU legislation is perfectly sensible, even though the problem may remain insufficiently addressed at the global level. Thus, for example, the adoption of the EU directive on race discrimination, in 2000, could be seen as an effective instrument for dealing with the 'internal' dimension of race discrimination, without prejudice to the possibility or the need for similar action at the global level. It must be remembered, in this respect, that the *potential* territorial coverage of an international instrument may be wider than that of EU law, but that the *actual* scope of application of global regulations will depend on how many, and which, countries, accept to be bound by the instrument.

The relative *ease of decision-making* is a third factor that may trigger the choice of one law-making venue rather than another. International law-making is often more flexible as regards the selection of the participants to the law-making process, and also allows—in the case of international treaties—for later modification between only some of the parties to the original treaty, although this possibility for differentiated evolution is not always available (think, for example, of the WTO Agreements whose revision is subject to pre-defined rules,[29] whereas a partial modification between a limited set of countries is not contemplated and indeed discouraged by the Most Favoured Nation (MFN) rules in the Agreements). In most cases, though, international treaty-making allows for the involvement of only those states that are willing to engage in regulating a certain subject matter. For example, the Schengen Agreement (1985) and Convention (1990) could be concluded between those EU states that were willing to engage in a new step of the integration process outside the participation constraints of the EU decision-making process. Indeed, within the EU system, the participating countries are pre-defined (with the exception of the enhanced cooperation mechanism[30] and of the flexible opt-out from which the UK

[26] Alpine Convention, Salzburg 1991. This is a Framework Convention whose provisions have been complemented by a series of Protocols of Implementation dealing with specific issues such as mountain farming, tourism and transport. See: <www.alpconv.org>.

[27] See Kenner's chapter in this volume.

[28] Energy Charter Treaty (1994); see: <www.encharter.org> for its text and state of ratifications. The hopes of involving energy producing countries were only partially fulfilled. Whereas Azerbaijan, Kazakhstan and Turkmenistan have ratified the Treaty, Russia has signed it but so far refused to ratify it. For the overall argument, see SS Haghighi, *Energy Security: The External Legal Relations of the European Union with Major Oil- and Gas-Supplying Countries* (Hart Publishing, 2007), particularly chs 4 and 5. On the deficiency of the Energy Charter Treaty as an energy security instrument, see PD Cameron, 'The EU and Energy Security: A Critical Review of the Legal Issues' in Antonis Antoniadis, R Schütze and E Spaventa (eds), *The European Union and Global Emergencies—A Law and Policy Analysis* (Hart Publishing, 2011) 125.

[29] Art X on Amendments of the Agreement Establishing the World Trade Organization: <http://www.wto.org/english/docs_e/legal_e/04-wto.pdf>. See the contribution by F Hoffmeister in this volume.

[30] Art 20 TEU; Arts 326–334 TFEU.

and Ireland benefit in the area of justice and home affairs),[31] and later amendments of directives and regulations must also, in principle, apply to all EU countries without the possibility of partial modifications applying to some countries only. This rigidity of the EU's participation rules is, however, compensated by the fact that, in most areas nowadays, the applicable decision-making rules provide for qualified majority voting in the Council so that reluctant Member States can be bound against their will, both in the original enactment of a directive or regulation, and in their later amendment. Also, the European Union provides to its Member States a permanent venue for law-making with tried and tested procedures and a social environment of 'repeat players' which tends to favour the adoption of compromise solutions. The very breadth of the EU's law-making powers favours decision-making also in another way, namely by allowing the building of 'package deals' across different law-making projects that are simultaneously considered by the EU institutions. Compromises can be struck not only within the text of a specific instrument (as is the case with one-off international treaty negotiations), but also more broadly between different sets of Council negotiations, so that a country that is forced to give in on, say, an immigration law directive can be compensated in a parallel legislative procedure dealing with, say, transport law.

The *effectiveness* of the law-making process in terms of its outcomes, and its compliance and dispute settlement regimes, is a fourth and very important factor in the choice of legal venue. In the statement quoted in the introduction of this chapter, Ludwig Krämer pointed out that international conventions 'lack the necessary authority on the one hand and effective enforcement on the other'. Although increasing efforts are made in international treaty practice to 'make treaties work'[32] through the use of more sophisticated non-compliance mechanisms,[33] judicial dispute settlement is still only rarely put in place by multilateral treaties and even more rarely used by the parties to those treaties.[34] EU law is rather different in this respect. The procedure of Articles 258 and following of the TFEU, through which the Commission can call the Member States to task for suspected infringements of EU law, as well as the principles of primacy and direct effect which require national courts to act as enforcement agencies of European law, lead to a situation in which states and private parties perform their obligations 'in the shadow of the courts', and in which compliance with legal obligations has become the norm, more so than for rules of public international law. In some cases, though, governments may prefer to avoid those constraints of EU law and opt for the more flexible compliance regime of international treaties. For example, the current resistance of the Member States against the 'unionization' of their bilateral investment treaties may be inspired also by their fear of losing the comfortable flexibility offered by the arbitration clauses of those bilateral treaties.[35]

[31] See n 23.

[32] See the title of a volume that discusses some recent advances in international practice: G Ulfstein (ed), *Making Treaties Work: Human Rights, Environment and Arms Control* (CUP, 2007).

[33] For an overview of compliance strategies under international legal regimes see Edith Brown Weiss, 'Rethinking Compliance with International Law' in Eyal Benvenisti and Moshe Hirsch (eds), *The Impact of International Law on International Cooperation—Theoretical Perspectives* (CUP, 2004) 134.

[34] The dispute settlement mechanism under the WTO Agreement is, of course, a major exception.

[35] H Wehland, 'Intra-EU Investment Agreements and Arbitration: Is European Community Law an Obstacle?' (2009) 58 *International and Comparative Law Quarterly* 297. For a discussion of the impact of the Lisbon Treaty, see J Chaisse, 'Promises and Pitfalls of the European Union Policy on Foreign Investment—How Will the New EU Competence on FDI Affect the Emerging Global Regime?' (2012) *Journal of International Economic Law* 1.

4. The Scope of Member States' Venue Choice: Political and Legal Constraints

Agenda-setting processes in the European Union have been the subject of important political science studies in recent years.[36] Those studies highlight that a decision-making process, on any given matter, is preceded by a phase of agenda-setting in which policies are *framed*, ie a set of social facts are identified as a problem requiring a policy response. This framing process is accompanied by discussion of the appropriate institutional framework (or *venue*) in which that policy response should be elaborated.[37] Once a decision-making process has started, questions of venue choice do not necessarily disappear from sight. The venue in which the process has started may still be contested by some of the participants. This happens frequently in the European Union.

The Member States, in particular, are leading actors of the EU process and can express their venue preferences within that context. The European Council and the EU Council of Ministers act as major 'signposting' institutions within the EU decision-making process. Since these institutions are composed of representatives of the EU Member States, they are in a perfect position to decide whether to pursue an EU law course of action proposed to them by the Commission[38] or, on the contrary, decide that an alternative international law-making project would be possible and preferable. Increasingly, though, the European Council does not limit itself to this passive signposting role but is itself the political source of EU legislation which it 'invites' the Commission to draft.[39] Given the particular institutional setting of the European Council, its participants are inclined to think that the EU legal order provides the best solution to a given problem, and will not often express their collective preference for some alternative, non-EU based, law-making venue. Thus, the European Council, in a somewhat paradoxical way, generally expresses a preference for law-making in an institutional context, that of the EU, which provides for a stronger role of non-state institutions in the decision-making and for stricter limits of national sovereignty once the law-making process has been achieved.

At a more day-to-day level, Council working groups act as the institutional settings in which the vast majority of Council decisions are effectively adopted, but they are also the settings in which Commission proposals occasionally get stranded so that they never reach the higher level echelons of Committee of Permanent Representatives (COREPER) and the Council of Ministers meetings. One of the reasons why Member State officials in those working groups may be unwilling to support a Commission initiative is because they may want to privilege an international law-making project in which their country is, or could be, involved. Since national officials representing their Member State in a Council working group are usually subject-matter specialists, they often simultaneously act as the national representatives in other international fora dealing with the same subject matter, and may behave as umpires who decide, together with their homologues from other Member States,

[36] B Guy Peters, 'Agenda-Setting in the European Union' in Jeremy Richardson (ed), *European Union: Power and Policymaking* (2nd edn, Routledge, 2001) 77; S Princen, *Agenda-Setting in the European Union* (Palgrave Macmillan, 2009); S Princen, 'Agenda-Setting Strategies in EU Policy Processes' (2011) 18(7) *Journal of European Public Policy* 927; J Tallberg, 'The Agenda-Shaping Powers of the EU Council Presidency' (2003) 10(1) *Journal of European Public Policy* 1; V Guiraudon, 'European Integration and Migration Policy: Vertical Policy-Making as Venue Shopping' (2000) 38 *Journal of Common Market Studies* 251; M Rhinard, *Framing Europe: The Policy Shaping Strategies of the European Commission* (Republic of Letters Publishing, 2010).

[37] See in particular S Princen, *Agenda-Setting in the European Union* (ibid), ch 2.

[38] The Commission initiates almost all EU legislation, and also produces documents that explain the reasons why, in its view, EU action is justified or necessary: explanatory memoranda accompany the proposal itself but, further upstream, the Commission often seeks to 'pave the way' for EU action by means of Green or White Papers.

[39] See eg the 'invitations' to propose new legislation which were addressed to the Commission by the European Council in its Conclusions of 23/24 June 2011, paras 4, 22, 25 and 29.

on whether it is worth pursuing a regulatory project in the EU context or rather diverting it to some alternative international law-making venue.

Other international organizations may, through the activity of their secretariats, try to 'occupy the field', by launching preparatory work on a law-making treaty and co-opting, for that purpose, the national government officials in charge of the subject matter. Those co-opted national officials may, in turn, feel reluctant towards rival initiatives that might arise from the side of the European Commission. This may seem to be a very mundane explanation, but as a matter of fact, it regularly happens that a subject matter is randomly embedded within an organization even though it could equally have been dealt with by another organization. Rivalries between universal organizations, such as the UN and the ILO, or the WTO and UNESCO, are well-known, but there are similar rivalries between the EU and other organizations that operate in the same policy fields. One important consideration, in this context, is that the EU itself is not a member of many global organizations, so it cannot effectively act to stop an initiative that is launched within those organizations. For example, the European Union, not being a member of the ILO, could not directly prevent the ILO from launching the process leading to the adoption, in June 2011, of the Convention No 189 Concerning Decent Work for Domestic Workers; it could only have counteracted this process by acting 'from the outside', that is, by submitting a Commission proposal for legislation on the same subject. Such a proposal would have been within the scope of EU legislative competences but it would likely have raised opposition within the Council working groups composed of national experts who were—at the same time—involved in the ILO law-making process. So, the Commission preferred not to act and the EU, as an organization, remained on the sidelines of this important law-making project.[40]

Looking at this question from the perspective of the EU Member States, we can see that their choice of venue is affected both by the dynamics of the EU's domestic legislative process and by the participatory structure of the competing international law-making venue. As long as the pertinent international setting does not allow for the EU itself to participate,[41] it is for the Member States to participate individually or jointly as subjects of the international legal order, and/or to allow for the EU to legislate on the same matter. However, that choice of the Member States is not only constrained by the *political* pressure that the Commission and the European Parliament may bring to bear in favour of the 'EU route', but also by the *legal* implications of the EU's internal competence allocation, which affects states' individual room for manoeuvre at the international level. In areas of EU exclusive competence, the choice of international or EU law-making venues depends on the EU institutions' decisions, possibly outweighing preferences of individual Member States. Where the EU is not itself represented in the international forum but holds exclusive competence under EU law with regard to (part of) the subject matter in question, Member States need to act as 'trustees' of the EU.[42] In Opinion 2/91 *(ILO Convention)*, the Court held that where constitutional rules of the international organization presented an obstacle to the EU's exercise of competence, such competence would need to 'be exercised through the medium

[40] EU support from the sidelines came in the form of a European Parliament resolution of 12 May 2011 'on the proposed ILO convention supplemented by a recommendation for domestic workers', P7_TA(2011)0237 which called on the EU Member States to ratify and implement the convention quickly (point 1 of the resolution).

[41] See eg Art 1 of the ILO Constitution, according to which ILO membership is only open to states; Art 19(5)(d) requires ILO Members to ratify Conventions, even where other authorities' consent is needed internally. Interestingly, although the EU is not a member of the Council of Europe, it does participate in most Council of Europe conventions by means of ad hoc participation clauses in those conventions. See, generally, F Hoffmeister, 'Outsider or Frontrunner? Recent Developments under International and European Law on the Status of the European Union in International Organizations and Treaty Bodies' (2007) 44 *CML Rev* 1.

[42] M Cremona, 'Member States as Trustees of the Union Interest: Participating in International Agreements on Behalf of the European Union' in A Arnull, C Barnard, M Dougan and E Spaventa (eds), *A Constitutional Order of States? Essays in EU Law in Honour of Alan Dashwood* (Hart Publishing, 2011) 435.

of the Member States acting jointly in the Community's interest'.[43] Following the choice of an international venue, this can oblige Member States to 'establish a joint negotiating position within the framework of the common institutions' which is binding on them.[44]

In addition to the existence of EU exclusive competence, there exist further legal constraints on the Member States' scope of venue choice precisely because of their EU membership. While the EU Treaties reiterate the Member States' retained room for manoeuvre on the international plane in a variety of areas,[45] the necessity to exercise their autonomous powers in the light of their EU membership is also highlighted.[46] Member States need to exercise retained competence 'in a manner consistent with [EU] law'.[47] In addition to Treaty obligations related primarily to the internal market,[48] the Court identified Member States' loyalty obligations under [now] Article 4(3) TEU, which affect their capacity of contributing to law-making in international fora,[49] even in the absence of EU exclusive competence.[50] Those loyalty obligations apply during the negotiation, conclusion, and fulfilment of international agreements.[51] Most relevant for our present assessment of the scope of their venue choice seems to be the Member States' 'special duties of action and abstention', which arise once there has been a 'point of departure for concerted [EU] action' in the context of international treaty negotiations.[52] In *PFOS*, the Court concluded that

[43] Opinion 2/91, *ILO Convention No 170* [1993] ECR I-1061, paras 5, 37; confirmed in Case C-45/07 *Commission v Greece (IMO)* [2009] ECR I-701, para 31.

[44] M Cremona, n 42, 439.

[45] The Member States explicitly retained competence to negotiate in international bodies and to conclude international agreements with third countries and international organizations in certain policy areas, for which they share competence with the EU; see eg Art 4(3) TFEU (research); Arts 4(4), 209(2) 2, 211, 212(3), 214(1)(3) TFEU (the exercise of EU competence in the areas of development cooperation and humanitarian aid to carry out activities and conduct common policy shall not prevent the Member States from exercising theirs); Art 191(4) TFEU (protection of the environment); Art 207(6) TFEU (Common Commercial Policy (CCP) shall not affect the delimitation of competences between the EU and the Member State, ie shall not affect other areas for which Member States retained competence). The Member States have also declared the retention of their powers 'in relation to the formulation and conduct of [their] foreign policy, [their] national diplomatic service, relations with third countries and participation in international organizations, including [their] membership of the Security Council of the United Nations' upon the adoption of the Lisbon Treaty (Declaration No 14).

[46] Arts 4(3), 20 TEU; Arts 222, 344, 347, 351(2) TFEU; see also Arts 24(3), 32, 34 TEU, even though compliance is to be ensured by the Council and the High Representative, not the ECJ (Arts 24(3), last sentence, 275 TFEU).

[47] Case C-124/95 *The Queen, ex parte Centro-Com Srl v HM Treasury and Bank of England* [1997] ECR I-81, para 25. For a detailed discussion of the ECJ's formula relating to the applicability of EU law where states exercise retained powers, see L Azoulai, 'The "Retained Powers" Formula in the Case Law of the European Court of Justice: EU Law as Total Law?' (2011) 4(2) *European Journal of Legal Studies* 192.

[48] eg Case C-466/98 *Commission v UK* [2002] ECR I-9427, para 41 (concerning the freedom of establishment, (now) Art 49 TFEU); Case C-205/06 *Commission v Austria* [2009] ECR I-1301, and Case C-249/06 *Commission v Sweden* [2009] ECR I-1335 (obligation to eliminate incompatibilities of pre-EU treaties with the EU Treaties, (now) Art 351(2) TFEU); Case C-459/03, *Commission v Ireland (MOX Plant)* [2006] ECR I-4635 (obligation to submit intra-EU Member State disputes to the ECJ, (now) Art 344 TFEU).

[49] Case C-45/07 *Commission v Greece (IMO)* [2009] ECR I-701; Case C-246/07 *Commission v Sweden* [2010] ECR I-3317.

[50] Case C-246/07 *Commission v Sweden* [2010] ECR I-3317, para 71, with reference to Case C-266/03 *Commission v Luxembourg* [2005] ECR I-4805, para 58, and Case C-433/03 *Commission v Germany* [2005] ECR I-6985, para 64.

[51] Case C-25/94 *Commission v Council (FAO)* [1996] ECR I-1469, para 48. The literature on this external duty of loyalty includes: M Cremona, 'Defending the Community Interest: the Duties of Cooperation and Compliance', in M Cremona and B De Witte (eds), *EU Foreign Relations Law: Constitutional Fundamentals* (Hart Publishing, 2008) 125; C Hillion, 'Mixity and Coherence in EU External Relations: The Significance of the "Duty of Cooperation"' in C Hillion and P Koutrakos (eds), *Mixed Agreements Revisited* (Hart Publishing, 2010) 87; E Neframi, 'The Duty of Loyalty: Rethinking its Scope through its Application in the Field of EU External Relations' (2010) 47 *CML Rev* 323; A Thies, 'The PFOS Decision of the ECJ: The Member States' Obligation to Refrain from Unilateral Action in Areas of Shared Competence', in J Díez-Hochleitner, C Martínez Capdevila and I Blázquez Navarro (eds), *Recent Trends in the Case Law of the Court of Justice of the EU (2008–2011)*, (La Ley, Grupo Wolters Kluwer, forthcoming).

[52] Case C-266/03 *Commission v Luxembourg* [2005] ECR I-4805, para 59, and Case C-433/03 *Commission v Germany* [2005] ECR I-6985, para 65. See also the wording of Art 4(3) TEU, which refers to the overall principle of 'sincere cooperation' in 'carrying out the tasks which flow from the Treaties' as well as the Member State obligations to: (a) 'ensure the fulfilment of the obligations arising out of the Treaties or resulting from the acts

Sweden had been under an obligation to refrain completely from unilateral action that could lead to the amendment of an Annex to the Stockholm Convention on Persistent Organic Pollutants.[53] While both the EU and its Member States are parties to this Convention—and share competence in the area of environmental policy in principle (see Article 4(2)(e) TFEU)—the Court held that Sweden's unilateral action interfered with an existing Council strategy, which arguably concerned both the content of the EU's own proposal under the Stockholm Convention and an envisaged sequence of EU and international law-making regarding the regulation of the substance in question.[54] The Court added that Sweden was in breach of its loyalty obligations, as its action could have consequences for the EU through the 'adoption of international legal rules', which are binding on all parties to the Convention.[55] In sum, the Court has identified far-reaching legal constraints of the Member States' international law-making activities where the EU and its Member States are both active in the same international forum. In this way, venue choices of the Member States are crucially affected by venue choices made—in the same subject area—by the European Union itself.

5. The European Union's Own Venue Choice: Between 'Domestic' Legislation and External Law-Making

To complete the venue choice panorama, this last section assesses the factors that may push the EU itself to participate in broader international law-making processes instead of focusing on internal EU legislation for a given subject matter. We suggest that the previously discussed policy considerations and factors influencing such venue choice (see section 3), namely path dependence, geographical nature of the subject, ease of decision-making and effectiveness, are as relevant for the choices made by the EU as an organization as they are for its Member States. However, given the EU's constitutional specificities—including the mixture of supranational and intergovernmental elements in its decision-making, the increased emphasis on its international role,[56] and the variable recognition of the EU as a 'global law-maker'—there are additional aspects worth addressing here. As in the previous section of this chapter, we propose to distinguish between legal and political considerations relevant for the EU's choice to participate in international law-making rather than legislating domestically, and vice versa.

What are the *legal* constraints or considerations concerning the EU's venue choice? It is important to highlight that the competence allocation under the Treaties does not distinguish, in principle, between internal and external competences of the EU[57] and therefore does not establish any 'venue preference'. In other words, where the EU has competence to legislate, it can do so in any accessible venue. The legal constraints in this context stem mainly from the international legal order that occasionally prevents the EU from contributing directly, as an organization, to international law-making (see previous section on the legal constraints of the EU Member States).[58] From an internal EU law perspective, the EU's scope of venue choice is constrained only marginally by the principle of proportionality and

of the institutions of the Union'; (b) to 'facilitate the achievement of the Union's tasks'; and (c) to 'refrain from any measure which could jeopardise the attainment of the Union's objectives'.

[53] Case C-246/07 *Commission v Sweden* [2010] ECR I-3317 (*PFOS*); M Cremona, 'Case Comment on C-246/07, *Commission v Sweden* (PFOS)' (2011) 48 *CML Rev* 1639.

[54] C-246/07 *Commission v Sweden* [2010] ECR I-3317, paras 85, 89, 91. On sequencing between EU and international law-making, see the next section of this chapter.

[55] Ibid, paras 100 et seq. The Court has since been criticized for establishing a Member States' 'duty to remain silent', which could lead to a stalemate in EU external action altogether and thus even negatively affect the attainment of external objectives. A Delgado Casteleiro and J Larik, 'The Duty to Remain Silent: Limitless Loyalty in EU External Relations' (2011) 36 *European Law Review* 524.

[56] Arts 3(5), 21, 22 TEU.

[57] Art 5(1) and (2) TEU, Title I of the TFEU (Categories and areas of Union competence).

[58] See text at n 41 and following.

the EU institutions' loyalty obligations towards the Member States. Accordingly, the EU should not bind or commit the Member States beyond 'what is necessary to achieve the objectives of the Treaties' (Article 5(4) TEU) through the conclusion of international agreements,[59] and possibly take account of their established international links and policy priorities (although, so far, the Court of Justice has not been particularly demanding in defining the EU's loyalty obligations towards its Member States).

In the particular context of the negotiation and conclusion of international agreements in areas not fully covered by EU competence, the use and implications of *mixed agreements* constitute a further legal consideration relevant for the EU's venue choice. Member States can make their authorization of the opening of negotiations by the Commission conditional upon the conclusion of the envisaged agreement as a 'mixed' one, thereby necessitating the ratification of that agreement by both the EU and all of its Member States.[60] Such condition can be included in the 'negotiating directives' that are adopted by the Council, normally acting by qualified majority (Article 218(2), (4), (8) TFEU). This enables Member States to influence the negotiation process and the content of the agreement; and even entrusting the Commission with the negotiation on behalf of the Member States does not pre-empt the national ratification process.[61] The use of mixed agreements might therefore facilitate the EU's choice of 'going external', as it allows for the involvement, input and 'control' by both the EU institutions and the Member States in the negotiation and conclusion of international agreements. At the same time, however, the use of mixed agreements may complicate the decision-making process. While internal law-making procedures now generally require only the support of a qualified majority of states, the conclusion of an international agreement—when it is mixed—requires consensus among all the Member States and the EU itself. Furthermore, the need for 28 decisions to conclude and ratify the agreement can lead to considerable delays in the law-making process.[62]

Turning to the *political* considerations relevant for the EU's venue choice, we can identify an EU-specific set of factors which lead the EU institutions to engage in international law-making. As discussed in other chapters of this book, the EU's 'governance mode' (de Búrca) as well as the EU's interest in securing its own global competitiveness (Cremona) are important factors that explain the Union's attempts to engage in international law-making in order to *export* existing EU law. This can happen in several ways, either by the EU and/or its Member States participating in multilateral negotiations in which they promote the adoption of pre-existing EU norms, standards and values;[63] or by means of bilateral agreements in which the EU seeks to incorporate its own regulatory norms (as is often

[59] See eg Arts 4(3), 5(4) TEU. While Art 5(4) TEU does not limit the application of the principle of proportionality to any particular kind of EU action, the Protocol (No 2) on the Application of the Principles of Subsidiarity and Proportionality focuses on 'legislative acts' only. We suggest, however, that the EU institutions need to 'consult widely', 'tak[ing] into account the regional and local dimension of the action envisaged' (Art 2, Protocol No 2) also before proposing the negotiation of, or accession to, an international agreement, and to provide a statement on the 'financial impact' and the 'implications for the rules to be put in place by Member States', and must 'take account of the need for any burden, whether financial or administrative, falling upon the Union, national governments, regional or local authorities, economic operators and citizens, to be minimized and commensurate with the objectives to be achieved' (Art 5, Protocol No 2).

[60] For a detailed study of mixed agreements see C Hillion and P Koutrakos (eds), *Mixed Agreements Revisited,* n 51.

[61] F Hoffmeister, 'Curse or Blessing? Mixed Agreements in Recent Practice' in Hillion and P Koutrakos (eds), *Mixed Agreements Revisited,* n 51, 249, 254.

[62] Ibid, 256.

[63] According to Arts 2 and 3(1) and (5) TEU, the EU is 'founded on the values of respect for human dignity, freedom, democracy, equality, the rule of law and respect for human rights', which are 'common to the Member States', and is committed to 'uphold and promote its values and interests and contribute to the protection of its citizens' in its relations with the wider world. For a discussion of categories of values, and ways for promoting them, see M Cremona, 'Values in EU Foreign Policy' in M Evans and P Koutrakos (eds), *Beyond the Established Legal Orders: Policy Interconnections between the EU and the Rest of the World* (Hart Publishing, 2011), 275.

the case with agreements with neighbouring countries and candidates of accession),[64] or, alternatively, seeks to incorporate pre-existing multilateral norms which the EU approves of (as is more often the case in agreements with more distant countries).

We find equally frequent examples of 'downstream' sequencing, whereby international law-making is followed by EU legal implementation rather than Member State implementation. Such downstream sequencing is made easier when the European Union is a member of the broader international organization and can therefore, with or without its Member States, influence the content of the international norm which will be implemented at EU level. This is, for example, the case with food standards which are set at the global level by the Codex Alimentarius Commission, of which the EU became a member in 2003, forty years after the Commission was created.[65] Similarly, the recent accession of the EU to the Hague Conference on Private International Law[66] allows the EU (in fact: the Commission) to be more directly involved in the coordination between the 'Brussels' and 'Hague' tracks of private international law harmonization. As the Commission put it in its explanatory memorandum of the accession decision, 'membership would enable the Community to fully participate in the negotiations of [Hague] conventions in areas of its competence by expressing its views and positions and ensuring the consistency and coherence between its own rules and envisaged international instruments'.[67]

Sequencing can also operate both ways, from the European to the international level and back again, within one and the same issue area. A recent example is offered by the protection of the rights of disabled persons. After having enacted, in 2000, a Directive which prohibits discrimination in employment on a number of grounds, including disability,[68] the EU claimed participation in the negotiation of a much broader UN instrument on the rights of disabled persons. In that negotiation arena, the EU was an active and influential participant. It sought to 'export' its own internal disability regime on the international stage, but was eventually pushed by a coalition of NGOs and some other states' delegates to accept a broader range of legal obligations which focuses on substantive entitlements rather than 'just' non-discrimination.[69] Thereby, the UN Convention, as adopted in 2006 and ratified by the EU, now forms the basis for new implementing measures at the EU level (as well as by the EU Member States separately).[70]

There are, in fact, many cases of 'co-evolution',[71] whereby law-making in the European Union develops in close connection with corresponding international law-making enterprises. Possibly the richest area of interplay between EU instruments and international

[64] eg the Agreement on the establishment of a European Common Aviation Area which the EC and its Member States concluded in 2006 with eleven European countries that were either candidates for accession or 'new neighbours' [2006] OJ L285.

[65] Council Decision (EC) 2003/822 of 17 November 2003 on the accession of the European Community to the Codex Alimentarius Commission [2003] OJ L309. See M Masson-Matthee, *The Codex Alimentarius Commission and Its Standards* (TMC Asser Press, 2007).

[66] Council Decision (EC) 2006/719 of 5 October 2006 on the accession of the Community to the Hague Conference on Private International Law [2006] OJ L297.

[67] European Commission, Proposal for a Council Decision on the accession of the European Community to the Hague Conference on Private International Law, COM (2005) 639 of 9 December 2005, 2.

[68] Council Directive (EC) 2000/78 of 27 November 2000 establishing a general framework for equal treatment in employment and occupation [2000] OJ L303.

[69] G de Búrca, 'The EU in the Negotiation of the UN Disability Convention' (2010) 35 *European Law Review* 174.

[70] The need for implementing measures by the EU is acknowledged in the Commission's communication *European Disability Strategy 2010–2020: A Renewed Commitment to a Barrier-Free Europe*, COM (2010) 636 of 15 November 2010.

[71] On that notion, see S Oberthür and T Gehring, 'Conceptual Foundations of Institutional Interaction' in S Oberthür and T Gehring (eds), *Institutional Interaction in Global Environmental Governance: Synergy and Conflict among International and EU Policies* (MIT Press, 2006), 19, 30.

regimes is that of environmental protection, where one finds all kinds of permutations.[72] A striking example, in a very different policy area, is that of the legal regulation of transfrontier television. In the late 1980s, with the advent of cable and satellite distribution of television programmes, the question arose of how to ensure the free flow of television programmes whilst allowing the single countries to preserve their autonomous media policies. The issue was put on the agenda of the Council of Europe and the European Community almost simultaneously. Parallel and rival law-making projects ensued, and it took a decision of the European Council at its Rhodes summit of 1998 to streamline both projects so that the resulting EC Directive on transfrontier television and the Council of Europe's Convention on Transfrontier Television would contain similar and mutually compatible rules.[73] Since that time, the European Union directive has been heavily amended on two occasions, and the Council of Europe sought to 'catch up' by adapting its own Convention to the changing regulatory regime of the European Union. In this case, the co-evolution is one in which the EU has acquired a clear leadership.[74] The autonomy of the EU legal order is, quite frequently, preserved by the use of disconnection clauses, which appear most frequently in Council of Europe conventions: those clauses state that EU law will prevail over the provisions of the convention in the internal relations between EU states, and thereby 'disconnect' the internal EU law regime from the content of the convention and allow that EU regime to develop autonomously in the future.[75]

6. Conclusion

The architecture of international cooperation[76] is complex and rather opaque. For European countries, the EU forms a central framework for their cooperation, which is relatively transparent and based on well-tested rules and routines. But the less obvious international venues for cooperation remain available, and may be preferred in many instances over the 'main route' of the EU. Venue choice is thus an important element of 'legal agenda-setting' and, more broadly, a pervasive question in the politics of institutional choice in European countries.

We have seen that the EU Member States are often able to choose between a variety of law-making venues, either in parallel or subsequently. The nature and legal framework of the EU also lends itself to venue choices which are not exclusive but complementary, in that they involve the combined use of various law-making venues in a given time sequence. The wide scope of the EU's domestic legislative competences, and the advanced level of harmonization (often based on existing national law of the Member States) establish a solid point of departure for the export of existing EU law to the international legal order. At the same time, the existing international law obligations imposed on individual EU Member States and the EU's growing ambitions to contribute to the development of international law increasingly give rise to the opposite phenomenon of import of international law into the

[72] See a collection of essays dealing with specific areas of environmental regulation from this perspective of overlapping regulatory regimes: S Oberthür and T Gehring (eds), ibid. See, further, the chapters by Marín Durán, Morgera and Scott and Rajamani in this volume, as well as D Kelemen, 'Globalizing European Union Environmental Policy' (2010) 17(3) *Journal of European Public Policy* 335–349.

[73] European Council Conclusions, Rhodes 2–3 December 1988, 8. See J Harrison and L Woods, *European Broadcasting Law and Policy* (CUP, 2007), ch 5.

[74] For a recent account of the co-evolution between the two legal regimes, see Udo Fink, T Keber and P Roguski, 'Die Zukunft der Medienregulierung im Europarat' (2011) *Zeitschrift für Urheber- und Medienrecht* 292.

[75] For an analysis and discussion of this practice, see M Cremona, 'Disconnection Clauses in EC Law and Practice' in C Hillion and P Koutrakos (eds), *Mixed Agreements Revisited*, n 51, 160; F Hoffmeister, 'The Contribution of EU Practice to International Law' in M Cremona (ed), *Developments in EU External Relations Law* (OUP, 2008) 37, 66; C Economides and A Kolliopoulos, 'La clause de déconnexion en faveur du droit communautaire: une pratique critiquable' (2006) 110(2) *Revue générale de droit international public* 273.

[76] We borrow the expression used by K Raustiala, 'The Architecture of International Cooperation: Transgovernmental Networks and the Future of International Law' (2002) 43(1) *Virginia Journal of International Law* 1.

EU domestic legal order. In many cases, the EU's multi-layered structure and the multitude of actors involved (EU institutions, Member States, third countries, international secretariats, NGOs) lead to simultaneous law-making activities in EU and international venues, with the resulting potential for synergy and danger of norm conflicts.[77] Looking at the EU's overall contribution to the making of international law, the prior adoption of EU legislation may either complicate or facilitate subsequent international standard-setting on the same issues. The existence of an 'EU template' may focus the international negotiation on the advantages and drawbacks of that existing piece of legislation, but it may also render the EU countries less flexible than they would otherwise be for fear of agreeing international standards that would require the subsequent amendment of existing EU laws, with all the political difficulties that may inhere in such amendments.

[77] See, for a general discussion of the consequences of multilevel regulation, R A Wessel and J Wouters, 'The Phenomenon of Multilevel Regulation: Interactions between Global, EU and National Regulatory Spheres' (2007) *International Organizations Law Review* 259.

3

EU External Relations: The Governance Mode of Foreign Policy

*Gráinne de Búrca**

1. Introduction

This chapter revisits the familiar question of the distinctive nature of EU foreign policy and external relations. It begins from a similar starting point from which much of the existing literature on the EU as a normative or civilian power begins, in assuming that there is something fairly distinctive about the way the EU conducts its external relations. But it departs from much of that literature in eschewing any claim that the EU is in some way more virtuous than other international actors, or that it is motivated mainly by values, principles or norms, rather than by its own interests.[1] Rejecting the assumption of a sharp distinction between the EU's promotion of values and its pursuit of interests, the analysis focuses instead on what I call the EU's *governance mode of foreign policy*, namely its tendency to act collectively rather than unilaterally, and to establish and institutionalize stable external governance systems on a wide range of issue areas. The first part explains in further detail what I mean by the governance mode of foreign policy. The second part briefly outlines the evolution of the EU's external role. The third part sets out a number of examples of the EU's governance mode of external relations, and the final part raises a number of questions about the impact of the governance mode in international relations.

2. Distinguishing the Governance Mode from Conceptions of 'Normative Power' Europe

There is a very large and rich international relations literature—mostly written by Europeans[2]—on the EU as a global actor. This literature in different ways interrogates the character of EU external power and policy, often distinguishing it from the foreign policy of states, and sometimes with the United States functioning as an implicit or explicit comparator. A range of different terms has been used to define the distinctive nature of the EU's international identity and the particular character of its external role. One of the most resilient and popular of these terms is that of the EU as a normative power. Although the notion of a normative power is itself a contested one, it is used to refer broadly to the

* Thanks to Marise Cremona, Ryan Goodman, Andy Hurrell, Bob Keohane, Benedict Kingsbury, Joris Larik, Gianluigi Palombella, Joanne Scott, Joseph Weiler, the students and participants at the NYU Straus Colloquium 2010, and the participants at the *Conference on The Legal Dimension of Global Governance: What Role for the EU?*, at the University of Copenhagen, 2011, for their valuable comments and suggestions.

[1] See also R Keohane, 'Governance in a Partially Globalized World' (2001) 95 *American Political Science Review* 1–13 on the necessary co-existence of norms and values with self-interest within governance institutions. For the European Court of Justice (ECJ)'s assertion that the EU is bound by the principles (values?) articulated in Art 3(5) TEU, see Case C-366/10 *ATAA v Secretary of State for Energy and Climate Change* (ECJ, 21 December 2011), para 101.

[2] On the perceptions of non-European actors about Europe's self-presentation as a normative actor, see A Gerrits (ed), *Normative Power Europe in a Changing World: A Discussion* (Netherlands Institute of International Relations Clingendael, 2009): <http://www.clingendael.nl/publications/2009/20091200_cesp_paper_gerrits.pdf>; D Sicurelli, *The EU's Africa Policy: Norms, Interests and Impact* (Ashgate Publishing, 2010) and S Lucarelli and L Fioramonti (eds), *External Perceptions of the European Union as a Global Actor* (Routledge, 2010).

EU's 'promotion of norms in a normative way'—ie the promotion of multilateralism and of values such as respect for international law, human rights and democracy, through non-coercive means.[3] A related term used to describe the EU's external role is as that of a *soft* power,[4] as well as a *structural* power which can shape and influence global structures and rules.[5] The EU is also described as a *civilian* power, in contrast to a military power,[6] while others have emphasized its *civilizing* power, in an adaptation of Norbert Elias's sociological idea of the civilizing process.[7] Other characterizations are of the EU as a global power,[8] a security regime,[9] an empire,[10] a normative empire[11] and a normative hegemon.[12]

Each of these different but related accounts captures something of what is believed or perceived to be the distinctive character of the EU's external role to date, emphasizing its resources, its goals, its ways of pursuing those goals, or some combination of the three. The argument I want to make shares certain premises of this literature, but aims to draw attention to a significant dimension of the EU's international relations character which differs from the emphasis of existing 'normative' or 'civilian' accounts. In describing the EU as pursuing a governance mode of foreign policy, the features I want to emphasize are: (1) the EU's preference for the creation of stable, long-term, institutionalized relationships with external states and entities; and (2) its frequent use of regulatory frameworks involving common articulated goals and relatively broad participation to coordinate policy externally in many of the same ways as it does internally. This preference seems to be partly a product of the EU's externalization of practices which developed internally as part of its original project of European transnational integration, although the EU's choice of external strategy is obviously also shaped by the international environment within which it acts.[13]

[3] I Manners, 'Normative Power Europe: A Contradiction in Terms?' (2002) 40 JCMS 235–58. H Sjursen, 'The EU as a normative power: How can this be?' (2006) 13 JEPP 235–251 and for a critical reflection see T Diez 'Constructing the Self and Changing Others: Reconsidering Normative Power Europe' (2005) 33 *Millenium: Journal of International Studies* 613–636. Also R Whitman (ed), *Normative Power Europe: Empirical and Theoretical Perspectives* (Palgrave, 2011). For a recent defence of the term as an ideal-type, see T Forsberg, 'Normative Power Europe, Once Again: A Conceptual Analysis of an Ideal-type' (2011) 49 JCMS 1183.

[4] The use of 'soft power' has been influentially defined as A's capacity to get B to want what A wants, as opposed to hard power, defined as A's capacity to get B to do something that B would not otherwise do: see JS Nye, *Soft Power: The Means to Success in World Politics* (Public Affairs, 2004). See also *The Future of Power* (Public Affairs, 2011), in which he defines smart power as the ability to combine hard and soft power resources into effective strategies. Also R Kagan, *Of Paradise and Power, America and Europe in the New World Order* (Knopf, 2003).

[5] On structural power see MN Barnett and R Duvall, *Power and Global Governance* (CUP, 2004), ch 1, and on the EU as exercising structural power, see S Keukeleire and J MacNaughtan, *The Foreign Policy of the European Union* (Palgrave Macmillan, 2008).

[6] See F Duchêne, 'The European Community and the Uncertainties of Interdependence' in M Kohnstamm and W Hager (eds), *A Nation Writ Large? Foreign Policy Problems before the European Community* (Macmillan, 1973); M Tèlo, *Europe: A Civilian Power?* (Palgrave Macmillan, 2006). For a critical commentary on the 'civilian' and 'normative' Europe debates, see J Orbie, 'Civilian Power Europe: Review of the Original and Current Debates' (2006) 40 *Cooperation and Conflict* 123.

[7] A Linklater, 'A European Civilizing Process' in C Hill and M Smith (eds), *International Relations and the European Union* (OUP, 2005).

[8] C Bretherton and J Vogler, *The European Union as a Global Actor* (2nd edn, Routledge, 2006) and J Rogers, 'From "Civilian Power" to "Global Power": Explicating the EU's "Grand Strategy" through the use of Discourse Theory' (2009) 47 JCMS 831–862. For an interesting approach which focuses on the distinctive political ethics of the EU, see R Howse and K Nicolaidis, 'This is my EUtopia' (2002) 40 JCMS 767–792.

[9] F Charillon, 'The EU as a Security Regime' (2005) 10 *European Foreign Affairs Review* 517–533.

[10] J Zielonka, *Europe as Empire: The Nature of the Enlarged European Union* (OUP, 2006).

[11] Z Laïdi, 'The Unintended Consequences of European Power' (2007) 5 *Les Cahiers européens de Sciences Po.*

[12] H Haukkala, 'The EU as a Regional Normative Hegemon: The Case of European Neighbourhood Policy', in RG Whitman (ed), *Normative Power Europe: Empirical and Theoretical Perspectives* (Palgrave Macmillan, 2011) 45–64.

[13] For other accounts which emphasize the EU's tendency to externalize its internal practices, see C Bretherton and J Vogler, *The European Union as a Global Actor* (2nd edn, Routledge, 2006), K Smith, *European Union Foreign Policy in a Changing World* (2nd edn, Polity, 2008) and its isomorphic tendencies, see F Bicchi, 'One Size Fits All: Normative Power Europe and the Mediterranean' (2006) 13 JEPP 286–303.

Type of Goal: Mode of Pursuit:	Possession	Milieu
Unilateralist	A	B
Collective	C	D

Figure 1

To sharpen the distinction between the governance analysis of EU foreign policy outlined in this chapter, and the broader premises of the normative and civilian power literature, the governance analysis does not rest on a claim that the EU pursues a generally liberal foreign policy, nor on the EU's lack of significant reliance on military power.[14] Neither does it focus on the question whether or not the EU is a more virtuous international actor than others.[15] As Laïdi puts it, Europe should be considered 'as a living, complex and contradictory actor and not as an idealized actor whose preference for norms is seen as a guarantee of its good faith and disinterestedness'.[16] Nevertheless, in keeping with much of the EU foreign policy literature, this chapter starts from the premise that there is something reasonably distinctive about the way the EU conducts its external relations, and seeks to elucidate that distinctiveness further.

In order to do so, it is useful to think of the pursuit of international relations, or foreign-policy making, in terms of a matrix with two axes. The first axis refers to the goals pursued (using Wolfers' distinction between possession goals and milieu goals)[17] and the second axis refers to the mode of pursuit (ranging from unilateralist to collective) of these goals. Possession goals, on Wolfer's analysis, are those which focus on the protection or strengthening of national possessions and resources, such as territory, trade advantages, and domestic sovereignty. The focus of milieu goals, on the other hand, is on shaping and stabilizing the surrounding and international environment. Milieu goals emphasize the promotion of long-term security, stability, sustainability, coöperation and peaceful international relations. These are depicted in the table below.

The difference between Wolfers' two types of goals is obviously a matter of degree since both can be understood as involving the pursuit of national interests. Nevertheless, it seems that milieu goals, unlike possession goals, generally require the collaboration of other actors and are unlikely to be capable of being unilaterally pursued or autonomously achieved (even if unilateral action may be used to trigger collaboration). States may attempt to secure regional peace, stability and democratization by using military might, but these goals are highly unlikely to be achieved through the unilateral use of force. And while the EU may attempt to promote action to combat climate change by adopting unilateral measures to

[14] See eg H Maull, 'Germany and Japan: The New Civilian Powers' (1990) 5 *Foreign Affairs* 91–106.

[15] In a recent book edited by N Tocci, *Who is a Normative Foreign Policy Actor: The EU and its Global Partners* (CEPS, 2008) a common analytical framework was applied to the EU and four other major powers (China, India, Russia and the US) to determine whether or not they were to be considered primarily as: (a) a normative power; (b) a realpolitik power; (c) an imperial power; or (d) a status quo power. The editors concluded that according to each of these actors, they were primarily a normative power, even though they had quite different accounts of how this was the case.

[16] Z Laïdi, 'European Preferences and their Reception' in Z Laïdi (ed), *European Foreign Policy in a Globalized World* (Routledge, 2009) 18.

[17] A Wolfers, *Discord and Collaboration: Essays on International Politics* (Johns Hopkins University Press, 1965) ch 5, in particular 73–76.

reduce the emissions of third-country aircraft, it is unlikely to achieve significant results until it secures the collaboration of third countries in its effort to reduce emissions.[18]

My argument about the distinctiveness of the EU's pursuit of external relations or foreign policy rests on two claims. The first is that the EU, in acting to advance its goals, generally seeks to act by collective (sometimes, but not always multilateral) rather than unilateral means. Again, I am not arguing that the EU seeks only or even mainly the pursuit of milieu rather than possession goals, as some accounts of the EU as a normative policy actor may imply. Rather, I suggest that while the EU's pursuit of external relations can be located to a significant extent—although not as much as the preferred self-image of the EU as a global actor would indicate—within Box D, involving the collective or multilaterialist pursuit of milieu-type goals, a substantial amount of EU external activity can also be located within Box C, involving the pursuit of possession goals, such as access to energy, trade preferences and migration control.[19] Nevertheless, the EU generally seeks to resort to collective action—ie to collaborate with other states and international actors—rather than unilateral means in pursuing both its possession goals and its milieu goals. Without engaging in a more detailed challenge to the sharp distinction drawn in much of the literature between the promotion of values on the one hand and the pursuit of interests on the other,[20] my argument proceeds on the assumption that the EU perceives it to be in its interests to secure both its milieu goals and its possession goals, and that the EU seems generally to consider it more feasible or desirable to pursue these goals in collaboration with other actors than to attempt them unilaterally.[21]

The second claim is that in its broadly collective pursuit of milieu and possession goals, the EU regularly seeks to replicate or externalize some of the modes of governance it has developed for similar policies in its internal realm. More specifically, the EU sets out to create and to institutionalize stable relationships with other states and entities, and to establish transnational, and broadly participatory regulatory frameworks to coordinate and govern various issue areas, often emphasizing longer-term rather than short-term goals, and pursuing proactive or preventative rather than mainly reactive strategies. While the typical or traditional instruments of foreign policy range from the tools of diplomacy at one end, through the use of economic and political incentives and sanctions of various kinds, to the use of military power and force at the other end, the EU's governance mode of foreign policy additionally focuses on the establishment of networks of stable, institutionalized and iterative relationships with other states, entities and regions, which often themselves entail the creation of other policy-making, norm-generating, coordinating and monitoring institutions, and which regularly resemble the kind of regulatory frameworks the EU has developed internally.[22] Further, while foreign policy has conventionally been understood as policy autonomously formulated and developed by state actors in pursuit of national interests, implemented by them in the external affairs of the state, and resting

[18] At the time of writing in April 2012, the EU's unilateral initiative is being fiercely opposed by many other states including China, India and the US, with calls for the International Civil Aviation Authority to intervene in the dispute. See the contribution by Scott and Rajamani to this volume.

[19] For an interesting discussion, see N Tocci, 'Can the EU Promote Democracy and Human Rights Through the ENP? The Case for Refocusing on the Rule of Law' in M Cremona and G Meloni (eds), *The European Neighbourhood Policy: A Framework for Modernisation?* (EUI, 2007) 21, EUI Working Paper.

[20] For an excellent analysis which challenges any simple dichotomy between the EU as a rational power in pursuit of its own interests and the EU as a normative actor promoting its values in the context of EU–Africa policy see Sicurelli, n 2.

[21] A preference for collective approaches is asserted in Art 3(5) TEU and also in some of the EU's own strategy documents.

[22] Cremona has suggested that 'there is a bias, inherent perhaps in the EU system, towards institutionalizing relationships and policy-making to a degree with which we are familiar in the regulatory state but less so in the sphere of foreign policy': 'Introduction' in *Developments in EU External Relations Law* (OUP, 2008), p 9.

mainly on specific rather than diffuse forms of reciprocity,[23] the EU's governance mode of foreign policy presupposes and promotes the intensification of interdependence and institution-building, and rests on the establishment of diffuse rather than specific forms of reciprocity.[24] Finally, the EU's external governance arrangements frequently pursue multiple goals, combining or integrating different issue areas and fields of policy within a given framework.

Below, the evolution of the external relations of the European Community and the European Union over time will briefly be outlined, and a number of possible reasons for the EU's development of its distinctive governance mode of international relations will be suggested. The chapter presents some specific examples of EU external policy with a view to exemplifying aspects of the governance mode in more detail. These examples include two broad regional policies: (i) the European Neighbourhood Policy (ENP) and (ii) the EU's promotion of inter-regionalism; as well as two more focused policy areas: (iii) the EU and climate change and (iv) EU policy towards the International Criminal Court (ICC).

3. The Evolution of EU International Relations

Over the last two decades, the EU has placed increasing emphasis on its role as a global actor and in so doing has given prominence to the international relations of the EU to a much greater extent than before. And as the EU's attention, following the preoccupation of the first four decades of its existence with developing the success and strength of its internal domain, has shifted to external affairs, scholars have similarly turned their attention to the task of understanding, characterizing, conceptualizing and critiquing this aspect of its role.[25]

Yet the EU (and previously the European Community (EC)) was engaged in international relations from the time of its inception in the 1950s,[26] even if the main focus of these relations for much of that time was on trade and development assistance respectively. The term 'external relations' consequently came to have a very specific meaning in the European

[23] R Keohane in 'Reciprocity in International Relations' (1986) 40 *International Organisation* 1–27 defines specific reciprocity as 'situations in which specified partners exchange items of equivalent value in a strictly delimited sequence. If any obligations exist they are clearly specified in terms of rights and duties of particular actors'.

[24] Keohane, ibid, p 4, explains diffuse reciprocity as entailing less a precise definition of equivalence, where 'one's partners may be viewed as a group rather than as particular actors, and the sequence of events is less narrowly bounded. Obligations are important. Diffuse reciprocity involves conforming to generally accepted standards of behavior'.

[25] For a selection of the many books on EU foreign policy, apart from those already cited, see F Bindi (ed), *The Foreign Policy of the European Union* (Brookings, 2010); K Smith, *European Union Foreign Policy in a Changing World* (2nd edn, Polity Press, 2008); Z Laïdi (ed), *EU Foreign Policy in a Globalized World* (Routledge, 2009); R Youngs, *The EU's Role in World Politics* (Routledge, 2010); S Keukeleire and J Macnaughtan, *The Foreign Policy of the European Union* (Palgrave Macmillan, 2008); C Hill and M Smith (eds), *International Relations and the European Union* (OUP, 2005); M Smith, *Europe's Foreign and Security Policy* (Cambridge University Press, 2004). For a useful synthesis of the difficulties of characterizing and evaluating European Union foreign policy, see B White, 'Foreign Policy Analysis and European Foreign Policy' in B Tonra and T Christiansen (eds), *Rethinking European Union Foreign Policy* (Manchester University Press, 2004). For some earlier analyses see J Zielonka (ed), *Paradoxes of European Foreign Policy* (Kluwer, 1998).

[26] For a small selection of the legal and other literature on EC external relations including early commentaries, see JF Deniau, 'The External Policy of the European Economic Community' (1961) 26 *Law and Contemporary Problems* 364–380; K Simmonds, 'The Evolution of the External Relations Law of the European Economic Community' (1979) 28 ICLQ 644, CWA Timmermans and ELM Volker (eds), *Division of Powers between the European Communities and their Member States in the Field of External Relations* (Kluwer Deventer, 1981); JJ Costonis, 'The Treaty-Making Power of the European Economic Community: The Perspectives of a Decade' (1967/68) 5 *CML Rev* 421–457; J Steenbergen, 'The Common Commercial Policy' (1980) 17 *CML Rev* 229–249; E Wellenstein, 'Twenty-five years of Community External Relations' (1979) 16 *CML Rev* 407–423; D O'Keeffe and HG Schermers, (eds), *Mixed Agreements* (Kluwer, 1981); S Konstantinidis and M Evans, *The Legal Regulation of the European Community's External Relations after the Completion of the Internal Market* (Ashgate, 1996); P Eeckhout, *The European Internal Market and International Trade: A Legal Analysis* (OUP, 1994); and more recently A Dashwood and C Hillion, *The General Law of EC External Relations* (Sweet & Maxwell, 2000).

Union context, being used to depict the fields of trade, aid and a number of other discrete, sectoral areas of Community international activity, as contrasted with what were understood to be the more specifically political dimensions of foreign policy. 'External relations' was understood to describe the areas of 'low politics' in which the new European Community was properly engaged, while matters of high politics were dealt with initially on an informal intergovernmental basis by the heads of state meeting within the context of European Political Cooperation (EPC) from 1970 onwards.[27] With the Single European Act and the Maastricht Treaty changes, however, there was a significant further push towards strengthening this formal framework for EU international relations, culminating most recently in the provisions of the Lisbon Treaty.

The Lisbon Treaty created a range of new institutions with a view to further bolstering the framework for and the conduct of EU international relations,[28] and bringing together the two fields which had developed separately—EC external relations on the one hand, and the more conventional dimensions of foreign policy on the other hand. The aim of the Lisbon changes seems to have been the wish to move towards a more coherent and unified EU international relations policy framework which is neither substantively nor institutionally fragmented, and which emulates or draws on some of the traditional foreign policy institutions of states.

But even before these latest formal institutional changes, various moves had been made to try to bring greater coherence to the conduct of EU international relations. The EU had begun to develop and use a range of strategies, instruments and policies which on the one hand avoided some of the legal and institutional complexities of its fragmented international relations framework, and which on the other hand addressed issues that could not readily be differentiated into the classic categories of high and low politics, in a more integrated way. Three significant examples of such integrated strategies, instruments and policies are: the enlargement and pre-accession strategy which the EU developed from the early 1990s onwards, after it was decided that a significant bloc of central and Eastern European states would be admitted as members;[29] the ENP, which was launched in 2003[30] and which was inspired by, but adapted some of the practices and strategies of the preceding enlargement process; and thirdly the policy of inter-regionalism pursued by the EU in its relations with other regional groupings.[31] The ENP and inter-regionalism will be discussed further below. These strategies relied on (at least nominally) collaborative governance techniques, created an array of new institutions with partner countries and regions involving networks of actors, and established broad regulatory frameworks covering a range of different policy fields and issue areas.

[27] On the development of institutional and procedural machinery for the EPC, see G Bonvicini, 'Mechanisms and Procedures of the EPC: More than Traditional Diplomacy?' in A Pijpers, E Regelsberger and W Wessels (eds), *European political cooperation in the 1980s: a common foreign policy for Western Europe?* (Kluwer Academic Publishers, 1988) 49–70.

[28] See R Gosalbo Bono, 'The Organisation of the External Relations of the European Union in the Treaty of Lisbon' in P Koutrakos (ed), *The European Union's external relations a year after Lisbon* (2011) CLEER Working Paper 3.

[29] 1993 European Council Conclusions, the 1997 launch of Agenda 2000.

[30] COM (2003) 104 of 11 March and COM (2004) 373 of 12 May.

[31] For some overviews, see the essays in the special issue of *The Journal of European Integration*: 'The EU as a Global Actor and The Role of Inter-regionalism' (2005) 27 JEI. See also M Telò (ed), *European Union and New Regionalism* (2nd edn, Ashgate, 2007), N Alecu de Flers and E Regelsberger, 'The EU and Inter-regional Cooperation' in C Hill and M Smith, *International Relations and the EU* (OUP, 2005) 317–342, B Hettne and F Söderbaum, 'Civilian Power or Soft Imperialism? The EU as a Global Actor and the Role of Inter-regionalism' (2005) 10 *European Foreign Affairs Review* 535–552, and A Hardacre and M Smith, 'The EU and the Diplomacy of Complex Inter-regionalism' (2009) 4 *Hague Journal of Diplomacy* 197, V Aggerwal, 'Explaining Trends in EU Inter-regionalism' in V Aggarwal and E Fogarty (eds), *European Union Trade Strategies: Between Globalism and Regionalism* (Palgrave, 2004).

To sum up this brief overview: while moves towards a more formally integrated and strengthened EU international relations framework for both the common foreign, security and defence policies on the one hand, and the other existing fields of external relations on the other, were taken in the Lisbon Treaty, the EU had already been developing what I have described as a governance approach to international relations in various spheres, institutionalizing its relationships with other states and entities, creating specific frameworks and regulatory processes to advance its goals, and seeking to establish an international presence of a particular kind. This governance approach seems to build on the ways in which EEC institutions had carried on externally oriented activities over many years, and includes the external extension of a range of governance methods—including aspects of so-called new and experimentalist modes of governance[32]—increasingly used by the EU in its internal domain to address complex policy problems, coordinating different interests and bringing a range of actors together into broadly non-hierarchical, iterative processes for advancing common interests or goals.

It was at one time asserted that the distinctiveness of the EU's international relations was largely attributable to the legally circumscribed external competences of the European Economic Community (EEC), which existed mainly in the fields of trade and aid, and hence resulted in a limited EEC engagement in international relations. A consequence of these limited competences and circumscribed engagements was said to be that the emphasis of EEC external relations was on issues which were conventionally categorized as matters of 'low' politics, rather than the matters of 'high' politics which are perceived to be the real meat of foreign policy. A different explanation for the EU's continued pursuit of a governance mode of international relations even as it began to broaden the scope of its international relations to include matters of 'higher' politics classically conceived, however, derives from the EU's own institutional characteristics, from the kinds of goals it has pursued and the instruments and processes it has typically relied on internally as well as externally.

There is a longstanding literature on the way in which the foreign policy of states is shaped by their domestic structures,[33] or by domestic politics.[34] And while the EU is not a state, lacking the centralized authority and institutions of a state, the EU's governance mode of foreign policy can also be considered in part as a reflection or extension of its internal ways of operating. It is notable, indeed, that the relationship between the internal modes of governing developed by the EU and its emerging foreign policy identity has been the subject of recent interest and analysis in the work of a growing range of EU scholars.[35] Hence the EU's governance mode of international relations might be explained by at least two kinds of

[32] See C Sabel and J Zeitlin, 'Learning from Difference: The New Architecture of Experimentalist Governance in the European Union' (2008) 14 *European Law Journal* 271, and *Experimentalist Governance in the European Union: Towards a New Architecture* (OUP, 2010).

[33] See eg Henry Kissinger, 'Domestic Structure and Foreign Policy', the first of the three essays in *American Foreign Policy: Three Essays* (Norton, 1969) and P Katzenstein, 'International Relations and Domestic Structures: Foreign Economic Policies of Advanced Industrial States' (1976) *International Organization* 1–45.

[34] For a review see J Fearon, 'Domestic Politics, Foreign Policy and Theories of International relations' (1998) Annual Review of Political Science 289–313.

[35] M Farrell, 'EU External Relations: Exporting the EU Model of Governance?' (2005) 10 *EFA Rev* 451–462; F Schimmelpfennig and W Wagner, 'External governance in the European Union' (2004) 11 JEPP 657–660; S Lavenex, 'EU External Governance in Wider Europe' (2004) 11 JEPP 680–700; B Rosamund, 'The EU model of governance in world politics' (2005) 10 *EFA Rev* 463–478; A Warleigh, 'Learning from Europe: EU Studies and the Rethinking of International Relations' (2006) 21 EJIR 31–51; A Myrjord, 'Governance Beyond the Union: EU Boundaries in the Barents Euro-Arctic Region' (2003) 8 *EFA Rev* 239–257; M Sicard Filtenborg, SG and E Johannsen, 'An Alternative Theoretical Approach to EU Foreign Policy: "Networked Governance" and the Case of the Northern Dimension Initiative' (2002) 37 *Cooperation and Conflict* 387 and T Diez, 'The Imposition of Governance: Transforming Foreign Policy Through EU Enlargement' (2000) *Copenhagen Peace Research Institute Working Paper*, <http://www.ciaonet.org/wps/dit04/>; S Keukeleire and S Schunz, 'Foreign Policy, Globalization and Global Governance: The European Union's Structural Foreign Policy' (2008) <http://www.jhubc.it/ecpr-riga/virtualpaperroom/102.pdf>.

reasons. The first is identity-driven: the EU has come to understand itself as a particular kind of actor based on its history, evolution and its mode of operating internally, and it tends to project that identity and mode of operating also into its external relations.[36] This takes the form both of projecting particular goals, norms, and objectives in its external relations, and of extending particular modes and processes of transnational cooperation and policy-making, into the external realm.[37] A second kind of reason is instrumental. The EU has (at least until the recent banking and sovereign debt crisis) enjoyed significant success as a regional economic and political system, and has found ways of governing in its internal domain that reconcile a significant degree of state sovereignty with the pursuit of common goals, and that manage the processes of interdependence well. Further, the effort to extend both its norms and ways of governing into international relations is likely to (or is perceived as being likely to) advantage the EU in those settings, or at least to prevent it from being disadvantaged vis-à-vis other actors and entities.[38] Finally, the EU's mode of conducting external relations is also significantly shaped by the possibilities and constraints of the external environment, and not only by its own internal processes and experiences.[39]

The next and more empirical part of the chapter suggests that the EU's distinctive governance mode of international relations can be seen clearly in some of the strategies adopted in recent years for engaging with its neighbouring and other regions, as well as on more focused issues like climate change and the establishment of the ICC. These strategies and policies exemplify central aspects of the EU's governance mode in their pursuit of both milieu and possession goals through the establishment of new institutions with the aim of creating ongoing relations of cooperation. They establish systems of governance which engage a wide network of actors, establishing broad goals and reasonably broad participation, and relying on diffuse forms of reciprocity. They are also strategies which to different degrees suggest the attempt by the EU to extend its own norms and methods of operation into its international relations.

4. The EU Governance Mode of International Relations: Some Illustrations

While elements of the governance mode have been evident in the policies and practices of EC external relations over many years, some of the EU's strategies in recent years bring together and exemplify its key features in striking ways. Below, the EU's ENP and its policy of inter-regionalism are used to illustrate central aspects of the governance mode in action. While these approaches, and indeed the prior process which inspired the ENP, the EU's accession strategy, have been criticized from a range of perspectives,[40] the aim of this

[36] F Bicchi expresses the point in sociological terms in saying that 'the EU promotes its own norms because institutions promote institutional isomorphism' in 'One Size Fits All: Normative Power Europe and the Mediterranean' (2006) 13 JEPP 286, at 293. The claim that European foreign policy is guided by the EU's own internal experience is made in the European Security Strategy, *A Secure Europe in a Better World* (December 2003).

[37] M Cremona in 'The Union as a Global Actor: Roles, Models and Identity' (2004) 41 *CML Rev* 553 draws attention to the EU's 'exportation of regulatory norms'.

[38] A humorous anecdotal example of this appeared in a commentary by G Rachman, 'Europe's Plot to Take Over the World' *Financial Times* (5 October 2009) on the proposal within the G20 summit for a form of economic peer review akin to the EU's 'open method of coordination'.

[39] B Rosamond has argued, in 'The EU model of governance in world politics' (2005) 10 *EFA Rev* 463–478, that 'there is no single EU mode of governance and, therefore, that the external projection of the EU's governance identity is far from straightforward. Moreover, in terms of governance models, the EU does not simply practice a weird, internally generated, path dependent mode, but rather its governance practice is part of a broader global exchange of governance methodologies'.

[40] eg the nature and operation of conditionality in the case of accession/enlargement; soft imperialism or 'the shadow of hierarchy' (Gänzle), and the absence of the membership incentive in the case of the ENP; the undeveloped nature of most regional partners in the case of inter-regionalism, and exploitation of asymmetrical relations in the case of the renegotiated African Caribbean and Pacific countries (ACP) agreements.

chapter is not so much to address these critiques as to use the examples to illustrate what I describe as the EU's governance mode of international relations. These two examples reflect certain features of the governance mode of external relations which have been emphasized above. One such feature is the inclusion of multiple issue areas, integrating policies that were conventionally considered to be matters of low and high politics respectively, covering eg trade and environment and economic matters as well as security and political cooperation. These strategies also clearly reflect the extension of some of the EU's distinctive internal modes of governance into the external domain. The third and fourth examples of the EU's governance mode of international relations which the chapter describes are the EU's international policy on climate change, and its policy towards the ICC.[41]

4.1. The European Neighbourhood Policy

In its background paper of 2003[42] and a follow-up strategy paper in 2004,[43] the European Commission introduced the idea of a European Neighbourhood Policy with countries neighbouring the EU, which would be distinct from the process of accession for candidate countries. Although inspired by the success of the previous enlargement strategy and building on several of its methodologies, the ENP was also deliberately designed as a somewhat different kind of process and strategy. According to the Commission, the neighbourhood strategy would go 'beyond existing relationships to offer a deeper political relationship and economic integration', and it 'remains distinct from the process of enlargement although it does not prejudge, for European neighbours, how their relationship with the EU may develop in future'.[44] The idea was to create a 'ring of friends', of 'well-governed countries' bordering the EU, which were not already the subject of integration arrangements with the EU (such as the European Economic Area) and which were not candidate states, but with whom there would be close cooperative relationships. There are now 16 countries covered by the neighbourhood strategy,[45] which does not include Russia.[46] The ENP is a framework for a more complex structure, and encompasses or overlaps with a range of other bilateral and regional or sub-regional relations, including the previous Barcelona Process,[47] the more recently created Union for the Mediterranean,[48] the Northern Dimension Initiative,[49] the Eastern Partnership[50] and the Black Sea Synergy.[51]

[41] This example could be extended to include international criminal tribunals more generally.

[42] COM (2003) 104 of 11 March, 'Wider Europe-Neighbourhood: A New Framework for Relations with our Eastern and Southern Neighbours'.

[43] COM (2004) 373 of 12 May, 'European Neighbourhood Policy Strategy Paper'.

[44] <http://ec.europa.eu/world/enp/policy_en.htm>.

[45] These are the EU's 'immediate neighbours' by land or sea—Algeria, Armenia, Azerbaijan, Belarus, Egypt, Georgia, Israel, Jordan, Lebanon, Libya, Moldova, Morocco, the Occupied Palestinian Territory, Syria, Tunisia and Ukraine.

[46] Russia had signed a Partnership and Cooperation Agreement in 1994, but rejected participation in the ENP. Instead a separate 'strategic partnership' based on four 'common spaces' was established with the EU in 2003. These four spaces are a common economic space, a space of freedom, security and justice, cooperation in the field of external security, and research, education and culture. The partnership has been criticized on the basis that these spaces cover mainly the areas in which the two share a common approach, and do not deal with the problematic issues such as the frozen conflicts in Georgia, the revolutions in Georgia and Ukraine. See S Blockmans, 'EU-Russia Relations through the Prism of the European Neighbourhood and Partnership Instrument' (2008) 13 *EFA Rev* 167–187.

[47] <http://ec.europa.eu/external_relations/euromed/index_en.htm>.

[48] Joint declaration of the Paris Summit for the Mediterranean, Paris, 13 July 2008: <http://www.ue2008.fr/webdav/site/PFUE/shared/import/07/0713_declaration_de_paris/Joint_declaration_of_the_Paris_summit_for_the_Mediterranean-EN.pdf>.

[49] <http://eeas.europa.eu/north_dim/index_en.htm>.

[50] <http://eeas.europa.eu/eastern/index_en.htm>.

[51] <http://eeas.europa.eu/blacksea/index_en.htm>.

At the outset of the ENP process, the Commission prepared Country Reports assessing the possibility of relations with each country and submitted these to the Council, which decided whether or not to proceed with each. The ENP is based on a 'single framework' for integration covering all aspects of bilateral relations. Bilateral ENP 'Action Plans' are agreed between the EU and each partner state, which set out an agenda of political and economic reforms with short and medium-term priorities. The action plans have been wide-ranging, covering political dialogue and reform, economic and social cooperation and development, trade-related issues and market and regulatory reform, cooperation in justice and home affairs, and sectors such as transport, energy, information society, environment, research and development. Amongst the incentives that were offered by the EU in return for progress on reforms were 'greater integration into European programmes and networks, increased assistance, enhanced market access'[52] and access to specific forms of cooperation such as 'twinning'.[53]

Financial support for the process and for the reforms identified was provided by the European Neighbourhood and Partnership Instrument (ENPI), established in 2007 to replace the various prior thematic and geographic programmes such as TACIS,[54] MEDA[55] and EIDHR.[56] According to the Commission, the ENPI is designed to target sustainable development as well as approximation to EU policies and standards, to support cross-border cooperation along land and maritime borders, and to strengthen cooperation between local and regional actors and civil society. Seven-year 'Country strategy papers' and three-year 'National Indicative Programs' are drawn up, based on guidance from the Action Plans.

The institutional structures for the ENP depend in part on the institutional framework under the existing Association Agreement or Partnership and Cooperation Agreement with each partner country. These generally establish a Cooperation Council or an Association Council, as well as a committee and a range of sub-committees set up under the Agreements. The working committees bring together relevant officials and experts in the corresponding fields from the partner countries and the Commission, and some of the committees have significant monitoring functions.

Although the macro-institutional dimension of the ENP has been described as weak and insufficiently developed and the elements of hierarchy as evident,[57] there is some empirical evidence to suggest that the networked forms of governance it establishes allow for more heterarchical relations and genuine co-ownership, at least in certain sectors.[58] Based on three case studies covering the sectors of air transport, trans-boundary water management, and immigration control respectively, Lavenex argues that there is in fact less shadow-hierarchy and more co-ownership at the micro level than some of the bleaker assessments of

[52] <http://ec.europa.eu/world/enp/howitworks_en.htm>.

[53] Twinning is described by the European Commission as 'a cooperation tool between a Public Administration in a Partner/Beneficiary Country and the equivalent institution in an EU Member State (which) aims at upgrading/modernising the institution in a Beneficiary Country through training, reorganisation as well as drafting of laws and regulations modelled after the EU... One of its key features is the concept of mandatory results: both the Beneficiary and the EU partners commit themselves to work towards a commonly agreed result, which should be measurable and precise': <http://ec.europa.eu/europeaid/where/neighbourhood/overview/documents/twinning_en.pdf>.

[54] The Technical Aid to the Commonwealth of Independent States (TACIS) programme was first established in 1991 to provide assistance to the former Soviet states.

[55] The MEDA programme was first established in 1996 to provide financial and technical assistance to support the economic and other transition reforms of Mediterranean states in the framework of the Euro-Mediterranean partnership between the EU and countries of the southern Mediterranean which were not Member States.

[56] The European Instrument for Democracy and Human Rights (EIDHR) came into force in 2007 to provide thematic funding for external aid to support projects promoting democracy and human rights internationally.

[57] Cremona and Hillion, n 70.

[58] See B Van Vooren, *EU External Relations Law and the European Neighbourhood Policy: A Paradigm for Coherence* (Routledge, 2012), 352.

the ENP have suggested.[59] More specifically she argues that 'commitments anchored in the so-called Action Plans are jointly agreed rather than unilaterally imposed, reflecting the ENP countries' different degrees of interest in deeper association' and also that:

> 'the ambiguous relationship to hierarchy and conditionality is complemented by the perspective for organizational participation in sectoral governance structures, including Community Programmes and Agencies. While it is true that such participation is part of the conditional incentives offered in the ENP Action Plans, prerequisites for participating in activities of Community agencies need not necessarily be "approximation with the Community" but instead "the establishment of relevant national institutions with sufficient capacities"'.[60]

She concludes that 'discussions within ENP subcommittees document a gradual approach towards co-operation with EU agencies and bodies which start with individual projects and later lead to more formal co-operation agreements' and that 'as a macro-policy, the ENP is in principle more open to more horizontal, co-owned governance structures', that extended network governance represents a 'hitherto neglected structural dimension of the ENP' and finally that 'these emerging webs of institutionalization... [point to] the advent of flexible integration beyond formal EU membership'.[61] In a larger study of the functioning of the ENP with particular emphasis on ascertaining its effectiveness or otherwise in relation to democracy promotion, Schimmelpfennig and Scholtz, despite their major finding that the prospects of success in the absence of full accession conditionality are weak, also found, using geographical proxies to control for transnational exchange as an alternative mechanism for democratization, that 'transnational exchange prove(s) robustly significant and positively correlated with the level of democracy in neighbouring countries' leading them to conclude that the 'general and diffuse cross-border exchanges do indeed matter'.[62]

It should be emphasized that the argument that the European Neighbourhood Policy usefully illustrates the governance mode of international relations does not entail a claim that this is the most successful of the EU's external policies, or that it does not need reform. On the contrary it has been widely acknowledged—including by the Commission[63]—that the ENP as it was originally established was significantly flawed.[64] However, the nature of its weaknesses and the recommendations which have been made for its reform—including greater clarity as to its aims, greater differentiation between countries and regions rather than a one-size-fits-all-approach,[65] a more realistic incentive structure in the absence of accession conditionality,[66] a stronger institutional dimension, greater involvement of civil society, the need to strengthen the conflict-resolution and crisis-management dimensions,[67] the need to integrate the interests of partner states in opening up the EU's textile markets

[59] S Lavenex, 'A Governance Perspective on the European Neighbourhood Policy: Integration Beyond Conditionality' (2008) 15 JEPP 938–955.

[60] Ibid.

[61] Ibid.

[62] F Schimmelpfennig and H Scholtz, 'EU Democracy Promotion in the European Neighbourhood Policy: Political Conditionality, Economic Development and Transnational Exchange' (2008) 9 European Union Politics 187, 202.

[63] For a previous reform attempt see 'Strengthening the European Neighbourhood Policy' COM (2006) 726

[64] See eg A Duleba, L Najšlová, V Benč and V Bilčík, 'The Reform of the European Neighbourhood Policy: Tools, Institutions and a Regional Dimension' (Research Center of the Slovak Foreign Policy Association, Bratislava, 2008): <http://www.pasos.org/www-pasosmembers-org/publications/the-reform-of-the-european-neighbourhood-policy-tools-institutions-and-a-regional-dimension>.

[65] Kochenov, n 71 also Cremona and Hillion, n 70.

[66] G Sasse, 'Conditionality-lite: The European Neighbourhood Policy and the EU's Eastern Neighbours', in C Musu and N Casarini (eds), *The Road to Convergence: European Foreign Policy in an Evolving International System* (Palgrave, 2006) 163–180.

[67] G Sasse, 'The European Neighbourhood Policy and Conflict Management: A Comparison of Moldova and the Caucasus' (2009) 8 *Ethnopolitics* 369–386 and D Helly, 'EU's Influence in Its Eastern Neighbourhood: The Case of Crisis Management in the Southern Caucasus' (2007) 7 *European Political Economy Review* 102–117.

rather than mainly pursuing EU security interests[68]—nonetheless support a continuation of the governance approach. The EU in 2011 published a review of the operation of the first stage of the ENP, and has proposed continuing with many of its existing strategies and features, although with a number of specific changes and reforms.[69] Continuation of the ENP with appropriate reforms and improvements, rather than its abandonment, has also been recommended by two prominent critics who argue that 'the ENP remains a valuable model of an integrated approach to EU external action, particularly from a policy making point of view'.[70] Significant blame for the weaknesses of the ENP has been laid on the lack of political consensus amongst the Member States on the underlying ENP vision,[71] and its being insufficiently linked to the Council for the purposes of better defining its strategic objectives.[72] But it has also been argued that the ENP is better understood less in conventional foreign policy terms with a clear hierarchy of goals and strategies and rather as 'the emergence of more horizontal, process-oriented modes of network governance allows for hitherto under-investigated forms of flexible integration for non-member states'.[73]

4.2. EU Inter-regional policy

By comparison with the European Neighbourhood Policy, EU inter-regional policy is less a well-defined and delimited strategy than a broad agenda which has characterized the international relations of the EU to varying degrees for many years. Karen Smith describes the fostering of regional integration and the oldest of the EU's five key foreign policy objectives.[74] She identifies two different practices in this respect, the first being the practice of classifying neighbouring countries together under regional strategies and the second being support and encouragement for regional groupings. From this perspective, the ENP itself can be considered as a part of the EU's broader 'regional cooperation' strategy.[75] However, the aspect of the EU's practice and strategy on which this chapter focuses is specifically that of promoting and fostering inter-regional cooperation between the EU and other world regions, in part by encouraging robust forms of integration in other regions and also by seeking to develop close and institutionalized relationships with them.

Inter-regional cooperation has been described as one of the most attractive frameworks for both the EU and for other countries to meet their respective foreign policy interests, as it corresponds to 'the EU's own wish to pool national resources and to resolve conflicts

[68] A Palacio, 'The Arab Spring and Europe's Turn' (*Project Syndicate*, 1 June 2011) <http://www.project-syndicate.org/commentary/palacio1/English>.

[69] 'A New Response to a Changing Neighbourhood: A Review of European Neighbourhood Policy', published in May 2011 by the Commission and the High Representative for Foreign and Security Policy: <http://ec.europa.eu/world/enp/pdf/com_11_303_en.pdf>. For an appraisal of the new approach, see S Wolff, 'Is the EU's New Neighbourhood Policy Fit for Purpose?' and S Blockmans, 'Reviewing EU Relations with its Neighbours Post-Lisbon' in P Koutrakos (ed), *The European Union's External Relations A Year After Lisbon* (CLEER Working Papers 2011/3) 113–124. See also the European Parliament resolution A7-400/2011 of 14 December 2011 on the review of the European Neighbourhood Policy (2011/2157).

[70] M Cremona and C Hillion, 'L'Union fait la force? Potential and Limitations of the European Neighbourhood Policy as an Integrated EU Foreign and Security Policy' (2006) 39 EUI Working Paper in Law. See also M Cremona, 'The European Neighbourhood Policy: More than a Partnership' in M Cremona and B De Witte (eds), *Developments in EU External Relations* (Hart Publishing, 2008).

[71] D Kochenov, 'The Eastern Partnership, the Union for the Mediterranean and The Remaining Need To Do Something With The ENP' (2010) CRCEES: <http://papers.ssrn.com/sol3/papers.cfm?abstract_id=1459560> and 'New Developments in the ENP: Ignoring the Problems' (2011) 9 *Comparative European Politics* 581–595.

[72] B Lippert, 'Beefing up the ENP: Towards a Modernisation and Stability Partnership' (2006) 41 *The International Spectator* 85–100.

[73] Lavenex, n 59.

[74] K Smith, *European Union Foreign Policy in a Changing World* (2nd edn, Polity, 2008), chs 1 and 4 in particular.

[75] The term inter-regionalism is also sometimes used to describe cooperation between regions and regional authorities *within* the EU, eg in the context of the structural funds, but this is not the kind of inter-regionalism I am interested in for the purposes of the current paper.

through dialogue and negotiation with all parties having an equal standing'.[76] Since regional 'actorness' has to be created by voluntary processes, it depends more on dialogue and consensus-building than on coercion, and hence corresponds to the model Europe claims to hold out as the preferred world order, given that this is the way the EU itself developed.[77]

Three different types of inter-regionalism have been identified.[78] The first is trans-regionalism, which refers to connections between or amongst transnational networks,[79] including private or public actors, across regions and not just intergovernmental connections.[80] The second is hybrid inter-regionalism, involving negotiation or cooperation between one organized region and with a group of countries from another non-organized or dispersed region; and the third is pure inter-regionalism involving cooperation and ties between two organized and integrated regional systems.[81]

Although it has been a longstanding policy of the EU, the last decade or two has seen increasing emphasis on inter-regionalism as a key aspect of EU foreign policy. The Commission regularly adopts strategy papers on regional or sub-regional cooperation, most recently for the period 2007–2013 or 2008–2013 with regions including the Andean Community,[82] Asia,[83] Central America,[84] the Euro-Med region,[85] the Balkans,[86] Latin America,[87] Mercosur,[88] Central Asia,[89] the ACP and West Africa,[90] amongst others.

The most developed of the EU's regional relationships in Latin America is EU–Mercosur (Mercado Común del Sur), with an Interregional Framework Cooperation Agreement in place since 1995 and negotiations for an Association Agreement underway at present. In Asia, the EU has a framework for inter-regional cooperation with the Association of South-East Asian Nations (ASEAN),[91] its main channel being the biennial Asia-Europe Meeting

[76] N Alecu de Flers and Elfriede Regelsberger, 'The EU and Inter-regional Cooperation' in C Hill and M Smith, *International Relations and the EU* (OUP, 2005) 317.

[77] B Hettne and F Söderbaum, 'Civilian Power or Soft Imperialism? The EU as a Global Actor and the Role of Inter-regionalism' (2005) 10 JEPP 535–552. See also T Börzel and T Risse, 'Diffusing (inter-) Regionalism: The EU as a Model of Regional Integration' (2009) KFG Working Papers <http://userpage.fu-berlin.de/kfgeu/workingpapers/WorkingPaperKFG_7.pdf>.

[78] A Hardacre and M Smith, 'The EU and the Diplomacy of Complex Inter-regionalism' (2009) 4 *Hague Journal of Diplomacy* 197. A list of some of the relevant EU relationships according to this tripartite classification:

- Transregional: Asia–Europe Meeting (1994); Europe–Latin America Summit (1999); EU–Africa Summit (2000).
- Hybrid Interregional: EU–Association of South East Asian Nations (ASEAN) (1980); EU–Gulf Cooperation Council (GCC) (1989); EU–South Asian Association for Regional Cooperation (SAARC) (1994); EU–South African Development Community (SADC) (1994); EU–Mediterranean (MED) (1995).
- EU–Rio Group (1999).
- Pure Interregional: EU–Central American Common Market (CACM) (1993); EU–Common Market of the South (Mercosur) (1995); EU–Community of Andean Nations (AC) (1996).

[79] See C Dent, 'From Inter-regionalism to Transregionalism: Future Challenges for ASEM' (2003) *Asia Europe Journal* 223–235.

[80] V Aggarwal and E Fogarty, 'Between Regionalism and Globalization: European Union Interregional Trade Strategies' in V Aggarwal and E Fogarty, *EU Trade Strategies: Between Regionalism and Globalism* (Palgrave Macmillan, 2004) 1–40.

[81] F Söderbaum and P Stålgren (eds), *The European Union and the Global South* (Lynne Rienner Publishers, 2010) 5–6.

[82] <http://ec.europa.eu/external_relations/andean/rsp/07_13_en.pdf>.

[83] The Regional Strategy Paper for EU–Asia Cooperation 2007–2013: <http://ec.europa.eu/external_relations/asia/rsp/07_13_en.pdf>.

[84] <http://ec.europa.eu/external_relations/ca/index_en.htm>.

[85] <http://ec.europa.eu/world/enp/pdf/country/enpi_euromed_rsp_en.pdf>.

[86] See S Blockmans, *Tough Love: The European Union's Relations with the Western Balkans* (TMC Asser Press, 2007), 251–253.

[87] <http://ec.europa.eu/external_relations/la/rsp/07_13_en.pdf>.

[88] <http://ec.europa.eu/external_relations/mercosur/index_en.htm>.

[89] <http://ec.europa.eu/external_relations/central_asia/rsp/07_13_en.pdf>.

[90] <http://www.delnga.ec.europa.eu/projects/EC-West%20Africa%20Regional%20Strategy%20Paper.pdf>.

[91] <http://ec.europa.eu/external_relations/asem/index_en.htm>.

(ASEM),[92] and with South Asian Association for Regional Cooperation (SAARC), in which the EU has observer status since 2006.[93] A similar emphasis on the importance of regional integration was clear in the EU's restructuring of its previous relationship with the African Caribbean and Pacific countries (ACP, mostly former colonies of EU Member States) in the Cotonou Agreement and the following Economic and Partnership Agreements,[94] and in its more recent relations with the African Union.

Hardacre and Smith argue that the EU has systematically attempted to create a distinctive focus in its external relations through the pursuit of pure inter-regionalism within the framework of what they call complex inter-regionalism. They suggest that despite the constant reviewing, restructuring and reiterating of the EU's dealings with third parties, the aims and objectives of EU external relations, including its inter-regionalism strategy, have remained fairly constant with a commitment to multilateralism at the centre.[95] They argue that the EU tries to create a model of international relations based on its own regional identity, with an 'equal partner association model' contrasting with the more direct US 'commercial/military model'. They describe an evolution in EU inter-regional strategy from early agreements based mostly on economic issues to much more comprehensive agreements which encompass political cooperation and dialogue on strategic issues as well as a wide range of other issues including sustainable development, poverty alleviation, democracy consolidation and respect for human rights. They suggest that as inter-regionalism develops, it generates a need for improved structures, defined forums and overarching aims and objectives, 'and thus in the broadest sense a need for a diplomacy that is focused on institution-building and the generation of stable expectations'.[96]

The institutional structures of EU inter-regional cooperation vary, but are broadly consistent across regions, resembling the structures described above in the European Neighbourhood Strategy, in creating a ministerial level Cooperation Council, Committee and sub-committees, as well as generating networks of other actors. The promotion by the EU of regional integration itself of course leads to the creation of new institutions and actors, as for example within the framework of robust regional arrangements such as Mercosur, ASEAN and the African Union. One of the main obstacles to stronger and more effective EU–interregional relations, however, is the relative strength and degree of integration of the EU's partner region,[97] which explains why promotion of regional integration remains a key objective in all of the EU's inter-regional relations.

Just as the claim that the ENP exemplifies the governance mode of international relations does not imply that many aspects of the ENP are not flawed or problematic in various respects, neither does the claim that the EU pursues inter-regionalism as part of its governance mode of international relations strategy make a claim about the virtues or substance of any particular instance of inter-regionalism. For example, the EU's renegotiation of ACP relationship—previously framed by the Lomé and Yaoundé Conventions—has been criticized from a developmental perspective and for exploiting the asymmetrical relations between the parties, undermining the aspiration of reciprocal accountability and collective governance in practice.[98] And it has been argued that elements of soft imperialism

[92] Which established subsidiary institutions and networks such as the Trans-EurAsia Information Network.

[93] <http://ec.europa.eu/external_relations/saarc/index_en.htm>.

[94] M Farrell, 'From Lomé to Economic Partnerships in Africa' in F Söderbaum and P Stålgren (eds), *The European Union and the Global South* (Lynne Rienner Publishers, 2010).

[95] A Hardacre and M Smith, 'The EU and the Diplomacy of Complex Inter-regionalism' (2009) 4 *Hague Journal of Diplomacy* 197.

[96] Ibid.

[97] V Aggerwal, 'Explaining Trends in EU Inter-regionalism', n 31.

[98] M Farrell, 'A Triumph of Realism over Idealism: Cooperation between the European Union and Africa' (2005) 27 JEI 263–283.

are creeping into other parts of the EU's inter-regional relationships.[99] More generally, it has been suggested that the nature of the EU's strategies are linked to the relative strength of the counterpart.[100]

The argument that the EU inter-regionalism strategy illustrates some of the main aspects of the governance mode of international relations is based on the features set out above. In the first place, the strategy represents a kind of extension of aspects of the EU's identity into its external relations. It is broad in its aims, integrating matters of high and low politics; it creates or triggers a range of new institutions and actors, and seeks to establish a horizontal network of close, stable relations, based at least in principle on the notion of partnership and the collective pursuit of common goals.

4.3. EU external climate change policy

Unlike the cases of the ENP and inter-regionalism, the example of the EU and climate change considers the EU's approach to a specific policy issue rather than a regional strategy.

The field of climate change is one in which the EU is seen to have exercised a degree of international leadership in recent years, contrasting with the approach of other major powers, including the US,[101] and also contrasting with the EU's much lower profile and influence in other fields of foreign relations such as security. Consistent with the premises of the governance approach to foreign policy, the EU in this field has pursued collective sustainability and other environmental goals by supporting and promoting multilateral negotiations for the creation of a stable, iterative international governance regime.[102] The EU attempted to exercise climate leadership during and after the original Kyoto Protocol negotiations, first by setting an example with its own internal policies—including the creation of an emissions trading system and the establishment of specific targets for the reduction of greenhouse gas emissions—and seeking to extend these policies into the external domain.[103] The EU has consistently been one of the key proponents and supporters of a multilateral climate change regime and has worked to bring reluctant states on board by offering additional incentives, such as the promise to Russia of EU's support for WTO membership.

[99] B Hettne and F Söderbaum, 'Civilian Power or Soft Imperialism? The EU as a Global Actor and the Role of Inter-regionalism' (2005) 10 JEPP 535–552 argue in relation to the Euro-med that 'although considerable dialogue and institution-building have taken place in order to go beyond the colonial legacy of inequality and dependence between the EU and its Mediterranean counterparts, little concrete progress has been achieved in transforming the underlying economic and political relationships'.

[100] F Söderbaum in 'African Regionalism and EU-African Regionalism' in M Telò (ed), *European Union and New Regionalism* (2nd edn, Ashgate, 2007).

[101] See C Piñon Carlarne on how the EU took over from the US in exercising climate leadership in, *Climate Change Law and Policy: EU and US Approaches* (OUP, 2010), and with an interesting analysis of the factors explaining the difference between the approaches of the two jurisdictions. Also M Schreurs and Y Tiberghien, 'Multi-Level Reinforcement: Explaining European Union Leadership in Climate Change Mitigation' (2007) 7 *Global Environmental Politics* 19–46, whose analysis bears out the external governance thesis in so far as they argue that EU leadership resulted from a 'process of mutual leadership reinforcement by different actors involved in the EU's process of multi-level governance'. Also on EU climate leadership, see the discussion in S Scheipers and D Sicurelli, 'Normative Power Europe: A Credible Utopia?' (2007) 45 JCMS 435–457. And finally, see J Szarka, 'The EU, The USA and The Climate Divide: Reappraising Strategic Choices' (2012) 11 *European Political Science* 31–40, emphasizing the EU's distinctive willingness—unlike the US—to give up or to pool sovereignty for these purposes.

[102] For an analysis of whether the EU promotes its interests or its normative preferences (which is similar to asking whether it pursues milieu or possession goals) in the context of its external climate change policy, see L Van Schaik and S Schunz, 'Explaining EU Activism and Impact in Global Climate Politics: Is the Union a Norm- or Interest-Driven Actor' (2012) 50 JCMS 169–186.

[103] See C Parker and C Carlsson, 'Climate Change and the European Union's Leadership Moment: An Inconvenient Truth' (2010) 48 JCMS 923–943, who examine the EU's 'structural', 'directional' and ideas-based leadership.

This policy was unsuccessful at the Copenhagen round of negotiations in 2009, at which the EU's conditional offer and its commitments to financial aid were rejected, and its attempts to obtain a binding instrument with binding targets failed.[104] Nevertheless, with the establishment of a new directorate general (DG Clima) on climate change with a specific mandate to lead international negotiations on the issue, the EU has continued to try to fill the international leadership gap, and has continued to establish binding internal measures first (currently an attempt to commit to a unilateral reduction of 30% of CO2 emissions against the 1990 benchmark), subsequently seeking to extend aspects of these into international negotiations.[105] Perhaps a clearer example of its climate leadership (given that the EU's emissions trading system was initially prompted by Article 17 of the Kyoto Protocol, which itself had been included as a result of US pressure, even though the US did not ultimately sign the accord).[106] The EU's more recent establishment of targets ('20/20/20') connected to its 2009 climate package, represented a clear attempt to agree such targets internally in the first instance, and to promote or even export these targets externally.[107]

Alongside its attempt to promote a multilateral regime, the EU has more recently sought to influence other countries in bilateral negotiations, such as in its partnership with China on climate change,[108] its 2008 Joint Work Programme on Energy, Clean Development and Climate Change with India, its Forum on Environmental and Sustainable Development with South Africa, and its multilateral Global Climate Change Alliance[109] with emphasis on regional cooperation,[110] mainstreaming climate change into other policies[111] and providing development aid to pursue sustainable development.[112] It has also—and more controversially—adopted what have been termed 'contingent unilateralist' policies,[113] such as its decision to include aircraft emissions from third country airlines within its emissions trading scheme, when the multilateral forum (the International Civil Aviation Organization) tasked with governing aircraft emissions had failed over ten years to act.[114] This form of unilateralism has been distinguished from the kind of conditionality that would simply impose the EU's own aims and objectives on third countries. It has been depicted instead as a kind of unilateralism which is multilateralism-forcing, or which at least aims by means of

[104] For a useful overview, see M Alessi, A Georgiev and C Egenhofer, 'Messages from Copenhagen: Assessments of the Accord and Implications for the EU' (2010) 9 *ECP Report*, available at: <http://www.ceps.eu/ceps/download/3054>.

[105] See N Purvis and A Stevenson, 'Rethinking Climate Diplomacy: New Ideas for Transatlantic Cooperation post-Copenhagen' (2010) *Brussels Forum Paper Series* <http://www.gmfus.org/brusselsforum/2010/docs/BF2010-Paper-Purvis-Stevenson.pdf>.

[106] See L Cass, 'Norm Entrapment and Preference Change: The Evolution of the European Union Position on International Emissions Trading' (2005) 5 *Global Environmental Politics* 38.

[107] <http://ec.europa.eu/clima/policies/package/index_en.htm>.

[108] SG de Cock, 'The European Union as a Bilateral Norm Leader on Climate Change vis-à-vis China' (2011) 16 *EFA Rev* 89–105. See also S Fischer and J Leinen, 'The European Union and International Climate Politics' (2010) <http://library.fes.de/pdf-files/id/ipa/07636.pdf>.

[109] <http://www.gcca.eu/pages/41_2-GCCA-Beneficiaries.html>.

[110] <http://www.gcca.eu/pages/22_2-Policy-Dialogues.html>.

[111] See Council Reg (EC) 2493/2000 [2000] OJ L288 (now replaced) to promote full integration of the environmental dimension in the development process of developing countries and the related Commission Communication COM (2000) 264 of 18 May. For criticism of the effectiveness of this attempt, see the Court of Auditors' Report: <http://eca.europa.eu/portal/pls/portal/docs/1/173653.PDF>. See J Gupta and N van der Grijp (eds), *Mainstreaming Climate Change in Development Cooperation: Theory, Practice and Implications for the European Union* (CUP, 2010) 196.

[112] See the somewhat older comparison of EU and US policies on development aid and aid for environmentally sustainable development, according to which the EU's development policy reflects its internal identity as a community of welfare states, while the US is less generous towards developing countries and towards poorer Americans.

[113] For an account see J Scott, 'EU Global Action on Climate Change and Regulatory Penalty Defaults' (2011) *SSRN Working Paper Series* <http://papers.ssrn.com/sol3/papers.cfm?abstract_id=1954667>.

[114] See the contribution by Scott and Rajamani to this volume.

the unilateral imposition of EU standards in the absence of equivalent protection, to prompt collective governance where there has been international unwillingness to act collectively.[115]

Most recently following the Durban conference of 2011, despite the equivocal outcome, the EU was again credited with exercising climate leadership by pressing for and securing, with the support of other international actors, a second commitment period for targets under the Kyoto Protocol, further action on the Green Climate Fund and related provisions, and agreement on a future binding agreement.[116] In sum, despite the painstakingly slow progress towards the kind of international agreement which the EU has sought since Kyoto, the EU has continued—by comparison with the US and despite some change in the US approach under the Obama administration—to pursue bilateral, regional, and multilateral strategies (and occasionally 'contingent' unilateral action aimed at triggering international cooperation) in pursuit of global environmental goods, mainstreaming climate change objectives within its other policies, and notably has been willing to yield or share sovereignty with a view to achieving collective goals.

4.4. EU policy towards the International Criminal Court

The fourth example, like the third, is more narrowly focused, as it concerns the EU's approach towards the establishment and operation of the ICC, and indeed towards the establishment and operation of international criminal tribunals more generally.[117]

The European Union has promoted the ICC fairly strongly since its establishment.[118] It has adopted a Common Position and an Action Plan on relations with the ICC and its policy towards the ICC is often (though not always) internally coherent.[119] The EU has used a variety of tools in pursuit of its support for the ICC, such as diplomatic pressure on states, economic, financial and technical assistance to states and NGOs, and mainstreaming of the ICC by including an ICC clause in trade and cooperation agreements.[120] Support for the ICC is arguably a good example of how the EU has pursued the goals of stability and pacific international relations through the creation and functioning of broad multilateral

[115] Scott, n 113, and Scott and Rajamani in this volume. Indeed, the same might be said of other bilateral initiatives of the EU, which some have criticized as a departure from its supposed commitment to multilateralism. Some of these bilateral initiatives might arguably be seen—as eg in the case of the EU's bilateral trade initiatives in the wake of the failed Doha round—as a response to the failures of multilateralism and as being premised on the assumption that bilateral action can be a spur towards increased collective and multilateral action. See the contribution of Hoffmeister to this volume.

[116] See eg the appraisal of the outcome of the Durban summit by a Harvard environmental economist: R Stavins, 'Assessing the Climate Talks—Did Durban Succeed?' (*An Economic View on the Environment*, 12 December 2011): <http://www.robertstavinsblog.org/2011/12/12/assessing-the-climate-talks-did-durban-succeed/>.

[117] For a suggestion that despite the EU's overall normative support for and engagement with the ICC, Member States have not always fully supported the ICC and the ICC Prosecutor in their actions and choices, and national interests often assert themselves in this context: E Aoun, 'The European Union and International Criminal Justice: Living up to its Normative Preferences' (2012) 50 JCMS 21–36.

[118] For a recent evaluation of the consistency and effectiveness of EU support for the Court, see M Mertens, 'The International Criminal Court: A European Success Story?' (2011) 1 *College d'Europe EU Diplomacy Papers*.

[119] Council Common Position 2003/444/CFSP of 16 June 2003 on the International Criminal Court. See recently Council Decision 2011/168/CFSP of 21 March 2011 on the International Criminal Court. Also the agreement between the EU and the ICC of 6 December 2005 on assistance and cooperation (the first agreement between the EU and another international organization): <http://register.consilium.eu.int/pdf/en/05/st14/st14298.en05.pdf>.

[120] The standard example is Art 11 of the Cotonou Agreement of 11 March 2009: '– In promoting the strengthening of peace and international justice, the Parties reaffirm their determination to:

- share experience in the adoption of legal adjustments required to allow for the ratification and implementation of the Rome Statute of the International Criminal Court; and
- fight against international crime in accordance with international law, giving due regard to the Rome Statute.

The Parties shall seek to take steps towards ratifying and implementing the Rome Statute and related instruments.'

institutions and regimes, and how it has integrated different issue areas within its external policies through strategies like mainstreaming.

As in the example of climate change, EU policy towards the ICC is often contrasted with that of the US,[121] which was opposed to the creation of the ICC and sought to weaken it by concluding bilateral treaties with individual states to ensure that US soldiers would not be brought before the ICC.[122] The EU has promoted ratification by other states of the Rome Statute establishing the ICC,[123] and acted to prevent the conclusion of 'Status of Forces' Agreements with the US by EU Member States and candidate countries.[124]

While the US has more recently begun to support the operation of the ICC in certain ways, as with its consent to the referral of Sudan to the Court, the EU and the US nonetheless continue to pursue rather different strategies towards international criminal tribunals. An example of the different kinds of conditionality used by the EU and the US in the context of the ICC's precursor ad hoc international criminal tribunals can be seen particularly in the cases of Croatia and Serbia before the International Criminal Tribunal for the former Yugoslavia (ICTY). While the US practice of conditionality is based on a positive evaluation by the US Secretary of State,[125] the EU chooses to base its practice of conditionality on the assessment of an independent (at least notionally) international institution, in the form of the ICTY prosecutor.[126]

To summarize, despite criticism of Member State interests which counter or undermine aspects of the EU's general support for the ICC and ICC processes,[127] the EU's governance approach to international relations is reasonably well exemplified in this particular field. The EU has fairly consistently promoted a multilateralist, institution-building strategy, supporting the creation of a new international governance system in the domain of serious criminal offences.

5. Conclusion

The analysis of the EU's 'governance mode' of foreign policy in this chapter has been primarily conceptual and descriptive. While sharing with much of the EU foreign policy literature an attempt to identify what is distinctive about EU external relations, it parts company with much of the 'normative power Europe' literature by eschewing any claim that the EU is a more virtuous international actor than others, that its distinctiveness depends on a lack of military capacity, or that it is motivated more by principles and values than by its interests. The chapter takes as a premise that it is unnecessary and indeed implausible to draw a sharp distinction between the EU's promotion of values and its pursuit of interests in the conduct of its foreign policy and suggests that the EU pursues both milieu goals and possession goals in its external relations. The main descriptive claim is that one of the most distinctive features of EU foreign policy is the *governance approach* which the EU adopts. This governance mode entails a preference for the creation of stable, long-term, institutionalized relationships with other states and entities, and frequent use of regulatory frameworks

[121] See P Pinto Soares, 'The ICC at Eight' (2010) CTR: <http://transatlantic.sais-jhu.edu/transatlantic-topics/Articles/homeland-security/THE_ICC_AT_EIGHT.pdf>.

[122] See in response the EU Guidelines on the Conclusion of Status of Forces Agreements with the US: <http://www.consilium.europa.eu/uedocs/cmsUpload/12134_02en.pdf>, 10.

[123] *The European Union and the International Criminal Court* (Council of the EU, 2010).

[124] J Kelley, 'Who Keeps International Commitments and Why? The International Criminal Court and Bilateral Non-Surrender Agreements' (2007) 101 *American Political Science Review* 573–589.

[125] <http://www.state.gov/r/pa/ei/bgn/5388.htm>.

[126] <http://ec.europa.eu/enlargement/candidate-countries/croatia/eu_croatia_relations_en.htm> and in the case of Serbia <http://news.bbc.co.uk/2/hi/europe/6728787.stm> and <http://ec.europa.eu/enlargement/potential-candidates/serbia/relation/index_en.htm>.

[127] See Aoun, n 117.

involving common articulated goals and broad participation to regulate and coordinate policy externally.

If this identification and depiction of this governance mode of foreign policy is correct, several different sets of questions may be asked about its implications and effect. A first is whether it is effective as a mode of conducting foreign policy, and indeed how its effectiveness may be measured. A second is whether the EU's governance mode involves the exportation (or attempted exportation) of its regulatory modes or its substantive rules.

In terms of the first question on effectiveness, it is sometimes suggested that there is a paradox in that the EU has been more effective globally as a trade and economic actor than as a political model. In other words, it is seen to achieve more as an international actor when it acts in its own material interests (in terms of trade, financial and economic interests, security and migration, etc) than when it attempts to pursue more diffuse milieu goals and to promote participatory governance systems to address collective concerns. But the answer to the effectiveness question depends largely on what the metrics of effectiveness are, and it is considerably more difficult to assess the effectiveness of the operation of an international governance system (eg the effectiveness of the Kyoto regime, which the EU has played a significant role in shaping, in addressing the causes and consequences of climate change, or the ICC regime in tackling impunity for the serious criminal offences, or the UN Convention on the Rights of Persons with Disabilities in tackling the marginalization of people with disabilities) than it is to assess whether the EU successfully negotiated a trade concession or concluded a trade deal which it wanted. The effectiveness of an international governance regime can only realistically be evaluated over time, and also by reference to a counterfactual assumption about how the problem or issue in question would have been addressed in the absence of the existence of the regime.

In terms of the second question, most of the literature on EU exportation of rules focuses on or examines the exportation of substantive EU rules and principles,[128] whereas the analysis of this chapter focuses instead on the proposition that the EU is exporting or spreading its processes and modes of governance to the international arena. A related question, however, is whether this alleged external extension of the EU's governance mode really does amount to an extension of its collective and broadly participatory decision-making processes from the internal to the external realm, or whether in fact it merely represents a more concealed attempt to export the content of its regulatory norms and standards internationally.[129] To put it slightly differently, the question is whether the apparent commitment to promote and participate in collective and participatory decision-making processes externally is meaningful in practice, or whether the EU in fact merely promotes its own interests, rules and agenda, albeit in the form of a governance system premised on partnership and collective decision-making. A satisfactory answer to this question requires substantial empirical investigation, but there is at least some interesting anecdotal evidence to the effect that when the EU attempts to export or extend its substantive rules externally, it encounters greater resistance and objection from other actors than when it promotes its governance model as one which may also be suitable for collective international or regional governance.[130] Further, even when the EU does purport to extend

[128] eg Z Laïdi, 'The Unintended Consequences of European Power' (2007) 5 *Les Cahiers européens de Sciences Po*, available online at <http://www.cee.sciences-po.fr/erpa/docs/wp_2007_5.pdf>, L Pech, 'Rule of law as a guiding principle of the European Union's external action' (2012) 2 CLEER Working Paper, available online at: <http://www.asser.nl/Default.aspx?site_id=26&level1=14467&level2=14468>, and A Bradford, 'The Brussels Effect' (forthcoming 2012/2013) 107 *Northwestern University Law Review* 1, available online at: <http://www.nyls.edu/user_files/1/3/4/15/276/BrusselsEffectBradford.pdf>.

[129] The editors of this volume, in their concluding chapter, suggest that the answer to this question may be that there are examples of both practices, namely the extension of EU substantive standards internationally, as well as an extension of the EU mode of collective decision-making into the international and global arena.

[130] See G de Búrca, 'The EU in the Negotiation of the UN Disability Convention' (2010) 35(2) ELR 174–196, on how the EU's attempt to export its substantive anti-discrimination rules internationally was unsuccessful in several

its collective governance processes and not merely its substantive rules and preferences, there seems to be some evidence that the EU's failure to live up to the explicit commitment to participation or partnership promised by that governance model becomes quickly evident and may generate resistance by the partner country or countries.[131] Another way of expressing this is that the EU's attempts to pursue its own material interests without regard to the interests of those with whom it is negotiating is more likely to be thwarted or at least exposed by the purported commitment to partnership and to collective governance on which is own preferred governance model is premised.

To conclude, this chapter has argued that what is distinctive about the EU as an international actor is not its promotion of values over interests, nor its use of soft versus hard power, nor its greater normative virtue as an international actor over others, but rather the governance mode of foreign policy which it pursues. Amongst the questions which arise from this argument are: (i) whether the governance approach to foreign policy is more effective in addressing collective global problems—or even certain kinds of global problem—than others; and (ii) whether the governance processes the EU promotes and participates in externally are genuinely collective and participatory rather than vehicles through which the EU seeks to export its own substantive rules or to promote its own particular interests without regard to those of other participants. For these questions to be satisfactorily addressed, further empirical analysis is required.

respects although the eventual UN Convention on the Rights of Persons with Disabilities exemplifies the kind of 'experimentalist governance' regime which the EU prefers for many internal policy issues, including anti-discrimination: see G de Búrca 'The EU Anti-Discrimination Regime: Stumbling into Experimentalism?' in Charles Sabel and Jonathan Zeitlin (eds), *Experimentalist Governance in the European Union* (OUP, 2010).

[131] See eg M Farrell, n 98, and B Hettne and F Söderbaum, n 31. See N Tocci and JP Cassarino, 'Rethinking the EU's Mediterranean Policies Post-1/11' (2011) 6 IAI, on what has occurred when the supposed EU commitment to 'joint ownership' has included only a very limited set of official participants, available online at: <http://www.iai.it/pdf/DocIAI/iaiwp1106.pdf>.

4

From the Nation State to the Market: The Evolution of EU Private Law as Regulation of the Economy beyond the Boundaries of the Union?

Hans-W. Micklitz and Dennis Patterson

1. Introduction

In this chapter we seek[1] to demonstrate how the European Union, being understood as a market state,[2] affects the private legal orders (*Privatrechtsordnung*) of the Member States and the design of the emerging European private legal order, first within the EU (the inner space of EU Statecraft) and second in the relations of the EU to the outside world (the outer space of European Statecraft or global governance). We argue that the national private legal orders may be equated with the pre-modern state nation and later with the nation state of the 20th century, whereas the emerging European private law may be equated with the EU market state. In the inner space of the internal market, the EU is smoothly but steadily building a genuine private law that must be kept distinct from nation state codifications. In the outer space the EU market state—and the Member State nation states—are engaged in using private law as a means to influence global governance processes.

We develop our argument in three steps. We begin by clarifying the notion and concept of the market state in its relation to the EU. We sketch out the concept of European private law as economic law[3] within the EU and outside the EU, before finally looking into the role of the EU market state in global governance through private law means.

2. The State

The State[4] exists to deliver security and welfare to its citizens. The 'State' is not a static entity. In the last five hundred years, the State has evolved through five distinct forms, which are properly characterized as 'constitutional orders.' As the State evolves, the grounds of its legitimacy vis-à-vis the nation changes. States produce legal systems consistent with the

[1] Although the text is a joint production, the prime responsibility for Part I lies with Dennis Patterson, for Part II with Hans-W. Micklitz.

[2] The legitimacy of the market state is grounded in its ability to provide economic opportunity for the citizenry. This is its purpose and its ethos.

[3] For clarification see H-W. Micklitz, 'The Visible Hand of European Private Law' in P Eeckhout and T Tridimas (eds), *Yearbook of European Law 2009*, volume 28 (OUP, 2010) 3–60.

[4] We use the word 'state' in two different senses. When we write 'State,' we are referring to the conceptual political entity that has evolved in the Western world over roughly the last 500 years. See JS McClelland, *A History of Western Political Thought* (Routledge, 1996) 280 (dating the birth of the modern state at 1500). The State is manifested in many territorially and politically distinct 'states', like Italy or the Republic of Latvia. When we refer to these individual states, we refer to them as a 'state'. For discussion of the various phases of the State's development, and their relation to a variety of constitutional orders, see Philip Bobbitt, *The Shield of Achilles: War, Peace and the Course of History* (Knopf, 2002) 69–347.

demands of legitimacy. As the grounds for the legitimacy of the State changes, so too does its legal system.[5]

Over the course of the last five hundred years, the State has evolved through a number of configurations. While the Peace of Westphalia is often identified as the point of origin for the State, we agree with those who locate the origins of the State in the mid-seventeenth century.[6] As the State evolves over time, its constitutive features change both in themselves and in relation to one another. At all times, the most important aspect of the evolution of the State is the degree to which the State responds to the demands of the nation[7] in the course of legitimizing itself.

The State has two faces, an inner and an outer. The outer dimension of the State is comprised of two principal features: strategy and trade. At all times, states have a strategic relationship to other states, the most basic of which are peace and war. Trade is the second dimension of the outer face of the State. Trade ideology (eg mercantilism or comparative advantage) follows the constitutional order of the society of states in that each form of the State is complemented by a particular trade regime.

The inner face of the State is law and welfare. With respect to welfare, the modern nation state provides support and protection for the nation. Additionally, the State improves the lives of citizens through law. The story of the nation state is one of the rise of law and regulation as the means for betterment of the daily lives of the citizenry.

'Statecraft' embodies the outer and the inner faces of the State. Our argument is that these two dimensions of Statecraft interact with one another over time, and that the legal regimes produced by states must be structured so as to accord with the ethos of the State.

The inner face of the State is law and 'welfare'. We understand welfare capaciously as both subventions by the State as well as the production of legal regimes designed to improve the lives of citizens. The latter is what we term 'regulatory welfare'. Regulatory welfare refers to the regulation of the economic and social aspects of the State. Health, labour, environmental regulations, resource conservation, worker safety, competition laws, consumer and investor protection are all examples of regulatory welfare. We call the subvention part of welfare 'entitlements welfare'. It encompasses the various regimes adopted by European states to ensure minimum standards of living for their subjects. These include unemployment benefits, retirement, health insurance, minimum income guarantees, housing aid, aid to families with children, education, and other welfare tools adopted by European states to ensure that their nation will not fall below a minimal safety net level.

Our theory posits that the inner constitutional dimension of the State, law, is directly linked to the outer face of the State; that the inner constitution of the State varies from one epochal manifestation to the next; and that the interaction between the inner and outer faces of the State ultimately brings about transformative patterns that, over time, usher in the next era of Statecraft.[8] Thus, the state nation's solidification enterprise, drawing on its subjects to consolidate the metropolis, wound up establishing a distinct 'nation' that became associated with the State and its boundaries. This nation would become the foundational interlocutor of the nation state, and the legitimating enterprise of the State would be to provide for its welfare.

[5] These ideas are elaborated in more detail in Dennis Patterson and Ari Afilalo, *The New Global Trading Order* (CUP, 2008).

[6] See Bobbitt, n 4 and Martin Van Creveld, *The Rise and Decline of the State* (CUP, 1999) 7.

[7] The 'nation' is an ethnographic construct or concept.

[8] Cooper writes: 'The kind of world we have depends on the kind of states that compose it: for the pre-modern world, success is empire and failure is chaos. For the modern, success entails managing the balance of power and failure means falling back into war or empire. For the post-modern state, success means openness and cooperation': R Cooper, The Breaking of Nations (Atlantic Monthly Press, 2003) 76.

In this essay, we seek to understand the European private law enterprise in light of a theory of Statecraft that views the State as undergoing successive epochal transformations. This theory holds that, in each era, a prevailing form of the State operates, characterized by foundational features that define the nature of its internal law and its relations with other states. We review the historical and legal background of the European collectivity in light of our Statecraft theory, and explain how Statecraft sheds light and insight into the political, legal and institutional evolution of Europe and its crises, both past and present.

2.1. Pre-modern era: no possible Europe

We posit that the pre-modern era started with the French Revolution, spanned the Industrial Revolution, and ended with World War I. In this age of Statecraft, the State focused on its own consolidation. Internally, the pre-modern era involved a foundational *laissez-faire* policy coupled with the growth of a legal system designed to protect private property and contract rights. Externally, the State adhered principally to a zero-sum game intended to amass wealth. Taken together, these policies had the design and purpose of strengthening the industrial base of the developing states.

The state nation[9] legitimated itself by bringing unity out of diversity. It arose from the unification into one entity of largely unrelated territories, such as dukedoms, feudal territories, and princely states. The state nation founded a single entity within discrete boundaries. Economically, it saw the rise of capital investment in the industrial base. Its ethos was to increase the power of the emerging sovereign. The internal legal system of the state nation enabled its essential purpose. The state nation adopted an economic legal structure designed to protect contractual and private property, rather than to extend entitlements to its subjects. Legal codes such as the Napoleonic Code were drafted.[10] They protected the expectations of capital holders, and they did so by ensuring that in the common cycles of 'boom-and-bust' policies that later in history came to be known as 'Keynesian' did not interfere with the free evolution of the market.

Another way to conceptualize this era of Statecraft is to think of it as a 'minimal welfare' constitutional era. A regime of entitlements welfare was inconsistent with the protection of capital. Industrialization and the concentration of capital required a freer market than a sophisticated system of welfare entitlements would permit. The same result was obtained for regulatory welfare. Here, as well, the state nation did not legitimize itself by providing protection to its nation. It had not even yet generated the concept of a nation. Instead, it drew on its subjects to amass resources and strengthen itself and, in the process, created the unified State resting on the nation that characterized the 20th century. In that context, regulatory systems like labour or consumer protection, environmental or resource conservation (generally, any of the 20th century administrative laws that we are familiar with) were not part of the internal legal fabric of the states. They would have burdened and hampered the solidification of the emerging industrial concerns at a time when the State derived its legitimacy from the protection of this very process.

[9] The state nation is the constitutional manifestation of a State characterized by a mobilization of a nation (a national, ethno-cultural group) to benefit the State. This form of the State, exemplified by Napoleonic France, dominated Europe and America in the nineteenth century and ultimately gave rise to the modern nation state with the advent of World War I. For a general description, see Bobbitt n 4, 144–204.

[10] A Grab, *Napoleon and the Transformation of Europe* (Palgrave Macmillan, 2003) 50–51. P van den Berg, *The Politics of European Codification: A History of the Unification of Law in France, Prussia, the Austrian Monarchy and the Netherlands* (Europa Law Publishing, 2007) 4–5, 206.

Externally, the state nation followed trade and strategic foundational policies that furthered a similar purpose: the consolidation of the state nation. The state nations of Europe colonized foreign territories and drew upon their resources to bolster their own commercial and industrial base.[11] These foreign territories were viewed as resources with respect to which they were in competition with their neighbours. The colonial map of Africa bears witness to these struggles. It was comprised of states that carved through traditional tribal boundary lines, lumping together ethnic groups that historically had never been part of the same polity, reflecting territorial struggles and compromises among England, France, Belgium, Germany, Italy and other European colonial powers.[12] The European state nations also followed a predominantly mercantilist policy, seeking to sell as much as possible and buy as little as possible from their trading interlocutors.[13]

In this environment, there was no foundation for a European Union. Each entity comprising the whole dedicated itself to consolidating its own base. The very ethos of the state nation was antithetical to unity. States could not engage in an economic and strategic zero-sum game to strengthen themselves while at the same time seeking collaboration. Whether in the colonial battlefield or in the realm of economic competition, the nature of Statecraft called for mustering the available resources to build a unified state.

The state nation needed to build its industrial and commercial base. The state nation process achieved that goal and, in the course of its enterprise, also created a nation associated with its physical boundaries. The Schuman Declaration may be read to perceptively understand that the European enterprise was not a matter of destiny. It described the failures of the nations of Europe, after World War I, to begin creating a unified whole. It did not argue, as Fukuyama or Ricardo did, that history had ended because we had reached a timeless and ultimate state of democratic rule or of economic organization. Instead, it acknowledged that the tragedy of Europe lay in its failure to recognize that, after World War I, a 'united Europe was not created and we had war'.[14] It recognized that in the post-World War I era, Europeans adopted a Treaty which reflected the state nation era values of competition, zero-sum game, lack of cooperation, and domination. The result was a foundational rupture between the architecture of a basic treaty defining the relations among European states and the Statecraft of the age.

World War II was a catalyst to the adoption of the treaties and programmes that shaped the world in the second half of the 20th century. Those treaties, as we explain below, are consistent with a nation state, modern age of Statecraft. The General Agreement on Tariffs and Trade (GATT) was signed at Bretton Woods and ushered in the trade liberalization enterprise, rejecting mercantilism and protectionism.[15] It 'embedded liberalism' in that each state participant enjoys, at least in theory, the sovereign right to establish and operate a welfare system of its choice, and at the same time removed barriers to trade and created a more efficient trading system. France could stay France and maintain programmes ranging from universal education to the supply of subsidized *metro* tickets to large families, all the while participating in a liberalized system of trade that generated more global resources to share. The Marshall Plan ensured that the European trading partners had sufficient economic strength to be meaningful commercial interlocutors for the United States. The new modern order relied on balance of powers, alongside liberalized trade and integration among sovereign equals, and the Marshall Plan fostered European powers so as to bring about greater balance.

[11] F Crouzet, *A History of European Economy, 1000–2000* (University of Virginia Press, 2001) 50–54, 165.

[12] T Pakenham, *The Scramble for Africa* (Avon Books, 1991) 21. H Wesseling, *Imperialism and Colonialism, Essays on the History of European Expansion* (Greenwood Press, 1997) 12–20. On the colonization of Africa see also V Khapoya, *The African Experience: An Introduction* (Prentice Hall, 2009).

[13] P Mathias and S Polland, *The Cambridge Economic History of Europe, Volume VIII* (CUP, 1989) 103.

[14] Schuman Declaration (1950).

[15] After the initiation of Bretton Woods, international trade proliferated six-fold from 1948–1973. *See* <http://econ2.econ.iastate.edu/classes/econ355/choi/bre.htm>.

Europe, because of its unique suffering during World War II, engaged in a deeply integrationist enterprise that went well beyond what any other free trade area would aspire to accomplish. Nevertheless, its roots can be traced to a modern enterprise, albeit amplified by historical circumstances.

2.2. Europe: the early years

By the end of World War I, after the adoption of the Treaty of Versailles, the European states had graduated to the early stages of the nation state era. During that era, the State would marshal its power to provide for the welfare of its nation. At that time, the seeds that had been sown for the establishment of a European collectivity based on free trade and common political institutions had yielded a collectivity of states ready to engage in the European endeavour.[16] The European Union was ready to proceed as a project of integration of discrete nations into a whole that would be inextricably bound but, at the same time, respect national sovereignty.[17]

The historical basis of Europe is succinctly expressed in the Schuman Declaration: 'A united Europe was not achieved, and we had war'. By binding France and Germany to a union and partnership for coal and steel, the resources of war, the community of Europe would make war not only 'unthinkable but materially impossible'. Europe would not be achieved overnight. It would focus on concrete achievements and, in leaps and bounds, become a polity that could in time fairly be labelled as the 'United States of Europe'. In the meantime, foundational treaties were designed to shelter the sovereign right of the Member State to engage in regulatory and entitlements welfare.

European exceptionalism joined Statecraft to create a highly integrated Europe.[18] The European treaties went well beyond the free trade treaties (eg the GATT) that were adopted after World War II. They included a commitment to a single, tariff-free market and the removal of non-tariff barriers to trade. The GATT, on the other hand, contemplated a gradual reduction of the applicable tariffs through a 'binding system' that capped the tariff each state could apply in any product category, and a most-favoured-nation system that (save for regional commitments) required that the lowest tariff extended by the GATT members to any trading partner be extended to all. The European Community, as successor to the European Coal and Steel Community (ECSC), also established common institutions mirroring those of the ECSC that the GATT and other integration systems did not come close to achieving. As explained in greater depth below, Europe attempted to replicate the institutional structure of modern liberal democracies by instituting legislative bodies, an executive-like agency, and a constitutional court. The Treaties also gave individuals a right of access to national courts to enforce rights granted under European law.[19]

While the European Treaties were bolder and more ambitious than any international treaty in force at the time, this overall design still provided a substantial level of protection of the Member States' ability to legislate both regulatory and entitlements welfare. Each Member State could, to a certain extent, remain a 'black box' in which it enjoyed freedom to determine how best to support the welfare of its nations, free from interference by European law.[20]

[16] A Sutcliffe, *An Economic and Social History of Western Europe Since 1945* (Longman Group, 1996) 106.

[17] D Chalmers, G Davies and G Monti, *European Union Law: Cases and Materials* (CUP, 2010) 7–9; N Nugent, *The Government and Politics of the European Union* (5th edn, Duke University Press, 2003) 9–16.

[18] As we explain below, the EU can be seen as one form of the market state. Conceived of as a distinct legal order, the EU produces legal regimes that not only regulate markets but enable them in ways that depart from the traditional nation state conception of the State. In the second half of this chapter, we provide examples that illustrate this point.

[19] See Case 14/83 *Sabine von Colson and Elisabeth Kamann v Land Nordrhein-Westfalen* [1984] ECR 1891.

[20] For quite some time the constitutional courts of the Member States contested the European Court of Justice's position on fundamental rights issues. Thus, in 1970 the German and Italian constitutional courts stated they would not apply provisions of EU law that failed to respect the fundamental rights and values set out in their

The initial challenges of Europe involved the familiar questions attendant to the integration of discrete nation states into a single market. When borders are open to trade, although formally regulatory welfare remains unaffected, the disparate regulatory levels travel along with the goods.

European judicial and political institutions reacted to this challenge of integration with a significantly greater pro-trade oriented approach than other integration projects that did not feature the European commitment to the creation of a new legal order.[21] In its early decisions, the European Court of Justice (ECJ) made certain that any measure that actually or potentially, directly or indirectly, hindered trade, would be subject to its judicial scrutiny.[22] In all cases, barriers to trade arose out of the disparity among national regulations.

The unbridled integrationist purpose of the ECJ thrust it in the midst of a European review of national measures. At the same time, the Court found that European law would have direct effect as long as it was clear and unconditional.[23] It implied a supremacy clause in the Treaties.[24] It also found an implicit 'Bill of Rights' in the common traditions of the Member States, thereby assuaging the national judicial fears that an all-powerful European law would trump national constitutional human rights provisions.[25] As Professor Weiler observed in his seminal article 'The Transformation of Europe',[26] the political institutions of the Member States (in particular, France) did not expect that the Treaties would be interpreted in such an aggressive integrationist manner.

As we explain below, every modern trade-liberalizing system ultimately erodes sovereignty and sows the seeds of its own demise. Modern Statecraft is based on sovereignty and the notion that liberalizing trade can be done without infringing sovereignty. While each trade system will, by definition, seek to balance these conflicting values (often choosing sovereignty protection), over time, the diffuseness and interloped nature of liberalized integrated markets erodes the black box nature of the participating states. This destroys the conditions that made modern trade interaction desirable, and necessitates a new system.

Owing to its unique history, Europe witnessed this phenomenon very early (at the height of the modern era), hence the significance and political sensitivity of the Empty Chair crisis.[27] The Member States rejected the combination of aggressive economic constitutional jurisprudence, passage to less-than-unanimity voting, and closure of selective exit through hardening of law because they could not fathom a situation where other States would outvote them and dictate welfare policy. The sensitivity to welfare and sovereignty, however, was no accident: it was a unique product of the modern age. As we explain later, the Member States had no issue abandoning the Luxembourg compromise whereby each State could veto European legislation that it disliked later in the 20th century, because by then they had graduated to a post-modern market state age. The protective reflex that led to the Luxembourg accords, thereby saving the European enterprise, stemmed from fundamental nation state constitutional principles: preservation of regulatory welfare, sovereign right to legislate

national constitutions. See in this respect Case 11–70 *Internationale Handelsgesellschaft* [1974] 2 *CML Rev* 540 and Frontini v Ministero delle Finanze[1974] *CML Rev* 386.

[21] See M Egan, *Constructing a European Market* (OUP, 2001) ch 4.

[22] See Case 41–74 *Van Duyn v Home Office* [1974] ECR 1337.

[23] See Case 26–62 *NV Algemene Transport- en Expeditie Onderneming van Gend and Loos v Netherlands Inland Revenue Administration* [1963] ECR 1.

[24] See Case 6–64 *Flaminio Costa v ENEL* [1964] ECR 585; Case 106/77 *Simmenthal II* [1978] ECR 629; Case C-106/89 *Marleasing* [1991] ECR 4135.

[25] Case 11–70 *Internationale Handelsgesellschaft* [1974] 2 *CML Rev* 540 and the so-called *Solange* case-law: Judgment of 29 May 1974, 37 *Entscheidungen des Bundesverfassungerichts* 271 (Solange I) and Judgment of 22 October 1986, 73 *Entscheidungen des Bundesverfassungerichts* 339 (Solange II).

[26] JHH Weiler, 'The Transformation of Europe' 100(8) *The Yale Law Journal*, Symposium: International Law.

[27] N Piers Ludlow, 'De-commissioning the empty chair crisis: The community institutions and the crisis of 1965–66' in J M Palayret, H Wallace, P Winand (eds), *Visions, Votes and Vetoes: The Empty Chair Crisis and the Luxembourg Compromise Forty Years On* (Peter Lang, 2006) 79–96.

in that area free of international and supranational interference, and sovereign limitation on the import of foreign standards into the domestic market.[28]

The closure of selective exit was unpalatable, because it would have established a foundational system more characteristic of the market state, where sovereignty is subordinate to international measures to solidify and protect markets. The European plan to install such a system was scheduled to take effect in the thick of the modern nation state era. This was inconsistent with the legitimacy demands on the State, and with its need to provide welfare unimpeded by international regulatory schemes.

2.3. Democracy deficit

Statecraft also explains the institutional challenges that arose in the formative years of Europe, and how those challenges were met. In the modern nation state age, the global collectivity of states agreed to open up borders to trade, all the while preserving in theory each individual state's ability to establish the welfare system of its choice.[29] France could remain France and extend half-price metro tickets to families with many children, England could continue to adhere to cradle-to-grave programmes, Japan could engage in indicative planning, and the United States could tax and spend.

Europe had to adopt a political decision-making structure for crafting laws that would harmonize the single market and that, in light of the decisions of the European Court on constitutional issues, would be binding throughout the Member States. This was another manifestation of European exceptionalism. One of its initial foundational challenges was how to design those institutions.

Europe quickly fell into the trap of trying to resolve this issue by replicating the political institutions of the nation state, attempting, in effect, to create a European 'super-nation state', one that would protect the welfare of the European collectivity. Europe adapted the institutions with which the Member States were familiar. Where it acted through its institutions for the whole, Europe would replicate the European modern liberal democratic state.

This is what led to what came to be known as the 'European democracy deficit'. The democracy deficit debate often took the form of a critique of Europe's failure to adopt institutions that better replicated those of modern liberal democracies.

Europe also sought to replicate the modern constitutional protections of minority rights. After it announced its supremacy jurisprudence, the European Court assuaged the fears of national judiciaries and other interlocutors by implying a Bill of Rights in the European treaties, which included none.[30] The fundamental rights guaranteed by this jurisprudence would be inspired by the common values of the Member States.

However, as more insightful observers commented, this nation state reflex to determine welfare by majority or other democratically endorsed voting quorum missed the core question of integration in the modern nation state era: how to craft rules for the whole all the while respecting national sovereignty. Whether an alliance of national members of Parliament voted down another set of Member State representatives directly elected by the people, or whether this happened through a vote of the executives delegated to the Council, the integrated area would overrule national choices that were the essence of Statecraft in action in the modern age. No matter how much representative democracy was infused in the system, the malaise caused by the democracy deficit would not dissipate.[31]

[28] Weiler, n 26, 2457.

[29] See JG Ruggie, 'International Regimes, Transactions, and Change: embedded liberalism in the postwar economic order' (1982) 36 *International Organization* 385–388.

[30] JHH Weiler, 'Eurocracy and Distrust: Some Questions Concerning the Role of the European Court of Justice in the Protection of Fundamental Human Rights within the Legal Order of the European Communities' (1986) 61 *Washington Law Review* 1105.

[31] Ibid, at pp 2466–2474.

2.4. From Luxembourg to Maastricht: accession to the age of the market state

The Empty Chair crisis both saved and tempered the integration enterprise of Europe. Bargaining 'in the shadow of the veto'[32] sheltered sovereignty but slowed the adoption of European integration measures. By the 1980s and 1990s, however, Europe picked up speed and moved rapidly ahead with the harmonization or approximation of its laws on a larger scale. Complementing the more perfect unification of its single market, Europe then proceeded to adopt a single currency, European citizenship, an agreement for the removal of border controls among Member States belonging to the Schengen zone, and other institutional and political breakthroughs that pushed Europe significantly along the integration road.

We posit that, while other factors surely contributed to it, the acceleration of the integration of Europe was made possible by the accession to the age of the market state. Nation states are bound to evolve into market states over time. Their inner ethos, welfare for the nation, corresponds to their outer face: integration through trade while preserving sovereignty. Trade in goods and services inevitably leads to capital flows and interloping ownership of global assets. This is true especially in an integrated area like Europe, where the movement of capital and people is ensured and encouraged to a much greater extent than in other trade regulatory schemes. The integrated area will then tend to become more diffuse and use its 'black box aggregation character'. Industries and other commercial sectors will tend to be dissociated from the nation. Regulatory welfare will be disrupted by the growing import of goods manufactured under other regulatory conditions. In time, jobs and production will be increasingly outsourced.

In this environment, the State loses control over regulatory and entitlements welfare. Traditional tools such as exchange rates become regulated by the market to a much greater extent than by the State. States gradually lose their ability to incur national debt because foreign debt holders gradually displace nationals. The free flow of goods carries with it disparate regulation. With the aging of a population that boomed after World War II, and with renewed birth rate and immigration, budgets for entitlements welfare come under excessive strain. In turn, the nature of sovereignty changes as the ethos of the State shifts away from providing top-down regulatory and entitlements welfare to fostering and preserving market conditions where economic opportunity can be maximized.

This is the legitimating ethos of the market state. Instead of providing top-down welfare, the post-modern market state unleashes its power to ground the market and maximize the enablement of economic opportunity for its citizens. This may translate into legislation that is similar to that found in the nation state. Securities disclosure or bank capitalization laws, for example, protect consumer welfare while fostering market stability. Even entitlements such as aid to education may belong to both ages, although vouchers and other market-based solutions may be more appropriate to the market state era. In the changed post-modern globalized terrain, market failures in one segment of the market can travel rapidly to threaten and infect other segments across borders. The collectivity of states must dedicate itself to create conditions that stabilize and solidify the enlarged market. The process is not unlike that of the state nation; even if it infringes on what would have been viewed as unassailable welfare sovereign rights in the middle of the 20th century, it is necessary to maintain the architecture of the 21st. This is the pattern that Europe followed.

We place the emergence of the market state toward the end of the 20th century,[33] when global economies started to integrate to such an extent that black box Statecraft eroded enough to give way to a more diffuse, interloped set of market states whose ethos focused on the preservation of the market and the maximization of opportunity, rather than top-down

[32] See Weiler, n 26, 2450.

[33] The emergence of market states is a global phenomenon. Our remarks in this chapter concentrate on Western nation states because we are elucidating a particular history, that of EU law.

welfare entitlements. Europe's expansion into market state regulatory territory coincided with this timetable. In effect, '[i]n the late 1980s the Single European Act was passed to facilitate the creation of a single market by streamlining the method by which harmonization laws were made. These laws were designed to complete the single market by the end of 1992.[34] Prior to 1993, over 300 measures were passed into law'.[35] Thereafter, hundreds more measures were adopted, thereby bringing the regulatory welfare landscape of Europe into substantial conformity. This was the birth of what we later call European Regulatory Private Law.

The Treaty of Maastricht built upon the Single European Act (SEA) by completing the single market and establishing the European Monetary Union in three successive stages. The Treaty requires the Member States to ensure 'a closer coordination of their economic policies'[36] (a significant move to which we will come back later in this essay), and to 'provide for multilateral surveillance of this coordination'. In addition, the States 'are subject to financial and budgetary discipline'. Monetary unification was an extremely significant step in the evolution of Europe, which was also consistent with accession to the market state. The objective of monetary policy is to create a single currency and to ensure this currency's stability by maintaining price stability, economic policy coordination, and respect for the market economy.

The convergence of economic policy that came with monetary unification goes to the heart of welfare entitlements. Although Europe did not adopt a common fiscal policy, it did not infringe on the welfare system of Member States in that it left them free to craft social security and health, education, retirement and other mainstays of welfare as they saw fit.[37] But entry to the Eurozone demanded that participating Member States adhere to specified macroeconomic goals.[38] These European requirements made sense in a market state age where protecting market opportunity becomes the ethos of the State and an animating principle of the relationship among states.

2.5. Lisbon—the market state takes shape

Lisbon is an eminently early market state era treaty.[39] While it continues the European tendency to replicate the structure of the nation state at the integrated area level, it does not hesitate to give the European polity powers that nation state Statecraft could never have

[34] Art 13 of the Single European Act (SEA), which entered into force in 1987 amended, inter alia, Art 8a of the Treaty Establishing the European Economic Community (EEC Treaty) so that it read: 'The Community shall adopt measures with the aim of progressively establishing the internal market over a period expiring on 31 December 1992. The internal market shall comprise an area without internal frontiers in which the free movement of goods, persons, services and capital is ensured in accordance with the provisions of this Treaty'. The SEA is available at: <http://ec.europa.eu/economy_finance/emu_history/documents/treaties/singleeuropeanact.pdf>.

[35] More at: <http://www.lavellecoleman.ie/cuuploads/editor/file/England%20and%20Wales%20pdfs/UsingEuropeanLaw2/5_%20Harmonistions%20of%20Laws.pdf>.

[36] Art 121 TFEU.

[37] Although certain case-law of the ECJ did start infringing on that prerogative of the Member States already in the pre-Lisbon era: eg confrontation of free movement and industrial relations in the European social model, such as Case C-341/05 *Laval and Partneri* [2007] ECR I-11767 and Case C-438/05 *The International Transport Workers' Federation and The Finnish Seamen's Union* [2007] ECR I-10779.

[38] These criteria, established by the Maastricht Treaty and referred to as the 'Maastricht Criteria', were enshrined in Arts 104 and 121(1) of the TEU, as well as in Protocol No 20 on the Excessive Deficit Procedure, and Protocol No 21 on the Convergence Criteria referred to in Art 121 of the Treaty on European Union. Such criteria may be summarized as follows: '1) inflation of no more than 1.5 percentage points above the average rate of the three EU member states with the lowest inflation over the previous year. 2) A national budget deficit at or below 3 percent of gross domestic product (GDP). 3) National public debt not exceeding 60 percent of gross domestic product. A country with a higher level of debt can still adopt the euro provided its debt level is falling steadily. 4) Long-term interest rates should be no more than two percentage points above the rate in the three EU countries with the lowest inflation over the previous year. 5) The national currency is required to enter the ERM 2 exchange rate mechanism two years prior to entry [to the Euro zone]': <http://glossary.reuters.com/index.php/Maastricht_Criteria>.

[39] We view the EU as a distinct legal order, separate from the Member States. As such, it has the makings of a market state.

tolerated being transferred from the nation. Lisbon gives Europe an important foreign policy unified voice. It consolidates it into a legal personality that will make it easier to accede to agreements and international institutions. It gives more power to the European Parliament while making qualified majority at the Council level the default. It transfers to the European Court jurisdiction over areas that are traditionally associated with the nation state's competence in the previous Statecraft age. It further europeanizes human rights by strengthening the legal status of the Charter of Fundamental Rights. It increases the coordination between national and European institutions, strengthens the concept of subsidiarity, and moves Europe theoretically further down the role of a quasi-Federal entity. But it did not properly lay the ground for the development of a European Civil Code, as we will demonstrate.

Altogether, these developments are consistent with the diffuseness of an integrated area that arose out of its nation state iteration, in the early age of the market state evolution. They reflect attempts to shore up the collective whole by strengthening the power of its institutions and loosening the decision-making capacities, all the while addressing some of the remnants of the nation stage age issues, such as the democracy deficit.

In this respect, Lisbon is most conspicuous for what it does not include: a coordination of budget and tax policies in the integrated single market for goods, services, capital, and persons. These aspects of integration are some of the last frontiers of the dismantlement of nation state welfare.[40] Welfare entitlements depend on the budget and tax choices made by the nation state. While the Eurozone nation states of Europe committed to a certain degree of convergence, Europe fell short of unifying or harmonizing budget and tax choices. The nation state's reflex, whether it is expressed in French strikes to protest the proposed lowering of the retirement age or Greek debt issuance, evidently does not allow Europe to strip its members of welfare entitlements sovereignty at this early market state age.

The situation just described is akin to the state nation reflex of the post-World War I era that prevented the emerging nation states from trading among themselves based on comparative advantage and the preservation of sovereignty. Architecturally, Europe had to shed its mercantilist skin in exchange for an economically collaborative one. Today, Europe must begin to shed its national welfare entitlements skin and trade it in for a market state budget and tax policy that will inevitably cut deep into the welfare entitlements programmes of the 20th century. Failure to do so will lead to existential crises akin to the trade wars of the 1920s and 1930s. The reason is this: in a diffuse and intertwined market, the welfare entitlements choices made by one national component reverberate and threaten those made by others. The Greek and Irish debt crises illustrate this claim.

3. European Private Law

Our argument is based on a particular understanding of private law (meaning 'economic law') that reaches beyond nation state categories of private legal orders. Only such a broadened frame opens the way to understanding this evolution. The transformation happens over time, takes various forms and it is not homogeneous. The process begins with the SEA. We use four parameters for getting to grips with the tensions between the nation state private legal orders and the market state European private law: conflict and resistance, intrusion and substitution, hybridization and convergence. The analysis clearly distinguishes between the inner space of the EU, the internal development of EU Statecraft and the outer space of the EU. The role and function the EU plays and might play in global governance through private law cannot be understood without taking the internal development into account: the making of a genuine European private law.

[40] While this dismantling will not spell the end of the nation state, it does mark the furthest point on the evolution of the state from a nation state to a market state.

3.1. Traditional nation state private law vs modern European market state private law

Private law is understood as economic law,[41] covering not only contract and tort or systematically speaking the continental codifications but also public and private regulation of the economy. The broad understanding of private law is crucial for the development of a deeper understanding of the ongoing transformation process in the EU. The traditional national private legal order, with its focus on contract and tort presents the *nation state variant of private law*. They have emerged and they are deeply rooted in the state nation and nation state building process of the 18th and 19th century in continental Europe. International private law formed the conceptual answer to decide on the applicable law in cross-border transactions.

European Union private law is different. The European Union is not a state, at least not a nation state or a state of nations. What makes the discourse on the European Constitution, with a big or a small 'c',[42] difficult is the fact that the conceptual design of the EU legal order is so deeply entrenched by nation state constitutional patterns, overlooking the potential of the ongoing transformation process, as has been shown above.[43] The debate (now over ten years old) over the feasibility of a European Civil Code[44] fits neatly into such a distorted perspective, which is just a mirror image of the constitutional debate. The 2001 document of the European Commission enumerated mainly European international private law and consumer contract law directives. The first category is conceptually speaking no more than a European variant of longstanding attempts at the international level to agree on common standards on how the applicable law should be determined. Consumer law had raised more awareness, being the gateway for the European Union to instrumentalize consumer contract law for completing the internal market, long before the discussion on a European Civil Code started. The second source of inspiration constituted the nation state private legal orders. Perhaps not thinking but discussing private law in categories of the nation state must cast a blind eye to the development of private law outside nation state formed categories. Not being a state, the European Union was never concerned with the underpinnings of national private law, with private autonomy or freedom of contract. In the completion of the internal market the European Union appears as a regulator, be it through the ECJ, which is challenging national economic rules that hinder free trade of products, services, capital or persons, or be it through the EU legislator, which is adopting horizontal or vertical market-related rules on private transactions, often by way of new modes of governance.[45] That regulatory private law, in its negative variant through the impact of the four freedoms on the private law and in its positive variant through the bulk of EU rules that have been adopted in the aftermath of the Single European Act outside Consumer and Anti-discrimination Law, serves the EU *market state* now becomes clear. *This* private law is different from national private legal orders which are based on private autonomy and free will; it is a private law which takes its form, its procedure and its content from being instrumentalized for building and shaping markets.[46]

[41] HD Assmann, G Brüggemeier, D Hart and C Joerges, 'Zivilrecht als Teil des Wirtschaftsrechts' in *Wirtschaftsrecht als Kritik des Privatrechts* (Athenäum Verlag, 1980).

[42] N Walker, 'Big "C" or small "c"' (2006) 12 ELJ 12–14.

[43] J Habermas, *Zur Verfassung Europas, Ein Essay* (Suhrkamp Verlag, 2011).

[44] The official start might be dated back to the Communication of the European Commission, although the European Parliament had been advocating for a European Civil Code since the early 1990s.

[45] F Cafaggi and H Muir-Watt (eds), *Making European Private Law* (Edward Elgar Publishing, 2008); same authors, *The Regulatory Functions of European Private Law* (Edward Elgar Publishing, 2010).

[46] In the German understanding of private law as economic law, *Privatrecht als Wirtschaftsrecht*, see for Europe: CU Schmidt, *Die Instrumentalisierung des Privatrechts durch die Europäische Union* (Nomos, 2010).

There is an obvious argument against such a distinction between *nation* states being equated with contract and tort law, with freedom of contract and private autonomy and *European* private law being regulatory in nature meant to design markets. Regulation in private law has already been discussed for more than hundred years. The distinction between formal private law of the pre-modern state and private law regulation, which contained the nucleus for what became the welfare state in the 20th century has been criticized in *Otto v Gierke*, amongst others.[47]

Regulatory law in the late 19th century was mainly labour and social law, which was kept outside the *Bürgerliches Gesetzbuch* (German Civil Code). Today's regulatory private law cuts across all sectors of economic policies. In particular, it lies at the heart of service contracts on financial services, on telecommunications, on energy (electricity, gas), on (the increasingly privatized) health care services, and last but not least on transport, which together amount for 70% of the gross income in the EU. The driving force behind all these rules that aim mainly at opening up markets, at establishing competition, at liberalizing former public services, at promoting privatization in former areas of public services, is undoubtedly the EU, more precisely the European Commission. Private law issues tie in only between other more 'important aspects' of the appropriate market design. This private law is regulatory law, but 'regulatory' should not be equated with rules that restrict private autonomy and freedom of contract. Their instrumental character shields them from easy classification. Regulatory private law may contain both elements, establishing market freedoms and therefore increasing private autonomy, while at the same time providing for rules that set boundaries to the newly created market autonomy.[48]

The regulator of hundred years ago was the nation state, which used its regulatory power to shape national markets for national economies. The establishment of the European Economic Community in 1957 changed the economic, political and social environments. Nowadays it is the EU that has garnered the necessary support at all institutional levels to adopt regulatory measures. The relevant pieces of secondary Community law address economic actors, business and consumers, who are ready to invest into a market that offers more opportunities and better choices on both sides. The legislative means and regulatory tools, not to speak of the particular content of the rules, inherently bear a cross-border dimension. This might explain why the EU has to 'invent' new devices that fit overall policy objectives.

3.2. Four parameters for analysing the transformation within the EU

The four categories are meant to capture the set of variants available in the relationship between nation state private law and market state European private law.[49] They share a common theoretical background in legal theories of private law as economic law,[50] theories analysing private law beyond the state,[51] and in institutional economics. We have identified four parameters which tentatively allow us to describe and analyse the interaction between nation state private law regimes and market state European private law regimes: conflict and resistance, intrusion and substitution, hybridization, and convergence. Without any attempt to explain the deeper reasons behind each category, we will use them in a rather pragmatic

[47] *Gierke, Otto v 1895–1917. Deutsches Privatrecht.* 3 vols. (Duncker and Humblot). Vol 1, Allgemeiner Teil und Personenrecht, 1895. Vol 2, Sachenrecht, 1905. Vol 3, Schuldrecht, 1917.

[48] As prominently designed in the *White Paper of the Completion of the Internal Market* COM (1985) 310 final.

[49] The following is no more than a snapshot of the theoretical background that guides our analysis. This is not the right place to explain the deeper reasons. For the purpose of this paper, we will simply 'use' and 'apply' what we have developed elsewhere. See n 3.

[50] L Raiser, *Die Zukunft des Privatrechts* (De Gruyter, 1971).

[51] R Michaels and N Jansen, 'Private Law Beyond the State? Europeanization, Globalization, Privatization' (2006) 54 *American Journal of Comparative Law* 843.

way to clarify the relationship between nation state private law and market state European private law.

(1) Conflict and resistance:[52] This is suggested as one of the possible reactions of the Member States. The perspective is that the Member States do not give way to the intruding European regulatory private law. Instead, they provoke a clash between the European regulatory private law and the national law and set limits to where the intruding law ends and where the national laws begin.

In defending the national private legal order, more precisely national civil codes, Member States defend nation state patterns. The political and academic reactions in the Member States on the feasibility of a European Civil Code provide ample evidence for such an understanding. Even the academic world is divided between the 'believers' and the 'opponents'. The discourse sometimes evinces a degree of hostility.[53] With the adoption of the draft Regulation on a Common European Sales Law (CESL), the remnants of the European civil code project reach the political agenda in the Council of Ministers, in the European and national Parliaments. Parliaments of seven Member States have raised objections to the draft Regulation, mainly for lack of competence. Whilst this does not suffice to stop the initiative under the rules of the Treaty, it provides evidence of strong resistance in a considerable number of Member States to any attempt by the EU to intervene into the core of the nation states private legal orders, ie into sales law.

(2) Intrusion and substitution:[54] This is suggested to be the perspective of the current EU law-making and law enforcement strategies, enshrined in the idea of a self-sufficient order composed of three major elements: (1) the horizontal and vertical sectoral rules; (2) the general principles enshrined in the horizontal and vertical sectoral rules; (3) the general principles of civil law.[55]

Regulatory private law is the blueprint for understanding the transformation process. The EU is bypassing the nation states and developing its own design for a market-based private legal order, an enabling legal order. The standard model for private law as a self-sufficient order is the sectorial rules on telecommunication, energy, financial services and transport. Self-sufficiency means that the whole process of law-making up to law enforcement follows sector-specific patterns. The Member States have given way to substitution and intrusion by adopting generations of secondary community law (1st, 2nd and 3rd between 1986 and 2010) rules which aim at establishing a European market for telecommunication, for energy and for transport. When the EU adopts secondary Community law in the area of private law, Member States keep the implementation of rules distinct from the codified national private

[52] For a deeper understanding see B Tamanaha, 'Understanding Legal Pluralism, Past to Present, Local to Global' (2007) 29 *Sydney Law Review* 375; D Caruso, 'The Missing View of the Cathedral: The Private Law Paradigm of European Legal Integration' (1997) 3 ELJ 3; L Niglia, 'The non-Europeanisation of Private Law' (2001) 4 ERPL 575.

[53] eg F Yves Leqeutte, 'Quelques remarques à propos du projet de code civil européen de Monsieur von Bar' (2002) *Receuil Le Dalloz* 2202–2214; B Fauvarque-Cosson, 'Faut-il un code civil européen?' (2002) *Revue Trimestrielle De Droit Civil* 463; also, 'Droit européen des contrats: première réaction au plan d'action de la Commission' (2003) *Receuil Le Dalloz* 1171; Ph Malinvaud, 'Réponse-hors délai- à la Commission européene: à propos d'un code européen des contrats' (2002) *Receuil Le Dalloz* 2542–2551; J Heut, 'Nous faut-il un "euro" droit civil?' (2002) *Receuil Le Dalloz* 2611–2614; P Legrand, 'Antivonbar' (2006) 1 *Journal of Comparative Law* 13.

[54] The link to system theory is obvious, though not sufficient: G Teubner, 'Self-subversive Justice: Contingency or Transcendence Formula of Law' (2009) 72 MLR 1.

[55] Case C-412/06 *Hamilton* [2008] ECR I-2383, para 42; Case C-489/07 *Messner* [2009] ECR I-7315, Opinion of A-G Trstenjak, paras 91 and 108; Case C-101/08 *Audiolux* [2009] ECR I-9823, at 29; Jürgen Basedow, 'Mangold, Audiolux und die allgemeinen Grundsätze des europäischen Privatrechts' in *Festschrift für Klaus J. Hopt zum 70. Geburtstag am 24. August 2010* (De Gruyter, 2010) 27; St Weatherill, 'The "principles of civil law" as a basis for interpreting the legislative acquis' (2010) ERCL 74; A Hartkamp, 'The General Principles of EU Law and Private Law' (2011) 75 RabelsZ 241.

legal orders. They are enshrined in national acts that leave the structure of the EU regulatory approach intact, which means market access rules and private law rules remain intact. Some Member States have compiled consumer law in a separate code; most of them integrate the relevant rules sector by sector into their national legislation.

(3) Hybridization:[56] This is suggested to be an overall normative model of a composite legal order, within which the European and the national legal orders both play their part in some sort of a merged European–national private legal order. Hybridization means that the legal character of the respective rule is neither European nor national. It bears elements of both legal orders and is therefore supposed to be hybrid.

From a historical perspective, this is an old form of the co-existence of different legal patterns. The colonial experience provides ample evidence for hybrid legal orders. In modern times hybridization characterizes the relationship between private legal orders and constitutions. In view of the envisaged analysis, one might understand hybridization as a means to leave space for nation state private legal orders and self-standing market state private legal order(s). Understood in this way, hybridization can be found mainly in the so-called 'constitutionalization' of private law. This development began decades ago in the Member States, when national courts referred to constitutional rights to intervene into classical private law cases, mainly in order to enhance the importance of social rights in private law matters.[57] The ECJ, as well as the European Court of Human Rights, has begun an ever stronger form to use human rights and since 2000 fundamental rights as a means to enhance the position of the individual, be it against his or her state, or be it horizontally in private law relations.[58] The result is a hybrid order, where nation state remedies form the ground which is be examined against European fundamental and human rights.

(4) Convergence:[59] This is suggested to be a process of mutual approximation of the two different legal orders, of nation state based legal orders and market based legal order(s). They are not merged as in the concept of hybridization, they still exist side by side, but they are drawing nearer to each other. Convergence is not bound to mandatory standards and default rules. It instead enshrines in particular the new modes of governance, co-regulation and self-regulation, which are enhanced by limited and limiting state powers.

The market state concept opens up space for private regulation, ie for private actors and private regulation.[60] The theoretical debate on convergence is very advanced, however it still focuses too much on statutory law-making or more precisely on EU law-making via directives and regulations. The inherent assumption of all EU law-making is that harmonization of private law rules via top-down binding directives and regulations increases

[56] T Duve, 'An Early Globalization of Justice? Historical observations on mechanisms of creating normative coherence in the Age of Discovery', paper presented at the University of Helsinki, September 2011; I-J Sand, 'Hybrid Law—Law in a Global Society of Differentiation and Change' in G-P Calliess, A Fischer-Lescano, D Wielsch and P Zumbansen (eds), *Soziologische Jurisprudenz: Festschrift für Gunther Teubner zum 65. Geburtstag* (Walter de Gruyter, 2009) 871–886.

[57] O Cherednychenko, *Fundamental Rights, Contract Law and the Protection of the Weaker Party: A Comparative Analysis of the Constitutionalisation of the Contract Law with Emphasis on Risky Financial Transactions, doctoral dissertation* (Utrecht University, 2008); C Mak, *Fundamental Rights in European Contract Law. A Comparison of the Impact of Fundamental Rights on Contractual Relationships in Germany, the Netherlands, Italy and England, Alphen aan den Rijin* (Kluwer Law International, 2008).

[58] N Reich, 'Horizontal Liability in EC Law—Hybridisation of Remedies for Compensation in Case of Breach of EC Rights' (2007) 44 *CML Rev* 704.

[59] W Van Gerven, 'Private Law in a Federal Perspective' in R Brownword, H-W. Micklitz, L Niglia and S Weatherill (eds), *The Foundations of European Private Law* (Hart Publishing, 2011) 337; P Legrand, 'The Impossibility of Legal Transplants' (1997) 4 Maastricht J European and Comparative L 111; T Wilhelmsson, 'The Contract Law Acquis—Towards More Coherence Through Generalisation' (2008) 4 *Europäischer Juristentag* 111–145.

[60] F Cafaggi (ed), *Reframing Self-regulation in European Private Law* (Kluwer, 2006).

	Conflict and resistance Nation state	Self-sufficiency Market state	Hybridization Nation state and market state side-by-side	Convergence State nation and market state (Co-state?)
Private/economic law	Maintenance of the national private legal orders	European regulatory private law	Constitutionalization of private law	Lex mercatoria, private regulation

Figure 2

convergence. The counter position is most prominently documented in the *Jus Commune* series edited by W Van Gerven. Here the idea is that the courts are the key players in paving the way for convergence via a mutual learning process. We start from the premise that convergence is easier to manage and to realise in areas where private actors dominate, eg standardization of services via national and European standards bodies. Private regulation is older than the state nation (lex mercatoria). That is why there is a link between the old state nation patterns (and its predecessors) and the new emerging market state.[61]

The current state of affairs—the intermingling of nation state private legal orders and the emerging EU market state—could be summed up in the following overview, which nicely demonstrates that we are observing an ongoing process of change where different patterns and different variations of the state stand side by side.

3.3. The interaction between the inner and the outer space of nation state private law and market state European private law

The answer to the question of the interaction between the inner and the outer space of private law in the EU market state might be a straightforward 'no', as Member States will claim that private law in the outer space of the EU lies in their hands, be it in the traditional or the modern variant. In traditional private law, Member States coordinate their private legal orders outside the EU within The Hague Conference of Private International Law,[62] or they unify contract law through international agreements such as the Vienna Convention. This clear picture becomes blurred through CESL which, if adopted, would compete with the Vienna Convention, similar to Latin American or ASEANplus (Japan, Korea, China) models of enhanced cooperation in nation state private law. It would make the EU an international player and competitor over the search for the best legal order, in an area where Member States today still hold competences. The picture seems similar in sector-related rules in areas such as telecommunications, financial services, transport, to some extent energy, or sports (football, Olympic Games), health and safety regulation in the area of pharmaceuticals (WHO), chemicals (Food and Agriculture Organization (FAO)/United Nations Environmental Programme (UNEP), pesticides (FAO/UNEP), foodstuff (FAO/Codex Alimentarius) and consumer goods (International Organization for Standardization/International Electrotechnical Commission). As in traditional nation state private law, Member States claim that any involvement at the international level, even under the integration of the EU, has to go through their hands, leaving the EU with a backstage role. Fortress Europe—the inner space of European (regulatory) private law—looks from the outside like a coherent block, whilst the outer space of European (regulatory) private law looks like an

[61] See on this issue N Jansen, 'Legal Pluralism in Europe, National Laws, European Legislation, and Non-legislative Codification' in L Niglia (ed), *Pluralism and European Private Law* (Hart Publishing, 2012, forthcoming).

[62] <http://www.hcch.net/index_en.php> (last consulted 29 April 2012).

integral part, if any, of an international legal order where the EU has no say. The result would be that the space for European private law remains limited to the inner world of the EU, whereas the outer space remains dominated by the Member States in both areas, ie traditional and modern private law. Whether and to what extent the EU is playing a role in global governance through private law remains to be clarified.

Competence is key. Whether or not the European Union may become involved in private law making and enforcement outside the EU depends on areas of *both* nation state private law and market state European law; on whether it has the competence to engage in negotiations and maybe even the conclusion of international agreements which bind the Member States. The EU law on external relations can be characterized as a long-standing battle over competences, with the EU constantly attempting to extend its powers via Treaty amendments and/or with the help of the European Court of Justice, whereas the Member States hesitate—to put it in cautious terms—to 'delegate sovereignty' to the EU level. The competence rules of the Treaty, read together with the relevant case-law of the ECJ, tell a different story, one where there could and might be much more coherence between the inner and the outer space of European regulatory private law; one where the market state has gained ground even outside the EU borders—silently promoted in particular by the European Commission, but where there is still room for nation state private legal orders in the traditional field of private law. In order to verify our thesis of the existing interlink we need to look into the EU powers in external relations, both in traditional nation state contract and tort law (the codifications), and the market state European regulatory private law. This requires a short excursion into competence rules, linked to the different substance of European private law (traditional and regulatory).

Within the EU, the scenario looks like this: traditional private law matters (eg the harmonization of contract and tort—the core of national private legal orders) are mainly and mostly subject to attempts by the EU to europeanize international private law rules via Article 81 TFEU (jurisdiction, applicable law and trans-border enforcement of judgments). The EU has no competence in the core areas of private law, contract, and tort. Measures to set common standards in the area of regulatory private law are based either on Article 114 TFEU (consumer law, telecommunications, energy, financial services) or Articles 91 and 100 TFEU (transport). CESL represents the first attempt to use Article 114 TFEU to regulate traditional private law matters, although in a trans-border context.

Outside the EU the situation is more complex. The implied power doctrine, as developed by the ECJ,[63] suggests that whenever the EU has succeeded in regulating (regulatory) private law matters *within* the EU under whatever competence rule (Articles 80, 91–100, 114 TFEU), it has also obtained the power to engage in negotiations and international agreements in *external* relations in that very same field. This power has to be shared with the Member States in so far as the measures adopted internally strive for minimum harmonization only. In *Lugano* the ECJ[64] confirmed the implied powers doctrine with regard to Article 81 TFEU, in the core area of Member States competences and of nation state private legal orders. Furthermore, the Lisbon Treaty extended the powers of the EU in the area of the Common Commercial Policy considerably: Article 207 TFEU grants the EU exclusive powers not only for the regulation of goods but now also for services, intellectual property and foreign direct investment. Setting aside the relationship between the implied powers doctrine and Article 207 TFEU, we assume that this extension must be regarded as another building block in shaping the EU as a market state.

[63] Case 22/70 *Commission v Council* (AETR/ERTA) [1971] ECR 263, para 19; generally M Cremona, 'External Relations and External Competence of the European Union: The Emergence of an Integrated Policy' in P Craig and G de Búrca (eds), *The Evolution of EU Law* (2nd edn, OUP, 2011) ch 9, pp 217, 219ff.

[64] Opinion 1/2003 (*Lugano II*) [2006] ECR I-01145 (7 February 2006).

Fields of private law in the Member States	EU internal powers	EU external powers	Fields of private law at the international level
Code Civil Code Civil, Codice Civile, Bürgerliches Gesetzbuch Contract and tort (common law)	Art 114 Mainly consumer law directives, product liability, few commercial law, but now CESL	Implied power Minimum harmonization (shared powers) Full harmonization (exclusive power)	Vienna Convention on Sales Law
International private law a) jurisdiction b) applicable law c) mutual recognition	Art 81 a) Reg 44/2001 b) Reg 864/2007; 593/2008 c) Reg 44/2001	Implied power *Lugano* 1/2006 (exclusive power)	The Hague Convention
Regulatory private law Energy,financial services, telecommunications, transport	Art 114 Art 114 (now Art 194) Art 114 Art 91/100	Competences a) Implied power doctrine Art 114 b) Art 133 services (exclusive powers)	Multilateral and bilateral sector-related international agreements

Figure 3

So far, only the regulation of investment services has raised the attention of the Member States with an interest in making sure in the Lisbon Treaty that the enlarged competences of the EU are not used to affect the existing bilateral investment treaties (BITS).[65] However, currently a regulation is being negotiated to ensure the 'orderly transition' from national BITS to EU-level BITS. The legislative developments in the economically most important area of services outside and beyond investments where the European Union has obtained powers internally via Article 114 TFEU and externally via the implied powers doctrine and now via Article 207 TFEU has not yet reached the political agenda, maybe because the European Commission has not yet clarified in which way and where it will use these powers. Looking into traditional private law and modern regulatory law and linking them to the powers of the European Union internally and externally, the interlink between the competences becomes clear. The divided world of traditional versus modern private law in the inner space is mirrored in the outer space of the EU. The way is free to develop a European private law that reaches beyond the territories of the EU, thereby circumventing the role and function of nation states private legal orders. We will come back to the crucial consequences for the EU in global governance in the third part of this article.

3.4. Four parameters for analysing the transformation outside the EU

The transfer of the four parameters of conflict and resistance, substitution and intrusion, hybridization and convergence from the inner to the outer world of the EU paves the way for a deeper understanding of conditions under which the EU is acting or may be acting as a market state and where it leaves space for traditional nation state patterns of behaviour. Our tentative hypothesis is that the EU takes a strong stand as a market state whenever it is truly

[65] See the strong statement of the German Constitutional Court in the Lisbon judgment at 370 et seq: <http://www.bundesverfassungsgericht.de/entscheidungen/es20090630_2bve000208en.html>, now the draft regulation <http://www.europarl.europa.eu/sides/getDoc.do?type=REPORT&reference=A7-2011-0148&language=EN> (last consulted 29 April 2012).

economically important, whereas it gives way to nation states behaviour in more ideologically charged fields.

Conflict and resistance: the counterpart to the established nation state private legal orders is the 'The Hague Convention on International Private Law'. The conventions adopted in that frame do not affect the substance of the nation state private legal orders. The general idea behind this is that the international rules shall balance out conflicts between different jurisdictions, the old Savigny ideal. The opinion of the ECJ in *Lugano* tilts the balance between the Member States and the EU. Granting exclusive competence to the EU must be understood as a big 'blow' to the finely tuned web of intertwined competences in the area of international private law. In a way it is the logical consequence of the harmonization of European international private law rules in the Brussels and the two Rome Regulations, although the latter two were adopted after the *Lugano* opinion.[66] Following this line of argument, the EU would become the sole actor in weaving the web that ties the nation state private legal orders together. However, the European Commission is not making use of that new power. On the first occasion offered to benefit from its exclusive power in the field of international private law, it behaved as if the EU and the Member States enjoy joint power.[67] One might argue that there is a difference between an established concept of joint power and a voluntary practice which leaves the last word and the last decision always in the hands of the European Commission. One might also argue that the European Commission intends to mitigate the heavy impact of the *Lugano* opinion, thereby avoiding new competence battles.[68] What matters much more, however, is that the European Commission is so generous because international private law issues do not rank highly on its policy agenda. The practical and economic importance is limited. Member States may defend their turfs; international private law does not really affect the task of the EU market state in the international economy. The EU is focusing on the regulation of services which currently are driving the economy.

Substitution and intrusion: in the area of telecommunications, energy and financial services, health and safety regulation, the European Commission keeps a rather low profile, although we know little about the role and function the European Commission is actually playing. Until now, it has not referred to the implied powers doctrine in these three sectors in order to claim competence in international agreements. Times are changing, however. The Commission now has a negotiating mandate for an agreement with Azerbaijan and Turkmenistan, and through the proposition of a decision 'coordinating' EU and Member State action the Commission is gently pushing the 'EU exclusive' approach in a way quite similar to what happened with the open skies agreements.[69]

Air transport, however, is the exception to the rule. The European Commission used the infringement procedure to claim and in the end to gain exclusive competence in that domain.[70] The visible result is the so-called Open Sky Agreements (OSA) concluded by the European Union, not only, but mainly with the US. One may wonder whether and to what extent the OSA can and might serve as a blueprint for action in the field of telecommunication, energy and financial services. Setting energy apart, the European Commission is already playing a key role in the external regulation of telecommunication, financial

[66] The ECJ decided on 7 February 2006, Rome II was adopted on 11 July 2007, and Rome I on 17 June 2008.

[67] Reg (EC) 662/2009 establishing a procedure for the negotiation and conclusion of agreements between Member States and third countries on particular matters concerning the law applicable to contractual and non-contractual obligations [2009] OJ L200/25; J-J Kuipers, 'The Exclusive Competence of the Community under Art 81 TFEU: Lugano re-opened' in M Cremona, J Monar and S Poli (eds), *The External Dimension of the Area of Freedom, Security and Justice* (Peter Lang, 2011) 287.

[68] This reading is stressed by my colleague Marise Cremona.

[69] We would like to thank Bart Van Vooren for this clarification and for the reference to COM (2011) 539 final (7 September 2011, at p 4).

[70] See A Heritier and Y Karagiannis, 'The New Institutions of Transatlantic Aviation' (2010) 2 *Global Policy* 152–162.

services as well as health and safety. This is independent of the questions of whether the European Commission is being granted exclusive or shared competence, whether the European Commission has no formal competence at all, or has obtained only an observer status. There is much research to be done in order to get a clear picture of the role and function of the EU in these market sectors. In all these areas the European Commission is involved in international (soft)law-making outside formal conventions. It is working as a catalyst all too often between the US (nearly always supported by the UK) and the other Member States of the EU. We would call this a typical market state behaviour. The European Commission is enabling the opening of markets, to the benefit of the companies in Europe, sometimes against the resistance or the reluctance of their host countries.

Hybridization: constitutionalization of private law in the external dimension of the EU is associated with the increasing role human rights/fundamental rights are playing. There is little knowledge available on the degree to which human rights are used to influence the external dimension of European private law issues, be it traditional nation state private law (international private law) or European regulatory private law. So far this question has never been systematically investigated. Case-law of the ECJ does not (yet) provide much guidance.[71] One striking, though rather old example, is the so-called export of hazardous products from the EU to non-EU Member States. At the culmination point of the debate in the 1980s the promoters of a home state responsibility for export outside national territories invoked human rights to justify and to legitimize the ex-territorial responsibility of nation states, be it as part of the national constitution or imposed via an international human right to safety.[72] Outside and beyond health and safety issues we do not have much evidence on the possible role and function of human rights in the external dimension of European (regulatory) private law. This might change once the EU has officially joined the European Convention for the Protection of Human Rights and Fundamental Freedoms. Hybridization would lead to a composite order of European private law rules in external relations combined with the Convention of Human Rights. In the past the EU played a rather active role in promoting human rights in external relations. Again, this is in line with the transformation process within the EU.[73]

Convergence: following the scenario at the inner EU level, one may start from the premise that the European Commission is playing and might play an ever-increasing role in the new modes of international governance that is so predominant in the regulation of services. In the aftermath of the 1985 'New Approach to Technical Standards and Regulation', the European Commission established a European standards body in the field of telecommunication, it developed and fine-tuned the comitology procedure, and invented the Lamfalussy procedure. These new forms of governance are particularly open to internationalization processes. The EU is well placed to connect the *inner* EU world to the *outer* international world. The very open and less legalized mechanisms leave substantial leeway for input from outside the EU, which could easily be organized by the European Commission. The new modes of governance have attracted great attention in particular within the EU. In the last couple of years, the transnational dimension of these new modes of governance have raised concern, theoretically under different headings such as 'private law beyond the state', global administrative law,[74]

[71] One might with some imagination read the *Kadi* logic (Case C-402/05 P and C-415/05 P *Kadi* [2008] ECR I-6351) into the *TNT* judgment Case C-533/08 *TNT v AXA* [2010] ECR I-nyr (4 May 2010), para 49, where the ECJ strongly argued that international commercial law rules must be 'equivalent' to the EU rules. However, in *TNT* the ECJ does not refer to *Kadi*.

[72] H-W. Micklitz, 'International Regulation and Control of the Production and Use of Chemicals and Pesticides: Perspectives for a Convention' (1992) 3 *Michigan Journal of International Law* 653–697.

[73] M Cremona and B De Witte (eds), *EU Foreign Relations Law—Constitutional Fundamentals* (Hart Publishing, 2008).

[74] B Kingsbury, N Krisch and RB Stewart, 'The Emergence of Global Administrative Law' (2005) 68 *Law and Contemporary Problems* 15.

transnational law,[75] lex mercatoria[76] or transnational private regulation.[77] These projects have in common that they link theoretical concepts to empirical evidence or empirical research. However, the EU and its role in the various areas of services remain under-investigated. These new forms of governance form the perfect ground for strengthening the market state profile of the EU.

4. Preliminary Conclusions on the Impact of the EU in Global Governance through Private Law

The distinction between traditional private law and European regulatory private law is crucial in order to get to grips with the role and function of the EU in global governance through private law. The Treaties set clear boundaries as to what the EU is able to achieve in the inner space of the EU. There is no room for harmonizing provisional private legal orders or even for replacing them via a European civil code. The lack of competence affects the way in which the EU can act in the outer space. Cooperation with the Member States is preferable even in areas where the ECJ has attributed exclusive competence to the EU, as in international private law matters. The EU keeps a low profile and leaves space for Member States in order to avoid conflict and resistance. In other words, it does not make use of its competences.

However, the EU has gained competences under the internal market rules to use private law as a means of regulating the European economy. Regulatory private law forms the core of what must be understood as the genuine European private legal order. Here the EU has developed a coherent body of rules, largely sector-related, which determines the economic activities on the internal market and which leaves very little space for national law, not to mention national private law. In sector-related areas the EU is entering in an ever stronger way into the outer space. A deeper analysis is necessary to get to know the role of the EU in the field of international telecommunication, energy, transport, financial services, health and safety regulation. What we know is that the European Commission is playing an increasingly strong role in international rule-making outside international treaties and formal agreements, and largely beyond whether it has competence or not and whether the competence is exclusive or shared.

In the long run the outer space (of Statecraft) could become a means of a more 'unified' approach to market state private law than is currently possible within the EU legal space due to the four competing parameters of Member State–EU private law. The development in the energy sector following air transport regulation seems to underpin such an assumption. With European private law being understood as economic law, the global governance dimension or the outer space turns into a means of circumventing the EU internal mechanic. European regulatory private law in the outer space is overhauling traditional national private law in the inner space. The EU market state is generating EU internal Statecraft through international legal means. This is by no means new. The most outspoken dicta on the 'constitutional character' of the EU have been formulated by the ECJ in external relations. However, now the EU discovers private law—the second pillar alongside of the constitutional charter—as a prominent field of action to strengthen its internal Statecraft. In our reading this is the direct consequence of the EU being conceived of as a market state.

[75] G-P Calliess and P Zumbansen, *Rough Consensus and Running Code: A Theory of Transnational Private Law* (Hart Publishing, 2009).

[76] JW Smith, *Mercantile Law* (ed, Hart and Simey, London Stevens, 1905); K-P Berger, *The New Law Merchant and the Global Market Place—A 21st Century View of Transnational Commercial Law* (<http://www.trans-lex.org/000002>).

[77] C Scott, F Cafaggi and L Senden (Hrsg), 'The Challenge of Transnational Private Regulation: Conceptual and Constitutional Debates' (2011) *Journal of Law and Society Special Issues*.

PART II

THE EU AND GLOBAL SECURITY GOVERNANCE

5

The European Union in the Global Security Architecture

*Panos Koutrakos**

1. Introduction

Whilst its genesis was focused on the economic dimension of market building, the whole process of European integration has always been, in essence, a security policy project. Seeking to ensure the impossibility of another war in Europe has been a central part of the DNA of the European polity. It was for this reason that the wars in the former Yugoslavia shocked the European Union (EU) system so profoundly. They also proved to be a powerful incentive for the development of the Union's foreign and security policy, both in terms of its legal grounding in primary rules and its increasingly prominent position in the rhetoric of the Union's elites.

However, to focus exclusively on its self-referential aspects is to ignore not only the direct interaction between the development of the EU's security and defence policy and the fundamental and constant changes of the international geopolitical landscape in the last twenty years, but also the distinct emphasis on the international outlook of the Union's strategic objectives and the relevant provisions of the Treaty of Lisbon. In terms of the geopolitical changes, whilst they have had an impact on the Union in various ways, two in particular are noteworthy. On the one hand, there has been a growing expectation by third parties, such as the United States, countries where EU missions are deployed and international organizations such as the African Union, that the EU shares the responsibility of monitoring international security. On the other hand, international organizations directly involved in global and regional security governance expect the EU to participate too.

This chapter explores the extent to which there is congruence between the current global security architecture and the Union's ambition to assert its identity on the international scene as a security actor. It identifies certain factors which are inherent in the genesis of the Common Security and Defence Policy (CSDP) and which have imposed a constraint on its development, preventing it from achieving the Union's ambition and meeting the expectations of other security actors.

2. Space for a Mutually Reinforcing Relationship

The last ten years have seen the EU attempt to define its security and defence identity in clearer strategic terms. Just three months after the terrorist attacks of September 11, 2001, the Laeken Declaration on the Future of the European Union, which initiated the process of reform of the Union's Treaties, refers prominently to 'Europe's new role in a globalized world' and raises the question: 'Does Europe not, now that it is finally unified, have a leading role to play in a new world order, that of a power able both to play a stabilizing role worldwide and to point the way ahead for many countries and peoples?'.[1] The role it seeks to

* I am grateful to Eileen Denza for comments on a previous draft of this chapter. The usual disclaimer applies.

[1] European Council, 14–15 December 2001, 2.

carve out is directly linked to 'its responsibilities in the governance of globalization' which 'Europe needs to shoulder'.[2]

The notion of responsibility becomes central in how the Union understands its international posture. The European Security Strategy, adopted in December 2003, states that: 'Europe should be ready to share in the responsibility for global security and in building a better world'.[3] Its introduction in the Union's vocabulary is coupled with an increased emphasis on effective multilateralism. The latter features prominently in the European Security Strategy, which refers to '[s]trengthening the United Nations, equipping it to fulfil its responsibilities and to act effectively' as 'a European priority'.[4] Both responsibility and commitment to effective multilateralism also feature prominently in the 2008 *Report on the Implementation of the European Security Strategy*, which refers to the Union's 'achievements' in the area of security as 'the results of a distinctive European approach'.[5]

This apparently outward emphasis of the Union's international action in general and CSDP in particular has found its way into the Lisbon Treaty. In relation to its revamped Common Foreign and Security Policy (CFSP) and the CSDP provisions, its preamble refers to its aim to 'reinforc[e] the European identity and its independence in order to promote peace, security and progress in Europe and in the world'.[6] In addition, there is an increasing emphasis in the EU's primary rules on the Union's commitment to multilateralism. By promoting its values, the Union 'shall contribute to peace [and] security in the world... as well as to the strict observance and the development of international law, including respect for the principles of the United Nations Charter'.[7] Setting out the principles which guide its external action in general as well as the CSDP in particular,[8] Article 21(1) of the Treaty on European Union (TEU) provides that the Union 'shall promote multilateral solutions to common problems, in particular in the framework of the United Nations', whereas one of its objectives is to 'promote an international system based on stronger multilateral cooperation and good global governance'.[9]

The emergence of these linked concepts of responsibility in the context of the international security system and commitment to effective multilateralism as central pillars of the Union's understanding of its role in the world may not be viewed beyond its proper political and economic context. On the one hand, the constant shifting of the dynamics of the global security architecture in the first decade of this century, the unilateralist reflexes of the United States administration, particularly during the Bush Presidency, and the emergence of terrorism as the main security challenge for the international community gave rise to a de facto wider distribution of power[10] and encouraged existing players to harbour greater ambition about their involvement in world affairs. It is striking that the then President of the European Commission Romano Prodi even suggested that George W Bush's close victory at the 2000 US presidential election would enable the EU to take centre stage and exercise a role akin to that of a world power.[11] On the other hand, the successful launch of the euro and the economic prosperity which appeared to prevail in the Union at the time spurred on the political elites to articulate a security role for the Union which would be commensurate to its perceived economic success.

[2] Ibid.

[3] *A Secure Europe in a Better World—European Security Strategy* (Brussels, 12 December 2003) 1.

[4] Ibid, at 9 which also refers to other international organizations such as the African Union.

[5] S407/08 (Brussels, 11 December 2008), p 2.

[6] Lisbon Treaty, 11th recital.

[7] Art 3(5) TEU. See M Cremona, 'Values in EU Foreign Policy' in M Evans and P Koutrakos (eds), *Beyond the Established Legal Orders—Policy Interconnections Between the EU and the Rest of the World* (Hart Publishing, 2011) 275.

[8] Art 23 TEU.

[9] Art 21(2)(h) TEU.

[10] See JS Nye Jr, *The Future of Power* (Public Affairs, 2011).

[11] *European Voice*, 5–11 April 2001, at 11–13.

The Union's appetite for a more pronounced role in the governance of international security, along with its apparent deference to the role of the United Nations as the main guarantor of international peace, may also be viewed against the political and legal framework within which the UN has carried out this function. Chapter VIII of the UN Charter sets out a role for 'regional arrangements or agencies for dealing with such matters relating to the maintenance of international peace and security as are appropriate for regional action provided that such arrangements or agencies and their activities are consistent with the Purposes and Principles of the United Nations'.[12] In accordance with Article 53 of the UN Charter, they may be relied upon by the UN Security Council 'for enforcement action under its authority'. The EU institutions have avoided referring to the Union as an organization within the meaning of Article 53 of the UN Charter, and the UN institutions have also avoided making such an inference.[13] However, the flexible and pragmatic approach which the latter has adopted to its interactions with international organizations in the security sphere[14] suggests that the legal framework set out in the UN Charter clearly offers scope for the security ambitions of the Union within the parameters set out in the Treaties.

Furthermore, the UN organs have developed over the years a security policy space in which regional organizations in general and the EU in particular may feature prominently. This became apparent in *An Agenda for Peace*, the report that the then UN Secretary General Boutros Boutros-Ghali drew up in response to a request from the UN Security Council.[15] Opening up the range and scope of actors who may assist the UN in its security tasks after the end of the Cold War, this Report referred expressly to the Union and its important role in tackling the Balkan wars in the 1990s. The emphasis on the role of regional organizations became gradually more specific, as, for instance, the UN authorities referred with approval to the development of EU battle groups,[16] the development of the Union's capabilities,[17] and the involvement of the Union in regional conflicts.[18]

The osmosis between the UN and the EU is not confined to statements made by each of the parties in official documents. Instead, it has developed along two distinct but interrelated tracks. The first emerges in relation to a number of military and police missions which the Union has carried out in the last decade. For instance, it is noteworthy, and not just in terms of semantics, that the very first security and defence operation of the Union, the European Union Police Mission in Bosnia and Herzegovina launched in 2003, assumed the tasks previously carried out by the United Nations International Police Task Force.[19] Whilst apparent, the link between the UN framework and the mandate of the CSDP missions may vary in its terms: for instance, the EU Police Mission in Bosnia and Herzegovina was welcomed rather than expressly authorized by the UN Security Council;[20] Operation Artemis in the Democratic Republic of Congo,[21] on the other hand, was authorized under Chapter VII of the UN Charter to be deployed in a city in the north-east Congo which was

[12] Art 52, UN Charter.

[13] See N White, 'The EU as a Regional Security Actor within the International Legal Order' in M Trybus and N White (eds), *European Security Law* (OUP, 2007) 329, 332–335.

[14] See J Wouters and T Ruys, 'UN–EU Cooperation in Crisis Management' in J Wouters, F Hoffmeister and T Ruys (eds), *The United Nations and the European Union: An Ever Stronger Partnership* (TMC Asser Press, 2006) 229, 231–232.

[15] A/47/277-S/24111 (17 June 1992).

[16] See Report of the Secretary General, A/59/2005, *In larger freedom: towards development, security and human rights for all* (21 March 2005), para 112.

[17] General Assembly Resolution A/60/L.1 *2005 World Summit Outcome* (24 October 2005), para 93(a).

[18] Report of the Secretary General A/61/204-S/2006/590, *A regional-global security partnership: challenges and opportunities* (28 July 2006), para 57.

[19] See Joint Action 2002/210/CFSP [2002] OJ L70/1.

[20] See UNSC Resolution 1396 (2002), para 5. Similarly, see EUFOR ALTHEA in Bosnia and Herzegovina under Joint Action 2004/570/CFSP [2004] OJ L252/10 and UNSC Resolution 1551 (2004), para 10. EUPOL Afghanistan under Joint Action 2007/369/CFSP [2007] OJ L139/33 and UNSC Resolution 1746 (2007), para 11.

[21] Joint Action 2003/423/CFSP [2003] OJ L143/50.

the epicentre of clashes between militias and forces originating in Uganda.[22] The link between a CSDP mission and the UN may give rise to considerable legal debate, as illustrated by the Union's Rule of Law mission in Kosovo.[23] Launched on 4 February 2008, that is two weeks prior to the unilateral declaration of independence by Kosovo, the mission had been prepared in anticipation of a political settlement under the aegis of the UN and pursuant to UN Security Council Resolution 1244(1999) which never materialized. In this context, it has been argued that its deployment lacked an express UN authorization.[24] The drafting of Joint Action 2008/124/CFSP and its emphasis on Resolution 1244 suggest that the EU Council was acutely aware of this charge. It is noteworthy that the UN Secretary General subsequently welcomed the mission.[25]

Growing from this ad hoc relationship which adjusts to the practical and political circumstances of the time, the second track on which an osmosis between the EU and UN has been developing is a process of more formalized interaction. In September 2003, the then UN Secretary General Kofi Annan and the EU Presidency signed a Joint Declaration on UN–EU Cooperation in Crisis Management which set up an institutional framework within which the two organizations would enhance the coordination and compatibility in civilian and military crisis management. They established a joint consultative mechanism at working level, known as 'the Steering Committee', to deal with planning, training, communication and best practices. This has given rise to some thinking within the EU as to the modalities of the provision of military capabilities by the Union to the UN.[26] It has also given rise to further consolidation of the consultation mechanisms between the two organizations.[27]

This section has focused so far on the positioning of the Union in the UN security system. This is by no means to suggest a paucity of interactions with other parts of the global security architecture. On the contrary, the links with NATO have been significant[28] and have given rise to considerable legal, political and practical controversies.[29] Furthermore, the considerable focus of CSDP in Africa has also given rise to interactions with the regional organizations in the area.[30] It is in the light of the central position which the UN system is afforded in the Union's primary rules, as well as the limited length of this chapter, that the analysis focuses on the UN system.

[22] UNSC Resolution 1484 (2003). Similarly, see EUFOR DR Congo under Joint Action 2006/319/CFSP [2006] OJ L116/98 and UNSC Resolution 1671 (2006); EUFOR Tchad/RCA under Joint Action 2007/677/CFSP [2007] OJ L279/21 and UNSC Resolution 1778 (2007), para 6.

[23] Joint Action 2008/124/CFSP [2008] OJ L42/92, last amended by Council Decision 2010/619/CFSP [2010] OJ L272/19.

[24] See E de Wet, 'The Governance of Kosovo: Security Council Resolution 1244 and the Establishment and Functioning of EULEX' (2009) 103 AJIL 83.

[25] See *Report of the Secretary-General on the United Nations Interim Administration Mission in Kosovo of 28 March 2008* (UN doc S/2008/211), para 5 and 12 June 2008 (UN doc S/2008/354), para 13.

[26] See *Elements of Implementation of the EU–UN Joint Declaration*, adopted by the European Council on 17–18 June 2004.

[27] See *Joint Statement on UN–EU Cooperation in Crisis Management* (Brussels, 7 June 2007) in which the UN 'recognizes the considerable contribution of human and material resources on the part of the European Union in crisis management' (para 1) and which refers to 'the achievements of the 2003 Joint UN–EU declaration' (para 50).

[28] See, for instance, *EUFOR ALTHEA in Bosnia and Herzegovina under Joint Action* 2004/570/CFSP [2004] OJ L252/10 which took over from a NATO-led Stabilization Force.

[29] See M Reichard, *The EU–NATO Relationship—A Legal and Political Perspective* (Ashgate, 2006).

[30] See, for instance, the EU Support AMIS II mission undertaken in support of the African Union mission to Sudan (Joint Action 2005/557/CFSP [2005] OJ L188/46). Over the years, the Union has channelled a considerable part of its energy in its broader security policy on Africa: in relation to non-proliferation, for instance, see P Koutrakos, 'The Non-proliferation Policy of the European Union' in Evans and Koutrakos, n 7 249, at 268–269. More generally, see A Abass, 'EU Crisis Management in Africa: Progress, Problems and Prospects', in S Blockmans (ed), *The European Union and Crisis Management: Policy and Legal Aspects* (TMC Asser Press, 2008), 327.

This brief overview suggests that the position of CSDP in the global security architecture is underpinned by a mutually reinforcing link between the international security structures and the EU: the former is willing to provide the legal and political space which would enable the latter to achieve its ambition to become a central security player. Whilst not fully formalized, relying on ad hoc arrangements and having to take into account not inconsiderable political and legal obstacles, this link sheds some light on the increasingly prominent commitment of the Union to effective multilateralism. However, the impact that this link has had on the security stature of the Union has been undermined by factors related to the Union's own approach to the development of its security and defence policy. These issues are examined in the following sections.

3. The State of CSDP after Lisbon

There has been more than a decade since the Union started focusing a considerable part of its energies on the development of its security and defence policy, and even though the rhetoric from both its official documents and officials appears to suggest a high level of activity, its relevance as a security and defence actor in practice is by no means apparent.

At the time of writing, the state of play is not encouraging. In terms of missions on the ground, the Union has only launched one operation since the entry into force of the Lisbon Treaty, namely Operation EUTM Somalia, a military mission of approximately 120 training approximately 2000 Somali soldiers.[31] There has also been planning for a military operation in Libya which has not been launched: its scope is envisaged to be narrow (support for humanitarian assistance) and its duration quite short, approximately four months.[32] Whilst this suggests a falling away in terms of CSDP missions, it is not accompanied by a general paucity of activity by Member States. In March 2011, a coalition of various states initiated a military operation against Libya under the authorization of United Nations Security Council Resolution (2011) 1973. This operation consisted of the enforcement of a no-fly zone and a naval blockade and led, controversially but inevitably, to strikes against forces remaining loyal to Gaddafi. The operation was not carried out by the EU but a number of individual states, most of which were European, led by the UK and France, whilst the US was for political reasons content to play second fiddle. It is worth noting that Germany abstained at the UN Security Council vote on Security Council Resolution 1973, in the company of China and Russia. It is also interesting that, in relation to this operation, British Prime Minister David Cameron, US President Barack Obama and former French President Nicolas Sarkozy wrote an article for *The Times*[33] in which there was no reference to the Union at all.

It has not been only in relation to CSDP activities that the Union's ambitions as a security player appear not to be borne out by its response in practice. In December 2010 and the first months of 2012, demonstrations and protests were organized in a number of countries in northern Africa and the Middle East.[34] Known as 'the Arab Spring', this led, amongst others, to regime change in Egypt, Tunisia, and Libya and bloody clashes in Yemen, Syria and Bahrain. The European Union has been criticized widely for tolerating the autocratic regimes ruling these countries and for failing to engage with the changes in a constructive way. Indicative of this approach is the title of an editorial in the *Financial Times*: 'Monstrous

[31] See Council Decision 2010/96/CFSP [2010] OJ L44/16, amended and extended by Council Decision 2011/483/CFSP [2011] OJ L198/37.

[32] Council Decision 2011/210/CFSP of 1 April 2011 on a European Union military operation in support of humanitarian assistance operations in response to the crisis situation in Libya (EUFOR Libya) [2011] OJ L89/17, repealed by Council Decision 2011/764/CFSP of 28 November 2011 [2011] OJ L314/35. See the contribution by De Baere to this volume.

[33] David Cameron, Barack Obama and Nicolas Sarkozy, 'Libya's Pathway to Peace' *The Times*, 15 April 2011, 25.

[34] At the time of writing, the demonstrations are escalating in Syria, and are ongoing in Egypt.

in size, feeble in action', accompanied by the subtitle 'Arab tumult exposes the ineptitude of EU foreign policy'.[35]

This is not the picture of a vibrant and dynamic security and defence policy which strives to achieve the grand objectives set out in the European Security Strategy. An unfortunate combination of circumstances may partly explain this state of affairs: not only do the actors at the helm of CSDP, including the High Representative, show disconcertingly little interest in security and defence, but the financial crisis has also focused the mind and energy of both the Union institutions and the Member States on other issues. Managing the distinct possibility of sovereign default within the eurozone, staving off the threat of contagion to economies which the euro members could not afford to save, seeking to tackle the political ramifications which the handling by the European powers of this extraordinary financial crisis has caused, all these are at the very centre of the current EU agenda. Their implications have been so profound that they have challenged further the much vaunted capacity of the foreign policy structures set out at Lisbon to transform the Union's action. This is even more so given the existential dimension which the crisis has taken for the EU elites.[36] And as if the lack of energy for CSDP activity has not been apparent enough, even the official rhetoric seems affected: in her speech in April 2011 to the European Parliament on the main choices on CFSP and CSDP, the High Representative of the Union for Foreign Affairs and Security Policy refers to security and defence only once and only in relation to the Libyan mission, which she views as an indication of 'how far we have come'.[37] There is a distinct dissonance between the underwhelming (and underwhelmed) tone of this statement and the earlier call for the Union to 'shoulder its responsibilities in the governance of globalization'.[38]

However, it is not only the current economic and political climate which explains the CSDP state of affairs. There are other reasons which are more deeply rooted and which are related to the genesis and development of the policy, as well as the deeply idiosyncratic constitutional framework in which it is carried out. These will be outlined in the following section.

4. A Process-centred Policy

The CSDP has been developed in the context of the Union's CFSP, and the Lisbon Treaty defines it as 'an integral part of CFSP'.[39] It is not surprising, therefore, that it shares the

[35] Editorial, 'Monstrous in size, feeble in action—Arab tumult exposes the ineptitude of EU foreign policy' *Financial Times*, 24 February 2011, 12. Following the strong criticism, the EU has responded by seeking to reframe and refocus its approach to the Southern Mediterranean in general, see COM (2011) 200 Final of 8 March 2011, Joint Communication by the High Representative and the European Commission, *A Partnership for Democracy and Shared Prosperity with the Southern Mediterranean* (Brussels) and COM (2011) 303 of 25 May 2011, Joint Communication by the High Representative and the European Commission, *A new response to a changing Neighbourhood* (Brussels). It has also established an EU–Tunisia Task Force aiming to coordinate the EU and international initiatives supporting the Tunisian transition to a fully functioning democracy. Co-chaired by the High Representative and the Tunisian Prime Minister, it met for the first time in September 2011.

[36] In his 2011 State of the Union address to the European Parliament, Commission President José Barroso referred to the crisis as the most important one in the Union's history: <http://ec.europa.eu/commission_2010-2014/president/pdf/speech_original.pdf>; German Chancellor Angela Merkel has stated time and again that the fight to save the euro is a fight to save the Union.

[37] Press Release A179/11 (Brussels, 11 May 2011), p 3 (the entire phrase is as follows: 'Or take Libya. There are members of this house who wish that the EU had a stronger defence and security policy. I say to them this—in the last weeks and months we've seen how far we have come in some ways, but in this, how far we have to go'). In December 2011, Baroness Ashton delivered a speech on CSDP in particular, the main theme of which was the need for the EU to use the financial crisis as a driver for closer cooperation (Press Release A512/11, Brussels, 13 December 2011). Countering the charge levelled at the EU for 'CSDP fatigue', she claims that '2011 has been a year of intensive work on CSDP with concrete results and ending with comprehensive, forward-looking Council conclusions'. The latter refers to the CSDP Conclusions of the Foreign Affairs Council of 1 December 2011 (17991/11) which referred to synergies between Member States, the latter and EU institutions, and the EU and NATO.

[38] Laeken Declaration, European Council, 14–15 December, 2001, 2.

[39] Art 42(1) TEU.

emphasis on rules and procedures which has characterized the development of the latter policy.[40] The position of CSDP in the evolving process which has shaped the Union's constitutional architecture in the last decade illustrates this clearly. All the milestones of this process (the 2001 Laeken Declaration, the drafting of the Treaty establishing a Constitution for Europe, the referendums which marked its long and painful death, the drafting of the Lisbon Treaty and its ratification process) have been characterized by a clear emphasis on the role of the Union as a security actor on the world scene. And the Lisbon Treaty, in so far as it may be defined as the tangible outcome of this process, bears out this emphasis by armouring the CSDP with an elaborate institutional framework and kitting it out with the appropriate rules and procedures. A detailed analysis of the Lisbon rules on CSDP is beyond the scope of this chapter.[41] Suffice it to point out the elevation of this policy not only in terms of semantics (as it is defined as 'common' rather than merely 'European' and its provisions are set out in a distinct section in Title V TEU), but also in terms of substance: the European Defence Agency is provided for in the field of defence capabilities development, research, acquisition and armaments;[42] flexibility is formalized pursuant to specific legal mechanisms;[43] the Member States undertake to improve their military capabilities[44] and commit them, along with their civilian capabilities, for the implementation of CSDP;[45] a mutual assistance clause is inserted.[46]

However, whilst these legal developments may appear to suggest progress in strengthening the CSDP machinery, their impact in practical terms is far from apparent. The European Defence Agency, for instance, had been established and was operative well before the Lisbon Treaty entered into force.[47] As the Treaty provisions were unnecessary for its establishment, they are similarly of little impact on its record. Given the position of military capabilities at the core of national sovereignty, any progress in the work of the Agency is bound to rely entirely upon the willingness of the Member States to engage in real cooperation in this area. Indeed, the limits of the actual work which the Agency has carried out as well as the continuing disagreements amongst national administrations about its budget further underline the impact of this major factor. Similarly, the improvement of national defence capabilities is unlikely to be achieved by means of a legal duty imposed by the Treaty. This is a political commitment which Member States may or may not implement in the light of a wide range of domestic factors, mainly of a political and economic nature. It would be exceedingly difficult to envisage a Treaty provision capable of changing this reality—and yet, the latter is central to the implementation of security and defence policy.

As for the issue of flexibility, it should not be forgotten that the membership of the various CSDP missions at present varies considerably, as does the contribution from different Member States.[48] Whilst the new 'willing and able' clause and the permanent structured

[40] See D Thym, 'The Intergovernmental Constitution of the EU's Foreign, Security and Defence' (2011) 7 EuConst 453.

[41] See P Koutrakos, 'The European Union's Foreign Affairs after the Lisbon Treaty' in D Ashiagbor, N Countouris, I Lianos (eds), *The EU After Lisbon* (CUP, 2012, 185); R Whitman and A Juncos, 'The Lisbon Treaty and the Foreign, Security and Defence Policy: Reforms, Implementation and the Consequences of (non-) Ratification' (2009) 14 *EFA Rev* 25.

[42] Arts 42(3) and 45 TEU.

[43] Art 42(5) and (6), as well as Arts 44 and 46 TEU.

[44] Art 42(3), subpara 2 TEU.

[45] Art 42(3) TEU.

[46] Art 42(7) TEU.

[47] See Council Joint Action 2004/551/CFSP [2004] OJ L245/17. For an early analysis, see S Ferraro, 'The European Defence Agency: Facilitating Defence Reform or Forming Fortress Europe' (2006–2007) 16 Transnat'l L and Contemp Probs 549, and M Trybus, 'The new European Defence Agency: a contribution to a common European security and defence policy or a challenge to the Community *acquis*?' (2006) 43 *CML Rev* 667.

[48] On the Lisbon provisions on flexibility, see S Biscop, 'Permanent Structured Cooperation and the Future of the ESDP: Transformation and Integration' (2008) 13 *EFA Rev* 431. During the second half of 2010, there were discussions amongst Member States about formalizing flexibility in CSDP, the tenor of which suggested that the relevant provisions merely provided some food of thought. For a different view, S Biscop and J Coelmont, 'CSDP

cooperation mechanism provide a framework which would allow for the formalization of different forms of the current realities, the rules they set out are quite vague as to their implementation[49] and, in any case, their impact would be in direct correlation to the willingness of the Member States to cooperate in the area of defence capabilities.

Similar considerations apply to the role of the mutual assistance clause which appears to impose a duty on Member States the scope of which is as broad as its nature rigorous. However, it is not a mutual defence clause and, in any case, there are questions as to how far Member States are required to go in order to comply with it, and how rigorous the enforcement of this duty can be. The significance of this clause is bound to be tested in such charged circumstances where its enforcement would be irrelevant. In fact, its presence in the Union's primary law is significant only at the level of rhetoric. The mutual assistance clause was regarded as key to the success of NATO, but was never actually invoked until the attacks of 9/11 on the United States.

This brief overview suggests that the importance of the much-praised provisions of the Lisbon Treaty on CSDP is in doubt on various grounds, not least the nature of the policy and the constitutional framework within which these provisions are applied. And yet, the Union institutions and the Member States have spent considerable energy drafting them and even greater political capital promoting them as a key that would enable the Union to assume its well-deserved place at the centre of the world stage. In that respect, the statement of President Sarkozy in August 2008 during the Russia–Georgia war is instructive: he argued that, had the Lisbon Treaty been in force, the Union would have had the institutions and tools which would have enabled it to act decisively and exert its influence.[50] This deeply held belief that it is institutions and procedures which an effective CSDP is missing also underpins the debate about the much-maligned role of unanimity in decision-making in this area. This emphasis on legal rules, principles and procedures may be explained in the light of the genesis of the CSDP in the Union's constitutional framework which had developed partly due to the considerable contribution of the law.[51] However, it fails to account for the role of the States as fully responsible for their defence and for prioritizing their defence spending and availability of resources, the differences in their strategic priorities, and the prevailing role of political and economic assessments made by national governments.[52] This affects both the principle and the practice of the development of CSDP in so far as it is entirely for each Member State to assess where, when and how to intervene and given that Member States have the capabilities which the Union needs in order to carry out CSDP missions. These considerations form the reality of security and defence policy and impose an inherent limit on the role of legal rules in the area.[53] Unless the specific underpinnings of these considerations are addressed, the CSDP will continue to be a deeply process-centred set of initiatives which hardly substitute for the absence of a unified policy. If anything, the post-Lisbon performance of the Union in CSDP illustrates with painful clarity how deeply misguided is the emphasis on rules and procedures in this area.

and the "Ghent Framework": The Indirect Approach to Permanent Structured Cooperation?' (2011) 16 *EFA Rev* 149.

[49] See, for instance, the protocol on permanent structured cooperation established by Art 42 of the Treaty on European Union.

[50] *Le Figaro*, 18 August 2008. See further the contribution by Blockmans to this volume.

[51] As Weiler puts it, '[i]n some ways, Community law and the European Court were everything an international lawyer could dream about: the Court was creating a new order of international law in which norms were norms, sanctions were sanctions, courts were central and frequently used, and lawyers were important': JHH Weiler, *The Constitution of Europe* (CUP, 1999), 205–206.

[52] 'Almost everything about defence in Europe remains resolutely national': *European Military Capabilities—Building Armed Forces for Modern Operations* (The International Institute for Strategic Studies, 2008) 149.

[53] See P Koutrakos, 'The role of law in Common Security and Defence Policy: functions, limitations and perceptions' in P Koutrakos (ed), *European Foreign Policy—Legal and Political Perspectives* (Edward Elgar Publishing, 2011) 235.

The analysis so far has highlighted the erroneous assumption that legal rules and procedures are the key to enabling the Union to become an effective security and defence actor. However, this is not to suggest that law is irrelevant in this area. In fact, when interpreted and applied properly, it may provide an impetus for development. A case in point is Article 346 of the Treaty on the Functioning of the European Union (TFEU): interpreted incorrectly for years for reasons of, amongst others, political sensitivity and institutional timidity, it was viewed as rendering the defence industries beyond the scope of application of EU law. It was only recently that a combination of judicial activity and initiatives by the Commission introduced a degree of normalization in the legal regime governing this sensitive sector.[54]

5. The Organic Link Between CSDP and Other Strands of EU External Action

The analysis so far has focused on the legal framework within which the Union carries its security and defence policy and the emphasis of the institutions and the Member States on legal rules and procedures in the area. This section will examine some other factors which are inherent in the development of CSDP and which may constrain its conduct. These may be better understood in the light of the objectives of the Union's external action in Article 21(3) TEU. It is recalled that one of the innovations of the Lisbon Treaty is the articulation in this provision of objectives common to all the different strands of the external policies. The wide range of these objectives and their overarching application to the Union's external action aim to enhance the coherence and effectiveness of the EU's international role.[55]

There are two interrelated developments which are worth examining. The first is the increasing securitization of the various strands of the Union's external action. This has become more pronounced since the terrorist attacks of 9 September 2001 as well as those in Madrid on 11 March 2004 and London on 7 July 2005. In the European Security Strategy, the wide definition of security is apparent in various ways: the range of threats facing the Union is understood as wide in both its sources and nature; there is a clear emphasis on the multifarious causes and implications of these threats (for instance, in relation to terrorism, reference is made to 'the pressures of modernization, cultural, social and political crises, and the alienation of young people living in foreign societies';[56] there is also a corresponding emphasis on what the Union traditionally does in the world, ie the other strands of external action such as development, trade, environmental policies, as well as the overarching requirement of coherence. The same view of security is apparent in the 2008 *Report on the Implementation of the European Security Strategy* which, if anything, underlines it further with its emphasis on cyber security, energy security, and climate change.

The other side of the coin reveals a similar picture. In the area of development, for instance, the link between development and security is pronounced in a distinct manner in the *European Consensus on Development*.[57] This is the case not only in terms of the general position of development within the broader context of the Union's security policy, but also regarding specific security challenges such as the non-proliferation of weapons. Similarly, the links between the Area of Freedom, Security and Justice (AFSJ) and security and defence policy are also quite pronounced.[58]

[54] See P Koutrakos, 'The Application of EC Law to Defence-related Industries—Changing Interpretations of Article 296 EC' in C Barnard and O Odudu (eds), *The Outer Limits of European Union Law* (Hart Publishing, 2009) 307.

[55] See the chapter by L Jorik in this volume.

[56] *The Stockholm Programme—An Open and Secure Europe Serving and Protecting Citizens* [2010] OJ C115/1.

[57] [2006] OJ C46/1.

[58] See P Koutrakos, 'The External Dimension of the Area of Freedom, Security and Justice and Other EU External Policies' in M Cremona, J Monar, and S Poli (eds), *The External Relations of the European Union's Area of Freedom, Security and Justice* (Presse Interuniversitaire Europeénne/Peter Lang, 2011) 139.

Therefore, in the different strands of its external action, the Union articulates a broad understanding of security with increasing clarity and confidence over the years. This is tied in with a second development, namely the link between internal and external security which has also become more pronounced over the years. This is apparent in various strands of EU policies, such as the AFSJ where the Stockholm Programme sets it out clearly,[59] as well as the European Security Strategy itself, and, even more so, in the Internal Security Strategy.[60]

Therefore, what emerges is an evolving process of interweaving policies and objectives which were originally developed in different contexts: the original European Security Strategy put forward a broad understanding of security based, amongst others, on the link between internal and external security, which is affirmed emphatically in the 2008 Report; this construction of security encompasses policies such as the AFSJ which are pursued on the external plane in order to achieve internal security objectives.

The broad understanding of security and the links between internal and external security are not confined to the level of principle. A considerable number of CSDP operations carried out so far have ingrained in them the DNA of other strands of the Union's external action. The rule of law missions, for instance,[61] seem as if they have grown organically from the Union's objectives in the AFSJ. They have also a very distinctive development dimension. The border assistance missions have a very clear AFSJ dimension too,[62] whereas the development aspect of security sector reform missions[63] is central to their design and deployment.[64]

The two interlinked premises set out above (the broad understanding of security and the links between internal and external security) are by no means unique to the Union. In *An Agenda for Peace*, for instance, the then UN Secretary General put forward a very wide definition of security which, he felt, would need to govern the policies of the states and organizations following the end of the Cold War.[65] Viewed from this angle, the general dimension of the Union's policy is entirely consistent with the general understanding of what the maintenance of security entails in these volatile times. What makes its relevance to the EU's posture interesting, however, is the specific political and constitutional context within which this understanding applies. Whilst it would be absurd to expect that security and defence missions would be carried out in a policy and legal vacuum, independently from what the Union does in its external policies, their organic link to them is so strong that the CSDP also inherits the legal and policy idiosyncrasies which define these policies. Put differently, even though the CSDP touches upon the very core of national sovereignty and its management is intergovernmental in nature, its DNA is deeply ingrained in the other, traditional features of the Union legal order and the policies which it has pursued over the years.

The profound impact that this inheritance has had on the conduct of CSDP may be illustrated by a number of interrelated themes which have emerged over the years. The first is about the choice of policy initiatives which the EU undertakes in the world, as CSDP operations are normally carried out in areas where the Union has been active in the context of its other policies. Whilst entirely consistent with the position of security within the

[59] [2010] OJ C115/1.

[60] 5942/2/10 (Brussels, 23 February 2010).

[61] EUJUST Themis in Georgia: Joint Action 2004/523/CFSP [2004] OJ L228/21; EUJUST Lex in Iraq: Joint Action 2005/190/CFSP [2005] OJ L62/37; EULEX Kosovo: Joint Action 2008/124/CFSP [2008] OJ L42/92.

[62] EUBAM Rafah: Joint Action 2005/889/CFSP [2005] OJ L327/28; EUBAM Moldova–Ukraine: Joint Action 2005/776/CFSP [2005] OJ L292/13.

[63] EUSEC RD Congo: Joint Action 2005/355/CFSP [2005] OJ L112/2; EU SSR Guinea–Bissau: Joint Action 2008/112/CFSP [2008] OJ L40/11.

[64] On the link between CSDP and development, see P Koutrakos, 'The nexus between the European Union's Common Security and Defence Policy and Development' in A Arnull, C Barnard, M Dougan and E Spaventa (eds), *A Constitutional Order of States: Essays in EU Law in Honour of Alan Dashwood* (Hart Publishing, 2011) 589.

[65] A/47/277 S/24111 (17 June 1992).

broader EU policy framework, this and the intrinsic link between the subject matter of CSDP missions and other EU actions raise legal questions. For instance, the distinction between projects managed under the Instrument for Stability[66] and police missions is not always immediately apparent.[67] This ambiguity provides fertile ground for inter-institutional disputes, breeds administrative inefficiencies and undermines the effectiveness of the Union's action.

Second, there is a distinct emphasis on internal coherence and coordination, a concern to manage the coexistence of CSDP and other EU initiatives in all documents which set out the main parameters of CSDP missions. This concern has two aspects: on the one hand, it relates directly to policy and is about the consistency between the implementation of a CSDP mission and other aspects of EU external action; on the other hand, it has a distinct legal dimension, as there is an underlying preoccupation to respect the competences of the various actors involved. This is played out in a context of a very considerable institutional and procedural density, not only within the CSDP context but also beyond it.[68] Coherence as a policy and legal imperative is tied in with what may be the strength of the Union's security posture: as it relates to its ability to have recourse to a wide range of policies and instruments, it touches upon what the 2008 *Report on the European Security Strategy* refers to as 'distinctive European approach to foreign and security policy'.[69] However, the management of coherence, and the policy and legal linkages which it entails is by no means straightforward, as it requires that the missions invest considerable energy and has a direct impact on their efficiency.[70] The European External Action Service (EEAS) was introduced in order to enhance the effectiveness of the Union's external action. Whilst it is premature to assess EEAS, it is worth noting that the inter-institutional squabbles which have marred its establishment, the compromises to which the agreement on its remit and management gave rise and the ambiguities resulting from the drafting of Council Decision 2010/427/EU[71] illustrate the very traits which the EEAS purports to address.[72]

Third, the choice of approaches adopted in the context of CSDP missions draws upon the methodology employed in other strands of EU action. The principle of local ownership, for instance, one of the cornerstones of the European Neighbourhood Policy, has been transplanted in CSDP missions and applied with varying intensity.[73] As it happens, in both contexts the relationship between the mission and the local authorities which emerges is considerably less mutual than the rhetoric of the term suggests.[74]

The fourth theme may have to do with the European Court of Justice. The role it plays in the development of EU external relations is so profound that, in the light of the increasing

66 Reg 1717/2006 [2006] OJ L327/1.

67 See, for instance, the activities set out in SEC (2009) 932 *Commission Staff Working Paper Accompanying Annual report from the European Commission on the Instrument for Stability in 2008* (COM (2009) 341), 7. On the relevance of actions supported by the Instrument for Stability to CSDP, see the Conclusions of External Relations Council Conclusions of 17 November 2009, para 127.

68 The role of EU Special Representatives and the various issues of coordination which their presence entails in areas where the EU carries out a CSDP mission is a case in point.

69 S407/08 (Brussels, 11 December 2008) 2.

70 See, for instance, A Juncos, 'Of Cops and Robbers: European Union Policy and the Problem of Organized Crime in Bosnia' in B Balamir-Coskun and B Demirtas-Coskun (eds), *Neighborhood Challenge: The European Union and its Neighbors* (Universal Publishers, 2009) 47.

71 [2010] OJ L201/30.

72 See S Duke, 'A difficult birth: the early days of the European External Action Service' in P Koutrakos, *The European Union's External Relations a Year after Lisbon*, 2011/3 CLEER Working Papers 69, and S Duke 'The European External Action Service: Antidote against Incoherence?' (2012) 17 *EFA Rev* 45.

73 See, for instance, the EU LEX Iraq: Joint Action 2005/190/CFSP [2005] OJ L62/37, amended and extended by Council Decision 2010/330/CFSP [2010] OJ L149/12 and, more recently, by Council Decision 2011/380/CFSP [2011] OJ L169/27 and EULEX Kosovo: Joint Action 2008/124/CFSP [2008] OJ L42/92, last amended by Council Decision 2010/619/CFSP [2010] OJ L272/19 missions.

74 See, for instance, S Keukeleire, A Kalaja and A Çollaku, 'The European Union's policy on Kosovo' in Koutrakos, n 53, 172.

congruence between CSDP and the other strands of EU external action, it raises questions about its potential impact on CSDP. Given the exclusion of this area from its jurisdiction, the ECJ may be called upon to adjudicate on a dispute about the legal basis of an external initiative as it did in *ECOWAS*.[75] Its approach in this case, along with the undiminished appetite of the Union actors for inter-institutional disputes and the increasingly pronounced nexus between security and development, may raise the question whether the temptation to interfere with the conduct of CSDP might be too strong for the ECJ to resist. This would add yet another layer of complexity in a legal and political context which needs it least.

The above themes, which seem to govern the links between CSDP and the other strands of EU external action, impose a considerable constraint on the ability of the Union to achieve its ambitions as a global security player. Does the complex DNA of the CSDP and the ways in which it has affected its missions impose too narrow a view on what the EU may do in the world? Whilst the scope of the operations which the Union may carry out is quite wide,[76] it is interesting how little the CSDP missions undertaken so far have to do with defence. Furthermore, it is not easy to assess the impact of the military operations carried out so far on the overall development of the CSDP identity, as their scope was limited and the security climate in which they were carried out was invariably favourable, given that the hard defence questions had already been answered by pre-existing forces and pursuant to other arrangements.

6. The Issue of Military Capabilities

It is not only the ambition of the security and defence missions which has been affected by the umbilical cord between CSDP and the other Union policies. The energy required to manage this coexistence, along with the constraints of legal rules and procedures, have somehow shifted the emphasis away from the factors which would actually make a difference to the conduct of the missions. A case in point is the area of military capabilities.

The grave problems facing the military capabilities of the Member States have by no means been new. Since the end of the Cold War, they have been plagued by, amongst others, decreasing defence budgets, duplication of resources, shortages in certain areas, and underinvestment in research and development. The perilous state of defence industries has a tangible impact on the ways in which the Union carries out its CSDP operations. On the one hand, and despite the grand pronouncements about the international role of the Union, Member States are reluctant to commit personnel and resources, not least because the cost of contributing, maintaining and replacing them is immense. This gives rise to delays in the deployment of missions and considerable problems in their management. It is indicative of the state of the Member States' military capabilities that, in EUFOR Chad, the Union had to rely upon Russian helicopters. The problem becomes more pronounced given that the Member States face similar difficulties in the context of other operations. In the Libya operation, for instance, the UK contributed about a dozen fighter aircraft, a couple of frigates and a submarine, and yet its military chiefs suggested that no more was possible and that they would have had serious problems had the operation lasted into the autumn of 2011; France faced similar problems.[77] And, even though the operation was not US-led, the United States provided 70% of all air support sorties.

A speech given in June 2011 by the then outgoing US Defence Secretary Gates on the future of NATO highlights the perilous state of the European military capabilities with

[75] Case C-91/05 *Commission v Council* [2008] ECR I-3651.
[76] See Art 43(1) TEU which formalizes pre-existing practice.
[77] *The Financial Times*, 25 March 2011, 13.

brutal honesty.[78] He refers to 'the very real possibility of collective military irrelevance' and argues as follows:

> 'The blunt reality is that there will be dwindling appetite and patience in the US Congress—and in the American body politic writ large—to expend increasingly precious funds on behalf of nations that are apparently unwilling to devote the necessary resources or make the necessary changes to be serious and capable partners in their own defense. Nations apparently willing and eager for American taxpayers to assume the growing security burden left by reductions in European defense budgets.
>
> Indeed, if current trends in the decline of European defense capabilities are not halted and reversed, future US political leaders—those for whom the Cold War was not the formative experience that it was for me—may not consider the return on America's investment in NATO worth the cost.'

The exasperation expressed in this statement does not bode well for the ambition of the Union to become an important global security player. This is even more so considering that factors extraneous to the Union's political agenda may exercise pressure on the Union to take the practical underpinnings of its security and defence policy more seriously. These include the shift of the US security interest in South East Asia and the Pacific region[79] and the decision of the US administration to cut its defence budget by $500 billion starting in 2012.

7. Conclusion

This chapter has highlighted the fit between, on the one hand, the increasing dispersal of power on the global scene and the willingness of the international security institutions to grant new players legal and political space and, on the other hand, the oft-repeated ambition of the EU to occupy that space and become a central security player. It examined the dissonance between this aim and the conduct of CSDP as a process-centred initiative whose organic links with the other strands of the Union's external action are both its strength and its weakness. It pointed out the heavy emphasis that the Union's institutions and the Member States put on rules and procedures and their failure to tackle the problems facing the practical underpinnings of security and defence.

It has been argued that what the Union needs in the current volatile and increasingly interdependent geopolitical climate is a grand strategy for its global role.[80] The analysis in this chapter has suggested that the function of such a strategy for the process-centred security policy of the Union would be irrelevant at best. The constraints on the Union's security role are internal and deeply embedded. If at all possible, addressing them would be very difficult at the best of times. And this is not the best of times. The ongoing financial crisis which has plagued the eurozone and the rest of the Union, and its implications for the international economy, are bound to have a profound impact on the role of the EU as a security actor. The pace of the deterioration of the financial stability of the eurozone is staggering, the political instability facing the countries seeking to avoid sovereign default tangible, and the risk of contagion unsettling. The interest of the Member States in the conduct of CSDP appears to be in inverse proportion to the energy which has been required to enable them and the Union institutions together to tackle the financial crisis. Furthermore, the crisis has led to further acceleration in the reductions which national governments have introduced in their defence budgets and which are bound to be further prolonged as

[78] Speech delivered on 10 June: <http://blogs.wsj.com/washwire/2011/06/10/transcript-of-defense-secretary-gatess-speech-on-natos-future/> (last accessed 26 January 2012).

[79] See the speech by President Obama in the Australian Parliament on 17 November 2011 (*The Economist*, 25 November 2011).

[80] J Howorth, 'Why the EU Needs a Grand Strategy' in Loukas Tsoukalis and Janis A Emmanouilidis (eds), *The Delphic Oracle on Europe—Is there a Future for the European Union?* (OUP, 2011) 149.

the Union struggles to extricate itself from the crisis.[81] In this context, the economic case for the rationalization of the military capabilities of the Member States appears even stronger and the potential benefits for the security role of the Union considerable. Whether the Member States will find the energy and courage to engage in such an exercise is a different matter.

[81] In March 2011 the NATO Secretary General stated that, whilst in 2002 the US accounted for about half of the defence spending of all NATO countries, that share is now closer to 75%. During 2010–2012, spending by the European members of NATO shrank by $45 billion, equivalent to the entire German defence budget: *The Financial Times*, 25 March 2011, 13.

6

The EU and the Responsibility to Protect

*Geert De Baere**

1. Introduction

In the first ever address of a permanent president of the European Council to the UN General Assembly, Mr Herman Van Rompuy recalled that when a bloodbath threatened to take place in Benghazi, Libya:

> 'European leaders... acted with swiftness and determination, diplomatically... and militarily... The principle of "responsibility to protect" was put into action – with perseverance and success. Now there is a "responsibility to assist" the new Libya with the political transition, the reconciliation and the reconstruction of a united country'.[1]

That statement arguably contains (at least) two ambiguous concepts: 'European leaders' and 'responsibility to protect'. Given that 'swiftness and determination' are perhaps not the qualifiers that first spring to mind to describe the European Union (EU)'s response to the humanitarian crisis in Libya, one might be forgiven for thinking that Mr Van Rompuy was, in fact, not referring to the EU at all, but to a broader and rather more protean category of 'European leaders' not necessarily acting within the framework of the EU. That, of course, raises the question of why the president of the European Council should feel compelled to do so. The explicit invocation of the responsibility to protect (R2P) is equally noteworthy. Developed by the International Commission on Intervention and State Sovereignty (ICISS)[2] R2P was unanimously endorsed on 15 September 2005 by the United Nations (UN) General Assembly when adopting the 2005 World Summit outcome.[3] Paragraphs 138 and 139 of the outcome document recognize the individual and collective responsibility of states to protect populations from genocide, war crimes, ethnic cleansing and crimes against humanity. The Security Council explicitly reaffirmed those paragraphs in UN Security Council Resolution (UNSCR) 1674 of 28 April 2006.[4] However, the precise content and scope of R2P remain nebulous. Nevertheless, the European Parliament has not only welcomed the recognition of R2P,[5] but also believes that, as defined in the 2005 World Summit Outcome Document, it should become one of the guiding principles for a coherent EU foreign policy strategy based

* Many thanks to Dr Frederik Naert, Dr Kimberley Trapp, and the editors of this volume for their valuable comments and suggestions. The usual disclaimer applies.

[1] General Assembly, Sixty-sixth session, 15th plenary meeting, Thursday, 22 September 2011, 11 a.m., New York, UN Doc. A/66/PV.15, p. 27–30.

[2] The International Commission on Intervention and State Sovereignty, *The Responsibility to Protect* (International Development Research Centre, 2001). On the history of the concept of R2P, see further eg G Evans, *The Responsibility to Protect: Ending Mass Atrocity Crimes Once and For All* (Brookings Institute Press, 2008); AJ Bellamy, *A Responsibility to Protect: The Global Effort to End Mass Atrocities* (Polity Press, 2008); L Axworthy, 'RtoP and the Evolution of State Sovereignty' in J Genser and I Cotler (eds), *The Responsibility to Protect: The Promise of Stopping Mass Atrocities in Our Time* (OUP, 2012) 3–16; and K Annan, Interventions. A Life in War and Peace (Allen Lane, 2012) 81–133.

[3] UN Doc A/RES/60/1. See Communication from the Commission to the Council and the European Parliament: *The 2005 UN Summit—Addressing the global challenges and making a success of the reformed UN*, COM (2005) 259, para 8.1.3., recommending that the EU should support the concept of R2P and make sure that it is translated into meaningful commitments and action on the part of states.

[4] UN Doc S/RES/1674 (2006) on the protection of civilians in armed conflict.

[5] European Parliament resolution on the outcome of the United Nations World Summit of 14–16 September 2005 [2006] OJ C227E/582, para 3.

on the objectives and principles established in Article 21 of the Treaty on European Union (TEU).[6] Conversely, the World Summit Outcome Document recognizes the important contribution to peace and security by regional organizations and supports the efforts of the EU in that regard.[7]

This chapter examines the significance of R2P for the EU's external relations and for the EU as a law-based system—bound to the protection of human rights and the respect for the principles of the UN Charter[8]—and the significance of the EU for the implementation of R2P. After a brief exploration of the content and the legal status of R2P, the present chapter looks at the role of regional organizations in its implementation. It analyses the role the EU could play in that regard, and offers suggestions on what the EU's most valuable contribution could be.

2. Obligations Flowing from the Responsibility to Protect

While the ICISS Report had characterized R2P as comprising the responsibilities to prevent, react, and rebuild, UN Secretary-General Ban Ki-moon's 2009 report to the General Assembly conceives of the responsibility to protect as resting on three pillars:[9]

> (i) 'the enduring responsibility of the State to protect its populations, whether nationals or not, from genocide, war crimes, ethnic cleansing and crimes against humanity, and from their incitement';
> (ii) 'the commitment of the international community to assist States in meeting those obligations', drawing on 'the cooperation of Member States, regional and subregional arrangements, civil society and the private sector, as well as on the institutional strengths and comparative advantages of the United Nations system';
> (iii) 'the responsibility of Member States to respond collectively in a timely and decisive manner when a State is manifestly failing to provide such protection...
>
> A reasoned, calibrated and timely response could... include pacific measures under Chapter VI of the Charter, coercive ones under Chapter VII and/or collaboration with regional and subregional arrangements under Chapter VIII.... In accordance with the Charter, measures under Chapter VII must be authorized by the Security Council. The General Assembly may exercise a range of related functions under Articles 10 to 14 of the UN Charter, as well as under the "Uniting for peace" process set out in its resolution 377(V)'.[10]

Former Australian Foreign Minister Gareth Evans, co-chair of the ICISS and one of the fathers of R2P, has described the obligations flowing from R2P as a three-layered cake 'labelled respectively, from the bottom up, "prevention", "reaction", and "rebuilding"—which is sliced vertically into three big wedges, labelled respectively Pillars One, Two, and Three'.[11]

[6] European Parliament resolution of 10 March 2010 on the annual report from the Council to the European Parliament on the main aspects and basic choices of the Common Foreign and Security Policy (CFSP) in 2008, presented to the European Parliament in application of Part II, Section G, para 43 of the Inter-institutional Agreement of 17 May 2006 (2009/2057(INI)) [2010] OJ C349E/51, para 1.

[7] A/RES/60/1, para 93.

[8] Arts 3(5) and 21(1) TEU.

[9] *Implementing the Responsibility to Protect*, Report of the Secretary-General, UN Doc A/63/677, 8–9.

[10] UN Doc A/RES/377 A. It provides for the General Assembly to make recommendations for collective measures to restore international peace and security in any case where there appears to be a threat to the peace, breach of the peace or act of aggression and the Security Council is unable to act because of lack of unanimity of the permanent members. The legality of the resolution has been implicitly accepted by the International Court of Justice (ICJ): see *Legal Consequences of the Construction of a Wall in the Occupied Palestinian Territory, Advisory Opinion* (2004) ICJ Reps 136, para 30; *Accordance With International Law of the Unilateral Declaration of Independence in Respect of Kosovo, Advisory Opinion of 22 July 2010*, para 42.

[11] G Evans, 'Lessons and Challenges' in J Genser and I Cotler (eds), *The Responsibility to Protect: The Promise of Stopping Mass Atrocities in Our Time* (OUP, 2012) 379.

Are these, however, legal obligations? The Secretary-General's 2009 report was followed by an extensive debate in the UN General Assembly, during the course of which some UN Member States explicitly denied the legal character of R2P, while others explicitly confirmed it.[12] In any event, the Secretary-General emphasized that the provisions of paragraphs 138 and 139 of the Summit Outcome that outline R2P are 'firmly anchored in well-established principles of international law'.[13] With the exception of 'ethnic cleansing', all crimes referred to in the R2P documents are codified in various international agreements such as the Geneva Conventions,[14] the Convention on the Prevention and Punishment of the Crime of Genocide,[15] and the Rome Statute.[16] Furthermore, the responsibility to protect civilians and to prevent mass atrocities could arguably be legally based on an expansive reading of the precautionary obligation to protect civilians under international humanitarian law.[17] Could R2P be said to already be part of general, ie customary international law? The conditions for that to happen, as succinctly spelled out in Article 38(1)(b) of the Statute of the International Court of Justice (ICJ) and recalled by that court in *North Sea Continental Shelf*, are that not only must:

> 'the acts concerned amount to a settled practice, but they must also be such, or be carried out in such a way, as to be evidence of a belief that this practice is rendered obligatory by the existence of a rule of law requiring it'[18]

Applying those two conditions to R2P, it appears that neither can be said to have been met.[19] While many would agree with the first pillar of R2P, ie that a state has the duty to protect citizens on its own territory, few would take the view that the same counted as regards a proposed duty to act for foreign entities in case of a failure to protect by the 'home state', ie the third pillar of R2P.[20] Indeed, there is almost no evidence that states view the third pillar of R2P as a positive duty to act under international law, at the very least not beyond Article 41 of the International Law Commission's Articles on State Responsibility (ASR).[21] By contrast to that Article, R2P is not limited to serious breaches of peremptory norms of general international law and therefore arguably constitutes a step beyond the ASR.[22] It is of course true that the ICJ has held that: '*opinio juris* may, though with all due caution, be deduced from, inter alia, the attitude of the Parties and the attitude of States towards certain

[12] UN Doc A/63/PV.98, 24–26.

[13] A/63/677, para 3. This was echoed in a number of UN Member States' contributions to the General Assembly debate on the report; eg Austria at A/63/PV.98, 1.

[14] Geneva Convention for the Amelioration of the Condition of the Wounded and Sick in Armed Forces in the Field, 75 UNTS 31; Geneva Convention for the Amelioration of the Condition of Wounded, Sick and Shipwrecked Members of Armed Forces at Sea, 75 UNTS 85; Geneva Convention relative to the Treatment of Prisoners of War, 75 UNTS 135; Geneva Convention relative to the Protection of Civilian Persons in Time of War, 75 UNTS 287.

[15] Convention on the Prevention and Punishment of the Crime of Genocide, 78 UNTS 277. cf *Application of the Convention on the Prevention and Punishment of the Crime of Genocide (Bosnia and Herzegovina v Serbia and Montenegro)* (2007) ICJ Reps 43, 221, para 430, on the extra-territorial application of the obligation to prevent genocide.

[16] Arts 6–8 of the Rome Statute of the International Criminal Court, UN Doc A/CONF 183/9; 37 ILM 1002 (1998); 2187 UNTS 90.

[17] See H Nasu, 'Operationalizing the "Responsibility to Protect" and Conflict Prevention: Dilemmas of Civilian Protection in Armed Conflict' (2009) 14 J of Conflict and Security L 227 and 230.

[18] *North Sea Continental Shelf* (1969) ICJ Reps 3, 44, para 77.

[19] cf eg C Stahn, 'Responsibility to Protect: Political Rhetoric or Emerging Legal Norm' (2007) 101 AJIL 110; S Zifcak, 'The Responsibility to Protect' in MD Evans (ed), *International Law* (3rd edn, OUP, 2010) 521–524.

[20] A Peters, 'The Responsibility to Protect: Spelling Out the Hard Legal Consequences for the UN Security Council and its Members' in U Fastenrath, R Geiger, D-E Khan, A Paulus, S von Schorlemer and C Vedder (eds), *From Bilateralism to Community Interest: Essays in Honour of Bruno Simma* (OUP, 2011) 304.

[21] 'The International Law Commission's Articles on the Responsibility of States for Internationally Wrongful Acts' *Yearbook of the International Law Commission* (2001) vol II (2) and Annex to General Assembly resolution 56/83 of 12 December 2001, corrected by UN Doc A/56/49 (vol I) Corr 4.; see C Stahn, n 19, 118–120.

[22] C Stahn, n 19, 116.

General Assembly resolutions'.[23] Nevertheless, it seems premature to view the World Summit Outcome Document as similarly reflecting general international law, especially in the light of the opinions expressed by various UN Member States on R2P's lack of legally binding force, as well as of the lack of state practice.[24] Or could the acceptance of R2P by the World Summit perhaps be seen as akin to the Continental Shelf Proclamation, issued by US President Truman on 28 September 1945, whereby he asserted the natural resources of the subsoil and sea bed of the continental shelf to be 'appertaining to the United States, subject to its jurisdiction and control'.[25] As Crawford and Viles point out, *opinio juris* in the traditional sense, ie pertaining to the state of existing law, was clearly lacking among those involved in drafting the proclamation. There was, however, *opinio juris* in the sense that the proclamation articulated a rule which the US was prepared to live by from that moment onwards, for itself and for others. The proclamation was variously welcomed or met with caution, but not condemned. Crawford and Viles therefore conclude that it was neither legal nor illegal.[26] Could R2P be compared to the Continental Shelf Proclamation? The answer depends on what precisely the concept of R2P encompasses. One of the more vexed aspects as regards the normative content of R2P is whether an intervention or other enforcement action could be undertaken without the authorization of the UN Security Council. It appears to be quite generally accepted that the admissibility of unilateral intervention is ruled out.[27] However, the increased practice of peacekeeping and enforcement action to protect the civilian population authorized by the UN Security Council appears to indicate that R2P may be regarded as aiming at nothing more than a flexible interpretation through which the Security Council can characterize grave human rights violations as a threat to the peace, as it did in UNSCR 1674,[28] and order enforcement action on that basis. In that respect, R2P can be regarded as a codification of a practice progressively developed since the early nineties.[29] UNSCR 1973[30] on Libya was in itself not ground-breaking and in fact consistent with a post-Cold War practice dating back at least to the adoption of UNSCR 794[31] in December 1992 and UNSCR 819[32] in April 1993, both of which authorize the use of 'all necessary means' to establish secure conditions for humanitarian relief and create safe havens in situations of internal conflict. Putting matters slightly more bluntly, perhaps the normative content of R2P amounts to no more than empowering the UN Security Council to authorize things that it had been authorizing for more than a decade,[33] though a confirmation of the vires

[23] *Military and Paramilitary Activities in and against Nicaragua (Nicaragua v United States of America) Merits, Judgment* (1986) ICJ Reps 14, 99–100, para 188.

[24] eg n 12.

[25] (1946) 40 AJIL Supp 46.

[26] J Crawford and T Viles, 'International Law on a Given Day' in J Crawford, *International Law as an Open System* (Cameron, May, 2002) 92. cf the Declaration of Judge Simma in *Kosovo Advisory Opinion*, n 10, para 9: '[T] he Court could have explored whether international law can be deliberately neutral or silent on a certain issue, and whether it allows for the concept of toleration, something which breaks from the binary understanding of permission/prohibition and which allows for a range of non-prohibited options. That an act might be "tolerated" would not necessarily mean that it is "legal", but rather that it is "not illegal"'.

[27] cf eg the Independent International Commission on Kosovo, *The Kosovo Report. Conflict, International Response, Lessons Learned* (OUP, 2000) 186, characterizing the intervention in Kosovo as 'illegal, yet legitimate'. Further: C Gray, *International Law and the Use of Force* (3rd edn, OUP, 2008) 39–51. See also Annan, n 2, 87–101.

[28] N 4, para 26. Further: D Shraga, 'The Security Council and Human Rights—From Discretion to Promote to Obligation to Protect' in B Fassbender (ed), *Securing Human Rights? Achievements and Challenges of the UN Security Council* (OUP, 2011) 11–14. cf R Higgins, *Problems and Process: International Law and How We Use It* (OUP, 1994) 255, describing such a characterization as a 'legal fiction'.

[29] cf O Corten, *The Law Against War* (Hart Publishing, 2010) 526.

[30] UN Doc S/RES/1973 (2011).

[31] UN Doc S/RES/794 (1992) on Somalia.

[32] UN Doc S/RES/819 (1993) on Bosnia and Herzegovina.

[33] S Chesterman, '"Leading from Behind": The Responsibility to Protect, the Obama Doctrine, and Humanitarian Intervention after Libya' (2011) 25 *Ethics and International Affairs* 279–280.

of that practice is in itself of value.[34] Therefore, if restricted to the possibility for the Security Council to qualify gross violations of human rights as a threat to the peace and to authorize enforcement action on the basis of Chapter VII of the UN Charter, R2P arguably has a clearer and more secure pedigree than the Continental Shelf Proclamation. Indeed, a good argument could be made that R2P as understood by the World Summit Outcome is a codification of state practice. If R2P is, however, understood more broadly as potentially allowing intervention without prior authorization by the Security Council, its status is precarious. Contrary to the Continental Shelf Proclamation, many states have clearly objected to such a doctrine, and continue to do so. At any rate, international law cannot be made by way of instant custom: 'Like good coffee, international law has to be brewed'.[35]

Be that as it may, it is important to emphasize that R2P pertains at least as much to preventing mass atrocities and post-conflict rebuilding than to military intervention. Indeed, the ICISS report itself lists prevention as the first priority under the core principles of R2P.[36] Prevention is also encapsulated in the basic obligations of the parties to the Genocide Convention[37] as outlined in Article I, and the ICJ has stressed the importance of prevention in its judgment in the *Bosnian Genocide Case*.[38] R2P must therefore not be reduced to the potential for coercive measures. In his address of 21 September 2011 to the General Assembly, Secretary-General Ban Ki-moon pleaded strongly in favour of more efforts for prevention and noted the relevance of R2P in that regard. To prevent violations of human rights, the Secretary-General argued, the UN must work for the rule of law and stand against impunity, noting also that 'development is ultimately the best prevention'.[39] The UN is increasingly cooperating with regional organizations to that end.[40]

3. The Role of the EU

3.1. The responsibility to protect and regional arrangements

Despite having been drafted at a time when they were largely things of the future, the UN Charter contains a surprising amount of language on regional arrangements.[41] Chapter VIII of the UN Charter addresses the role of regional arrangements in the maintenance of international peace and security.[42] It comprises a system described by Secretary-General

[34] Note that those in favour of the Office of the Special Adviser on the Prevention of Genocide considered its mandate as an unprecedented recognition of the relationship between massive human rights violations and threats to peace and security: P Akhavan, 'Report on the Work of the Office of the Special Adviser of the United Nations Secretary-General on the Prevention of Genocide' (2006) 28 *Human Rights Quarterly* 1047.

[35] Crawford and Viles, n 26, 93.

[36] ICISS Report, n 2, XI.

[37] See n 15.

[38] *Bosnian Genocide Case* n 15, 222, para 431. However, the ICJ was careful to specify that it did not 'in this case, purport to establish a general jurisprudence applicable to all cases where a treaty instrument, or other binding legal norm, includes an obligation for States to prevent certain acts. Still less does the decision of the Court purport to find whether, apart from the texts applicable to specific fields, there is a general obligation on States to prevent the commission by other persons or entities of acts contrary to certain norms of general international law': at 220, para 429. cf also *Application of the International Convention on the Elimination of all Forms of Racial Discrimination (Georgia v Russian Federation), Provisional Measures, Order of 15 October 2008* (2008) ICJ Reps 353, 392, para 126: 'whereas the Court considers that it is not appropriate, in the present phase, for it to pronounce on the issue of whether Arts 2 and 5 of CERD imply a duty to prevent racial discrimination by other actors'.

[39] General Assembly, Sixty-sixth session, 11th plenary meeting, Wednesday, 21 September 2011, 9 a.m., New York, UN Doc. A/66/PV.11, p. 2.

[40] *The role of regional and subregional arrangements in implementing the responsibility to protect*, Report of the Secretary-General, UN Doc A/65/877-S/2011/393.

[41] This has been described by Secretary-General Ban Ki-moon as 'visionary': 'Human Protection and the Twenty-First Century United Nations', 2011 Cyril Foster Lecture, delivered by UN Secretary-General Ban Ki-moon at Oxford University on 2 February 2011, SG/SM/13385.

[42] cf P Koutrakos, in the present volume.

Ban Ki-moon as 'a dual bottom-up top-down relationship', underlining 'the value of ongoing working relationships among global, regional and sub-regional organizations for prevention and protection purposes'.[43] Furthermore, Article 33(1) of the UN Charter provides that the parties to 'any dispute, the continuance of which is likely to endanger the maintenance of international peace and security, shall, first of all, seek a solution by... resort to regional agencies or arrangements...'.[44] The UN has already collaborated with various regional organizations in a number of missions aimed at preventing conflict, but equally missions aimed at terminating conflict or restoring societies in the aftermath of conflict. Examples include the EU's military operations in support of the UN operation in the Democratic Republic of the Congo in 2003 and 2006.[45]

Following an expression of interest by many UN Member States in having a dialogue within the framework of the General Assembly on the role of regional and sub-regional dimensions of R2P, the Secretary-General prepared a report on the matter in June 2011, in which he describes fostering 'more effective global–regional collaboration' as a 'key plank' of his strategy for 'fulfilling the promise embodied in the responsibility to protect'. That strategy consists of what the Secretary-General, as mentioned above, describes as 'three pillars': 'pillar one, on the protection responsibilities of the State; pillar two, on international assistance and capacity-building; and pillar three, on timely and decisive response'.[46]

The goal of the first pillar is to have states institutionalize, and societies internalize, the principles of the UN Charter and of international law in a purposeful and sustainable manner. 'The more progress that States make towards the inclusion of these principles in their legislation, policies, practices, attitudes and institutions, the less recourse there will be to the third pillar (response)'.[47] Regional and sub-regional arrangements can encourage governments to recognize their obligations under relevant international conventions and to identify and address sources of friction within their societies before they lead to violence or atrocities. The report lists a number of examples, such as the Association of Southeast Asian Nations (ASEAN) Intergovernmental Commission on Human Rights, the Office of the High Commissioner on National Minorities of the Organization for Security and Co-operation in Europe (OSCE), and the EU.[48]

The second pillar involves efforts, either of a structural or of an operational nature, to help the state bolster its capacity to prevent or curb mass atrocities.[49] The added value of regional and sub-regional arrangements in terms of strengthening the structural–prevention component of the second pillar is mainly twofold: (i) the regional and sub-regional development of norms, standards and institutions that promote tolerance, transparency, accountability, and the constructive management of diversity; and (ii) in the area of preparedness and planning, which can make a difference in reducing the ill effects of both man-made and natural disasters. Given the fact that mass atrocities often have consequences for neighbouring countries and that they are sometimes committed by non-state actors, which tend to operate on a transnational basis, humanitarian and natural resource implications of large-scale refugee flows, preparedness, planning, and response should be undertaken both at the cross-border and the country levels, as well as regional or sub-regional levels.[50] This approach ties in with the idea that the key to successful peace-building lies within state

[43] A/65/877-S/2011/393, para 5.

[44] See also Art 47(4) of the UN Charter.

[45] KM Haugevik, 'Regionalising the Responsibility to Protect: Possibilities, Capabilities and Actualities' (2009) 1 *Global Responsibility to Protect* 349.

[46] A/65/877-S/2011/393, para 9.

[47] Ibid, para 11.

[48] Ibid, paras 17–18.

[49] Ibid, para 21: 'Structural prevention seeks to change the context from one that is more prone to such upheavals to one that is less so. Its timeline is more extended and its results harder to perceive or measure. Operational prevention, on the other hand, strives to avert what appears to be the imminent threat of an atrocity'.

[50] A/65/877-S/2011/393, para 23.

building. Possibly the most difficult challenge faced by peace-builders is the fact that they have to cope with the failure or indeed the absence of a functioning state apparatus.[51] If a failed state is what R2P is there to remedy, surely the most obvious remedy would seem to consist of state building or, in the context of the EU, Member State building.[52]

The Secretary-General is somewhat less clear on the role of regional arrangements as regards the third pillar, which starts from the acknowledgement that no broad strategy for implementing the responsibility to protect could be complete without some reference to Chapter VII methods. However, the quiet responses undertaken with the tools of investigation, fact-finding, good offices, mediation, personal persuasion and conflict resolution laid out in Chapters VI and VIII of the Charter remain of crucial importance. The Secretary-General emphasizes the need for an early and flexible response tailored to the circumstances of each case, rather than any generalized or prescriptive set of policy options, and advocates 'natural synergies' between the UN and its regional and sub-regional partners when it comes to gathering and exchanging information, comparing notes and sharing assessments of situations of common concern.[53]

In particular, several regional organizations strengthened their capacity for preventive action after the *Brahimi Report*,[54] and they could play an important role in the implementation of the preventive aspect of R2P.[55] Moreover, as Secretary-General Ban Ki-moon points out, while R2P is a universal principle, its implementation should respect institutional and cultural differences, without diluting the national and international responsibilities flowing from it,[56] thereby putting forward an argument often heard in the context of the implementation of human rights.[57] The Security Council has also recognized that regional organizations 'are well positioned to understand the causes of armed conflicts owing to their knowledge of the region which can be a benefit for their efforts to influence the prevention or resolution of these conflicts'.[58] For example, the League of Arab States and the African Union both played a crucial role in establishing a consensus on stopping atrocities in Libya.[59] Both the 2009 and the 2011 reports of the Secretary-General[60] explicitly mention the experience of the EU.

3.2. The EU and the implementation of the responsibility to protect

Gareth Evans has remarked that the EU has the greatest potential fully to operationalize R2P, both because of its standing as a 'normative power' and as a primary model for conflict prevention across its own territory, and because the Union already has a large set of practical instruments and policies in the realm of prevention and rebuilding.[61] The EU has the organizational capacity for early warning and prevention, which is currently further developed through the common security and defence policy (CSDP).[62] Since 2004, the EU

[51] R Paris, *At War's End. Building Peace after Civil Conflict* (CUP, 2004) 46–47.

[52] cf S Blockmans, 'EU Enlargement as a Peacebuilding Tool' in S Blockmans, J Wouters, and T Ruys (eds), *The European Union and Peacebuilding. Policy and Legal Aspects* (TMC Asser Press, 2010) 77.

[53] A/65/877-S/2011/393, paras 30–31.

[54] *Report of the Panel on United Nations Peace Operations*, UN Doc A/55/305–S/2000/809.

[55] D Carment and M Fischer, 'R2P and the Role of Regional Organisations in Ethnic Conflict Management, Prevention and Resolution: The Unfinished Agenda' (2009) 1 *Global Responsibility to Protect* 263.

[56] A/65/877-S/2011/393, para 8.

[57] eg P Carozza, 'Subsidiarity as a Structural Principle of International Human Rights Law' (2003) 97 AJIL 38–79.

[58] UN Doc S/RES/2033 (2012) on cooperation between the United Nations and regional and subregional organizations in maintaining international peace and security, 4th recital.

[59] MS Helal, 'Middle East' in J Genser and I Cotler (eds), *The Responsibility to Protect: The Promise of Stopping Mass Atrocities in Our Time* (OUP, 2012) 229.

[60] A/63/677, para 4; A/65/877-S/2011/393, paras 18, 27, 34 and 40.

[61] Evans, n 2, 183–184.

[62] Arts 42 and 43 TEU. See Carment and Fischer n 55, 282.

has also been developing so-called 'rapid reaction battle groups',[63] modelled on the Union's first autonomous military operation in the Democratic Republic of Congo in 2003.[64] Then UN Secretary-General Kofi Annan referred to these battle groups as 'a very valuable complement to our own efforts' and urged heads of state and government to support the efforts by, inter alia, the EU 'to establish standby capacities as part of an interlocking system of peacekeeping capacities'.[65] Indeed, while not well-equipped for large-scale and long-term interventions, the EU is arguably better equipped than the UN for small-scale rapid deployment actions.[66]

Furthermore, the concept of R2P has been appearing in a growing number of EU documents. For example, in the June 2005 Presidency Conclusions, the European Council emphasized 'the importance which it attributes to the concept of responsibility to protect, which must be implemented by the Security Council' in the context of remarks on the preparation for the September 2005 United Nations Summit.[67] The 2006 *European Consensus on Development* emphasizes the Union's support for R2P in its point 37 and stresses its intention to contribute to a 'strengthened role for the regional and sub-regional organizations in the process of enhancing international peace and security'.[68] The conception of R2P to which the EU adheres appears to be the one espoused by the World Summit Outcome Document. In its December 2008 report on the implementation of the European Security Strategy,[69] the Council explicitly confirmed that with respect to 'core human rights, the EU should continue to advance the agreement reached at the UN World Summit in 2005, that we hold a shared responsibility to protect populations from genocide, war crimes, ethnic cleansing and crimes against humanity'.[70] The *European Consensus on Humanitarian Aid* confirms that the EU endorses the commitment to R2P in accordance with the 2005 World Summit Outcome.[71] Finally, the EU's priorities for the 66th session of the UN General Assembly welcomed the references to R2P in UN Security Council Resolutions (UNSCR) 1970,[72] 1973[73] and 1975,[74] and provided:

> 'The EU will strive for the operationalization of the concept of Responsibility to Protect (R2P) on the basis that the concept is not open for renegotiation. The EU will apply a "narrow but deep approach" to R2P-related policies and will particularly focus on its preventive pillar.'[75]

However, to what extent can the EU be said to have already operationalized R2P? While a number of examples could arguably be regarded as an operational implementation of R2P by the EU,[76] this chapter considers the 'third pillar' example of Libya, as it featured so

[63] eg Haugevik, n 45, 356; S Duke, 'Peculiarities in the Institutionalisation of CFSP and ESDP' in S Blockmans (ed), *The European Union and Crisis Management: Policy and Legal Aspects* (TMC Asser Press, 2010) 95–99.

[64] Council Joint Action 2003/423/CFSP of 5 June 2003 on the European Union military operation in the Democratic Republic of Congo [2003] OJ L143/50.

[65] *In larger freedom: towards development, security and human rights for all*, Report of the Secretary-General, UN Doc A/59/2005, para 112 and Annex, para 6(j).

[66] MV Vlasic, 'Europe and North America' in J Genser and I Cotler (eds), *The Responsibility to Protect: The Promise of Stopping Mass Atrocities in Our Time* (OUP, 2012) 181.

[67] Presidency Conclusions of the Brussels European Council, 16 and 17 June 2005, 10255/1/05, para 37.

[68] *The European Consensus on Development* [2006] C46/01 7.

[69] *A Secure Europe In A Better World, European Security Strategy*, Brussels, 12 December 2003.

[70] Council of the European Union, *Report on the Implementation of the European Security Strategy: Providing Security in a Changing World*, S407/08, 2 and 12.

[71] Joint Statement by the Council and the Representatives of the Governments of the Member States meeting within the Council, the European Parliament and the European Commission [2008] OJ C25/1, para 17.

[72] UN Doc S/RES/1970 (2011) on peace and security in Africa.

[73] See n 30.

[74] UN Doc S/RES/1975 (2011) on the situation in Côte d'Ivoire. See also UN Doc S/RES/2045 (2012) on Côte d'Ivoire, 13th recital.

[75] Council Doc 11298/11, para 6.

[76] eg the Union's Rule of Law Mission in Kosovo: UN Doc S/RES/1244 (1999), paras 5 and 17; Council Joint Action 2008/124/CFSP of 4 February 2008 on the European Union Rule of Law Mission in Kosovo, EULEX Kosovo [2008] OJ L42/92 (last amended by Council Decision 2012/291/CFSP of 5 June 2012 [2012] OJ

prominently in Herman Van Rompuy's first address to the UN General Assembly,[77] and because it provides a rare example of the Security Council explicitly referring to R2P in the relevant UNSCRs 1970 and 1973.

In UNSCR 1970, the Security Council had recalled 'the Libyan authorities' responsibility to protect its population', and taken various measures under Chapter VII, including a referral of the situation to the International Criminal Court (ICC), an arms embargo, a travel ban, and an asset freeze.[78] In UNSCR 1973, the Security Council reiterated 'the responsibility of the Libyan authorities to protect the Libyan population' and reaffirmed 'that parties to armed conflicts bear the primary responsibility to take all feasible steps to ensure the protection of civilians'.[79] Crucially, the Security Council also authorized 'Member States that had notified the Secretary-General acting nationally or through regional organizations or arrangements, and acting in cooperation with the Secretary-General, to take all necessary measures . . . to protect civilians and civilian populated areas under threat of attack in the Libyan Arab Jamahiriya, including Benghazi, while excluding a foreign occupation force of any form on any part of Libyan territory'.[80]

Likewise, the Security Council authorized Member States that had notified the Secretary-General and the Secretary-General of the League of Arab States, 'acting nationally or through regional organizations or arrangements, to take all necessary measures to enforce compliance with the ban on flights'.[81]

At its spring meeting held on 24 and 25 March 2011, the European Council discussed the situation in Libya. Recalling its 11 March Declaration on the developments in Libya and the Southern Neighbourhood Region, the European Council expressed its satisfaction with the adoption of UNSCR 1973, and underlined its determination to contribute to its implementation. It also welcomed the Paris Summit of 19 March 2011, which marked the start of a military operation against the Libyan regime, as a decisive contribution to its implementation.[82] While that may be so, there is not even a hint of acknowledgement of the irony of an EU institution hailing a decision seemingly taken with the intention of avoiding the direct involvement of the EU. Meanwhile, apart from various statements by the President of the European Council and the High Representative of the Union for Foreign Affairs and Security Policy (HRUFASP), the Union remained absent from international action as regards Libya. However, on 1 April 2011, the Union finally managed to adopt Council Decision 2011/210/CFSP on a military operation in support of humanitarian assistance operations (EUFOR Libya).[83] While the decision did not explicitly refer to R2P,

L146/46), which acknowledged the need 'to prevent, on humanitarian grounds, possible outbreaks of violence, acts of persecution and intimidation in Kosovo, taking account, as appropriate, of the responsibility towards populations as referred to in Resolution 1674 by the United Nations Security Council on 28 April 2006' (recital (3)); and the Union's military operation in Chad and the Central African Republic (EUFOR Chad/RCA): UN Doc S/RES/1706 (2006) para 12; UN Doc S/RES/1769 (2007) paras 1 and 23; *Report of the Secretary-General on Chad and the Central African Republic*, UN Doc S/2007/488; UN Doc S/RES/1778 (2007) para 6; Council Joint Action 2007/677/CFSP of 15 October 2007 on the European Union military operation in the Republic of Chad and in the Central African Republic [2007] OJ L279/21 (repealed by Council Joint Action 2009/795/CFSP of 19 October 2009 [2009] L283/61); Council Decision 2008/101/CFSP of 28 January 2008 on the launching of the European Union military operation in the Republic of Chad and in the Central African Republic (Operation EUFOR Tchad/RCA) [2008] L34/39; European Parliament resolution 2009/C 259 E/20 of 24 April 2008 on the situation in Chad [2009] C259E/106, para O.

77 See n 1.

78 S/RES/1970 (2011), 9th recital and paras 1–21.

79 S/RES/1973 (2011), 4th recital.

80 Ibid, para 4.

81 Ibid, para 8.

82 Paris Summit For The Support To The Libyan People, 19 March 2011 (see the communiqué at <www.elysee.fr>). cf P Koutrakos in the present volume.

83 Council Decision 2011/210/CFSP of 1 April 2011 on a European Union military operation in support of humanitarian assistance operations in response to the crisis situation in Libya (EUFOR Libya) [2011] OJ L89/17 (Corrigendum [2011] OJ L203/36).

it did refer to UNSCRs 1970 and 1973. It also expressed its determination to ensure the protection of civilians and civilian populated areas and the rapid and unimpeded passage of humanitarian assistance and the safety of humanitarian personnel.[84] The EU mission aimed to support humanitarian assistance in the region. EUFOR Libya was to be conducted at the request of the United Nations Office for the Coordination of Humanitarian Affairs (OCHA) with a view to underpinning the mandates of UNSCRs 1970 and 1973.[85] In support thereof, EUFOR Libya was to 'contribute to the safe movement and evacuation of displaced persons', and 'support, with specific capabilities, the humanitarian agencies in their activities'.[86] The UN Security Council in the meantime adopted UNSCR 2009 of 16 September 2011, whereby it reaffirmed that the UN 'should lead the effort of the international community in supporting the Libyan-led transition and rebuilding process aimed at establishing a democratic, independent and united Libya', but also welcomed 'the efforts of the African Union, Arab League, European Union and the Organization of the Islamic Cooperation'.[87] However, a request by OCHA was not forthcoming and, as the situation on the ground in Libya evolved, the planned EU mission was overtaken by events. Rather anticlimactically, EUFOR Libya was therefore never launched and Council Decision 2011/210/CFSP was quietly repealed in November 2011.[88]

In any event, the EU had to tread carefully, as Germany's abstention on UNSCR 1973 indicates that the support for R2P among EU Member States may not be as unanimous as hoped for.[89] That abstention also casts doubt on possible arguments to the effect that the Union's rather frequent references to the concept of R2P may be taken into account as state practice or as evidence for *opinio juris* in the quest for a customary international law status of R2P.[90]

However, one should not rush to the conclusion that the EU's role in the implementation of R2P is marginal verging on the non-existent. Indeed, with respect to both Libya[91] and Syria,[92] the Union has pursued the tried and tested route of imposing restrictive measures on the regime in question. Such targeted sanctions are explicitly mentioned in the UN Secretary-General's 2009 report as one of the means to implement R2P's third pillar on timely and decisive response, to be considered 'on a case-by-case basis and in cooperation with relevant regional organizations'.[93]

More generally, the Union has developed a number of policies that support different pillars of R2P, including contributing to the objective of the widest possible participation in

[84] Recital 2.

[85] Art 1(1).

[86] Art 1(2).

[87] UN Doc S/RES/2009 (2011), 11th recital.

[88] Council Decision 2011/764/CFSP of 28 November 2011 [2011] OJ L314/35.

[89] J Wouters, P De Man, M Vincent, 'The Responsibility to Protect and Regional Organisations: Where Does the EU Stand?' (2011) Leuven Centre for Global Governance Studies, Policy Brief 18, 13 and 24–25.

[90] Compare F Hoffmeister, 'The Contribution of EU Practice to International Law' in M Cremona (ed), *Developments in EU External Relations Law* (OUP, 2008) 97–98, arguing that various declarations on the NATO intervention in Kosovo may contribute to the *opinio juris* that a humanitarian intervention is lawful under international law under strictly limited circumstances.

[91] Council Decision 2011/137/CFSP of 28 February 2011 concerning restrictive measures in view of the situation in Libya [2011] OJ L58/53 (last amended by Council Decision 2011/867/CFSP of 20 December 2011 [2011] OJ L341/56) and Council Reg (EU) 204/2011 of 2 March 2011 concerning restrictive measures in view of the situation in Libya [2011] OJ L58/1 (last amended by Council Reg (EU) 1360/2011 of 20 December 2011 [2011] OJ L341/18).

[92] Council Decision 2011/782/CFSP of 1 December 2011 concerning restrictive measures against Syria and repealing Decision 2011/273/CFSP [2011] OJ L319/56 (last amended by Council Decision 2012/420/CFSP of 23 July 2012 [2012] OJ L196/59) and Council Reg (EU) 36/2012 of 18 January 2012 concerning restrictive measures in view of the situation in Syria and repealing Reg (EU) 442/2011 [2012] OJ L 16/1 (last amended by Council Reg (EU) 867/2012 of 24 September 2012 [2012] OJ L 257/1).

[93] A/63/677, para 57.

the Rome Statute on the ICC,[94] promoting compliance with international humanitarian law,[95] the protection of civilians in CSDP missions and operations,[96] and institution-building under the Instrument for Stability.[97]

Furthermore, in his 2011 report on the role of regional organizations in the implementation of R2P, the Secretary-General mentions the EU a number of times, twice explicitly referring to its enlargement process and the applicable conditions. The EU helps to discourage 'conditions that could serve as a breeding ground for atrocities'. It does so partly 'through its rigorous standards for membership accession'. For example, some observers 'have suggested that the arrest of former Bosnian Serb General Ratko Mladić in May 2011 is evidence that such policies can aid the cause of accountability for atrocities under certain circumstances'.[98] Nevertheless, the transfer of suspects such as Mladić[99] and Hadžić[100] is only part of the issue, and the EU would be well-advised to focus more on the willingness and preparedness of domestic institutions to promote tolerance and reconciliation.[101]

Further in the report, the Secretary-General adds that the requirements for entry into the EU may also be helpful in encouraging countries to meet human rights standards. 'Such efforts at collective peer pressure may not always constitute timely and decisive action, but they have symbolic and political value'.[102] He thus appears to regard EU enlargement as its greatest contribution to R2P. That may be quite an accurate observation. The EU was set up as a means for tackling a situation of states that did not manage to guarantee the safety of their population. It is perhaps the most successful example of conflict prevention and of the rebuilding of broken states after a conflict.[103] Put differently, the EU is a 'peace-building process *an sich*'.[104]

The EU's most valuable contribution to R2P could therefore be precisely that: consolidating reconciliation within Europe through its accession process, and at the same time sharing its experiences in post-conflict rebuilding with other regions in the world through the externalization of practices developed internally as part of its original project:[105] its neighbourhood policy,[106] its development cooperation,[107] its economic, financial and technical cooperation with third countries,[108] and its humanitarian aid policy.[109] However, the

[94] Council Decision 2011/168/CFSP of 21 March 2011 on the International Criminal Court and repealing Common Position 2003/444/CFSP [2011] OJ L76/56.

[95] Updated European Union Guidelines on promoting compliance with international humanitarian law (IHL) [2009] OJ C303/12.

[96] Draft Revised Guidelines on the Protection of Civilians in CSDP Missions and Operations, Council Doc 15091/10. See also Council Doc 14940/10, in which the Political and Security Committee (PSC) invites the Permanent Representatives Committee (COREPER) to recommend that the Council adopt the Draft Revised Guidelines on the Protection of Civilians in CSDP Missions and Operations, as set out in the document 15091/10, which the Foreign Affairs Council did on 25 October 2010.

[97] Reg (EC) 1717/2006 of the European Parliament and of the Council of 15 November 2006 establishing an Instrument for Stability [2006] OJ L327/1.

[98] A/65/877-S/2011/393, para 18.

[99] See International Criminal Tribunal for the former Yugoslavia, Case IT-09-92-I, *The Prosecutor v Ratko Mladić*, pending.

[100] See International Criminal Tribunal for the former Yugoslavia, Case IT-04-75-I, *The Prosecutor v Goran Hadžić*, pending.

[101] cf Blockmans, n 52, 98–99.

[102] A/65/877-S/2011/393, para 34.

[103] cf Address by President Herman Van Rompuy at the High-Level Meeting on Libya, New York, 20 September 2011 (EUCO 76/11), emphasizing that it is 'time for justice, rule of law and human rights and for reconciliation' and noting that 'Europe was built on reconciliation'. See also Herman Van Rompuy, President of the European Council, Address to the 67th General Assembly of the United Nations, New York, 26 September 2012, (EUCO 178/12) 5.

[104] Blockmans n 52, 77.

[105] See de Búrca in the present volume.

[106] Art 8 TEU. See also the Commission Proposal for a Regulation of the European Parliament and of the Council establishing a European Neighbourhood Instrument COM (2011) 839 final.

[107] Arts 208–211 TFEU.

[108] Arts 212–213 TFEU.

[109] Art 214 TFEU.

international community, including the EU and the UN, must not assume that their combined power and capabilities suffice to substitute themselves for the failing state. Indeed, the willingness of Western states to do so has been rather underwhelming, resulting in inevitable disillusionment. That said, as Blockmans argues, European integration and EU enlargement constitutes one of the few unambiguously positive achievements of the post-Cold War era. In little over a decade, the prospect of accession to the EU has provided the impetus needed to transform the post-Communist states of Central and Eastern Europe into functioning democracies. Nonetheless, he highlights two problematic aspects of the EU pre-accession process. On the one hand, the reinforcement of executives almost inevitably engendered by the pre-accession process in turn has the predictable effect of weakening legislatures. On the other hand, the pre-accession process is, true to the original paradigm of European integration,[110] largely a technical process of building or rebuilding regulatory capacities of the state to accompany a functioning market.[111] Moreover, the EU must not assume that its remedies can be applied universally without any need for adaptation to the specific socio-economic circumstances of the state or region to which they are to be applied, so as not to run the danger of actually upsetting potential economic recovery or growth.[112] Finally, if pre-accession conditionality is to remain one of the EU's most valuable contributions to R2P, internal monitoring and supervision of human rights must be organized in a manner that prevents the 'post-accession regression' we are currently witnessing in certain Member States.[113]

What is more, performing its role in the implementation of R2P properly would seem to require a rethinking of the disunited structure of EU foreign policy, making as it does a distinction between political and socio-economic foreign policy. R2P, as we have seen, is not merely about the possibility of intervention if things go irredeemably wrong. It is also and perhaps more importantly about conflict prevention and rebuilding. An integrated and effective implementation of R2P therefore requires the EU to be able to offer an integrated foreign policy based on aspects of development cooperation and other forms of peaceful cooperation on the one hand and elements of the CFSP on the other. As argued elsewhere, such a unified policy was probably made more difficult by the ECJ's judgment in the *Small Arms and Light Weapons* case,[114] and it remains unclear whether Lisbon has changed that situation much.[115]

Both R2P and the EU as such are often regarded as challenges to what is commonly (and arguably rather inaccurately)[116] referred to as the 'Westphalian' conception of state sovereignty, as 'necessarily exclusive and absolute' and 'susceptible of no limitation not imposed by itself',[117] bearing in mind that 'the right of entering into international engagements is an attribute of State sovereignty'.[118] However, the ICJ has made it quite clear that the whole of international law still rests on 'the fundamental principle of State sovereignty'.[119]

[110] G De Baere, 'European Integration and the Rule of Law in Foreign Policy' in J Dickson and P Eleftheriadis (eds), *Philosophical Foundations of European Union Law* (OUP, forthcoming, 2012).

[111] cf H-W. Micklitz and D Patterson in the present volume.

[112] Blockmans, n 52, 80, 91–92, and 100.

[113] See Editorial Comments, 'Fundamental rights and EU membership: Do as I say, not as I do!' (2012) 49 *CML Rev* 481–488.

[114] Case C-91/05 *Commission v Council* [2008] ECR I-3651.

[115] G De Baere, *Constitutional Principles of EU External Relations* (OUP, 2008) 283–98; E Sharpston and G De Baere, 'The Court of Justice as a Constitutional Adjudicator' in A Arnull, C Barnard, M Dougan and E Spaventa (eds), *A Constitutional Order of States? Essays in EU Law in Honour of Alan Dashwood* (Hart Publishing, 2011) 144–147. For some possible indications, see Case C-130/10 Parliament v Council [2012] OJ C295/2.

[116] See A Osiander, 'Sovereignty, International Relations, and the Westphalian Myth' (2001) 55 *International Organization* 251–287.

[117] *The Exchange v McFaddon*, 11 US (7 Cranch) 116, 136 (1812).

[118] *Case of the SS 'Wimbledon'* PCIJ 1923, Series A, No 1, 15, 25.

[119] *Nicaragua case*, n 23, 133, para 263. Further: J E Alvarez, 'State Sovereignty is not Withering Away: A Few Lessons for the Future' in A Cassese (ed), *Realizing Utopia. The Future of International Law* (OUP, 2012) 26–37; and J Crawford, 'Sovereignty as a legal value' in J Crawford and M Koskenniemi (eds), *The Cambridge Companion to International Law* (CUP, 2012) 117–133. Compare: A Peters, 'Humanity as the A and Ω of Sovereignty' (2009) 20 EJIL 513–544; and P Eleftheriadis, 'Law and Sovereignty' (2010) 29 L and Philosophy 535–569.

Furthermore, the EU's failures in the implementation of R2P in that regard are no more than an illustration of its continuing difficulties in integrating high politics foreign policy within its constitutional framework and the tendency of the Member States to affirm their continuing sovereignty in defence matters by setting up ad hoc forms of cooperation (such as through the Paris Summit called by President Sarkozy)[120] outside the Union in defence matters. It is only through coming to terms with that fact that the EU may start to take up its role as a natural ally of the UN in operationalizing R2P.

If the Union is serious about R2P and about its unique position as a privileged partner of the UN in its implementation, it will need to rethink the fundamental structure of its foreign policy. The jury is still out on whether the European External Action Service (EEAS) constitutes a significant step forward in that respect. The EEAS was established to assist the HRUFASP in fulfilling her mandate.[121] It would appear that it provides a rather decent basis to start from in building a more unified EU foreign policy, but it is important to note that much will depend on the legal and practical implementation of its workings and policies and hence on the commitment and common vision of the individuals involved.[122] Specifically with respect to R2P, the EEAS has indicated that it is firmly committed to ensuring that it becomes an accepted international norm.[123] However, France and the UK's seemingly unstoppable urge to play *cavalier seul* in Libya indicates that the EEAS has a fairly long and winding road ahead of it in further operationalizing a comprehensive approach to EU external relations by linking EU conflict prevention, mediation, conflict resolution and development cooperation policies.[124] The UN Secretary-General, meanwhile, appears to be hopeful. In his report on the role of regional arrangements, he specifically mentions that the 'civilian capacities to help inform regional and sub-regional policies with regard to emerging crises', such as through the EEAS, 'could make a more significant contribution to the prevention of atrocities, especially in the near term'.[125]

4. Concluding Observations

The lack of agreement on what precisely R2P entails by way of international obligations and international responsibility is evidently a major obstacle in the way of its operationalization.[126] Indeed, the European Parliament has explicitly recommended to the Council 'to fully support the efforts of the UN Secretary General to better define the notion of the principle of the Responsibility to Protect (R2P), to stress its importance in preventing conflicts while encouraging its implementation'.[127] It is hard to implement a norm, the

[120] See n 82. See P Gourevitch, 'No Exit' *The New Yorker* (12 December 2011) 60, describing the intervention in Libya by the French-led coalition as 'an opportunity to represidentialize'.

[121] Art 27(1) TEU.

[122] B Van Vooren, 'A Legal–Institutional Perspective on the European External Action Service' (2011) 48 *CML Rev* 490 and 501–502, professing to be 'cautiously optimistic' on the role of the EEAS. See also *Report by the High Representative to the European Parliament, the Council and the Commission*, 22 December 2011 (available at: <http://www.eeas.europa.eu/images/top_stories/2011_eeas_report_cor.pdf>), para 33, noting that the 'political and economic context for the launch of the EEAS has been particularly challenging'. See, further L Erkelens and S Blockmans, 'Setting Up the European External Action Service: An Act of Institutional Balance' (2012) 8 Eur Constitutional L Rev 246–279.

[123] 'International Justice, Peace and Crisis Management—Experiences and Reflections from Africa, Middle East and EU 50 years after Dag Hammarskjöld', speech by Kristin de Peyron, Head of Division, Multilateral Relations, European External Action Service, High-level Seminar organized by the Swedish Embassy to the Netherlands, The Hague, 9 November 2011.

[124] S Blockmans, 'The European External Action Service one year on: First signs of strengths and weaknesses' (2012) 2 Asser Institute, CLEER Working Paper 31.

[125] A/65/877-S/2011/393, para 29.

[126] H Cuyckens and P De Man, 'The Responsibility to Prevent: On the Assumed Legal Nature of Responsibility to Protect and its Relationship with Conflict Prevention' in J Hoffmann and A Nollkaemper (eds), *Responsibility to Protect: From Principle to Practice* (Amsterdam University Press, 2012) 113.

[127] European Parliament recommendation to the Council of 25 March 2010 on the 65th Session of the United Nations General Assembly (2010/2020(INI)) (2011/C 4 E/08) [2011] OJ C4E/49, para n.

normative status of which itself is contested and the contours of which appear to be made up entirely of what HLA Hart called the 'penumbra' of a norm.[128] Its inherent vagueness allows for significantly diverging interpretations, such as the duty to prevent nations run by rulers without internal checks on their power from acquiring or using weapons of mass destruction, as suggested by Feinstein and Slaughter.[129] As Alvarez put it: 'It means too many things to too many different people'.[130]

Many have therefore argued that the significance of R2P is more political and rhetorical than legal. Put differently, the legal significance of R2P is conceptual and consists of the pulling together of pre-existing norms of international law and placing them in a novel framework.[131] Gareth Evans has, however, noted that those arguing that R2P is nothing more than 'old wine in new bottles' are missing the point,[132] and has revealed that the model that the ICISS expressly had in mind was the World Commission on Environment and Development and its introduction of the concept of 'sustainable development'.[133] Perhaps R2P's true significance, as with Article 99 of the UN Charter,[134] lies not in creating new rights or positive obligations, but in making it harder to act wrongly or to do nothing at all.[135] Akin to Article 99 of the UN Charter, R2P does not impose a duty or obligation on the Secretary-General, but provides a mandate to undertake executive action. The mere existence of R2P arguably makes it politically more costly for states to perpetrate atrocities or allow them to be perpetrated unhindered.[136]

Nevertheless, what is potentially new about R2P is not that sovereignty implies responsibility and that, as a consequence, legitimacy can be lost if the state neglects its responsibility,[137] but the subsidiarity-based logic[138] that the international community consequently has the responsibility to step into the breach. However, the R2P concept *prima facie* does not appear to take account of the democratic or otherwise grounding of the authority that performs the duty to protect, uncomfortably echoing Hobbes: 'The obligation of Subjects to the Soveraign, is understood to last as long, and no longer, than the power lasteth, by which he is able to protect them'.[139] The 2009 Secretary-General's report on implementing R2P does not help in that regard, addressing as it does mostly ways and means to systematize, integrate and expand international executive authority. If authoritarian tendencies are to be avoided, the institutionalization of R2P must involve not just the legitimization of new forms of authority, but also of delineating the precise limits to those authorities.[140] Successful state building requires the balancing of building a functioning government capable of upholding the law and protecting its citizens on the one hand, and limiting governmental power in order to preserve individual liberty.[141] That is an issue integral to the rule of law,[142]

[128] See HLA Hart, 'Positivism and the Separation of Law and Morals' (1958) 71 Harvard LR 607.

[129] L Feinstein and AM Slaughter, 'A duty to prevent' (2004) 83 *Foreign Affairs* 136–150.

[130] JE Alvarez, 'The Schizophrenias of R2P' in P Alston and E MacDonald (eds), *Human Rights, Intervention, and the Use of Force* (OUP, 2008) 277.

[131] Peters, n 20, 302.

[132] Evans, n 11, 377.

[133] World Commission on Environment and Development, *Our Common Future* (OUP, 1987).

[134] This article provides that the Secretary-General 'may bring to the attention of the Security Council any matter which in his opinion may threaten the maintenance of international peace and security'.

[135] Chesterman, n 33, 282. cf Peters, n 20, 323–324.

[136] WW Burke-White, 'Adoption of the Responsibility to Protect' in J Genser and I Cotler (eds), *The Responsibility to Protect: The Promise of Stopping Mass Atrocities in Our Time* (OUP, 2012) 34–35, describing R2P as a 'social norm' (cf C Sunstein, 'Social Norms and Social Roles' (1996) 96 Columbia L Rev 914) of the international community; and cf Annan, n 2, 132–133, referring to 'a norm that gives nations and peoples a yardstick - a standard by which they can hold their government to account'.

[137] D Miller, 'The Responsibility to Protect Human Rights' in LH Meyer (ed), *Legitimacy, Justice and Public International Law* (CUP, 2009); cf AL Bannon, 'The Responsibility to Protect: The UN World Summit and the Question of Unilateralism' (2006) 115 Yale LJ 1162.

[138] Peters, n 119, 535.

[139] T Hobbes, *Leviathan* (Andrew Crooke, 1651) 114.

[140] A Orford, *International Authority and the Responsibility to Protect* (CUP, 2011) 112, 137, and 192–195.

[141] Paris, n 51, 50. [142] See De Baere, n 110.

which both the UN and the EU need to examine closely in order not to undo the positive effects of the development of R2P and of its institutional operationalization by regional and global actors.

At the level of the UN, UNSCR 2040 on the situation in Libya, for example, arguably gives proof of the awareness of the need for such an integrated approach in both reiterating 'the need for the transitional period to be underpinned by a commitment to democracy, good governance, rule of law, national reconciliation and respect for human rights and fundamental freedoms of all people in Libya' and underscoring 'the Libyan authorities' primary responsibility for the protection of Libya's population, as well as foreign nationals'.[143]

For the EU, the development of such an integrated and balanced approach could perhaps be its most valuable contribution to the development of R2P, bearing in mind that, as the Court of Justice of the EU recalled in *Air Transport Association of America and Others*, under Article 3(5) TEU, the EU 'is to contribute to the strict observance and the development of international law'.[144] The EU's action in that regard is to be guided, pursuant to Article 21(1) TEU, 'by the principles which have inspired its own creation, development and enlargement', and which have made it possibly the most successful example of post-conflict rebuilding. It is therefore unsurprising that the UN Secretary-General mentioned the role of those principles twice in his report on the role of regional organizations.[145] As listed in Article 21(1) TEU, these are 'democracy, the rule of law, the universality and indivisibility of human rights and fundamental freedoms, respect for human dignity, the principles of equality and solidarity, and respect for the principles of the United Nations Charter and international law'. In other words, while the EU has some way to go in developing a balanced approach to R2P, the EU Treaty itself mandates its pursuit.

143 UN Doc S/RES/2040 (2012), paras 2 and 4.
144 Case C-366/10 *Air Transport Association of America and Others* [2012] OJ C49/7, para 101.
145 A/65/877-S/2011/393, paras 18 and 34.

7

EU Global Peace Diplomacy: Instruments to Support Status Processes

Steven Blockmans

1. Introduction

The central question of this book is to what extent the European Union can shape the ongoing reorientation of the legal structures and substance of global governance regimes in a multi-polar world in line with its rule-of-law based mission statement in Article 21 of the Treaty on European Union (TEU). This Article, in paragraph 2(c),[1] resonates the Member States' preambular resolve to implement a Common Foreign and Security Policy '... in order to promote peace, security and progress in Europe and in the world'. Further to the previous chapters in this part of the book, this contribution examines the legal and institutional contribution of the EU—as an international actor, above and beyond its Member States—to the global governance of peaceful settlement of disputes (hereinafter also: PSD). In doing so, the analysis follows the language of Article 33(1) of the UN Charter (UNC) and analyses the European Union's diplomatic tools to peacefully settle disputes 'out-of-area', ie beyond the borders of the EU: 'negotiation, enquiry, mediation, conciliation, ... or other peaceful means'.[2] The EU's use of the legal methods mentioned in Article 33(1) UNC (arbitration and judicial settlement) will largely remain outside of the scope of this chapter.[3] Status processes, ie mechanisms devoted to resolve disputed claims of statehood, will serve as case studies to evaluate the Union's contribution to global peace diplomacy.

This chapter will first present the current international legal framework for the peaceful settlement of disputes, and the status of the EU in it (section 2). It will make a geographical quick scan of the peace processes in which the EU has been actively involved in order to tackle the root causes of armed conflict (section 3). Special attention will be paid to the different means and methods employed by the EU to peacefully resolve status disputes in the Western Balkans. In many ways, the Balkans have formed the testing ground for the development of the Union's Common Foreign and Security Policy; so too in the field of PSD. The geographical quick scan of the EU's handling of the protracted transition of *de facto* states to fully fledged subjects of international law is illustrative of the diplomatic ways and means by which the Union, as a regional arrangement under Chapter VIII of the UN Charter, could contribute to the global governance of peaceful

[1] 'The Union shall define and pursue common policies and actions, and shall work for a high degree of cooperation in all fields of international relations, in order to: ... preserve peace, prevent conflicts and strengthen international security, in accordance with the purposes and principles of the United Nations Charter, with the principles of the Helsinki Final Act and with the aims of the Charter of Paris, including those relating to external borders'. The prevention of conflicts was added to the objectives by the Lisbon Treaty.

[2] With the exception of F Hoffmeister, 'The European Union and the Peaceful Settlement of International Disputes' (2012) 11 Chinese JIL 77–105, there is a desert of literature on this issue. Hoffmeister focuses primarily on the Union's use of international litigation to peacefully settle international disputes. Where he deals with the softer means prescribed by Art33 UNC, Hoffmeister describes and analyses the role of the EU in bringing an end to the Russo-Georgian war of August 2008, and the Union's efforts in resolving two pre-accession disputes: the Cyprus problem and the maritime border dispute between Croatia and Slovenia. These three case studies will therefore remain largely outside the scope of this chapter.

[3] An exception will be s 3.1.

dispute settlement.[4] Finally, the chapter will offer some insights into the Union's new structures to engage as a global peace broker. The focus here will be on the capacity of the European External Action Service (EEAS) to legally and institutionally shape the 21st century's global system of PSD governance and match the Lisbon Treaty's ambitions in this respect (section 4).[5] The chapter will conclude with an overall evaluation of the Union's contribution to the global system of governance in the area of peaceful dispute settlement (section 5).

2. International Legal Framework for the Peaceful Settlement of Disputes

2.1. Semantic clarifications

In order to assess the European Union's contribution to the global governance of peaceful dispute settlement, one ought to distinguish between non-binding and binding means of settlement of disputes. Arbitration and adjudication are binding methods in which independent experts apply the law to a dispute, resulting in a judgment that the parties are bound to respect. On this basis, binding means of settlement are often also called legal methods of dispute settlement, even though other binding means are possible that are not based on law, such as judicial settlement *ex aequo et bono*.[6] Non-binding dispute settlement, on the other hand, as a whole employed much more frequently than any form of binding settlement, comprises all forms of settlement in which each of the parties legally retains the last word in accepting a finding, compromise or ruling. This classification is irrespective of the pressures that may in practice compel a party to comply with the outcome of the settlement method. The outcome of such 'diplomatic' dispute settlement mechanisms is not legally binding upon a state. The elaboration in the 20th century of the dispute settlement method of conciliation arose in part as a consequence of the intentions of states to qualify certain disputes as suited only for diplomatic treatment.[7]

As to the definition of a 'dispute', there is both legal and political importance to a shared understanding of the term. Certain dispute settlement mechanisms allow one party to put a matter to a third party body unilaterally, provided the matter constitutes a 'dispute'. Even if there is no such mechanism available, parties can be sensitive to the qualification of a 'dispute'. To agree to call something a dispute may seem to some to imply recognition of a competing legal claim, or at least recognition of the status of an opponent to pursue a competing claim. Thus, the dispute arising out of the division of Cyprus, involving strongly divergent views on the status of the Turkish political representatives, is officially called 'the Cyprus problem'.[8]

The International Court of Justice (ICJ) and its predecessor the Permanent Court of International Justice (PCIJ) have made several pronouncements on the understanding of a 'dispute' in the sense of a 'legal dispute'. It held that the existence of an international dispute is a matter for objective determination.[9] In the classic *Mavrommatis Palestine Concessions*

[4] For an account on the Union's impact on the development of substantive norms in the context of status processes, see S Blockmans, 'EU Global Peace Diplomacy: shaping the law on statehood' in F Amtenbrink and D Kochenov (eds), *European Union's Shaping of the International Legal Order* (CUP, 2013, forthcoming).

[5] See further S Blockmans, 'EU Global Peace Diplomacy: institutional framework', in C Stahn and H Melber (eds), *Peace Diplomacy, Global Justice and International Agency: Rethinking Human Security and Ethics in the Spirit of Dag Hammarskjöld* (CUP, 2013, forthcoming).

[6] cf Art 38(2) ICJ Statute. See generally, MN Shaw, *International Law* (CUP, 2008) 1010–1024. See more in general United Nations, *Handbook on the Peaceful Settlement of Disputes between States* (UN, 1992); JG Collier and AV Lowe, *The Settlement of Disputes in International Law* (OUP, 1999); and JG Merrills, *International Dispute Settlement* (4th edn, CUP, 2005).

[7] See S Koopmans, *Diplomatic Dispute Settlement: The Use of Inter-State Conciliation* (TMC Asser Press, 2008).

[8] See generally, 'Report of the Secretary-General on his Mission of Good Offices', UN Doc S/2004/437.

[9] ICJ, *Interpretation of Peace Treaties with Bulgaria, Hungary and Romania (Advisory Opinion) (First Phase)* (2004) ICJ Rep 36, 37.

(Jurisdiction) case, the PCIJ held that a dispute is 'a disagreement over a point of law or fact, a conflict of legal views or of interests between two persons'.[10] The formulation chosen by the ICJ in the *East Timor* case suggests that the denial by one party of another's complaints of *facts* only can also be a legal dispute.[11] In a slightly broader definition, it is suggested that a dispute on the existence or meaning of facts is a 'legal dispute' if these facts are relevant to the determination of rights.[12] Conversely, non-legal disputes are thus controversies in which parties have claims not based on an interpretation of the law but on a conception of the good or the belief in the existence of certain facts, provided these facts do not affect the other's rights. 'Political disputes' are disputes 'of such a nature as to arouse national political passions, irrespective of whether they are capable or not of settlement in conformity with international law'.[13] Conceptually, however, these definitions are much too broad for the purpose of this chapter.

Arguably, the link between the type of dispute and the kind of settlement became less pronounced with the conclusion of the United Nations Charter. In fact, it is fair to say that the peaceful settlement of disputes forms the core objective of the post-1945 international legal order.[14] Article 33 UNC recognizes disputes, 'the continuation of which is likely to endanger the maintenance of international peace and security'. On the understanding that disputes threatening the peace are also political disputes, it follows from the UN Charter that legal disputes can at the same time be political disputes. By consequence, the Security Council may call upon the parties to settle such disputes by various means. Apart from adjudication procedures, the peaceful settlement of disputes has a number of political or diplomatic means at its disposal (negotiation, fact-finding, mediation, good offices and conciliation), often used in combination, and states and regional agencies or arrangements have a free choice as to the mechanisms adopted for settling their disputes. In the absence of binding Security Council resolutions, all methods available are operative only with the consent of the particular states.

Whereas the definition of a 'dispute' is generally distinguished from that of a 'conflict', a term which is used to signify a general state of hostility between the parties,[15] the present chapter will follow the link provided by Article 33 UNC and narrow the definition of 'dispute' down to controversies in which international peace and security are at stake.

2.2. Means and actors of PSD, with a special focus on the EU

The above-mentioned instruments of Article 33 UNC returned in the 1970 *Declaration on Principles of International Law Concerning Friendly Relations and Co-operation among States*: 'states shall accordingly seek early and just settlement of their international disputes by negotiation, inquiry, mediation, conciliation, arbitration, judicial settlement, resort to regional agencies or arrangements or other peaceful means of their choice'.[16] A fuller enumeration would also include consultation and good offices. Whereas the obligation to seek settlement of their disputes is directed to states, 'resort to regional agencies or arrangements' is one of the means available to them.[17] Indeed, this is where regional economic integration organizations (REIOs) may come in. Some constitutive treaties of

[10] PCIJ (1924) Series A no 2, 11.

[11] (1995) ICJ Rep 22. This appears to be contradicted by Art 36(2) of the ICJ Statute.

[12] ITLOS, *Southern Bluefin Tuna* case (*Australia and New Zealand v Japan*) (*Provisional Measures*) (1999) ILM 1624, 1632.

[13] JHW Verzijl, *International Law in Historical Perspective* (Springer, 1976) Vol VIII, 18.

[14] Art 2(3) UNC: 'All members shall settle their international disputes by peaceful means in such a manner that international peace and security and justice are not endangered.'

[15] JG Collier and AV Lowe, *The Settlement of Disputes in International Law* (OUP, 1999) 1.

[16] UNGA Res 2625 (XXV) of 24 October 1970, UN Doc A/8082, GA 25th session 121.

[17] On the concept of regional arrangements, see A Abass, *Regional Organizations and the Development of Collective Security: Beyond Chapter VIII of the UN Charter* (Hart Publishing, 2004).

REIOs explicitly foresee a PSD role for their organizations.[18] In Europe, the European Convention for the Peaceful Settlement of Disputes[19] lays down the agreement that legal disputes are to be sent to the ICJ and that other disputes are to be solved through conciliation and/or arbitration.[20] The Organization on Security and Cooperation in Europe (OSCE) established a number of conventions and mechanisms related to early warning, conflict prevention and crisis management—allowing, for instance, to send observer and mediation missions to participating states. What is striking, however, is that these (pan-) European organizations and mechanisms are primarily directed at preventing or solving conflicts between members of those organizations only.

The central question of this chapter pertains to the diplomatic contribution of the European Union to the *global* governance of peaceful dispute settlement. Against the international legal background sketched out in this section, the question that should be answered first is whether the EU can be seen as a regional agency or arrangement in the sense of the UN Charter and the Declaration on Friendly Relations. Without any doubt, this question should be answered in the affirmative.

Chapter VIII (Article 53) of the UN Charter allows the Security Council to 'utilize... regional arrangements or agencies for enforcement action under its authority'. According to Akehurst, 'the difference between an agency and an arrangement would appear to be that an *agency* possesses an institutional superstructure... whereas an *arrangement* does not... In other words, an agency is simply a more highly developed form of an arrangement'.[21] With regard to the EU, the existence of an 'institutional superstructure' is beyond doubt.[22] The question, however, to which extent the institutional structure may also be used to fulfil a role as a 'regional agency' is less easy to answer.[23] Whereas regarding the EU as a regional agency would explain the way in which the Union intends to attain its objective to 'preserve peace, prevent conflicts and strengthen international security, in accordance with the purposes and principles of the United Nations Charter' (Article 21(2)(c) TEU),[24] the TEU at this moment does not provide any additional clues for the Union to function as a regional agency. Neither did the Treaty expressly claim to fall within the ambit of Chapter VIII UNC. On the other hand, the concept of 'regional arrangements and agencies' is not defined by the Charter, and according to the (former) UN Secretary-General this was intentional:

> 'The Charter deliberately provides no precise definition of regional arrangements and agencies, thus allowing useful flexibility for undertakings by a group of States to deal with a matter appropriate for regional action which also could contribute to the maintenance of international peace and security. Such associations or entities could include treaty-based organizations, whether created before or after the founding of the United Nations, regional organizations for mutual security and defence, organizations for general regional development or for cooperation

[18] eg the Protocol Relating to the Establishment of the Peace and Security Council of the African Union, adopted on 9 July 2002. Similarly, the Economic Community of West African States (ECOWAS), South African Development Community (SADC), the Arab League and the Organization of American States (OAS) proclaim themselves as a 'regional arrangement or agency'. In NATO, mechanisms have been set up to act as a regional arrangement or agency, outside of the allied territory. See G Nolte, 'Die "neuen Aufgaben" von NATO und WEU: Völker- und verfassungsrechtliche Fragen' (1994) 95 *ZaöRv* 107. See, generally, C Dominicé, 'Co-ordination between Universal and Regional Organizations', in NM Blokker and HG Schermers (eds), *Proliferation of International Organizations: Legal Issues* (Kluwer Law International, 2001) 65–84.

[19] Council of Europe, 1957.

[20] UNTS (1958), no 320, 243–256. See further the Commission on Security and Cooperation in Europe (CSCE) Convention on Arbitration and Conciliation of 1992 (1993) 32 ILM 553.

[21] M Akehurst, 'Enforcement Actions by Regional Organizations with Special Reference to the Organization of American States' (1967) 42 *British Yearbook of International Law* 177. Emphases added.

[22] See also L Vierucci, 'WEU: A Regional Partner of the United Nations?' *Chaillot Paper* (1993) No 12, who argued that the Western European Union (WEU) (at the time the 'military arm' of the EU) could be seen as a regional arrangement.

[23] See also the contribution by Koutrakos to this volume.

[24] The Union's ambitions in this area are formulated in the so-called 'Petersberg tasks', captured by Art 43 TEU.

on a particular economic topic or function, and groups created to deal with a specific political, economic or social issue of concern.'[25]

The Secretary-General at the time even explicitly hinted at the possible 'emergence' of new regional arrangements in Europe.[26] In his *Agenda for Peace*, the UN Secretary-General thus stressed the need for flexibility in the post-Cold War era, and the purpose of establishing closer links with regional organizations was not to set forth 'any formal pattern of relationship between regional organizations and the United Nations, or to call for any specific division of labour'.[27]

The many references to the UN in the EU Treaties, including the implicit competence in Protocol 10 to act in response to a request of the UN to participate in the peaceful settlement of disputes ('the United Nations Organisation may request the Union's assistance for the urgent implementation of missions undertaken under Chapters VI'), point to new characteristics of the European Union to act as a global peace broker.[28] Based on this, as well as on the above-mentioned objectives in the EU Treaties, it would be difficult for the EU to deny that it is subject to Chapter VIII UNC.[29]

The implications of the acceptance of a role for the EU as a 'Chapter VIII organization' are not to be brushed aside too easily. According to Article 52 of the UN Charter, the activities of regional arrangements or agencies are to be consistent with the purposes and principles of the United Nations. Moreover, regional arrangements and agencies have a primary function in the pacific settlement of local disputes;[30] they shall make every effort in that respect before referring the dispute to the Security Council, but they 'have autonomy in diplomacy, in peaceful settlement, and implicitly in the case of consensual peacekeeping, subject to a reporting requirement'.[31] Currently, nothing in the EU Treaties seems sufficient to enable the EU to fulfil this task internally. The unresolved status issue of Cyprus is a case in point. The Union's policies in this area are primarily (if not exclusively) related to threats to or breaches of the peace within or by states that are *not* members of the EU. This clearly distinguishes the EU from other regional arrangements and agencies, which see as their primary task the settling of disputes among their Member States.[32]

3. Mapping the EU's Role as a Global Peace Broker

Since the end of the Cold War, the EU has acted as a diplomatic agent on a number of occasions. The following brief geographical overview of the Union's engagement in PSD—in the context of Chapters VI and VIII UNC—gives a sense of the extent to which the EU has acted externally and the instruments it has employed when doing so. Again, it should be emphasized that this study does not go beyond the role of the EU in PSD related to status

[25] Report of the Secretary-General, *Agenda for Peace*, UN Doc A/47/277–S/24111.

[26] Report of the Secretary-General on the Work of the Organization, *Secretary Gen Rep 21* (1990), 21.

[27] No 25, at 10.

[28] A similar competence to act 'in response to requests from the United Nations Organisation' may be found in relation to the permanent structured cooperation ex Art 42(6) TEU.

[29] See also ND White, 'The EU as Regional Security Actor within the International Legal Order', in M Trybus and ND White (eds), *European Security Law* (OUP, 2007) 329–349.

[30] Local disputes are commonly understood as disputes exclusively involving states which are parties to the regional arrangement or agency (cf also Arts 34 and 35 UNC).

[31] Art 54 UNC provides that the Security Council shall at all times be kept fully informed of activities which are undertaken or are being contemplated under regional arrangements by regional agencies for the maintenance of international peace and security. This would include all activities by the EU related to the peaceful settlement of disputes.

[32] Of course, Art 21(1) TEU refers to the 'principles which have inspired [the EU's] own creation'. In a way, therefore, the historic stablizing role played by the European integration process is externalized.

processes. It is for this reason that the Union's role in, for instance, non-proliferation talks with Iran, will remain outside this chapter's analysis.[33]

3.1. Western Balkans

In the Western Balkans, the testing ground par excellence for the development of the Common Foreign and Security Policy (CFSP) and Common Security and Defence Policy (CSDP), the EU has been actively involved in the peaceful settlement of status disputes.[34] The first instance concerns the pre-Maastricht failed attempt of the European Community (EC) to act as a peace broker and international arbiter in the context of the violent disintegration of the Socialist Federal Republic of Yugoslavia (SFRY). In the absence of direct initiatives or involvement from the UN, NATO, CSCE, Council of Europe and the United States at the outset of the war, the EC found itself sitting alone in the front row to address the implosion of the SFRY.[35] The EC assumed leadership and responsibility and tried to call a halt to the conflict by imposing a comprehensive solution on the warring parties. It sent a troika to Belgrade and Zagreb which leveraged a ceasefire accord by threatening the belligerents to block trade and withdraw economic aid, for which the SFRY was a major beneficiary.[36] It was the success of this first European intervention in the Slovenian crisis which led Jacques Poos to boast the phrase that would haunt him forever after,[37] for it soon proved that the assurances that the troika had received in Belgrade and Zagreb were the first of a long series of (dis)illusions. The adoption of sanctions and intensive diplomatic pressure led the parties to sign a ceasefire agreement for Slovenia on the island of Brioni. But whereas the Brioni Accord of 7 July 1991 was hailed as a triumph of European diplomacy, it left every important item of contention unresolved, pending a three-month cooling-off period.[38] By turning its offensive against Croatia, and later Bosnia-Herzegovina, Yugoslavia's 'federal' army (JNA) tore the heart right out of the proud, confident, new Europe. A pattern of negotiated ceasefires facilitated by EC mediation—and mostly broken by the Serbian dominated JNA—was accompanied by a series of threats by the EC to impose economic sanctions on Serbia and recognize the other republics seeking independence.[39] In response to the factions' failure to honour the ceasefires and accept a comprehensive peace plan put on the table by the EC at the Conference on Yugoslavia which it organized in The Hague in the Autumn of 1991,[40] the twelve Ministers of Foreign Affairs on 8 November decided to unilaterally suspend all coordinated assistance to and relations with Yugoslavia, including

[33] See S Blockmans, 'Beyond Entrenchment over Iran: Can the EU Offer a Framework for Regional Security?' CEPS Commentary, 3 September 2012; M Tocha, 'The EU and Iran's Nuclear Programme: Testing the Limits of Coercive Diplomacy' *College of Europe EU Diplomacy Paper* 1/2009; W Posch, 'Iranian challenges', *Chaillot Paper* No 89 (2006), 1–135; E Denza, 'Non-Proliferation of Nuclear Weapons; the EU and Iran' (2005) 10 *EFA Rev* 289–311; AZ Borda, 'The Iranian nuclear issue and EU3 negotiations', *FORNET Working Paper* (2005) 1–24.

[34] See S Blockmans, *Tough Love: The European Union's Relations with the Western Balkans* (TMC Asser Press, 2007) 111–175, 189–220.

[35] Javier Pérez de Cuéllar, then Secretary-General of the UN, did not want to put the matter to the Security Council, fearing that an intervention by the UN would be perceived as 'une sorte d'ingérence dans les efforts européens'. Reported in *Agence Europe*, No 5527, 4 July 1991. See a similar comment made by Thomas Pickering, the US Ambassador to the UN at the time, reported in *Le Monde* of 5 July 1991: 'Les Etats-Unis n'ont aucun rôle à jouer en Yougoslavie, sauf si les efforts des Européens échouaient'.

[36] A declaration of the European Council, which was strangely enough only published in *Agence Europe*, No 5523, 29 June 1991, served as the mandate for the troika.

[37] 'The hour of Europe has dawned'. Declaration of Jacques Poos, Luxembourg's Foreign Minister to the international press, 29 June 1991.

[38] Brioni Accord, reproduced in S Trifunovska, *Yugoslavia through Documents: From its Creation to its Dissolution* (Springer, 1994), at 311.

[39] See European Political Cooperation (EPC) Statements of 6 August 1991 (EPC, No P 73/91), 27 August 1991 (EPC, No P 82/91), followed by some sort of ultimatum on 6 October 1991 (EPC, No P 98/91), and the final ultimatum on 28 October 1991 (EPC, No P 106/91).

[40] The Conference opened in the Peace Palace in The Hague on 7 September 1991. It lasted until August 1992, without any significant achievement.

the 1980 Cooperation Agreement—a precedent.[41] It was obvious that, with the latter, the aim of the Community was not merely to economically sanction the country—or rather those parts of the Federation supporting war, but to take account of the factual dissolution of Yugoslavia as a state. This observation is confirmed by a tangible demonstration of support for those republics in favour of the EC peace initiative. First, in their statement of 6 October 1991, the twelve Foreign Ministers expressed their intention to apply a differentiated treatment to the different parties to the conflict, the adoption of which 'inevitably' had to lead to the recognition of those republics wishing to be independent and the adoption of restrictive measures against those parties that would continue to flout the desire of the other Yugoslav parties for a successful outcome of the Conference on Yugoslavia.[42] Secondly, on 2 December 1991, the EC restored trade links, the Generalized System of Preferences (GSP), economic and financial aid terms with all Yugoslav republics, except Serbia and Montenegro.[43] And thirdly, on the morning of 17 December, the eleven Ministers of Foreign Affairs succumbed to what amounted to an ultimatum by their German colleague Hans-Dietrich Genscher and agreed to invite those republics seeking diplomatic recognition to submit applications by 24 December or else lose the opportunity.[44] The Council of Ministers formulated original Guidelines on the recognition of new states emerging from the dissolution of the Soviet Union and Yugoslavia, and set up the Badinter Arbitration Commission to offer legal advice to the Conference on Yugoslavia.[45] Four republics (Bosnia-Herzegovina, Croatia, Macedonia and Slovenia) rose to the occasion and requested to be recognized as sovereign states. On 11 January 1992, the EC's 'Arbitration Commission' charged with the task of deciding on these applications opined that two out of the four republics (Macedonia and Slovenia) met all criteria to be recognized as new states. The political impact of these measures on the dissolution of and the war in former Yugoslavia was significant because EC action isolated and punished the Serbian/Montenegrin-dominated federal authorities in Belgrade; it also ended the sole European stewardship of the international efforts to negotiate a peaceful settlement to the conflict in Croatia because the EC had to acknowledge the collapse of the peace talks at The Hague as well as Serbia's distrust of the EC as a mediator.

All in all, the combination of diplomatic methods (ie the Conference on Yugoslavia—as the primary political vehicle through which the disputing parties would meet, and the shuttle diplomacy of the troika) and a legal instrument (ie the Badinter Arbitration Commission) was an imaginative but unsuccessful attempt to stop the violence from spiralling out of control.[46] The failure to prevent all-out war in Bosnia and Herzegovina condemned the EU, freshly endowed with a Common Foreign and Security Policy under the Maastricht Treaty, to take the back bench in the international efforts to force peace upon the warring parties in the Balkans.

[41] See EPC Statement of 8 November 1991, Bull EC 11-1991, point 1.4.4.

[42] EPC Statement of 6 October 1991 (EPC, No P 98/91), Bull EC 10-1991, point 1.4.7. This view is supported by H-D Genscher, *Erinnerungen* (iedler Verlag, 1995) at 954: 'unvermeidlichen Konsequenz'. See also European Parliament, 'Rapport de la commission politique sur la proposition relative à une décision concernant la dénonciation de l'accord de coopération entre la CEE et la RSFY', Rapporteur: Cassanmagnago Ceretti, Doc A3-0323/91, 18 November 1991, at 6.

[43] Council Reg (EEC) No 3567/91 of 2 December 1991 concerning the arrangements applicable to the import of products originating in the Republics of Bosnia–Herzegovina, Croatia, Macedonia and Slovenia [1991] OJ L342/1.

[44] While some states—notably Britain and the US—argued that premature recognition could derail the peace process, political opinion in Germany was contemptuous. Bonn argued that the peace process had been derailed already—by Belgrade. Genscher made it clear that if the EC did not move towards recognition, then Germany would break ranks and recognize some of the republics (especially Croatia and Slovenia) unilaterally. Needless to say that this was a bitter blow to the spirit of common purpose which had prevailed during the pre-Maastricht Inter-Governmental Conference.

[45] See S Terrett, *The Dissolution of Yugoslavia and the Badinter Arbitration Commission: A Contextual Study of Peace-making Efforts in the Post-Cold War World* (Ashgate Publishing, 2000).

[46] The Member States' implementation of the Guidelines and Arbitral Awards was erratic and unsatisfactory. See E Denza, 'European practice on the recognition of states' (2011) 36 EL Rev 321–338.

After the Union was sidelined in the US-led negotiations which led to the adoption of the Dayton Peace Accords, the political leaders of the EU Member States sharpened up the treaty mechanisms to engage the Union in global peace diplomacy. The innovations of the Treaty of Amsterdam in Title V TEU concerned both the scope and objectives of the CFSP, the instruments and the decision-making procedures. It was, however, the upgrading of the position of the Secretary-General of the Council, since then also designated 'High Representative for the CFSP', which really triggered a more active diplomatic role for the EU on the international scene. In spite thereof, the EU played only a modest role in the international efforts to reach a peaceful settlement over the violent secession of Kosovo from the Federal Republic of Yugoslavia (FRY). But elsewhere in the Balkans, the European Union was instrumental in brokering a peace deal between the government and the Albanian separatists in Macedonia in 2001[47] and in hammering out the 2002 Belgrade Agreement to prevent the FRY from violently falling apart and having a knock-on effect on the precarious balance reached in Kosovo.[48] In both cases, the EU's High Representative—who played a key role in the settlement of the disputes—used the prospect of the conclusion of a Stabilization and Association Agreement and eventual EU membership as a strong lever to persuade the adversarial parties in each country to engage in negotiations to reform the Constitution and establish equal rights for their respective communities. The same drivers are now pulling Serbia and Kosovo together in an EU-facilitated dialogue.[49]

3.2. Eastern neighbourhood

The Union's eastern neighbourhood is littered with potential and actual flash points triggered by status issues. Yet, the EU—as an international actor, above and beyond its Member States—has been surprisingly absent as a peace broker in its own neighbourhood.[50] With respect to the disputed statelet of Nagorny Karabakh, Russia, France and the US, which under the auspices of the OSCE serve as co-chairs of the so-called 'Minsk Group',[51] are relatively united and have advanced proposals to resolve the conflict between Azerbaijan and Armenia. Whereas the peaceful settlement of the dispute over Nagorny Karabakh is a 'key strategic interest of the European Union', the EU does not form part of the 'Minsk Group' and is only informed by the co-chairs of their work.[52]

With regard to the 'frozen' conflict of Transnistria, the EU has participated in the so-called '5 + 2 talks' since 2006.[53] Yet, its observer status limits the Union's leverage over the parties to the dispute. While the EU, by way of two Special Representatives mandated (from March 2005 until February 2011) to assist in the resolution of the conflict,[54] has tried to raise its stake in the international efforts to settle the status dispute, its impact has been

[47] See S Blockmans, *Tough Love: The European Union's Relations with the Western Balkans* (TMC Asser Press, 2007), 189–199.

[48] Ibid, 199–207.

[49] See S Blockmans, 'EU Global Peace Diplomacy: institutional framework', in C Stahn and H Melber (eds), *Peace Diplomacy, Global Justice and International Agency: Rethinking Human Security and Ethics in the Spirit of Dag Hammarskjöld* (CUP, 2013, forthcoming).

[50] See S Blockmans and RA Wessel, 'The European Union and Peaceful Settlement of Disputes in its Neighbourhood: The Emergence of A New Regional Security Actor?' in A Antoniadis, R Schütze and E Spaventa (eds), *The European Union and Global Emergencies: Law and Policy Aspects* (Hart Publishing, 2011), 73–103.

[51] EU Member States Germany, Italy, Portugal, the Netherlands, Sweden and Finland are also participating in the process.

[52] Speech by High Representative Catherine Ashton on Nagorny Karabakh at the European Parliament, SP11-055EN, 6 July 2011.

[53] The five being Russia, Ukraine, OSCE, the EU and the US, the two being Moldova and Transnistria.

[54] One of the EU Special Representative's tasks was to oversee the activities of the EU Border Assistance Mission deployed on the Ukrainian/Moldovan border since November 2005 to support efforts in fighting smuggling and trafficking through Transnistria.

limited due to the conflict's own dynamics and Moscow's opposition to engage in a more concrete plan for common action in the shared security space.[55] After a breakdown in negotiations, the '5 + 2' talks were resumed in September 2011. The EU has reaffirmed its readiness to assist the conflicting parties in both the negotiations and the implementation of a settlement.[56]

Judgments about the EU's reaction to the flare-up of conflict over the breakaway regions of Abkhazia and South Ossetia, Russia's incursion into Georgia, and Moscow's unilateral recognition of the two de facto states have varied—from the cartoon of EU leaders held together in a wobbly red jelly on the cover of the *Economist* of 6 September 2008, to the assessment that '[w]ithout the European Union's intervention and rapid reaction on the part of the French president the Russians would already have made Tbilisi theirs'.[57] The reference here is to the diplomatic initiative of Nicolas Sarkozy, who—as holder of the EU's Presidency in the second half of 2008—visited Moscow and Tbilisi, brokered the initial ceasefire agreement on 12 August 2008, and then pushed hard for Russia to observe the terms. In a rare display of unity, the EU Member States followed up at their emergency summit on 1 September—only the third in its history—by sticking together in an unprecedented condemnation of Russian aggression.[58] While it was in Russia's own interest to withdraw its forces from the self-declared buffer-zone in Georgia and start a programme of damage control in international relations, Moscow—otherwise used to a squabbling and uncritical EU—will have taken note of the Union's strong reaction. Arguably, the EU's mediating role in the conflict was all the more effective because it was backed by a growling US that openly supported Georgia's President, Mikheil Saakashvili. Washington found it easier to be firm and critical precisely because it could rely on the EU Presidency to do the actual negotiations. The European Union has since supplemented its high-level diplomacy in an attempt to mitigate the consequences of the war on the ground by sending a European Union Monitoring Mission in Georgia to replace Russian troops in the buffer-zone,[59] and giving aid to help the reconstruction of the devastated Georgian economy.[60] On the whole, however, the disputes over the breakaway republics have been resolved, not in a peaceful manner by the EU but by way of armed force by Russia. When the sense of urgency over the Georgian crisis dissipated, the divisions between EU Member States over how to deal with Russia reappeared.[61] Regrettably, the differences in positions between EU Member States—from the 'new cold warriors' (eg Lithuania and Poland) to Russia's 'Trojan horses' in the EU (eg Bulgaria and Cyprus)—are so far apart that building a common framework on settling the status disputes in the eastern neighbourhood will be a long and arduous process.[62] The EU will thus need to continue its debate about the kind of tools it has at its disposal to resolve (potential) conflicts in its neighbourhood, as indeed in other parts of the world.

[55] Many observers have been critical of Moscow's apparent deviousness in evading any serious peace and reconciliation negotiations, either under UN or OSCE auspices. N Popescu, '"Outsourcing" De Facto Statehood: Russia and the Secessionist Entities in Georgia and Moldova' (2006) 109 *CEPS Policy Brief* 6.

[56] Statement by High Representative Catherine Ashton at the UN High Level Symposium on the resumption of official negotiations on the settlement of the Transnistria conflict, Press release A 369–11, 22 September 2011; and Statement by High Representative Catherine Ashton on the '5 + 2' meeting in Vienna on 17–18 April 2012, Press release A 183/12, 18 April 2012.

[57] See J-D Giuliani, 'Editorial: Europe and Russia', *Fondation Robert Schuman Newsletter*, 24 August 2008, available at: <www.jd-giuliani.eu/en/article/cat-2/101_LEurope-et-la-Russie.html>.

[58] Presidency Conclusions, Extraordinary European Council, Brussels, 1 September 2008, doc 12594/08, 11.

[59] Council Joint Action 2008/736/CFSP of 15 September 2008 on the European Union Monitoring Mission in Georgia, EUMM Georgia [2008] OJ L248/26 (as amended).

[60] GAERC, Council Conclusions of 15–16 September 2008, Press Release no 13030/08 (Presse 255), 9.

[61] eg, P Runner, 'Lithuania complicates French rapprochement with Russia', *EU Observer*, 7 November 2008; and R Goldirova, 'EU resumes Russia talks, isolating Lithuania', *EU Observer*, 11 November 2008.

[62] For the conceptualization and categorization of EU Member States' positions on Russia-related topics, see M Leonard and N Popescu, 'A Power Audit of EU–Russia Relations' (2007) *ECFR Policy Paper* 2.

3.3. Southern neighbourhood

Although the Arab world has seen a lot of turmoil recently and the EU has claimed to play 'an important part' in the handling thereof,[63] the uprisings in Tunisia, Egypt, Libya, Syria and Yemen fall outside the scope of this contribution as these disputes did not and do not (as of yet)[64] revolve around claims of statehood. Rather, the issues connected to the uprisings centre on the legitimacy of the governing authorities and the (international) recognition of their successors.[65]

There is, however, one dispute in the Union's southern neighbourhood that does fall within the ambit of the current analysis: the dispute between Morocco and the Saharawi Arab Democratic Republic (SADR) over the Western Sahara. Backed by Algeria, the SADR is a de facto state which currently controls about 20% of the entire territory of the Western Sahara, which it claims. Recognitions have over the past two decades been extended and withdrawn according to changing international trends.[66] In April 2007, the UN—which has had a peacekeeping force on the ground since 1991—asked the parties to enter into direct and unconditional negotiations to reach a mutually accepted political solution to the conflict.[67] So far, these efforts remain without result. Quiet diplomacy goes on, with the EU Head of Delegation in Morocco taking an active interest but not an official role.

3.4. Middle East

The proposed establishment of an independent state for the Palestinian people in the Gaza Strip, which is currently controlled by Hamas, and parts of the West Bank, which is administered by the Palestinian National Authority, is caught in a protracted negotiation process under US leadership of the Quartet on the Middle East (including Russia, the EU and the UN). The precise borders of this state are subject to debate with Israel. The right of the Palestinian people to a state is recognized by approximately 100 countries.[68] Armed conflict is almost a daily reality in the region. Since 2011, the EU has taken a more central role in the Quartet's efforts to get the Middle East peace process unstuck. Of course, being a 'player' as well as a 'payer' also means a heightened risk of mediatized failure. Still, the High Representative of the Union for Foreign Affairs and Security Policy, supported by the EEAS and the EU's international partners, is occupying a policy space otherwise left to the other members of the Quartet. So far, however, the High Representative's only success has been to prevent a complete fall-out of EU Member States over Palestine's application for UN membership in September 2011. The EU's internal agreement to disagree collapsed barely one month later when Member States voted differently over the admission of Palestine to the United Nations Educational, Scientific and Cultural Organization (UNESCO).[69] Given its internal divisions, it is unlikely that the EU will soon be able to take applause for having forged an agreement on the issue of statehood of Palestine.

[63] Dixit Pierre Vimont at the University Association for Contemporary European Studies (UACES) conference in Cambridge, 6 September 2011, pointing to, eg, the role played by the EU in support of the Transitional National Council in Libya.

[64] Libya may fall apart if the creation of the federation does not succeed.

[65] eg S Talmon, 'Recognition of the Libyan National Transitional Council' (2011) 15 ASIL Insights No 16.

[66] See T Whitfield, *Friends Indeed? The United Nations, Groups of Friends, and the Resolution of Conflict* (US Institute of Peace Press, 2007) 191.

[67] Report of the Secretary-General on the situation concerning Western Sahara, UN Doc S/2007/202, 13 April 2007.

[68] 'How many countries recognize Palestine as a state?' (Institute for Middle East Understanding, 2008), available at: <http://imeu.net/news/article0065.shtml>.

[69] See A Rettman, 'Unesco vote highlights EU split on Palestine' *EU Observer*, 1 November 2011.

3.5. Beyond wider Europe

Outside of the wider Europe region, the EU's diplomatic clout has so far been used only once in a deciding fashion, namely in the resolution of the dispute over Aceh.[70] Under the auspices of Martti Ahtisaari and his non-governmental organization (NGO) Crisis Management Initiative, secret negotiations between the government of Indonesia and the separatist Free Aceh Movement (GAM) took place in Helsinki in the early months of 2005. The negotiations were partly funded by European Commission instruments.[71] The negotiations were concluded with the signing of a Memorandum of Understanding on 15 August 2005.[72] Under the peace agreement, GAM agreed to end its armed struggle and hand over its weapons in exchange for broad autonomy, including the right to form local political parties, and local control over a portion of the revenues from natural resources in the oil and gas-rich province. As the negotiations appeared to be leading to a tangible agreement, the parties and Ahtisaari sought to identify a suitable monitoring body for the eventual agreement. After the experience of East Timor, Jakarta did not want the United Nations to oversee the implementation of the peace process and GAM were uncomfortable with a purely Association of South-East Asian Nations (ASEAN) mission, which, it was felt, would be partial towards the Indonesian authorities. Ahtisaari suggested that the European Union could play a role. Their discussions resulted in the proposal for an Aceh Monitoring Mission (AMM) to be established by the European Union and ASEAN contributing countries with the mandate to monitor the implementation of the commitments made by the parties in the Memorandum of Understanding (MoU).[73] This unusual coalition of EU and ASEAN countries[74] was an untried and untested formation in international peacekeeping. In the MoU, both GAM and Jakarta agreed to fully support the implementation of the mandate of AMM. For the EU, it was the first complex European Security and Defence Policy (ESDP) mission with an executive mandate undertaken at such a distance, in such a potentially dangerous environment, and at such short notice.[75]

Elsewhere in the world, the EU has been largely absent, or only acting below the radar, in the peaceful settlement of status disputes. One notable exception, though, concerns South Sudan. Whereas the EU did not play any significant role in negotiating the 2005 Comprehensive Peace Agreement (CPA) between the two Sudans,[76] it has been active in efforts to secure a peaceful transition under the CPA. In August 2010 the Council appointed Rosalind Marsden, until then British Ambassador to the Republic of Sudan, as EU Special Representative (EUSR) to work with the Sudanese parties, the African Union (AU), the UN and other national, regional and international stakeholders to achieve the transition, including the organization of credible referenda on the disputed oil-rich region of Abyei and on self-determination of South Sudan in January 2011.[77] The EUSR's mandate includes actively

[70] See J Davies, 'The Aceh Monitoring Mission: Securing Peace and Democracy', in S Blockmans, J Wouters and T Ruys (eds), *The European Union and Peacebuilding: Policy and Legal Aspects* (TMC Asser Press, 2010) 375–386.

[71] The costs of the mission were financed from the EU budget (EUR 9.3 million) and by contributions from EU Member States and participating countries (EUR 6 million). See the Council Secretariat's Factsheet on AMM ACEH/07, 15 December 2006.

[72] Memorandum of Understanding between the Government of the Republic of Indonesia and the Free Aceh Movement, signed in Helsinki, 15 August 2005, available at: <http://www.consilium.europa.eu/uedocs/cmsUpload/MoU_Aceh.pdf>.

[73] Council of the EU, Press Release 10813/05 (Presse 177), 18 July 2005, at 3.

[74] Brunei, Malaysia, the Philippines, Singapore and Thailand.

[75] For a detailed examination of the establishment of AMM, see P-A Brand and G Grevi, *The EU Mission in Aceh: Implementing Peace*, Occasional Paper No 61 (Institute of Security Studies, 2005).

[76] See International Crisis Group (ICG), 'The Khartoum–SPLM Agreement: Sudan's Uncertain Peace', *Africa Report* No 96, 25 July 2005, at 11; ICG, 'Sudan's Comprehensive Peace Agreement: The Long Road Ahead', *Africa Report* No 106, 31 March 2006.

[77] Council Decision 2010/450/CFSP of 11 August 2010 appointing the European Union Special Representative for Sudan [2010] OJ L211/42, Arts 2 and 3.

contributing to the full and timely implementation of the CPA and the negotiation of arrangements necessary to foster stability, security and development in the post-referendum period, as well as efforts in the area of institution-building in South Sudan. It also attributes a role for the EUSR in facilitating the international efforts to reach a political solution to the conflict in Darfur, by supporting the work of the Joint UN/AU Mediator and the AU High-Level Implementation Panel for Sudan. The dynamics of the border conflicts between the Sudans have impeded progress on reaching lasting peace arrangements.[78] It remains to be seen whether the agreements signed in Addis Ababa in September 2012 will hold and whether they will allow the EU to secure return for its bigger investment in aid and trade since 2011.[79]

3.6. Concentric circles

The picture that emerges from the geographical quick scan of EU diplomatic involvement in PSD is one of concentric circles emanating from the Union's bureaucratic centre: as the ripple effect expands, the impact thereof weakens. In general, the alluring promises of future membership and the conclusion of an Association Agreement serve the EU's strategic interests in sustainable conflict resolution. Such prospects have helped to increase prosperity and growth opportunities in destitute countries and regions, improve links with vital transport and energy routes across borders, and to increase the EU's weight in the immediate neighbourhood, as indeed in the world. The Cyprus issue stands out as a notable exception to the Union's success story in wielding its 'soft power' to impose durable peace on aspirant members. This is, however, not due to the EU's lack of trying. But years of engagement, most intensively in the pre-accession period in the framework of the Annan Plan,[80] have not yet brought the parties to an agreement.[81]

The consistent implementation of the renewed consensus on enlargement[82] gains importance in the light of recent challenges to stability in the eastern neighbourhood of the EU, most notably the Southern Caucasus. While the 'carrot' of future EU membership is lacking in the context of the European Neighbourhood Policy (ENP), those 'European' states that could theoretically fulfil all EU membership conditions mentioned in and attached to Article 49 TEU could perhaps be swayed more easily and effectively than their non-European brethren in the ENP to resolve their internal and/or cross-border disputes.

Further afield, the influence of the EU as an independent peace broker wanes. Arguably, its power of attraction is lost beyond the European periphery and remains only defined in terms of development assistance and trade relations. With a history of colonial domination, the EU's diplomatic slate is less clean than that of the Swiss and the Norwegians. However, some Member States' familiarity with previously held overseas territories may play to the Union's advantage in bringing a political *savoir faire* to the negotiation table.

[78] eg, Statement by the Spokesperson of the EU High Representative on the talks between Sudan and South Sudan, Press release A 110/12, 8 March 2012; and Statement by the Spokesperson of EU High Representative, Catherine Ashton, on armed border clashes between Sudan and South Sudan, Press release A 166/12, 11 April 2012.

[79] Statement by the High Representative Catherine Ashton on the agreements concluded between Sudan and South Sudan in Addis Ababa, Press release A 425/12, 27 September 2012. See D Helly (ed),'Post-2011 Scenarios in Sudan: What Role for the EU?', *ISS Report* No 66, November 2009.

[80] For historical backgrounds, political realities and legal analyses, see F Hoffmeister, *Legal Aspects of the Cyprus Problem: Annan Plan and EU Accession* (Martinus Nijhoff Publishers, 2006).

[81] On the legal problems pertaining to the situation where only one part of the island is effectively in the EU, see N Skoutaris, *The Cyprus Issue: The Four Freedoms In A Member State Under Siege* (Hart Publishing, 2011); and M Brus, M Akgün, S Blockmans, S Tíryakí, T van den Hoogen and W Douma, *A Promise to Keep: Time to End the International Isolation of the Turkish Cypriots* (TESEV, 2008).

[82] The renewed consensus on enlargement, agreed by the December 2006 European Council (see *EU Bulletin*, December 2001, point I.25.1), and based on the principles of consolidation of commitments, fair and rigorous conditionality and good communication with the public, combined with the EU's capacity to integrate new members, remains the framework for the EU's 'new approach' to its enlargement policy. See Enlargement Strategy and Main Challenges 2011–2012, COM (2011) 666 final, 12 October 2011.

4. The Union's New Structures to Engage in Peaceful Dispute Settlement

What transpires from the analysis above is that the EU is engaged in the entire spectrum of mediation, facilitation and dialogue processes mentioned in Article 33 UNC. Such processes are often identified with outstanding personalities who play a key and visible role. Peaceful dispute settlement is, however, a team effort which requires substantial expertise, knowledge, technical capacity, engagement at different levels over time as well as cooperation with other actors in order to be effective and to improve its chances of success. In addition to EU involvement at the highest political level, CSDP missions, EUSRs, EU delegations and the Presidency have been frequently engaged with local political and civil society actors in activities of a mediating and confidence-building nature. These EU activities on the ground play an important role in consolidating and sustaining peace processes and their outcomes, inter alia, by strengthening the rule of law and democratic governance, promoting disarmament, demobilization and reintegration and security sector reform,supporting confidence-building measures, and establishing a link between processes at the government and community levels. By supporting local mechanisms for mediation and dialogue, these EU activities on the ground help transform relationships between conflict parties, leading to genuine and sustainable solutions in conflict-prone environments.

While this chapter has found that, in practice, fact-finding, mediation, conciliation and other instruments are already an integral part of the EU's external action toolbox, the EU has so far used these diplomatic tools in a rather ad hoc fashion. On the basis of a concept floated at the end of 2009, the EU aims to develop a more systematic approach to its peaceful dispute settlement efforts and to strengthen its mediation support capacity to allow it to contribute in a more efficient and effective way to preventing and resolving conflicts.[83] It is the Union's ambition to strive to establish and promote the use of mediation as a tool of first response to emerging or ongoing crisis situations. As such, mediation could also be mainstreamed into other EU conflict prevention and crisis management activities, wherever relevant.

Strengthening the Union's mediation support capacity involves the provision of operational support to ongoing mediation and dialogue initiatives, assessment of lessons learned, identification of best practices and, as appropriate, the development of guidelines for the EU practice in the area of mediation, developing training and capacity building in the area of mediation as well as networking and coordination with other actors in crisis management. Here, the focus is on the newly established EEAS, which is expected to support, inter alia, the High Representative in carrying out his (her, when considering the current incumbent) tasks.[84] Arguably, it is still early days to draw firm conclusions on the organization and functioning of the EEAS. The EU external actors which it is supposed to serve are only now beginning to find their feet and the EEAS itself is still in establishment mode: in the wake of the January 2011 transfer of entire departments (and their officials) of the Commission and the Council General Secretariat, staffing decisions, especially on the secondment of national diplomats, continue to be made. A first thorough review of the Service is only foreseen to take place mid-2013 and may lead to amendments to the EEAS Council Decision, thus having repercussions on the organization and functioning of the Service. Establishing a firm

[83] See Council General Secretariat, 'Concept on Strengthening EU Mediation and Dialogue Capacities', doc.15779/09, 10 November 2009.

[84] According to Art 2(2) of Council Decision 2010/427/EU of 26 July 2010 establishing the organization and functioning of the European External Action Service OJ [2010] L201/30 (hereinafter: EEAS Council Decision), the Service is expected to also 'assist' the President of the European Council (pursuant to Art 15(6) TEU), the President of the Commission, and the Commission as a whole in the exercise of their respective functions in the area of external relations (pursuant to Art 17(1) TFEU). See L Erkelens and S Blockmans, 'Setting Up the European External Action Service: An act of institutional balance' (2012) 8 *European Constitutional Law Review* 246–279.

and effective EU diplomatic service which is able to join up the different strands of EU external action is therefore a long-term project. Nevertheless, some initial comments pertaining to the EU's new structures for PSD can be made.

First, the creation of a Division for Conflict Prevention, Mediation and Peacebuilding within the EEAS' Directorate for Conflict Prevention and Security Policy should be welcomed. With the right resources and clout, this Division could contribute expertise on conflict, peace and security issues to the full range of EU policies, programmes and activities in conflict-affected countries and fragile situations by, eg, providing support to the High Representative and EUSRs in the preparation and conduct of peace negotiations, organizing training on conflict and peaceful dispute settlement issues for the regional managing directorates, and using the Instrument for Stability (or its successor as part of the new multi-annual financial framework) to support mediation and conciliation efforts. The second comment flows from the latter point. Whereas there exists already a close cooperation between the EEAS's Division for Conflict Prevention, Mediation and Peacebuilding and the Commission's Foreign Policy Instruments Directorate General (DG) (for assistance in the short-term) and DG Development Cooperation (DEVCO)'s security policy unit (for longer term aid), the precise boundaries of portfolios, competences and responsibilities remain to be settled.[85] A third and final comment relates to the form in which the EEAS will provide mediation support. Under the Instrument for Stability, a sum of EUR 1 million was earmarked by the European Parliament in the 2011 budget, allowing the EEAS to spend EUR 600,000 in 2012 to start up a pilot project on building up the EU's own mediation support capacity. The choice to spend these funds on training, coaching, and building on best practices as a resource for EUSRs seems to indicate that the idea to set up a roster of experts in mediation processes and related thematic areas, ie a standing team of EU mediators, has been put on the back burner. While understandable from a budgetary perspective, this decision does translate into the necessity to organize a proper check of the negotiation abilities of personalities before they are appointed as EUSRs with a mediation mandate. Ultimately, a combination of a training capability and a flexible and useable roster of civilian experts will be the best way forward to equip the EU with the necessary deployment mechanisms for expert mediators to assist third parties in the short run, as well as the appropriate tools (offered by the EEAS) to prepare and equip EUSRs to engage in longer term peaceful dispute settlement.[86]

When strengthening its PSD capacities, the EU will arguably make best use of the resources and expertise which are already available in the EU, including its Member States, as well as with the United Nations, regional organizations such as the OSCE and the AU, national, local and civil society actors. The initial aim for the EU is to optimize the use of existing tools and instruments in the area of peaceful dispute settlement by ensuring close cooperation and coordination, internally and with other actors, leading to coherence and complementarity.

5. Concluding Remarks

Given the multitude of potential actors in the global governance of peaceful dispute settlement, close coordination is essential in order to determine who, in a given mediation

[85] This is a point of more general concern. See S Blockmans, 'The European External Action Service One Year On: First signs of strengths and weaknesses' *CLEER Working Papers* 2012/2.

[86] eg organizing (de-)briefings to secure continuity; the ability to draw on human resources more quickly, as indeed the ability to coordinate the use of financial resources more directly; compiling lessons learnt; and drawing up analyses of the 'anthropology' of conflicts. Current EUSRs De Soto, Fouéré, Marsden and Otte expressed these needs at a conference devoted to 'Regional actors as vectors of peace. What role for the EU?' organized by the Crisis Management Initiative, an NGO headed by Martti Ahtisaari, at the European Parliament in Brussels on 25 April 2012.

initiative, would take on the lead role and who would play a supportive role. This decision would have to be taken depending on considerations of comparative advantage for the lead role in a particular case. The United Nations is the most important actor in the area of international peaceful dispute settlement and has, over the years, developed a high level of expertise. The report of the Secretary-General on 'Enhancing Mediation and its Support Activities' summarizes this experience, provides guidance for action and examines future challenges, both for the UN and other actors involved in mediation.[87] Even though the UN plays a pre-eminent role in PSD, other actors, like the European Union, have important roles to play, either as a regional security arrangement or agency in the sense of Chapter VIII UNC or as a mediator upon the invitation of (third parties) engaged in a dispute.

So far, however, the EU has played only a minor role as a successful mediator on the global scene. In less than a handful of cases, the Union has been able to resolve status disputes in a sustainable manner (cf the 2001 Ohrid Framework Agreement, the 2002 Belgrade Agreement and the implementation of the 2005 Aceh Peace Agreement). This modest track record is not, however, the result of a lack of trying. The EU's role in PSD activities and their mandates include a host of mediation- and dialogue-related tasks: supporting stabilization and conciliation processes, contributing to initiatives leading to settlement of conflicts and to negotiation and implementation of peace and ceasefire agreements, facilitating and maintaining close contact with all the parties, etc. EU actors at the highest political level (two High Representatives, a handful of EU Presidencies, and a raft of EU Special Representatives) have been sent to South East Europe, the southern Caucasus, the Middle East, the Sudans and further flung places to work towards the peaceful settlement of status disputes; CSDP missions of various kinds have been deployed to keep or build the peace; financial and technical assistance has been given; restrictive measures have been adopted upon parties unwilling to cooperate in the search for a peaceful solution; and much more. Yet, for all the initiatives, good offices, 'carrots' and 'sticks', none of these instruments appears as strong a leverage for securing sustainable dispute settlement as the EU's own power of attraction in its immediate neighbourhood. And even then, the instruments of the Union's enlargement policy only seem to work if local players can fit EU demands in their own political agendas.[88] Cyprus is a case in point. The same observation applies to the European Neighbourhood Policy, which serves as the European Security Strategy's regional sub-set for the neighbouring countries to the east and the south of the EU's borders, but is—by the Union's own admission—not a dispute resolution mechanism.

Yet, the EU is a global actor and its political, developmental and security interests go well beyond its neighbourhood. Also, with a wide field presence and a broad range of instruments at its disposal, the EU has a lot to offer as an actor in the global governance of peaceful dispute settlement. It will therefore continue to use its mediation (support) services whenever relevant and as part of its comprehensive approach to conflict prevention and resolution. This, of course, needs to be done in full coordination with other international actors. The development and consolidation of the European Union's PSD capacities and mediation support tools will lead to additional entry points for third party peaceful dispute settlement and contribute to the strengthening of the overall capacity of the international community, and indeed the international legal order, in this area. Other regional actors, including the African Union and the League of Arab States, are playing an increasingly active role. In many instances they are the first to respond to cases of dispute, based on the advantage of being knowledgeable on local and regional dynamics and credible third parties in the regional context. The EU will therefore have to continue to cooperate closely with the UN and its Mediation Support Unit, including in such areas as training and support to regional

[87] UN doc S/2009/189, 8 April 2009.

[88] See S Blockmans, 'EU Enlargement as a Peacebuilding Tool', in S Blockmans, J Wouters and T Ruys (eds), *The European Union and Peacebuilding: Policy and Legal Aspects* (TMC Asser Press, 2010) 77–103, at 81–82.

organizations in their efforts to strengthen their mediation capacities. Acting as part of a comprehensive approach to conflict prevention and resolution also requires effective coordination and communication between all relevant EU actors to ensure that the EU can respond quickly to rapidly evolving situations. The EEAS plays a particularly important role in this coordination. Further strengthening of its Division for Conflict Prevention, Mediation and Peacebuilding will be crucial if the EU wants to live up to expectations. A revision of the 2009 Concept of Mediation is also necessary in order to operationalize the ideas and proposals held therein. Seeing that the EU is not exactly over-performing in the global governance of peaceful dispute settlement, this is not the time to be complacent about revising the EU's mediation and dialogue capacities.

8

International Responsibility for EU Military Operations: Finding the EU's Place in the Global Accountability Regime

*Aurel Sari and Ramses A Wessel**

1. Introduction

The Lisbon Treaty has reconfirmed the EU's intention to advance its interests and values on the international scene in a more proactive manner, including through the conduct of crisis management missions in third countries as part of its Common Foreign and Security Policy (CFSP).[1] Although most missions launched by the Union so far have been relatively modest in their size and objectives,[2] even small-scale operations may give rise to a breach of international law or cause damage and injury to private parties. Yet holding EU missions accountable for their activities is hampered by a range of legal and practical difficulties.[3] One particularly thorny issue concerns the attribution of the wrongful acts committed by EU military operations: since they are composed of personnel made available to the Union by its Member States and third states, it is not immediately obvious which party—the EU, the contributing states or both—should bear responsibility for their conduct. This question is of great practical significance, for accountability cannot be discharged effectively if it is unclear where responsibility lies. The purpose of this chapter is to revisit this issue and establish what rules govern the attribution of wrongful acts committed by EU military operations.

In line with the general topic of this book, the present chapter aims at investigating an area in which the EU's contribution to global governance is highly visible and which affords the Union with considerable opportunities for shaping the pertinent regulatory frameworks. Due to the complex division of competences between the EU and its Member States in the field of foreign and security policy, a matter which the Lisbon Treaty did little to rectify, the attribution of conduct in the context of EU crisis management missions is arguably even less clear than in the case of military operations led by other international organizations. With the expanding role of the EU in global security governance,[4] a better understanding of the allocation of responsibility between the Member States and the Union therefore becomes ever more important, especially since the Member States have underlined in Article 21 of the Treaty on European Union (TEU) that the EU's actions on the international scene shall be guided by international law and the principles of the UN Charter. This solemn commitment to the international rule of law raises the question whether the rules of international law governing the responsibility of international organizations laid down in the Draft Articles

* Some of the ideas developed here were first presented at the Second ESIL Research Forum held in Budapest in September 2007.

[1] See Frederik Naert, *International Law Aspects of the EU's Security and Defence Policy* (Intersentia, 2010) 15–191.

[2] See Koutrakos in this volume, notably sections three and four on 'The state of CSDP after Lisbon' and 'A process-centred policy'.

[3] eg it is not fully settled to what extent the EU is bound by the pertinent rules of international law, including those applicable during armed conflict. See Naert, n 1, 463–540.

[4] M Emerson *et al*, *Upgrading the EU's Role as Global Actor: Institutions, Law and the Restructuring of European Diplomacy* (Centre for European Policy Studies (CEPS), 2011).

on the Responsibility of International Organizations (DARIO)[5] adopted by the International Law Commission (ILC) at second reading in June 2011 can accommodate the Union's constitutional complexity and enable it to contribute to global security in an accountable manner.

Between 2003 and 2011, the European Commission has actively participated in the ILC's work with the aim of ensuring that the DARIO would 'allow sufficient room for the specificities of the European Union'.[6] It has been argued that the European Commission's contribution to shaping of international law in this area 'has had demonstrable effects on the final outcome of the ILC's work and should be regarded as a success on the part of the EU's external identity'.[7] This assessment appears overly generous. The ILC's reluctance to fully embrace the European Commission's demands to accord special treatment to the EU has led the latter to suggest that 'the draft articles, even taking account of the commentaries,... do not adequately reflect the situation of regional (economic) integration organizations such as the European Union'.[8] This hardly sounds like a ringing success in asserting the EU's external identity. Moreover, it is important not to lose sight of the fact that the European Commission's efforts to influence the development of the DARIO centred exclusively on the 'Community' parts of the Union, rather than on the Union's foreign, security and defence policy.[9] Nor were the 'post-Lisbon' global ambitions of the EU, which form the focus of the present contribution, part of the main discussion.

Accordingly, we begin our analysis by noting that no special considerations justify the application of *lex specialis* rules of attribution to EU crisis management missions. While this means that such missions are subject to the general rules of attribution laid down in the DARIO, we argue that the way in which the ILC purports to apply these rules to peacekeeping operations is too narrow. Contrary to the approach adopted by the ILC, any attempt to establish where responsibility lies for the wrongful conduct of EU missions must first of all clarify their position within the legal order of the EU. To this end, we assess the legal framework and practice of EU military operations in order to establish whether they constitute either *de jure* or de facto organs of the Union. Based on this analysis, we submit that to be able to contribute to the governance of global security the EU should accept that the wrongful conduct of its crisis management missions is, in principle, attributable to it, and seize the opportunity to contribute to the development of the law of international responsibility in this area.

2. International Responsibility and the EU

As an international legal person,[10] the EU bears responsibility under international law for any violations of its international obligations.[11] The applicability of this principle is

[5] Draft Articles on the Responsibility of International Organizations, with Commentaries, in Report of the International Law Commission, Sixty-third Session (2011), UN doc A/66/10, 52.

[6] Comments and Observations received from International Organizations, 14 February 2011, UN doc A/CN.4/637, 7.

[7] S McArdle and PJ Cardwell, 'EU External Representation and the International Law Commission: An Increasingly Significant International Role for the European Union?', in S Blockmans and RA Wessel (eds), *EU External Representation after Lisbon: Legal Challenges*, CLEER Working Paper series, 2012/5, 83–101.

[8] Comments and Observations, n 6, 38. While the Commission's comments related to the DARIO as adopted at first reading, it is unlikely that the changes made at second reading have prompted it to change its mind.

[9] E Paasivirta and PJ Kuijper, 'Does one size fit all? The European Community and the responsibility of international organizations' (2005) 36 NYIL 169.

[10] Art 47 TEU. This provision is widely understood to endow the EU with legal personality under international law: eg M Cremona, 'Defining Competence in EU External Relations: Lessons from the Treaty Reform Process', in A Dashwood and M Maresceau (eds), *Law and Practice of EU External Relations: Salient Features of a Changing Landscape* (CUP, 2008) 34, 38.

[11] The application of this principle to international organizations is well-established: M Hirsch, *The Responsibility of International Organizations Toward Third Parties: Some Basic Principles* (Nijhoff, 1995) 7–10.

reinforced by Article 3(5) TEU, which provides that in its relations with the wider world, the Union shall contribute to 'the strict observance and the development of international law'. A narrow reading of this provision may suggest that promoting the strict observance of international law is merely what in the words of Arnold Wolfers may be called a 'milieu goal' of EU external relations, that is a goal aimed at shaping the environment in which the EU as a foreign policy actor operates.[12] However, the more detailed objectives of EU external action laid down in Article 21 TEU make explicit what already seems to be implied by Article 3(5) TEU, namely that the Union itself must observe international law when it acts on the international scene.[13] The relevant provisions of the TEU therefore not only express a preference for an international system based on multilateral cooperation and the rule of law,[14] but they also recognize that international law imposes certain constraints on EU external action.[15]

In addition, the fact that Articles 3(5) and 21(2)(b) TEU direct the EU to contribute to the development of international law and to consolidate and support its principles hints at the Union's ambition to shape the international legal order in its own image, including by exporting its regulatory standards and models to the international level as discussed by Gráinne de Búrca in this volume.[16] In principle, this engagement may take two main forms. On the one hand, it may lead to a growing convergence between international law and EU law[17] to the extent that European law as a highly effective mode of legal governance offers a 'possible horizon' for the development of the international legal system.[18] On the other hand, it may also lead to greater differentiation and pluralism should the EU's institutions choose to emphasize the autonomy and distinct features of the European legal order, as the European Court of Justice (ECJ) has done on successive occasions,[19] notably in *Kadi*,[20] and demand special treatment for the Union on these grounds. The European Commission has adopted exactly this position with regard to the international responsibility of the EC.

2.1. Lex specialis rules of attribution

In a series of comments concerning the ILC's work on the responsibility of international organizations, the European Commission underlined that the EC 'was not the "classic" type of international organization'.[21] Unlike classical inter-governmental organizations, the Community constituted 'a legal order of its own, with comprehensive legislative and treaty-making powers, deriving from transfer of competence from the Member States to the Community level'.[22] While certain principles of the law of international responsibility applied to all international organizations, the Commission argued that in other areas account had to be taken of the special supranational features of the EC.[23] One such area

[12] A Wolfers, *Discord and Collaboration: Essays on International Politics* (John Hopkins Press, 1962) 73. The promotion of international law is one of the milieu goals specifically mentioned by Wolfers at 74.

[13] Art 21(1) and (3) TEU.

[14] See Koutrakos in this volume, notably s 5.

[15] cf Case C-366/10, *Air Transport Association of America and Others v Secretary of State for Energy and Climate Change*, Judgment of 21 December 2011 (Grand Chamber), not yet reported, para 101.

[16] See de Búrca in this volume.

[17] For examples, see E Denza, 'Two Legal Orders: Divergent or Convergent?' (1999) 48 ICLQ 257, 269–283.

[18] C Leben, 'Hans Kelsen and the Advancement of International Law' (1998) 9 EJIL 287, 296–298.

[19] N Krisch, *Beyond Constitutionalism: The Pluralist Structure of Postnational Law* (OUP, 2010) 201–206.

[20] Joined Cases C-402/05 P and C-415/05 P, *Kadi and Al Barakaat v Council and Commission* [2008] ECR I-6351. For a critique of the court's 'robust pluralism', see G de Búrca, 'The European Court of Justice and the International Legal Order After *Kadi*' (2010) 51 Harvard ILJ 1, especially at 26–48.

[21] Sixth Committee, Summary record of the 14th meeting, 22 December 2003, UN doc A/C.6/58/SR.14, para 13.

[22] Comments and Observations received from International Organizations, 25 June 2004, UN doc A/CN.4/545, 18.

[23] Ibid, 5.

concerned the attribution of measures adopted by its Member States in the implementation of Community law.

Even in fields where the EU enjoys exclusive competence, the implementation of its decisions is normally left to the Member States.[24] However, such implementing measures are not attributable to the EU since the Union does not exercise a sufficient degree of control over its Member States that would justify imputing their acts to it.[25] From the perspective of EU law, this non-attributability may create difficulties in cases where national implementing measures contravene an international agreement to which both the EU and the Member States are parties. In such instances, the EU may enjoy an exclusive competence under its internal law to regulate the conduct of the Member States, yet it is their responsibility, not that of the EU, which is engaged under international law. This outcome sits somewhat uneasily with the requirement of unity in the international representation of the Union[26] and the autonomy of its legal order.[27] The European Commission has therefore adopted the position, in particular in the context of WTO litigation, that measures of the Member States adopted in the implementation of exclusive Community competences should be attributed to the Community and engage its international responsibility.[28]

Based on this practice, the European Commission reasoned that the ILC should incorporate special rules of attribution of conduct, special rules of responsibility or a special exception or saving clause into the DARIO in order to address the distinct features and situation of the EC and similar organizations.[29] However, as neither Special Rapporteur Giorgio Gaja nor the ILC saw the need for special rules of attribution or responsibility,[30] the DARIO attempts to address the Commission's concerns in a savings clause which stipulates that its provision do not apply, amongst other things, where and to the extent that the content or implementation of the international responsibility of an international organization are governed by special rules of international law.[31]

2.2. The Common Foreign, Security and Defence Policy

The European Commission's position regarding the attribution of national measures adopted in the implementation of exclusive Community competences raises the question whether similar considerations apply in the field of the Common Foreign and Security Policy (CFSP) and the Common Security and Defence Policy (CSDP), in particular with respect to EU crisis management missions. Clearly, some parallels between these different policy areas exist. As already noted, the EU must rely on its Member States and third parties to conduct military operations in third countries, just as the Community had to rely on the national authorities of the Member States in order to put its decisions into practice. However, these parallels do not run much deeper.

[24] Paasivirta and Kuijper, n 9, 183.

[25] P Klein, *La Responsabilité des Organisations Internationales dans les Ordres Juridiques Internes et en Droit des Gens* (Bruylant, 1998) 85; S Talmon, 'Responsibility of International Organizations: Does the European Community Require Special Treatment?', in M Ragazzi (ed), *International Responsibility Today: Essays in Memory of Oscar Schachter* (Nijhoff, 2005) 405, 414.

[26] Opinion 1/94, *Agreements Concerning Services and the Protection of Intellectual Property* [1994] ECR I-5267, para 108. See also Paasivirta and Kuijper, n 9, 179–183.

[27] cf Opinion 1/91, *Treaty on a European Economic Area* [1991] ECR I-6079, paras 32–36; Opinion 1/00, *European Common Aviation Area* [2002] ECR I-3493, para 16. See also Case C-459/03, *Commission v Ireland (Mox Plant)* [2006] ECR I-4635, paras 175–177.

[28] Comments and Observations, n 22, 19–20. See also Paasivirta and Kuijper, n 9, 189–191; P Eeckhout, 'The EU and its Member States in the WTO—Issues of Responsibility' in L Bartels and F Ortino (eds), *Regional Trade Agreements and the WTO Legal System* (OUP, 2006) 449, 453–455.

[29] Sixth Committee, Summary record of the 21st meeting, 18 November 2004, UN doc A/C.6/59/SR.21, 5.

[30] Third Report on Responsibility of International Organizations, UN doc A/CN.4/553, 13 May 2005, 4–6.

[31] Art 64 DARIO.

In its observations on the ILC's work, the European Commission was careful to confine its comments to the EC and to Community law without expressing any view on the international responsibility of the EU within its specific areas of activity, including the CFSP. This self-restraint no doubt stemmed from the Commission's limited competence in these areas.[32] Indeed, the Commission expressly declined the ILC's invitation to comment on the attributability of the conduct of peacekeeping forces on the basis that this question did not relate to Community law.[33] However, it is likely that the Commission's silence on the international responsibility of the EU was also motivated by the fact at the time the Union constituted a separate legal regime[34] which did not share the supranational features of the Community legal order.[35] Most importantly, the activities carried out in the context of the EU, including the CFSP and CSDP, were generally understood not to involve a transfer of competence by the Member States to the EU resulting in a loss of authority on their part: in other words, the Member States did not endow the EU with an exclusive competence in its specific areas of activity.

Although the entry into force of the Lisbon Treaty has clouded rather than clarified the exact division of competences between the EU and its Member States in the field of the CFSP/CSDP,[36] it is beyond doubt that the EU has not acquired an exclusive competence in the conduct of foreign, security and defence policy following the entry into force of the Lisbon Treaty.[37] This is a significant point, for the exclusive nature of the EC's competence lay at the heart of the arguments advanced by the European Commission in its quest to see special rules of attribution applied to national measures adopted in the implementation of Community law.[38] Given that the Union's competence over the CFSP/CSDP is not exclusive, the reasoning and precedents invoked by the Commission to justify the special treatment sought for the EC do not apply directly to the conduct of EU crisis management missions. In fact, as Esa Paasivirta and Pieter Jan Kuijper have pointed out, the EU 'is in many ways a classical intergovernmental organization with problems similar to the UN in respect of peace-keeping and police action'.[39] The attribution of wrongful conduct committed by EU military operations must therefore, primarily, be determined with reference to the general rules of attribution laid down in the DARIO and any contribution of the EU to global security governance take place within that general regulatory framework.

3. Attribution of Conduct in Peace Operations: The Missing Link

In recent years, the rules governing the attribution of wrongful acts committed in the context of peace support operations have been the subject of intense discussion, in particular in the aftermath of the widely criticized decision of the European Court of Human Rights in *Behrami* and *Saramati*.[40] Although this debate has demonstrated that academic opinion insists on a high level of factual control for holding states and international organizations

[32] cf Art 18(4) TEU (Nice).

[33] Comments and Observations, n 22, 16.

[34] *Kadi*, n 20, para 202.

[35] See R Gosalbo Bono, 'Some Reflections on the CFSP Legal Order' (2006) 43 *CML Rev* 337.

[36] G De Baere, *Constitutional Principles of EU External Relations* (OUP, 2008) 108–112; A Sari, 'Between Legalization and Organizational Development: Explaining the Evolution of EU Competence in the Field of Foreign Policy' in Cardwell (ed), *EU External Relations Law and Policy in the Post-Lisbon Era* (Springer, 2012) 59.

[37] This is so despite the somewhat ironic fact that international agreements in the field of the CFSP are concluded exclusively by the EU without any provision for mixed agreements.

[38] See Comments and Observations, n 22, 14; F Hoffmeister, 'Litigating against the European Union and its Member States—Who Responds under the ILC's Draft Articles on International Responsibility of International Organizations?' (2010) 21 EJIL 723, 743. See also RA Wessel and L den Hertogh, 'EU Foreign, Security and Defence Policy: A Competence–Responsibility Gap?', forthcoming in M Evans and P Koutrakos (eds), *International Responsibility: EU and International Perspectives* (Hart Publishing, 2012).

[39] Paasivirta and Kuijper, n 9, 174.

[40] *Behrami and Behrami v France* and *Saramati v France, Germany and Norway* (2007) 45 EHRR SE10.

responsible for the conduct of peace operations,[41] it has stopped short of addressing the underlying question of whether factual control is the only relevant ground of attribution in this context. In this section, we argue that the DARIO provides too narrow an answer to this question.

3.1. Dual organ status and the DARIO

Since no international organization, including the EU, enjoys the competence to raise its own armed forces by way of direct recruitment, international organizations conducting military operations have to rely on personnel made available to them by their Member States or third countries. In placing members of their armed forces at the disposal of international organizations, states do not detach them from their body politic and divest them of their status as state officials. If that were the case, assigning troops to international organizations would be tantamount to disbanding them. To avoid this effect, states usually transfer only limited powers of operational control over their forces to international organizations,[42] and retain supreme authority, known as full command,[43] for themselves.[44] The armed forces of a state thus never lose their institutional status as state organs during their secondment to an international organization.[45]

However, none of this precludes an international organization from temporarily incorporating national contingents into its own institutional structure with the consent of the contributing states. The UN offers some lessons in this respect: beginning with the United Nations Emergency Force (UNEF), peacekeeping operations conducted by the UN have been established as subsidiary organs of the General Assembly or the Security Council in exactly this manner. In the case of UNEF, this arrangement was recognized in express terms in the status of forces agreement concluded between the UN and Egypt, which described UNEF 'as an organ of the General Assembly of the United Nations established in accordance with Article 22 of the [UN] Charter'.[46] This precedent was followed in subsequent operations and is reflected in their legal instruments, including the applicable force regulations[47] and status of forces agreements.[48] The International Court of Justice (ICJ) has confirmed the

[41] eg Kjetil Mujezinović Larsen, 'Attribution of Conduct in Peace Operations: The "Ultimate Authority and Control" Test' (2008) 19 EJIL 509.

[42] UN Department of Peacekeeping Operations, *United Nations Peacekeeping Operations: Principles and Guidelines (Capstone Doctrine)* (UN, 2008) 68. See also Command and Control of United Nations Peace-keeping Operations: Report of the Secretary-General, UN doc A/49/681, 21 November 1994, 2–3; Report of the Special Committee on Peace-keeping Operations, UN doc A/50/230, 22 June 1995, 11.

[43] NATO Military Committee, 'Overall Organization of the Integrated NATO Forces', MC 57 (Final), 11 October 1957, 10 (on file with the authors).

[44] B Cathcart, 'Command and Control in Military Operations' in T Gill and D Fleck (eds), *The Handbook of the International Law of Military Operations* (OUP, 2010) 235. See also C Jean, 'Il Controllo degli Stati sulla partecipazione delle loro Forze Armate alle Operazioni di Pace' in N Ronzitti (ed), *Comando e Controllo Nelle Forze di Pace e Nelle Coalizioni Militari* (Franco Angeli, 1999) 129, 136–142.

[45] L Condorelli, 'Le Statut des forces de l'ONU et le droit international humanitaire' (1995) 78 RDI 881, 885–888. But see the more ambiguous position of M Bothe, *Streitkräfte internationaler Organisationen: Zugleich ein Beitrag zu völkerrechtlichen Grundfragen der Anwesenheit fremder Truppen* (Heymann, 1968) 37–49 and 'Peacekeeeping', in B Simma and others (eds), *The Charter of the United Nations: A Commentary*, vol 1 (2nd edn, OUP, 2002) 648, 691.

[46] Exchange of Letters constituting an Agreement concerning the Status of the United Nations Emergency Force in Egypt, 8 February 1957, 260 UNTS 62. Art 22 of the UN Charter entitles the General Assembly to 'establish such subsidiary organs as it deems necessary for the performance of its functions'.

[47] eg Art 6, Regulations for the United Nations Force in Cyprus (UNFICYP), UN doc ST/SGB/UNFICYP/1, 25 April 1964, reprinted as Annex II to Exchange of Letters Constituting an Agreement between the UN and Canada, 21 February 1966, 555 UNTS 119.

[48] eg Art IV(14), Agreement on the Status of the United Nations Protection Force in Bosnia and Herzegovina, 15 May 1993, 1722 UNTS 78; Art IV(15), Agreement between the UN and the African Union and the Government of Sudan (UNAMID), 9 February 2008 (on file with the authors).

legality of these institutional arrangements in the *Certain Expenses* case.[49] Consequently, it is a well-established aspect of UN peacekeeping practice that national contingents serving in UN operations hold a dual institutional status as organs both of their contributing state and of the UN.[50]

The dual organ status of UN peacekeeping operations poses a dilemma in so far as their wrongful conduct may be attributed to more than one party. Whilst recognizing that 'the question of attribution of conduct is not clear-cut',[51] Special Rapporteur Gaja proposed a straightforward solution to this problem in his Second Report on the Responsibility of International Organizations, suggesting that the 'decisive question in relation to attribution of a given conduct appears to be who had effective control over the conduct in question'.[52] The ILC agreed, but went one step further by declaring this to be the only relevant factor. The Commentary to the DARIO thus distinguishes between state organs that are 'fully seconded' to an international organization on the one hand and state organs which to a certain extent still act in a national capacity during their secondment, such as national contingents participating in UN peacekeeping operations, on the other hand.[53] The DARIO accordingly applies two distinct and mutually exclusive rules of attribution to these two situations: it treats the conduct of fully seconded state organs as an act of the receiving organization under Article 6, but applies the test of effective control to not fully seconded state organs under Article 7 in order to determine whether their conduct should be attributed either to the contributing state or to the receiving organization.

The sharp distinction that the DARIO attempts to draw between fully and not fully seconded state organs is artificial. A state will always retain a substantial degree of authority over any organs it makes available to an international organization, otherwise they would cease to be state organs by definition. Even in the European Union this starting point is undisputed. Since *every* secondment of a state organ requires the seconding state and the receiving organization to share their authority in some form, it is difficult to follow the ILC's argument that national contingents forming part of peacekeeping operations are in a class apart from other seconded state organs. The difference is at best one of degree, not one of principle. If no precise distinction can be drawn between fully and not fully seconded organs, the possibility must be accepted that entities enjoying a dual organ status, such as national contingents serving in UN operations, could fall under Article 6 DARIO.[54]

3.2. A rebuttable presumption

The DARIO discount the legal and institutional ties that bind national contingents to an international organization in favour of attributing their conduct solely on the basis of factual criteria. This approach is highly problematic, since it deliberately ignores the institutional law of the international organization concerned. Rather than giving effect to the rules of the international organization in determining whether any person or entity possesses the status of an organ of that organization—which according to Article 2(c) DARIO should be the decisive factor[55]—the ILC has in effect reserved that decision for itself. Moreover, in the case

[49] *Certain Expenses of the United Nations (Article 17, paragraph 2, of the Charter)*, Advisory Opinion (1962) ICJ Rep 151, 177.

[50] eg Seyersted, 'United Nations Forces: Some Legal Problems' (1961) 37 BYIL 351, 410; JW Bridge, 'The Legal Status of British Troops Forming Part of the United Nations Force in Cyprus' (1971) 34 MLR 121, 180. K Schmalenbach, *Die Haftung internationaler Organisationen im Rahmen von Militäreinsätzen und Territorialverwaltungen* (Peter Lang, 2004), 103–106.

[51] Second Report on Responsibility of International Organizations, UN doc A/CN.4/541, 2 April 2004, 17.

[52] Ibid, 19.

[53] DARIO Commentary, n 5, 85.

[54] cf the position of INTERPOL in relation to seconded officials, in Comments and Observations received from Governments and International Organizations, 12 May 2005, UN doc A/CN.4/556, 24.

[55] See also the European Commission's observations in Comments and Observations, n 22, 13.

of the UN, this approach flies in the face of long-standing and consistent practice whereby the UN has accepted responsibility for the wrongful acts of its peacekeeping operations. As the Office of Legal Affairs made clear in a Memorandum submitted to the ILC in 2004, the UN takes the view that its responsibility arises in such circumstances because '[a]s a subsidiary organ of the United Nations, an act of a peacekeeping force is, in principle, imputable to the Organization'.[56]

It is important to underline that the justification for attributing the acts of peacekeeping forces to the UN is based on their legal and institutional status as subsidiary organs of the organization. As Dan Sarooshi has shown, UN law and practice defines a subsidiary organ as an entity established by a principal organ of the UN and operating under its authority and control.[57] The exercise of control therefore forms one of the preconditions for the establishment and continued existence of a subsidiary organ. However, control in this context is a requirement of the institutional law of the UN ('the rules of the organization') and must not be confused with control as a distinct basis of attribution of wrongful conduct.[58] This means that the degree of control to be exercised over a subsidiary organ does not necessarily have to equate to 'effective control'. In the case of UN peacekeeping forces, the exercise of overall authority and control by the Security Council is sufficient to permit their establishment as a subsidiary organ of the UN.[59] In addition, it must be borne in mind that contributing states relinquish certain powers of control over their national contingents whenever they make them available to the UN to be incorporated into a peacekeeping operation.[60] This transfer of authority creates a presumption that national contingents act exclusively on behalf of the UN during their assignment and that their conduct is therefore attributable to the organization, rather than the contributing state.[61] This presumption may be rebutted, however, whenever national contingents operate under the direct instructions of their contributing state and thereby in fact fall outside the reach of the UN's effective control.[62]

The advantage of this rebuttable presumption is that it gives effect to the status of UN peacekeeping operations as subsidiary organs of the organization, and thus fully respects the constitutional rules and practice of the UN, but recognizes that the dual institutional status of national contingents leaves contributing states with considerable authority over their troops. However, the reasons for attributing the acts of national contingents to the UN are purely normative: it is the institutional status of UN peacekeeping operations as subsidiary organs which necessarily entails the attributability of their acts to the UN and it is the formal transfer of legal authority over national contingents which gives rise to a presumption that they act exclusively on behalf of the UN in the exercise of their mandates.[63]

[56] Inter-office Memorandum regarding the topic Responsibility of International Organizations, 3 February 2004 (2004) UNJYB 352.

[57] D Sarooshi, 'The Legal Framework Governing United Nations Subsidiary Organs' (1996) 67 BYIL 413. See also Santiago Torres Bernárdez, 'Subsidiary Organs' in R-J Dupuy (ed), *Manuel sur les organisations internationales: A Handbook on International Organizations* (2nd edn, Nijhoff, 1998) 109.

[58] This would amount to repeating the Grand Chamber's mistake in *Behrami*, but in reverse: see A Sari, 'Jurisdiction and International Responsibility in Peace Support Operations: The *Behrami* and *Saramati* Cases' (2008) 8 HRLR 151, 164.

[59] Sarooshi, n 57, 440–441.

[60] *Out-of-area-Einsätze*, BVerfGE 90, Judgment of 12 July 1994, 286, 351–353. See also Bothe (2002), n 45, 691.

[61] SR Lüder, *Völkerrechtliche Verantwortlichkeit bei Teilnahme an 'Peace-keeping'-Missionen der Vereinten Nationen* (BWV, 2004), 102–105; M Zwanenburg, *Accountability of Peace Support Operations* (Nijhoff, 2005) 100ff; U Häußler, 'Human Rights Accountability of International Organisations in the Lead of International Peace Missions' in J Wouters and others (eds), *Accountability for Human Rights Violations by International Organisations* (Intersentia, 2010) 215, 243–251. See also DW Bowett, *United Nations Forces: A Legal Study of United Nations Practice* (Stevens, 1964) 245.

[62] Inter-office Memorandum, n 56, 355.

[63] cf *Stephens v Cyprus, Turkey and the UN*, Admissibility Decision (Application No 45267/06), 11 December 2008.

4. The Institutional Status of EU Military Operations

The evidence suggests that the UN has accepted that the wrongful conduct of national contingents serving in its peacekeeping operations is attributable to it on the basis of general legal principles.[64] The rules of attribution applied to UN peacekeeping operations therefore may be applied to other international organizations. Consequently, if it can be established that EU military missions constitute subsidiary organs of the EU, a rebuttable presumption may be said to exist in favour of attributing their wrongful conduct to the Union, rather than to the contributing states. In order to be able to assess the responsibility issues flowing from the EU's ambitions in global security governance, we need to take short 'internal examination' into the institutional position of military operations within the EU. Section 3 has shown that two basic conditions must be satisfied for our presumption to arise in the present context: the contributing states must transfer their legal authority over national contingents to the EU and the contingents must be incorporated into the institutional structure of the EU as its organs.

The first condition is undoubtedly satisfied. Although no document affecting a transfer of authority by a Member State to the EU is in the public domain, the available evidence suggests that contributing states confer operational control over their personnel on the EU Operation Commander.[65] This is confirmed by the participation agreements concluded with third countries contributing to EU operations, which typically declare that all forces and personnel remain under the full command of their national authorities, but provide for the transfer of operational and tactical command and/or control to the EU Operation Commander.[66] However, such a transfer of authority does not transform the national contingents concerned into a *de jure* organ of the EU.[67] To satisfy the second condition, a separate step in the form of a legal instrument or another expression of will is required whereby the EU formally incorporates the assembled military personnel and assets into its own institutional structure.[68] The fact that the legal acts establishing EU military operations do not expressly designate them as subsidiary organs is not determinative of this question, since their institutional status within the EU is a substantive and not a terminological matter.[69] Whether or not they form part of the Union therefore depends, first, on whether the EU enjoys the necessary competence to incorporate national contingents into its institutional framework and, second, whether the legal acts establishing EU operations evidence an intention to do so in individual cases.

4.1. Competence and legal basis

Although the Lisbon Treaty has left the nature of the EU's competence in the field of foreign, security and defence policy unclear in important respects,[70] here we are concerned not with the nature of the EU's competence, but its scope. According to Article 24(1) TEU, '[t]he

[64] eg Financing of the United Nations Protection Force, the United Nations Confidence Restoration Operation in Croatia, the United Nations Preventive Deployment Force and the United Nations Peace Forces headquarters: Report of the Secretary-General, UN doc A/51/389, 20 September 1996, para 8.

[65] EU Military C2 Concept, Council doc 11096/03 EXT 1, 26 July 2006, 14. cf Art 5, Joint Action 2003/681/CFSP of 29 September 2003 on the EU Police Mission in FYROM (EUPOL 'Proxima') [2003] OJ L249/66. The Member States' duty to make civilian and military capabilities available to the Union under Art 42(3) TEU does not entail such a transfer of authority: see *Lissabon*, BVerfGE 123, Judgment of 30 June 2009, 267, 422–425. See also Sebastian von Kielmansegg, *Die Verteidingungspolitik der Europäischen Union: Eine Rechtliche Analyse* (2005) 323–325.

[66] eg Art 13, Agreement between the EU and the Government of the Swiss Confederation (EUFOR RD Congo), 10 August 2006, [2006] OJ L276/111.

[67] Although it may transform them into a de facto organ: see S 5.

[68] Sarooshi, n 57, 438–446. cf Seyersted, n 50, 462–463.

[69] DARIO Commentary, n 5, 82.

[70] cf Cremona, n 10, 65.

Union's competence in matters of common foreign and security policy shall cover all areas of foreign policy and all questions relating to the Union's security, including the progressive framing of a common defence policy that might lead to a common defence'. While the material scope of the EU's competence in the field of foreign and security policy could hardly be broader, its competence in defence questions is more limited.[71] However, the specific provisions on the Common Security and Defence Policy (CSDP) laid down in Section 2 of Title V of the TEU confirm in express terms that the *Union* may conduct military operations drawing on capabilities provided by the Member States.[72] Consequently, there is no doubt that the Member States have clothed the EU with the legal capacity to dispose over military assets made available to it for the purposes specified in the TEU.[73]

Since all legal acts relating to the launch, conduct and termination of EU military operations are adopted by the Council of the EU,[74] the latter is the only EU institution capable, in principle, of establishing military operations as its subsidiary organs. Pursuant to Article 240 of the Treaty on the Functioning of the European Union (TFEU), the Council enjoys the power to determine the organization of its General Secretariat. In the past, the Council has relied on the predecessor of this provision to create new military bodies within the General Secretariat, in particular the EU Military Committee and Military Staff,[75] and to lay down rules applicable to national military staff on secondment to the General Secretariat.[76] The adoption of these instruments demonstrates that the Council enjoys the competence to temporarily incorporate military personnel belonging to the Member States into its own institutional structure.[77]

Matters are nevertheless complicated somewhat by the fact that the Council has never relied on Article 240 TFEU to establish military operations. Instead, it has always based itself on Article 28 TEU and its predecessor, which enables the Council to adopt decisions in situations where operational action by the Union is required.[78] The operational nature of EU crisis management missions seems to have been the key consideration leading the President of the General Court to deny in the case of *H v Council and Commission* that the EU Police Mission (EUPM) in Bosnia and Herzegovina could be classified as a body, office or agency of the Union subject to judicial review under Article 263 TFEU.[79] In his view, the EUPM was merely 'a "mission", in other words, a simple activity' of limited duration, which unlike the European Defence Agency had not been accorded the legal status of an agency and enjoyed no legal personality.[80] Notwithstanding the President's assessment, the fact that the Council established the European Defence Agency under what is now Article 28 TEU[81] shows that this provision is perfectly capable of serving as a legal basis for decisions having institutional

[71] P Eeckhout, *EU External Relations Law* (2nd edn, OUP, 2011) 168.

[72] Art 42 TEU.

[73] von Kielmansegg, n 65, 130–133.

[74] Arts 42(4) and 43(2) TEU.

[75] Council Decision 2001/79/CFSP of 22 January 2001 setting up the Military Committee of the EU [2001] OJ L27/4; Council Decision 2001/80/CFSP of 22 January 2001 on the establishment of the Military Staff of the European Union [2001] OJ L27/7, as amended. The EU Military Staff has since been transferred to the European External Action Service.

[76] Council Decision 2001/496/CFSP of 25 June 2001 on the rules applicable to national military staff on secondment to the General Secretariat of the Council in order to form the European Union Military Staff [2001] OJ L181/1, since replaced by Council Decision 2007/829/EC of 5 December 2007 [2007] OJ L327/10.

[77] At least this is how the Council has applied Art 240 TFEU and its predecessor for almost a decade, without ever being challenged in this interpretation.

[78] See A Sari, 'Art 28' in Hermann-Josef Blanke and Stelio Mangiameli (eds), *Commentary on the Treaty on European Union* (Springer, 2013, forthcoming).

[79] Case T-271/10 R, *H v Council and Commission*, Order of the President of the General Court, 22 July 2010, unreported, para 20.

[80] Ibid, para 19.

[81] Joint Action 2004/551/CFSP of 12 July 2004 on the establishment of the European Defence Agency [2004] OJ L245/17.

implications:[82] if the Council has the power to establish independent agencies under Article 28 TEU, it must have the power to create subsidiary organs in this area too. While the absence of separate legal personality may disqualify EU crisis management missions from being classified as bodies or agencies of the EU within the meaning of its internal law,[83] the conferral of legal personality is not a necessary requirement for the establishment of a subsidiary organ.[84] Nor is it necessary for subsidiary organs to be established on a permanent basis.[85] Both the relevant Treaty provisions and past practice therefore confirm that the Council enjoys the capacity to incorporate military personnel within its own structure as subsidiary organs.[86]

4.2. Are EU military operations subsidiary organs of the Council?

Since the Council has not developed its own rules to guide the establishment of subsidiary organs, the criteria developed by the UN may be applied by analogy.[87] These require that a subsidiary organ must be established by a principal organ and operate under its authority. In addition, the creation of a subsidiary organ must not violate the competences of other principal organs and the functions entrusted upon it may not be broader than the competences of the international organization of which it forms a part. EU military operations satisfy all of these conditions. All military operations launched so far have been established by the Council, which is one of the institutions, or principal organs, of the EU.[88] All operations perform their tasks under the overall authority and control of the Council, exercised by the Political and Security Committee on its behalf.[89] The creation of EU military operations does not violate the prerogatives of any other EU institution, since only the Council enjoys the power to adopt legal acts concerning the launch and conduct of EU crisis management missions.[90] Finally, the functions carried out by EU military operations do not exceed the competences of the EU. As we have seen, the EU enjoys the express competence to conduct military operations in third countries. Nothing therefore precludes the relationship between the Council and EU military operations from being classified as a relationship between a principal and a subsidiary organ.

Still, the status of an entity as a subsidiary organ cannot be simply presumed, but requires formal recognition of some sort.[91] Neither the Council decisions establishing EU military operations nor any related instruments, such as the status of forces agreements concluded with host states, describe EU operations as subsidiary organs or otherwise evidence the Council's intention that they should form part of its institutional structure.[92] This may be contrasted with the clear language adopted in the Joint Action establishing the European Defence Agency, which provides that the 'Agency shall act under the Council's authority... *within*

[82] See also Joint Actions 2001/554/CFSP of 20 July 2001 on the establishment of a EU Institute for Security Studies [2001] OJ L200/1 and 2001/555/CFSP of 20 July 2001 on the establishment of a EU Satellite Centre [2001] OJ L200/5. See Naert, n 1, 347–355.

[83] S Andoura and P Timmerman, 'Governance of the EU: The Reform Debate on European Agencies Reignited', EPIN Working Paper No 19, October 2008, 4–5. See also G Schusterschitz, 'European Agencies as Subjects of International Law' (2004) 1 IOLR 163.

[84] While subsidiary organs must enjoy a degree of *functional* independence from their principal organ, separate legal personality is not essential. See Sarooshi, n 57, 416–417.

[85] UN peacekeeping operations are established only for a limited period: Bothe (2002), n 45, 688.

[86] It is noteworthy that in *H v Council and Commission*, the President of the General Court held that the 'Council retain[ed] responsibility for the action of the EUPM in several respects' and that the decisions taken by the Head of EUPM therefore may have been attributable to the Council: see n 79, paras 24 and 25.

[87] Sarooshi, n 57, 416.

[88] For a detailed account of the legal framework of EU missions, see Naert, n 1, 97–191.

[89] Art 38 TEU.

[90] Art 43(2) TEU.

[91] cf *Case concerning the United States Diplomatic and Consular Staff in Tehran* (1980) ICJ Rep 41, para 58.

[92] See also Schmalenbach, n 50, 572.

the single institutional framework of the European Union'.[93] Various signs suggest that EU military operations too fall within the single institutional framework of the EU, including their international nature,[94] the fact that they are conducted under the authority of the Council and the language of the relevant Treaty provisions more generally.[95] Yet none of this can substitute for the absence of a clear expression of will on the part of the Council to establish military operations as its subsidiary organs. The absence of such formal recognition, which is the hallmark of a *de jure* organ, militates against the view that EU military operations constitute *de jure* organs of the EU. For this reason, no presumption can be said to exist to the effect that the wrongful conduct of national contingents serving in such operations should be attributed to the EU on these grounds.

5. EU Military Operations as de facto Organs

States may exercise such comprehensive control over persons or entities not forming part of their institutional structure that the latter may be regarded as their de facto organs and be treated as acting on their behalf. There is no reason why international organizations should not be capable of acquiring de facto organs under similar circumstances. Accordingly, if it can be shown that the EU exercises the requisite level of control, this creates a presumption that the activities of its military missions must necessarily be attributed to it in the same way as if they were its *de jure* organs.[96] However, while the notion of a de facto organ is reasonably well-established, it is not recognized as a distinct ground of attribution in either the Draft Articles on State Responsibility or the DARIO. For the purposes of the present analysis, two understandings of de facto organs may be distinguished: one based on factual and one based on normative control.

5.1. The 'complete dependence' test

The ICJ has defined and applied the concept of de facto organ in a strict manner. According to the *Nicaragua* and *Genocide* cases, persons, groups of persons or entities not holding the status of a formal state organ may be equated with one of its organs for the purposes of international responsibility provided that they act in 'complete dependence' of that state so that, ultimately, they are merely its instrument.[97] The ICJ has emphasized that a finding to this effect would be exceptional and 'requires proof of a particularly great degree of State control'.[98] Adapting this to international organizations, a person, group of persons or entity may be considered a de facto organ of an international organization provided they act in complete dependence of the latter and under its particularly high level of control.

At first sight, EU military missions may appear to satisfy these requirements. After all, the EU establishes a single chain of command for all operations,[99] running from the political level down to the military–strategic, operational and tactical levels. Overall responsibility for the conduct of EU missions lies with the Council:[100] it is for the Council to launch and

[93] Art 1(2), Joint Action 2004/551/CFSP, n 81 (emphasis added).

[94] cf Art 4, Agreement between the EU and the Government of the Swiss Confederation, n 66.

[95] eg the image created by Art 42 TEU is that EU operations are 'owned' by the Union.

[96] cf M Milanović, 'State Responsibility for Acts of Non-state Actors: A Comment on Griebel and Plücken' (2009) 22 LJIL 307, 312.

[97] *Case Concerning Military and Paramilitary Activities in and against Nicaragua*, Merits (1986) ICJ Rep 14, para 109; *Application of the Convention on the Prevention and Punishment of the Crime of Genocide*, Judgment (2007) ICJ Rep 15, para 392.

[98] *Genocide*, ibid, para 393.

[99] EU Military C2 Concept, n 65, 9. cf Art 10(2), Joint Action 2003/92/CFSP of 27 January 2003 on the EU military operation in FYROM [2003] OJ L34/26. See von Kielmansegg, n 65, 308–370.

[100] Art 43(2) TEU.

terminate operations,[101] to determine their mandate,[102] to appoint the Operation and Force Commanders[103] and to approve key documents, such as the Operation Plan and the Rules of Engagement.[104] Acting under the authority of the Council, the Political and Security Committee exercises political control and strategic direction of EU missions on a day-to-day basis.[105] In particular, it sets political–military objectives and, acting through the EU Military Committee, translates these into military guidance and directives for the Operation Commander. Since the Operation Commander and any subordinate levels in the chain of command act under the exclusive direction of the political and military bodies of the EU and must report back to these in the performance of their tasks,[106] EU military missions may be said to be completely dependent on the EU from a political and military–strategic point of view.

Nevertheless, it is difficult to see how national contingents and other assets, including international headquarters, made available to the EU act in complete dependence of the Union within the meaning of the *Nicaragua* and the *Genocide* cases. What the ICJ seems to have had in mind was factual dependence and not a relationship of strategic or legal subordination. In both cases, the court was concerned with establishing whether the persons and entities concerned were completely dependent on the practical assistance and support of the respondent states.[107] Clearly, national contingents and other assets made available for EU crisis management operations do not depend on the EU in this sense. Bearing in mind that the financing, transportation and logistic support of assets is the responsibility of the contributing states and third parties,[108] it is actually the other way around: the EU depends completely on the support of its Member States and third parties to conduct military missions. Consequently, while EU crisis management missions are completely dependent on the EU in terms of their mandate and strategic direction, this is not sufficient to allow them to be classified as de facto organs of the Union pursuant to the strict test espoused by the ICJ.

5.2. Alternative approaches

The test employed by the ICJ has not gone unchallenged. In particular, the validity of the high threshold of control it entails has been questioned by the Appeals Chamber of the International Criminal Tribunal for the Former Yugoslavia (ICTY) in the *Tadić* case.[109] Considering the significant legal consequences attached to a finding that an entity is a de facto organ of an international organization, lowering the threshold of control along the lines proposed in *Tadić* does not seem appropriate.[110] However, it does not seem

[101] eg Art 5, Joint Action 2006/319/CFSP of 27 April 2006 on the EU military operation in support of MONUC during the election process [2006] OJ L116/98.

[102] eg Arts 1 and 2, Joint Action 2008/851/CFSP of 10 November 2008 on a EU military operation to contribute to the deterrence, prevention and repression of acts of piracy and armed robbery off the Somali coast [2008] OJ L301/33.

[103] eg Arts 2 and 4, Joint Action 2004/570/CFSP of 12 July 2004 on the EU military operation in Bosnia and Herzegovina [2004] OJ L252/10. The Council may delegate this power: see Art 6, ibid.

[104] eg Council Decision 2003/432/CFSP of 12 June 2003 on the launching of the EU military operation in the DRC [2003] OJ L147/42.

[105] Art 38 TEU.

[106] EU Military C2 Concept, n 65, 17–18. eg Arts 7(2)–(3) and 8(2), Joint Action 2003/423/CFSP of 5 June 2003 on the EU military operation in the DRC [2003] OJ L143/50.

[107] *Nicaragua*, n 97, para 109; *Genocide*, n 97, para 392.

[108] See EU Concept for Logistic Support for EU-led Military Operations, Council doc 8641/11, 4 April 2011.

[109] *Prosecutor v Tadić*, ICTY Appeals Chamber, Judgment, 15 July 1999 (Case No IT-94-1-A), paras 98–144.

[110] Ibid, para 117. Besides, *Tadić* has rightly been criticized for misreading *Nicaragua* on this point: AJJ de Hoogh, 'Articles 4 and 8 of the 2001 ILC Articles on State Responsibility, the Tadić Case and Attribution of Acts of Bosnian Serb Authorities to the Federal Republic of Yugoslavia' (2001) 72 BYIL 255, 279–281; M Milanović, 'State Responsibility for Genocide' (2006) 17 EJIL 553, 576–581.

unreasonable to relax the threshold as regards the *type* of control required.[111] The notion of a de facto organ is a hybrid rule of attribution which combines factual and institutional considerations into one: if a person or entity is subject to the comprehensive control of an international organization in fact, it must be considered as part of its institutional structure in law. Nothing suggests or demands that the evidence of such factual control must be based entirely on casual links to the exclusion of all normative relations. In other words, what needs to be demonstrated is complete dependence in fact, but the evidence for such dependence does not necessarily have to be deduced exclusively from factual considerations. In principle, a particularly high degree of normative control may also suffice.

The *Geographical Indications Dispute* case offers a precedent for this approach, where the WTO Dispute Panel accepted the position put forward by the European Commission that in the execution of Community law, the Member States 'act *de facto* as organs of the Community, for which the Community would be responsible under WTO law and international law in general'.[112] Clearly, in a narrow factual sense it is the EU which is dependent on the Member States for the execution of EU law, rather than the other way around.[113] Nonetheless, what justifies treating the Member States as de facto organs of the EU in this context is that they have transferred their respective competences upon the EU and consequently exercise Union powers in the implementation of its laws. Their dependence on the EU and its corresponding control is therefore based on legal, not factual, considerations. Understood in this way, the attribution of implementing measures adopted by the Member States of the EU in the exercise of its exclusive competences does not have to be conceived as a *lex specialis* rule as the European Commission has argued,[114] but can be derived from the general principles of attribution.

A similar argument may be made in relation to EU military operations. As we have already indicated, the reasoning adopted by the European Commission in the *Geographical Indications Dispute* case does not apply directly to the activities carried out in the context of the CFSP/CSDP, since in this field the EU continues to share its competence with the Member States.[115] However, Member States and third parties contributing to EU missions nevertheless find themselves in a broadly analogous situation. By placing their forces at the disposal of the EU, contributing states not only transfer certain powers of command and control to the EU, but also undertake a series of corresponding commitments which limit their freedom to exercise control over those forces themselves. In particular, all contributing states are bound by the relevant legal instruments establishing the mission,[116] including any agreements with third states concluded by the EU, while EU Member States are also subject to a general duty of loyal cooperation, which includes the obligation to refrain from any steps which are contrary to the interests of the Union or likely to impair its effectiveness.[117] The position of national contingents serving in EU operations therefore differs dramatically from the position of the Nicaraguan rebels and their relationship with the United States forming the basis of the proceedings in the *Nicaragua* case. Bearing in mind the applicable

[111] cf R Wolfrum, 'State Responsibility for Private Actors: An Old Problem of Renewed Relevance', in Ragazzi, n 25, 423, 427–431.

[112] WTO Panel Report, *European Communities—Protection of Trademarks and Geographical Indications for Agricultural Products and Foodstuffs*, DS174, 15 March 2005, paras 7.98 and 7.269.

[113] See n 25.

[114] S 2.1.

[115] S 2.2.

[116] For EU Member States, this obligation results from Art 28 TEU, while in the case of contributing third states it is based on the applicable participation agreements, eg Art 1, Agreement between the EU and the Russian Federation on the participation of the Russian Federation in the EU military operation in the Republic of Chad and in the Central African Republic (EUFOR Tchad/RCA), 5 November 2008 [2008] OJ L307/16.

[117] Art 24(3) TEU. See C Hillion and RA Wessel, 'Restraining External Competences of EU Member States under CFSP' in M Cremona and B De Witte (eds), *EU Foreign Relations Law: Constitutional Fundamentals* (Hart Publishing, 2008) 79.

legal arrangements, it seems justified to conclude that the EU acquires a 'particularly great degree of control' over national contingents participating in its missions, albeit be it on a temporary basis, and that the contingents are completely dependent in their action upon the EU during their assignment. On this reasoning, EU military missions should be classified as de facto organs of the EU.[118]

6. Conclusion

As Piet Eeckhout has aptly observed, the EC's eagerness to assume international responsibility for implementing measures adopted by its Member States which contravene its treaty obligations is counter-intuitive: normally, one would expect an international actor to minimize or evade its exposure to legal liability.[119] The EC's practice is of course entirely consistent when seen from the perspective of the Community legal order. Since the rules of international law governing the attribution of wrongful conduct do not necessarily reflect the division of competences between the EC and its Member States, the European Commission has insisted that the Community should be subject to special rules of attribution which better respect its internal law. Yet this practice poses a direct challenge to the idea that the international responsibility of international organizations is governed by a single set of rules which applies in a uniform manner. As such, it also exposes a possible tension between the promotion of 'multilateral solutions to common problems'[120] as a milieu goal of EU external action and the advancement on the international level of the EU's more narrowly defined constitutional values and principles.[121]

The conduct of military operations by the EU raises a similar question: taking account of the EU's ambitions laid down in the current Treaties to contribute to global security governance, do the rules of attribution laid down in the DARIO provide an adequate system for allocating responsibility between the EU and contributing states? Whereas the European Commission played a visible role in the debate on the DARIO by pointing to the special nature of the Community, its contribution did not extend to the complex questions emerging from the role of the EU as a global security actor. We have suggested that the way in which the ILC purports to apply the rules on the allocation of responsibility to peace operations is too narrow. By focusing exclusively on factual control as a ground for attribution, the Commentary to the DARIO deliberately disregards the institutional and legal ties which may exist between national contingents and international organizations. This approach is inappropriate in cases where an international organization incorporates national contingents into its own institutional structure, since such an act of incorporation gives rise to a rebuttable presumption that the conduct of national contingents is attributable to the international organization rather than to the contributing states.

Whether or not such a presumption of attribution exists in the case of EU military operations depends on their status within the institutional and legal order of the EU. We have found that the picture is a mixed one. The EU certainly enjoys the competence to incorporate military assets into its institutional structure and the Council is competent to establish military operations as its subsidiary organs. However, none of the legal acts adopted in relation to EU military operations provide clear evidence of the Council's intention to confer the status of a subsidiary organ on them. Since this intention cannot be presumed, we were led to conclude that EU military operations are not *de jure* organs of

118 Provided one ignores the Commentary's instructions to deal with peacekeeping operations under Art 7, as we have suggested earlier, this position is compatible with Art 6 DARIO, which covers the conduct of both organs and agents and thereby combines, or rather conflates, the institutional and agency paradigms. See DARIO Commentary, n 5, 84.

119 Eeckhout, n 28, 456.

120 Art 21(1) TEU.

121 See n 16 and the accompanying text.

the EU.[122] However, they may still be classified as de facto organs, provided that the Union exercises the necessary degree of control over them. Although EU operations do not satisfy the high threshold of complete dependence demanded by the ICJ in its case-law, a strong argument can be made that they are subject to a particularly high degree of normative control by the EU and may be considered as its de facto organs on this basis. Accordingly, if our analysis is correct, a presumption exists in favour of attributing the conduct of EU military operations to the EU on the grounds that they constitute de facto organs of the Union.

Nevertheless, we believe that there are significant benefits to be had in formalizing this presumption by granting EU military operations the status of *de jure* subsidiary organs of the Council in the legal acts establishing them. For a start, this would eliminate any doubts about the institutional status of EU operations and remove the incentive created by Article 7 DARIO to contest which party exercised effective control over the wrongful conduct in each particular case.[123] The presumption of attributability would therefore help to avoid potentially distracting disputes between the EU and contributing states and indicate to prospective claimants that their remedy lies with the Union. To borrow a term used by the Editors in the Introduction to this volume: it would be an 'external projection of an internal reality'. For example, pursuant to the decision of the European Court of Human Rights in *Behrami*,[124] any breaches of the European Convention for the Protection of Human Rights and Fundamental Freedoms committed by EU military operations would be attributable to the EU alone if such operations were subsidiary organs of the Council.[125] Formally recognizing that the conduct of EU military operations is attributable to the EU would also create a sound basis for the development of a coherent claims settlement practice by the EU. In the past, claims brought by private parties suffering injury or damage at the hands of EU operations would normally receive compensation from the authorities of the national contingent involved in the incident. However, in the absence of binding standards shared by all contingents, this quickly leads to inconsistencies and the fragmentation of claims settlement practice along national lines, in particular in large operations. If the responsibility to settle claims lies with the EU, this would allow the Union and contributing states to develop a coherent set of principles and procedures to be applied in all EU crisis management operations. Of course, this requires that the contributing states provide the EU with the financial and other resources to meet its liabilities.

More generally, a formal recognition by the Council that the conduct of EU military operations is attributable to the EU would signal to the international community that the EU is ready to accept that its growing global engagement as an international security actor brings with it a duty to act in an accountable manner.[126] The EU cannot entrust the implementation of its security and defence policy to its Member States and other parties and disavow responsibility for its adverse effects[127] or hide behind the effect control test set down in Article 7 DARIO. Accepting that the wrongful conduct of its crisis management missions engages the Union's international responsibility would not only better reflect the spirit of the principles laid down in Article 21 TEU, but it could also serve as an example for other international organizations, including NATO,[128] and thereby make a broader contribution to the development of the law of international responsibility in this particular field.

[122] cf N Tsagourias, 'EU Peacekeeping Operations: Legal and Theoretical Issues', in M Trybus and ND White (eds), *European Security Law* (OUP, 2007) 102, 122; Naert, n 1, 355–357.

[123] cf Zwanenburg, n 3, 403–405; von Kielmansegg, n 65, 330–331.

[124] *Behrami*, n 40.

[125] See also *Stephens*, n 63.

[126] See also ND White, 'The EU as a Regional Security Actor within the International Legal Order', in M Trybus and ND White (eds), *European Security Law* (OUP, 2007) 329, 348.

[127] cf Wolfrum, n 111, 431.

[128] See Häußler, n 61, 231.

PART III

THE EU AND GLOBAL TRADE GOVERNANCE

9

Institutional Aspects of Global Trade Governance from an EU Perspective

*Frank Hoffmeister**

1. Introduction

Meeting on 4 November 2011 in Cannes, the heads of states and governments of the Group of Twenty (G20) declared their resolve to refrain from adopting protectionist trade measures. Moreover, they directed their trade ministers to pursue 'fresh, credible approaches' to furthering world trade negotiations held under the auspices of the world trade organization (WTO). They concluded that they should draw on the progress achieved so far in the Doha Development Agenda (DDA) and specifically address the needs of the least-developed countries (LDCs).[1]

At the 8th Ministerial WTO conference, held from 15–17 December 2011 at Geneva, the Chairman of the Conference summarized the state of affairs of the Doha Round by a statement, most of which was already agreed by consensus at the General Council of 30 November that year.[2] Ministers approved the accession of Russia, Samoa, Vanuatu and Montenegro to the organization and granted a waiver enabling WTO members to give preferential treatment to services and service suppliers of LDCs deviating from the most-favoured nation principle under Article II:1 of the General Agreement on Trade in Services (GATS). Moreover, they extended: (1) the transitional period for LDCs to comply with obligations under the Agreement on Trade Related Aspects of Intellectual Property Rights (TRIPS); (2) an existing practice of not imposing customs duties on e-commerce services; and (3) a moratorium on non-violation and situation complaints under the TRIPS. Finally, ministers of the 15 parties to the Government Procurement Agreement (GPA) agreed on an updated rule book and increased their reciprocal market access offers.

Leaving aside the debacle of Seattle in 1999, this is probably one of the least impressive packages to ever came out of the bi-annual ministerial gatherings at the WTO since its inception in 1995. In particular, it reflects the fact that the over 150 members are not willing to take further steps towards liberalizing trade at a time of economic crisis. Moreover, the latest WTO report on G20 trade measures complained that out of a total of 674 measures that can be considered as restricting or potentially restricting trade taken by the strongest trading nations since October 2008, only 19% had been eliminated by September 2011.[3] On the other hand, there is no widespread retrogression either. Between 2008 and 2011, governments pursued a mix of trade restrictions with an increasing resort to non-tariff measures, but also pursued some bilateral trade liberalization and trade promotion.[4]

In this contribution, we will take a closer look at the institutional aspects of global trade governance. In the first section, we examine how decision-making functions in the WTO,

* The views expressed are personal.

1 G20 Cannes summit, Final declaration, paras 65–66.

2 WT/MIN(11)/W/2.

3 WTO Report on G20 Trade Measures (May–mid-October 2011), Geneva, 25 October 2011, available on the WTO homepage: <www.wto.org>.

4 M Datt, B Hoekman, M Malouche, 'Taking Stock of Trade Protectionism since 2008, Economic Premise (The World Bank)', No 72 of December 2011, pp 1–9 (6 et seq).

and how WTO-related decisions are taken within the EU. The second section conducts a similar inquiry in the context of G20 decision-making. On that basis, and in light of the research objective of this volume, we examine the following question: can the European Union, under the current institutional structure of the international trading system—which the then EU Trade Commissioner Pascal Lamy has referred to as 'medieval' in the aftermath of the DDA collapse in Cancun 2003[5]—live up to its constitutional commitment to contribute to 'free and fair trade' as laid down in Article 3(5) of the Treaty on European Union (TEU)? In light of the analysis of WTO and G20 decision-making, we will present a critical assessment on the need to reform the respective governance structures, in light of ambitions stated in the EU Treaty.

2. Governance Structures in the WTO

As a so-called 'member-driven organization', the WTO works in general by consensus—for example, at the above-mentioned 8th Ministerial Conference 2011 no single vote was taken. Rather, in line with footnote 1 to Article IX (1) of the WTO Agreement, which defines consensus,[6] the Chairman concluded the respective agenda points by simply verifying that no delegate voiced an objection. However, the legal foundation for this practice is much more nuanced. Article IX:1, first sentence, of the WTO Agreement acknowledges consensus as the preferred way of taking decisions, but at the same time allows for voting in a considerable number of cases. Although these rules are currently 'dormant in the background',[7] it is nevertheless useful to recall them, as their mere existence poses a number of theoretical and practical questions.[8]

2.1. Amendments to covered agreements

a) General rules for multilateral agreements

Covered WTO agreements can be amended by a rather complicated procedure. In the first step, the Ministerial Conference (or the General Council) adopts a decision which contains the amendment. If no consensus is reached within 90 days, an amendment can also be voted by a two-thirds majority of members.[9] In the second step, ratifications (called 'acceptance') are required. Unless certain hardcore provisions are affected which trigger a need for unanimous acceptance under Article X:2 of the WTO Agreement, an amendment enters into force if a two-thirds majority of members has formally declared that it accepts the amendment. The amendment will become binding only on those members who have declared such acceptance, if the amendment affects rights and obligations of the members. If, however, the amendment is neutral to such rights, ratification by a two-thirds majority is sufficient to make the amendment binding to the entire membership.

In practice, this procedure has been used once, and only the first phase has been completed so far. Replacing the earlier Declaration by the Ministerial Conference (2001) and the respective waiver on that matter (2003), the General Council adopted in August 2005 by consensus an amendment to the TRIPS agreement, which would affect the rights

[5] 'Brussels urges shakeup of "medieval" WTO' *The Guardian* (16 September 2003), available at: <http://www.guardian.co.uk/business/2003/sep/16/europeanunion.wto>.

[6] The definition reads: 'The body concerned shall be deemed to have decided by consensus on a matter submitted for its consideration, if no Member, present at the meeting when the decision is taken, formally objects to the proposed decision'.

[7] M Hahn, 'Die zukünftige Rolle der Mitgliedstaaten in der WTO' in M Bungenberg and C Hermann (eds), *Die gemeinsame Handelspolitik der Europaeischen Union nach Lissabon*, (Nomos Verlag, 2011), pp 13–24 (15).

[8] For an early assessment see T Cottier and S Takenoshita, 'The Balance of Power in WTO Decision-Making: Towards Weighted Voting in Legislative Response' (2003) *Aussenwirtschaft* 171.

[9] WTO Agreement, Art X:1, 6th sentence.

and obligations of members on compulsory licensing.[10] In particular, the new Article 31bis of TRIPS was designed to achieve a fair balance between the interests of those members with a strong pharmaceutical industry and those members with a weak manufacturing capacity of certain pharmaceuticals deemed important for the health of their population. However, despite the consensus on the substance of this amendment, it has still not entered into force because the actual number of formal 'acceptance' declarations fell far short of expectations. Within the first two years—a deadline set originally by the General Council—only 13 other members and the EU declared their acceptance.[11] From 2007 to 2009—the next deadline from the General Council—another 13 members followed suit, and up to the end of 2011 the WTO registered 16 more deposits of declarations of acceptance. This brings the number of total acceptances to 42 members plus the European Union out of 153 members (including the EU).

b) *The weight of an EU acceptance*

Although it is clear that this ratio does not meet by far the two-thirds threshold as laid down in Article X:3 of the WTO Agreement, an important question is how to exactly calculate the number of necessary acceptances. The method is far from obvious because the acceptance from the European Union can be calculated in different ways: does it count for one member only (the EU itself) or does it also have the weight of all the EU Member States? In the latter hypothesis, the EU instrument could count for 27 members (all EU Member States) or even 28 members (all EU Member States plus the EU itself).

Following a traditional international law approach, a former senior lawyer at the WTO Secretariat argues in favour of the first hypothesis.[12] In his view, Article IX of the WTO Agreement counts the EU and all its Member States as separate members of the WTO. Since none of the Member States has expressed a will to be bound by the TRIPS amendment they are not bound by it under international law.[13] Also pointing to the formulation in the TRIPS Amendment itself (The European Community '*with* its Member States', rather than '*and* or *on behalf* its Member States'), for him there is only one 'acceptance' which could be counted under Article X:3 of the WTO Agreement, namely the one expressed by the EU.[14]

In my view, this line of reasoning does not take sufficiently into account that the EU is not a normal member both under WTO law and European law. In contrast to other subjects of international law, the EU has the capacity to prevent Member States from acting within the WTO when the subject matter falls under its exclusive competence. With respect to the TRIPS amendment that is exactly what happened: When the Commission submitted a proposal to the Council to accept the amendment on behalf of the EU,[15] it was debated whether or not the amendment fell within exclusive EU competence under the then Article 133(5) EC. Despite some initial hesitations of certain Member States, the Council finally accepted the Commission proposal. Hence, at EU level it was agreed that Member States lacked competence to submit separate national declarations of acceptance (with the exception of overseas territories to which the EU Treaty does not apply).[16] The EU's instrument

[10] Decision of the General Council of 6 December 2005, WTO/L/641 of 8 December 2005 and the Protocol hereto, introducing a new Art 31bis to the TRIPS agreement.

[11] The instrument of acceptance from November 2007 referred to the European Community. However, under the Art 1(3) TEU, as amended by the Treaty of Lisbon, the European Union replaced the European Community. This succession was also communicated to the WTO by note verbale (see WT/L/779).

[12] M Kennedy, 'When will the Protocol Amending the TRIPS Agreement Enter into Force?' (2010) 13(2) *Journal of International Economic Law* 459–473.

[13] Ibid, at 467.

[14] Ibid, at 468.

[15] COM (2006) 175 final of 27 April 2006.

[16] Hence, the Netherlands was able to submit an instrument of acceptance with respect to its overseas territories (the Netherlands Antilles and Aruba). This instrument does not count as an additional acceptance, but should be

submitted to the WTO on 30 November 2007 reflected this point, stating that under Article 300(7) EC (currently 216(2) of the Treaty on the Functioning of the European Union (TFEU)) the Member States are also bound by the EU's international commitments.[17] Since the EU's acceptance has the effect of binding 27 Member States under European law, and since this fact has been clearly expressed in the EU's instrument of acceptance, there is good reason to apply by analogy the voting rule contained in Article IX:1 of the WTO Agreement. This rule takes account of the specificities of the EU by counting a vote by the EU in areas of its competence as 27 votes. Applying this rule for the TRIPS amendment would not upset the institutional balance in the WTO either: the EU would not get 'additional' influence since the EU's instrument would *not* count as 27 plus 1,[18] but as 27. Otherwise, the EU Member States would be counted in the denominator of WTO members (making up the total figure to 153), but they could never be counted on the other side of the equation. This would dramatically increase the two-third threshold and run counter to the *effet utile* of Article X:3 of the WTO Agreement, which made the entry into force of amendments decidedly not dependent on acceptance of virtually the entire membership.

In the alternative, if one really does count the EU's instrument of acceptance as counting for one member only, the logical consequence would be to exclude the EU Member States also from the denominator. The WTO would only have 126 members for the purpose of this particular TRIPS amendment (153 minus the 27 EU Member States), and consequently only 84 acceptances would be necessary to bring the amendment into force. This idea would probably be even more straightforward, as it would count the EU acceptance as any other acceptance and eliminate the Member States from the entire picture as they have lost competence on the issue *tout court*. However, from an international law point of view, this interpretation would be even more far reaching, as it would suppose that the membership in the WTO would alter depending on whether an amendment falls into EU exclusive competence or not. The consequence would be that not only the notion of 'like products' could be understood differently in different places of the WTO agreements,[19] but also the fundamental notion of a 'member' itself. Given the systemic implications of such an approach, it seems more prudent to keep the EU Member States on both sides of the equation: on the one hand, their separate WTO membership brings the denominator to the high number of 153, but on the other hand, the fact that they transferred competence to the EU on the TRIPS amendment gives the EU acceptance the weight of 27 ratifications in analogy to Article IX:1 of the WTO Agreement.

c) No need for EU Member State acceptance

More generally, the TRIPS amendment shows that Article X of the WTO Agreement does not require that all WTO members participate in the amendment procedure. In particular, in the case of the Union, EU acceptance may be enough if the subject matter of the amendment is covered by EU exclusive competence. It follows that EU Member States are not necessarily involved in treaty amendments just because of the fact that they are WTO

seen as a geographical extension of the acceptance from the Netherlands, made through the EU (see n 12, pp 465–466).

[17] Under the instrument of acceptance, the President of the Council of the European Union cites as legal basis Art 133(5) in conjunction with Art 300(2) and (3), second subpara EC, notifies the acceptance 'by the European Community' and 'confirms, in accordance with Art 300(7) EC that the Protocol will be binding on the Member States of the European Union'.

[18] Probably some of the problems on counting were raised by the spokesperson of the former EU Trade Commissioner, Cronin, who opined that the EU instrument would count as 28 ratifications, namely those of the European Union's 27 Member States and that of the EU as a whole. This would, however, exactly lead to undesired additionality, which fn 2 of the WTO agreement excludes when counting votes for the EU.

[19] AB Report, Japan, Alcoholic Beverages, WT/DS 8/AB/R,WT/DS10/AB/R, WT/DS11/AB/R, S 21.

members. This may become even more important when the Doha package might be concluded, entailing a number of amendments to existing WTO agreements, which may entirely fall within EU competence, whether exclusive or shared in nature.

d) Special rules for plurilateral agreements

Finally, there are special rules to amend plurilateral agreements, as those are only binding a restricted circle of WTO members. Article X:10 of the WTO Agreement refers to the special rules contained in the two remaining texts, namely the Agreement on Trade in Civil Aircraft and the Agreement on Government Procurement (GPA). The agreements on dairy and bovine meat are irrelevant in this context as they were terminated at the end of 1997.

The Agreement on Trade in Civil Aircraft of 1980 contained in Section 9.5.1 only a rough indication about future amendments, stating essentially that the responsible Committee should establish the respective procedure. In 2001, the Agreement was indeed amended by a Protocol, which updated the relevant annex in order to bring it into line with the Harmonized Commodity Description and Coding System.[20] Meeting within the Committee on Trade in Civil Aircraft, signatories to the original text drew up the protocol and opened it for acceptance. According to point 3 of the Protocol, it entered into force on 1 January 2002 for those signatories who had accepted it, and for each other signatory on the date on which it accepted it later on—hence no minimum number of acceptances was required. This procedure looks very light and convenient.

Under Article XXIV:9 of the GPA 1994, amendments thereto are again negotiated on the basis of procedures to be established by consensus in GPA committee. The text also makes it clear that no amendment shall bind a party without its acceptance. Against that background, GPA parties negotiated plurilaterally on the modernization of the text and bilaterally on their respective market access offers. A provisional agreement on a revised text was reached in 2006, but there was no agreement about expanding its coverage. As of 2010, such negotiations were conducted for the EU by the Internal Market Commissioner, Barnier, in consultation with the Trade Commissioner, De Gucht.[21] Prior to the Geneva Conference, the EU submitted its third revised offer. Intensive negotiations by the two Commissioners and their staff with the United States and Japan focusing on the railroad sector took place on 14 and 15 December 2011, and allowed closing the market access chapter in time for the Ministerial Conference. Moreover, the EU accepted the US request that the new rules are formally treated as amendments to the GPA rather than as a new agreement. Subsequently, the GPA committee adopted a protocol revising the GPA by consensus.[22] The Protocol itself will enter into force upon acceptance by two-thirds of the 1994 GPA parties.

2.2. Accessions

a) WTO rules

When a new member is admitted to the WTO, such decision may *de iure* also be taken by a vote. Indeed, Article XII:2 of the WTO agreement foresees a decision in the General Council by two-third majority of members. In the early practice of the organization, this rule was also applied as follows. When the accession of Ecuador was on the agenda in July 1995, the Chairman of the General Council received consensus in the room to proceed to a vote. He submitted the decision to a vote by postal ballot in line with the Rules of Procedure of the

[20] WTO doc TCA/4 of 23 November 2001.

[21] The division between the two Commissioners dates back to a gentleman's agreement of 1996, according which the Internal Market Commissioner and his services are competent within the Commission for GPA matters, whereas the Trade Commissioner negotiates public procurement chapters in bilateral FTA negotiations.

[22] For the revised GPA see WTO doc GPA/113 of 2 April 2012.

General Council.[23] However, it turned out that a not insignificant number of states took their time to cast the vote. Any 'missing' vote, however, would de facto be counted as a negative vote, since such votes did not count to passing the required two-thirds threshold from the entire membership. Inter alia, in order to prevent such occurrences in the future, the membership agreed to equally apply consensus for accession decisions. A Declaration from the Chair of November 1995 formalized this understanding,[24] while at the same time underlining that every member retains the right to ask for a vote under Article XII:2 of the WTO Agreement. This Decision had two effects: on the one hand, it simplified the accession procedure as consensus of members actually present sufficed; on the other hand, it allowed each current member to temporarily oppose accession of a new member, thereby making it more difficult to enter the organization and creating the risk of a blockage for bilateral political reasons.

In the case of Russia's accession, these intricacies of WTO decision-making played an important role. Indeed, 18 years after the initial request to join the organization in 1993, the Russian Federation had finally secured the support of all the main WTO members in bilateral talks. In particular, Washington and Brussels had come to an agreement with Moscow by early October 2011. More specifically, after intensive negotiations between EU Trade Commissioner De Gucht and the Russian Deputy Prime Minister Shuvalov, the EU had hammered out four bilateral agreements with the Russian Federation settling the following four controversies:

(1) the Russian investment scheme for cars;
(2) the administration of tariff-rate quotas applying to Russian exports of woods and the technical modalities for those wood exports (one agreement and a protocol thereto);
(3) the introduction or increase by the Russian Federation of export duties on raw materials; and
(4) preservation of existing trade relations in maritime services.

Moreover, the 2006 Agreed Principles to adjust over-flight fees paid by EU airlines flying over Siberia were confirmed in a joint letter between the Russian side and the two EU Commissioners for trade and transport. Finally, certain multilateral issues which not only interested the EU but also other members such as on meat exports and Russian SPS standards (negotiated on the EU side by Agriculture Commissioner Ciolos) were recorded in the draft working party report to the satisfaction of the EU and the US.

However, one important outstanding point remained unresolved between Russia and Georgia. In particular, Georgia insisted on establishing an international monitoring system over the trade flows involving the breakaway regions of South Ossetia and Abkhazia. As this demand had a clear diplomatic overtone connected with sovereignty issues, it had the potential to unravel the trade-related progress made. The two protagonists had already agreed to ask the Swiss Confederation to mediate between them as of March 2011. Swiss mediation was conducted confidentially in several rounds. When the informal deadline rapidly approached, namely the working party meeting scheduled for 10–11 November 2011, Georgia formally protested against the scheduling of this meeting on 14 October 2011.[25] This alarm bell made the High Representative/Vice President of the European Commission, Mrs Ashton, and the European External Action Service (EEAS) press both sides for a compromise. Coincidentally, when the competent EEAS Director visited Tbilisi

[23] WTO, Rules of Procedure for Sessions of the Ministerial Conference and Meetings of the General Council, WT/L/161, 25 July 1996.

[24] General Council, Statement by the Chairman as agreed by the General Council on 15 November 1995, WTO doc WT/L/93 of 24 November 1995.

[25] See Letter from the Georgian Ambassador Tchiaberashvili to the Working Party on the Accession of the Russian Federation, WT/ACC/RUS/66 of 14 October 2011.

during the last week of October, the *Wall Street Journal* reported that he did not exclude that the EU would resort to voting on Russian accession.[26] On the next day however, this report was corrected by the newspaper as being wrongly attributed to the said EEAS official.[27] In sum, the episode showed clearly that the 'shadow of voting' could become more visible if diplomatically necessary.

It remains speculative whether an eventual EU request to proceed to voting would have found support by the rest of the WTO membership. In particular, the US is known to be principally opposed to finding itself potentially out-voted. Moreover, it resists the relative gain of influence of the EU from one player for consensus to a bloc of 27 votes under a voting exercise. In any case, it is remarkable that Georgia and Russia reached a breakthrough under Swiss mediation shortly after the Swiss Foreign Minister visited Moscow in early November. Both sides communicated their agreement to the Swiss in early November, in which the two sides entrusted a private Swiss company, supervised by the Swiss Federation, to exercise the relevant monitoring at the relevant crossings.[28] In that way, both sides could save their respective position under international law on the status of the contested territories. Following the adoption of the working party report on 10–11 November, the Ministerial Conference finally adopted the decision on Russian accession and the Russian Accession Treaty by consensus on 16 December 2011.[29]

b) EU rules

Within the EU, joining such consensus on accession is certainly no easy matter. As the entry of a new member creates rights and obligations of the EU vis-à-vis this member, the Council decides on the EU position following a Commission proposal under Article 218(9) TFEU. This EU position is represented by the Commission at the Ministerial Conference—implying that the Commission welcomes the accession on behalf of the EU. It is however less clear whether the EU Member State can also join the consensus, since that would presuppose that accession of a new member also touches upon their remaining national competences. To date, Member States are equally present in the WTO meeting room during accession decisions, creating the impression that they participate in the consensus as well. Whether this external 'joint' presence of the Commission and the Member States complies with domestic division of competences is, however, not settled. Similarly to the preceding cases of Vanuatu and Samoa in October 2011, the Member States added to the EU position on Russian accession[30] a 'decision of the representatives of Member States convening in the Council' to that effect.[31] The Commission disagreed and added a statement to the Committee of Permanent Representatives (COREPER) minutes, stating that an EU-only decision would have been sufficient. The final word on this matter will have to come from the European Court of Justice (ECJ) sooner or later. There are strong arguments favouring an EU-only decision since the Lisbon Treaty has done away with the highly confusing wording of the former Articles 133 (5) and (6) EC, which had triggered

[26] JW Miller, 'EU Pushes Georgia to Accept Russian Membership in the WTO' *The Wall Street Journal* (26 October 2001), at: <http://online.wsj.com/article/SB40001424052970204644504576653302881291070.html>.

[27] *The Wall Street Journal*, 27 October 2011.

[28] The agreement is not public. A detailed description is given at the Georgian news website of 18 November 2011 at: <http://www.civil.ge/eng/article.php?id=24158>.

[29] <http://www.wto.org/english/news_e/news11_e/acc_rus_16dec11_e.htm>.

[30] Council Decision of 14 December 2011 establishing the position to be taken by the European Union within the relevant instances of the World Trade Organization on the accession of the Russian Federation to the WTO [2012] OJ L6/6.

[31] This decision is not mentioned in the minutes of the Council meeting of 14 December 2001 (EU Council Document 550/11), as it has been taken at COREPER level, whose proceedings are not published.

mixity on many issues.[32] Due to this treaty change, services and trade-related aspects of intellectual property rights are now fully within the scope of EU competence. Old arguments formulated at the time the WTO was concluded are no longer valid, and the fact that a Member State will bear some expenses of the WTO does in itself not justify its participation in the conclusion of an agreement at the WTO.[33] Hence, it is difficult to see how accession of a new WTO member would allow a separate decision of each EU Member State.

In contrast, concluding the relevant side-agreements with a new member causes less controversy within the Union. Here, the ordinary treaty-making procedures apply, giving the Council a right to sign the agreement, as was done by the Foreign Affairs Council with respect to the EU–Russia agreements on 14 December 2011.[34] Later in the Article 218 TFEU procedure, the Council can conclude the agreement after having received consent from the European Parliament.

2.3. Waivers

a) WTO rules

Another important area where the WTO rule book allows for voting is waivers. Under Article IX:3 of the WTO agreement a decision to relieve a member of any WTO obligation can be taken by three-quarters majority of the Ministerial Conference if consensus has not been reached beforehand. Responding to a request from the US during the Uruguay round negotiations, footnote 4 specifies that a waiver to prolong transition periods granted to certain (developing) members can in any case only be taken by consensus. In addition to this partial derogation from the rule, the above-mentioned Chairman's Decision of November 1995 re-established consensus as the ordinary decision-making method also with respect to waivers. It thus follows that, again, decisions in this area do not go against the will of any member. There are clear instances where this has led to a considerable slowing of the process. First, the Ministerial Conference at Doha 2001 took considerable time to adopt a declaration on compulsory licensing under the TRIPS agreement. Even after that breakthrough the formulation for a legally binding waiver could only be agreed in August 2003 when the American delegation was satisfied,[35] thereby exceeding the December 2002 deadline set by the Doha TRIPS Declaration. Although the question at issue was presented by some to be one of life or death for thousands of people in Africa, no Member considered requesting a vote to accelerate the process.[36]

A more recent example concerns temporary preferences to Pakistan to help rebuilding the economy after the devastating floods in summer 2010. When the EU request to waive its most-favoured nation obligation under Article I:1 of the General Agreement on Tariffs and Trade (GATT) was presented to the WTO Council on Goods in December 2010, a number of WTO members expressed reservations, arguing that trade should not be used as a humanitarian policy tool. It cannot be excluded that behind this principled stance manifest commercial interests were hidden. In any case, the EU request was vetoed by at least three

[32] See in this respect the opinion of Advocate-General Kokott of 26 March 2009 in the case C-13/07, *Commission v Council* on the accession of Vietnam to the WTO. The opinion concluded that the former Art 133 EC did not cover the entire accession package of Vietnam. However, as the Lisbon Treaty extended the EU's powers on commercial policy, this opinion is not relevant anymore for current practice.

[33] ECJ *Opinion 1/94 WTO* [1994] ECR I-5267, para 21.

[34] Council decisions of 14 December 2011, [2012] OJ L57/1, 14, 43, and 53 respectively.

[35] General Council Decision of 30 August 2003, Implementation of para 6 of the Doha Declaration on the TRIPS Agreement and public health, WTO/L/540. For a succinct overview of the political battles surrounding this decision see F Abbott, 'The WTO Medicines Decision: World Pharmaceutical Trade and Public Health' (2005) 99 AJIL 317–358.

[36] C-D Ehlermann and L Ehring, 'Decision-Making in the World Trade Organization—Is the Consensus Practice of the World Trade Organization Adequate for Making, Revising and Implementing Rules on International Trade?' (2005) 8(1) *Journal of International Economic Law* 51–75, at 64.

WTO members during the entire year 2011. Only after a shift in the Indian position at the Council on Trade in Goods meeting in November 2011 and the submission of a second revised (slimmed down) request,[37] the relevant waiver was finally granted on 1 February 2012.[38] This can hardly be regarded as swift and effective help to counter a humanitarian urgency, as originally intended by the EU.

b) EU rules

To be fair, procedures within the EU to approve such waivers are not very expedient either. Unlike other WTO members, where the executive simply defines the national position, the EU position is found in collaboration between the Commission and the Council. Under Article 218(9) TFEU, any position to be adopted on the Union's behalf in a body set up by an agreement when that body is called upon to adopt acts having legal effects, with the exception of acts supplementing or amending the institutional framework of the agreement, had to be adopted by the Council upon a proposal from the Commission. The original version of this subparagraph in the Treaty of Amsterdam[39] was designed to safeguard the Council's legislative prerogatives for decisions taken by joint EU/treaty partner bodies established under bilateral Association Agreements.[40] Such secondary association law should be treated as a simplified international agreement, and since the Council had the right to decide on the conclusion of the original international agreement, by extension it was also given the right to decide on any derived law with legal effects on the Union. With the Treaty of Nice, the reference to Association Agreements was deleted in the text, and the Council henceforth had the right to define the EU position for all treaty bodies to which the EU was a party, provided that such body took a substantive decision with legally binding effect. The extension was probably designed to catch other bilateral agreements of the EU with third countries, such as the Partnership and Cooperation Agreements that the EU concluded with Eastern European and Central Asian States, without resorting to the legal basis of Article 310 EC (currently Article 217 TFEU). Against that background, EU practice with respect to waivers in the WTO did not change after 2000. As before, the Commission simply joined the relevant consensus in the WTO without formally resorting to the Council to that effect.

However, the text of Article 218(9) TFEU in its Nice version[41] did not contain any restriction on bilateral agreements, as under the Amsterdam Treaty. A strict reading thereof could therefore have led to the conclusion that decisions by the WTO General Council (a body set up by an agreement to which the EU is a party) which waive obligations of a member (hence producing legal effects) should be decided by the Council. After the entry into force of the Lisbon Treaty in December 2009, where Article 218(9) TFEU confirmed the broad Nice language, the Commission thus changed its practice on waivers. Starting with the Pakistan waiver request in December 2010, the Commission hitherto adopted proposals to the Council to define the relevant EU position on a given WTO waiver.[42] The Council has

[37] WTO Doc G/C/W/640/Rev. 2.

[38] <http://www.wto.org/english/news_e/news12_e/good_02feb12_e.htm>.

[39] Art 300(2), second subpara EC, in the version of the Treaty of Amsterdam 1997.

[40] Under Art 300(2) second subpara EC (1997) the Council had the right to define the EU position only for bodies established under agreements 'according to Article 310', ie the former treaty article relating to association agreements.

[41] Art 300(2), second subpara EC, Nice version.

[42] See eg the Commission proposal on a European Union position concerning the decision of the WTO General Council on the extension of the WTO waiver in order to implement the EU autonomous trade preferential regime for the Western Balkans, COM (2011) 716 final of 31 October 2011.

accepted this,[43] although at times it is only able to do so immediately before the WTO meeting. For example, when the text for the LDC waiver was stabilized in a special session of the Council for Trade in Services on 28 November 2011, very few days were left for the internal EU procedure. The EU position to join this waiver at the 8th WTO Ministerial Conference was defined by the Foreign Affairs Council on 14 December 2011,[44] ie one day before the Geneva Conference, upon a proposal from the Commission of 2 December.[45] According to Article 218(10) TFEU the Parliament was immediately informed thereafter.

This new practice is not without legal interest from a constitutional point of view as the precise substantive legal basis for such Council decisions needs to be identified. For example, in the LDC services waiver, Articles 91, 100 and 207(4), first subparagraph TFEU were cited, as the waiver concerned all services including transport services. This may constitute an important precedent for the view that under the Lisbon Treaty the EU is indeed competent to address all kinds of services by an EU-only decision, contradicting those who still derive a need to keep mixed decisions on services from Article 207(6) TFEU.[46]

Finally, it should be mentioned that parallel preparations are launched with Council and Parliament under the ordinary legislative procedure when a waiver directly concerns EU legislation. For example, the Commission proposal on the Pakistan preferences from October 2010[47] was substantially watered down by the European Parliament in its plenary meeting in May 2011: the duration of the waiver was shortened from two to one year and all leather products were eliminated from the proposal due to Pakistan's maintenance of export duties on raw leather. Hence, even after having completed the waiver process in Geneva in early 2012, the EU's measure will be quite different from the one originally presented.

2.4. Other secondary law

As has recently been observed,[48] the legal nature of other WTO secondary law is uncertain. Only a few bodies, in particular some of the Committees of the Agreements on Trade in Goods, as well as the Councils for Trade in Services and for TRIPs, are equipped, at least *prima facie*, with the power to produce decisions. Although the terminology 'decision' in contrast to 'recommendation' speaks in favour of assuming that such acts are binding on the Members,[49] the US-Poultry (China) Panel did not reach that conclusion with respect to decisions of the Sanitary and Phytosanitary (SPS) Committee.[50] Given that Article 12.1 of the SPS Agreement mandates the SPS Committee, not only to 'exercise the necessary functions for the implementation of the provisions of the present agreement and for the

[43] Council decision of 30 November 2011 on the position to be taken by the European Union within the General Council of the World Trade Organization on the extension of the WTO waiver in order to implement the EU autonomous preferential trade regime for the Western Balkans [2011] OJ L324/28.

[44] Council Press Release on the Foreign Affairs Council meeting of 14 December 2011 (Doc No 18685/11), p 8.

[45] See COM (2011) 871 final of 2 December 2011. Proposal for a Council Decision establishing the position to be taken by the European Union within the Ministerial Conference of the World Trade Organization (WTO) as regards a request for granting a waiver in order to give preferential treatment to services and service suppliers of Least-Developed Countries.

[46] See below on the future legal basis for a potential Doha agreement.

[47] COM (2010) 522 final of 7 October 2010. For more background see F Hoffmeister, 'The European Union's common commercial policy a year after Lisbon—Sea change or business as usual?' in P Koutrakos (ed), *The European Union's External Relations A Year After Lisbon*, CLEER working papers 2011/3, (TMC Asser Press, 2011), 83–95 (88).

[48] PJ Kuijper and F Hoffmeister, 'The impact of WTO law on the European Union' in RA Wessel and S Blockmans (eds), *The Influence of International Organizations on the European Union domestic legal order* (TMC Asser Press, 2012, forthcoming).

[49] PJ Kuijper, 'WTO Institutional Aspects' in D Bethlehem et al (eds), *The Oxford Handbook of International Trade Law* (OUP, 2009) 79–128. Contra P Holmes, 'The EU and the WTO: Some Constitutional Comparisons' in G de Búrca and J Scott, *The EU and the WTO: Legal and Constitutional Issues* (Hart Publishing, 2001), p 66: '[the] WTO cannot really make secondary law'.

[50] Panel Report, DS 392 US-Poultry (China), WT/DS 392/R, para 7.136.

realization of its objectives', but also to 'take its decisions by consensus', this view of the panel is not self-evident. Leaving aside this uncertainty about the legal effect of such decisions, the organization is often incapable of taking decisions at all because of the well-known and continuing practice of consensus. The consequence is that there is generally very limited 'true' WTO secondary law in existence.

If, nevertheless, such WTO secondary law comes into being, there is no particular challenge from an EU perspective. Hortatory soft law does not have to be formally accepted and is simply incorporated in administrative practice, if deemed useful.[51]

2.5. Judicial decisions

In sharp contrast to the above-mentioned decision-making procedures, the judicial branch of the WTO is characterized by reverse consensus laid down in the Rules and Procedures Governing the Settlement of Disputes.This means that reports of a panel or the appellate body are regularly adopted by the Dispute Settlement Body, unless there is consensus not to adopt them. As the winning party (be it the complainant or the defendant) always participates in the Dispute Settlement Body (DSB) meeting, such negative consensus has never occurred in practice. Judicial decisions in the WTO are hence quasi-automatically adopted by a political body. This can be seen as one of the real strengths of the WTO, which makes it particularly attractive as a forum to settle disputes. From its inception in 1995, the dispute settlement system has thus been confronted with over 450 cases, out of which roughly one-third are decided by a final judicial decision.

From an EU perspective this system does not pose particular legal challenges. For a long time the ECJ has accepted that the EU can submit itself to binding dispute settlement procedures. This entails, of course, also a duty to abide by decisions in which the EU loses. Politically, it is thus all the more important to be able to have sufficient influence on the composition of the dispute settlement bodies. For the appellate body, the EU and the US traditionally support a candidate of the other side, selected from a list of two potential candidates.[52] At panel stage however, an EU official is almost never selected as a panellist for disputes between other trading nations. One reason for this was the EU's constant intervention as third party in any other dispute with a view to influence the evolving jurisprudence. While the know-how of EU officials is certainly no less impressive than that of a nominee from other WTO members, there is no good reason why the New Zealand WTO ambassador or a Swiss expert can sit on the bench for cases involving the EU, while the EU ambassador or an EU expert is never asked to do the same in cases involving New Zealand or Switzerland.

Finally, it is worth recalling that the decision to launch a case before a WTO Panel or to bring an appeal before the appellate body within the EU is a prerogative of the Commission. This situation has not been changed by the Lisbon Treaty. While the Parliament and the Council became the joint legislator in the Common Commercial Policy, they are nevertheless not empowered to take administrative decisions. Rather, under Article 207(2) TFEU, their task is confined to adopting *framework regulations*. Hence, when the existing basic regulations on importation,[53] exports,[54] anti-dumping,[55] anti-subsidies,[56] and trade barriers in third countries[57] will have to be updated, the Parliament will indeed become the

[51] See the examples given by Kuijper and Hoffmeister, n 48, in the field of anti-dumping.

[52] From the inception, the EU thus always had a judge on the appellate body's bench, namely Claus-Dieter Ehlermann (Germany), Giorgio Sacerdoti (Italy) and Peter Van den Bossche (Belgium).

[53] Reg 260/2009 [2009] OJ L84/1.

[54] Reg 1061/2009 [2009] OJ L291/1.

[55] Reg 1225/2009 [2009] OJ L343/51.

[56] Reg 597/2009 [2009] OJ L188/93.

[57] Reg 3286/1994 [1994] OJ 349/71.

co-legislator, together with the Council.[58] However, individual decisions to launch a WTO case are not legislative in nature. They neither define the framework of EU action, nor do they require the legal form of a Regulation. Accordingly, the view that under the Lisbon Treaty the European Parliament should be involved in launching WTO cases against third countries[59] does not withstand closer scrutiny. This is confirmed by post-Lisbon practice, where the Commission continued to launch on its own new WTO cases against the United States,[60] China,[61] and Canada[62] under Article 17(1) TEU.

2.6. New agreements

a) WTO rules

Finally, a brief word on the negotiation method of the so-called WTO 'rounds'. So far, such rounds were always based on a political mandate agreed between the GATT Contracting Parties before 1995 and between WTO members thereafter. Such mandates famously contained the 'single undertaking', according to which all members had to accept the entire negotiation package, except for very few areas (the plurilateral agreements). The negotiation dynamics in earlier days was essentially bipolar: when the US and the EU were able to agree on tariff reductions, most others would profit from those additional openings through the most-favoured nation principle, while themselves not pressured to lower their own tariffs drastically. While this logic still functioned in the Uruguay Round (which received its decisive push from the Blairhouse Agreement between the US and the EU in 1992), the situation has become considerably more complex today. After the launch of the broad Doha Development Agenda in 2001, there were at least four protagonists, namely the EU, the US, India and Brazil. The latter claimed to represent, inter alia, the interests of the developing world. Later on, roughly starting from 2006, China joined this club and the G4 grew to G5. Moreover, Japan and Canada still considered themselves important players (G7), let alone Australia, South Africa and representatives for the least developed countries and the African Caribbean and Pacific countries (ACP) countries (G11). This complex cluster has created entirely different negotiation dynamics and often leads to 'negotiations about negotiations', ie discussions about the proper forum to pursue certain issues on the negotiation table.

b) EU rules

Inside the EU, a possible agreement on the DDA would have to be concluded by the Council upon a proposal from the Commission as the negotiator (Article 218(3) TFEU). In addition, the European Parliament would have to give its consent to the agreement under Article 218 (6) TFEU, as trade policy falls into ordinary legislation under the Lisbon Treaty.[63] Moreover, next to the Trade Policy Committee (the trade body assembling the Director-Generals of Trade from the Member States), the Parliament is to be fully and immediately informed

[58] T Müller-Ibold, 'Die gemeinsame Handelspolitik nach Lissabon—Sekundärrechtsabhängigkeit der gemeinsamen Handelspolitik' in M Bungenberg and C Hermann (eds), *Die gemeinsame Handelspolitik der Europäischen Union nach Lissabon* (Nomos Verlag, 2011), pp 75–93 (86).

[59] A Serdarcevic, *The European Union as a collective actor in the WTO*, PhD thesis, Vrije Universiteit of Brussels (unpublished manuscript of November 2011), p 274.

[60] DS424 *United States—Anti-Dumping Measures on Imports of Stainless Steel Sheet and Strip in Coils from Italy*. This case was soon settled with the US who acknowledged the obvious calculation error in that measure.

[61] DS407 *China—Provisional Anti-Dumping Duties on Certain Iron and Steel Fasteners from the European Union* (this case was discontinued after consultations); DS425 *China—Definitive Anti-Dumping Duties on x-ray security inspection equipment from the European Union* (the case is pending).

[62] DS426 *Canada—Measures Relating to the Feed-in Tariff Program*.

[63] On the scope of this new European Parliament power see M Krajewski, 'Die neue handelspolitische Bedeutung des Europäischen Parlaments' in Bungenberg and Hermann (eds), *Die gemeinsame Handelspolitik der Europäischen Union nach Lissabon* (Nomos Verlag, 2011), pp 55–74 (63–64).

about the progress in the negotiations. In practice, and in line with the 2010 framework agreement between the Commission and the Parliament,[64] the Commission accepts observer delegations from the Parliament for the relevant negotiations. For example, during the 8th Ministerial Conference, a delegation of six MEPs from the European Parliament Committee on International Trade was present in Geneva and regularly briefed by the Commissioner on Trade and his staff. Through meeting parliamentarians of other WTO members in informal or formal settings[65] they might also have revitalized the somewhat dormant parliamentary dimension of the WTO itself.

Whether or not the EU Member States would become a party to a Doha agreement as well is an open question. In contrast to the pre-Lisbon situation where the ECJ explicitly found that the competence on three of four modes of services under the GATS and on trade-related aspects of intellectual property rights is shared,[66] the post-Lisbon treaty has integrated these fields into the EU's exclusive competence. Hence, with the potential exception of transport services, all current topics dealt with in the Doha round are *a priori* covered by Article 207 TFEU.[67] Only when the Doha package would contain new rules on criminal sanctions for intellectual property rights in the TRIPS could there be room to discuss whether such rules go beyond the EU's trade competence, given that Article 207(1) TFEU refers to the 'commercial aspects' of intellectual property rights only, thus excluding criminal sanctions. However, even under this scenario, any such new WTO rule could still come under EU competence when the Council decides to exercise the EU's shared competence under Article 83(2) TFEU. Finally, the point has been made that any new Doha rule on health, education or cultural services would trigger mixity, as such services would be excluded from the EU's external competence under Article 207(6) second alternative TFEU.[68] This is not convincing. The intention of the Lisbon Treaty was exactly to do away with the cumbersome division of powers in the area of services. In contrast to the Nice version of the Treaty, the new Article 207(6) TFEU does not call explicitly for mixed agreements in the said services areas, but says instead that the '*exercise* of the competence conferred by this Article' shall not lead to harmonization. This can only mean that the EU has the full competence in the field of services, as has recently again be confirmed by the Council decision on the LDC services waiver. Article 207(6) TFEU thus only calls upon the negotiator to refrain from agreeing to a Doha rule which would lead to *harmonization* of health, culture and educational services at international level,[69] which is at any rate a rather long-term perspective.

Hence, many arguments favour the thesis that the Doha package can be concluded as an EU-only agreement. From a Member State perspective, not being a party to the Doha agreement would not pose any insurmountable legal problem, as their membership status in the WTO itself would remain intact.[70]

[64] [2010] OJ L304/47.

[65] The European Parliament and the Inter-Parliamentary Union have together organized a 'Parliamentary Conference on the WTO' with standing rules of procedure adopted in 2004. Those rules foresee that the Conference should meet at least once a year, but no such meetings were held in 2007, 2009 and 2010. The last Conference took place in March 2011 at the premises of the WTO, Geneva (see H Rommetvedt, 'The institutionalization of a *parliamentary* dimension of an inter*governmental* organization: the WTO' (2011) 10:4 *World Trade Review* 423–446 (438–439)).

[66] ECJ, Opinion 1/94 *WTO* [1994] ECR I-5267.

[67] Hahn, n 7, p 23.

[68] For this thesis see W Weiss, 'Unionale Handelspolitik im Europäischen Verfassungsverbund: Aussenhandelskompetenz und die Lissabon-Entscheidung des Bundesverfassungsgerichts' in M Bungenberg and C Hermann (eds), *Die gemeinsame Handelspolitik der Europäischen Union nach Lissabon* (Nomos Verlag, 2011), pp 35–51 (39–45).

[69] C Herrmann, Die Zukunft der mitgliedstaatlichen Investitionspolitik nach dem Vertrag von Lissabon' (2010) EuZW 207 (2010).

[70] Note that the German Constitutional Court regarded Germany's membership of the WTO as an essential feature of the 'identity clause' in Art 79(3) of the German Basic Law. It therefore found that the German constitution would not authorize further integration steps under the European Treaties which would question that status (BVerfGE 123, 267, at pp 418–420). For a critical analysis of this finding see R Raith, 'The Common

3. Governance Structures in the G20

3.1. Structure of G20

The G20 is a relatively new forum for international economic governance. Originally, it was a group of twenty finance ministers and central bank governors meeting since 1999 to bring together important economies from both the industrialized and the developing world to discuss key issues of global finance. In 2008, at the height of the first financial crisis, the G20 gathered for the first time also the leaders of the G8 countries, enlarged by emerging economies such as China, India, Brazil and representatives of international economic organizations. The G20 does not work on the basis of a constituent instrument, it has no secretariat and there is no formalized voting mechanism.[71] Rather, its work is coordinated by the members themselves, who entrust the preparations of respective meetings to a Presidency which is rotating each half year. The Presidency sets the agenda and convenes preparatory meetings at different levels. For the summits, the political advisors of the heads of state and governments ('Sherpas') act as preparatory body.

3.2. G20 summit statements on trade

Starting with the Washington summit of November 2008, the G20 included trade matters in its deliberations. Combating a general fear that a protectionist spiral could be set in motion, the heads of states pledged not to adopt WTO-inconsistent measures to overcome the crisis. This important commitment was solemnly repeated at the next summit in spring 2009 in London. Gathering in Pittsburgh in September 2009, the leaders also gave specific directions for the Doha Development Agenda in order to 'bridge the gaps'. In particular, they asked their ministers to seek progress by early 2010 on agriculture, non-agricultural market access (NAMA), services, rules, trade facilitation and all other remaining issues.[72] In Toronto (June 2010) the leaders tasked the WTO, the Organization for Economic Cooperation and Development (OECD) and the United Nations Conference on Trade and Development (UNCTAD) to prepare joint reports on their commitment to refrain from raising trade barriers, and repeated language at the Doha round stressed the importance of aid for trade.[73] Moreover, the Seoul Declaration from November 2010 contained a commitment to bring the Doha round to conclusion, as 2011 would be a 'critical window of opportunity'. In particular, the leaders expressed their common belief that they 'now need to complete the end game'.[74]

Drawing on this language, the EU started a diplomatic initiative in early 2011. Following a G7 ministerial gathering in the margins of the World Economic Forum at Davos in late January, the EU made a proposal in May 2010 on three sectoral agreements in the 'NAMA' basket of Doha (machinery, electronics and chemicals). While the EU had asked the emerging countries to lower their tariffs in addition to the cuts foreseen by the Swiss formula—although not as much as the EU and the US—the United States insisted on full equal treatment of all partners. However, such a proposition was not acceptable to any of the other partners. Hence, when the G20 leaders met in November 2011, the optimism of Doha had faded away, and some members were even tempted to declare the Doha round 'dead'. Moreover, British Prime Minister Cameron was tasked to present a report on economic

Commercial Policy and the Lisbon Judgment of the German Constitutional Court' (2009) *Zeitschrift für Europarechtliche Studien* 12, 613 (614 et seq).

[71] B Van Vooren, 'The EU as a global Robin Hood: Proposal for a multilateral convention on a global financial transaction tax' CLEER working papers 2011/4, p 18.

[72] G20 Pittsburgh summit declaration of 24–25 September 2009, paras 48 and 49.

[73] G20 Toronto summit declaration of 26–27 June 2010, paras 35–39.

[74] G20 Seoul summit declaration, para 9.

governance, which also could have contained critical language on Doha. In this situation, following a suggestion from the Trade Commissioner, the EU Commission President's Sherpa, Cabral, took the initiative. Drawing from the EU position as expressed at the Foreign Affairs Council (trade configuration) in mid-October, he reminded his Sherpa colleagues about the need not to unravel the Doha package. Rather, it would be important to build on the progress achieved so far, and find topics for a broader WTO agenda. Such issues, for example, energy, climate change, competition and investment, should not become part of the Doha negotiating mandate, but could usefully be explored by WTO members in 2012. While this initiative caused at first some irritation to WTO ambassadors in Geneva of certain G20 members, as it did not contain the usual diplomatic caveats for developing countries, it nevertheless served the important purpose to streamline the position of EU Sherpas in the meeting, and to impress the non-EU Sherpas as a well-thought through contribution. At the summit itself, the leaders did not discuss trade issues in depth and agreed on the compromise language cited in the introduction.

4. Institutional Reform Issues

Under Article 3(5) TEU, the European Union is to contribute to the strict observance and the development of international law. From the first part ('strict observance') the European Court of Justice recently deduced that the Union has to abide by international customary law when it adopts internal acts.[75] Less clear, however, is how strongly the second part ('contribute to the development of international law') influences the reform agenda of the European Union. In the trade field, the EU's political institutions generally follow a cautious approach towards the WTO and G20. Rather than simply transposing the EU's own image onto the international scene and trying to build strong institutions everywhere, the EU would argue for a more 'effective' multilateral system. This notion allows a more tailor-made approach, duly taking account of the EU's commercial (self-) interests and its political (altruistic) interest in striving for a fair and free world trade order for all. Against this backdrop, we can identify at least three fundamental issues for possible reforms in the WTO and the G20.

4.1. Decision-making method

First, there is the well-known tension between consensus and majority voting. Much can be said in favour of the first method. Decisions taken by consensus have high legitimacy and enjoy better chances of implementation. Moreover, they avoid diplomatic frictions and the risk of marginalization. Sometimes, high majorities are difficult to find in the meeting room or by postal ballots, and consensus may thus add to expediency. At the same time, consensus has number of drawbacks. It gives a veto right to any player, who can use it for non-trade related issues, as demonstrated with the examples of certain accessions and waiver decisions in the WTO. Consensus slows down the process when swift action might be warranted. And finally, it may lead to a deadlock or even paralysis, where simply no progress is possible at all.

Would it therefore make sense to give more weight to majority voting in the future? After all, such decisions are also legitimate since the concerned states have agreed in advance to such a method of decision-making. What is more, the judicial decisions from the WTO demonstrate that even those who are outvoted in a given case might still have a systemic interest to implement such decisions as they might stand on the other side of the fence in the next case. They thus have an interest that majority decisions are enforced as a matter of principle to ensure the efficiency of the system as such. Moreover, the under-use of the

[75] Case C-366/10 *Air Transport Association of America (ATAA)*, ECJ, Judgment of 21 December 2011, para 101.

political decision-making mechanisms results into an ever stronger dispute settlement system, which is in the long run unhealthy for the WTO as a whole.[76] All this speaks in favour of making the 'shadow of voting' more visible in the WTO,[77] in particular with respect to accessions, waivers or amendments. As can be seen from the 2011 Russian accession experience, a 'threat' to resort to voting might even be stronger than its actual implementation, where uncertainties on the outcome of such a vote do always exist.

These considerations are not relevant for political directions taken at G20 summit level or discussed by WTO trade ministers with respect to new agreements. Here, consensus remains an essential element of decision-making, as there is no legal basis to make a country accept a proposal against its will. The only remedy to overcome blockages in these *fora* might be to restrict the participants of the round. This might be a temporary solution to bring forward certain dossiers in which not all WTO or G20 members have sufficient interest. In the long run, 'going plurilateral' cannot, however, provide a proper institutional solution for global trade governance.

4.2. Decision-making level

Second, there is a certain tension between decision-making at head of state and government level at the G20, and ministerial and ambassadorial level in the WTO. G20 summit declarations may spread some imperial glamour, but their practical effect is limited in the absence of a proper monitoring system, let aside an implementation machinery. For example, when the relevant monitoring report from the WTO, the OECD and UNCTAD found that certain measures violated the pledge not to introduce protectionist measures, no real follow-up could be observed except some public naming and shaming. Moreover, from an EU point of view, speaking with one voice is easier at ministerial level through the EU Commissioner for Trade rather than at G20 level, where the EU Commission President is surrounded by the heads of states and governments of a number of EU Member States, speaking in their national capacity.

Accordingly, there are good reasons *not* to call upon the G20 to turn itself into a new forum for world trade governance.[78] Rather, the existing mechanisms of the WTO—robust monitoring, an experienced forum for negotiations and effective dispute settlement—must remain at the centre stage. In all likelihood the WTO itself must realize that only by strengthening its institutional capacities further will it bring home this point. When a G20 pledge to refrain from trade-restrictive measures is ineffective, WTO members may enforce it by resorting more often to the binding WTO dispute settlement system. Markets will likely remain open only if measures to close them do not remain unsanctioned.

4.3. Relevant decision-makers

Third, the politically very sensitive question arises of which countries should be regarded as 'relevant' decision-makers on global trade matters and thus be included in different configurations of decision-making. Of course, a rough estimate can be made by resorting to the respective trade volumes of each trading nation. However, this cannot solve the underlying problem of representativeness, especially when a trading round is said to serve the developing countries. Here, neither the WTO nor the G20 seem to have found stable configurations that are both representative and efficient. Leadership from the WTO Director-General or

[76] L Bartels, 'The Separation of Powers in the WTO: How to Avoid Judicial Activism' (2004) 53 *International Comparative Law Quarterly* 861, 866.

[77] Ehlermann and Ehring, n 36, p 72.

[78] For a proposal to that effect see J Vestergaard, 'The G20 and Beyond: Towards Effective Global Economic Governance' *DIIS Report 2011:4* (Danish Institute for International Studies).

some key WTO members might thus be required to establish a relevant circle of decision-makers which could make first progress *inter se* and convince the larger membership. Such a steering group could also save time which is otherwise lost in rather useless negotiations about negotiations and probably tackle the key question of the Doha round: 'what constitutes a fair distribution of rights and obligations within the trading system, among Members with different levels of development'.[79]

5. Conclusion

In conclusion, the institutional architecture of the global trading system can be said to work sufficiently, but certainly not splendidly. The consensus principle has produced some important substantive results under the auspices of the WTO, but its limits could also be felt on a number of occasions. As the G20 is built on the very same principle, it cannot provide for a solution either—on the contrary, the relevant commitments at the G20 have proven to be relatively useless as the G20 is lacking a proper machinery of compliance control. The most promising avenue to overcome probable blockages thus seems to be to identify a steering group of relevant trading nations, who could provide for guidance in WTO negotiations. At the same time, WTO members should be prepared to use the existing majority voting systems for issues such as accessions, waivers or amendments, if blockages for non-trade-related issues cannot otherwise be prevented.

Being endowed with a constitutional objective to contribute to the development of international law in general and to strive for 'free and fair' trade in particular, the European Union tries to take up these reform challenges. In the current discussions on the future of world trade, the EU presented a non-paper in advance of the G20 meeting of trade and economic ministers in Mexico in April 2012. It argued for the strengthening of the monitoring system on newly introduced protectionist measures, reaffirmed the narrative on the benefits of free trade, and proposed to enlarge the trade agenda with 'new topics', such as trade and climate protection, trade and investment or trade and currency rates. Moreover, world trade governance rules in the WTO should be revisited. Whether this new initiative will fall on fertile ground with the other G20 members—and the larger WTO membership—remains to be seen.

Inside the EU, it has been shown that the Commission most of the time plays the leading role, while the Council and the Parliament are involved for the concluding amendments or new agreements. Under the Lisbon Treaty, however, there is also the new practice to adopt EU positions for WTO waivers by the Council upon a proposal from the Commission. In return, Parliament is stepping up its presence during negotiations through presence of International Trade (INTA) committee members. When compared to Geneva, the institutional house in Brussels thus seems to be in relatively good order.

[79] See report of WTO Director-General Lamy to the 8th Ministerial Conference, WT/MIN(11)/5, p 2.

10

Expanding the Internal Market: An External Regulatory Policy for the EU?

Marise Cremona

1. Introduction

Within the internal market, market integration in the sense of creating the 'area without internal frontiers' within which the fundamental freedoms are enjoyed has implied both negative and positive integration, both liberalization and regulatory measures as a basis for market access. By 'regulatory measures' in this context we might include all measures which impact on the state's autonomy in adopting and setting regulatory standards, including mutual recognition of conformity assessment ('home country control'), controls over the introduction of new regulations, and harmonization—whether minimum or complete.

The Common Commercial Policy (CCP), while asserting liberalization as a primary objective (Article 206 of the Treaty on the Functioning of the European Union (TFEU)), has no corresponding explicit regulatory dimension. Nevertheless, the uniform principles which it mandates (Article 207(1) TFEU), together with powers derived from the internal market provisions, have provided a basis for the development of an external regulatory policy through both autonomous measures and the conclusion of international agreements. In a recent policy document the Commission recognizes the need to 'examine how to strengthen the mutual links between internal and external regulatory actions and to explore how to improve coordination between the two'.[1] This chapter will attempt to outline the components of this external regulatory policy: (i) the basis and scope of EU external regulatory competence, and (ii) the EU's objectives in developing an external regulatory policy. It will (iii) take as an example the Anti-Counterfeiting Trade Agreement (ACTA) with a view to examining the part played in the shaping of EU external regulatory policy by a plurilateral/multilateral agreement which is designed to contribute to the governance of trade, and the way in which the interaction between the EU's internal and external regulatory policy affects the EU's policy choices in contributing to global governance.

2. The Basis and Scope of EU External Regulatory Competence

The original CCP as it appeared in the Treaty of Rome covered only goods. It was not clear from its wording whether only issues of market access, or also regulatory policy such as technical regulations and standards were included in this competence. However the Tokyo Round Agreements of 1979 were concluded by the European Economic Community (EEC) under CCP powers,[2] and legislation was adopted based on the old Article 113 EEC regarding the application of technical regulations and standards to third country goods.[3]

[1] COM (2010) 612 on 'trade policy as a core component of the EU's 2020 strategy', 9 November 2010, p 7.

[2] Council Decision 80/271/EEC of 10 December 1979 concerning the conclusion of the Multilateral Agreements resulting from the 1973 to 1979 trade negotiations [1980] OJ L71/1.

[3] Council Decision 80/45/EEC of 15 January 1980 laying down provisions on the introduction and implementation of technical regulations and standards [1980] OJ L14/36. The decision is still in force. Where standards have not been harmonized at Union level, Member States are to apply national standards on a national treatment basis; harmonized standards of course apply equally to goods of non-EU origin, however where the EU establishes only minimum harmonization, direct imports from third countries will be subject to the relevant national regulations

In *Opinion 1/94* the European Court of Justice (ECJ) dismissed an argument that the Technical Barriers to Trade (TBT) and Sanitary and Phytosanitary Measures (SPS) agreements fell outside the scope of (then) Article 113 EC.[4] The fact that the implementation of the SPS Agreement may require internal measures to be adopted on the basis of agricultural policy powers did not prevent the international commitments from being based on CCP powers.[5] As regards the TBT Agreement the Dutch government had argued that, since harmonization of technical standards was incomplete, Member States retained competence in the field. The court held that since the TBT Agreement was designed to ensure that technical regulations and standards and conformity assessment procedures do not create unnecessary obstacles to international trade, it fell within the scope of the CCP.[6] So, in so far as regulatory measures are directly concerned with trade, in the sense of promoting, facilitating or governing trade, they may be adopted on the basis of the CCP.[7] However, the fact that goods or services of third country origin are covered by an EU regulatory provision does not *require* the use of Article 207 TFEU, or prevent that measure from being adopted on an internal market legal basis. Thus, to take the example of tobacco control (an issue where there has been an attempt at regulation through international agreement as well as internally in the EU): Directive 2001/37 on the production, marketing and labelling of tobacco products was based on Articles 114 and 207 TFEU (ex-Articles 95 and 133 EC).[8] Its predecessors were based on an internal market legal basis alone but since Directive 2001/37 also covered tobacco products to be exported from the EU, it was decided to add a trade legal basis.[9] The court however took the view that this additional trade legal basis was unnecessary, since although certain provisions did affect exports to third countries, the main objective was the protection of the internal market from illegal re-imports.[10] In contrast, the WHO Convention on Tobacco Control was concluded by the Community (now Union) on the joint legal bases of Articles 114, 207 and 168 TFEU (ex-Articles 95, 133 and 152 EC).[11] It contains provisions on trade in tobacco products.[12]

With the amendments made to Article 207 TFEU by the Lisbon Treaty, this provision may now form the basis for external regulatory measures concerning services, 'commercial aspects' of intellectual property rights (IPR) and foreign direct investment (FDI), which includes aspects of establishment and capital movements.[13] However, some uncertainty

which may go beyond the minimum: the right of market access on the basis of the EU minimum standards is applicable only to third country goods already in free circulation in the EU.

[4] Opinion 1/94 [1994] ECR I-5267.

[5] Ibid, para 29.

[6] Ibid, para 33.

[7] eg Council Reg 1383/2003/EC of 22 July 2003 concerning customs action against goods suspected of infringing certain intellectual property rights and the measures to be taken against goods found to have infringed such rights [2003] OJ L196/7. In *Kadi*, the court held that a measure falls within the CCP 'only if it relates specifically to international trade in that it is essentially intended to promote, facilitate or govern trade and has direct and immediate effects on trade in the products concerned': Case C-402/05 P *Kadi v Council and Commission* [2008] ECR I-06351, para 183.

[8] Directive 2001/37/EC of the European Parliament and of the Council of 5 June 2001 on the approximation of the laws, regulations and administrative provisions of the Member States concerning the manufacture, presentation and sale of tobacco products [2001] OJ L194/26.

[9] See Directive 2001/37, recital 11, and Art 3 which sets maximum tar, carbon monoxide and nicotine yields for all cigarettes manufactured in the EU, whatever their destination.

[10] Case C-491/01 *R v Secretary of State for Health ex parte: British American Tobacco (Investments) Ltd and Imperial Tobacco Ltd* [2002] ECR I-11550, paras 81–97. The court went on to find, however, that since the co-decision procedure had in fact been used to adopt the directive, the addition of Art 133 EC as a legal basis had not vitiated the procedure nor invalidated the directive.

[11] Council Decision 2004/513/EC of 2 June 2004 concerning the conclusion of the WHO Framework Convention on Tobacco Control [2004] OJ L213/8. All EU Member States are also parties.

[12] WHO Framework Convention on Tobacco Control, Art 15 on illicit trade in tobacco products.

[13] Art 207(1) TFEU. For a discussion of the precise scope of the CCP since the Lisbon Treaty, see P-C Müller-Graff, 'The Common Commercial Policy enhanced by the Reform Treaty of Lisbon?' in A Dashwood and M Maresceau (eds), *Law and Practice of EU External Relations—Salient Features of a Changing Landscape*

remains about the precise boundary between Article 207 and other 'internal' legal bases for regulatory measures. Although it is clear that Article 207 covers both international agreements and autonomous measures concerned with liberalization of imports, exports, and trade protection, it is not so clear to what extent it would cover regulations applied to third country service providers or companies wishing to establish themselves in the EU.

From the case-law on goods it would seem that international agreements fall within Article 207 where they concern the 'development, adoption and enforcement' of standards, so as to avoid 'unnecessary obstacles to international trade'.[14] The court, by saying in Opinion 1/94 that the TBT and SPS Agreements were 'confined to' these issues, suggested that agreements which included substantive harmonization of standards could not be concluded on the basis of Article 207 alone, but would require an internal market legal basis as well. Indeed, the WHO Convention on Tobacco Control, which does establish some harmonized rules (inter alia) on the packaging and labelling of tobacco, was based also on Article 114 TFEU. However, we should note the stipulation in Article 207(6) that the exercise of the competence conferred by Article 207 'shall not lead to harmonization of legislative or regulatory provisions of the Member States in so far as the Treaties exclude such harmonization'. *A contrario*, it would appear that in so far as the Treaties do *not* exclude such harmonization, Article 207 can be used as a basis for external measures involving harmonization, and this would apply to services, IPR and FDI as well as goods. However, other legal bases may be used alongside Article 207; the decision on the signature of the FTA with South Korea, for example, is based on CCP powers, alongside legal bases for transport (excluded from Article 207) and culture.[15] The use of the latter is significant since it emphasizes the shared nature of this competence despite the inclusion of trade in cultural services within Article 207 TFEU (and indeed the FTA is a mixed agreement).

As far as autonomous measures are concerned, where imports or exports of goods from or to third countries, or services offered by external providers, are only affected incidentally, an internal legal basis alone is used. So, for example, Regulation 1007/2009 on trade in seal products is based on Article 95 EC (now Article 114 TFEU) alone and is framed as essentially an internal market measure, applying to seal products imported from third countries '[i]n order to ensure that the harmonized rules provided for in this Regulation are fully effective'.[16] The consolidated banking directive is based on Article 53 TFEU (ex-Article 47 EC) and contains a Title on relations with third countries including provisions relating to the establishment of third country banks in the EU and providing a legal basis for possible agreements with third countries on both authorization and consolidated supervision of credit institutions.[17] On the other hand, where the predominant purpose of

(CUP, 2008); F Van den Berghe, 'The EC's Common Commercial Policy Revisited: What does Lisbon Add?' (2009) 4 *Global Trade and Customs Journal* 275; M Krajewski, 'The Reform of the Common Commercial Policy' in A Biondi, P Eeckhout and S Ripley (eds), *EU Law After Lisbon* (OUP, 2011); Y Devuyst, 'The European Union's Competence in International Trade After the Treaty of Lisbon' (2011) 39 *Georgia Journal of International and Comparative Law* 639.

[14] Opinion 1/94, n 4.

[15] Council Decision 2011/265/EU of 16 September 2010 on the signing, on behalf of the European Union, and provisional application of the Free Trade Agreement between the European Union and its Member States, of the one part, and the Republic of Korea, of the other part [2011] OJ L 127/1. It is based on Arts 91, 100(2), 167(3) and 207 TFEU (transport, culture and CCP legal bases).

[16] Reg 1007/2009/EC of the European Parliament and of the Council of 16 September 2009 on trade in seal products [2009] OJ 6 L286/3, recital 13.

[17] Directive 2006/48/EC of the European Parliament and of the Council of 14 June 2006 relating to the taking up and pursuit of the business of credit institutions [2006] OJ L177/1, Title IV, Arts 38–39. The directive proposed to replace Directive 2006/48 will also be based on Art 53 TFEU: COM (2011) 453 final; for the provisions on relations with third countries see Title VI, Arts 47–48. Other recent legislation regulating the financial services sector and adopted on internal market legal bases also covers institutions established in third countries and offering services in the EU: eg Reg 513/2011/EU of the European Parliament and of the Council of 11 May 2011 on credit rating agencies [2011] OJ L145/30; Proposal for a Directive of the European Parliament and of the Council on markets in financial instruments, COM (2011) 656 final, Arts 41–50.

the measure is the regulation of (for example) the post-establishment treatment of third country service providers, it could be argued that Article 207 would be the appropriate legal basis, either alone or (perhaps more likely) together with an internal legal basis such as Article 53 or 114 TFEU. However, such practice as there is since the Treaty of Lisbon rather suggests that internal legal bases are used alone also in these cases.[18]

The competence picture is more fragmented even than would appear from this discussion. First, many aspects of regulatory policy are clearly excluded from Article 207 and must find their legal bases elsewhere in the Treaties: transport by virtue of Article 207(5),[19] competition policy, recognition of qualifications, employment and social policy, environmental protection. As the experience of trade and environment legal basis disputes shows, it is not always easy to decide whether a measure is predominantly trade, or predominantly concerned with (for example) environmental or social policy—or both equally.[20]

Second, we have already noted one of the exclusionary clauses of Article 207(6), that relating to harmonization. There is also the further provision in Article 207(6), that the exercise of powers conferred by Article 207 'shall not affect the delimitation of competences between the Union and the Member States'. What exactly does this mean? Since the exclusivity of the CCP is now treaty-based (Article 3(1) TFEU) it cannot refer to that aspect of the delimitation of competences. Piris argues that it means that the scope of Article 207 cannot be interpreted so as to extend EU external powers beyond the scope of internal powers granted elsewhere in Treaty, thereby excluding (for example) expropriation from CCP FDI powers, as a result of Article 345 TFEU, or limiting CCP powers in certain service sectors such as health where internal powers are only supporting or coordinating.[21]

Gosalbo Bono, on the other hand, suggests that such an interpretation would render the prohibition on harmonization in the same paragraph redundant.[22] He also argues that this reading would conflict with Article 207(4)(b) since Article 207 does here grant an external competence beyond that which is given internally, ie to conclude agreements which may affect the responsibility of Member States to deliver health services.[23] The sentence in Article 207(6) may thus more feasibly be intended to preclude the extension of internal powers as a result of the exercise of external powers under Article 207, and also to prevent a 'reverse AETR effect' ie to prevent the operation of pre-emption internally as a result of external EU action.[24] As Gosalbo Bono points out, the provision thus does not affect the existence of EU competence under the CCP but rather the consequence of its exercise.[25] This is important, since the exclusivity attached to Article 207 is not based on pre-emption (the existence of

[18] See eg Council Decision 2011/467/EU of 19 July 2011 on the position to be taken by the European Union within the EU–Swiss Joint Committee established by Art 14 of the Agreement between the European Community and its Member States, of the one part, and the Swiss Confederation, of the other, on the free movement of persons, as regards the replacement of Annex III (Mutual recognition of professional qualifications) thereto [2011] OJ L195/7. The substantive legal bases for the Decision are Arts 46, 53 and 62 TFEU.

[19] See eg Proposal for a Council Decision on the conclusion of a Memorandum of Cooperation between the EU and the International Civil Aviation Organization, COM (2011) 107 final, which has Art 100 TFEU as its substantive legal basis. So too does Decision 2011/181/EU of the Council and of the Representatives of the Governments of the Member States meeting within the Council on the signature and provisional application of the Euro Mediterranean Aviation Agreement between the EU and its Member States and The Hashemite Kingdom of Jordan [2011] OJ L79/1.

[20] Opinion 2/2000 [2001] ECR I-9713; C-281/01 *Commission v Council* [2002] ECR I-12049; C-178/03 *Commission v Parliament and Council* [2006] ECR I-107; C-411/06 *Commission v European Parliament and Council* [2009] ECR I-7585. On trade and environment, see further the chapter by Marín Durán in this volume.

[21] J-C Piris, *The Lisbon Treaty: A Legal and Political Analysis* (CUP, 2010), pp 282–283.

[22] R Gosalbo Bono, 'The Organization of the External Relations of the European Union in the Treaty of Lisbon' in P Koutrakos (ed), *The European Union's external relations a year after Lisbon*, CLEER Working Paper 2011/3.

[23] cf Art 168(7) TFEU.

[24] J Wouters, D Coppens and B De Meester, 'The European Union's External Relations after the Lisbon Treaty', in S Griller and J Ziller (eds), *The Lisbon Treaty—EU Constitutionalism without a Constitutional Treaty?* (Springer, 2008), p 143.

[25] R Gosalbo Bono, n 22, p 17.

internal legislation) but operates *a priori* from the Treaty itself.[26] Article 207(6) thus confirms that although exclusive competence over the CCP now extends into fields (such as IPR) not entirely covered by internal EU rules, and although the CCP is based on uniform principles (Article 207(1) TFEU), Article 207 does not require the EU to adopt uniform rules over all fields covered by the CCP regardless of whether internal rules have yet been adopted.[27] Nor does the conclusion of an agreement under CCP powers necessarily imply that the implementation of that agreement will take the form of internal EU regulation.[28]

This point draws attention to the reason why it matters that the EU's external regulatory competence is based not solely on Article 207, but also on other internal powers (such as Article 114 TFEU) which are shared powers, leaving room for the Member States to regulate in so far as the EU has not done so. In the case of trade in goods, the general regulations on import and export of goods include a provision based on Article 36 TFEU (ex-Article 30 EC) which allows the Member States to regulate as long as the Union has not yet dealt with the issue.[29] However there is no general equivalent in the case of trade in services, trade-related aspects of IPR, or FDI, authorizing the Member States to regulate in so far as no Union regulation exists.[30]

We may conclude from this brief account that the EU possesses competence to regulate goods and services either coming from or destined for a third country, as well as the competence to engage in external regulatory activity affecting trade in goods and services, IPR and FDI: regulatory dialogue and cooperation, participation in the formation of international standards, and even harmonization of standards. We have also seen that although competence under Article 207 TFEU is exclusive, it is by no means certain when Article 207 should be included as a legal basis for regulatory measures or even agreements, and when other legal bases (especially internal market legal bases) should be used.

In the next section we will take a look at how this EU competence may be used in practice. We will first turn to the EU's objectives in engaging in this external regulatory activity, and in particular the strong emphasis on coherence between internal and external policy. When the EU engages in international regulatory activity in the context of trade and external commercial policy, it does so with a clear 'internal' perspective; at the fore is the promotion of EU competitiveness but there are of course other policy objectives in the frame, including sustainable development. We will turn to the EU's involvement in the negotiation of ACTA as a specific example of the interaction between internal and external policy in the trade field, and of the EU's external regulatory strategy in practice. As we shall see, the presence (or absence) of internal rules may well be a factor in the EU's decision to participate in an international initiative designed to establish rules at an international level.

[26] Art 3(1) TFEU.

[27] A Dimopoulos, 'The Effects of the Lisbon Treaty on the Principles and Objectives of the Common Commercial Policy' (2010) 15 *EFA Rev* 153, at 159.

[28] Y Devuyst, n 13, pp 659–660; see also M Krajewski, 'Of Modes and Sectors: External Relations, Internal Debates and the Special Case of (trade in) Services' in M Cremona (ed), *Developments in EU External Relations Law* (OUP, 2008).

[29] Council Reg 260/2009/EC on the common rules for imports (Codified version) [2009] OJ L84/ 1, Art 24(2)(a); Council Reg 1061/2009 EC establishing common rules for exports [2009] OJ L291/ 1, Art 10. This is subject to the measure already mentioned which requires Member States to apply national standards in the non-harmonized sectors to third country origin goods on the basis of national treatment: see n 3.

[30] As far as FDI is concerned, the Commission has proposed a Regulation that would authorize the Member States, under certain conditions, to maintain and conclude Bilateral Investment Treaties (BITs): Proposal for a Regulation of the European Parliament and of the Council establishing transitional arrangements for bilateral investment agreements between Member States and third countries COM (2010) 344 final (7 July 2010).

3. How is this External Regulatory Competence Used? Objectives and the Internal and External Dimensions of Regulation

The Treaty of Lisbon makes an explicit link between internal and external policy objectives. Article 21(3) TEU provides that the Union's general external policy principles and objectives should be respected and pursued also in 'the development and implementation... of the external aspects of its other policies'. Thus the EU's internal regulatory policy must take into account the EU's general external policy objectives, including sustainable development, abolition of restrictions on international trade, environmental protection, and the promotion of an international system based on stronger multilateral cooperation and good global governance.[31] On the other hand, Article 207(3) TFEU provides that the EU's CCP agreements (as well as pursuing these general external objectives)[32] shall be 'compatible with internal Union policies and rules'. Presumably this means that in addition to taking internal policy objectives into account, and although internal rules may require amending, international agreements should not be concluded which directly contradict an established EU policy framework.[33] This obviously has implications for the EU in developing an external regulatory strategy.

The Commission, the Council (in particular the Competitiveness Council), the European Council and the European Parliament have all recently—in discussing the future of the Single Market—emphasized the need to enhance coherence between internal and external policy, and more specifically between the internal market and external commercial policy. In its Conclusions in December 2009, the Competitiveness Council included among its priorities for the Internal Market in the next decade the need to build an external dimension into the impact assessment of EU legislative proposals, 'to ensure coherence between internal regulation and external competitiveness'. In other words, the impact of new regulatory proposals on the external competitiveness of EU business should be taken into account, and this includes, for example, the promotion of international standards which play a 'crucial role' in market access and removing barriers to trade. The Council also stated that 'the renewed EU strategy for growth and jobs must contain an explicit external agenda', including 'promoting EU access to third markets on the basis of internationally agreed rules, in particular as concerns fair competition and the protection of intellectual property rights'.[34] The European Council said in September 2010 in the context of its discussion of the Single Market Act, that 'the European Union should further enhance the coherence and complementarity between its internal and external policies'.[35] While coherence in the sense here given to it by the institutions implies that the EU's external regulatory strategy should be designed to further internal competitiveness objectives, it is also the case—as the reference to international standards illustrates—that internal regulation needs to take account of the international regulatory context.

[31] Art 21(2) TEU; the concept of 'good global governance' is not defined and as the controversy over the ACTA (see below) demonstrates, opinions may well differ as to its meaning. In her discussion of the EU's 'governance mode of foreign policy' in this volume, de Búrca emphasizes the EU's preference for the creation of stable, long-term, institutionalized relationships with external states and entities, and its frequent use of regulatory frameworks. For a discussion of the institutional aspects of global trade governance see Hoffmeister's contribution to this volume, and for a discussion of the significance of the EU's general external objectives, see the chapter by Larik.

[32] Arts 205 and 207(1) TFEU.

[33] It might also refer to the fact that the EU's international treaty commitments do not take precedence over the EU Treaties themselves or over the general constitutional principles of the EU, including fundamental human rights: Joined Cases C-402/05 P and C-415/05 P *Yassin Abdullah Kadi and Al Barakaat International Foundation v Council and Commission* [2008] ECR I-06351, para 308. However, the phrase 'internal Union policies and rules' is not an obvious reference to primary Union law.

[34] Conclusions on 'Priorities for the Internal Market in the next decade'—contribution by the Competitiveness Council to the post-2010 Lisbon agenda, 4 December 2009.

[35] European Council Conclusions of 16 September 2010, Annex I, para (a).

In its Communication on 'trade policy as a core component of the EU's 2020 strategy',[36] the key issues for trade policy identified by the Commission are almost all directly related to the internal market. They include market access for services and investment, opening public procurement, better agreements on and enforcement of protection of IPR, and overcoming regulatory barriers, including via the promotion of international standards. The Commission's 2010 Communication on the Single Market Act includes a section on 'Being competitive in global markets', containing two of the 50 initiatives put forward for discussion, one on regulation, one on procurement.[37] The Council's Conclusions on the Single Market Act also include a reference to coordination of internal and external policies and a section on strengthening the external dimension of the Single Market:

> 'In particular, in the field of international standardization, the EU has to play a central role in order to facilitate trade relationships for its enterprises with the rest of the world; [the Council] also deems [it] necessary to promote regulatory convergence with third countries...'[38]

The Conclusions of the Competitiveness Council of 30 May 2011 on the priorities for re-launching the Single Market also make reference to the importance of trade policy, with a focus on 'promoting free, fair and open trade', the need to reinforce the external dimension of the Single Market and 'to further enhance the coherence and complementarities between the EU's internal and external policies'.[39] Despite all this emphasis, among the 12 'levers' identified in the Commission's 2011 Communication on the Single Market Act,[40] only one—public procurement—expressly mentions an external dimension. But in that document the Commission makes a more general point about the importance of regulatory convergence and its aim to promote the wider adoption of international standards.[41]

Thus, more attention is being paid to the regulatory dimension of trade policy, and to the external dimension of internal regulatory policy-making. Trade policy objectives, including liberalization and market access, are increasingly linked to competitiveness and growth objectives (the 2020 strategy). Global Europe, the Lisbon Strategy, the 2020 strategy, and the Single Market Act share the same objective: increasing the competitiveness of EU business and industry both on the home market and on third country markets. As far as regulation is concerned, EU policy has been directed at seeking to lessen regulatory barriers for EU exporters, supporting the adoption of intellectual property and competition policies and more generally a rule-based approach to trade and investment, and improving discipline on the enforcement of (for example) IPR and state aid rules, as well as assisting the development of and promoting international standards.

Are the objectives of EU external regulatory policy entirely focused on EU competitiveness and the interests of EU enterprise overseas, on building an EU-friendly regulatory environment and protecting EU IPR-holders? Perhaps not entirely. In its Communication on trade policy and the EU's 2020 strategy, the Commission does put some emphasis on the greening of trade and the social dimension, both internal and external (sustainable development, supporting 'green growth' in energy and biodiversity protection, the promotion of international labour standards).[42] Of course this starts from the position that trade helps development and liberalizing trade helps development more: 'integrating developing countries into the global economy helps poverty eradication and fosters better working

[36] 'Trade, Growth and World Affairs—Trade Policy as a core component of the EU's 2020 strategy' COM (2010) 612, 9 November 2010.

[37] 'Towards a Single Market Act' COM (2010) 608 final/2, 11 November 2010, s 1.6.

[38] Council Conclusions on the Single Market Act of 10 December 2010, para 18.

[39] Conclusions of the Competitiveness Council, 30 May 2011.

[40] 'Single Market Act—Twelve levers to boost growth and strengthen confidence' COM (2011) 206, 13 April 2011.

[41] Ibid, pp 21–22.

[42] COM (2010) 612, n 36.

conditions'.[43] In this way it can be claimed that trade policy helps further the broader general external policy objectives of Article 21(2) TEU.

In November 2010 the European Parliament adopted three resolutions on human rights, social and environmental standards in international trade agreements,[44] on corporate social responsibility in international trade agreements,[45] and on international trade policy in the context of climate change imperatives.[46] In the first of these, the Parliament called for the EU's future trade strategy not to envisage trade as an end in itself, but as a tool for the promotion of European values and commercial interests and as an instrument for fair trade that can bring into general practice the effective inclusion and implementation of social and environmental standards with all EU trade partners.

More concretely, the Parliament emphasized the need for cooperation between the WTO, the UN and the International Labour Organization (ILO); it supported the systematic inclusion of human rights clauses in new EU Free Trade Agreements (FTAs), with improved enforcement provisions modelled on Article 96 of the Cotonou Convention; it also supported the systematic inclusion of trade and sustainable development chapters in new bilateral FTAs. It called on the Commission to include in all FTAs a series of social and environmental standards, including: (a) a list of minimum standards that must be respected by all the EU's trading partners;[47] and (b) a list of other conventions 'that should be implemented gradually and flexibly, taking account of developments in the economic, social and environmental situation of the partner concerned'.

How are these external regulatory objectives to be realized? Dating from the Global Europe trade strategy of 2006,[48] the EU has revised its approach to bilateral relations, which during the 1990s had been dominated by pre-accession and neighbourhood agreements, the negotiation of the Cotonou Convention and the Economic Partnership Agreements with developing country partners. It has initiated two types of activity. It seeks to negotiate new generation FTAs with important trading partners including South Korea, Singapore, India, Canada, Mercosur, Peru and Columbia; and it seeks to upgrade its trade dialogue with 'strategic' partners with whom an FTA is not so far planned, including the US, Japan and China. Relations with strategic partners could include regulatory cooperation, mutual recognition agreements and participation in international standard-setting. These bilateral relationships are seen as providing a foundation for the EU's desired leadership role in international regulation.

The new 'deep and comprehensive FTAs' include the promotion of international standards and provisions on regulatory convergence and cooperation. The FTA with South Korea, which is regarded as a trailblazer,[49] is the first of the new generation agreements to have extensive provisions on services, establishment, investment and capital movements, IPR, competition, as well as specific chapters on TBT and SPS measures, with extensive provision for regulatory cooperation. In aiming to reduce 'behind the border' barriers to trade and investment, it thus connects with the regulatory policy underpinning the Single Market. However we need to be careful; the Korea FTA does not at all extend the Single Market *acquis* to Korea, nor does it adopt a Single Market approach. It does not envisage harmonization of standards or regulation, nor is there any presumption of mutual

[43] Ibid, p 8.
[44] P7_TA(2010)0434.
[45] P7_TA(2010)0446.
[46] P7_TA(2010)0445.
[47] The Parliament suggests that these should correspond to the ILO's eight Core Labour Standards as well as the list of conventions on the environment and the principles of good governance included in the EU scheme of generalized tariff preferences (see Council Reg 732/2008 [2008] OJ L211/1, as extended by Reg 512/2011 [2011] OJ L145/28).
[48] Commission communication 'Global Europe: Competing in the World' COM (2006) 567, 4 October 2006.
[49] See n 15.

recognition; the approach is based on the TBT and SPS agreements, international conventions (eg on IPR, environment and labour standards) and regulatory cooperation, and this is characteristic of current EU external regulatory policy outside the group of accession and neighbourhood states. The agreement recognizes each party's 'right to regulate' environmental and labour standards, and makes reference to international conventions, including ILO core conventions and multilateral environmental agreements.[50] Again we see the bilateral relationship not as a way of directly exporting the EU's own standards through harmonization, but rather as a framework for cooperation on global standard-setting.

4. Global Standard-setting: The ACTA

The Commission's Global Europe policy set as an objective of EU trade policy 'to play a leading role in sharing best practice and developing global rules and standards'.[51] This objective has two dimensions: on the one hand, the EU must take account of global 'best practice' when developing regulatory and other standards. On the other hand, the EU should engage in cooperation at multilateral as well as bilateral level to ensure that European norms are a reference for global standards. The Commission has argued that EU regulatory standards are well-placed to become a reference point for global standards for a number of reasons: they are relatively modernized; they set high standards; they draw upon different regulatory traditions in the Member States; they also draw upon international standards and best practice of non-EU regulators; they are suited to application in different regulatory environments; they are trade-friendly; they already exist in a number of different languages; they operate within the EU which is the world's largest import market; and capacity-building with a view to compliance with EU standards is part of EU development policy.[52] But EU regulatory leadership cannot be taken for granted outside its neighbourhood.[53] Regulatory partnerships with respect to specific sectors and key partners will become more important. In this section we will take only one example, that of enforcement of IPR, to illustrate the EU's involvement in international regulatory initiatives. Enforcement of IPR has been identified as a priority for EU trade policy at least since 2004. EU policy has operated—as with regulatory policy more generally—at a number of levels: working with accession countries (eg Turkey) and neighbourhood states (eg Ukraine); seeking to include chapters on IPR enforcement in bilateral trade agreements; reinforcing cooperation and dialogue on IPR enforcement; capacity building within the context of development policy.[54] Among these initiatives, the EU has taken part in the negotiations for an international Anti-Counterfeiting Trade Agreement (ACTA).[55]

The ACTA negotiations were launched in June 2008 and concluded in November 2010. The EU participated with 10 other countries: Australia, Canada, Japan, Korea, Mexico, Morocco, New Zealand, Singapore, Switzerland and the United States.[56] The ACTA builds

[50] See further the chapters by Marín Durán and Kenner in this volume.

[51] Global Europe, n 48, p 7.

[52] 'The external dimension of the single market review' SEC (2007) 1519, Commission staff working document accompanying the Commission's Communication on 'A single market for 21st century Europe' COM (2007) 724 final.

[53] 'Trade as a Driver of Prosperity' SEC (2010) 1269, Commission staff working document accompanying the Commission's Communication on 'Trade, Growth and World affairs', n 36, p 40.

[54] Global Europe, n 48, p 13; see also 'Trade, Growth and World Affairs—Trade Policy as a core component of the EU's 2020 strategy' COM (2010) 612, p 14.

[55] In what follows, references to provisions of the ACTA will be to the finalized text, Anti-Counterfeiting Trade Agreement between the European Union and its Member States, Australia, Canada, Japan, the Republic of Korea, the United Mexican States, the Kingdom of Morocco, New Zealand, the Republic of Singapore, the Swiss Confederation and the United States of America; Council doc 12196/11, 23 August 2011, available at: <http://register.consilium.europa.eu/pdf/en/11/st12/st12196.en11.pdf>.

[56] The Council adopted a decision on the signing of the ACTA on 15–16 December 2011 (Council doc 12192/1/11, REV 1) and the Agreement was signed by the EU and 22 of its Member States on 26 January 2012. The

upon the Agreement on Trade Related Aspects of Intellectual Property Rights (TRIPS), and its focus is on enforcement of IPR. It contains provisions on customs, civil and criminal enforcement mechanisms, and the internet. It is not supposed to be concerned with defining (or creating) IPR, although the distinction between defining IPR and defining the scope of protection may not be easy to draw: if a particular action is declared under specific circumstances not to be an infringement, is this a restriction of the right, or of the remedy?[57] This distinction may be important in relation to liability of internet service providers,[58] in relation to trade in generic drugs,[59] where domestic laws and/or TRIPS provide specific exemptions, and also in the context of 'fair usage' exceptions.[60]

In the Commission's view, the agreement will not need implementation at EU level since IPR enforcement standards in the EU *acquis* are equal to or higher than those in the ACTA.[61] While intended to be reassuring, of course this also implies that the EU has not persuaded all its negotiating partners to accept its own standards for IPR enforcement. However, there is disagreement over whether the ACTA will require amendment of the EU *acquis*. The ACTA has been controversial, both in the US and in the EU. A group of European academics issued an opinion on the draft agreement in February 2011, which calls upon the EU institutions, and in particular the European Parliament, to consider a number of issues relating to fundamental rights and to trade in generic drugs.[62] The significance of this type of public lobbying is demonstrated by the decision of the Commission to refer the ACTA to the Court of Justice for an opinion on its compatibility with the Treaties,[63] as well as by the debate within the European Parliament which voted to refuse its consent to the conclusion of the ACTA.[64] It is argued that the ACTA is not precise enough on issues which concern the balance between the protection of intellectual property rights and fundamental

Agreement was to be concluded by the EU and its Member States as a mixed agreement (see further below). In February 2012 the Commission decided to refer the ACTA to the Court of Justice of the EU (CJEU) under Art 218 (11) TFEU for an opinion on its compatibility with the Treaties and the Charter of Fundamental Rights. The European Parliament needs to give its consent to the conclusion of the Agreement and on 4 July 2012 the Parliament refused its consent (European Parliament legislative resolution of 4 July 2012 on the draft Council decision on the conclusion of the Anti-Counterfeiting Trade Agreement, 12195/2011–C7-0027/2012–2011/0167 (NLE) P7_TA-PROV(2012)0287) leaving the future of the Agreement in doubt.

57 BT Yeh, Memorandum to Senator Wyden, 29 October 2010, p 3. See also P Velasco Martins, DG Trade, Civil Society Meeting on the ACTA, 25 March 2011, tra_doc.147947, 'Exceptions and derogations consist in lawful uses and not infringements to IPR. They can hence not be affected by the agreement'.

58 Directive 2000/31/EC (E-Commerce Directive) [2000] OJ L178, 17/ 1, Arts 12–15; Directive 2001/29/EC (Copyright in the Information Society Directive) [2001] OJ L167, Art 8. See also Art 27.2 and fn 13 ACTA.

59 Where TRIPS provides exceptions: Doha Declaration on TRIPS and Public Health, 14 November 2001; Decision of 30 August 2003 on the implementation of para 6 of the Doha Declaration. Here the ACTA allows some flexibility since parties are not required to introduce customs controls or criminal sanctions for patent infringements: Art 13, fn 6 and Art 23. In addition, Art 1 of ACTA is a 'non-derogate' clause with respect to TRIPS obligations, and Art 2.3 provides that the objectives and principles of Part I of TRIPS, especially Arts 7 and 8, will apply to the ACTA.

60 Fair usage has been an issue in the context of the provision for criminal enforcement in cases of an IPR infringement 'on a commercial scale'. In response to criticism that this is not specific enough in excluding fair usage, it is argued by the Commission that fair usage activities are encompassed in the definition of an infringement: they are considered 'legitimate "exceptions" and therefore do not fall under the scope of the criminal enforcement provisions of ACTA, since this applies only to certain illegal activities (piracy and counterfeiting), practiced wilfully and on a commercial scale. In fact, these exceptions are totally outside the scope of ACTA, which, as an enforcement agreement, only applies to infringing activities, not to legal ones'. Commission response to Academics' Opinion, tradoc. 147853, 27 April 2011.

61 P Velasco Martins, DG Trade, Civil Society Meeting on the ACTA, 25 March 2011, tradoc.147947.

62 The academics' opinion is available here: <http://www.iri.uni-hannover.de/tl_files/pdf/ACTA_opinion_110211_DH2.pdf>. For the Commission's response, see tradoc. 147853, 27 April 2011.

63 In announcing the Commission's legal submissions to the CJEU on 4 April 2012, Commissioner de Gucht said: 'Considering that tens of thousands of people have voiced their concerns about ACTA, it is appropriate to give our highest independent judicial body the time to deliver its legal opinion on this agreement. This is an important input to European public and democratic debate'.

64 The European Parliament commissioned a report on the ACTA: 'The Anti-Counterfeiting Trade Agreement (ACTA): An Assessment' EXPO/B/INTA/FWC/2009-01/Lot7/12, published June 2011. A draft recommendation to the Parliament's International Trade Committee by rapporteur David Martin recommended that the ACTA should not be accepted by the Parliament as it stands (doc 2011/0167(NLE) PE486.174v02-00, 12 April 2012), and in July 2012 the Parliament refused its consent to the agreement: n 56.

freedoms, including those on criminal sanctions, giving rise to the risk of 'unintended consequences'.[65]

This is not the place for a detailed assessment of ACTA.[66] But what does its negotiation tell us about the ability of the EU to develop and prosecute effectively an external regulatory policy? What does it tell us about the EU as a player in global governance?

5. The ACTA and Internal/External Policy Coherence

In this section we shall examine the extent to which the ACTA reflects (i) EU external policy on IPR enforcement and (ii) EU internal rules.

5.1. EU external policy on IPR enforcement

The EU's external policy on IPR enforcement illustrates clearly the links already identified between the current objectives of EU trade policy and the competitiveness of EU industry.[67] In a Communication on IPR of May 2011 the Commission declared:

> 'The increase in international trade has put the spotlight on the international dimension of IPR. Globalisation provides Europe with immense opportunities to export and trade in its IP intensive products, services and know-how to third-countries. At the same time, the growth in IP infringements creates the need to focus on a robust global enforcement strategy, in accordance with fundamental rights.' Thus '[t]he consolidation and streamlining of the governance of IPR should go hand in hand with strengthening enforcement tools both on the EU and international levels.'[68]

The Commission's approach to the enforcement of intellectual property rights in third countries was first elaborated in its 2004 Strategy for the Enforcement of IPR in Third Countries ('the Strategy'),[69] followed by the 2006 Global Europe Communication,[70] and the Communication on Trade, Growth and World Affairs in November 2010.[71] The ACTA is a major plank of this policy. Other elements include IPR enforcement chapters in new FTAs (eg Korea); dialogue with key countries (eg China,[72] Thailand,[73] Russia[74]); regulatory cooperation with the US and Japan; and allocating technical assistance resources to enforcement.[75] The Strategy incorporates both multilateral and bilateral dimensions, while declaring that it is not intended to impose the EU's approach on third countries, nor to propose a one-size-fits-all approach; nor does it wish to adopt another state's model, nor to create

[65] D Martin, Explanatory Statement to draft recommendation to the Parliament's International Trade Committee, doc 2011/0167(NLE), PE486.174v02-00, 12 April 2012, p 6. Martin concludes: 'Given the vagueness of certain aspects of the text and the uncertainty over its interpretation, the European Parliament cannot guarantee adequate protection for citizens' rights in the future under ACTA'.

[66] See eg K Weatherall, 'ACTA as a New Kind of International IP Law-Making' PIJIP Research Paper 2010 no 12, American University Washington College of Law, Washington, DC; AX Fellmeth, 'The Anti-Counterfeiting Trade Agreement in the Public Eye' *Insights: American Society of International Law* (2011) 24(8), 24 June 2011.

[67] See eg Commission Communication, *Trade, Growth and World Affairs*, 9 November 2010, COM (2010) 612 final, p 14.

[68] Commission Communication, *A Single Market for Intellectual Property Rights: Boosting creativity and innovation to provide economic growth, high quality jobs and first class products and services in Europe*, 24 May 2011, COM (2011) 287 final.

[69] Strategy for the enforcement of intellectual property rights in third countries [2005] OJ C129/3.

[70] COM (2006) 567 final.

[71] COM (2010) 612 final, n 67.

[72] Action plan on customs cooperation regarding IPR enforcement signed with China in 2009.

[73] Report on the First EU–Thailand IPR Dialogue, Bangkok, Thailand, 25 February 2011, tradoc 147855; the second IPR dialogue meeting was held on 24 February 2012.

[74] Within the framework of the EU–Russia Common Economic Space and more recently the Partnership for Modernization launched at the EU–Russia Summit in June 2010.

[75] For a summary of technical cooperation activities carried out between August 2009 and August 2010 by the European Union and individual Member States in favour of developing countries, see EU Communication to WTO TRIPS Council, IP/C/W/550/Add.7, 1 June 2011.

alliances against 'certain countries'.[76] The EU's approach to the ACTA exemplifies this approach and perhaps also the EU's desire, if not to create alliances *against*, rather to create alliances *with* other countries on IPR enforcement.

5.2. EU internal rules[77]

There has been debate over the extent to which the ACTA may require modification of the current EU *acquis*.[78] The Commission is adamant that it does not.[79] The ambiguity in part results from what ACTA does not contain as much as what it does: for example over due process, or 'fundamental principles such as freedom of expression, fair process, and privacy' in relation to enforcement in the digital environment. The Commission argues that there is nothing to prevent the EU from inserting (as it does) due process requirements into its own legislation, but the point made by the critics is that these safeguards are not written into ACTA itself, nor are the 'fundamental principles' fully defined, although there are general provisions on due process (Article 6.2) and proportionality (Article 6.3). So, the ACTA permits such 'good practice' but does not require it.

There are also the criminal provisions. Since the proposed EU directive on criminal remedies for IPR was abandoned, there were hints that the conclusion of ACTA based on Article 207 TFEU might lead to harmonization by stealth, or so-called 'policy laundering'. The Commission argues that this competence balance will not change: 'There is not yet an EU *acquis* in terms of penal sanctions for IPR infringements, but instead 27 national laws and this will not be modified by ACTA'.[80] The ACTA was negotiated, and will be concluded, as a mixed agreement. The criminal provisions were negotiated not by the Commission but by the Presidency on the basis of common positions of the Member States adopted unanimously. The proposal for signature of the ACTA by the EU is based on Article 207 TFEU (CCP powers). According to the Commission the EU will not exercise its shared competence under Article 83 TFEU and therefore the agreement will be mixed.[81]

None of this precludes, of course, a future decision to revive the criminal enforcement directive and—were the ACTA ever concluded—to implement it at EU level. It may be felt to be necessary to align national legislation, especially if ACTA-based provisions of criminal enforcement are included in FTAs, and third countries expect a uniform approach to implementation from the EU side. Aside from this issue, a revision of the Border Regulation is currently underway.[82] More generally, the Commission has argued that 'further harmonizing IP rules within the EU would enhance the Commission's capacity to

[76] See further DG Trade Report on Evaluation of the Intellectual Property Rights Enforcement Strategy in Third Countries, November 2010. Tradoc. 147053.

[77] In particular, Reg 1383/2003 on customs action against goods suspected of infringing certain intellectual property rights [2003] OJ L 196/7, and Directive 2004/48/EC on the enforcement of intellectual property rights [2004] OJ L195/16. A proposal for a Directive on criminal enforcement of IPR (COM (2006) 168 final) was ultimately withdrawn. Other relevant directives are the Copyright in the Information Society Directive (Directive 2001/29) and the E-Commerce Directive (Directive 2000/31/EC). See also Council resolution of 25 September 2008 on a comprehensive European anti-counterfeiting and anti-piracy plan [2008] OJ C253/1.

[78] Academics' Opinion, n 62.

[79] Commission response to Academics' Opinion, n 62.

[80] P Velasco Martins, DG Trade, Civil Society Meeting on the ACTA, 25 March 2011, tra_doc.147947.

[81] Proposal for a Council Decision on the conclusion of the Anti-Counterfeiting Trade Agreement between the European Union and its Member States, Australia, Canada, Japan, the Republic of Korea, the United Mexican States, the Kingdom of Morocco, New Zealand, the Republic of Singapore, the Swiss Confederation and the United States of America, COM (2011) 380 final. See F Hoffmeister, 'The European Union's common commercial policy a year after Lisbon—Sea change or business as usual?' in Koutrakos (ed), *The European Union's external relations a year after Lisbon*, CLEER Working Paper 2011/3, p 84.

[82] Council Resolution of 16 March 2009 on the EU Customs Action Plan to combat IPR infringements for the years 2009 to 2012 [2009] OJ C71/1; proposal for a Regulation of the European Parliament and of the Council concerning customs enforcement of intellectual property rights COM (2011) 285 final.

negotiate on behalf of the EU stronger IP commitments with our key trading partners'.[83] Thus, while the extent of existing EU internal regulation influences its ability to negotiate externally, regulatory norms agreed at an international level will of course impact on internal EU regulatory policy: the EU may be an importer of norms as well as an exporter.

6. The ACTA and Global Governance of IPR

6.1. Link to bilateral agreements

The argument that bilateral agreements have paved the way for the ACTA is probably more demonstrable in the case of recent US FTAs[84] than for the EU, since it is only in the Caribbean Forum (CARIFORUM) Economic Partnership Agreement and the South Korean FTA that substantial IPR chapters have been included (and the CARIFORUM states were not ACTA negotiators). Chapter 10 of the EU–South Korean FTA is to 'complement and specify the rights and obligations between the Parties under the TRIPS Agreement'. It refers to a number of international conventions on IPR, and contains provisions on enforcement, including criminal enforcement, which reflect the ACTA. It also goes further than ACTA in containing substantive provisions relating to duration of authors' rights and the scope of broadcasting rights, as well as provisions on geographical indications. For other ACTA parties with whom the EU has an earlier generation FTA with limited IPR provisions, such as Morocco and Mexico, the ACTA would represent a significant upgrading of commitment on IPR enforcement. The EU insisted that it would not put pressure on third countries to sign up to ACTA as a condition of concluding a FTA (unlike membership of the WTO, which has de facto become a pre-condition for a FTA with the EU), nor seek to include accession to ACTA as a commitment in the FTA itself (unlike, for example, the World Intellectual Property Organization (WIPO) Copyright Treaty or the Berne Convention).[85] But its statements have referred carefully only to 'on-going free-trade agreement negotiations'.[86]

On the other hand, where an FTA partner is a party to ACTA (eg South Korea), the Commission argues that the ACTA will 'complement and reinforce' the commitments in the FTA.[87] It may be easier to negotiate an IPR chapter in a future FTA with countries that have already committed to ACTA (eg Singapore). It might even be possible to persuade countries that are not parties to the ACTA that it represents a new 'global standard' which could provide a basis for an IPR chapter in an FTA, as a more palatable alternative to using the EU *acquis* as a model.

6.2. Contribution of ACTA to the IPR enforcement ratchet?

Both the US and the EU have stressed that the ACTA will not require any change to their own domestic laws,[88] and this does (given the likely parties) raise issues as to its purpose.

[83] COM (2010) 612 final, n 67, p 14.

[84] Weatherall, n 66, p 10: several parties to ACTA negotiations have FTAs with the US (Singapore, Morocco, Australia, Korea). Weatherall argues that in the case of Australia, the changes already made to Australian IPR enforcement as a result of the US–Australian FTA made it easier to accept the ACTA—and also made it easier to accept a US (as opposed to EU) approach to ACTA.

[85] eg see EU–Albania SAA, Art 73 and Annex V; EU–CARIFORUM EPA, Arts 143.1 and 147.1.

[86] Question E-1654/2011 by David Martin (S&D), answer given by K De Gucht on behalf of the Commission, 31 March 2011. See also Commission's reply to the Academics' Opinion, on this point relating to 'pressure', n 62.

[87] Answer given by Mr De Gucht on behalf of the Commission to Question E-6187/10 by Elisabeth Köstinger (PPE), 15 September 2010.

[88] The EU argues that it follows closely the EU *acquis*: 'the content of ACTA is either in line or less demanding than the EU *acquis*, therefore the Agreement is already fully implemented by the current EU legislation. This means that ACTA will not require the adoption or modification of EU legislative acts'. Answer given by Mr De Gucht on behalf of the Commission to Question P-9179/10 by Françoise Castex (S&D), 15 December 2010.

Countries that pose real problems of IPR infringement (such as China) are perhaps not likely to become parties. But in the Commission's view, the ACTA will help to establish an agreed minimum—more extensive than TRIPS and based on both US and EU regulatory approaches—on which to base any further international regulation:

> The Anti-Counterfeiting Trade Agreement aims to establish a comprehensive international framework—a catalogue of 'best practices'—that will assist its members to effectively combat the infringement of IPRs. When agreed and implemented, ACTA will effectively introduce a new international standard, building on the WTO TRIPS agreement.[89]

Thus, one view would present the IPR enforcement ratchet as working through a cycle of bilateral—multilateral/plurilateral (TRIPS then ACTA)—bilateral agreements.[90] Not only might the ACTA help to include IPR enforcement in new bilateral FTAs, it might also, as a plurilateral agreement, help progress towards a multilateral agreement that would bind more countries, including those that are the major sources of counterfeit goods, such as China.[91]

However, the flexibility of ACTA and its number of optional ('may' as opposed to 'shall') provisions may be regarded as a weakness. The Commission has argued that these represent a 'catalogue of best practices'. They may also be regarded—in so far as they are controversial—as an 'international political incitement to implement these clauses into contracting Party's [sic] law'.[92] But at least for the US and the EU, the ACTA does not 'ratchet up' IPR protection—Weatherall argues that the chapter of ACTA on enforcement in the digital environment, which was originally drafted by the US and based on its FTA model, was significantly amended to bring it closer to the EU model.[93] And the EU, as we have seen, was keen to ensure—and boasted—that no change to its own IPR *acquis* would be needed.

The ACTA may be innovative in providing a framework of international rules on enforcement of IPR (albeit so far only agreed to by 37 states: EU27 + 10).[94] But it does not really provide innovative solutions to the challenge IPR faces from (for example) the digital environment; it does not seek to challenge the IPR paradigm. It was not intended to do so. The EU has proved relatively successful in helping to shape these new rules in such a way that they 'fit' already-existing EU rules. It can help to make existing rules work better. But the factors which assisted the EU in meeting its negotiating objectives for the ACTA make it very difficult for the EU easily to propose or guide the creation of a new paradigm for IPR in external fora.

7. Conclusion

It is clear that the EU has the competence to develop an external regulatory policy, whether based on CCP powers, or on internal (in particular internal market) powers. Despite the

The US has put some stress on Art 2.1 of ACTA whereby 'Each Party shall be free to determine the appropriate method of implementing the provisions of this Agreement within its own legal system and practice', arguing that this allows the US to continue to apply existing domestic exceptions and limitations to IPR enforcement.

89 COM (2010) 612 final, n 67, p 14.

90 Weatherill, n 66, p 9.

91 Weatherall, n 66, p 15.

92 Academics' Opinion, n 62, preamble, para (g).

93 Weatherall, n 66, pp 17–18, citing Michael Geist, 'US Caves on Anti-Circumvention Rules in ACTA', Michael Geist Blog (19 July 2010), available at: <http://www.michaelgeist.ca/content/view/5210/125/>. An example would be the definition of 'technological protection measure' in the anti-circumvention provisions: Art 27.5, fn 14, as well as the scope of the criminal provisions.

94 It should be noted that although they agreed the final text in December 2010, some EU Member States have subsequently indicated unwillingness to sign it, at least for now: the Agreement was signed by the EU and 22 of its Member States on 26 January 2012.

Lisbon Treaty's expansion of the scope of the CCP, external regulatory competence is not concentrated solely in Article 207 TFEU. International agreements such as free trade agreements are by their nature concerned with third country goods and services and in general the CCP will provide the legal basis also for the regulatory dimension of the agreement. Still, even here other legal bases may be needed, or chosen. And where autonomous regulatory measures deal both with domestic and third country goods or services, internal powers tend to be used as the legal basis. Indeed, the need to use (or choice of) legal bases other than the CCP implies that the EU's external regulatory competence does not always exclude the Member States.

The second part of the chapter turned to the principles and policy that guide the use by the EU of its external regulatory competence. It is clear that even where the EU contemplates 'deep integration' with a third country, including a regulatory dimension, this does not necessarily imply harmonization based on EU internal market standards.[95] The link between the internal and external dimensions of regulation, increasingly emphasized by the EU institutions, is of a different nature. The EU seeks to ensure that EU trade policy supports EU exporters of goods and services, and that internal regulatory policy does not put EU enterprises at a disadvantage on third country markets. These goals have led to an emphasis on extending the regulatory dimension of trade agreements; on regulatory cooperation and where possible mutual recognition; on the promotion of existing international standards in the context of bilateral agreements, dialogue and cooperation; and EU leadership in developing new international standards which are at least consistent with EU standards.

The EU's involvement in the negotiation of the ACTA is an example of such leadership. The EU was keen to get an agreement which would build upon the TRIPS, in particular as regards enforcement of IPR. It identified weaknesses in IPR enforcement as a major problem for EU exporters and IPR-holders. At the same time it saw the need to ensure that the concerns of developing countries, especially over patents and imports of generic medicines, were addressed (whether they have been adequately reflected in the final text is still subject to debate). Thus the EU in practice adopted a conception of the EU interest (a 'balanced agreement') that encompassed development needs as well as its direct commercial interests. The EU was also keen to ensure that the agreement would follow as closely as possible existing EU legislation on enforcement, and would not interfere with accepted EU exceptions, although it did not see the need to ensure that EU 'best practice' was incorporated in the agreement itself. The EU *acquis* provided a solid ground on which the EU could base its negotiating position, its sometimes hard-won compromises making the Commission negotiators unwilling to re-open already-fought battles. While this perhaps strengthened the EU position, it may make it difficult for the EU to launch a really innovative approach to regulation at the international level. The balance between EU and Member States plays a role here too: aspects of ACTA (criminal enforcement) fall within Article 83(2) TFEU, and thus shared competence. Since there is (as yet) no EU internal *acquis* on criminal enforcement measures against counterfeiting and intellectual property piracy, it has been decided that the EU should not exercise its potential external competence in this area, but that the ACTA should rather be concluded (as it was negotiated) as a mixed agreement.[96] We can conclude that the EU will find it easier to exercise its external regulatory competence where it has already worked out a position at the internal level, and once that position has been worked

[95] In some cases, notably within the EU's close neighbourhood, harmonization of standards may indeed be an objective; however this is not an intrinsic part of the 'global' policy of the Union.

[96] COM (2011) 380 final, 24 June 2011, Explanatory Memorandum, para 6: 'the Commission has opted not to propose that the European Union exercise its potential competence in the area of criminal enforcement pursuant to Art 83(2) TFEU. The Commission considers this appropriate because it has never been the intention, as regards the negotiation of *ACTA to modify the EU acquis or to harmonize EU legislation as regards criminal enforcement of intellectual property rights*' (emphasis in the original).

out, the EU will have an incentive not to engage in international commitments which represent a significant departure from the policy balance achieved internally.[97] The dynamic between internal and external regulatory policy is an essential ingredient in the EU's ability to contribute to global governance.

[97] Indeed the Parliament's rapporteur, David Martin, in recommending rejection of the ACTA, suggests that the Commission should instead bring forward new proposals to meet the challenge of ensuring effective IPR protection and its balance with fundamental rights; an 'internal' regulatory approach is an alternative to external action especially where, as here, renegotiation to meet the European Parliament's concerns is not a realistic option: see n 64.

11

Access to Raw Materials: The EU's Pursuit of Trade Disciplines on Export Control

Chien-Huei Wu

1. Introduction

In response to surging commodity prices and shortages of raw materials, the European Commission in 2008 adopted its Raw Materials Initiative (RMI)[1] with the aim of securing sustainable supplies of raw materials for the EU economy. The RMI is to be founded on three pillars consisting of access to raw materials on world markets, sustainable supplies from European sources, and the reduction of European consumption.[2] External trade policy constitutes an essential element of RMI-related policy. The EU is not only a major player in the raw materials market, but is also trying to create disciplines in that respect.[3] The EU attempts to ensure access to raw materials through different fora and venues, including multilateral frameworks and bilateral negotiations, and ranging from rule-making to law-enforcement.

Multilaterally, the EU keeps raising this issue in such fora as G8, Organization for Economic Cooperation and Development (OECD), and United Nations Conference on Trade and Development (UNCTAD) and seeks cooperation with international organizations such as the World Bank and the International Seabed Authority.[4] The EU has also submitted a proposal under the auspices of the Doha Development Agenda (DDA) within the WTO with a view to strengthening disciplines on export restrictions. It has additionally taken the opportunities offered by WTO accession negotiations to secure commitments from acceding members to eliminate or phase out their export restrictive measures. Regarding law enforcement, it has filed complaints against Argentina and China on certain export restrictive measures on hides, leather and raw materials via the WTO dispute settlement mechanism. Bilaterally, the EU consistently included trade rules on export restrictions in its external economic agreements. Such practices are present in EU external economic agreements such as the EU–Korea Free Trade Agreement (FTA),[5] EU–CARIFORUM Economic Partnership Agreement (EPA),[6] EU–Columbia–Peru Trade Agreement,[7] and so on.

The EU's pursuit of disciplines in export restrictions faces a number of challenges. First, the existing trade regulatory regime led by the General Agreement on Tariffs and Trade (GATT)/WTO system focuses mainly on the liberalization of import restrictions and has little regulation on export restrictions. The rationale underpinning the GATT/WTO system is to secure market access to other countries through tariff reduction and the elimination of

[1] COM (2008) 699 final of 4 November 2008.
[2] Ibid, at 5–11.
[3] On the role of EU as a market player and rule-generator, see M Cremona, 'The Union as a Global Actor: Roles, Models and Identity' (2004) 41 *CML Rev* 553, 553–565.
[4] RMI, n 1, 6.
[5] Free Trade Agreement between the European Union and its Member States, of the one part, and the Republic of Korea, of the other part, [2011] OJ L127/6, 14 May 2011.
[6] Economic Partnership Agreement between the CARIFORUM States, of the one part, and the European Community and its Member States of the other part [2008] OJ L289/3, 30 October 2008.
[7] Council Decision proposed, but not yet approved, COM (2011) 570 final of 22 September 2011.

non-tariff barriers.[8] Secondly, whereas commitments on export restrictions are undertaken by some new WTO members, these commitments only bind the members concerned and do not extend to other members. A law-making process resulting in specific obligations applicable only to a limited subset of WTO members may undermine the multilateral nature of the WTO rules. Thirdly, in pursuing trade rules on export restrictions in its FTA negotiations, the EU may further marginalize the role of the WTO in global trade governance, and thus deviate from the spirit of the second subparagraph of Article 21(1) of the Treaty on European Union (TEU), which instructs the Union to 'promote multilateral solutions to common problems'.

In this context, this chapter aims to explore the EU's contribution to new trade rules pertaining to export restrictions with a view to securing its access to raw materials. This chapter examines both the EU's position within the multilateral WTO framework (section 2) and its bilateral negotiations with other trade partners (section 3). Within the WTO forum, this chapter first, by contrasting the EU's proposal relating to export taxes with that of Japan and the US, focusing mainly on procedural transparency on export licensing, illustrates the EU's aim to advance rule of law and respect for international law in the wider world and its regulatory ambition to 'promote multilateral solutions to common problems'.[9] Secondly, it investigates whether and how the EU can successfully secure commitments on export restriction from new WTO members during bilateral accession negotiations. It will examine the EU's complaints lodged via the WTO dispute settlement mechanism with regards to Argentina and China on their export restrictive measures. With regard to the bilateral aspect, this chapter will examine those provisions pertaining to export restrictions in selected EU external economic agreements. This chapter concludes with an evaluation of the EU's success in pursuing trade disciplines on export restrictions through law-making and law enforcement in multilateral frameworks and bilateral negotiations (section 4).

2. Export Restrictions under the Multilateral WTO Framework

2.1. Export restrictions and the WTO agreement

Export restrictions may take the form of an export ban, export taxes, export quotas, export licensing, minimum export price or reduction of value-added taxes rebates.[10] The most important provision pertaining to restrictive export measures in the existent WTO framework is the general elimination of quantitative restrictions. As Article XI:1 of the GATT 1994 states, 'no prohibitions or restrictions other than duties, taxes, or other charges, whether made effective through quotas, import or export licenses or other measures shall be instituted or maintained'.[11] This general obligation to eliminate quantitative restrictions applies both to the importation and exportation of goods. Export bans, export quotas and minimum export price may be held to be WTO-incompatible in terms of Article XI:1. In contrast, however, export taxes fall outside the realm of the Uruguay Round Agreements,[12] and it is also debated whether the Schedules of Concessions as contained in Article II of the GATT 1994 extends to export taxes.[13]

The Uruguay Round Agreements address import licensing, but not export licensing, and thus leave great leeway for members to escape WTO disciplines. In the absence of a

[8] M Matsushita, 'Export Controls of Natural Resources and the WTO/GATT Disciplines' (2011) 6 *Asian Journal of WTO and International Health Law and Policy* 281, 283–284.

[9] TEU, Art 21.1. On this point, see the contributions of Larik and de Búrca to this volume.

[10] J Kim, 'Recent Trends in Export Restrictions on Raw Materials' in OECD (ed), *The Economic Impact of Export Restrictions on Raw Materials* (OECD Publishing, 2010) 14.

[11] Art XI:1 of the GATT 1994.

[12] Kim, n 10, 23.

[13] Matsushita, n 8, 288–291.

WTO agreement on export licensing procedures, Article X of the GATT 1994, on the publication and administration of trade regulation, may be a subsidiary instrument to regulate the granting and distributing of export licenses. In particular, Article X:3 of the GATT 1994 dictates that Members 'administer in a uniform and impartial and reasonable manner all its laws, regulations, decisions, and rulings of general application'. Whereas Article X relates mainly to the administration of laws and regulations in general, it is used in these two cases as a weapon to challenge the incompatibility of WTO export licensing procedures.[14]

2.2. Rule-making and market access for non-agricultural goods

Filling in the gaps in WTO disciplines on export restrictions, Japan, at the negotiating group on Market Access for Non-Agricultural Products (NAMA) proposed a WTO Agreement on Export Licensing Procedures, with the aim of enhancing the transparency of export licensing.[15] In contrast, the EU proposed a WTO Agreement on Export Taxes.[16] While Japan's proposal was revised and transformed into a protocol to the GATT 1994, and has gained some limited support from other WTO members; no other member has joined the EU to sponsor the proposed WTO Agreement on Export Taxes.

2.2.1. Proposed protocol on transparency in export licensing: a procedural approach

Japan's proposal for a WTO Agreement on Export Licensing Procedures was adapted from the WTO Agreement on Import Licensing Procedures. Therefore, the legal text of the draft Agreement on Export Licensing Procedures mirrors that of the Agreement on Import Licensing Procedures, though substituting the term 'export' for 'import'. The proposed Agreement on Export Licensing Procedures aims to address three issues: publication of the rules and administration of export restrictions; notification to the WTO; and publication of domestic statistics.[17] In its proposal, Japan emphasizes that the proposed agreement aims mainly to enhance procedural transparency. Thus, it neither curtails legitimate export restrictions in compliance with the WTO Agreement, nor introduces any new substantive rule.[18] A revised version of this proposed agreement was presented by Japan and the US in 2008, in the form of a protocol attached to the GATT 1994.[19] The draft protocol has only five articles addressing the definition of export licensing; notification; request for information; confidential information; and review.

Article 1 of the proposed protocol defines export licensing as 'any administrative procedures involving the submission of an application or other documentation (ie other than customs purposes) to the relevant administrative body or bodies as a prior condition for exportation from the customs territory of the exporting Member'.[20] The pertinent point of this definition is that export licensing constitutes a prior condition for exportation for non-customs purposes. It may, nonetheless, result in ambiguity since ultimately the export

[14] Kim, n 10, 23–24

[15] Text-based Proposal for Negotiation on Enhanced Transparency on Export Restrictions, *Communication from Japan*, TN/MA/W/15/Add.4 (18 April 2006).

[16] Negotiating Proposal on Export Taxes, *Communication from the European Communities*, TN/MA/W/11/Add.6 (27 April 2006).

[17] TN/MA/W/15/Add.4, para 2.

[18] TN/MA/W/15/Add.4, para 3.

[19] Protocol on Transparency in Export Licensing to the General Agreement on Tariffs and Trade 1994 (hereinafter the Proposed Protocol on Transparency on Export Licensing), *Communication from Japan and the United States*, TN/MA/W/15/Add.4/Rev.1 (11 April 2008).

[20] Proposed Protocol on Transparency on Export Licensing, Art 1.

license would be required by the customs for shipping activities. Finding a means to separate customs purposes from non-customs purposes may be thus subject to dispute.[21]

Article 2 of the proposed protocol regulates notifications of export licensing. Members are obliged to notify the Committee on Market Access (the Committee) within sixty days after the entry into force of this protocol. A Member imposing new measures on export licensing should also notify the Committee within sixty days after the entry into force of the new measures.[22] In view of the fact that many members do not spontaneously notify the WTO under the current practices, the proposed protocol introduces a novel practice. According to Article 3.4 of the proposed protocol, an interested member who believes that another member is failing to give notice of new or existent export licensing measures may bring this matter to the attention of that member. If that particular member still fails to promptly notify the Committee, the interested member may notify the pertinent new or existent export licensing measures to the Committee. This counter-notification mechanism offers other members the possibility of bringing the pertinent measures to the attention of the Committee and may thus contribute to the transparency of export licensing measures.

Article 3 of the proposed protocol identifies the information relating to export licensing to be supplied upon request of a member. However, a member is not obliged to provide such information if its disclosure would impede law enforcement, be contrary to the public interest or security interest, or would prejudice the legitimate commercial interests of particular enterprises.[23] Aware of such possibilities, Article 5 of the proposed protocol instructs the Committee to review the implementation and operation of this protocol at least once every two years.[24]

2.2.2. Proposed WTO agreement on export taxes: a substantive approach

In contrast to the procedural approaches of Japan and the US, the EU aimed to substantively address the legal vacuum into which export taxes fall. According to the EU, export taxes remain a policy instrument not subject to GATT/WTO disciplines due to the traditional focus of those organizations on import policies.[25] With a view to redressing their distortions of international trade, the EU thus proposed regulating export taxes, which have the effect of transferring the gains of trade between WTO members; which create an unfair advantage for domestic industries at the expense of the producers of other WTO members; or which evade existing WTO rules on export restrictions by resorting to prohibitive export taxes on the exportation of goods.[26]

Article 1 of the proposed Agreement on Export Taxes regulates two kinds of levies imposed on the exportation of non-agricultural goods. The first relates to the duties, taxes or other charges collected upon, or in connection with, their exportation from the territory of one member to that of another. The second deals with internal taxes and other charges imposed on exporting products that are in excess of those imposed on like products for internal sale. The former is normally collected by the customs agency while the latter is generally imposed by other administrative agencies such as the ministry of finance. These two levies against the exportation of non-agricultural products are prohibited under the proposed Agreement on Export Taxes.

[21] Enhanced Transparency on Export Licensing, *Communication from the Separate Customs Territory of Taiwan, Penghu, Kinmen and Matsu; Japan; Republic of Korea and the United States*, TN/MA/W/130 (11 December 2009), p 3.

[22] Proposed Protocol on Transparency on Export Licensing, Article 2.1.

[23] Ibid, Art 4.

[24] Ibid, Art 5.1.

[25] Non-Tariff Barriers, *Communication from European Communities*, TN/MA/W/11/Add.3 (1 April 2003), para 13.

[26] TN/MA/W/11/Add.6, p 1.

Article 2 of the proposed Agreement on Export Taxes provides special and differential treatment for developing country members and least developed country (LDC) members in particular. Article 3 prescribes two conditions for developing country members to maintain low levels of export taxes on a limited number of products listed in their schedules. The first condition is a 'necessity' test, which dictates that the imposition of the export taxes should be necessary for two purposes: to maintain fiscal stability or to facilitate economic diversification.[27] The second condition is an 'adverse trade effects' test. The imposition of export taxes should not adversely affect international trade either by limiting the availability of the goods subject to export taxes to the WTO members, or by raising the world price of such goods. The maintenance of export taxes should not seriously prejudice the interests of other developing country members.[28] When imposing export duties, the rules on customs valuation as set out in Article VII of the GATT 1994 should be followed.[29] Article 3.2 of the proposed Agreement on Export Taxes also makes it clear that the obligation associated with MFN treatment applies wherever export taxes are maintained by a developing country member.

2.2.3. *Comparison*

The Proposed Protocol on Transparency on Export Licensing and the Proposed Agreement on Export Taxes address two important issues associated with export restrictions which are largely left untouched in the Uruguay Round Agreements: export licensing and export taxes. Japan and the US chose to focus on the procedural transparency of export licensing and include no substantial obligations in their proposal. The only obligation incumbent upon members is to notify the WTO of their export licensing measures, with a possibility of the counter-notification by other interested members: when a member maintains or adopts export licensing procedures, other interested members may bring the subject matter to the member concerned and may notify the WTO themselves.

In contrast, the EU's proposed Agreement on Export Taxes is more ambitious in laying down substantive obligation. It aims to eliminate all export taxes maintained by developed country members. While developing country members are entitled to maintain or institute export taxes, stringent criteria must be fulfilled. The principle of MFN treatment has to be complied with for a developing country member to impose export taxes. The proposed agreement is also wider in scope: it covers both export duties, taxes and other charges which are imposed on, or in connection with exportation, and internal taxes and other charges on exported products which are excessive to those on products for domestic consumption. The proposed Agreement is situated within the framework of the WTO Agreement, and thus affirms the applicability of relevant provisions of the GATT 1994, such as the general exception and special and differential treatment, and the dispute settlement mechanism.

Although the ambition of the EU to lay down disciplines on export taxes should be applauded in view of the principles that guide the Union's action on the international scene as enshrined in Article 21(1) of the TEU, the far-reaching proposal has had great difficulty garnering support from other members. Whereas the Japanese/US Proposed Protocol on Transparency on Export Licensing has won some limited support from other members, the EU remains the only sponsor for the proposed Agreement on Export Taxes. Notwithstanding its high aim, the EU's proposal may lose its relevance during the negotiation processes in the end. As the Chairman of the NAMA negotiation group stated as regards the Draft Modalities for Non-Agricultural Market Access,[30] members do not have sufficient incentives to engage in discussions of export taxes

[27] Proposed Agreement on Export Taxes, Art 3.1(a).
[28] Ibid, Art 3.1(b). [29] Ibid, Art 6.
[30] Draft Modalities for Non-Agricultural Market Access, TN/MA/W/103 (8 February 2008).

because this issue would overburden developing country members.[31] Since export taxes constitute a tariff, it may be argued that export taxes fall outside the mandate of the NAMA on non-tariff barriers. It also runs counter to the objectives of the DDA, which prioritizes development objectives. The imposition of disciplines on export taxes leading to their reduction or elimination may adversely impact the economic development of developing country members.

Such concerns can also be seen in the Dar Es Salaam Declaration, issued by the sixth LDC trade ministers' meeting in Dar Es Salaam, Tanzania in 2009. The LDC members called upon the WTO members to agree not to 'impose any disciplines on export taxes, as these are legitimate tools for development'.[32] The African Caribbean and Pacific countries (ACP) group voiced similar concerns in the ACP Declaration on the seventh session of the WTO Ministerial Conference. The ACP group stressed the need for maintaining export restrictive measures to promote industrial development[33] and urged that the proposal on export taxes be excluded from NAMA negotiations.[34]

Whereas the EU sees export taxes as 'a distortion of international trade', developing country members view them as 'legitimate tools for development'. The differences in characterizing export taxes between the EU and developing Members effectively prevents them from reaching any agreement on this subject. While the proposed Agreement on Export Taxes provides for special and differential treatment of developing country members, the conditions are too strict. The imposition of export taxes, in conjunction with the domestic measures adopted by developing country members, ought to be possible in a limited set of conditions and should also not adversely affect international trade. But these over-strict requirements make it impossible to sufficiently address the needs of developing country members. In light of the development aims of the DDA, it would be difficult for the EU to justify its proposal on export taxes under the NAMA negotiation group, and to find sufficient support for the proposal.

Further, it is also questionable whether the EU's proposal carefully accommodates trade policies with development objectives, both of which are to be conducted 'in the context of the principles and objectives of the Union's external action'. As will be seen below, the EU has been rather successful in writing into trade rules on export restrictions via bilateral negotiations on WTO accessions, EPAs or FTAs. However, this success was achieved by sacrificing the EU's development objectives, which may run counter to the principle of equality and solidarity as put forward in Article 21(1) of the TEU.[35] This is even so when it comes to the EU's EPA negotiations with ACP countries.

2.3. Bilateral negotiations in the accession of new members to the WTO[36]

During bilateral negotiations for the accession of new members to the WTO, the EU has tried to secure commitments relating to the elimination of export restrictions from these newly-acceded or acceding members. While ferrous and non-ferrous scrap and metals have been the focus of negotiations between the EU and Vietnam and Ukraine, the EU paid

[31] Ibid, at 16.

[32] WT/MIN(09)/2 (21 October 2009), para 26. South Centre, an inter-governmental policy think tank of developing countries advanced four arguments based on economic rationale to exclude export taxes and export restrictions from NAMA negotiations, namely 'terms of trade', 'economic diversification' and 'tariff revenue' and 'countervailing monopsony power'. South Centre, 'Some Reasons not to Negotiate Export Taxes and Restrictions in the WTO NAMA Negotiations', SC/AN/TDP/MA/6 May 2006, 4–8.

[33] WT/MIN(09)/7 (27 November 2009), para 43.

[34] Ibid, para 42.

[35] See also the contribution by Larik to this volume.

[36] See also the contribution by Hoffmeister to this volume.

greater attention to energy issues in its negotiations with Saudi Arabia and Russia.[37] The EU succeeded in obtaining commitments from Vietnam and Ukraine on export taxes, but failed to win commitments on dual-pricing from Saudi Arabia and Russia.

On 4 January 1995, Vietnam applied for WTO membership and bilateral negotiations between the EU and Vietnam began on 9 October 2004. The EU expressed its concerns over Vietnamese export duties on ferrous and non-ferrous scrap and metals, and requested commitments from Vietnam on that point.[38] In its proposal for a Council Decision on the position of Vietnam's WTO accession, the European Commission stated that: 'Vietnam will reduce its current export duties of 35% on ferrous scrap to 17% within 5 years of the accession, and its current export duties of 45% on non-ferrous scrap to 22% within 5 years of the accession and Vietnamese export duties on ferrous and non-ferrous scrap metal will be reduced'.[39] The EU successfully secured commitments from Vietnam on ferrous and non-ferrous scraps and metals.

Such an approach extended to bilateral negotiations with Ukraine. According to the World Bank, the EU was aggressive in its bilateral negotiations with Ukraine, demanding that Ukraine eliminate all export duties upon its accession.[40] The Global Analysis Report for the EU–Ukraine Trade Sustainability Impact Assessment (TSIA) also highlights Ukraine's elimination of export bans on non-ferrous metals and its efforts to gradually reduce export duties on ferrous and non-ferrous metals, live cattle and raw leather.[41] Before the completion of Ukraine's accession process, the EU reportedly threw up a last-minute hurdle. The EU regarded export taxes on scrap as a very important issue that had to be resolved before the process was concluded.[42] The EU's demand was largely met, as is reflected in the Ukraine's Working Party Report, in particular paragraphs 236 and 240.[43] As explained by the European Commission in its proposal for a Council Decision on its position on the accession of Ukraine to the WTO: 'Ukraine has taken on a commitment to gradually reduce its export duties imposed on scrap metal, hides and skins, live cattle and oil seeds significantly within the periods of 5 to 8 years. The reduction schedules and the reduced levels of duties will be bound upon accession'.[44]

As regards Saudi Arabia, while it committed to lift its export ban on scrap metal and eliminate export duties on iron and steel scrap,[45] the major issue during bilateral negotiations with the EU was related to dual-pricing of energy. Petroleum products are sold at an administered price significantly lower than international prices with the aim of promoting the industrialization of Saudi Arabia.[46]

[37] Given that the EU has filed a complaint against China based on China's accession commitments, which will be dealt with in great detail in the following section, this section will not examine the accession negotiations between the EU and China.

[38] Press Release, DG Trade, 'EU says Vietnam has fulfilled requirements for WTO accession', Brussels (7 September 2006), available at: <http://trade.ec.europa.eu/doclib/docs/2006/september/tradoc_130100.pdf> last accessed 23/09/2011.

[39] COM (2006) 659 final of 27 October 2006, pp 4–5.

[40] World Bank, Ukraine Trade Policy Study, Vol II, Main Report, Report No 29684-UA, 16 November 2004, para 5.30.

[41] ECORYS Global Analysis Report for the EU–Ukraine TSIA, Commissioned by the European Commission, DG Trade, Ref: TRADE06/D01, Rotterdam, 30 August 2007, p 23.

[42] BS Klapper, 'EU Slows Ukraine's Entry into the WTO' (27 November 2007), available at: <http://trade.ecoaccord.org/english/news/2007/60.htm> last accessed 19 September 2009.

[43] Report of the Working Party on the Accession of Ukraine to the World Trade Organization, T/ACC/UKR/152 (25 January 2008), para 236.

[44] COM (2008) 24 final of 23 January 2008, p 4.

[45] Report of the Working Party on the Accession of the Kingdom of Saudi Arabia to the World Trade Organization, WT/ACC/SAU/61 (1 December 2005), paras 181 and 184.

[46] M Chirullo and P Guerrieri, 'GCC–EU Relations and Trade Integration Patterns' (2005) The Robert Schuman Centre's Policy Paper Series, 02/05, 6.

When concluding their bilateral agreement, the EU announced that the two parties had solved this problem and that Saudi Arabia had abolished the double-pricing of gas.[47] However, such a commitment was not reflected in Saudi Arabia's Working Party Report. According to Quick, Saudi Arabia withdrew this commitment in the end due to the fact that the EU did not insist on the same commitment from Russia.[48] The EU did not insist on the same commitment from Russia mainly due to geopolitical concerns.[49] The EU originally demanded that Russia triple its domestic gas price, but soon softened its position. Zimmermann argues that this is the consequence of the EU seeking a leadership role on climate change policy, which led to non-trade concerns outweighing trade interests.[50]

The EU's pursuit of trade disciplines on export restrictions through bilateral negotiations with newly-acceded, or acceding, members has been largely successful. This may be attributed to the fact that in WTO accession negotiations individual members may effectively block the accession decision if bilateral agreements are not reached. Nonetheless, geopolitical concerns may outweigh trade interests and thus weaken the EU's bargain power in demanding commitments from the acceding members. The softening of the EU's position against one country may also affect its negotiations with another country, as can be seen by the impact of its negotiations with Russia on its negotiations with Saudi Arabia.

2.4. Law enforcement within the WTO Dispute Settlement Mechanism

Two complaints filed by the EU help to illustrate the EU's pursuit for disciplines on export restriction through law enforcement: *Argentina—Hides and Leather* and *China—Raw Materials*.[51] In *Argentina—Hides and Leather*, the EU contended that Argentina maintained a de facto export prohibition on raw and semi-tanned bovine hides and acted in a manner inconsistent with Article VIII:1 and X:3(a) of the GATT 1994. In *China—Raw Materials*, the EU argued that China violated its obligations under both the WTO Agreement and its Accession Protocol by imposing export duties and export quotas, maintaining minimum export prices and giving broad discretionary powers to competent authorities in its export licensing procedures. *Argentina—Hides and Leather* relates to existing trade rules under the WTO Agreement, while *China—Raw Materials* deals with China's 'WTO-plus' obligations under China's Accession Protocol and commitments undertaken in its Working Party Report, which exist apart from the provisions of the WTO Agreement. These two complaints thus offer good examples for an examination of the EU's approach to enforcing trade rules on export restrictions and clarify how the EU contributes to the establishment of a rule-based trading regime.

[47] Press Release, 'Accession of Saudi Arabia to the WTO: Conclusion of the EU–Saudi Arabia bilateral market access deal', Reference: IP/03/1188, 1 September 2003, p 2.

[48] R Quick, 'Further Liberalisation of Trade in Services—Can the DDA Deliver? A Summary of the Chemical Industry's Position on the Doha Development Agenda' in H Hohmann (ed), *Agreeing and Implementing the Doha Round of the WTO* (CUP, 2008), 173.

[49] Ibid, 174.

[50] H Zimmermann, 'Realist Power Europe? The EU in the Negotiations about China's and Russia's WTO Accession' (2007) 45 *Journal of European Public Policy* 813, 825–827.

[51] In addition to these two complaints, the EU has also requested for consultation with India and Pakistan with respect to their measures affecting the exportation of, inter alia, raw hides and skins. As mutually agreed agreements were reached between the EU and India as well as between the EU and Pakistan, the WTO Dispute Settlement Body (DSB) did not establish a panel to examine these two disputes. WT/DS107/1 (20 November 1997); WT/DS120/1 (23 March 1998). Moreover, after the DSB adopted the panel and appellate body reports on *China—Raw Materials*, the EU, in conjunction with the US and Japan, again requested for consultation with China on the export restrictions of raw materials. This is the first case where the EU, the US and Japan, acting together, lodged a complaint against another WTO member. WT/DS341/1, WT/DS342/1, WT/DS/343/1 (15 March 2012).

2.4.1. Argentina—Hides and Leather

In *Argentina—Hides and Leather*, the EU argued that whereas Argentina did not overtly impose export restrictions, Argentinean export procedures, which allowed for the presence of representatives of the Association of Industrial Producers of Leather, Leather Manufactures and Related Products (ADICMA), constituted a de facto export prohibition. The EU asserted that given the ADICMA's access to confidential information and its concentrated market power, the participation of representatives of the ADICMA in export procedures effectively prevented the export of bovine hides.[52] Nonetheless, these arguments were not accepted by the panel. According to the panel, while the discipline of Article XI does extend to restrictions of a de facto nature,[53] the EU had not provided the panel with sufficient evidence to prove there was indeed a de facto export restriction.[54] As the panel stated, in case of an assertion of a de facto restriction on trade, a factual analysis becomes especially important.[55] Greater weight should be thus attached to the trade impact of the alleged de facto restriction.[56] The panel, after reviewing all the evidence before it, did not find the existence of a de facto export restriction by Argentina.

The EU also relied on Article X of the GATT 1994 to challenge the WTO-compatibility of Argentinean export procedures, claiming that the presence of representatives of ADICMA and its access to confidential information breached Argentina's obligation under Article X:3 (a). In responding to this argument, the panel pointed to 'the presence of private parties with conflicting commercial interests in the customs process',[57] and the advantage that any interested party may take in this process to 'obtain confidential information to which they have no right'.[58] Given the presence of the ADICMA and the advantage arising thereof, the Argentinean export procedures deviated from the requirement of impartial administration as put forward by Article X:3(a). The panel thus found that Argentina acted inconsistently with Article X:3(a) of the GATT 1994.[59]

In light of the panel's reasoning in *Argentina—Hides and Leather*, there may well exist a de facto export quota; nonetheless, its existence should be supported by stronger evidence of the impact on trade of this alleged de facto export quota. Further, the discipline of impartial administration of laws and regulation as set out in Article X:3(a) of the GATT 1994 can be extended to export procedures. The key to evaluate the impartiality of the Argentinean export procedures lies in whether an interested party has been given an advantage to which it has no right. In this complaint, the pertinent obligations are general in nature, which makes it more difficult for the EU to make its case. In contrast, as will be seen below, by virtue of the detailed obligations provided in the China's Accession Protocol and Working Party Report, the EU has little difficulty in establishing a prima facie case in *China—Raw Materials*.

2.4.2. China—Raw Materials

In *China—Raw Materials*, the EU challenged the WTO-consistency of Chinese export restrictive measures relating to, inter alia, export licensing, minimum export prices, export quotas and export taxes. The EU argued that China's export licensing system is 'non-automatic' as it endorses a great discretion to the export licensing agencies and is thus inconsistent with Article XI:1 of the GATT 1994.[60] The EU further argued that China

[52] Panel Report, *Argentina—Hides and Leather*, para 11.8.
[53] Ibid, para 11.17.
[54] Ibid, para 11.55.
[55] Ibid, para 11.14.
[56] Ibid, para 11.20.
[57] Ibid, para 11.99.
[58] Ibid, para 11.100.
[59] Ibid, para 12.2.
[60] Panel Report, *China—Raw Materials*, para 7. 923.

coordinated export prices through China Chamber of Commerce of Metals Minerals and Chemicals Importers and Exports, and that exporters not following the coordinated price scheme were penalized, as were licensing authorities that allocated export licenses to those who deviated from the coordinated pricing schedule.[61] The panel was thus called upon to address whether minimum export pricing constitutes a form of quantitive restriction prohibited by Article XI:1 of the GATT 1994.

Regarding export taxes, the existing provisions under the WTO Agreement do not regulate export taxes, and the panel on *China—Raw Materials* is the first example of a panel being called upon to examine the legality of export taxes imposed by a member based on its Accession Protocol and Working Party Report. By virtue of the clear language of Section 11.3 of China's Accession Protocol, the EU in the panel proceedings has little difficulty in establishing a prima facie case for the inconsistency of export duties with the WTO regime. Nonetheless, a difficult legal issue arises when China refers to Article XX, instead of Article XI of the GATT 1994, to justify the imposition of export duties. The EU further maintained that China imposed export quotas upon several raw materials, a fact that China did not contest. Nonetheless, China invoked Articles XI:2 and XX(b) or XX(g) as a defence.

In order to justify its export quota on refractory-grade bauxite, China asserted that the export restrictive measures were applied to prevent or relieve a critical shortage of essential products.[62] The panel first agreed with China that bauxite was a product essential to China in view of its use as an intermediary in the production of iron and steel, which play an important role in Chinese employment and economic development.[63] The panel nonetheless noted that it saw no evidence of a critical shortage of bauxite. Further, the panel stressed that Article XI:2(a) permits quantitative restrictions or prohibitions only on a temporary basis. This provision does not permit long-term conservation; were that the case, Article XX(g) would lose its meaning.[64] As the panel observed, the export quota on bauxite was in place at least as early as 2000. If China intended to maintain this export quota until the exhaustion of its reserve, such a period could not be interpreted as a temporarily application in terms of Article XI:2(a) of the GATT 1994.[65]

The panel continued to examine China's defence on the basis of Article XX(g) and XX(b).[66] China claimed that its export quotas on refractory-grade bauxite and fluorspar were aimed at managing and protecting these two exhaustible natural resources, and thus ought to be permitted by Article XX(g).[67] However, this argument was rejected by the panel. According to the panel, three conditions must be satisfied for China to justly invoke Article XX(g). First, there must be 'a close and genuine relationship of ends and means' between the export restrictions and the conservation of bauxite and fluorspar.[68] Secondly, the export restrictions should be made effective 'in conjunction with restrictions on domestic production or consumption', which requires export restrictions and related domestic restrictions to operate simultaneously.[69] Thirdly, there must be an 'even-handedness' between export restrictions and restrictions on domestic production or consumption.[70]

The panel opined that the export quotas on refractory-grade bauxite and fluorspar did not contribute to the conservation of these two exhaustible resources, as it made no difference

[61] Ibid, para 7.997.
[62] Ibid, para 7.283.
[63] Ibid, para 7.340.
[64] Ibid, paras 7.348–7.349.
[65] Ibid, paras 7.351 and 7.354.
[66] Whereas the panel concludes that Art XX is not applicable to China's obligation to eliminate export taxes, it nonetheless examines *arguendo* China's defence on general exception relating to export taxes.
[67] Panel Report, *China—Raw Materials*, para 7.356.
[68] Ibid, para 7.416.
[69] Ibid, para 7.398.
[70] Ibid, para 7.402.

whether they were consumed domestically or abroad.[71] It thus saw no clear link between the export restrictions and any conservation objective.[72] Additionally, China failed to prove that other measures were put into place to restrict domestic production or the consumption of bauxite and fluorspar,[73] which led to the imposition of uneven burdens on foreign and domestic consumers.[74]

China also claimed that its export restrictions on coke, manganese, magnesium and silicon carbide were aimed at reducing the pollution emitted during the extraction and production of these metals, and could thus protect the health of the Chinese population.[75] In addressing China's argument, the panel examined five pertinent issues: the purpose and objective of the export restrictions; the importance of the interests and values involved; the contribution of the export restrictions to the protection of human health; the severity of the export restrictions; and the availability of less restrictive alternative measures.[76] After examining these five issues, the panel concluded that China's export restriction could not be justified by Article XX(b) of the GATT 1994.[77]

Regarding export duties, the panel first declared that China's Accession Protocol constitutes an integral part of the WTO Agreement and that the commitments included in the Working Party Report and incorporated into the accession protocol by cross-reference are binding and enforceable under the WTO dispute settlement mechanism.[78] The panel examined the ordinary meaning of the legal text of Section 11.3 of China's Accession Protocol, which specifies two exceptions to the obligation to eliminate export taxes: the 84 products listed in Annex 6, and measures adopted in accordance with Article VIII of the GATT 1994.[79] The panel also compared the legal text of Sections 5.1, 11.1, 11.2 and Section 11.3 of China's Accession Protocol and found that there was no similar stipulation to 'without prejudice China's right to regulate trade in a manner consistent with the WTO Agreement' or 'in conformity with the GATT 1994' in Section 11.3.[80] The panel thus held that whereas Sections 5.1, 11.1 and 11.2 of China's Accession Protocol incorporate a general exception, Section 11.3 does not. The general exception as set out in Article XX of the GATT 1994 is thus inapplicable to China's obligation to eliminate export taxes.[81]

Owing to the detailed regulations in China's Accession Protocol, the EU succeeded in making its case that China was in violation of its WTO obligation on export taxes. However, this development may not be as positive as it appears, as it may undermine the EU's efforts to promote 'multilateral solutions to common problems' and damage the EU's image in advancing environmental or public health objectives. First, given the absence of disciplines on export taxes in the Uruguay Round Agreements, the obligation relating to export taxes is only applicable to a limited set of newly-acceded members, which results in an unfair allocation of rights and obligations between existent and new WTO members. More importantly, these 'WTO-plus' obligations, as the export taxes in this present case suggests, seem incongruent with the WTO legal system. Whereas the panel's conclusion on the inapplicability of general exception to China's obligation on export taxes may be technically correct from a textual perspective, that same finding may undermine the coherence of WTO rules. A closer look of the panel's reasoning would evince this.

The backbone of the panel's reasoning, which is supported by the Appellate Body, is based on the legal text of Section 11.3 of China's Accession Protocol, as contrasted to Sections 5.1, 11.1 and 11.2. However, this reasoning may be problematic. As Matsushita points out, Article XX of the GATT 1994 provides that 'nothing in this Agreement' prevents a member from adopting measures satisfying the conditions set out thereafter. However, the panel's ruling effectively excludes the application of general exceptions to other Annex 1A

71 Ibid, para 7.428. 72 Ibid, para 7.432. 73 Ibid, para 7.458.
74 Ibid, para 7.466. 75 Ibid, para 7.470. 76 Ibid, paras 7.478–493.
77 Ibid, paras 7.615–616. 78 Ibid, paras 7.112–7.114. 79 Ibid, paras 7.122–7.123.
80 Ibid, paras 7.118–7.120 and 7.136–7.138. 81 Ibid, paras 7.159.

agreements to the WTO Agreement that contain no explicit reference to the GATT 1994. Matsushita further notes that in appreciating the relationship between GATT 1994 and other Annex 1A agreements, emphasis should be placed more on continuity than on separation.[82] The same rationale should be followed in relation to existent WTO agreements and accession protocols.

Taking a holistic perspective, if one agrees that export taxes are regulatory measures falling within the scope of the GATT 1994, it would be paradoxical to exclude from the application of the general exception provided therein. It is thus doubtful whether the EU does pursue a rule-based trade regime and respect the consistency of the WTO as it claims. Admittedly, from a purely 'legalist' perspective, the EU had a right to argue against the application of Article XX to China's obligation on export taxes, and the EU had also made a good case in persuading the panel on this point. However, this success is not without a price. First, the EU's positions are contradictory between law-making and law-enforcement. On the law-making front, it proposed the general exception applicable to export taxes.[83] But on the law enforcement front, it argued that China could not rely upon Article XX to justify its export taxes. Secondly, this undermines the EU's creditability in advancing rule of law and promoting 'multilateral solutions to common problems' in light of the threat to the consistency of the WTO law. Thirdly, it also has an adverse policy impact upon China's environment and heath policies, given that China would be prevented from referring to Article XX when China does wish to use export taxes as a policy instrument for these legitimate objectives rather than 'disguised restriction on international trade'. These developments run counter to Article 21.1 of the TEU and present the EU as incoherent actor in the international trading regime.

3. Export Restrictions in Bilateral EU External Agreements

In pursuing trade rules on export restrictions, the EU relies not only upon the multilateral WTO framework, but also upon its bilateral trade agreement negotiations. This section examines provisions pertaining to export restrictions as contained in the EU's external economic agreements.[84] After the launch of the Global Europe strategy, the EU has concluded several important bilateral agreements with its trade partners, including CARIFORUM states, South Korea, Peru and Columbia. The EU–CARIFORUM EPA was the first EPA concluded under the auspice of the Cotonou Agreement, while the EU–Korea FTA is the first FTA which the EU successfully concluded with the targeted countries identified in the Global Europe strategy. The EU–Columbia–Peru Trade Agreement is a multiparty trade agreement, and although Ecuador participated in the negotiations in the beginning, it later suspended its participation. This multiparty agreement is a substitute for the region-to-region agreement between the EU and the Andean Community. As will be seen below, the legal obligations relating to export restrictions have become increasingly precise and the subject matters covered gradually expand. While the EU may wish to promote 'multilateral solutions to common problems', it seems that the EU is more effective in pursuing trading rules on export restrictions through bilateral negotiations.

Export taxes and quantitative restrictions remain two major restrictions in the EU–CARIFORUM EPA. The EU–CARIFORUM EPA first clarifies that a customs duty covers 'any duty or charge of any kind, including any form of surtax or surcharge, imposed in connection with the importation or exportation of goods', but excludes internal taxes and other internal charges; contingency measures; and fees and charges for the services

[82] Matsushita, n 8, 301–302.
[83] cf Proposed Agreement on Export Taxes, Art 5.
[84] See also the contribution by Cremona to this volume.

rendered.[85] It sets out a timetable for the elimination of customs taxes on imports and exports for the parties. Whereas the EU–CARIFORUM EPA instructs the parties to eliminate customs duties applicable to exports, it nonetheless provides a three-year implementation period for Guyana and Suriname on a certain products, such as precious stones, bauxite, unrefined cane sugar and wood.[86] The EU–CARIFORUM EPA prohibits restrictions on imports and exports other than customs duties, taxes, fees or other charges, which cover quotas, import or export license or other measures.[87] This obligation basically copies the legal text of Article XI:1 of the GATT 1994.

As for the EU–Korea FTA, it first instructs the parties to eliminate 'any duties, taxes or other fees and charges imposed on, or in connection with, the exportation of goods'.[88] It further dictates the parties to refrain from imposing 'any internal taxes, fees and charges on goods exported to the other party that are in excess of those imposed on like goods destined for internal sale'.[89] The latter requirement mirrors the language of the EU's proposal Agreement on Export Taxes. The EU effectively wrote into the EU–Korea FTA what it aimed, but failed, to achieve in the multilateral framework. In addition to export duties, the EU–Korea FTA reiterates the importance of the elimination of quantitative restrictions and incorporates Article XI of the GATT 1994 and its interpretative notes, which by reference *mutatis mutandis* constitute part of the EU–Korea FTA.[90] A difference in detail may be seen between the EU–CARIFORUM EPA and the EU–Korea FTA in their treatment of quantitative restrictions. The EU–CARIFORUM EPA borrows the language of Article XI:1 from the GATT 1994 but does not include the exceptions as provided in Article XI:2. In contrast, the entirety of Article XI is incorporated into the EU–Korea FTA. This poses a question whether or not the exceptions as provided in Article XI:2 are available for the EU–CARIFORUM EPA.

In addition to export duties and quantitative restrictions, the EU–Peru–Columbia Trade Agreement also touches upon export licensing procedures. The EU–Peru–Columbia Trade Agreement in Article 25 regulates export taxes, prohibiting the parties from adopting or maintaining 'any duty or tax, other than internal charges' inconsistent with the obligation of national treatment, unless the agreement provides otherwise.[91] Regarding quantitative restrictions, the EU–Peru–Columbia Trade Agreement follows the model of the EU–Korea FTA by incorporating Article XI of the GATT 1994 and its interpretative notes into the legal text.[92] The EU–Peru–Columbia Trade Agreement goes on to address the third discipline on export restrictions: export licensing procedures. According to Article 26.2 of the EU–Peru–Columbia Trade Agreement, provisions contained in the Import Licensing Procedures should be, *mutatis mutandis*, applied to any licensing procedures for exports to another party. The obligation to notify the WTO regarding the import licensing procedures is recast as an obligation to notify the parties of export licensing procedures.[93] So far, the EU–Peru–Columbia Trade Agreement contains the most stringent disciplines on export restrictions, covering the elimination of export duties, prohibition of quantitative restrictions and transparency and notification requirements for export licensing procedures. The EU–Peru–Columbia Trade Agreement thus covers both the EU's proposal relating to substantive obligation and the Japan and US's proposal on procedural transparency in the WTO forum. From the perspective of negotiation strategy, this might not be so surprising, since the procedural requirement is not as threatening as the substantive obligation. As long as the EU has successfully imposed substantive obligations, it would have little difficulty in including procedural norms altogether. Interestingly however, from the perspective of the 'EU as a rule-generator', what the EU included in the EU–Peru–Columbia Trade Agreement

[85] EU–CARIFORUM EPA, Art 11.
[86] EU–CARIFORUM EPA, Art 14.
[87] EU–CARIFORUM EPA, Art 14.
[88] EU–Korea FTA, Art 2.11.
[89] Ibid, Art 2.11.
[90] Ibid, Art 2.9.
[91] EU–Peru–Columbia Trade Agreement, Art 25.
[92] Ibid, Art 23.
[93] Ibid, Art 26.2.

covers both its proposal and that of Japan and the US. In this rule-generating process, a combination and co-existence of norms from different sources may be visible.

Overall, in its external economic agreements, the EU has been rather successful in exerting provisions on export restrictions, in particular with developing countries. Nonetheless, this aggressive approach has brought resentment from its trade partners, notably, its counterparts in EPA negotiations. According to Lazzari, export duties are one of the few trade policies available to developing countries, since most policy space has been significantly reduced by Structural Adjustment Programmes imposed by the International Monetary Fund (IMF) and the World Bank in the 1980s and 1990s, and WTO negotiations.[94] When the EU imposes rules in EPAs, African countries are effectively stripped of important policy instruments. African countries may not effectively achieve specific policy goals and respond to economic challenges, such as value addition, infant industry development and promotion of industrialization in general.[95] In short, whereas the EU enjoys greater bargaining power in bilateral trade agreement negotiations and may easily succeed in including disciplines on export restrictions, this approach may compromise the objectives of its development policy. Similar weaknesses can be seen in the law-making and law-enforcement processes in the multilateral WTO forum. The EU's proposed Agreement on Export Taxes, regardless of its exception for developing country members, fails to address the concerns of developing country members. As a consequence, the EU's proposal has not won support from these members. In the complaint against China, the EU has made the imposition of export taxes completely impossible, even where they are truly for the purposes of environmental protection or public health objectives. It may thus be safe to say that in pursuing trading disciplines, trade interests generally override development objectives or environmental concerns.

4. Conclusion

This chapter finds that the EU has had, at best, limited success in negotiating new rules on export restrictions in NAMA negotiations. This is mainly due to the multilateral framework of the WTO wherein developing country members may act as a bloc to compete with developed country members in negotiations. If the EU aggressively pursues trade rules on exports, this might frustrate the objective of the DDA to balance rights and obligations between developing and developed country members, to make the multilateral framework fairer and to respond to the needs of developing country members. To developing country members, proposals to eliminate export taxes mean, in effect, allowing the EU's access to their natural resources and constraining their policy space, instead of correcting market distortions. The EU's effort to pursue trade rules on export restrictions through NAMA negotiations is doomed to futility. By contrast, in bilateral negotiations for WTO accession of new members, the EU has generally succeeded in securing commitments pertaining to export restrictions, for example, in negotiations with Ukraine and Vietnam. Whereas the EU would like to see similar commitments by Saudi Arabia and Russia, other political agendas overrode trade interests. As a consequence, the EU did not insist on the abolishment of the practices of dual-pricing on energy products in Saudi Arabia and Russia.

The law-enforcement aspect of the WTO dispute settlement mechanism has been rather successful, but nonetheless poses a threat to the coherence of the multilateral trade rules. More specifically, the EU's victory in *China—Raw Materials* relies mainly on China's 'WTO-plus' obligations. The EU has little difficulty in making a prima facie case on China's

[94] Thomas Lazzeri, 'EPAs and the European Raw Materials Initiative', available at: <http://www.aefjn.org/index.php/352/articles/epas-and-the-european-raw-materials-initiative.html> last accessed 4 October 2011.

[95] I Ramdoo, 'Shopping for Raw Materials: Should Africa be worried about EU Raw Materials Initiative?' ECDPM Discussion Paper No 105, February 2011, 39.

violation of WTO obligations. However, the aggrandizement of 'WTO-plus' obligations may endanger the inherent coherence of WTO rules. Most importantly, the EU argues, and the panel and the Appellate Body agree, that the general exception as provided in Article XX of the GATT 1994 is not applicable to China's obligation to eliminate export taxes. The EU's contention and the panel's holding have effectively undermined the general applicability of supposedly general exceptions. Moreover, the EU's interpretation of the inapplicability of Article XX of the GATT 1994 to China's obligation on export taxes is inconsistent with its position in the proposed WTO Agreement on Export Taxes where a general exception would apply to export taxes.

With regard to bilateral negotiations, the EU successfully included trade rules on export restrictions in its FTAs. Nonetheless, the author is not certain whether this is a positive development, as the proliferation of bilateral trade rules on export restrictions may further reduce the incentives of members to engage into multilateral rules and thus marginalize multilateral frameworks. Besides, channelling the issue of export restrictions to bilateral venues may weaken the negotiating position and bargaining power of the EU's developing country trade partners. The EU may gain on the trade front, but lose goodwill and soft power on the development front. It is thus essential to ensure that the objectives of the EU's development policy not be compromised by EU trade interests.

Policy coherence may be the key, but this seems not to be the case with regard to the EU's efforts in shaping global rules on export restrictions. Whereas the EU is instructed to advance in the wider world rule of law and 'principles of equality and solidarity' and 'promote multilateral solutions to common problems', it has not consistently adhered to these principles and objectives. We have seen an incoherent Union in proposing legal norms on export taxes with general exception, but arguing against the applicability of general exception in China's obligation to export taxes. We have also witnessed that the EU undermines the coherence of the WTO with the inclusion of 'WTO-plus' obligations on export restrictions in bilateral accession negotiations and marginalizes the multilateral WTO framework by exerting trading rules in bilateral trade agreements, which contradicts the aim to advance rule of law and promote 'multilateral solutions to common problems'. Finally, development objectives and environment concerns have not always been duly taken into consideration when pursuing the trading rules in the multilateral or bilateral framework. In most cases, trade interests outweighed development objectives or environment concerns.

PART IV

THE EU AND GLOBAL ENVIRONMENTAL GOVERNANCE

12

Ambition, Complexity, and Legitimacy of Pursuing Mutual Supportiveness Through the EU's External Environmental Action

Elisa Morgera[1]

1. Introduction

The role of the EU as environmental norm generator and exporter is increasingly being supported by complex interactions between EU internal regulation with extraterritorial implications,[2] as well as unilateral and bilateral external action, in a combined attempt to influence ongoing multilateral environmental negotiations. This is part of the EU's strategy to act as a global environmental leader against the background of fragmented international environmental law, and in particular the need for mutual supportiveness between the international climate change regime and the international biodiversity regime.

This contribution aims to identify the strengths and weaknesses of the EU's external action in pursuing holistic environmental protection outside its borders. In the first section the ambition of the EU's external environmental action will be illustrated, in its objective to support environmental multilateralism and contribute to shaping a holistic approach in international environmental law, in light of the Treaty requirement of environmental integration (Article 11 Treaty on the Functioning of the European Union (TFEU)) and the emerging international principle of mutual supportiveness. The second section examines the complexity of the EU's external environmental action, by looking at the plethora of external relations tools used by the EU to achieve its global environmental objectives. The third and central part of the paper will assess the legitimacy of EU external environmental action against the international environmental principle of common but differentiated responsibility, taking recent EU initiatives on sustainable forest management and biofuels as case studies. The concluding section will point to the diversity of approaches currently deployed by the EU and their characteristics that are most promising to ensure that EU external environmental action fully respects EU and international law.

2. The Ambition of the EU's External Environmental Action

The new Treaty-based framework of the EU's external action clearly emphasizes the EU's external *environmental* agenda and its various levels, by providing that all external activities of the Union should foster the sustainable environmental development of developing countries, with the primary aim of eradicating poverty; helping to develop international measures to preserve and improve the quality of the environment and the sustainable

[1] The author wishes to thank James Harrison, Gracia Marín Durán, Rok Zvelc and another anonymous reviewer from the European Commission for their valuable comments on previous drafts of this paper; and Riccardo Beltrame for his editorial assistance. The author also gratefully acknowledges the financial support provided by the Christie Law Fellowship 2009/2010.

[2] As opposed to measures with an extraterritorial 'effect': see the distinction drawn by AG Kokott with regards to EU internal measures that do not embody a concrete rule of conduct for subjects beyond the territory of the EU, but still create an indirect incentive for them: Opinion, C-366/10 *Air Transport Association of America and Others*, 6 October 2011, paras 145–147.

management of global natural resources;[3] and promoting an international system based on stronger multilateral environmental cooperation and good global environmental governance.[4] This confirms the pre-existing Treaty-based requirement of environmental integration, which provides that the more specific objectives, principles and criteria for the EU environmental policy[5] should be applied in all other EU policies, be these external or internal, in the same way as they must be applied in the environmental policy.[6] Conversely, the EU's external environmental action is expected to contribute to the other objectives of the Union's external relations, such as supporting human rights, preventing conflicts and encouraging the integration of all countries into the world economy.[7] In addition, the EU is under a general obligation to 'promote multilateral solutions to common problems, in particular in the framework of the United Nations',[8] which encompasses multilateral solutions to common environmental problems devised through relevant UN environmental initiatives and instruments.

While these broadly framed objectives already represent a challenging external agenda for the EU, the requirement of environmental integration adds a further layer of ambition. Aside from the greening of non-environmental policies, Article 11 TFEU also entails that EU environmental law itself is to be construed and interpreted broadly, taking into consideration all of the EU environmental objectives, principles and criteria[9]—in essence requiring a holistic approach to EU environmental law-making. This dimension of environmental integration is becoming increasingly relevant as climate change is steadily receiving political priority at the international and EU level,[10] because of its prominent position in the global development agenda,[11] its securitization,[12] its increasingly sophisticated rules, as well as high-profile climate finance.[13] On the other hand, possible negative impacts of climate change response measures on other areas of environmental protection and cooperation are increasingly identified by the international community, particularly in the area of biodiversity.[14]

[3] Art 21(2)(d) and (f) TEU. See contribution by Joris Larik to this collection.

[4] Art 21(2)(h) TEU, read in conjunction with the above-mentioned provisions and Art 11 TFEU on environmental integration ('Environmental protection requirements must be integrated into the definition and implementation of the Union policies and activities, in particular with a view to promoting sustainable development').

[5] Art 191 TFEU.

[6] N Dhondt, *Integration of Environmental Protection into Other EC Policies* (Europa Law Publishing, 2003), at 84; and discussion in G Marín Durán and E Morgera, *Environmental Integration in the EU's External Relations: Beyond Multilateral Dimensions* (Hart Publishing, 2012) ch 1.

[7] For a discussion, see M Cremona, 'Coherence and EU External Policy' in E Morgera (ed), *The External Environmental Policy of the European Union: EU and International Law Perspectives* (CUP, 2012); and specifically on human rights obligations concerning the EU's external environmental action, see D Augenstein, 'The Human Rights Dimension of Environmental Protection in EU External Relations Post-Lisbon', in the same collection.

[8] Art 21(1), second sentence, TEU.

[9] N Dhondt, n 6, at 179, on basis of Joined Cases C-175/98 and C-177/98 *Criminal proceedings against Paolo Lirussi and Francesca Bizzaro* [1999] ECR I-6881; Joined Cases C-418 and 419/97 *ARCO Chemie Nederland Ltd v Minister van Volkshuisvesting, Ruimtelijke Ordening en Milieubeheer and Vereniging Dorpsbelang Hees, Stichting Werkgroep Weurt + and Vereniging Stedelijk Leefmilieu Nijmegen v Directeur van de dienst Milieu en Water van de provincie Gelderland* [2000] ECR I-4475; and Case C-318/98 *Criminal proceedings against Giancarlo Fornasar, Andrea Strizzolo, Giancarlo Toso, Lucio Mucchino, Enzo Peressutti and Sante Chiarcosso* [2000] ECR I-4785.

[10] As reflected in the specific mention of climate change in Art 191(1) TFEU, which reads: 'Union policy on the environment shall contribute to pursuit of the following objectives:... promoting measures at international level to deal with regional or worldwide environmental problems, and in particular combating climate change'. For an earlier discussion about the political priority attached to climate change by the EU, see E Morgera and G Marín Durán, 'The UN 2005 World Summit, the Environment and the EU: Priorities, Promises and Prospects' (2006) 15 RECIEL 1–18.

[11] E Morgera, 'The 2005 UN World Summit and the Environment: The Proverbial Half-Full Glass?' (2006) 15 *Italian Yearbook of International Law* 53–80.

[12] F Sindico, 'Climate Change: A Security (Council) Issue?' (2007) 1 *Carbon and Climate Law Review* 26–31.

[13] C Streck, 'Ensuring New Finance and Real Emission Reduction: A Critical Review of the Additionality Concept' (2011) 2 *Carbon and Climate Law Review* 158.

[14] The parties to the Convention on Biological Diversity (5 June 1992, 1760 UNTS 79; hereinafter, CBD) have been increasingly addressing the environmental sustainability of response measures to climate change: E Morgera,

The need for a holistic interpretation of what can be perceived as fragmented[15] international environmental law is expressed in the principles of *pacta sunt servanda* and sustainable development, and more clearly articulated in the emerging principle of mutual supportiveness.[16] The latter requires, at the interpretative level, that states disqualify solutions to tensions between competing regimes involving the subordination of one regime to the other; and, at the law-making level, that states exert good faith efforts to negotiate and conclude instruments that clarify the relationship between competing regimes, when interpretative reconciliation efforts have been exhausted.[17] While this principle is usually invoked in the context of the trade and environment nexus,[18] the increasing tensions between the international climate change regime and the international biodiversity regime equally call for a mutually supportive approach to the further development and implementation of the two legal frameworks.[19] Mutual supportiveness may thus have similar implications to those of the EU Treaty-based requirement of environmental integration in the context of tensions between the international climate change regime and the international biodiversity regime. Namely, it calls upon the EU to address climate change as a threat to biodiversity (proactively addressing the negative impacts of climate change, and of climate responses, on biodiversity and community livelihoods); and as a response that contributes to biodiversity conservation and sustainable use (ensuring the adoption of mitigation and adaptation measures with biodiversity co-benefits).[20] Thus, both in light of the requirements of EU primary law and the Union's international obligations, EU external environmental action is to take a holistic approach, ensuring that other sectoral environmental initiatives (be they external or internal) consider climate change implications,[21] and at the same time that broader environmental concerns are fully accounted for in devising and implementing climate change measures (that is, that climate change response measures are environmentally sustainable).[22]

To achieve these objectives, the Union has put in place three modalities to support the development and implementation of international environmental law. First, the EU seeks to use its external action to politically, technically and financially support the implementation of existing multilateral environmental agreements beyond its borders, particularly in developing countries. Second, the EU is also using its external action tools to build alliances with third countries, regions or groups of countries with a view to influencing ongoing international environmental negotiations. Third, the EU is also using these tools to make progress on environmental issues on which the international community has been unable to

'Far Away, So Close: A Legal Analysis of the Increasing Interactions between the Convention on Biological Diversity and Climate Change Law' (2011) 2 *Climate Law* 85–115; and CBD Secretariat, 'Connecting Biodiversity and Climate Change Mitigation and Adaptation: Report of the Second Ad Hoc Technical Expert Group on Biodiversity and Climate Change' (Technical Series, No 41, 2009).

[15] H van Asselt, F Sindico and M Mehling, 'Global Climate Change and the Fragmentation of International Law' (2008) 30 *Law and Policy* 423; E Morgera, No Need to Reinvent the Wheel for a Human Rights-based Approach to Tackling Climate Change: The Contribution of International Biodiversity Law in E Hollo, K Kulovesi and M Mehling (eds), *Climate Change and the Law* (Springer, forthcoming).

[16] R Pavoni, 'Mutual Supportiveness as a Principle of Interpretation and Law-Making: A Watershed for the WTO-and-Competing-Regimes Debate?' (2010) 21 EJIL 649, at 662.

[17] Ibid, at 661–669.

[18] See contribution by Marín Durán to this collection.

[19] This argument is fully developed in Morgera, 'Far Away, So Close...', n 14, at 87–90.

[20] These objectives have already been emphasized by the European Parliament (Resolution of 22 May 2007 on halting the loss of biodiversity by 2010 (2006/2233(INI)), paras 6 and 67–68); and more recently by the Council, 'Conclusions on the EU Biodiversity Strategy 2020', 23 June 2011, paras 3 and 16.

[21] Climate change mainstreaming has become an explicit Treaty requirement, based on a combined reading of Art 11 TFEU and Art 191(1), where climate change is for the first time explicitly mentioned as a result of the amendment introduced by the Lisbon Treaty.

[22] For such an assessment in the context of the EU climate policy, see K Kulovesi, E Morgera and M Muñoz, 'Environmental Integration and the Multi-faceted International Dimensions of EU Law: Unpacking the EU's 2009 Climate and Energy Package' (2011) 48(3) *CML Rev* 829–891.

launch negotiations towards an international legally binding agreement: in the absence of multilateral environmental negotiations, the EU wishes to pursue certain environmental goals with other willing countries with a view to building international consensus from the bottom up.[23] This strategy clearly aims at proactively addressing cases in which multilateralism appears slow or ineffective, while also having the potential to promptly respond to the changing multilateral landscape, so that EU external environmental action switches from one of the above-outlined modalities to the other, depending on progress or lack thereof at the multilateral level. The EU therefore aims to use its unilateral and bilateral approach as a *complement*, rather than as an alternative, to multilateralism.

3. The Complexity of EU External Environmental Action

The strategy just illustrated is traditionally carried out by the EU and its Member States as a powerful negotiating block in multilateral environmental negotiations, and as one of the world's largest providers of funding for multilateral environmental protection initiatives and instruments. More recent are the EU's more systematic efforts to support its global environmental leadership through its external relations tools at the unilateral, bilateral and inter-regional level.

Trade-related instruments include sophisticated clauses on environmental cooperation in bilateral and inter-regional agreements, which increasingly rely on international environmental standards. While these agreements have different denominations and objectives, their environmental clauses are notably similar.[24] In particular, the bilateral agreements concluded by the EU with third countries or regions since 2005 ('post-Global Europe agreements')[25] establish obligations to effectively implement and enforce key multilateral environmental agreements (MEAs) in the context of trade and sustainable development chapters. In addition, environment-specific cooperative monitoring and dispute-resolution mechanisms are set up in that context, requiring the involvement of environmental experts and allowing also for advice to be sought from MEA Secretariats.[26] The negotiations of these agreements are preceded by Sustainability Impact Assessments (SIAs), which contribute to identify trade-offs between the trade component of the agreement under negotiation and environmental protection in the EU and in the partner country: SIAs thus often serve to address global environmental issues or instruments.[27] For countries that have no trade agreement in place with the EU, the Generalized System of Preferences (GSP) unilaterally offers developing and least-developed countries trade incentives that are made conditional upon the ratification and effective implementation of key MEAs.[28]

In terms of development aid, the EU practice of integrating environmental concerns in external assistance is also increasingly targeting the implementation of key MEAs, as well as contributions to the reform of global environmental governance with the explicit objective of shaping it by the external dimensions of the EU's own environment and climate change

[23] Marín Durán and Morgera, *Environmental Integration in the EU's External Relations*, n 6, ch 7.

[24] Ibid, ch 2.

[25] As their negotiations were launched by the Commission, 'Communication—Global Europe: Competing in the World: A Contribution to the EU's Growth and Jobs Strategy' COM (2006) 567 final of 4 October 2006. See Marín Durán and E Morgera, n 6, at 133–142, and for an insider's perspective, R Zvelc, 'Environmental Integration in EU Trade Policy: The Generalized System of Preferences, Trade Sustainability Impact Assessments and Free Trade Agreements', in Morgera (ed), n 7.

[26] This is the case of association agreements (Art 217 TFEU), partnership and cooperation agreements, as well as free trade agreements between the EU and individual third countries or groups of third countries. For a comprehensive assessment, see Marín Durán and Morgera, n 6, ch 2.

[27] Marín Durán and Morgera, n 6, ch 6.

[28] Marín Durán and Morgera, n 6, ch 3. This is the 'GSP-plus' under Reg (EC) 732/2008 of 22 July 2008 applying a scheme of generalized tariff preferences for the period from 1 January 2009 to 31 December 2011 [2008] OJ L 211/1.

policies.[29] In addition, the EU institutionalizes a plethora of policy dialogues with various individual developed and developing countries, and with various groups of third countries, for the periodic exchange of views on environmental priorities and respective negotiating positions. These exercises, which are mainly organized at the initiative of the EU, serve to develop specific action plans that also address global environmental issues.[30]

These instruments are inter-linked in a complex and somewhat obscure manner: SIAs feed into the negotiations of bilateral agreements, but their outcomes should also be taken into account in the implementation of these agreements, particularly because some of the recommendations emerging from SIAs may be addressed through other EU external relations tools, such as financial and technical assistance. The implementation of bilateral agreements is followed up on through policy dialogues, which produce action plans to attract funding on certain priority activities falling under the broad scope of the environmental cooperation clauses included in bilateral agreements. The allocation of EU external funding, however, remains separate from dialogue processes and in the vast majority of cases, also from bilateral agreements: generally it is up to the EU regulations on each funding instrument to set the principles and procedures for integrating environmental requirements in EU external funding.[31] Enhanced dialogue is, in turn, seen as an objective of the Union's external funding, as well as a means to increase the visibility of EU financial and technical assistance supporting environmental protection in partner countries. Furthermore, dialogues are expected to be informed by SIAs and ex-post SIAs, and are used by the EU to support the understanding beyond its borders of certain pieces of EU internal environmental legislation with extraterritorial implications.

The complexity of such a toolbox is self-evident, and there appears to be no systematic monitoring and assessment of its combined effectiveness. The Commission has already noted that even international consultants carrying out SIAs are not aware of the full breadth of external relations tools used by the EU to address trade-offs between environmental protection and socio-economic development.[32] It is therefore quite likely that such complexity puzzles outsiders, fuelling a lack of trust or at least limited understanding in third country governmental counterparts and stakeholders. It may also be unmanageable for the various EU institutional actors involved, with obvious risks of duplicated efforts, wasted resources and overlapping or even conflicting results as a consequence. The credibility and coherence of the EU external environmental action may therefore be victims of its complexity.[33]

4. The Legitimacy of EU External Environmental Action?

In the face of the high level of ambition and growing complexity of EU external environmental action, an analysis of the legitimacy[34] of relevant initiatives seems warranted for at

[29] Commission, 'Environment and Natural Resources Thematic Programme—2011–2013 Strategy Paper and Multiannual Indicative Programme', 29 October 2010, at 25.

[30] Marín Durán and Morgera, n 6, ch 5.

[31] G Marín Durán, 'Environmental Integration in EU Development Cooperation: Responding to International Commitments or Its Own Policy Priorities?' in Morgera (ed), n 7.

[32] Commission, 'Position Paper: Trade SIA of the Negotiations of a PCA between the EU and China' February 2009, at 5; Commission, 'Position Paper: Trade Sustainability Impact Assessment of the Euro–Mediterranean Free Trade Agreement' June 2009, at 6; Commission, 'Position Paper on the SIA of the EU–Cooperation Council of the Arab States of the Gulf (GCC) SIA' March 2006, at 6.

[33] The now defunct Cardiff process—a European Council-led exercise to closely monitor environmental integration in the work of sectoral Council formations—could be revived or inspire another periodic process to track and assess renewed environmental integration efforts at the internal/external action interface. On the Cardiff process, see Commission, 'Communication on Partnership for Integration: A Strategy for Integrating Environment into EU Policies' COM (1998) 333 final and Commission, 'Working Document on integrating environmental considerations into other policy areas—A stocktaking of the Cardiff process' COM (2004) 394 final.

[34] This contribution will refer both to input legitimacy, as a transparent, participatory and expertise-inclusive process, and output legitimacy, as the legality and effectiveness of the result of decision-making: for a discussion

least two reasons. From an EU law standpoint, it seems necessary to ascertain whether and under what conditions the Union's significant resources devoted to unilateral, bilateral and inter-regional action are effectively used for the pursuit of multilateral environmental objectives as required by the Treaties. And from an international law standpoint, it seems necessary to consider whether these EU initiatives comply with general principles of international law, such as mutual supportiveness, as well as the objectives and principles of the multilateral environmental agreements to which the EU and its Member States are parties, and to which the EU unilatral and bilateral external relations initiatives are explicitly linked.

The concept of common but differentiated responsibility,[35] which is a key feature of international environmental law, provides an ideal lens to further explore these concerns. Leaving aside questions related to the status of this concept (as a general principle of international law or just a recurring feature of treaty law in the area of environmental protection),[36] common but differentiated responsibility will be used in this chapter as a useful conceptual benchmark to assess the legitimacy of the EU external environmental action, with the very pragmatic purpose of testing the outside credibility of EU initiatives as an essential precondition for their effectiveness.

The concept essentially justifies the design of different international obligations on the basis of differences in the current socio-economic situations of countries and their historical contribution to a specific environmental problem, thus 'reconcil[ing] the tensions between the need for universalism in taking action to combat global environmental problems and the need to be sensitive to individual countries' relevant circumstances' and thereby responding to concerns of legitimacy, equity and effectiveness.[37] Several of its corollaries may be employed to analyse EU external environmental action.[38]

First, the concept supports the role of developed countries in taking the lead in addressing global environmental issues,[39] which is certainly one of the main motivations of EU pioneering environmental legislation with extraterritorial implications. Secondly, the concept entails the respect on the part of developed countries of the allocation of less burdensome obligations on developing countries:[40] therefore, in the context of the EU unilateral and bilateral external relations tools, this prevents the Union from subverting globally determined allocation of international responsibility, particularly through trade-related instruments. Third, in terms of development aid, the concept is usually translated in developed countries' obligations to transfer technology and 'new and additional' financial means to developing countries, to enable them to implement international environmental obligations.[41] In that respect, it serves as a 'test for the seriousness of efforts and willingness

from an EU internal environmental regulation perspective, see M Lee, *EU Environmental Law: Challenges, Change and Decision-Making* (Hart Publishing, 2005), at 117–148.

[35] Rio Declaration on Environment and Development (1992) UN Doc A/CONF.151/26 vol 1, Annex 1, Principles 6–7. See generally, L Rajamani, *Differential Treatment in International Environmental Law* (OUP, 2006). See also contribution by Scott and Rajamani in this collection.

[36] E Hey, 'Common but Differentiated Responsibilities' in R Wulfrum (ed), *Max Planck Encyclopedia of Public International Law* (OUP, 2010, online edition), considers it a general principle of international law; C Stone, 'Common but Differentiated Responsibilities in International Law' (2004) 98 AJIL 276, concludes that it is not 'a customary principle of international law'.

[37] T Honkonen, 'The Principle of Common but Differentiated Responsibility in Post-2012 Climate Negotiations' (2009) 18 RECIEL 257, at 259.

[38] To that end, I find particularly useful the schematic identification of the implications of this principle proposed by Hey, n 36.

[39] United Nations Framework Convention on Climate Change (UNFCCC), 4 June 1992, 1771 UNTS 107, entered into force for the EU on 21 March 1994, Art 3.

[40] There are various examples in MEAs of differentiated responsibilities: the most notable is the Kyoto Protocol, which provides for quantified and time-bound obligations to mitigate climate change only for so-called 'Annex-I countries', ie developed countries.

[41] This is a common obligation across MEAs, although it is most clearly expressed in the Convention on Biological Diversity (CBD), Art 20(4).

to cooperate' of developed countries.[42] The amounts of assistance, as well as its priorities and modalities, therefore need to be closely scrutinized. It has been argued, for instance, that the EU should limit itself to procedural guarantees for environmental integration in its external assistance (through improved prior assessments, follow-up, monitoring and evaluation), leaving substantive and output-oriented environmental integration to recipient countries.[43]

On this premise, two case studies have been selected to test whether EU external environmental action can be considered legitimate under EU law and international law in the way it addresses issues at the intersection of climate change and biodiversity. The case studies will thus seek to determine whether the EU is living up to its ambition of being a global environmental leader through norm creation and export by pursuing a holistic approach to environmental protection in its external action. By doing so, it will also be investigated whether the Union fulfils its international obligations in light of mutual supportiveness and its Treaty obligations related to environmental integration, while fully respecting common but differentiated responsibility. The purpose of the following two examples is to show the intricate network of domestic regulation with extraterritorial implications and external action, as well as the different strategies that the EU has put in place to complement and contribute to multilateralism.[44]

4.1. Biofuels

The EU has prominently attempted to demonstrate its global environmental leadership by unilaterally setting the first supra-national standards for the sustainable production of biofuels, in the face of protracted and inconclusive multilateral negotiations.[45] Biofuels provide an ideal testing ground for mutual supportiveness in international environmental law. They are fuels of renewable and biological origin that may help supplant fossil fuels and therefore help the fight against climate change, but that have been associated with alleged negative impacts on the environment (particularly in terms of deforestation), indigenous and local communities, and small-hold farmers.[46]

The EU's 2009 Renewable Energy Directive introduced sustainability criteria for biofuels, including imported ones, to protect high-value biodiversity land and high-value carbon-stock land, as well as ensuring delivery of substantial reductions in greenhouse gas emissions. The criteria have thus been unilaterally set by the EU, but were expressly based on international reference documents.[47] Lack of compliance with these criteria does not lead to a ban on imports or use within the EU, but rather to a series of disincentives.[48] This is explicitly motivated by the concern that biofuels production in third countries might not respect minimum environmental or social requirements and by the desire to promote the

[42] Streck, n 13, at 159–160 and 168.

[43] A Persson, 'Environmental Policy Integration and Bilateral Development Assistance: Challenges and Opportunities with an Evolving Governance Framework' (2009) 9 *International Environmental Agreements* 409.

[44] See generally contribution by De Witte and Thies in this collection.

[45] The question of biofuels' sustainability standards is currently being discussed in multiple international fora such as the Convention on Biological Diversity (eg CBD Decision X/37, Biofuels and Biodiversity (2010)); and the Food and Agriculture Organization of the UN. The FAO hosts the Global Bioenergy Partnership, which brings together public, private and civil society stakeholders and adopted in May 2011 the first global, government-level consensus set of voluntary, science-based indicators for assessing the sustainable production and use of bioenergy (see: <www.globalbioenergy.org>). See also E Morgera, K Kulovesi and A Gobena (eds), *Case Studies on Bioenergy Policy and Law: Options for Sustainability*, FAO Legislative Study No 102 (FAO, 2010), at 15–34.

[46] CBD Subsidiary Body on Scientific, Technical and Technological Advice, 'New and emerging issues relating to the Conservation and Sustainable Use of Biodiversity: biodiversity and Liquid Biofuel Production' UN Doc UNEP/CBD/SBSTTA/12/9 (2007).

[47] Directive (EC) 2009/28 of the European Parliament and of the Council on the Promotion of the Use of Energy from Renewable Sources [2009] OJ L140/16 (Renewables Directive), preambular paras 69, 73 and 77.

[48] See detailed discussion in Kulovesi *et al*, n 22, at 883–884.

production of biofuels and bioliquids worldwide,[49] in a move towards 'contingent unilateralism'.[50] Notably, the Directive indicates that the EU will endeavour to conclude bilateral or multilateral agreements with third countries containing provisions on the sustainability criteria.[51]

In terms of mutual supportiveness, the Directive adopts a three-tiered approach. First, it requires that biofuels and bioliquids must not be made from raw material obtained from land with high biodiversity value and protected areas, or highly biodiverse grassland.[52] Second, for other biodiversity dimensions that are not explicitly covered by the sustainability criteria, the Directive provides complementary monitoring requirements: the Commission is expected to report on possible broader impacts in third countries that are a significant source of raw material for biofuels consumed within the Union as to their ratification and implementation of other relevant MEAs.[53] While noting the importance of broader land use issues,[54] land-related environmental or social concerns, however, were not included in the sustainability criteria, regardless of lengthy negotiations in the context of the CBD with regard to biofuels impacts on indigenous and local communities' rights.[55] Instead, the Commission is tasked with biannual reports on the impact on the respect of land-use rights in third countries.[56] Thus, the matter is kept under review for the time being, with the possibility for the Commission to propose 'corrective action'.[57] Third, the Renewables Directive calls upon the Commission to maintain dialogue with third countries and biofuels producers, consumer organizations and civil society concerning the general implementation of the Directive.[58] This is particularly significant in light of the extensive monitoring tasks assigned to the Commission vis-à-vis third countries, thus possibly injecting a sense of partnership in an otherwise unilateral exercise.[59]

Not only has the EU systematically referred to the Directive in its negotiating position under the CBD when biofuels were discussed at the multilateral level,[60] hoping to contribute to developing international standards 'at least consistent with EU standards',[61] but it has also used the Directive in combination with bilateral tools of external relations as a basis for building alliances with individual third countries with a view to arriving at a common/closer negotiating position at the multilateral level or inspiring domestic action beyond its borders. Dialogues between the EU and third countries or regions[62] have provided an avenue for the discussion of respective negotiating positions on biofuels and sometimes led to commitments to hold bilateral high-level meetings in the run-up to key negotiating sessions.[63] In addition, the Sustainability Impact Assessments have addressed the issue of certification

[49] Renewables Directive, n 47, recital 74.

[50] J Scott, 'The Multi-Level Governance of Climate Change' (2011) 4(1) *Carbon and Climate Law Review* 25, 28 and 32. See also, in reference to other EU external environmental action, the contribution by Scott and Rajamani to this volume.

[51] Renewables Directive, n 47, Art 18(4).

[52] Ibid, Art 17(3).

[53] Ibid, Art 17(7).

[54] Ibid, recitals 85 and 89, also referring to relevant questions of land degradation and desertification.

[55] 'Summary of the Fourteenth Meeting of the Subsidiary Body on Scientific, Technical and Technological Advice to the CBD: 10–21 May 2010' (2010) 9(514) ENB 12, at 12–14.

[56] Renewables Directive, n 47, Art 17(7).

[57] Ibid, Art 17(7), last subpara. The analysis of the EU biofuels sustainability criteria from a biodiversity perspective is based upon Kulovesi *et al*, n 22, at 879–880.

[58] Renewables Directive, n 47, Art 23(2).

[59] Ibid, Art 17(7).

[60] eg, ENB summary, n 55, at 12.

[61] Contribution by Cremona to this collection.

[62] EUROLAT—Resolution of 15 May 2010, 'Tackling Climate Change Challenges Together: For an EU–LAC Coordinated Strategy in the framework of the UNFCCC Negotiations' (2010), paras 37–38.

[63] 'Third European Union–Brazil Summit, Stockholm, 6 October 2009—Joint Statement' (14137/09 (Presse 285) 2009) paras 2–12.

for biofuels among policy recommendations to ensure sustainability,[64] occasionally making express reference to the EU criteria as guidance for third countries.[65] The Commission has thus pointed to the opportunity to discuss the applicability of the EU biofuels sustainability criteria to processes carried out in third countries as a means to prevent negative environmental and social impacts arising from the EU's bilateral trade negotiations,[66] thereby taking an additional opportunity (besides the incentives created by its own Renewables Directive) to present EU internal regulation as a source of inspiration in third countries.

On the face of it, therefore, the EU has attempted, in a phased manner, to take an environmentally holistic approach to biofuels with a view to ensuring gains for climate change mitigation, as well as avoiding negative impacts on biodiversity, and thus satisfying its own environmental integration requirement as well as its international obligations under various MEAs. The actual environmental benefits and scientific soundness of the EU legal framework have, however, been subject to continued criticism.[67] In terms of common but differentiated responsibility, the EU is certainly taking the lead on a matter that is difficult to tackle at the multilateral level, but it remains to be clarified whether the different circumstances of developing countries are fully taken into account in exporting the EU approach, and whether appropriate assistance is provided to facilitate developing countries' compliance with the criteria. Further research is also needed to ascertain whether developing countries' circumstances are reflected upon in the context of dialogues and participatory monitoring.

Bilateral and inter-regional dialogue may thus be critical for taking stock of third countries' needs and concerns on multilateral negotiations and domestic regulatory preferences, particularly because at the multilateral level the EU proposal on sustainability criteria for biofuels has not yet received sufficient support.[68] The impact of these exercises could be tested in the Commission's reports and its proposal for review of the Directive in the coming years from an inward perspective, and in evolutions of country negotiating positions in relevant multilateral negotiations from an outward perspective. The ultimate effect of the EU's approach remains in fact difficult to be assessed: by way of illustration, although the EU and Brazil have agreed to review bilaterally the state of the multilateral discussions on biofuels,[69] at the multilateral level Brazil continues to adamantly oppose the development of biofuels sustainability standards.[70]

4.2. Sustainable forest management

Sustainable forest management has been a long-standing international concern for the EU and as such it has been addressed at the multilateral level with support for the development

[64] IARC, Institute for Development Policy and Management, 'Trade Sustainability Impact Assessment of the Association Agreement under Negotiation between the European Community and MERCOSUR' (Final Report, 2009) 99; ECORYS Research and Consulting, 'Trade Sustainability Impact Assessment of the Association Agreement to be negotiated between the EU and Central America' (Draft Final Report, 2009) 90–91.

[65] ECORYS Research and Consulting, 'Trade Sustainability Impact Assessment of the FTA between the EU and ASEAN' (Final Report, 2009) Vol I, Main Findings and Recommendations, 60–61.

[66] Commission, 'Position Paper on the Trade Sustainability Impact Assessment of the EU–ASEAN FTA', June 2010, at 9; Commission, 'Position Paper on the of the EU–Central America Association Agreement', June 2010 at 4 and 6; Commission, 'Position Paper on the SIA of the EU–MERCOSUR Association Agreement' July 2010, at 5.

[67] 'UK scientists launch scathing criticism of EU biofuel targets' *The Ecologist* (2 June 2011); see also letter by Greenpeace and other leading NGOs to the President of the European Commission, 'Addressing indirect impacts of biofuels' (22 September 2011), at: <www.euractiv.com/sites/all/euractiv/files/biofuels%20letter.pdf >.

[68] At the 2010 meeting of the CBD Conference of the Parties, it was merely agreed to analyse 'information on tools for voluntary use' on sustainable biofuel production: CBD Decision X/37 *Biofuels and Biodiversity* (2010), para 11.

[69] Fourth EU–Brazil Summit, 'Joint Statement' Brasília, 14 July 2010, paras 5–8.

[70] See Brazil's minimalist negotiating position at the latest round of negotiations on biofuels in the CBD context: S Jungcurt et al, 'Summary of the Tenth Meeting of the Conference of the Parties to the Convention on Biological Diversity: 18–29 October 2010' (2010) 9:544 ENB at 22 (under 'CBD future work').

of a legally binding agreement on forests.[71] In the absence of such a development, sustainable forest management has also been addressed under the CBD, and increasingly under the international climate change regime.[72] At the unilateral and bilateral level, the EU has consistently provided external funding for the protection of tropical forests.[73]

In addition, the idea of a global approach to deforestation has been supported by the EU through a combination of domestic regulation with extraterritorial implications[74] and bilateral external tools that have been explicitly linked to the EU's multilateral agenda. The EU has first developed an action plan and enacted a series of regulations to tackle this global problem in the immediate term, in the face of limited progress at the multilateral level.[75] The EU approach is explicitly based on global soft law commitments,[76] and made clearly compatible with ongoing, albeit partial, multilateral efforts.[77] The underlying policy clearly points to an EU-explicit agenda of gradually furthering a global multilateral forest agreement, or at least the linking of regional forest agreements, through concerted unilateral and bilateral action to address deforestation by exporter and importer countries.[78]

The EU has thus clearly articulated its strategy for gradually building international consensus on sustainable forest management from the bottom up: it proposes to work with willing third countries on the legality of the trade of timber as a neutral concept rather than the politically charged sustainable forest management[79]—a term that has resisted international definition thus far.[80] To this end, the EU first enacted in 2005 the Forest Law Enforcement, Governance and Trade (FLEGT) Regulation setting up a licensing scheme for imports of timber based on bilateral agreements, called Voluntary Partnership Agreements (VPAs) to be concluded between the EU and timber-exporting third countries. The verification of the legality of harvests of timber imported into the EU is to be checked against compliance with the national law of the third state 'as set out in the VPA'—the latter reference points to a joint evaluation by the third country and the EU of the alignment of third-country national forest law with relevant multilateral standards.[81] The VPA

[71] The EU advocated the development of a global, legally binding instrument on forests at the fifth session of the United Nations Forum on Forests ('Summary of the Fifth Session of the United Nations Forum on Forests' (2005) 13(133) ENB, at 4). See G Reischl, 'The EU and the UN Forest Negotiations: A Case of Failed International Environmental Governance?' (Paper presented to Marie Curie European Summer School on Earth System Governance, Vrije Universiteit, Amsterdam, 24 May–6 June 2007).

[72] C Streck and S Scholz, 'The Role of Forests in Global Climate Change' (2006) 82 *International Affairs* 861; and (2008) 1 *Carbon and Climate Law Review* 52 (Special issue on forests).

[73] Reg (EC) 2494/2000 on Measures to Promote the Conservation and Sustainable Management of Tropical Forests and Other Forests in Developing Countries [2000] OJ L288/6; Reg (EC) 1905/2006 of the European Parliament and of the Council establishing a financing instrument for development cooperation [2006] OJ L378/41, Arts 6(e) and 7(e).

[74] First on the Common Commercial Policy legal basis (Reg 2173/2005, [2005] OJ L347/1) and then on the environmental legal basis (Reg 995/2010, [2010] OJ L295/23).

[75] Commission, 'Forest Law Enforcement, Governance and Trade (FLEGT): Proposal for an Action Plan' COM (2003) 251 final, 3; endorsed by the Council, 'Conclusions—Forest Law Enforcement, Governance and Trade (FLEGT)' [2003] OJ C268/1.

[76] Ibid, at 5; WSSD Plan of Implementation (2002) UN Doc A/CONF.199/20, Resolution 2, para 45(c).

[77] Namely, timber species listed under Convention on International Trade in Endangered Species of Wild Fauna and Flora, 3 March 1973, 993 UNTS 243: FLEGT Action Plan, n 75, at 20.

[78] Ibid, at 9 and 11.

[79] Although references to sustainable forest management remain in the bilateral agreement concluded by the EU under FLEGT: eg Voluntary Partnership Agreement between the EC and Ghana, [2010] OJ L70/3 (Ghana VPA): its objective is 'consistent with the Parties' common commitment to the sustainable management of all types of forests' (Art 1).

[80] The most recent attempt to do so, the Non-Legally Binding Instrument on All Types of Forests (UNGA Resolution 62/98 of 2008) only indicates that 'sustainable forest management, as a dynamic and evolving concept, aims to maintain and enhance the economic, social and environmental values of all types of forests, for the benefit of present and future generations' (para 3) and provides seven 'thematic elements' for global monitoring, para 6(b) and related fn. See also Non-legally Binding Authoritative Statement of Principles for a Global Consensus on the Management, Conservation and Sustainable Development of All Types of Forests (1992) UN Doc A/CONF.151/26 Vol III (Rio Forest Principles), preambular para c.

[81] Recitals 3–4, Ghana VPA, point to the multilateral instruments of reference.

negotiations notably touch upon all elements of sustainability: they thus emphasize the links between disparate pieces of national law that are needed to achieve sustainable forest management on the ground.

The main incentive for third countries to participate in the FLEGT VPA process is receiving priority assistance for the upgrading of their legal and administrative framework related to forest management: the VPA thus provides, on the one hand, for the need for a 'joint arrangement on financing and technical contributions from the EU and its Member States'[82] and market incentives, such as encouragement of public and private procurement policies and market promotion.[83] Significantly, support is also provided by an independent, specialized international organization, namely the Food and Agriculture Organization (FAO) of the UN who is managing a global project funded by the EU to support African, Caribbean and Pacific countries in the review of their legislation and upgrading of their forest governance and law enforcement capacities.[84] FAO has a long-standing and well-respected tradition of providing expert and independent advice on the reform of national forest laws.[85] In the continued 'absence or slow pace of multilateral progress' on an international forest treaty,[86] however, the EU decided to set up an additional incentive for third countries to engage in VPA negotiations, by creating an obligation of due diligence on operators placing timber and timber products on the EU market to ensure the legal origin of their timber products,[87] and establishing a presumption of compliance for timber originating from a VPA country and licensed accordingly.[88]

The specialized track of bilateral negotiations leading to the conclusion of VPAs is noteworthy for its cooperative approach. VPAs are expected to include a series of common elements, namely the commitment to developing credible legal structures that are supportive of sustainable forest management practices and procedures to licence the export of legally harvested wood—that is, in accordance with third country national laws as revised to ensure alignment with relevant multilateral standards.[89] Linking legality to the forest-related legislation of the exporting country arguably aims to ensure the third country's ownership of the initiative, as well as to demonstrate respect for its national sovereignty over its forest resources.[90] It is coupled with a commitment from the third country to review its national legal framework when it does not support international standards on sustainable forest management,[91] thus opening the door for a bilateral dialogue on the definition of this concept using the national legislation of the third country as a departure point. An annex to the VPA includes the definition of legal harvest as agreed with local stakeholders, which details standards of compliance with national forest legislation, social responsibility agreement, relevant cultural norms, occupational and health safety legislation, and also outlines areas in which national legislation should be improved.[92] Another notable feature of the

[82] eg Art 15(4) Ghana VPA.

[83] eg Art 18 Ghana VPA.

[84] See <www.fao.org/forestry/acp-flegt/en>. Note that while there is no formal link between the FAO FLEGT Programme and the VPAs, FAO assistance specifically targets countries depending on 'their level of interest in the FLEGT Action Plan and in negotiating a VPA' through support for national and regional FLEGT/VPA workshops to share information, knowledge and lessons learnt, feasibility studies on VPA-related issues and support for national multi-stakeholder committees in charge of VPA negotiations and for the participation of local stakeholders: FAO, *Improving Forest Governance in Africa, the Caribbean and the Pacific* (FAO, undated) 6 and 9, at: <http://foris.fao.org/static/data/acpflegt/4087Forestgovernance_en.pdf>.

[85] See FAO Legal Office, 'Legal Advisory Services: Forestry and Wildlife', at: <http://www.fao.org/legal/advserv/forest-e.htm>.

[86] Commission, 'Proposal laying down the Obligations of Operators who Place Timber and Timber Products on the Market' COM (2008) 644/3, at 3.

[87] Reg (EU) 995/2010 of 20 October 2010 laying down the Obligations of Operators who Place Timber and Timber Products on the Market [2010] OJ L295/23, Art 4.

[88] Ibid, Art 3.

[89] FLEGT Action Plan, n 75, at 12–13.

[90] See Rio Forest Principles, n 80, para 1a.

[91] FLEGT Action Plan, n 75, at 5.

[92] eg, Ghana VPA, Annex II.

FLEGT approach is therefore the systematic involvement of third-country stakeholders in the definition of the legality of timber with a view to setting out a broad-based understanding about the areas in which national legislation should be improved.

The FLEGT approach has already made visible inroads in the general bilateral tools of the EU's external relations, although the negotiations of VPAs remain a separate bilateral process. The initiative is explicitly mentioned[93] or hinted at[94] in clauses on trade in forest products in post-Global Europe bilateral agreements. The EU's external funding for environment explicitly emphasizes the implementation of the FLEGT Action Plan at the national, regional and international policy development level; as well as the need to promote on the ground community-based forest management, respect for local and indigenous peoples' rights over forest land, private sector investment in sustainable forest management, and design of financial instruments for forest conservation.[95]

The FLEGT initiative is also notable for demonstrating EU responsiveness to changed international landscapes. Deforestation issues are increasingly addressed in the context of the negotiations on a post-2012 climate change regime under the so-called REDD-plus item.[96] An incipient strategy by the EU is in fact emerging, to use FLEGT to influence forest-related negotiations as part of its broader agenda on the post-2012 international climate change regime.[97] The EU is thus considering capitalizing upon agreement on key concepts related to forest governance emerging from FLEGT, as well as the lessons learnt in the multi-stakeholder processes leading to the conclusion of VPAs. Both can provide inputs into multilateral negotiations on REDD-plus,[98] which have proven particularly complex in ensuring mutual supportiveness between climate change mitigation objectives, on the one hand, and biodiversity conservation and respect for the rights of forest-dwelling communities on the other hand.[99] The EU's FLEGT approach may thus contribute to mutual supportiveness within the international climate change regime.

Overall, the EU has shown willingness to take the lead in tackling sustainable forest management in a holistic way, accounting both for its biodiversity and climate change dimensions. In terms of common but differentiated responsibility, the FLEGT initiative can

[93] Agreement establishing an Association between the EU and its Member States, on the one hand, and Central America on the other (initialed 22 March 2011), Art 289.

[94] Economic Partnership Agreement between the CARIFORUM States, of the one part, and the European Community and its Member States, of the other part [2008] OJ L/289/I/3, Art 189; Free Trade Agreement between the EU and its Member States, on one side, and Colombia and Peru, on the other (initialed 24 March 2011), Art 273; Framework Agreement between the European Union and its Member States, on the one part, and the Republic of Korea, on the other part (signed 10 May 2010), Art 25 and Free Trade Agreement between the European Union and its Member States of the one part, and the Republic of Korea, of the other part (signed 6 October 2010), Art 13.11.

[95] Commission, 2011–2013 strategy paper, n 29, at 22.

[96] REDD-plus means 'reducing emissions from deforestation and forest degradation, conservation of forest-carbon stocks, sustainable management of forests, and enhancement of forest-carbon stocks'. For a discussion, see H van Asselt, 'Managing the Fragmentation of International Environmental Law: Forests at the Intersection of the Climate and Biodiversity Regime' (forthcoming) *NYU Journal of International Law and Politics*; A Savaresi, 'Reducing Emissions from Deforestation in Developing Countries under the UNFCCC. Caveats and Opportunities for Biodiversity' (2011) 21 *Yearbook of International Environmental Law* (online version).

[97] Commission proposal, n 86, at 5; and Central America Association Agreement, n 93, Art 20; EU–Colombia and Peru FTA, n 94, Art 286; Second Revision of the Cotonou Partnership Agreement—Agreed Consolidated Text (11 March 2010), Art 32bis.

[98] For a more detailed discussion, see A Savaresi, 'FLEGT and REDD: Interactions between EU Bilateral Cooperation and the Development of International Law' in Morgera (ed), n 7.

[99] This relates to the international debate on the so-called 'safeguards' for REDD-plus concerning biodiversity and forest-dependent communities. See Environmental Council Conclusions of 20 December 2010 on the Nagoya Conference of the Parties to the CBD, where Member States and the Commission are invited to 'actively contribute to the preparation of advice on the application of relevant safeguards for biodiversity in relation to REDD +, in line with the CBD COP 10 decision, and facilitate the development and implementation of such safeguards under REDD +'. This is already the case for the EU–Africa partnership: Third EU–Africa Summit, 'Joint Africa–EU Strategy Action Plan (2011–2013)' Tripoli, 30 November 2010.

be usefully contrasted with the EU biofuels sustainability criteria: FLEGT is markedly more partnership-oriented, with its reliance on third country legislation and multilateral standards, consultation with third-country stakeholders and involvement of expert and impartial international organizations. Thus, in the FLEGT context, the EU explicitly combines trade incentives and external assistance. It acts as a co-creator of norms rather than an exporter, by using third country legislation as the starting point and relying on the expertise of an independent, specialized UN organization. The EU also has provided a clear explanation of its intentions in relation to the ultimate objective vis-à-vis the evolution of international environmental law.

5. Conclusions

Against its ambitious agenda for supporting environmental multilateralism and contributing to environmental sustainability beyond its borders, the EU has certainly taken action as a norm generator and exporter in devising holistic solutions to pressing global environmental challenges. This responds to its Treaty requirement of environmental integration and the international principle of mutual supportiveness. The Union has done so in a creative and complex manner, relying on a combination of domestic regulation with extraterritorial implications, various unilateral and bilateral external relations tools, and corresponding negotiating positions in multilateral environmental fora.

Due to the complexity of this strategy, however, the effectiveness, coherence and credibility of EU external action cannot be taken for granted. In particular, developing countries may mistrust or at least misunderstand the EU's tools and intentions.[100] In particular they may fear that higher environmental standards than they have the human, technical and financial capacity to implement are imposed upon them unilaterally or bilaterally.[101] With a view to proving the legitimacy of EU external environmental action, therefore, several lessons can be drawn from comparing the experience of the EU biofuels sustainability criteria and FLEGT in light of the common but differentiated responsibility principle. Complexity should be systematically tackled by explicitly justifying the use of Union unilateral and bilateral tools against the goal of supporting environmental multilateralism, as in the case of the FLEGT Action Plan. In addition, input legitimacy is better ensured through specific provisions for dialogue and joint monitoring with third countries, which were only alluded to in the context of biofuels. Conversely, joint activities were fully fleshed out under the FLEGT VPA process, and coupled with structured stakeholder involvement and the participation of expert and independent international entities. Output legitimacy could in turn be achieved by the EU and its partner countries acting as co-generators of norms, jointly identifying solutions to multilateral impasses, based on their respective internal frameworks and relevant international instruments, as in the VPA process.

Furthermore, accountability mechanisms should be put in place by the Union to clearly demonstrate the extent to which partner countries benefit from trade incentives and external assistance offered by the EU,[102] and whether these effectively avoid any negative impacts on

[100] For instance, on the unclear relationship between general bilateral agreements concluded by the EU with third countries and specialized bilateral relations under VPAs: Ronnie Hall, 'Undercutting Africa: Why EPAs Threaten the World's Forests and Forest Peoples' (2009) 8(1) *Trade Negotiations Insights* at: <www.ictsd.org/i/news/tni/39374/>; and response by Peter Thompson (DG Trade), 'EPAs and Natural Resources: The European Sustainability Agenda' (2009) 8(4) *Trade Negotiations Insights* at: <www.ictsd.org/i/news/tni/45717>.

[101] B Chaytor, 'Environmental Issues in Economic Partnership Agreements: Implications for Developing Countries' ICTSD Issue Paper 1 (September 2009).

[102] It remains true, for instance, that limited progress has been made in biodiversity mainstreaming in the EU development cooperation: Commission, 'Impact Assessment for the Communication Halting the Loss of Biodiversity by 2010 and Beyond' SEC (2006) 607, at 37 and 76–77; and Commission, 'Impact Assessment for the Communication Our Life Insurance, Our Natural Capital: an EU Biodiversity Strategy to 2020', SEC(2011) 540, at 16.

the environment.[103] The principle of common but differentiated responsibility in that respect entails that EU external assistance is provided in accordance with the increasing number of multilateral standards on financial assistance and technology transfer.[104] As the CBD governing body is developing more specific guidance, particularly on synergetic climate and biodiversity financing,[105] it becomes critical to demonstrate mutual supportiveness in the EU unilateral and bilateral external relations instruments by respecting relevant international guidelines[106] or going above them, without however disregarding multilateral determinations as to the equitable relations between states with different financial and technical capacities.

Ultimately, the legitimacy of the EU external environmental action, in its complexity and ambition, depends on the good-faith efforts of the EU on the multilateral scene,[107] its openness in having recourse to unilateral and bilateral tools when multilateral progress is out of reach,[108] and its responsiveness to intervening developments in global fora. The linkage recently established by the EU between its FLEGT initiative and multilateral progress on deforestation in the international climate change regime is certainly an indication of such responsiveness. EU domestic regulation with extraterritorial implications can also provide specific guarantees to this end, such as review clauses expressly triggered by developments at the multilateral level and inputs from third countries at the bilateral level. In addition, dialogue with third countries can be used to build trust in ongoing multilateral environmental negotiations, as well as to nurture regulatory experience-sharing, thus becoming a tool that specifically tackles risks of 'unhealthy competition between various jurisdictions for legal influence or retaliation'.[109]

What emerges from the comparison of the biofuels and FLEGT initiatives, furthermore, is that the EU is experimenting with a *variety* of models of engagement with third countries based on a variety of interactions between different tools and different levels of environmental regulation. While fully understanding the complex reasons of this differentiation and assessing the comparative effectiveness of different initiatives goes beyond the realm of a legal enquiry, it certainly shows the merit and necessity of analysing the contribution of the EU to global governance not only through the lenses of EU law, but also of international and transnational law.

[103] The Court of Auditors, for instance, has unveiled the lack of a consistent system for the environmental screening of new projects, finding evidence that environmental impact assessments had not always been carried out where needed in EU external assistance (Special Report 6/2006 concerning the Environmental Aspects of the Commission's Development Cooperation [2006] OJ C235/1).

[104] Hey, n 36.

[105] Note for instance that the Commission had indicated the need to apply the CBD Akwé: Kon Guidelines for environmental and socio-cultural impact assessments prior to projects affecting the lands of indigenous and local communities in third countries. (Commission, 'Impact Assessment for the Communication Halting the Loss of Biodiversity by 2010 and Beyond', n 102, at 81). Several other guidelines have been produced by the CBD governing body on mutually supportive climate and biodiversity finance (see Morgera, 'Far Away, So Close', n 14, at 110–113).

[106] Particularly as the EU environment-specific funding is made available to developing countries (as defined by the EU) whose environmental activities meet the priorities unilaterally established by the EU on the basis of an assessment of the international context and geographic funding that, with the exception of the European Development Fund, is also largely dominated by the EU': Marín Durán n 31. The Commission has pointed to a commitment to support developing countries in evaluating their biodiversity funding needs 'according to CBD guidelines' (Commission, 'Impact Assessment for the Communication Halting the Loss of Biodiversity by 2010 and Beyond', n 102, at 53–54).

[107] K Kulovesi, '"Make Your Own Special Song, Even if Nobody Else Sings Along": International Aviation Emissions and the EU Emissions Trading Scheme' (2011) 2 *Climate Law* 535.

[108] AG Kokott, n 2, paras 185–186, noted that the EU 'could not reasonably be required to give . . . [multilateral] bodies unlimited time in which to develop a multilateral solution': I am grateful to Marise Cremona for having drawn my attention to this point.

[109] Kulovesi, n 107.

13

Contingent Unilateralism—International Aviation in the European Emissions Trading Scheme

*Joanne Scott and Lavanya Rajamani**

1. Introduction

The European Union is a self-conscious leader in the 'fight' against climate change and an active proponent of an ambitious global climate regime. Nonetheless, to a significant degree its efforts have been in vain. A global agreement to extend or replace the Kyoto Protocol has not been put in place and prospects for an ambitious and comprehensive global climate agreement seem slim. It is against this backdrop of global climate inertia that the EU has started to change its tack. Fuelled by both environmental and competitiveness concerns, the EU is acting to extend the global reach of its 'domestic' climate change law. It is engaging in climate change unilateralism, albeit unilateralism of a particular and interesting kind. The EU's climate change unilateralism is 'contingent' in the sense that the global extension of EU climate change law depends upon there being no adequate international agreement or third country climate action in place. As such the EU should be viewed as a reluctant unilateralist and as deploying contingent unilateralism as a means of incentivizing urgently needed climate action elsewhere. In keeping with the theme of this volume as a whole, the EU is shaping the legal structures of global governance in a multi-polar world by testing the boundaries of permissible unilateral action and by experimenting with a form of action-forcing contingent unilateralism that conceives unilateralism as a necessary policy option but one which, ultimately, is second best.

2. EU Contingent Unilateralism in the EU–ETS

The EU's contingent unilateralism comprises two core elements. First, it extends the reach of EU climate change law to include emissions that are embodied in imported services or goods; for example as a result of the production or transportation process. Second, it sets out the conditions under which the imported services or goods may be exempted from the application of EU climate change law on the basis that they fall within a sector that is subject to adequate climate change regulation internationally or on the part of third states. Where adequate climate change regulation has been put in place, the relevant imported goods and services may be able to 'escape' from the EU's provisionally applied 'regulatory penalty default.'[1] The EU's contingent unilateralism is most apparent in the recent revisions to the EU's emissions trading scheme (ETS). Four examples of this are set out below.

* The authors would like to thank Anu Bradford, Gráinne de Búrca, Dan Cole, Maria Lee, Jürgen Lefevere, Jacob Werksman, Harald Winkler, Michael Zammit Cutajar and the participants at the Conference on *The Legal Dimension of Global Governance: What Role for the EU?*, at the University of Copenhagen, 2011, for their very helpful comments on an earlier version of this paper. For a much fuller and considerably developed presentation of the argument laid out in the second part of this paper, concerning the principle of common but differentiated responsibilities, see J Scott and L Rajamani, 'EU Climate Change Unilateralism' (2012) 23(2) EJIL 469.

[1] For a fuller discussion from the perspective of regulatory penalty defaults see J Scott, 'EU Global Action on Climate Change and Regulatory Penalty Defaults' (4 November 2011). Available at SSRN: <http://ssrn.com/abstract%20=%201954667>.

First, against a backdrop of global climate inaction in the aviation sector, and notwithstanding its own considerable efforts to promote multilateral action in the International Civil Aviation Organization (ICAO), the EU decided in 2008 to include aviation emissions in the ETS, and to include all emissions generated by flights that arrive in or depart from the EU.[2] This includes emissions that are generated outside of EU airspace and consequently airlines will be obliged to acquire emissions allowances also for those parts of their journeys that take place abroad. It is said that on a flight from San Francisco to London, 29% of emissions will occur in US airspace, 37% in Canadian airspace and 25% over the High Seas. Less than 9% of emissions will take place in EU airspace.[3] Nonetheless, the airline will be obliged to surrender allowances under the ETS for each tonne of carbon that they emit, regardless of where these emissions take place. This decision to include aviation in the ETS is the EU's 'regulatory penalty default'.

An airline operator may be exempted from the requirement to surrender emissions allowances for flights landing in the EU (but not for flights taking off from the EU), where the airline comes from a country which has itself taken measures to reduce the climate change impact of flights departing from it which land in the EU.[4] Exemptions may also be granted following consultation with the third country concerned and the EU has insisted that it is 'ready to engage constructively in such consultations so as to reach agreement'.[5] The emissions trading directive also provides that if a global agreement to reduce greenhouse gas emissions from aviation were to be concluded, the Commission shall consider whether amendments to the directive are required.[6] The aviation directive thus sets out circumstances in which it is possible to 'escape' from the EU's regulatory penalty default.

The elements that make up this example of contingent unilateralism are captured by the table below:

Objectives	Regulatory Penalty Default	Escape Route
To reduce global emissions; to create a level playing field for EU carriers; to leverage global or third country climate action.	Foreign airlines to surrender emission allowances for the whole journey in respect of flights taking off from or landing in the EU.	A global agreement to reduce aviation emissions or third country measures to reduce the climate change impact of flights.

Figure 4 Contingent Unilateralism: The Example of Aviation

In the second example of contingent unilateralism, the EU is actively contemplating the inclusion of maritime transport emissions in the ETS in a similar way. In keeping with the contingent quality of its climate unilateralism, unless the international community has

[2] See Directive 2008/101/EC of 19 November 2008 amending Directive 2003/87/EC of 13 October 2003 so as to include aviation activities in the scheme for greenhouse gas emission allowance trading within the Community [2008] OJ L8/3; Consolidated version of Directive 2003/87, Arts 3a–3g and 25a: <http://ec.europa.eu/clima/policies/ets/documentation_en.htm> accessed 9 March 2012.

[3] See Statement of Nancy N Young, Vice President of Environmental Affairs, Air Transport Association of America Inc (ATA) before the Subcommittee on Aviation of the House Transportation and Infrastructure Committee, 'The European Union's Emissions Trading Scheme: A Violation of International Law' (27 July 2011) 4–5: <http://republicans.transportation.house.gov/Media/file/TestimonyAviation/2011-07-27-%20Young.pdf> accessed 9 March 2012.

[4] Consolidated version of Directive 2003/87, n 2, Art 25a.

[5] See 'Written Statement of Reservation by Belgium on behalf of the EU, its 27 Member States, and the 17 Other States Members of the European Civil Aviation Conference on Resolution A37–17/2: Consolidated Statement of continuing ICAO policies and practices related to environmental protection—Climate Change': <http://www.icao.int/icao/en/assembl/A37/Docs/10_reservations_en.pdf> accessed 12 March 2012.

[6] Consolidated version of Directive 2003/87, n 2, Art 25a(1).

approved an agreement by the end of 2011 (which it did not) that includes international maritime emissions in its reduction targets, the Commission *should* put forward a proposal to include these emissions in the EU scheme.[7] The framework for measuring and assigning emissions has yet to be agreed.

As concerns the third example of contingent unilateralism, the recently revised emissions trading directive creates a legal framework for its possible extension to imported products in energy-intensive industries in the event of carbon leakage.[8] It falls to the European Commission to assess the situation for sectors exposed to a significant risk of carbon leakage and to put forward appropriate proposals to include the relevant imported products in the ETS. Although no proposals of this kind have as yet been introduced, a framework for a possible extension of this kind is already in place.[9] In making a determination about whether to include imported energy-intensive products in the ETS, and again consistent with the contingent quality of the EU's climate unilateralism, the Commission is required to take into account the prior existence of binding sectoral agreements which lead to global greenhouse gas emission reductions of the magnitude required to effectively address climate change.

In the final example of contingent unilateralism arising in the context of the ETS, the EU has prohibited, from the start of 2013, the use of Certified Emissions Reductions (CERs) from new Clean Development Mechanism projects, except in so far as these projects are situated in Least Developed Countries or originate in a country that has (contingently) concluded an agreement with the EU regulating the level of their use.[10]

In each of these examples, EU climate unilateralism is contingent rather than absolute. This is because the geographical extension, or externalization, of the ETS to foreign goods or services can be avoided if the goods or services are subject to adequate climate regulation elsewhere. For example, the extension of the ETS to maritime transport depends upon there being no suitable international agreement in place. For imported products in sectors exposed to carbon leakage, geographical extension of the ETS may be avoided if binding sectoral agreements are concluded which lead to global greenhouse gas emission reductions of the magnitude required to address climate change effectively.[11]

The contingency that characterizes EU climate unilateralism is key to understanding and evaluating the EU's approach. We will look at EU climate unilateralism more closely and provide an initial evaluation by looking at the aviation example in more depth. While a number of environmental NGOs have spoken out in favour of the EU's approach, the EU's aviation decision has provoked a vocal and in the main critical reaction from the private sector and by many powerful states.[12]

[7] See Directive 2009/29 of 23 April 2009 amending Directive 2003/87/EC so as to improve and extend the greenhouse gas emission allowance trading scheme of the Community [2009] OJ L140/63, recital 3. The stated aim is that the proposed measure should enter into force by 2013. See Roadmap: Measures to include maritime transport emissions in the EU's greenhouse gas reduction commitment if no international rules agreed, Version 2, 1: <http://ec.europa.eu/governance/impact/planned_ia/docs/2012_clima_001_greenhouse_maritime_transport_en.pdf > accessed 24 February 2012.

[8] Consolidated version of Directive 2003/87, n 2, Art 10b(1)(b). Carbon leakage occurs when there is an increase in emissions in one country as a result of steps taken to reduce emissions in another country.

[9] See Communication from the Commission to the European Parliament, the Council, the European Economic and Social Committee and the Committee of the Regions, 'Analysis of options to move beyond 20% greenhouse gas emission reductions and assessing the risk of carbon leakage' COM (2010) 265 final of 26 May 2010.

[10] Consolidated version of Directive 2003/87, n 2, Art 11a(4).

[11] Directive 2003/87, n 2, Art 10, final sub-para.

[12] D Keating, 'Trade war looms over aviation emissions' (*European Voice*, 21 December 2011): <http://www.europeanvoice.com/article/imported/trade-war-looms-over-aviation-emissions/73021.aspx> accessed 12 March 2012. The Aviation Law Prof Blog is a good place to keep up with what states and other actors are saying about the EU's aviation decisions: <http://lawprofessors.typepad.com/aviation/> accessed on 12 March 2012.

3. EU Climate Unilateralism: The Example of Aviation

3.1. Background

Aviation produces around 2.5% of the world's greenhouse gas emissions (2007),[13] with international aviation responsible for around 55% of this.[14] Aviation emissions are increasing rapidly, at a rate of around 3–4% per year.

International aviation emissions are essentially unregulated at the international level. While for developed countries domestic aviation emissions are counted as part of that country's emissions for the purpose of their international emission reduction commitments, international aviation emissions are not. There is not even a settled framework at the international level for assigning responsibility for international aviation emissions to specific countries.

The Kyoto Protocol states that developed countries shall pursue limitation or reduction of international aviation emissions working through the International Civil Aviation Authority (ICAO).[15] Progress in ICAO has been exceedingly slow. While ICAO recently endorsed an 'aspirational goal' of annual fuel efficiency improvements in aviation of 2%, still no binding emission targets have been agreed.[16]

In view of the glacial pace of global action to combat aviation emissions, the EU decided to include aviation in its emissions trading scheme from the start of 2012.[17] In order to ensure that European airlines were not placed at a competitive disadvantage and to enhance the environmental ambition of the scheme,[18] all flights arriving in or departing from an EU airport are covered in the scheme. Because of its broad scope, the European emissions trading scheme has the potential to cover emissions amounting to around 60% of international aviation emissions.

During the first year of the aviation sector's inclusion in the emissions trading scheme, an overall emissions cap of 97% of historic emissions will be set.[19] After that, the cap will be set at 95%. In the first instance, 85% of allowances will be issued free of charge, with the remaining 15% to be sold at auction by the individual Member States.[20]

3.2. Analysis

The EU's aviation decision has been broadly greeted with dismay. A 25-nation meeting was held in Delhi on 29–30 September 2011 to protest against the EU measure. India has signalled its opposition to the scheme in the context of its proposed agenda item on 'unilateral trade measures' at the seventeenth Conference of Parties to the Framework Convention on Climate Change (FCCC) (COP-17) in Durban.[21] The US Government has expressed 'strong concern' about the aviation decision and has said that it is working to have

[13] International Transport Forum, *Reducing Transport Greenhouse Gas Emissions: Trends and Data 2010* (OECD, 2010), 5.

[14] Ibid, 10.

[15] Kyoto Protocol to the United Nations Framework Convention on Climate Change, 10 December 1997, reprinted in (1998) 37 ILM 22, Art 2.2.

[16] See ICAO: Resolution A37/19, Consolidated statement of continuing ICAO policies and practices related to environmental protection—Climate change, for a taste of the limited progress so far.

[17] Directive 2008/101/EC, n 2.

[18] See Consolidated version of Directive 2003/87, n 2, Annex I, laying out the various exemptions that apply.

[19] The baseline for calculating historic emissions is the average annual emissions during the year 2004–2006. See ibid, Art 3c.

[20] See ibid, Art 3d(1).

[21] Proposals by India for inclusion of additional agenda items in the provisional agenda of the seventeenth session of the Conference of the Parties, Note by the secretariat, FCCC/CP/2011/INF.2/Add.1 (7 October 2011).

US airlines exempted from it.[22] In a radical role reversal, the US House of Representatives and the Senate have passed a Bill to resist the application of the EU measure in the United States.[23] This prohibits US aircraft operators from participating in the ETS, and instructs US officials to negotiate or take any action necessary to ensure US aviation operators are not penalized by any unilaterally imposed EU scheme. The US Bill condemns the EU's aviation decision as unilateral, extra-territorial and as infringing directly upon the sovereignty of the United States. We will use these three concepts to frame our analysis of the EU decision.

Unilateral: While the EU's aviation decision operates in pursuit of an internationally agreed objective,[24] it is unilateral nonetheless. The decision was adopted autonomously by the EU with only limited input by other states, and the EU decision occupies a policy space in which decision-making authority had already been allocated—albeit on a non-exclusive basis—to an international organization (ICAO).[25] As noted previously, over a period spanning more than fifteen years, this international organization has failed to take any meaningful steps to regulate international aviation emissions.

By including aviation in its ETS, the EU has adopted a unilateral measure of far-reaching significance. The EU has acted to define unilaterally the 'system boundary' to govern aviation emissions.[26] In the absence of international agreement, the EU has settled upon a framework that allocates responsibility for aviation emissions to the departure state. Where a departure state fails to take responsibility for regulating aviation emissions, by adopting measures to reduce the climate change impact of ETS-covered flights, the EU as the arrival state asserts a right to step in. It is for the EU to decide, following consultation with the relevant state, whether to grant an ETS-exemption for EU-arriving flights. It is because of the way in which the EU has chosen to draw the system boundary for aviation that its decision is controversial. It is because of this that the measure is said by some to be extra-territorial and to infringe the sovereignty of other states.

Extra-territorial: The dominant system boundary in the global regulation of greenhouse gas emissions is production-based.[27] This allocates responsibility for greenhouse gas emissions to the state where these emissions are generated or produced. If emissions are generated in the production of steel in China, it is China that incurs responsibility for these, regardless of where the resulting steel is consumed. The influence of this production-based system boundary is apparent in the claim that the EU's aviation decision is extra-territorial. The EU's emissions trading scheme now extends to emissions that are generated abroad. Hence, viewed through the lens of a production-based system boundary, which posits the place in which the emissions are generated as the relevant territorial connecting factor, the EU's decision adopts an extra-territorial approach.

However, as is clear from the discussion of unilateralism above, the EU has (rightly)[28] rejected a production-based system boundary for aviation, in favour of an alternative

[22] P Clark, 'US Rejects EU Emissions Zone' *Financial Times* (22 June 2011).

[23] European Union Emissions Trading Scheme Prohibition Act of 2011 (HR 2594) passed on 24 October 2011: and European Union Emissions Trading Scheme Prohibition Act of 2011 (S 1956) passed on 22 September 2012. The EU has previously adopted 'blocking statutes' to guard against the extra-territorial effects of US legislation, most notably the Helms-Burton Act. See J Huber, 'The Helms-Burton Blocking Statute of the European Union' (1996) 6 Fordham Int'l L J 699.

[24] The Copenhagen Accord recognizes 'the scientific view that the increase in global temperature should be below 2 degrees Celsius' and that in order to achieve this 'deep cuts in global emissions are required'. See Decision 2/CP.15, 'Copenhagen Accord', in FCCC/CP/2009/11/Add.1 (30 March 2010).

[25] Kyoto Protocol, n 15, Art 2.2.

[26] The idea of a system boundary in this setting is drawn from GP Peters, 'From Production-Based to Consumption-Based National Emission Inventories' (2008) 65(1) *Ecological Economics* 13.

[27] This is by no means uncontested. There is increasing pressure to integrate an element of consumption-based accounting into climate change. See, eg SJ Davis and K Caldeira, 'Consumption-based accounting of CO_2 emissions' (2010) 107(12) PNAS 5687.

[28] There is widespread recognition that a production-based system boundary is not adequate in relation to aviation as many emissions are generated in areas which are not subject to the jurisdiction of any state, eg over the High Seas.

approach. While this alternative approach does seek to allocate responsibility for aviation emissions even where these occur above the High Seas, it does not eschew territoriality but insists rather upon the relevance of a different territorial factor than that privileged by the dominant production-based approach. The territorial connecting factor to which the EU attaches importance is access to the EU aviation market, whether as a departing or a landing flight. Only flights that depart from or land at an EU airport will be covered in the emissions trading scheme. The aviation decision is extra-territorial when viewed through the lens of a production-based system boundary. However, it is merely differently territorial when viewed through a system boundary that posits market access as key.

This argument is in keeping with the approach adopted by both the Advocate General and the European Court of Justice (ECJ) in the recent action for judicial review.[29] The Advocate-General concluded that the assertion that the EU has created an extra-territorial rule is 'based on an erroneous and highly superficial reading' of the emissions trading directive.[30] Likewise, the ECJ found that the aviation decision does not infringe the principle of territoriality (or sovereignty) in customary international law. In reaching this conclusion, the ECJ emphasizes two different types of territorial connection between the measure and the EU. It points out first that the EU measure only applies to 'those aircraft . . . physically in the territory of one of the Member States of the European Union and are thus subject on that basis to the unlimited jurisdiction of the European Union'.[31] Second, drawing analogies with competition law and other areas of environmental law, the ECJ makes it clear that even though the event being regulated by EU law occurred in part outside of the territory of the EU, it was capable of contributing to pollution inside the territory of the EU Member States.[32] The fact that the court lays emphasis upon these two different kinds of territorial connection leaves open the question of whether just one form of territorial connection alone would suffice to ground the jurisdiction of the EU. The language of the ECJ is emphatic when it confirms the sufficiency of the territorial connection based on the presence of the regulated aircraft, and in view of this it seems probable that this form of territorial connection would alone suffice.

Sovereignty-Infringing: As with the claim that the EU's aviation decision is extra-territorial, the argument that the decision is sovereignty-infringing rests upon a prior, and at least in the case of aviation inappropriate, decision to privilege a production-based system boundary. Viewed from this perspective, emissions generated in the territory of one country necessarily fall within the exclusive jurisdiction and sphere of sovereignty of that state. Any attempt by the EU to regulate these emissions amounts to an illegitimate external encroachment and an attempt to sap the sovereignty of the relevant state.

Viewed from the EU's perspective, however, the position is different but no less clear. In the absence of an international agreement establishing the system boundary for aviation emissions, the EU has made its own choice. It is this choice that determines the geographical scope of the EU's regulatory jurisdiction and the global reach of its regulatory powers. The EU's choice of system boundary may be viewed as 'polity-defining',[33] in that it serves to delineate the boundaries of the EU.

It is therefore the case that both the EU and the US can put forward a credible claim to jurisdiction over the contested aviation emissions. These two polities have settled upon different system boundaries and consequently they demarcate the limits of their sovereign

[29] Case C-366/10, *The Air Transport Association of America, American Airlines Inc, Continental Airlines Inc, United Airlines Inc v The Secretary of State for Energy and Climate Change*, judgment of Court of Justice of 21 December 2011 and opinion of Advocate General Kokott of 6 October 2011.

[30] Case C-366/10, Opinion of Advocate General Kokott, ibid, para 144.

[31] Case C-366/10, judgment of Court of Justice, n 29, para 125.

[32] Ibid, para 129.

[33] We are drawing here upon Neil Walker's work and his writing on the concept of 'late sovereignty'. See especially N Walker, 'Late Sovereignty in the European Union' in N Walker (ed), *Sovereignty in Transition* (Hart Publishing, 2003) 22.

authority in very different ways. As a result, the sovereignty claims of the EU and the US clash and overlap, giving rise to 'border conflicts' of a kind that are all too familiar inside the EU.[34] These border conflicts cannot be settled through recourse to the concept of sovereignty, because they emerge as a result of there being more than one, plausible and overlapping, sovereignty claim.[35] They may be managed in a variety of different ways: through the exercise of material power (for example, through the imposition of economic sanctions), through litigation (for example, the case before the Court of Justice), and through dialogue which is actively encouraged by the strategy of contingent unilateralism that was highlighted above.

Thus, in contrast to some other observers, we are not willing to condemn the EU on the basis that its aviation decision is unilateral, extra-territorial or sovereignty-infringing. In a policy domain that is essentially unregulated at the international level, the EU is using its market power to avoid regulatory 'lift-off' and to achieve 'juridical touchdown'.[36] It is doing so in an area where 'domestic' EU regulation can achieve a substantial global reach and in a way that may encourage similar regulatory action elsewhere. We are, however, critical of the EU's approach in one important respect. Contrary to the European Commission's recently expressed view, we believe that the principle of 'Common but Differentiated Responsibilities and Respective Capabilities' (CBDRRC) is relevant in relation to the EU's aviation decision and that there is a danger that this decision will be interpreted and applied in a manner that is not in keeping with it. Needless to say, the contours of this principle remain ill-defined and as a result the EU would enjoy substantial discretion in defining what this principle requires and means. The principle of CBDRRC forms the focus for the next part of this paper.

4. Common but Differentiated Responsibilities and Respective Capabilities

In a statement, the China Air Transport Association condemned the EU scheme as contrary to the principle of common but differentiated responsibilities.[37] India has also in a recent submission to the FCCC levelled this charge against the scheme.[38] In the discussion that follows, we will examine the concept of CBDRRC, consider whether it is relevant in the context of the EU's aviation decision, consider whether this decision sufficiently reflects this principle, and explore how best the decision may be adjusted to ensure that it does. We will conclude this discussion by looking briefly at the nature of the non-discrimination principle and by considering the constraints that this may impose on the EU when determining how to ensure respect for CBDRRC.

4.1. The principle

The principle of common but differentiated responsibilities and respective capabilities (CBDRRC) has underpinned global efforts to address climate change from the very start. The principle finds expression in the FCCC, and is the basis of the burden-sharing arrangements crafted under the FCCC and its Kyoto Protocol. It is also highlighted in numerous

[34] Ibid. Of course there is a vigorous debate about whether the EU as opposed to its Member States can enjoy sovereignty.

[35] For a similar argument in a similar setting see N McCormick, 'The Maastricht-Urteil: Sovereignty Now' (1995) 1 ELJ 259.

[36] These terms are taken from the article by R Wai, 'Transnational Liftoff and Juridical Touchdown: The Regulatory Function of Private International Law in an Era of Globalization' (2002) 40 Columbia J Int'l L 209.

[37] 'Statement by CATA on Inclusion of International Aviation in the EU ETS' (WCARN, 3 October 2011): <http://www.wcarn.com/list/13/13140.html> accessed 12 March 2012.

[38] Proposals by India, n 21, 6.

decisions of the FCCC Conference of the Parties (COP), the controversial and non-binding Copenhagen Accord, 2009,[39] as well as the Cancun Agreements, 2010.[40] While there is strong agreement on the relevance of the principle, there is little agreement about its meaning, application and legal status.[41] Given these disagreements, it is unlikely that the principle of CBDRRC has acquired the status of customary international law, however, given its frequent invocation, as well as the pervasive differential treatment in evidence in the climate treaties, it seems equally clear that it is a key pillar in the conceptual architecture of the climate regime, and ought at least to be 'taken into consideration' and 'given proper weight'.[42]

At the heart of the concept of CBDRRC in relation to climate change is the idea of the differential treatment of different countries. In keeping with this, both the FCCC and the Kyoto Protocol require that developed countries take the lead in assuming ambitious greenhouse gas mitigation targets. In line with this, only developed country parties have agreed to binding emission reduction commitments under the Kyoto Protocol. In this setting, CBDRRC is predicated upon differentiation in favour of all developing states and upon the uniform treatment of developing states.

The future implications of the CBDRRC principle are contested and unclear. As a result of disagreements over its application, this principle does not find explicit reference in the text of the Durban Platform, 2011, which launched a negotiation process to reach a post-2020 climate agreement.[43] Nevertheless, the fact that this new process is intended to be 'under the Convention',[44] both endorses the relevance of and implicitly engages the principles and provisions of the FCCC. Many developed countries are in favour of a new legally binding instrument that would substitute a regime of *differentiation in favour of developing countries* with a regime of *differentiation between all countries*. This would imply a more flexible and evolving categorization of countries that would permit differences within the developed and developing country blocs to be taken into account in fashioning obligations under a future climate regime. Thus, the US for example insists that CBDRRC 'inherently recognizes a spectrum or continuum of effort among all countries, not just between categories of countries'.[45] In the context of the post-2020 climate agreement, the EU notes that 'responsibilities and capabilities are differentiated but evolve over time and that the agreement should reflect those evolving realities by including a spectrum of commitments in a dynamic way.[46] Some developing countries, on the contrary, would prefer to continue with the Kyoto model that imposes binding emission reduction targets on developed countries alone.

The EU accepts that developed countries must lead the way in cutting greenhouse gas emissions, but it also insists that '[a] significant contribution from developing countries, and in particular from economically more advanced developing countries, is also essential, as many of them are quickly becoming important emitters'.[47] It proposes that developing

[39] Copenhagen Accord, n 24.

[40] See Decision 1/CP.16, 'The Cancun Agreements: Outcome of the work of the Ad Hoc Working Group on Long-term Cooperative Action under the Convention', in FCCC/CP/2010/7/Add.1 (15 March 2011).

[41] See L Rajamani, 'The Reach and Limits of the Principle of Common but Differentiated Responsibilities and Respective Capabilities in the Climate Change Regime' in NK Dubash (ed), *Handbook of Climate Change and India: Development, Politics and Governance* (Earthscan, 2011).

[42] See the judgment of the International Court of Justice in *Gabčíkovo—Nagymaros (Hungary/Slovakia)* [1997] ICJ Rep 7, 78, at para 140 discussing the role of the principle of sustainable development.

[43] Dec. 1/CP.17, 'Establishment of an Ad Hoc Working Group on a Durban Platform for Enhanced Action', in FCCCP/CP/2011/9/Add.1 (15 Mar. 2012).

[44] Ibid, para 2.

[45] Submission by the United States of America, in FCCC/AWGLCA/2010/MISC.2 (30 April 2010) 79, at 80.

[46] Submission by Denmark and the European Commission on behalf of the European Union and its Member States, 'Options and ways for further increasing the level of ambition', 1 March 2012: <http://unfccc.int/bodies/awg/items/6656.php> accessed on 12 March 2012.

[47] Communication from the Commission to the European Parliament, the Council, the European Economic and Social Committee and the Committee of the Regions, 'Towards a comprehensive climate change agreement in Copenhagen' COM (2009) 39 final of 28 January 2009, 3.

countries should limit the increase in their greenhouse gas emissions through nationally appropriate actions to 15–30% below a 'business-as-usual' baseline by 2020, insisting that 'differing national circumstances and stages of development in developing countries require differentiated actions and levels of ambition'.[48] On this basis, it should not be assumed that CBDRRC will imply that developing countries should not incur any emission reduction obligations, but that developing countries should incur obligations when they are able, which in turn will be determined in the light of criteria still to be agreed.

4.2. Does the principle of CBDRRC apply?

While the Commission Staff Working Document that accompanied the proposal for the aviation decision acknowledged the relevance of this principle, it argued that the proposal was 'fully in line with the principle of "common but differentiated responsibilities" under the UNFCCC'.[49] More recently, however, the Commission has suggested that the principle of CBDRRC is not engaged by the EU's aviation decision.[50] It argues that this principle applies to states and to the climate measures they take and that the EU–ETS, by contrast, applies to businesses active in the EU market and not to states.

It is our view that this argument is flawed, both in general and specifically in relation to the inclusion of aviation in the ETS. Our first argument is that the EU's aviation decision applies not only to businesses but also to states. Our second argument is that, in so far as the EU's aviation decision does apply to businesses, this is not a reason to exclude the application of CBDRRC. In other settings, the EU acknowledges that CBDRRC does apply to state measures, even where these state measures regulate or steer business activities.

Our first argument rests upon the proposition that, contrary to the Commission's recent claim, the EU's aviation decision applies not only to businesses but also to states. This is because it provides for the possibility that EU-arriving flights may be exempted from inclusion in the ETS where their state of departure has itself taken measures to reduce the climate change impact of flights. Thus, the nature of the burden imposed by the ETS on businesses will depend in part upon the behaviour of states and upon whether developed and developing countries have themselves taken measures to reduce the climate change impact of flights. The EU's aviation decision is thus also addressed to states.

As regards our second argument, it should be stressed that neither the nature nor the scope of the EU's CBDRRC argument is absolutely clear. The Commission accepts that CBDRRC applies to states and to the climate measures that they take. And yet, it does not accept that it applies in the case of the ETS, even though this is a measure adopted by an entity exercising state-like powers with a view to influencing the behaviour of business. By contrast, the EU does accept that the principle of CBDR is relevant when developing countries take climate measures, even where these developing country climate measures aim similarly to influence the behaviour of business. Thus, for example, the EU accepts that CBDRRC would apply when developing countries set or agree to a sectoral emissions baseline for the purpose of a Sectoral Crediting Mechanism.[51] Here, the EU stresses that

[48] Ibid, 5. The EU thus situates itself in the differentiation between all countries camp.

[49] Commission of the European Communities, 'Impact Assessment of the inclusion of aviation activities in the scheme for greenhouse gas emission allowance trading within the Community' SEC (2006) 1684 of 20 December 2006, 52.

[50] Presentation by A Runge-Metzger, 'Aviation and Emissions Trading', ICAO Council Briefing (29 September 2011) 40: <http://ec.europa.eu/clima/policies/transport/aviation/docs/presentation_icao_en.pdf> accessed 12 March 2012.

[51] The EU seems to accept that the principle of CBDRRC would remain applicable even where developing countries regulate business activity directly by setting or agreeing to a sectoral emissions baseline in the context of a Sectoral Crediting Mechanism. The EU stresses that higher capability developing countries would be expected to set more ambitious sectoral baselines and that this would be in accordance with the principle of CBDRRC. See Ad Hoc Working Group on Long-term Cooperative Action under the Convention (AWG-LCA), 'Views on the

higher capability developing countries would be expected to set more ambitious sectoral baselines and that this would be in accordance with the CBDRRC.[52] To reiterate, the EU accepts that CBDRRC applies to developing country climate measures even where these measures are closely tied to the regulation of business activities within the state.

The implications of the EU's position may be teased out by way of an example. If the EU were to decide to include imported steel in the ETS, thus imposing a burden on steel manufacturers in both developed and developing countries, the EU would consider that CBDRRC does not apply. By contrast, if states were to conclude a global sectoral agreement for steel, the EU would endorse the relevance of CBDRRC and accept that different countries should be treated differently within this agreement depending upon their respective capabilities. In this example, both the ETS and the global sectoral agreement would impose a burden on developing country steel manufacturers but where the burden flows from the EU measure rather than from the global sectoral agreement, according to EU logic, CBDRRC would not apply.

It is difficult to articulate what the normative basis underpinning the EU's CBDRRC position might be. If *developing country* measures imposing a burden on developing country businesses implicate the principle of CBDRRC, it is not clear why *EU* measures which similarly impose a burden on developing country businesses do not. Differentiation in the case of the former would result in the different treatment of businesses from different states. An absence of differentiation in the case of the latter would result in the equal treatment of businesses from different states. It is not clear to us how the origin of the state measure—EU or developing country—could serve to justify this different result.

There is perhaps one argument that the EU could make. This argument would have to be narrowly tailored to aviation and maritime transport and would not be susceptible to generalization in relation to other business sectors such as steel. The EU argues that its aviation decision does not implicate CBDRRC because it applies to businesses 'active in the EU'. It is possible that the underlying claim is that the EU measure is a developed country measure that only applies to developed country businesses; with this latter concept being construed by the EU as those businesses that are active in the EU.

An argument of this kind would be difficult to make in relation to an extension of the ETS to imported steel. For steel, the 'system boundary' for allocating responsibility for business emissions to individual states has been globally agreed. Whether one agrees or not, the settled system boundary is 'production-based' and accordingly emissions generated in the course of producing steel are allocated to the country of production, regardless of where the steel is ultimately consumed. Consequently, an EU measure imposing a financial or regulatory burden on steel imported from a developing country would impose a burden in respect of emissions which are seen as developing country emissions and businesses which are seen as developing country businesses.

For international aviation (and maritime transport) the situation is less clear. As noted previously, no system boundary for international aviation has as yet been agreed. Consequently, there is no agreement on what constitutes a developing country business, developing country emissions or a developing country flight. It is therefore arguably open to the EU to draw up a unilateral system boundary which defines all emissions from EU-departing *and* EU-arriving flights as *EU* emissions, and all ETS-covered flights as EU flights. On this basis, it would be open to the EU to argue that its aviation decision does not apply in respect of developing country businesses, developing country emissions or

elaboration of market-based mechanisms', Submission by Hungary and the European Commission on behalf of the European Union and its Member States, in FCCC/AWGLCA/2011/MISC.2 (21 March 2011) 48, at 55.

52 Ibid.

developing country flights. If developing country businesses are not implicated, CBDRRC does not apply.

In the absence of a settled system boundary it is impossible to refute conclusively an argument of this kind. Nonetheless two sceptical observations may be made. First, if this is the basis of the EU's argument that CBDRRC does not apply, it would be helpful for this to be clearly and unequivocally expressed. This argument would imply that the EU is asserting that around 60% of all international aviation emissions are to count as 'EU emissions' for the purpose of its argument about the scope of application of CBDRRC. It would be important for the EU to maintain a consistent position on this issue when a system boundary for international aviation is finally agreed, and consequently for the EU to accept that more than half of the world's international aviation emissions should appear on its emissions account.

Second, although there is no settled system boundary in place, according to the Intergovernmental Panel on Climate Change (IPCC) Guidelines for the preparation of greenhouse gas inventories and the FCCC reporting guidelines on annual inventories, emissions from international aviation should be calculated as part of the greenhouse gas inventories of Annex I Parties, although they are excluded from national totals and are reported separately.[53] The reporting of international transportation emissions is based upon the volume of fuel sold in that country for international transportation by air or by sea (bunker fuels). In the case of aviation, because aircraft do not carry more fuel than required, there is a close correlation between this and the emissions generated by *departing* flights. While a bunker fuel sales methodology would not yield identical results to a methodology based on the place of departure or arrival of a flight, IPCC recourse to a bunker fuel methodology does serve to highlight that any EU claim that emissions from flights arriving in the EU, as well as flights departing from the EU, should count as EU emissions would be out of step with current international practice in this respect.

At any rate, whatever the EU's explanation as to why CBDRRC is not relevant in the context of its unilateral action, we do not accept this claim. We consider that this principle forms a fundamental part of the conceptual apparatus of the climate change regime and that state parties are obliged not just to interpret current obligations and fashion new ones in keeping with the CBDRRC principle but also to take this principle into account in their unilateral actions vis-à-vis other parties.

4.3. Does the EU's aviation decision respect the principle of CBDRRC?

The final Impact Assessment accompanying the EU proposal to include aviation in the ETS states that the measure is 'fully in line with the principle of common but differentiated responsibilities under the UNFCCC'.[54] There are, however, reasons to doubt this conclusion and to question the arguments that the Impact Assessment makes.

It was argued above that the EU's aviation decision applies both to businesses and to states. As a first step, it is necessary to ask whether this decision leaves any room for differential treatment of developed and developing country businesses or developed and developing states.

The aviation decision is premised upon the equal treatment of all airlines, regardless of the nationality of the airline, and of the point of departure or arrival or the ETS-covered flight. All airlines whose activities fall within the scope of the aviation decision will incur the same obligation in the form of a requirement to surrender one allowance for each tonne of

[53] See the Revised 1996 IPCC Guidelines for National Greenhouse Gas Inventories: <http://www.ipcc-nggip.iges.or.jp/public/gl/invs4.html> accessed 12 March 2012.

[54] Impact Assessment, n 49, 52.

carbon that they emit. While a proportion of these allowances will be issued free of charge,[55] a significant number will have to be bought at auction. Thus, the burden of surrendering allowances will bring with it a financial cost.[56] This financial cost will be borne in part by developing country airlines and by ETS-covered flights which depart from or arrive in the territory of a developing country. The revenues generated by the purchase of allowances at auction will accrue to the administering EU Member State.[57]

In so far as the aviation decision applies to states as opposed to businesses, the matter is less clear-cut. As was noted previously, for a third country to gain exemption from the ETS for EU-arriving flights, it is obliged to take to take measures to reduce the climate change impact of these flights.[58] This requirement is noticeably vague. While the Commission's original proposal suggested that exemption should be conditional upon the adoption of measures which are at least equivalent to the requirements laid down in the directive, this reference to equivalence was dropped by the Council when it reached political agreement on 21 December 2007,[59] and it does not appear in the Common Position adopted on 18 April 2008. It does, nonetheless, remain the case that a reference to equivalence remains in the directive's preamble which provides:

> 'If a third country adopts measures, which have an environmental effect at least *equivalent* to that of this Directive, to reduce the climate impact of flights to the [EU], the Commission should consider the options available in order to provide for optimal interaction between the Community scheme and that country's measures, after consulting with that country.'[60]

In light of this, the correct interpretation of the directive is far from clear. On the one hand, it can be argued that the main body of the directive should be read in the light of its preambular text. On the other hand, it can be argued that given the decision of the legislature to remove this reference to equivalence from the main body of the text, it would be contrary to legislative intent to interpret this instrument in a way that suggests that the equivalence requirement remains.

It is our suggestion that if equivalence is the parameter to be used by the Commission in assessing whether to exempt EU-arrival flights, this has the potential to be contrary to the principle of CBDRRC. Equivalence can be understood in a wide variety of different ways. For example, equivalence may be evaluated on the basis of an effort commensurate with resources or on the basis of outcome regardless of the relative effort made. The preamble to the directive seems to exhibit a preference for an outcome-based approach, premised as it is upon equivalence in terms of environmental effect. Although the concept of CBDRRC is vague, the idea that all countries should contribute in equal measure to the environmental goal of climate change mitigation is clearly out of step with it.

We recognize that in its application to states, the emissions trading directive can be read in a variety of different ways, and any final evaluation of the EU's aviation decision from the

[55] See Consolidated version of Directive 2003/87, n 2, Art 3d(2). In the first instance 85% will be issued free of charge. This can only be increased as a result of an amendment to the directive.

[56] Merrill Lynch estimates that the EU's aviation decision will cost airlines around US$4.3 billion by 2015. See Merrill Lynch, 'Aviation in the EU ETS: an incentive for efficiency' (8 September 2008), 15: <http://www.ml.com/media/113530.pdf> accessed 12 March 2012.

[57] See Consolidated version of Directive 2003/87, n 2, Art 3d(4) stating merely that Member States *should* (but not shall) use aviation revenues to tackle climate change in the EU and abroad.

[58] Ibid, Art 25a.

[59] See Commission of the European Communities, Communication from the Commission to the European Parliament pursuant to the second subparagraph of Art 251(2) of the EC Treaty concerning the common position of the Council on the adoption of a Directive of the European Parliament and of the Council amending Directive 2003/87/EC so as to include aviation activities in the scheme for greenhouse gas emission allowance trading within the Community, COM (2008) 221 final of 22 April 2008 where it is observed that: 'The Commission's proposal provides for flights arriving from third countries to be exempt if they are covered by equivalent measures in those countries. The Council's common position provides for a more *flexible* approach to finding the best option to ensure interaction between the Community scheme and measures taken in a third country. The Commission supports this approach' (emphasis added), at 4.

[60] Directive 2008/101/EC, n 2, recital 17.

point of view of CBDRRC will depend upon how the criteria for exemption are defined and applied. No exemption has been granted thus far and no guidance has been issued setting out how the Commission will exercise its powers in this regard. While there are tentative signs that the Commission may regard equivalence in terms of environmental effect as the key parameter in this respect,[61] we reserve judgment on this point until the relevance and meaning of this concept in this setting become clear.

4.4. How could the EU reform its aviation decision to ensure respect for the principle of CBDRRC?

Given the uncertain and contested content of the principle of CBDRRC, the EU enjoys broad discretion in defining this principle and in designing mechanisms to ensure its respect. Different mechanisms for instilling respect for CBDRRC will offer different advantages and disadvantages and a number of key considerations should be kept in mind. Among the most important would be the extent of the emissions reach of the EU scheme, its capacity to 'encourage' action on the part of other states, competitiveness and leakage considerations and concerns, and fairness in terms of the ability of the EU measure to respond appropriately to the very different economic and emissions profile of vastly differently situated developing states.

As a preliminary matter, the EU would have to decide which countries are to count as developing countries, and which airlines, emissions or flights are to count as developing country airlines, emissions or flights.

There is no simple answer to the question of how to classify countries as developing countries or not. In view of the arguments that follow, it is our suggestion that this concept be broadly defined to include all countries other than those included in Annex I of the Kyoto Protocol.[62] One result of this is that a number of large, rapidly developing, economies would be included in this list. This broad definition of developing countries is only realistic because of our preferred method for ascertaining which flights are to be considered developing country flights for the purpose of integrating CBDRRC into the ETS. In a manner that is in keeping with existing IPCC international aviation reporting guidelines as well as with the distinction between departing and arriving flights inherent in the EU–ETS itself, it is our suggestion that developing country flights should be understood as those flights which depart from a developing country en route to the EU, regardless of the nationality of the airline operating the flight. On this basis, all flights that depart India for the EU would be classified as developing country flights; including flights operated by Air India and flights operated by Air France. This definition of developing country flights would serve to placate competitiveness concerns, as it is premised upon the equal treatment of all airlines regardless of whether they are registered in a developed or developing country.

Preliminary issues aside, there would be a number of options available to the EU in seeking to address CBDRRC concerns. Three options will be set out and evaluated below. It is crucial to emphasize here that none of the three options set out below is based upon the differential treatment of developing country airlines.

First, the EU could choose to exempt all developing country flights from inclusion in the ETS; exempting all flights that depart from a developing country and land in the EU. This option would score well from the point of view of competitiveness concerns as all airlines flying the same route would be treated in an identical way. It would, however, greatly reduce the emissions coverage of the EU–ETS and it would undermine the action-forcing quality of

[61] See eg 'EN E-005387/2011, Answer given by Ms Hedegaard on behalf of the Commission' (European Parliament Register, 15 July 2011): <http://www.asd-europe.org/site/fileadmin/user_upload/news/EU_news_150711a.pdf> accessed 12 March 2012.

[62] See Kyoto Protocol, n 15.

the directive, by removing any incentive for developing countries to take their own steps to reduce the climate change impact of departing flights. The broader the definition of developing countries, the more pronounced these concerns would be.

Second, the EU could interpret and apply the existing exemption for EU-arriving flights on the basis of different thresholds for climate action on the part of different states. In keeping with the idea of CBDRRC, these thresholds could be elaborated on the basis of a country's historic and current responsibility for greenhouse gas emissions and its capabilities in terms of wealth.

This second option, based upon differentiation in the conditions for exemption, has much to commend it. The exemption of developing country flights would be partial rather than absolute, and dependent upon appropriate climate mitigation measures being put in place by other states. This option would be complex and contested nonetheless. The question of how to share the climate mitigation burden is at the heart of the disagreement that impedes progress in global climate negotiations and, as things stand, no operational principles or criteria to guide the distribution of the climate mitigation burden have been agreed. In the absence of internationally agreed principles and criteria, it would fall to the EU to elaborate its own framework for determining what is to count as an appropriate policy contribution on the part of different categories of states. As such, this second option would necessitate the EU making another unilateral determination; this time about the climate mitigation burden in international aviation that should be distributed between different states.

Third, the EU could ensure that all revenue generated as a result of the inclusion of developing country flights in the ETS reverts to developing countries in order to assist them in addressing the causes and/or the effects of climate change. As things stand, this is not the case. There is at present no *obligation* attaching to EU Member States to hypothecate ETS revenues. Further, there are currently strict limits on the use of Certified Emissions Reductions in the aviation sector, implying that at least a proportion of the bought allowances required by airlines will have to be bought at auction rather than 'earned' through investment in Clean Development Mechanism (CDM) projects situated in developing states.[63] Given the concentration of CDM projects in a small number of developing countries, including China which is an upper middle-income country experiencing sustained and rapid growth, we would favour an hypothecation approach. More concretely, we would favour an approach that commits the revenue generated as a result of developing country flights in the ETS to a global fund dedicated to assisting developing countries to tackle the causes and/or effects of climate change. At the Cancun climate talks a decision was taken to establish a Green Climate Fund; this would be the type of destination that we have in mind for international aviation revenue of this kind.[64] What is crucial here is that this solution would imply a degree of redistribution of resources as between different developing countries. The availability of funding would not depend upon the specific contribution made by a single developing country as a result of the inclusion of international aviation in the ETS, but would depend upon the funding priorities and criteria of the funding instrument itself.

5. Conclusion

EU climate change unilateralism represents an important shift in the EU's leadership style. Having previously led by example, the EU is now relying more on its structural power. It is

[63] See Consolidated version of Directive 2003/87, n 2, Art 11a(8).

[64] At COP 16 held in Cancun, Mexico, from 29 November to 10 December 2010, the COP adopted decision 1.CP/16 in which it decided to establish a Green Climate Fund. See Decision 1/CP.16, 'The Cancun Agreements: Outcome of the work of the Ad Hoc Working Group on Long-term Cooperative Action under the Convention', FCCC/CP/2010/7/Add.1 (15 March 2011), para 100.

using market access as a lever to make climate-related demands.[65] It is doing so both to level the competitive playing field and in a bid to serve as a catalyst for climate action elsewhere. It is an ambitious strategy that tests the jurisdictional boundaries set by public international law; although not to breaking point, according to the recent aviation decision of the ECJ.[66]

One way or another, the EU's strategy of contingent unilateralism can be expected to alter the background conditions for national and international action on climate change. In a best case scenario it could encourage individual states to pursue more effective climate action in the sectors concerned. Equally, it could help destabilize those dynamics of the multilateral negotiations on climate change that are action-suppressing. In keeping with this, there are signs that the International Civil Aviation Organization may put forward a proposal for a global strategy to combat aviation emissions by the end of 2012.[67] We have focussed in this paper on the controversial aviation example. This may be viewed as a test-case for the EU's multi-pronged strategy of contingent unilateralism. And for this reason, it will be important to examine closely, and over time, the policy impact that the EU's aviation directive has had.

[65] For a discussion of earlier examples of EU unilateralism in relation to the regulation of aviation see: J Chiavari, S Withana and M Pallemaerts, 'The Role of the EU in Attempting to Green the ICAO' (EPIGOV Paper 35, Ecologic—Institute for International and European Environmental Policy 2008) at: <http://ecologic.eu/projekte/epigov/documents/epigov_paper_35_chiavari_et_al.pdfhttp://ecologic.eu/projekte/epigov/documents/epigov_paper_35_chiavari_et_al.pdf> accessed 12 March 2012.

[66] See n 29.

[67] Transport and Environment, 'Firm EU Stance on Aviation Emissions Confirms ICAO Promise for Global Proposal': <http://www.transportenvironment.org/news/firm-eu-stance-aviation-emissions-confirms-icao-promise-global-proposal> accessed 24 March 2012.

14

The Role of the EU in Shaping the Trade and Environment Regulatory Nexus: Multilateral and Regional Approaches

Gracia Marín Durán

1. Introduction

Over the past two decades, the European Union (EU) has increasingly sought to assert itself as a leading player in ensuring the 'mutual supportiveness' between trade and environment enshrined in, among others, the 1992 Rio Declaration[1] and the 1994 Agreement establishing the World Trade Organization (WTO),[2] as a means to achieve 'sustainable development'. Until recently, the EU had largely confined its efforts to the multilateral level, being the leading proponent of including environmental issues in the 2001 Doha agenda of multilateral trade negotiations and playing an active role in the relevant discussions within the WTO Committee on Trade and Environment (CTE). And yet, against the backdrop of scant progress at the multilateral level, the EU seems now determined to use the free trade agreements it has with a growing number of countries or regions more actively to advance its trade and environment agenda. But does 'mutual supportiveness' between trade and environment have the same meaning for the EU in the multilateral and bilateral/regional contexts? And to what extent, if at all, are the two approaches 'mutually supportive' in enhancing the Union's capacity to shape the trade and environment regulatory nexus at the global level?

In an attempt to address these questions, the chapter is structured as follows. Following this introductory section, section 2 will briefly introduce the trade and environment nexus to identify the key regulatory issues that will inform our analysis of the EU's approaches to the global governance of these issues. Section 3 will examine the extent to which the *EU legal framework* enables 'mutual supportiveness' between EU external trade and environmental policies –in other words, which is the Treaty basis for integrating environmental protection objectives into the formulation and implementation of the common commercial policy? Section 4 will explore the *EU's multilateral approach* to the trade and environment nexus, focusing on one key regulatory issue of particular interest to the EU but still divisive among WTO members, namely: the clarification of the relationship between WTO rules and specific trade obligations (STOs) contained in multilateral environmental agreements (MEAs). The EU's position on this contentious issue will be examined on the basis of internal policy documents and negotiating proposals submitted to the CTE. Section 5 will turn to the *EU's regional approach* to the trade and environment interface, drawing attention to an emerging shift in EU practice towards incorporating specific chapters on 'trade and sustainable development' in regional trade agreements (RTAs). A number of agreements concluded after 2008 will be analysed as the first instances of this new trend, which the EU

[1] Rio Declaration on Environment and Development (12 August 1992) UN Doc A/CONF.151/26 vol 1 Annex I (Rio Declaration), Principle 12; see also, 'Agenda 21' (12 August 1992) UN Doc A/CONF.151/26/Rev.1, vol 1 Annex II, ch 2, paras 2.3(b), 2.9(d), 2.19–2.22.

[2] Agreement establishing the World Trade Organization (Marrakesh, 15 April 1994), Preamble, para 1; see also, Doha Ministerial Declaration (14 November 2001) WT/MIN(01)/DEC/1 (Doha Declaration), Preamble, para 6.

wants to pursue in future RTA negotiations. It will be shown that the EU's regulatory ambitions at the regional level go beyond the current multilateral trade and environment agenda, particularly with regards to preventing the use of environmental standards for trade/investment promotion purposes. The chapter concludes by offering some reflections on the EU's role and influence in shaping the trade and environment regulatory nexus at the global level.

2. The Trade and Environment Nexus: Key Regulatory Issues

Regulatory linkages between trade and environment are by no means new and were in fact embedded in the original text of the General Agreement on Tariffs and Trade (GATT) adopted in 1947 as the basis for the post-war global trading system.[3] Yet, the trade and environment relationship has evolved over time and grown more complex as parallel developments have taken place since the 1970s in both international trade (notably, with the establishment of the WTO in 1995)[4] and environmental law (notably, with the conclusion of MEAs containing trade-related provisions).[5] The inclusion of environmental issues into the agenda of the ongoing round of multilateral trade negotiations, launched at the Doha Ministerial Conference in 2001,[6] has moved this relationship into the spotlight. While this chapter will not contribute to the widely documented trade and environment debate,[7] it is here necessary to identify the key regulatory links between trade and environment. Broadly speaking, the trade and environment nexus can be looked at from two regulatory angles.

The first, and oldest, has a *permissive* nature and relates to the use of trade measures for environmental protection purposes. These measures can be based on domestic standards of environmental protection or taken to implement trade obligations set out in MEAs, and may have an impact (partly or totally) outside the jurisdiction of the regulating state.[8] By their very nature,[9] such measures can often restrict or distort trade and thus run against basic trade disciplines, such as the principle of non-discrimination or the prohibition of quantitative restrictions. This tension is usually addressed through 'exception clauses' in trade liberalization agreements, including in the WTO,[10] which recognize a *right* of parties

[3] Art XX GATT 'General Exceptions', paras (b) and (g). The GATT Contracting Parties also established a Group on Environmental Measures and International Trade in 1971.

[4] While formally established by the Marrakesh Agreement of 1994, n 2, the WTO became fully operational on 1 January 1995.

[5] For an overview, see H Cameron, 'The Evolution of the Trade and Environment Debate at the WTO' in A Najam, M Halle and R Meléndez-Ortiz (eds), *Trade and Environment—A Resource Book* (ICTSD/IISD/The Ring, 2007), 3–8: <http://ictsd.org/i/environment/11235/> accessed 12 April 2012.

[6] Doha Declaration, para 31 contains the trade and environmental issues of the Doha 'negotiating' mandate, namely: (i) the relationship between existing WTO rules and STOs set out in MEAs; (ii) observer status of MEA Secretariats in the WTO and procedures for regular information exchange; (iii) trade liberalization of environmental goods and services. The Doha Declaration (paras 32, 33 and 51) also includes other 'non-negotiating' trade and environmental issues to be considered by the CTE, such as: the effect of environmental measures on market access; the relationship between the WTO Agreement on Trade-related Intellectual Property Rights (TRIPS) and the Convention on Biological Diversity (n 92); eco-labelling; technical assistance and capacity-building; and environmental review.

[7] See generally, Najam, Halle and Meléndez-Ortiz, n 5; J Wiers, *Trade and Environment in the EC and the WTO—A Legal Analysis* (Europa Law Publishing, 2002).

[8] For an overview of STOs under MEAs, see United Nations Conference on Trade and Development, *Trade and Environment Review 2003* (UNCTAD/DITC/TED/2003/4, 2004) 13–39; WTO Secretariat, 'Matrix on Trade Measures Pursuant to Selected Multilateral Environmental Agreements' (15 June 2011) WT/CTE/W/160/Rev.5. According to the WTO Secretariat, 20 out of the 250 MEAs currently in force contain implementation provisions that can affect trade.

[9] These generally take the form of import/export bans, tariffs, taxes and other fiscal charges, but can also include government procurement and domestic support measures (eg the environmental support programmes that fall within the 'green box' (Annex 2) of the WTO Agreement on Agriculture).

[10] Art XX(b) and (g) GATT; Art XIV(b) of the General Agreement on Trade in Services (GATS); Arts 27.2 and 27.3 TRIPS.

to adopt trade measures aimed at protecting the environment under certain conditions. One of the key aspects of the Doha trade and environment mandate is in fact to consider whether WTO rules would need to be revised in order to *permit* WTO members to implement their (specific) trade obligations set out in MEAs.[11] It should be noted, however, that the majority of developing countries remain wary of these measures being used as tools of 'disguised protectionism'. Another, more positive, aspect of this first dimension of the trade and environment nexus relates to the use of trade liberalizing measures (eg reduction of tariffs) to encourage trade in certain goods and services that are considered beneficial from an environmental standpoint. This is also part of the Doha negotiating mandate,[12] and has been equally addressed within some regional trade agreements recently concluded by the EU.[13]

The other side of the trade and environment nexus has a *prescriptive* nature and concerns the possible impact of national differences in environmental regulations on the international competitiveness of traded goods and services. This has been a concern primarily of developed countries which fear the prospect of so-called 'pollution heavens', whereby (developing) countries try to encourage trade and investment by lowering or not enforcing domestic environmental standards leading to a 'race to the bottom' in environmental regulation.[14] Such a weakening of environmental regimes is perceived as creating an 'unfair' competitive advantage, particularly if the costs of reduced environmental regulation are partly or fully externalized outside the territory of the de-regulating state. Some countries with more stringent environmental laws have sought to address this matter in their bilateral/regional trade agreements—the United States being a prominent example—through the inclusion of provisions that prevent regulatory competition in the environmental domain and ensure a 'level playing field' between the parties as regards environmental standards.[15] Such provisions can take the form of a *prohibition* to lower existing domestic environmental standards (through changes in law or lack of enforcement), and/or an *obligation* (whether in mandatory or 'best endeavour' terms) to enhance or harmonize standards of environmental protection. However, and importantly, this prescriptive dimension of the trade and environment nexus is not part of the Doha agenda. In line with the principle of common but differentiated responsibility,[16] it is generally recognized that each WTO member has the right to set its own standards of environmental protection at the level it considers appropriate in light of its environmental and development context, and it would be arguably beyond the WTO mandate (not being an environmental agency) to require otherwise.

Differences in national standards of environmental protection have, of course, been also a major cause of concern for developing and least-developed countries. In many instances, high environmental standards or related product requirements (for instance, eco-labelling) in developed country markets—no matter how legitimate from an environmental policy viewpoint—can hinder exports from less developed countries that simply lack the capacity

[11] Doha Declaration, para 31(i), which however states that: 'The negotiations shall be limited in scope to the applicability of such existing WTO rules as among parties to the MEA in question. The negotiations shall not prejudice the WTO rights of any Member that is not a party to the MEA in question'.

[12] Doha Declaration, para 31(iii).

[13] For an examination, see G Marín Durán and E Morgera, *Environmental Integration in the EU's External Relations—Beyond Multilateral Dimensions* (Hart Publishing, 2012) 99 and 121.

[14] This is based on the premise that, under free trade, firms will migrate to countries where environmental regulations are less stringent, as using cheaper but environmently costly production and processing methods will give them a competitive edge. See Organization for Economic Cooperation and Development, *Environment and Regional Trade Agreements* (OECD, 2007) 110–111.

[15] See the discussion on system boundaries in the contribution by Scott and Rajamani to this volume.

[16] Rio Declaration, Principle 7: 'States shall cooperate in a spirit of global partnership to conserve, protect and restore the health and integrity of the Earth's ecosystem. In view of the different contributions to global environmental degradation, States have common but differentiated responsibilities'; and Principle 11: 'Environmental standards, management objectives and priorities should reflect the environmental and development context to which they apply'.

to meet them. In addition, developing country WTO members are generally wary of 'green protectionism', whereby high environmental standards are used as an excuse for protectionism rather than for legitimate policy objectives. This dimension of the trade and environment nexus is usually addressed through *supportive* non-trade measures, such as technical assistance and capacity building, in order to enable developing country exporters to meet higher standards of environmental protection. This is an issue that is receiving particular attention within the work of CTE, although it is not formally part of the Doha negotiating mandate,[17] and to which the EU has shown some responsiveness at both multilateral and regional levels.[18]

3. An Enabling EU Legal Framework

The common commercial policy (CCP) is the oldest among the EU's external policies, introduced by the original Treaty of Rome as the necessary external dimension of establishing the then European Economic Community (EEC) as a customs union.[19] From the start, the Community actively sought to promote and defend its trade (and other) interests through a network of autonomous and contractual measures,[20] and as a result the CCP is also amongst the most developed EU policies. Overall, the impact and effectiveness of the CCP go largely undisputed, being often considered a successful means to assert the EU's identity on the international scene.[21] Against this background, one may have expected the CCP to also be amongst the most clearly defined policies in EU primary law. On the contrary, until the Lisbon amendments, the Treaty provisions on the CCP were strikingly silent regarding its objectives and principles: the only clear constitutional requirement for the conduct and formulation of the CCP was that it be based on 'uniform principles',[22] coupled with an aspirational commitment to trade liberalization.[23] This constitutional construct has been taken by the European Court of Justice (ECJ) as a ground for non-interference with political and executive discretion in the definition of the 'Community interest' (now 'Union interest') in this policy arena.[24] In other words, the EU political institutions enjoy considerable freedom—as a matter of EU primary law at least—in using trade policy measures to pursue non-trade policy objectives, including environmental protection goals.

[17] Doha Declaration, para 32(i). Among the measures being discussed in the CTE are: transparency, notification, early warning, consultation, impact assessment, technical assistance and capacity building. Regarding the latter, there is growing consensus among WTO members on the need to deliver an outcome on technical assistance and capacity building as part of the Doha negotiations (see n 112).

[18] For an examination of EU environment-related external assistance: G Marín Durán, 'Environmental Integration in EU Development Cooperation: Responding to International Commitments or Own Policy Priorities?' in E Morgera (ed), *The External Environmental Policy of the European Union: EU and International Law Perspectives* (CUP, 2013 forthcoming).

[19] EEC Treaty, Art 9 and ch 3 of Title II provided for the adoption of a common external tariff and the development of a common commercial policy.

[20] See generally, P Eeckhout, *External Relations of the European Union—Legal and Constitutional Foundations* (OUP, 2011) ch 10; S Inama and E Vermulst, *Customs and Trade Law of the European Community* (Kluwer, 1999).

[21] M Cremona, 'The Common Commercial Policy' in C Saunders and G Triggs (eds), *Trade and Cooperation with the European Union in the New Millennium* (Kluwer, 2002) 43.

[22] Art 133(1) EC Treaty.

[23] Art 131 EC Treaty stated: 'By establishing a customs union between themselves Member States *aim to contribute*, in the common interest, to the harmonious development of world trade, the progressive abolition of restrictions on international trade and the lowering of customs barriers' (emphasis added). Note the slightly different version of current Art 206 TFEU: 'the Union *shall contribute*...' (emphasis added).

[24] Case C-150/94 *UK v Council* [1998] ECR I-7235, paras 53–54: 'the Community institutions enjoy a margin of discretion in their choice of the means needed to achieve the common commercial policy... In a situation of that kind, which involves an appraisal of complex economic situations, judicial review must be limited to verifying whether the relevant procedural rules have been complied with, whether the facts on which the contested choice is based have been accurately stated, and whether there has been a manifest error in the appraisal of those facts or a misuse of powers'.

EU treaty law does not only enable, but purposely supports, the integration of environmental protection considerations in EU external trade policy-making. Since the Single European Act of 1986, the CCP has figured amongst the Union policies to which the environmental integration requirement enshrined in Article 11 TFEU applies,[25] and the ECJ has accepted that CCP instruments (including trade restrictions) can serve environmental protection purposes.[26] With the Lisbon Treaty, the interplay between EU external trade and environmental policies has been recognized more explicitly.[27] The CCP is now also subject to the common set of non-prioritized objectives for EU external action found in Article 21(2) TEU, which contains several environmental protection goals, including pledges to: 'help to develop international measures to preserve and improve the quality of the environment and the sustainable management of global natural resources, in order to ensure sustainable development';[28] and 'foster the sustainable economic, social and environmental development of developing countries, with the primary aim of eradicating poverty'.[29]

The new Article 21(2) TEU could thus be seen as reinforcing the function hitherto played only by Article 11 TFEU of constitutionally underpinning 'mutual supportiveness' between EU external trade and environmental policies, by requiring the EU political institutions to take account of environmental policy objectives when defining and implementing the CCP. That being said, it is unlikely to see the ECJ interpreting any of these Treaty provisions as entailing a strictly enforceable obligation for the EU legislator to effectively integrate, or give priority to, environmental considerations within external trade policy-making. The ECJ can instead be expected to maintain its position that the EU political institutions enjoy a great margin of discretion in balancing the various (and at times conflicting) policy objectives established in the EU Treaties when conducting the CCP. In other words, it is difficult to imagine a EU trade measure (whether autonomous or contractual) being successfully challenged before the ECJ solely on grounds that it does not, or not sufficiently, support environmental protection objectives.[30] Still, the key point for our purposes is that there is a clear basis in the EU Treaties for action by the Union to shape the trade and environment regulatory nexus at the global level. Yet, the precise extent to which the Union does so in practice, and the approaches it uses, are ultimately a matter of political appreciation and choice. In this regard, one important change introduced by the Lisbon Treaty of relevance for our purposes is the new power of the European Parliament to act as a co-legislator with the Council in CCP matters,[31] enabling the European Parliament to influence the EU's approaches to the trade and environment nexus in both the multilateral and the bilateral/regional contexts.

4. Shaping the Trade and Environment Nexus: Multilateral Approach

4.1. Policy basis: 1996 Communication on Trade and Environment

The EU has been taking an active part in international discussions on the relationship between trade and environment that have followed the Rio commitment to make trade and

[25] Art 11 TFEU (former Art 6 EC Treaty): 'Environmental protection requirements must be integrated into the definition and implementation of the Union's policies and activities, in particular with a view to promoting sustainable development'.

[26] For an overview with reference to relevant ECJ case-law, see Eeckhout (n 20) 39–56.

[27] See the contribution by Larik to this volume.

[28] Art 21(2)(f) TEU.

[29] Art 21(2)(d) TEU. Art 207 TFEU reiterates the need for the CCP to be conducted 'in the context of the principles and objectives of the Union's external action'.

[30] While no cases have dealt with Art 21(2) TEU at the time of writing, see discussion of the jurisprudence on former Art 6 EC Treaty (now Art 11 TFEU) in Marín Durán and Morgera, n 13, 28–33. For a similar view, see M Cremona, 'Coherence and EU External Environmental Policy' in Morgera, n 18.

[31] Art 207(2) TFEU (for the adoption of EU regulations in accordance with the ordinary legislative procedure) and Art 218(6)(v) TFEU (for the conclusion of international agreements).

environmental policies 'mutually supportive', and which have taken place primarily within the WTO Committee on Trade and Environment that was established at the conclusion of the Uruguay Round of multilateral trade negotiations in April 1994.[32] Only one year after the CTE formally began its work, the European Commission put forward its first Communication on Trade and Environment in 1996, which established the key priorities for the EU in these multilateral discussions ahead of the WTO Ministerial Conference in Singapore of December 1996.[33]

The 1996 Communication was anchored on three basic premises. First, the Commission maintained that trade and environmental policies 'can play a mutually supportive role in favour of sustainable development', and that the EU ought to remain committed to a 'high-level of environmental protection and to an open, equitable and non-discriminatory trading system'.[34] Second, the Commission acknowledged that all states have a sovereign right to set their own standards of environmental protection at the level they consider appropriate, and argued that national differences in environmental standards can constitute an 'entirely legitimate source of comparative advantage' in international trade relations.[35] Back then, the Commission was not concerned by the prospect of a 'race to the bottom' in environmental regulation, pointing to the lack of conclusive evidence 'of countries deliberately resorting to low environmental standards to gain competitive advantages or to attract investments',[36] nor did it fear possible negative effects of stringent environmental standards on the location decisions and international competitiveness of European companies.[37] Third, the 'EU should remain strongly committed to the multilateral approach as the most effective way to tackle global and transboundary environmental problems',[38] avoiding the use of unilateral measures in line with the Rio Declaration.[39]

As to EU priorities in the CTE discussions, the Communication placed particular emphasis on the interplay between WTO rules and trade-related measures under MEAs. In this regard, the Commission considered that the multilateral trading system should accommodate, under 'clear and predictable rules', the use of trade measures taken in the framework of MEAs, arguing that the multilaterally agreed character of such measures is the 'best guarantee against the risk of protectionist abuses'.[40] The Commission recognized nonetheless the need to introduce safeguards against the application of unnecessary trade restrictions on WTO members that are not parties to the MEAs.[41] On this basis, the EU became an active *demandeur* as regards the clarification of the relationship between existing

[32] WTO Ministerial Decision on Trade and Environment (Marrakesh, 15 April 1994). The CTE was given the broad mandate of identifying 'the relationship between trade and environmental measures in order to promote sustainable development' and of making 'appropriate recommendations on whether any modifications of the provisions of the multilateral trading system are required, compatible with the open, equitable and non-discriminatory nature of the system'. On the CTE, see G Shaffer, 'If Only We Were Elephants: The Political Economy of the WTO's Treatment of Trade and Environment Matters' in DLM Kennedy and JD Southwick (eds), *The Political Economy of International Trade Law: Essays in Honor of Robert E Hudec* (CUP, 2002).

[33] Commission, 'Communication on Trade and Environment' COM (1996) 54 final of 28 February (Communication Trade and Environment) 9.

[34] Ibid, 22.

[35] Ibid, 6 and 8, expressing a clear stance against the notion of 'eco-dumping' and against the introduction of duties or export rebates as a means to compensate domestic industries for the cost of complying with more rigorous environmental protection requirements than those faced by their foreign competitors.

[36] Ibid, 5.

[37] Ibid, 5–6, arguing that cost of compliance with environmental regulatory requirements are not a significant factor in the cost structure of most EU companies (between 1% and 2% of overall costs) and have little influence on their location decisions.

[38] Ibid, 7.

[39] Rio Declaration, Principle 12: 'Trade policy measures for environmental purposes should not constitute a means of arbitrary or unjustifiable discrimination or a disguised restriction on international trade. Unilateral actions to deal with environmental challenges outside the jurisdiction of the importing country should be avoided . . .'.

[40] Communication Trade and Environment, 12.

[41] Ibid, 13.

WTO rules and trade-related provisions in MEAs, which is now one of the three issues in the Doha trade and environment negotiations, but only in so far as the '*specific* trade obligations' in these agreements are concerned and as among the WTO members that are parties to the MEAs in question.[42] The EU has also supported the inclusion of the liberalization of trade in environmental goods and services (particularly those that it views as beneficial in tackling climate change) as part of the Doha negotiating mandate,[43] whilst also pressing for the recognition of eco-labelling in WTO agreements.[44]

4.2. The EU in the Doha negotiations on the MEA–WTO relationship

Doha negotiations on the MEA–WTO relationship take place in the special sessions of the CTE and have dealt with both the substantive (paragraph 31(i)) and the procedural (paragraph 31(ii)) elements of the Doha mandate. In substantive terms, the negotiations have addressed five aspects of the MEA–WTO linkage: (a) the identification of the MEAs at issue; (b) the definition of specific trade obligations in these MEAs; (c) the relationship between WTO rules and the specific trade obligations in MEAs; (d) MEA party/non-party issues; (d) the outcome of the negotiations.[45] In addition, negotiations have focused on procedures for regular information exchanges between MEA and WTO bodies, including the criteria for the granting of observer status to MEA Secretariats. As a key proponent of the negotiations, the EU has generally favoured a broad approach to the scope of the Doha MEA–WTO mandate, but its enthusiasm has only been shared by a few other WTO members, such as Norway or Switzerland. Not being *demandeurs* in this particular aspect of the Doha agenda, developing countries have for the most part engaged in the MEA–WTO negotiations rather reluctantly, hoping that this would bring concessions on other issues of particular interest to them, such as the reduction of agricultural subsidies or a strengthening of special and differential treatment, as part of a wider Doha deal. These countries have therefore taken a largely defensive position in the negotiations and advocated a narrow interpretation of the Doha MEA–WTO mandate with a view to avoiding further regulatory space for environment-related trade measures that could restrict their exports. They have been sided in their position by the United States, albeit for different motivations.[46] As a result, progress in the negotiations has been slow and modest, particularly in relation to substantively clarifying the MEA–WTO relationship.

Looking at its first submission in 2002, the EU has sought agreement among WTO members on the extent to which STOs under MEAs 'should be considered to be automatically in conformity'[47] with WTO rules, thus without being subject to the regular analysis under Article XX GATT. In this regard, the EU has pressed for a flexible definition of the terms 'specific trade obligations set out in MEAs' that would not be limited to those that are explicitly provided for and mandatory[48] (as proposed, for example, by the US), but could also include other trade measures that are not specifically identified, nor strictly required,

[42] See nn 6 and 11.

[43] See nn 6 and 12. EU proposals are available at: <http://www.wto.org/english/tratop_e/envir_e/envir_negotiations_e.htm> accessed on 12 April 2012.

[44] See n 6, as one of the issues discussed in the regular sessions of the CTE. EU proposals are available at: <http://www.wto.org/english/tratop_e/envir_e/wrk_committee_e.htm> accessed on 12 April 2012.

[45] WTO Secretariat, 'Compilation of Submissions under Paragraph 31(i)' (23 April 2003) TN/TE/S/3/Rev.1 (WTO Secretariat Compilation, 2003) 4.

[46] Ibid, for an overview of the different positions; and also Cameron, n 5, 9–13.

[47] WTO CTE Special Session, 'Multilateral Environmental Agreements: Implementation of the Doha Agenda—Submission by the European Communities' (21 March 2002) TN/TE/W/1 (EU Submission, 2002) 7.

[48] Ibid, 5. Examples of this include: the Convention on International Trade in Endangered Species of Wild Fauna and Flora (CITES, 3 March 1973, 993 UNTS 243), which creates a system that restricts and regulates trade in species whose survival is threatened to varying degrees, involving the use of bans or quotas for more threatened species listed in Appendix I; the Stockholm Convention on Persistent Organic Pollutants (POPs Convention, 22 May 2001, 2256 UNTS 119) which (inter alia) prohibits the import and export of certain POPs with some

under such agreements.[49] Similarly, the EU has proposed to broaden the scope of MEAs to be given explicit recognition in WTO law as including not only agreements negotiated under the aegis of the UN, but also any other treaty between at least three parties that aims to protect the environment, and which is negotiated under procedures that are open to all WTO members.[50]

Besides these definitional issues that dominated discussions in the CTE until 2004 and remain largely unresolved, the EU has advocated pursuing a more holistic approach in the negotiations that would establish the general principles to govern the MEA–WTO relationship within the broader 'global governance system' on sustainable development.[51] Emphasis is placed above all on multilateral institutions and processes (particularly, MEA Secretariats and WTO bodies), and no reference is made to regional regimes as a possible additional component of that global governance system.[52] Pursuant to its latest written submission made in 2006,[53] the first of such principles would be 'mutual supportiveness', understood as ensuring that no WTO member is prevented from taking measures for the protection of the environment at the level it considers appropriate, and that all WTO bodies interpret and apply WTO rules taking due account of the provisions of MEAs. Mutual supportiveness is accompanied by principles of 'no subordination' (recognizing that the WTO and MEAs represent equal bodies of international law), deference (recognizing the distinct competences and expertise of the WTO and MEAs),[54] and transparency (emphasizing the importance of close coordination, information exchanges and expertise-sharing at both national and international levels).[55] According to the EU, these principles are aimed in particular at ensuring that the WTO is part of the global governance system on sustainable development and 'does not operate in isolation from international developments and agreements in other fields that are more specific but nevertheless trade-related',[56] such as multilateral environmental processes.

Elaborating further on the procedural dimension of the Doha MEA–WTO mandate, the EU sees the strengthening of cooperation between MEA Secretariats and the CTE as an essential means to ensure conflict prevention and synergies between the two international

exceptions; the Cartagena Protocol on Biosafety (Cartagena Protocol, 29 January 2000, 2226 UNTS 208) as regards the obligatory advanced informed agreement procedure for the first shipment of living modified organisms.

[49] EU Submission 2002, 5–6 referring to more discretionary trade measures that states can decide to implement as an '*obligation de résultat*' of the MEAs, or pursuant to a general provision found in some MEAs allowing parties to adopt more stringent measures in accordance with international law. Examples of the latter include: Art 2.11 of the Montreal Protocol on Substances that Deplete the Ozone Layer (Montreal Protocol, 16 September 1987, 1522 UNTS 3); Art 15.4 of the Rotterdam Convention on the Prior Informed Consent Procedure for Certain Hazardous Chemicals and Pesticides in International Trade (Rotterdam Convention, 10 September 1998, 2244 UNTS 337). See also, WTO CTE Special Session, 'The Relationship between MEAs and the WTO Agreements: "set out in MEAs"—Submission by the European Communities' (14 May 2003) TN/TE/W/31, submitting that this term should not be interpreted as being limited to the treaty itself, as originally adopted, but should also cover all subsequent decisions by the Conference of the Parties.

[50] WTO Secretariat Compilation 2003, 14; EU Submission 2002, 2.

[51] The notion of sustainable development is not a monolithic well-defined notion in international law and policy-making, rendering it difficult to identify precisely which regulatory issues fall within the remit of that 'global governance system'. While it certainly includes the trade and environment nexus discussed here, it also encompasses other economic, environmental and social issues. For a brief examination of this concept in EU and international law, see Marín Durán and Morgera, n 13, 34–42 and references therein.

[52] EU Submission 2002, 4; see also WTO CTE Special Session, 'Proposal for a Decision of the Ministerial Conference on Trade and Environment—Submission by the European Communities' (30 June 2006) TN/TE/W/68 (EU Submission 2006) 2.

[53] EU Submission 2006, ibid.

[54] See also WTO CTE Special Session, 'The Relationship between WTO Rules and MEAs in the Context of the Global Governance System—Submission by the European Communities' (24 March 2004) TN/TE/W/39 (EU Submission 2004) 4, emphasizing that multilateral environmental policy should be done within MEAs.

[55] See also WTO CTE Special Session, 'Putting MEA/WTO Governance into Practice: the EC's Experience in the Negotiation and Implementation of MEAs—Submission by the European Communities' (4 July 2005) TN/TE/W/53, describing internal policy coordination on MEA and WTO issues as an example of experience-sharing.

[56] EU Submission 2004, 6.

legal regimes, and has called for the granting of permanent observer status to such MEA bodies.[57] The EU has also submitted that an additional means to avoid conflict is effective policy coordination in the negotiation and implementation of trade-related provisions in MEAs at national level as, in principle, countries which are parties to both an MEA and to the WTO covered agreements would strive to fulfil both sets of obligations in a consistent way.[58] Should conflicts arise nonetheless, the EU's position is clearly deference: WTO committees and/or panels examining 'issues with an environmental content' related to a particular MEA 'shall call for and defer to' the institutional expertise under the MEA in question.[59]

The draft Ministerial Decision on Trade and Environment of April 2011[60] captures the progress thus far made in the trade and environment negotiations and points to some convergence among WTO members, but mainly on the procedural elements of the Doha mandate and falling short of effecting definitive clarity in the overall MEA–WTO relationship.[61] The draft Decision underscores the importance of coordination at the national level in the negotiation and implementation of STOs under MEAs and of continued sharing of domestic experiences in this regard within the CTE.[62] It also contains some compromise language on cooperation between the WTO and MEA Secretariats and on the criteria for granting permanent observer status to MEA Secretariats in the CTE, indicating, however, that consensus is still lacking over pending requests for observer status by MEA Secretariats with current ad hoc participation in the CTE.[63] In essence, this means that the outcome of the negotiations would be (as per the draft decision) to create institutional mechanisms for managing the MEA–WTO relationship, rather than establishing 'clear and predictable rules' on the WTO-compatibility of trade measures taken in the framework of MEAs as initially sought by the EU. Instead, the draft decision reflects the view that such clear rules are not needed in light of the fact that no formal disputes have arisen in the WTO challenging the implementation of STOs set out in an MEA, and thus prescriptive language in this respect should be avoided.[64] Similarly, the EU does not seem to have succeeded in securing support from the majority of WTO members on mandatory deference to MEA expertise in WTO dispute settlement.[65]

But should this lead us to conclude that the EU lacks the capacity to effectively shape WTO rules on 'mutual supportiveness' between trade and environment, and should therefore turn to other fora to influence the development of global rules on this issue? Such a conclusion would seem premature, particularly if one considers the relative economic and

[57] See the latest submission in this regard: WTO CTE Special Session, 'Continued Work under Paragraph 31(ii) of the Doha Declaration—Submission by the European Communities' (15 May 2006) TN/TE/W/66, proposing inter alia the granting of observer status (automatic or by strong presumption) to MEA Secretariats with long-standing participation in the CTE.

[58] Ibid, 7.

[59] EU Submission 2006, preamble stating also that 'if a dispute arises between WTO members which are Parties to an MEA over trade measures they are applying pursuant to that MEA, they shall endeavour to resolve it through the dispute settlement mechanism available under the MEA'. See also EU Submission 2002, 7 stating that 'the fact that we are currently only considering the applicability of WTO rules as among Parties to MEAs does not mean that MEAs should not be an important element of interpretation of WTO law in disputes involving non-Parties'.

[60] WTO CTE Special Session, 'Report by the Chairman to the Trade Negotiations Committee' (21 April 2011) TN/TE/20 (2011 Draft Decision).

[61] The draft decision in fact reflects the combined outcome of negotiations under paras 31(i) and (ii) of the Doha Declaration, and most of it deals with the latter.

[62] 2011 Draft Decision, 9.

[63] Ibid, 9–10.

[64] Ibid, 5 and 8. See also WTO CTE Special Session, 'Report by the Chairman to the Trade Negotiations Committee' (22 March 2010) TN/TE/19, 1–2 conveying the same view even though there was some convergence among WTO members in identifying STOs in the following MEAs: CITES; Montreal Protocol; Basel Convention on the Transboundary Movements of Hazardous Wastes and their Disposal (Basel Convention, 22 March 1989, 1673 UNTS 57); Cartagena Protocol; Rotterdam Convention; and POPs Convention.

[65] 2011 Draft Decision, Annex I.B; cf with fn 2 therein the mandatory language proposed by the EU.

political weight of the EU in the WTO—as a single customs territory representing (as of yet) 27 countries—vis-à-vis that of other members. To be sure, the EU has had to lower its initial ambitions in relation to the Doha MEA–WTO negotiations, but this is to some extent inevitable in a multilateral negotiating process which requires consensus among over 150 WTO members and follows a 'single undertaking' approach, and that has moreover been dragging on for over ten years due to more fundamental disagreements over other aspects of the Doha negotiating agenda. A less ambitious outcome of the Doha MEA–WTO negotiations would not necessarily mean that the Union has been incompetent to affect legal and institutional change at WTO level, but that it needs to act within the inherent constraints of the Doha negotiating process just like any other WTO member. At the same time, and precisely because of these constraining characteristics of the Doha negotiations, any substantive or procedural change to the trade and environment regulatory nexus which the EU manages to secure through this multilateral track will enjoy the recognition and endorsement of most other global actors, and thus a degree of international reach and legitimacy that is far from guaranteed through other courses of EU external action (ie bilateral/regional or unilateral). Furthermore, slow and insufficient progress at the multilateral level is not the only factor to have prompted a shift in the focus of EU action towards the bilateral/regional level which, as will be shown next, is instead reflective of changing policy priorities of the Union with regards to (inter alia) the trade and environment regulatory nexus.

5. Shaping the Trade and Environment Nexus: Regional Approach

5.1. Policy basis: 2006 Sustainable Development and Global Europe Strategies

Until 2006, the EU had largely confined its initiatives to shape the trade and environment regulatory nexus to the multilateral level, while the only direct linkage between trade and environment found in EU regional trade agreements was in the form of a general exception clause, usually modelled after Article 36 TFEU, which is considered more flexible than Article XX GATT in allowing countries to pursue environmental protection objectives.[66] However, a shift in the EU's approach is starting to be noticed following the endorsement of its renewed Sustainable Development Strategy in June 2006,[67] where the European Council gave a clear mandate for the integration of environmental (and social) concerns in bilateral and inter-regional trade and cooperation agreements.[68] In the particular case of trade agreements, a new policy strategy named 'Global Europe—Competing in the World' was also adopted in November 2006,[69] which announced the launch of negotiations on

[66] Given that Art 36 TFEU allows for the adoption of measures that are more broadly justified on grounds of 'public policy': see A Cosbey et al, 'The Rush to Regionalism: Sustainable Development and Regional/Bilateral Approaches to Trade and Investment Liberalisation' (IISD, 2005), 12: <http://www.iisd.org/publications/pub.aspx?id=670> accessed 12 April 2012. For an overview of the trade and environment provisions in these earlier EU agreements, see Marín Durán and Morgera, n 13, 72–73, 80–81 and 114–115.

[67] European Council, 'Review of the EU Sustainable Development Strategy (EU SDS)—Renewed Strategy' Brussels, 15–16 June 2006 (Brussels Council Conclusions, 2006); see also the preceding Commission 'Communication on the 2005 Review of the EU Sustainable Development Strategy: Initial Stocktaking and Future Orientations' COM (2005) 37 final of 9 February.

[68] Brussels Council Conclusions 2006, 21 stating: 'the Commission and Member States will increase efforts to make globalization work for sustainable development by stepping up efforts to see that international trade and investment are used as a tool to achieve genuine global sustainable development. In this context, the EU should be working together with its trading partners to improve environmental and social standards and should use the full potential of trade or cooperation agreements at regional or bilateral level to this end'.

[69] Commission, 'Communication on Global Europe—Competing in the World. A Contribution to the EU's Growth and Jobs Strategy' COM (2006) 567 final of 4 October (Global Europe Strategy); endorsed by the Council, 'Conclusions on Global Europe—Competing in the World' (14799/06) 13 November 2006. For an assessment, see SJ Evenett, '"Global Europe": An Initial Assessment of the European Commission's New Trade Policy' (18 December 2006): <http://www.imd.org/uupload/EvianGroup/PUBLICATIONS/1456.pdf> accessed 12 April 2012.

new 'competitiveness-driven' RTAs, aimed at 'the highest possible degree of trade liberalization'[70] (including of services and investment) and incorporating new 'cooperative provisions in areas related to labour standards and environmental protection',[71] alongside other trade-related regulatory issues (eg intellectual property rights, public procurement, competition).

Whereas the Global Europe Strategy does not elaborate on the content of such novel provisions, it is indicative of a change in the EU's approach to the trade and environment regulatory nexus in two particular respects. First, the Global Europe Strategy is above all motivated by the desire to put EU external trade and investment policies 'at the service' of its competitiveness and economic reform agenda as presented in the renewed Lisbon Strategy[72] and, unlike the 1996 Communication on Trade and Environment discussed earlier, is not based on a thorough assessment of the trade and environment relationship.[73] The Global Europe Strategy instead tackles trade and environmental issues as part of the broader objective of using the CCP more actively to enhance the Union's competitiveness in a changing global economic order. In other words, the integration of environmental considerations in the post-Global Europe RTAs appears to be primarily concerned with the prescriptive dimension of the trade and environment nexus seen earlier: avoiding a 'race to the bottom' in environmental regulation and ensuring a 'level playing field' between regional partners as regards environmental standards.[74]

Second, these changing policy priorities flowing from the Global Europe Strategy are accompanied by a shift in the focus of EU action. Whereas in the 1996 Communication EU action was focused on the multilateral trading system and on how WTO rules should be adapted to accommodate environmental protection objectives (including the implementation of STOs under MEAs),[75] this multilateral dimension is largely absent in the Global Europe Strategy. Notwithstanding rhetoric statements that 'there will be no European retreat from multilateralism' and that concluding the Doha Round negotiations remains the EU's 'first priority',[76] the emphasis in the Global Europe Strategy is clearly placed on how the new RTAs can serve EU competitiveness interests in the meantime, including with regards to the trade and environment nexus. As will be further illustrated below, the EU's regulatory ambitions at the bilateral/regional level go beyond the Doha negotiating mandate to encompass the competitiveness-driven prescriptive dimension of the trade and environment nexus.

5.2. Trade and sustainable development (T&SD) chapters in new RTAs

At the time of writing, the EU has concluded four RTAs since the endorsement of the Global Europe Strategy,[77] all aimed (inter alia) at establishing a free trade area between the parties:

[70] Global Europe Strategy, ibid, 9.

[71] Ibid.

[72] European Council, 'Presidency Conclusions' Lisbon, 23–24 March 2000, which was re-launched by the Commission on 2 February 2005. See also, Commission 'Press Release—New strategy puts EU trade policy at the service of European competitiveness and economic reform' Brussels, 4 October 2006.

[73] Communication Trade and Environment, part 2 (analysing the key issues in the trade and environment debate) and part 3 (considering the interests of developing countries in these issues); cf with scant references to the environment in the Global Europe Strategy, 5, 6, and 9.

[74] See s 2.

[75] Communication Trade and Environment, part 4 (detailing issues that arise in the context of environmental protection and the multilateral trading system, including dispute settlement) and part 5 (on the way forward within the CTE and other multilateral bodies).

[76] Global Europe Strategy, 2 and 8; see also Commission, 'Working Document—Report on Progress achieved on the Global Europe Strategy 2006–2010' SEC (2010) 1269 (Report Global Europe Strategy) 3.

[77] Note that, while only South Korea was explicitly designated as a priority partner within the Global Europe Strategy, all four agreements contain similar trade and environment provisions, and were also included in the later report on the Global Europe Strategy (n 76).

the Economic Partnership Agreement (EPA) with the CARIFORUM States,[78] the Free Trade Agreement with South Korea;[79] the Association Agreement with Central American countries;[80] and finally the Free Trade Agreement with Colombia and Peru (COPE FTA).[81] All these four agreements contain specific chapters that seek to promote 'mutual supportiveness' between trade and sustainable development,[82] and which deal (inter alia) with trade and environment regulatory linkages. In the CARIFORUM EPA for instance, the parties 'reaffirm their commitment to promoting the development of international trade in such a way as to ensure sustainable and sound management of the environment, in accordance with their undertakings in this area including the international conventions to which they are a party'.[83] The agreements often identify several international instruments as providing the context of the T&SD chapter, including the 1992 Rio Declaration and its Agenda 21,[84] as well as the 2002 World Summit on Sustainable Development Declaration and its Plan of Implementation,[85] but notably none refers to the WTO Agreement and/or the Doha Declaration. So what exactly does 'mutual supportiveness' entail in this regional context?

Unlike the Doha negotiations, the purpose of the T&SD chapters is not limited to reconciling possible tensions between trade liberalization commitments and the implementation of trade-related obligations under MEAs. In fact, these RTAs add little to the existing WTO provisions in terms of clarifying the extent to which trade measures may be used for environmental protection purposes. Three of them incorporate a GATT Article XX-type exception clause, which recognizes a right of parties to adopt (or maintain) measures 'necessary to protect human, animal, or plant life or health' (Article XX(b) GATT), and/or 'related to the conservation of exhaustible natural resources' (Article XX(g) GATT), subject to the requirement that such measures are not applied in a manner that would constitute 'a means of arbitrary or unjustifiable discrimination' or a 'disguised restriction' on trade between the parties (GATT Article XX chapeau).[86] Subject to these conditions, only the agreements with Latin American countries also include a reference to the right of parties to adopt trade measures to implement their obligations under MEAs.[87] The CARIFORUM EPA, on the other hand, provides for a specific 'environmental exception clause' that is broader in scope as it incorporates a mention of the 'protection of the environment' (and not only 'the conservation of exhaustible natural resources'), but the application of which is subject to the same requirements as in GATT Article XX chapeau.[88]

[78] Economic Partnership Agreement between the CARIFORUM States, of the one part, and the European Community and its Member States, of the other [2008] OJ L/289/I/3 (CARIFORUM EPA). For a more detailed examination, see Marín Durán and Morgera, n 13, 95–108.

[79] Free Trade Agreement between the European Union and its Member States of the one part, and the Republic of Korea, of the other part, signed on 6 October 2010, [2011] L127/6 (South Korea FTA). It has been provisionally applied since 1 July 2011: 'Notice concerning the provisional application of the Free Trade Agreement between the European Union and its Member States, of the one part, and the Republic of Korea, of the other part' [2011] OJ L168/1.

[80] Agreement establishing an Association between the EU and its Member States, on the one hand, and Central America on the other, initialled on 22 March 2011 (Central America AA): <http://trade.ec.europa.eu/doclib/press/index.cfm?id=689> accessed 12 April 2012.

[81] Free Trade Agreement between the EU and its Member States, on one side, and Colombia and Peru, on the other was initialled on 23 and 24 March 2011 (COPE FTA): <http://trade.ec.europa.eu/doclib/press/index.cfm?id=691> accessed 12 April 2012.

[82] CARIFORUM EPA, Part II, Title IV, ch 4 (exclusively devoted to the environment); South Korea FTA, chapter 13; Central America AA, Title VIII; COPE FTA, Title IX (all three also addressing labour issues).

[83] CARIFORUM EPA, Art 183(4).

[84] See n 1.

[85] World Summit on Sustainable Development, 'Political Declaration' (4 September 2002) UN Doc A/CONF.199/20, Resolution 1 (WSSD Declaration); 'Johannesburg Plan of Implementation' (4 September 2002) UN Doc A/CONF.199/20, Resolution 2, (JPOI).

[86] South Korea FTA, Art 2.15(1); Central America AA, Art 203(1)(b)–(c); COPE FTA, Art 178.

[87] Central America AA, Art 287(5); COPE FTA, Art 270(4).

[88] CARIFORUM EPA, Art 184(3).

The T&SD chapters are instead motivated by a desire to enhance standards of environmental protection as a means to achieve sustainable development, as well as a fear—particularly on the part of the EU—of a 'race to the bottom' in environmental regulation. These policy goals of promoting environmental protection per se and ensuring a 'level playing field' in environmental standards for competitiveness considerations are to some extent intertwined and reflected in two sets of prescriptive provisions found in all four RTAs. First, the agreements lay down an obligation—albeit couched in best-endeavour language and subject to the parties' right to regulate—to 'strive to ensure' that domestic laws and policies provide for a 'high level'[89] of environmental protection. All four RTAs embrace international environmental standards as the benchmark for assessing domestic environmental performance, but only two of them actually specify the standards in question.[90] In the COPE FTA and the Association with Central American countries, a high level of environmental protection is defined as 'consistent with' the following core MEAs (all containing trade-related provisions):[91] the Montreal Protocol, the Basel Convention, the POPs Convention, CITES, the Convention on Biological Diversity[92] and its Cartagena Protocol, the Kyoto Protocol,[93] and the Rotterdam Convention.[94] To a large extent, this first set of provisions can be seen as reiterating in a regional context commitments that both parties have undertaken at the multilateral level to ratify and implement core MEAs as part of the global agenda on sustainable development.[95]

A second set of provisions is found in all four RTAs establishing an obligation to 'uphold levels of protection', this time using bold mandatory language. Taken as an illustrative example, the South Korea FTA provides:

> 'A Party shall not fail to effectively enforce its environmental and labour laws, through a sustained or recurring course of action or inaction, in a manner affecting trade or investment between the Parties.
>
> A Party shall not weaken or reduce the environmental or labour protections afforded in its laws to encourage trade or investment, by waiving or otherwise derogating from, or offering to waive or otherwise derogate from, its laws, regulations or standards, in a manner affecting trade or investment between the Parties.'[96]

It is in this obligation to uphold protection levels where we see most clearly the influence of the Global Europe Strategy: regional partners are explicitly prevented from weakening environmental protection standards *as a means to* encourage trade and investment. Competitiveness considerations are thus the main rationale behind one of the few legally binding commitments found in the T&SD chapter. Furthermore, in the CARIFORUM EPA, the undertaking to uphold protection levels is reinforced in the separate investment chapter, where parties are more forcefully required to ensure that foreign direct investment is not

[89] This language may be inspired by the EU's objective in Art 191(2) TFEU, which has been interpreted as not necessarily implying the highest technically possible level of protection: Case C-284/95 *Safety Hi-Tech Srl v S and T Srl* [1998] ECR I-4301.

[90] The CARIFORUM EPA (Arts 184(1) and 185) and the South Korea FTA (Art 13.3) instead make open-ended references to 'internationally recognized standards' and 'multilateral environmental agreements to which they are a party'.

[91] See nn 8 and 64.

[92] Convention on Biological Diversity (CBD), 5 June 1992, 1760 UNTS 79.

[93] Kyoto Protocol to the United Nations Framework Convention on Climate Change, 11 December 1997, 2303 UNTS 148.

[94] Central America AA, Arts 285 and 287; COPE FTA, Arts 268 and 270. Note that in the Association with Central America the Rotterdam Convention is not included in the list but in a separate provision in which parties undertake to ratify the Convention (Art 287(4)).

[95] These MEAs are for instance explicitly referred to in the JPOI (n 85), see for a commentary: M-C Cordonier-Segger and A Khalfan, *Sustainable Development Law: Principles, Practices, and Prospects* (OUP, 2004), at 32–36 and tables 2.2 and 2.3.

[96] South Korea FTA, Art 13.7; see similar provisions in CARIFORUM EPA, Art 188(1); Central America AA, Art 291(2)–(3); COPE FTA, Art 277.

encouraged by lowering domestic environmental standards.[97] A provision titled 'behaviour of investors' goes into further detail on enforcement and mandates the parties, 'within their own respective territories',[98] to take 'such measures as may be necessary' in order to ensure that (inter alia) 'investors do not manage or operate their investments in a manner that circumvents international environmental... obligations arising from agreements' to which the EU and/or the CARIFORUM States are parties.[99]

Taken together, these innovative provisions seem to indicate that national differences in environmental standards are now seen by the EU only up to a certain point as an 'entirely legitimate source of comparative advantage' in trade relations between countries at different levels of development, thus departing from its initial position in the 1996 Communication.[100] While countries are still recognized as possessing a sovereign right to regulate in these post-Global Europe RTAs, and national regulatory differences may emerge as a result, this right is significantly restrained by the obligation to ensure a high level of environmental protection (anchored upon international environmental standards), coupled with a prohibition to use environmental standards as a means to promote trade and/or investment. Performing such obligations can be challenging, particularly for developing countries such as the CARIFORUM states, which may find that they are called upon to enforce through their agreements with the EU higher environmental standards than they have the human, technical and financial capacity to implement.[101] Yet to what extent may the EU actually enforce these provisions against its RTA partners?

In response to that question, another significant novelty of these recent RTAs relates in fact to the creation of institutional mechanisms to deal specifically with the T&SD chapter, which are distinct from the general institutional provisions of the agreement. Joint specialized committees (or sub-committees) are established under the agreements to oversee the implementation of such a chapter, and decisions in this regard are taken by consensus and with guarantees for public participation.[102] Similarly, special procedures are laid down for settling trade and environment disputes, requiring the involvement of environmental experts and allowing also for advice to be sought from MEA Secretariats. As a general rule, dispute settlement by consultations within the specialized committee is favoured, although third-party arbitration is also possible through the establishment of a panel of experts. However, the implementation of the panel's recommendations is monitored by the specialized committee and no kind of sanction is available to enforce the trade and environment provisions.[103]

Therefore, with one exception only,[104] the EU has (as yet) maintained a cooperative and non-confrontational approach in its quest to ensure a certain 'level playing field' as regards environmental standards in the post-Global Europe RTAs, by promoting compliance with

[97] Ibid, Art 73.

[98] This specification seems to exclude home state regulation, whereby the EU would adopt legal measures to regulate extra-territorially the activities of its private investors in the CARIFORUM States.

[99] CARIFORUM EPA, Art 72.

[100] See s 4.1: Communication on Trade and Environment, 6 and 8.

[101] Note that the CARIFORUM EPA (Art 189), as well as the Central America AA (Art 63) and the COPE FTA (Art 286), recognize and address this through provisions on cooperation and capacity building (including with regard to MEA ratification and implementation), but it remains to be seen whether, and how, this important cooperative element of the trade and environment nexus is given meaningful effect in practice.

[102] CARIFORUM EPA, Arts 189(2)–(3) and 232(1); Central America AA, Arts 294 and 295; COPE FTA, Arts 280–282; South Korea FTA, Arts 13.12, 13.13 and 15.1.

[103] CARIFORUM EPA, Arts 189(4)–(6); Central America AA, Arts 296–301; COPE FTA, Arts 283–285, South Korea FTA, Arts 13.14–13.15.

[104] CARIFORUM EPA, Arts 72 and 73 (including the obligation upon parties to ensure that investors do not circumvent international environmental standards), because these provisions are situated in another chapter of the CARIFORUM EPA (Part II, Title II, chapter 2) which is fully subject to the general dispute settlement procedure, and thus theoretically enforceable through sanctions. See further, L Bartels, 'Comments on CARIFORUM–EU Economic Partnership Agreement' (13 February 2008) 3: <http://trade.ec.europa.eu/doclib/docs/2008/february/tradoc_138072.pdf> accessed 12 April 2012.

international environmental standards rather than seeking to impose its own standards of environmental protection upon (less developed) regional partners as a strictly enforceable obligation. This is a welcome step given the inherent limitations of enforcing environmental standards through trade sanctions, and particularly when countries at different levels of development (and thus of economic strength) are involved. In this regard, the EU has distanced itself from US practice under the North American Agreement on Environmental Cooperation associated to the North American Free Trade Agreement (NAFTA)[105] and other RTAs concluded thereafter,[106] where the enforcement of trade and environment clauses is subject to dispute settlement procedures that include the possibility of sanctions.[107] Against this background, T&SD chapters have the potential to act as a laboratory for an alternative, less controversial, model to address the prescriptive dimension of trade and environment regulatory nexus within RTAs.

Yet, there are a number of factors that may constrain the EU's capacity to shape the trade and environment nexus at the global level through this regional approach. First, RTAs are by definition selective and exclusive, and thus rules on trade and environment developed within these regional regimes are *a priori* of limited global significance in terms of the third parties reached. While the EU has in place RTAs with a significant number of countries or regions,[108] T&SD chapters are not found in those agreements concluded before the endorsement of the 2006 Global Europe Strategy.[109] Furthermore, even in future RTA negotiations, the degree of acceptance of T&SD chapters by third countries is likely to vary in light of the negotiating dynamic and bargaining position of the EU vis-à-vis each regional partner. In fact, it remains to be seen whether more advanced 'emerging economies', such as Brazil (as part of Mercado Común del Sur: MERCOSUR), China, India or South Africa currently engaged in RTA negotiations but less dependent on securing preferential access to the EU market and/or its development assistance, would accept the inclusion of such chapters as part of their agreements.

Second, the European Parliament, now a co-legislator in the conclusion of RTAs, has been advocating a shift towards a binding and sanction-based enforcement mechanism along the lines of US practice.[110] Such an enforcement mechanism could however increase reluctance among partner countries against including clear trade-and-environment obligations, or indeed the T&SD chapter itself, in their agreements with the EU. Third, acceptance of T&SD chapters is deemed to depend on the degree to which the EU takes account of the principle of common but differentiated responsibility and is willing to 'level the playing field' also for its regional partners by supporting their capacity, and that of their exporters, to meet higher standards of environmental protection. However, the EU has remained reluctant to undertake bold and concrete commitments on financial and technical assistance as part of

[105] See inter alia S Charnovitz, 'The NAFTA Environmental Side Agreement: Implications for Environmental Cooperation, Trade Policy and American Treatymaking' (1994) 8(2) *Temple International and Comparative Law Journal* 257.

[106] See eg 2004 US–Chile Free Trade Agreement, ch 19 ('Environment') subject to dispute settlement procedures (ch 22); 2004 US–Dominican Republic-Central America FTA, ch 17 ('Environment') subject to dispute settlement procedures (ch 20) following 'collaborative environmental consultations'. All US FTAs are available at: <http://www.ustr.gov/trade-agreements/free-trade-agreements> accessed 12 April 2012.

[107] See B Chaytor, 'Environmental Issues in Economic Partnership Agreements: Implications for Developing Countries' *ICTSD Issue Paper* 1, September 2009, 15–24: <http://ictsd.org/i/publications/61864/?view=document> accessed 12 April 2012.

[108] As per the notifications made to the WTO at the time of writing, the EU has 34 RTAs in force and another three under negotiation. For an overview, see M Cremona, 'The European Union and Regional Trade Agreements' in C Herrmann and JP Terhechte (eds), *European Yearbook of International Economic Law* (Springer, 2010).

[109] See n 69.

[110] European Parliament, 'Resolution on Human Rights and Social and Environmental Standards in International Trade Agreements' Strasbourg, 25 November 2010 (P7_TA(2010)0434), para 22(c).

the T&SD chapter of its regional/bilateral agreements,[111] even though such supportive measures are a key instrument in achieving environmental protection objectives under MEAs and are gaining increasing support within the Doha trade and environment negotiations.[112] Moreover, as recognized by the Commission itself, the overall amount of EU funding allocated to the environment remains modest: the yearly average financial commitments by the EU for the environment over the period 2007–2010 was around €295 million, representing roughly 4.3% of all EU external assistance.[113]

6. Conclusions—Assessing the EU's Role

This chapter has illustrated the interplay between the EU's global role as a 'market player' and as a 'rule generator'[114] in relation to the trade and environment regulatory nexus, distinguishing between its multilateral and regional approaches. Within the WTO, the EU has successfully used its market size and bargaining power to place an environmental mandate on the Doha negotiating agenda, and has sought to build consensus around what it considers are core issues in ensuring 'mutual supportiveness' between the international trade and environmental regimes. In parallel to this multilateral process, and as the prospects for concluding the Doha negotiations in the short-to-medium term have become increasingly bleak, the EU has more decisively used its market power to advance its 'mutual supportiveness' agenda at the regional/bilateral level through the inclusion of T&SD chapters in regional trade agreements negotiated on the basis of the 2006 Global Europe Strategy. The EU intends, furthermore, to continue including such chapters systematically into its ongoing and future RTA negotiations.[115] Regional trade agreements, therefore, can be expected to become an increasingly important element of the EU's role in shaping the trade and environment regulatory nexus at the global level.

Besides this shift in the focus of EU action, we have also seen that 'mutual supportiveness' between trade and environment has different meanings in the multilateral and regional/bilateral contexts, which are the product of distinct policy priorities. The Doha mandate on the MEA–WTO relationship is confined to clarifying what WTO members *can do* in terms of implementing their STOs under MEAs, as well as to establish procedures for enhanced cooperation between WTO and MEA bodies. The post-Global Europe agreements are not only concerned with this permissive dimension of the trade and environment nexus. Instead, these agreements are aimed at establishing what parties *should do* in terms of promoting a 'high level' of environmental protection, and in particular what parties *should not do* in terms of lowering environmental standards as a means to promote trade and investment–that is, the prescriptive dimension of the trade and environment nexus.

While the EU has seized the opportunity to place its mark on the shaping of global governance regimes in this field, its influence as a 'rule generator' has thus far been greater at the bilateral/regional level where it has managed to have T&SD chapters accepted by the regional partners concerned. Conversely, a number of EU proposals in the Doha MEA–WTO negotiations do not seem to have garnered broad support among WTO members, at

[111] See eg CARIFORUM EPA, Art 7: 'Commensurate with their respective roles and responsibilities, [the Parties] shall take all necessary measures to ensure the effective mobilization, provision and utilization of resources aimed at facilitating development cooperation activities under this Agreement'.

[112] 2011 Draft Decision, 11 and Annex I.A.

[113] Commission, 'Working Paper on Improving Environmental Integration in Development Cooperation' SEC (2009) 555 final of 21 April, 4.

[114] M Cremona, 'The Union as a Global Actor: Roles, Models and Identity' (2004) 41 *CML Rev* 566, 557.

[115] See Commission, 'Communication on Trade, Growth and World Affairs—Trade Policy as a Coherent Component of the EU's 2020 Strategy' COM (2010) 612 of 9 November, 8 (emphasizing the implementation of trade and sustainable development chapters in current agreements) and 9 (reiterating the ambition to include these chapters in future RTAs); and Report Global Europe Strategy, 15.

least when judging by the results of the CTE discussions. At the same time, it was argued that this is largely reflective of the different negotiating dynamics and bargaining leverage of the EU in the multilateral and bilateral/regional contexts, and that each entails different challenges and opportunities for the EU to affect substantive and institutional change in relation to the trade and environment regulatory nexus. The *degree* of influence at the bilateral/regional level may have been greater in matching the EU's regulatory ambitions, but the *global scope* of that influence would not easily match that of any, even if less ambitious, outcome of the Doha MEA–WTO negotiations. An 'European retreat' from these multilateral negotiations should, therefore, be truly avoided and EU's efforts as a 'rule generator' should not become exclusively focused on the bilateral/regional level.

In this regard, a fundamental question arises as to the implications of the shift in the focus of EU action towards generating rules on the trade and environment nexus at the bilateral/regional level for its self-proclaimed commitment to 'promote an international system based on multilateral cooperation and good global governance' (Article 21(2)(h) TEU). In fact, how, if at all, are the two EU approaches on 'mutual supportiveness' interconnected? This question is not, regrettably perhaps, of concern to the EU (and particularly the Commission) which has often claimed that its multilateral and regional trade agendas are 'mutually supportive' because its RTAs would serve as a 'stepping-stone' (and not a 'stumbling block') for multilateral discussions.[116] From this viewpoint, the T&SD chapters could serve as a laboratory for defining the trade and environment regulatory nexus and prepare the ground for subsequent agreement on this issue at the multilateral level.

And yet, it is far from clear how this 'mutual supportiveness' between the two approaches can be ensured, when EU negotiations on the trade and environment nexus at the bilateral/regional level seem to be entirely detached from parallel multilateral processes. As we have seen, the Doha negotiations on the MEA–WTO relationship are absent from the T&SD chapters. In terms of the permissive dimension of the trade and environment nexus, T&SD chapters do not (as yet) seek to serve as a laboratory for developing new rules to those existing in WTO law to deal with potential tensions between trade liberalization commitments and MEA trade-related implementation measures.[117] Conversely the prescriptive dimension of the nexus which is mostly elaborated by the T&SD chapters lies outside WTO competence altogether. In addition, there has been little consideration by the EU of how the institutional mechanisms being established at the regional level to oversee the implementation of T&SD chapters (including in terms of assessing consistency of domestic laws with international environmental standards) will interact, if at all, with existing monitoring mechanisms at the international level, or/and affect the coordination and expertise-sharing arrangements being discussed under the Doha negotiations.

In sum, the Union's influence in shaping the trade and environment regulatory nexus at the global level—both multilaterally and regionally—ultimately depends on its bargaining position vis-à-vis negotiating partners, and even when the relationship is one of equals, on the extent to which its intentions are shared by the third parties concerned. A trade and environment agenda that is acceptable to third parties at large needs therefore to look beyond the competitiveness and commercial self-interests of the Global Europe Strategy and reflect more thoroughly on the implications for partner countries, as well as on how exactly the EU multilateral and regional approaches can be made 'mutually supportive' in shaping global rules on the trade and environment.

[116] See eg Global Europe Strategy, 8; and more generally M Cremona, 'Rhetoric and Reticence: EU External Commercial Policy in a Multilateral Context' (2001) 8(2) *CML Rev* 359.

[117] See, in contrast, NAFTA (Art 104) establishing a clear precedence of specific trade-related MEAs (CITES, the Basel Convention and the Montreal Protocol) in the event of conflict, while other agreements subsequently concluded by the US (eg US–Chile FTA, Art 19.9) postpone a decision on this matter pending the outcome of the Doha negotiations.

PART V

THE EU AND GLOBAL FINANCIAL GOVERNANCE

15

What Role for the European Union in Shaping Global Financial Governance?

Fabian Amtenbrink

1. Introductory Remarks

The global financial and economic crisis has not only revealed the insufficiency of domestic regulatory and supervisory systems, but by and large also the interconnectedness of national economies and financial markets on a global scale and the lack of a corresponding transnational legal regime. As the world's largest integrated (financial) market, arguably the European Union has a responsibility to ensure the stability of the Union's financial system and by doing so to contribute to, if not take the lead in, setting global financial governance standards.[1] Since 2009 the EU has been seen to be overhauling its financial market regulatory and supervisory regime in major ways. Moreover, the EU has initiated a major reform of its system of economic governance as a consequence of the severe financial difficulties in several euro area Member States that have resulted in what is sometimes referred to as the euro area debt crisis.

Rather than dealing with the strategies that may result in a cohesive Union position on financial governance in relevant international (in-)formal policy-making and standard-setting fora, such as the International Monetary Fund (IMF), G20 and the Financial Stability Board (FSB),[2] the present contribution zooms in on the EU's approach to financial and economic governance following the global financial and economic crisis. It explores the extent to which the EU's regulatory approach can contribute to global financial governance either directly by setting standards or more indirectly through the scope of its legal framework. While in the EU context the generic term governance has not only been associated with rules, but also processes and behaviour that influence the way in which power is exercised,[3] the present analysis focuses on the former aspect. Moreover, the discussion of EU regulatory activities will take place at a rather aggregate level as it is not possible within the limited space available to provide an in-depth analysis or even overview of the specific regulatory regime applying to financial institutions.

This contribution is composed of three parts. First, we identify the causes that have contributed to the global financial and economic crisis and that—at least in parts—have also formed the rationale for the Union's legislative activities. Thereafter the main institutional arrangements of the new approach to financial and economic governance in the EU are reviewed. Finally, the contribution turns to the role of the EU in shaping global financial governance. The hypothesis of this contribution is that the Union's potential to shape global financial governance may not so much lie in the scope of its regulatory and supervisory framework as such, but rather in the multi-level approach to European financial regulation and supervision and its increasing role in promoting the (global) financial governance agenda.

[1] Art 3 iunto 21 of the Treaty on European Union (TEU). On the EU's constitutional objectives and its model of global governance see the contribution by Joris Larik to this volume.

[2] This equally important issue is addressed in the contribution by Jan Wouters, Sven Van Kerckhoven and Jed Odermatt to this volume.

[3] European Commission, 'European Governance. A White Paper' COM (2001) 428.

2. The Global Financial and Economic Crisis—A Wake-up Call for the European Union

Since 2009 the EU has been seen to have taken an active role in financial and also economic governance. As a result of the global financial and economic crisis legislative (hyper-)activity can be observed in policy fields which in the past were characterized by a lack of political consensus on the necessity and direction of European measures. For a long time this has seriously hampered progress towards more effective regulatory and supervisory structures. Indeed, in many regards this crisis has been a wake-up call for domestic and international policy and lawmakers that economic globalization taking the shape of 'the opening of markets and the rapid expansion of trade, but moreover also of the removal of financial market restrictions and free capital flow on a global scale'[4] is anything but risk-free. Arguably the opening of capital markets, be it unilaterally or as part of a process of regional economic integration, can potentially come at severe private and societal costs, if a regulatory and supervisory system that can detect and address undesirable developments with potentially far-reaching consequences for the viability of the economic system as a whole is absent.

The 2009 de Larosière Report, among others, has analysed the factors that have contributed to the global financial meltdown.[5] It has been argued that a loose monetary policy, especially by the United States Federal Reserve, contributed to the housing bubble that eventually resulted in the subprime mortgage crisis.[6] It was not only individual and institutional investors who acted based on the illusion that a permanent and sustainable high level of growth is possible, but also in many instances governments had made little effort to consolidate their finances and to take the necessary structural reforms in good economic times. As a case in point—certainly in the European context—government debts and deficits could be seen to rise. In the face of—in some instances repeated—bail-outs of financial institutions and measures to stimulate economies at the brink of recession, government deficits and—eventually—government debts could be seen to skyrocket in the euro area.[7] Across the Atlantic a similar picture has emerged as the US national debt has risen to unprecedented heights.[8] The most affected euro area countries were pushed to the brink of a quasi-insolvency, as they were effectively no longer able to service their debts. Major financial institutions with a large exposure in quasi-insolvent countries, especially in the shape of sovereign debt bonds, can destabilize the whole financial system. The 2010–2011 events in the euro area surrounding Greece and the reportedly large exposure of especially French and German banks in Greek sovereign debt bonds are a case in point. The example of Greece also highlights how uncertainty about the line of action at the European level can result in financial market volatility that spreads throughout the whole internal market. This

[4] F Amtenbrink and RM Lastra, 'Securing Democratic Accountability of Financial Regulatory Agencies—A Theoretical Framework' in R De Mulder (ed), *Mitigating Risk in the Context of Safety and Security. How Relevant is a Rational Approach?* (ESL/OMV 2008) 5. With regard to capital flows see eg J-C Trichet, 'The role of central banks in a globalised economy' (Speech held on the occasion of the 13th Conference de Montréal, 18 June 2007), 1.

[5] The High-Level Group on Financial Supervision in the EU, chaired by J de Larosière, 25 February 2009, p 7 et seq, hereafter referred to as de Larosière Report. Other analyses include, inter alia, International Monetary Fund, 'Containing Systemic Risks and Restoring Financial Soundness', Global Financial Stability Report (IMF, April 2008); European Commission, 'Economic Crisis in Europe: Causes, Consequences and Responses' (European Economy 7/2009); S Claessens, RJ Herring and D Schoenmaker, 'A Safer World Financial System: Improving the Resolution of Systemic Institutions' *Geneva Reports on the World Economy 12* (International Center for Monetary and Banking Studies and Centre for Economic Policy Research, 2010).

[6] De Larosière Report, ibid.

[7] See the statistical data on government debts and deficits provided by Eurostat, available at: <http://epp.eurostat.ec.europa.eu/portal/page/portal/eurostat/home/> accessed 5 April 2012.

[8] See White House Office of Management and Budget, Historic tables, Table 7.1, available at: <http://www.whitehouse.gov/omb/budget/Historicals> accessed 5 April 2012.

highlights how financial governance cannot be viewed in isolation from macroeconomic governance.

In search of profitable investment opportunities, excess liquidity fuelled market innovation and especially the engineering of more and more complex structured financial instruments, such as 'asset-backed securities'. In order to assess the risk of such financial products and, moreover, the creditworthiness of their issuers, individual and institutional investors have relied on the professional opinion of Credit Rating Agencies (CRAs).[9] CRAs have been criticized for having under-estimated the credit risk associated with structured credit products thereby having at least contributed to the extent of the crisis.[10] Given the institutionalized (over-)reliance on such credit ratings, such as through the contractual requirement for institutional investors to invest in investment-grade rated products only, the sudden large-scale downgrading of previously investment-grade rated products sent earthquakes through the global financial system and triggered large-scale (automated) selling. Yet investors may not only have been let down in their trust in credit ratings. They may also have mitigated other risks not even covered by such assessments, such as market risks and liquidity risks.[11]

Yet, not only individual and institutional investors rely on credit ratings. Ratings are also utilized for regulatory purposes on a major scale. Both in the EU and in the US CRAs are a de facto part of the financial market regulatory system and as such arguably serve a public function.[12] The reason for this is that minimum capital requirements for financial institutions are determined based on external credit ratings. The decisions on the size of the buffers against unexpected losses, a crucial instrument in safeguarding the stability of the financial system, is effectively in the hands of commercial and hence profit-oriented entities, which—until recently—to a large extent fell outside any real supervisory framework.[13] In the EU this use of credit ratings for regulatory ends can be found most prominently in the so-called Capital Requirements Directive, which effectively implements the Basel framework and which until recently provided for a rather marginal system of recognition of credit ratings for regulatory purposes that had to ensure the quality of such ratings.[14]

What is more, until recently the regulatory framework in place to assess risks was almost exclusively geared towards individual financial market participants, that is financial institutions, rather than towards the stability of the financial system as a whole. Put differently, not enough attention has been paid to systemic risks.[15] This has certainly been the case in the EU where, despite the central place of financial market integration, neither the European

[9] Generally with regard to CRAS: F Amtenbrink and J de Haan, 'Credit Rating Agencies' DNB Working Paper No 278 (De Nederlandse Bank, 2011).

[10] Ibid, at 1 et seq, with further references, among others, to the observations in a 2010 *IMF Global Financial Stability Report*.

[11] Respectively, the risk involved with an unfavourable movement in market prices and the risk that a given security or asset cannot be traded quickly enough in the market to prevent a loss.

[12] For the US see Senate Committee on Governmental Affairs, 'Financial Oversight of Enron: The SEC and Private-Sector Watchdogs' Staff Report (Washington DC, 8 October 2002).

[13] With regard to the controversial 'issuer pays' business model of CRAs see Amtenbrink and De Haan, n 9, with further references.

[14] Especially Directive 2006/48/EC of 14 June 2006 relating to the taking up and pursuit of the business of credit institutions [2006] OJ L177/1 and Directive 2006/49/EC of 14 June 2006 on the capital adequacy of investment firms and credit institutions [2006] OJ L177/201. See recently European Commission, 'Proposal for a Directive of the European Parliament and of the Council on the access to the activity of credit institutions and the prudential supervision of credit institutions and investment firms and amending Directive 2002/87/EC of the European Parliament and of the Council on the supplementary supervision of credit institutions, insurance undertakings and investment firms in a financial conglomerate' COM (2011) 453 final.

[15] See eg Claessens, Herring and Schoenmaker, n 5. With regard to the definition of systemic risks in the EU context see s 3.2 of this contribution.

Central Bank (ECB) nor any other Union institution or body was explicitly charged with monitoring systemic risks.[16]

System stability has been rightly described as a necessary functional condition that amounts to an important public good.[17] Indeed, the global financial and economic crisis and especially its effects on the financial markets across the globe are the proof of the pudding that in today's global financial marketplace without borders, a crisis in any one (geographic) part of the system, such as the default of a large bank, bears the risk of contagion of other parts of the system.[18] Given the high degree of global financial networking and the interdependencies resulting therefrom, any insistence on separate and independent systems may actually be either idealistic or naïve. Yet, it is this fiction that national and supranational legislators seem to have maintained in their regulatory approach to financial market supervision. Indeed, in the EU context the regulatory and supervisory system in place at the time the US subprime crisis spilled over to Europe hardly matched the stage of development of European market integration. The existing legal framework has been rightly criticized for its 'serious limitations in the existing supervisory framework globally, both in a national and cross-border context' and for: 'Insufficient supervisory and regulatory resources combined with an inadequate mix of skills as well as different national systems of supervision'.[19]

With the liberalization of capital movements, first by means of secondary legislation and the implementation of the Financial Services Action Plan,[20] and moreover supported by the internal market jurisprudence of the Court of Justice of the European Union (CJEU), a European financial area has been created that does not only allow for cross-border transactions and investments, but also for cross-border financial services and the setting up of agencies, branches and subsidiaries.[21] In the case of the free movement of capital, restrictions on capital mobility are in principle abolished between Member States and third countries.[22] The creation of a European legal framework for financial services has contributed to greater integration of financial markets. This has allowed, for example in the banking sector, for the mutual recognition of national rules governing the registration and supervision of financial institutions, thereby allowing for the exercise of banking services throughout the Union based on the regulatory and supervisory system of one Member State (the so-called European passport).

Initially the European Commission focused on the completion of the internal market for financial services (through harmonizing measures approximating diverging national legislation), while paying less attention to the regulatory and supervisory challenges linked to the creation of such a financial area.[23] In financial market regulation and supervision, the fiction of national financial markets has been upheld for a long time in the shape of the so-called Lamfalussy structure.[24] This did not, however, lead to the Europeanization of financial

[16] Generally critical on the role of central banks: AS Roberts, 'The Failure of the Guardians: Central Banking Reform and the Financial Crisis', Suffolk University Law School Legal Studies Research Paper Series, Research Paper 09-54, 21 December 2009.

[17] Author's translation from: W Bayer, D Dietrich *et al*, 'Konstitutionelle Grundlagen globalisierter Finanzmärkte—Stabilität und Wandel', Working Papers on Global Financial Markets No 1 (University Jena/University Halle, November 2008) 3.

[18] See eg C-P Georg, 'The Effect of the Interbank Network Structure on Contagion and Financial Stability', Working Papers on Global Financial Markets No 12 (University Jena/University Halle, September 2010).

[19] De Larosière Report, n 5, at p 10.

[20] European Commission, 'Implementing the Framework for Financial Markets: Action Plan' COM (1999) 232.

[21] With regard to this development see John A Usher, *The Law of Money and Financial Services in the EC* (2nd edn, OUP, 2000).

[22] Art 63(1) of the Treaty on the Functioning of the European Union (TFEU).

[23] Generally on the development of European (economic) integration see the contribution by H-W. Micklitz and D Peterson to this volume.

[24] RM Lastra, 'The Governance Structure for Financial Regulation and Supervision in Europe' (2003) 10 Colum J Eur L 49.

supervision and the transfer of responsibilities from the national to the supranational level, as most notably the Lamfalussy committees, the predecessors of today's European Supervisory Authorities (ESAs), had no real regulatory or supervisory powers.[25] On the basis of the principle of home state supervision, regulatory tasks in the internal market remained allocated at the Member State level, while at the same time the national regulatory and supervisory authorities saw their scope of action diminish in the face of the internationalization of financial markets beyond European borders. Calls to improve upon the existing regulatory regime remained largely unheard for some time.[26]

The global economic and financial crisis has not only highlighted the limited capability of the EU to deal with crisis situations even within its own territory, but also the absence of any adequate global mechanisms to deal with the consequences of a crisis, such as with regard to preventing the 'wild fire' from spreading throughout the whole financial system.

3. The New Approach to Financial and Economic Governance in the EU—Setting Viable Standards?[27]

Against the background of the findings of the previous section, the question is whether the EU's regulatory response to the global financial and economic crisis has addressed the shortcomings of the old system and can show the way forward in financial and economic governance beyond the state level. In this context two main aspects of the Union's recent regulatory activities that are worth highlighting are the new institutional framework for micro- and macro-prudential oversight and, considering that this may have an impact on the stability of the financial system, the Union's new approach to economic governance in the European Monetary Union (EMU).

3.1. Multilevel financial market regulation and supervision in the internal financial market

Considering the previous passivity in this area in responding to the global financial and economic crisis, the European legislator has been relatively swift in drawing conclusions and translating them into regulatory responses. However, as the European Commission seemed eager to go on the record as acting quickly in the face of crisis, its proposals and the subsequent legislative acts were not in all instances characterized by a systematic and coherent approach.

A case in point is the regulation of the activities of CRAs. In 2009 the Council and European Parliament passed a regulation that has introduced a registration and supervision regime for CRAs.[28] However, as this regime was introduced under the old Lamfalussy structure, it had to be revised only one year later in the context of the 2010/2011 general reform of the European System of Financial Supervision (ESFS), thereby recognizing the competences of the newly established European Securities and Markets Authority

[25] The level 3 Lamfalussy committees.

[26] See eg European Commission, 'Inter-institutional Monitoring Group proposes improvements to the development of financial services regulation' Press release (IP/07/108) of 30 January 2007, that calls for further measures to improve cooperation between national supervisory authorities.

[27] This section of the paper builds on F Amtenbrink, 'Legal Developments' (2011) *Journal of Common Market Studies* 49, 165–186 and, by the same author, 'Institutionelle Aspekte der neuen europäischen Finanzmarktregulierung und -aufsicht' in Ludwig Gramlich und Cornelia Manger-Nestler, *Europäisierte Regulierungsstrukturen und -netzwerke* (NOMOS, 2011), 119–120.

[28] Reg 1060/2009 of 16 September 2009 on credit rating agencies [2009] OJ L302/1.

(ESMA).[29] Less than a year after this first amendment, the European Commission was preparing a second overhaul of the regulatory system applying to CRAs.[30]

In establishing the ESFS the European legislator has to a large extent followed the recommendations of the de Larosière Report.[31] The ESFS is aimed at providing for better coordination and communication between national supervisors and to overcome the problems arising from the 'complicated arrangements' that result from having 'to take account of the patchwork of regulatory and supervisory requirements' in the Member States.[32] The institutional framework that has been put in place with effect from 2011 consists in principle of three new ESAs at the European level, including the European Banking Authority (EBA), the European Insurance and Occupational Pensions Authority (EIOPA) and the above-mentioned ESMA.[33] These three new authorities do not only have to coordinate their activities among each other and with the competent national supervisory authorities, but also with a newly created European Systemic Risk Board (ESRB), to be discussed below.[34]

While the ESFS is a significant improvement on the old Lamfalussy structure, the notion of decentralized financial market supervision has not been abandoned altogether. The ESFS arguably does not constitute a centralized European supervisory system, as the preambles to the legal bases of the three ESAs describe the aim of the framework as the creation of an integrated network of national and Union supervisory authorities. Rather than to be in charge of the day-to-day supervision of, among others, financial institutions, the ESAs' primary task is to provide for a higher convergence of the rules applicable to financial market participants through the creation of a single rulebook.[35] This is not to say, however, that the powers of the ESAs are limited to the coordination of the activities of national supervisory authorities, to advise national and European institutions, and to the development of implementing technical standards, guidelines and recommendations.[36] ESAs also have a task in the realization of delegated acts and implementing acts and, as part of their supervisory powers, can take legally binding measures.[37]

In circumstances of an insufficient application of technical regulation and operating standards to financial market participants, ESAs are authorized to enforce those European

[29] Reg 513/2011 of 11 May 2011 amending Reg (EC) No 1060/2009 on credit rating agencies [2010] OJ L145/30.

[30] European Commission, 'Proposal for a Reg of the European Parliament and of the Council amending Reg (EC) No 1060/2009 on credit rating agencies' COM (2011) 747 final. See also s 4.1 of this contribution.

[31] See the preamble to Reg 1093/2010 of 24 November 2010 establishing a European Supervisory Authority (European Banking Authority), amending Decision No 716/2009/EC and repealing Commission Decision 2009/78/EC [2010] OJ L331/12, consideration 8, which recognizes the shortcomings of the country-based system of financial supervision.

[32] Ibid.

[33] Reg 1093/2010, Reg 1094/2010 of 24 November 2010 establishing a European Supervisory Authority (European Insurance and Occupational Pensions Authority), amending Decision No 716/2009/EC and repealing Commission Decision 2009/79/EC [2010] OJ L331/48; Reg 1095/2010 of 24 November 2010 establishing a European Supervisory Authority (European Securities and Markets Authority), amending Decision No 716/2009/EC and repealing Commission Decision 2009/77/EC [2010] OJ L331/84. See also Directive 2010/78/EU of 24 November 2010 amending Directives 98/26/EC, 2002/87/EC, 2003/6/EC, 2003/41/EC, 2003/71/EC, 2004/39/EC, 2004/109/EC, 2005/60/EC, 2006/48/EC, 2006/49/EC and 2009/65/EC in respect of the powers of the European Supervisory Authority (European Banking Authority), the European Supervisory Authority (European Insurance and Occupational Pensions Authority) and the European Supervisory Authority (European Securities and Markets Authority) [2010] OJ L331/120.

[34] Reg 1092/2010 on European Union macro-prudential oversight of the financial system and establishing a European Systemic Risk Board [2010] OJ L331/1; Council Reg 1096/2010 conferring specific tasks upon the European Central Bank concerning the functioning of the European Systemic Risk Board [2010] OJ L331/162.

[35] See eg Preamble to Reg 1093/2010, consideration 22.

[36] See respectively Art 15–16 of Reg 1093/2010, Reg 1094/2010 and Reg 1095/2010.

[37] On the implications of the new agency structure see N Moloney, 'EU Financial Market Regulation after the Global Financial Crisis: "More Europe" or more Risks?' (2010) 47 *CML Rev* 1317–1383, 1344; thereafter Amtenbrink, 'Legal Developments', n 27.

provisions that are directly applicable to financial market participants.[38] Moreover, in the event of a crisis, under certain circumstances ESAs have the right to issue instructions to national competent authorities, which become obliged to take supervisory action.[39] Previously a prohibition of certain market activities could only be unilaterally decided upon by a Member State competent authority, which has resulted in irritations on the part of other Member States and of the European Commission, as the example of the 2010 German ban of naked short selling highlights.

The new ESFS is also aimed at addressing two issues which pose particular challenges in the context of financial market integration, that is cross-border disputes between national supervisory authorities and cross-sectorial consistency of the regulatory and supervisory regime. With regard to the former, the competent ESA is given the role of a mediator in the case of disagreements between competent national authorities in cross-border situations on the appropriate course of action in a given case. If the national authorities fail to reach an agreement, the competent ESA is authorized to decide the matter by obliging the national authorities to take specific action or to refrain from action in order to settle the matter.[40]

Given the increasing importance of financial conglomerates it is of vital importance that the new ESFS also provides for a dispute settlement mechanism in the case of cross-sectorial disagreements between national authorities.[41] What is more, at the level of the ESFS, a Joint Committee of European Supervisory Authorities consisting of the chairs of the three ESAs has been set up to ensure close cooperation between the three ESAs, especially in the area of financial conglomerates, micro-prudential analyses of cross-sectorial developments, risks and vulnerabilities for financial stability, and retail investment products.[42]

While the overriding and the dispute settlement mechanisms signify the denationalization of financial governance to some degree, this is not to say that the predominantly intergovernmental nature of financial market regulation has been fully replaced by a supranational system. Despite its pretentious name, the ESFS falls short of a comprehensive transfer of regulatory and supervisory powers to the European level and thus a centralizing of these functions. It is telling that even for cross-border operating systemically important financial institutions such a transfer of authority to the European level has not been achieved. An examination of the organizational structure of the three ESAs highlights the multi-level structure of European financial market governance that arguably reflects the current state of European integration. The main decision-making body of each ESA is the Board of Supervisors on which the heads of the competent national supervisory authorities participate in a voting capacity.[43] While decisions are foreseen to be usually taken by simple majority, those decisions involving the setting of regulatory technical standards, as well as guidelines and recommendations, are subject to a qualified majority vote similar to that applicable in the Council of the European Union.[44] This can hamper a fast regulatory response to undesirable market developments. The fact that emergency measures by the ESAs are subject to a Council decision highlight that parts of the supervisory process are politicized.[45] This is reminiscent of the European excessive deficit procedure, as part of EMU shows that in the last instance Member States have not been prepared to fully transfer the power of financial market supervision to the EU. In a case of emergency, this procedure could prove to be the Achilles heel of the new regulatory system.

In contrast to the institutional structure of European financial supervision, for the time being, the scope of financial market supervision has yet to become subject to major revision.

[38] See respectively Art 17(6)–(7) Regs 1093/2010, 1094/2010 and 1095/2010.
[39] Ibid, Art 18. [40] Ibid, Art 19.
[41] Ibid, Art 20. [42] Ibid, Art 54.
[43] Ibid, Art 40(1).
[44] See respectively Art 44(1) of Reg 1093/2010, Reg 1094/2010 and Reg 1095/2010.
[45] See respectively Art 18(2) of Reg 1093/2010, Reg 1094/2010 and Reg 1095/2010.

Despite recent measures to regulate short selling and Credit Default Swaps,[46] the global financial and economic crisis has yet to result in a holistic approach to the reassessment of the types of financial market activities that are considered desirable. One area where a more inclusive approach emerges is CRAs and the function of credit ratings. Here, since 2011, ESMA is in charge of the registration and supervision of CRAs. While the EU's initial regulatory approach fell short of effectively addressing some fundamental problems of credit ratings,[47] the European Commission has issued proposals for a further regulation of CRAs with the aim of addressing a number of important omissions of the 2009 regulation. This concerns mainly 'the risk of overreliance on credit ratings by financial market participants, the high degree of concentration in the rating market, civil liability of credit rating agencies vis-à-vis investors, conflicts of interests with regard to the issuer-pays model'.[48]

3.2. Monitoring systemic risks in the EU

In addition to an insufficient regulatory and supervisory system, the absence of proper instruments for macro-prudential supervision has been identified as having contributed to the global financial and economic crisis.[49] The European regulatory response to this criticism comes in the shape of the new ESRB. Its objective is to contribute to the prevention or mitigation of systemic risks to the financial stability in the Union that result from developments within the financial system.[50] Systemic risks are defined as 'a risk of disruption in the financial system with the potential to have serious negative consequences for the internal market and the real economy'. The legal basis of the ESRB points out that: 'All types of financial intermediaries, markets and infrastructure may be potentially systemically important to some degree'.[51] Together with the ESRB, the ESAs have to develop criteria to detect and measure systemic risks and to develop stress tests. Moreover, the powers of the ESRB reach beyond a simple monitoring and reporting of systemic risks. In the event of a detection of significant systemic risks the ESRB has the power to issue warnings and recommendations for remedial action.[52]

The fact that the task of systemic risk monitoring has been assigned to a separate body at the European level could in itself be considered quite significant, as one of the issues vividly discussed in the economic literature in the past has been whether monetary policy authorities should be entrusted with such a task.[53] For proponents of a separation of these tasks, the ESRB will be considered too close for comfort to the ECB, as for the time being the ECB president serves as the chair of the ESRB.

What is more, the composition of the main decision-making body of the ESRB once more reflects the multi-level system of financial governance in the EU.[54] Participation and input from all government stakeholders in the decision-making process may enhance the information basis of the ESRB. Yet, whether the same holds true for the decision-making process is questionable. For the actual signalling of systemic risks, arguably the most important task of

[46] Reg 236/2012 on short selling and certain aspects of Credit Default Swaps [2012] OJ L86/1.

[47] F Amtenbrink and J de Haan, 'Regulating Credit Ratings in the European Union: A Critical First Assessment of Regulation 1060/2009 on Credit Rating Agencies' (2009) 46 *CML Rev* 1915–1949.

[48] Commission Proposal, n 30, Explanatory Memorandum, 2. See also s 4.1.

[49] International Monetary Fund, 'Global Financial Stability Report. Responding to the Financial Crisis and Measuring Systemic Risks' (IMF, April 2009), ch 3. See also O Merrouche and E Nier, 'What Caused the Global Financial Crisis?—Evidence on the Drivers of Financial Imbalances 1999–2007' IMF Working Paper WP/10/265.

[50] Reg 1092/2010 and Reg 1096/2010.

[51] Art 2 Reg 1092/2010.

[52] Arts16–18 Reg 1092/2010.

[53] See F Amtenbrink, 'Central Bank Challenges in the Global Economy', in C Herrmann and JP Terhechte (eds), *European Yearbook of International Law 2011* (Springer, 2011), 19–42, 37, with reference to relevant economic literature.

[54] Amtenbrink (JCMS), n 27, at 171.

the ESRB, an impressive two-thirds majority vote is required to issue recommendations to the EU, to the Member States or to European or national supervisory authorities.[55]

3.3. The link between financial and economic governance

The current euro area sovereign debt crisis highlights how the lack of effective economic governance, especially in the context of a common currency area, can threaten financial stability on a global scale. Indeed, economic imbalances and excessive government deficits that have become too large to service through capital market financing (not least as a result high interest rates resulting from a loss of creditworthiness) can have large-scale (spill-over) effects on the financial system. What is more, through the obligation included in primary Union law to finance government deficits at market conditions, economic governance and financial governance are interconnected and thus, should not be considered in isolation.

While the deteriorating budgetary position of Member States was initially mainly attributed to the global financial and economic crisis and the rescue measures that countries had to take to keep their financial markets afloat, it has since been recognized that economic coordination in EMU falls short of ensuring the Union's objective of sound public finances and a sustainable balance of payments.[56] The existing primary and secondary Union law framework, combining soft and hard law measures with peer review and politicized decision-making, has failed to avoid the emergence of excessive government deficits in a vast majority of Member States and, moreover, has not prevented the emergence of major economic imbalances in EMU.[57]

In 2010, the EU reacted by adopting a set of secondary Union law measures geared towards addressing shortcomings in the multilateral surveillance and excessive deficit procedure pursuant to Articles 121 and 126 TFEU and to the 1997 Stability and Growth Pact.[58] An analysis of this complex new regulatory framework reveals that despite some innovations, such as the reinforced focus on government debt levels, the requirement for Member States against whom an early warning has been issued to place a non-interest bearing deposit,[59] the requirement of sanctions immediately upon the decision on the existence of an excessive deficit,[60] and the application of reversed voting of the Council for parts of the multilateral surveillance and excessive deficit procedure,[61] unwilling or unable Member States can arguably still hardly be forced to pursue prudent economic policies.[62]

In addition to the reinforcement of the existing procedures, new procedures to further strengthen economic coordination, such as the European (budgetary) Semester, more

[55] Art 10 Reg 1092/2010. This also applies to the publication of warnings and recommendations.

[56] Art 119(3) TFEU.

[57] See eg F Amtenbrink, J de Haan and O Sleijpen, 'Stability and Growth Pact: Placebo or Panacea?' *EBL Rev* (1997) 202–210 and 233–238; F Amtenbrink and J de Haan, 'Reforming the Stability and Growth Pact' *EL Rev* (2006) 31(3), 402–413.

[58] Consisting of two Regulations: Reg 1466/97 on the strengthening of the surveillance of budgetary positions and the surveillance and coordination of economic policies [1997] OJ L209/1, last amended by Council Reg 1055/2005, [2005] OJ L174/1; Reg 1467/97 on speeding up and clarifying the implementation of the excessive deficit procedure [1997] OJ L209/6, last amended by Council Reg 1056/2005 [2005] OJ L174/5. Reg 1175/2011 of 16 November 2011 amending Council Reg 1466/97 on the strengthening of the surveillance of budgetary positions and the surveillance and coordination of economic policies [2011] OJ L306/12; Council Reg 1177/2011 of 8 November 2011 amending Reg 1467/97 on speeding up and clarifying the implementation of the excessive deficit procedure [2011] OJ L306/33.

[59] Especially under the new Reg 1173/2011 of 16 November 2011 on the effective enforcement of budgetary surveillance in the euro area [2011] OJ L306/1.

[60] Ibid.

[61] See Arts 6(2) and 10(2) of the revised Reg 1466/07 and Arts 4(2) and 5(2) of Reg 1173/2011.

[62] For a more detailed assessment see F Amtenbrink, 'Naar een effectievere economische governance in de Europese Unie?' (2011) 10(10) *SEW.Tijdschrift voor Europees en economisch recht* 429–443.

uniform requirements for the budgetary frameworks of the Member States,[63] and a new regulatory framework to address macroeconomic imbalances, have been introduced.[64] With regard to the latter, Regulation 1176/2011 defines imbalances as 'any trend giving rise to macroeconomic developments which are adversely affecting, or have the potential adversely to affect, the proper functioning of the economy of a Member State or of the economic and monetary union, or of the Union as a whole'.[65] Such imbalances are considered to be excessive and thus are caught by the new regulatory regime if they are severe, that is to say if they 'jeopardize or risks jeopardizing the proper functioning of the economic and monetary union'.

The detection of an excessive imbalance results in the application of a so-called excessive imbalances procedure in the context of which the Council decides on 'a set of policy recommendations to be followed and a deadline within which the Member State concerned is to submit a corrective action plan'.[66] In the case of non-compliance a non-interest-bearing deposit can be imposed in order to enforce the corrective measures.[67]

Whether the new legal framework will provide for more robust economic governance in the Union remains to be seen. Skepticism in this regard does not only exist in the financial markets but apparently also among European political leaders. As the economic situation continued to deteriorate in a number of European countries in recent months and the trust in the European system of economic governance has not recovered despite the above-described measures, a more far-reaching reform requiring an amendment of primary Union law was debated. However, as the required consensus for an amendment of central provisions of primary Union law on economic coordination could not be reached, 25 of the 27 Member States of the EU signed the Treaty on Stability, Coordination and Governance in the Economic and Monetary Union (Fiscal Compact) on 2 March 2012.[68] Among the main features of this intergovernmental agreement outside the EU Treaty framework is the obligation on parts of the signatory states to have a balanced or surplus budgetary position and to enshrine a rule of a binding and permanent character to that effect in national legislation, which also must state that annual structural deficit may not exceed 0.5% of GDP.[69] Moreover, an automatic corrective mechanism must be foreseen in national legislation, in case a significant deviation from the medium-term objective is observed in a Member State. Member States with a government debt above 60% of GDP are obliged to reduce that debt at an average rate of 0.05% per year.[70] Member States that do not adjust their national legislation accordingly can become subject to a procedure before the ECJ.[71] What is more, financial assistance under the European Stability Mechanism[72] is conditional on ratification of and, thereafter, compliance with the Fiscal Compact.[73]

63 Council Directive 2011/85/EU of 8 November 2011 on requirements for budgetary frameworks of the Member States [2011] OJ L306/41.

64 Reg 1176/2011 of 16 November 2011 on the prevention and correction of macroeconomic imbalances [2011] OJ L306/2; Reg 1174/2011 of 16 November 2011 on enforcement measures to correct excessive macroeconomic imbalances in the euro area [2011] OJ L306/8.

65 Art 4(3) Reg 1176/2011.

66 Ibid, Art 7.

67 Ibid, Art 3. In the case of continued non-compliance this deposit is turned into a fine, which amounts to 0.1% of GDP of the Member State concerned.

68 Art 3, Treaty on Stability, Coordination and Governance in the Economic and Monetary Union. Great Britain and the Czech Republic did not sign. It is foreseen that the Treaty is reviewed after 5 years with the aim of incorporating it into the EU framework.

69 Ibid, Art 3.

70 Ibid, Art 4.

71 Ibid, Art 8.

72 Treaty establishing a European Stability Mechanism, signed by the euro area Member States on 2 February 2012.

73 See preamble to the Treaty on Stability, Coordination and Governance in the Economic and Monetary Union.

All in all, the current legal framework pertaining to economic governance is far-reaching compared to what can be found elsewhere with regard to macroeconomic policy cooperation between states. At the same time the Member States of the EU, and in particular those countries that have irrevocably fixed their exchange rates vis-à-vis each other and have replaced their national currencies with the euro, have long surpassed the stage at which a mere cooperation without any real engagement suffices. The ineffective system of economic coordination that was introduced by the Treaty of Maastricht at this juncture affects the stability of the financial system and even the independent monetary policy of the ECB that finds itself forced into financial market interventions.[74] In the long term monetary union is hardly sustainable without further substantial centralization of economic policy decision-making. Yet, as the Fiscal Compact highlights, for the time being there is no consensus among the Member States for a further substantive deepening of (economic) integration within the framework of the existing Union Treaties.

4. Contributing to Global Financial Governance

The question arises whether and to what extent the EU does or potentially can shape global financial governance through the establishment of this framework. This could either be the case because its governance standards have the potency to set trends at a global level and/or by employing strategies to promote or extend the scope of the financial governance regime beyond the borders of the EU.

4.1. Frontrunner in, or follower of, emerging global standards?

Legislators, regulators and central banks around the globe have in principle recognized the need to strengthen financial market regulation and supervision, to better monitor systemic risk and to provide for better tools for crisis management. To the extent that this results in concrete action, it could be argued that these regulatory activities are the sign of an emerging global understanding of the basic pillars of financial governance. Indeed, since November 2008 financial market regulation and supervision has featured prominently in six consecutive G20 summits,[75] and are also reflected in the so-called key standards for sound financial systems, set up by the FSB and broadly endorsed by international organizations and bodies dealing with different policy areas linked to financial and economic governance, such as the IMF,[76] the World Bank,[77] the Organization for Economic Co-operation and Development, the Basle Committee on Banking Supervision,[78] and the International Organization of Securities Commissions (IOSCO).[79]

Determining whether, in the context of emerging global standards, the EU can be seen as a frontrunner or rather as a follower is anything but straightforward. The exact impact which the Union's approach to financial governance has or can have for global financial governance can only be reliably assessed based on the outcomes of a qualitative and—to the extent possible—empirical study on a case-by-case basis and separately for each of the existing international (informal) policies and decision-making fora, which goes beyond the scope of this contribution. What is more, this may actually amount to a chicken and egg debate, as international fora and standard-setting bodies in their current composition regularly include EU representatives and in any event representatives of the Member States.

[74] Reference is made here to the Securities Market Program of the ECB.

[75] Including the Mexico Summit of June 2012, the Cannes Summit of November 2011, the Seoul Summit of November 2010, the Toronto Summit of June 2010, the Pittsburgh Summit of September 2009, the London Summit of April 2009 and the Washington Summit of November 2008.

[76] eg the IMF Code of Good Practices on Transparency in Monetary and Financial Policies.

[77] eg the World Bank Principles for Effective Insolvency and Creditor Rights Systems.

[78] eg the Core Principles for Effective Banking Supervision.

[79] eg the IOSCO Objectives and Principles of Securities Regulation.

What can be safely stated is that given the size of its integrated financial market, the impact of any regulatory activities employed by the EU will reach beyond what can normally be expected from any one jurisdiction. After all, of the ten largest economies in the world, in 2011 four belonged to the EU, including Germany, United Kingdom, France and Italy. Moreover, an analysis of the G20 Summit statements reveals that the EU in several areas is certainly acting in line with the priority areas identified at the global level when it comes to the strengthening of regulatory regimes, prudential oversight, and risk management, such as the monitoring of macro-prudential risks across the financial system.[80] Other examples of issues identified at the level of the G20 that have been addressed by the new EU regulatory framework include the issue of cross-border resolutions[81] and the registration and supervision of CRAs whose ratings are used for regulatory purposes.[82] The EU thus does not establish new standards in isolation or independently from the global discourse on the financial regulatory and supervisory regime required to ensure financial stability. Moreover, the EU is not the only main economic player to reinforce financial governance. In the United States a new focus on ensuring financial stability can be witnessed as well, especially in the shape of the 2010 Dodd-Frank Act,[83] which includes an increased emphasis on monitoring systemic risks[84] and a reinforced oversight over CRAs.[85]

In the case of the regulation of CRAs the European legislator has at least initially rather heavily relied on pre-existing international standards. The legal framework to be found in the original Regulation 1060/2009 resembled, to a considerable extent, the principles of the non-binding IOSCO Code of Conduct for Credit Rating Agencies.[86] To be sure, the EU, represented by the European Commission, is a so-called affiliated member of IOSCO. While the European Commission does not as such participate in the decision-making of IOSCO, it does take part in the exchange of information on regulatory regimes and related enforcement issues.[87] This adoption of international standards can hardly be considered a recent phenomenon, as prior to the recent reform efforts international bodies, such as the Basel Committee on Banking Supervision,[88] the Bank for International Settlements (BIS) and the FSB, to name only a few, have had a notable impact on the shape of the Union's financial governance regime.

Having said that, the above-mentioned Commission proposal to amend Regulation 1060/2009[89] highlights the EU's determination, based on its own assessment, to further develop the existing framework to address major systemic issues. On the point of over-reliance on credit ratings, it is inter alia proposed that certain financial institutions should make their own credit risk assessment and that the three ESAs should avoid references to credit rating

[80] See the declaration at the end of the Summit on Financial Markets and the World Economy (Washington Summit) of 15 November 2008, available at: <http://www.canadainternational.gc.ca/g20/summit-sommet/g20/declaration_111508.aspx?view=d> accessed 5 April 2012.

[81] Leaders' Statement at the end of the Summit on Strengthening the International Financial Regulatory System (Pittsburgh Summit) of 24–25 September 2009, available at: <http://www.canadainternational.gc.ca/g20/summit-sommet/g20/declaration_092509.aspx?view=d> accessed 5 April 2012.

[82] Leaders' Statement at the end of the Summit, Declaration on Strengthening the Financial System (London Summit), declaration of 2 April 2009, available at: <http://www.canadainternational.gc.ca/g20/annex1-annexe1_-fin_2009.aspx?view=d> accessed 5 April 2012.

[83] Dodd-Frank Wall Street Reform and Consumer Protection Act [HR 4173.IH].

[84] For this, the Financial Stability Oversight Council has been set up.

[85] See in this regard the US Credit Rating Agency Reform Act of 2006, which introduced a registration process for CRAs.

[86] Code of Conduct Fundamentals for Credit Rating Agencies, published by the technical committee of IOSCO, revised version of May 2008: <http://www.iosco.org/library/pubdocs/pdf/IOSCOPD271.pdf> accessed 5 April 2012. IOSCO is mainly made up of representatives of national central banks and financial market regulatory and supervisory agencies.

[87] In the framework of the so-called SRO Consultative Committee. Ordinary members of IOSCO are usually national public authorities that are charged with securities regulation.

[88] Most importantly the Capital Requirements Directive.

[89] See n 30.

to the extent that this could result in mechanical reliance on ratings by supervisory authorities or market participants.[90] In the future, issuers that intend to solicit a credit rating of a structured finance instrument must mandate at least two CRAs, which must thereafter provide their own independent rating.[91] Moreover, CRAs become liable for damages caused by infringements of their obligation under Regulation 1060/2009, such as the requirement to report actual or potential conflicts of interests and to immediately assess whether there are grounds for re-rating or withdrawing an existing credit rating. This liability is conditional upon the establishment of the fact that the infringement had an impact on a credit rating that an investor relied upon when purchasing a rated instrument.[92] Finally, special requirements for the issuing of sovereign ratings are foreseen, aimed at greater transparency in the rating process and more frequent reassessments of such ratings.[93] As will be explained in the following section, the EU can be expected to actively pursue exporting these standards abroad once they have been adopted.[94]

The EU is a good example of the kind of political and legal challenges that are linked to the establishment of a global system of financial governance beyond the mere exchange of best practice and supervisory information of national regulatory and supervisory bodies. The missing centralization of supervisory power for cross-border operating systemically important financial institutions is arguably a case in point. As such, it is doubtful whether the European solution can lead the way globally. In fact, even more so than in the EU, at the global level a unique challenge lies in the absence of 'a coherent and streamlined international financial regulatory and surveillance system' that makes use of existing international institutions.[95] It is difficult to see how such a coherent system of financial governance could come into existence without a solid institutional framework that goes beyond a mere coordination and exchange of information between national and regional regulatory and supervisory authorities. Yet it is doubtful whether countries whose economies are not even linked by an internal market and a single currency are willing in the short to medium term to delegate the corresponding powers onto a supranational/international authority.

In the absence of (the prospect of) such a coherent global system of financial governance, despite or rather because of the absence of a centralized system, the EU may still provide inspiration for the future design of global structure, especially with regard to dealing with cross-border disputes between national supervisory authorities and the cross-sectorial consistency of the regulatory and supervisory regime. The same holds true for the introduction of a mechanism to override national supervisory authorities in case of an emergency. In fact, the EU is effectively putting into operation arrangements that are also being debated on the global level, such as the designing of macro-prudential policy tools, the link between macro- and micro-prudential policy, and cross-border cooperation on crisis management.[96]

Moreover, the EU can be considered a forerunner when it comes to recognizing the link between financial and economic governance. While it has been observed above that economic governance in EMU is far from perfect, the reinforced system by which Member States commit themselves to budgetary discipline and addressing macroeconomic imbalances is certainly setting new standards. In fact, the link between financial governance and economic governance has also implicitly been recognized at the global level, where the FSB, IMF and the BIS have stated that 'Macroprudential policy is a complement to

[90] Commission Proposal, n 30, s 6, introducing Art 5a and b.
[91] Ibid, s 11, introducing Art 8b.
[92] Ibid, s 20, introducing Art 35a, and Annex III.
[93] Ibid, s 10, amending Art 8, and the new Part III in Annex 1, S D.
[94] See s 4.2.
[95] As observed in the de Larosière Report, n 5, 59.
[96] FSB, IMF and BIS, n 97. Financial Stability Forum, 'Principles for Cross-Border Cooperation on Crisis Management' (2 April 2009).

microprudential policy and . . . interacts with other types of public policy that have an impact on financial stability'.[97]

For the time being, in the absence of a global system, financial governance will not only be shaped by global agreement on financial governance standards, but also by the potentially competing models of financial governance of major economies and trading blocks, in the first place, but certainly not exclusively, the EU and the United States. The European Commission frequently calls for more global coherence and its regular consultations with key regulatory and supervisory authorities in third countries, such as the United States and Japan, are not only fuelled by the desire to contribute to the emergence of global best practice, but also by the aim to ensure a level playing field, especially in those policy areas where the EU is taking the lead.[98]

4.2. Exporting the European regulatory framework

A somewhat different approach to contributing to global standards and practices can be found in a number of the recently adopted legislative measures in the context of the ESFS. European legislation is in some instances effectively geared towards extending its reach beyond the territory of the EU, while in other areas providing openings for regulatory and supervisory cooperation on a global level.

An example of such an extension of the scope of the Union's financial market supervisory regime can be found in Regulation 1060/2009 on Credit Rating Agencies. While it is in principle envisaged that a CRA that issues ratings that are used for regulatory purposes is established and registered in the EU, it is also possible for EU-established CRAs to endorse third country ratings.[99] For this the credit rating activities by the third country credit rating agency must in principle comply with the conditions set out in the EU regulation for issuing credit ratings. ESMA is in the position to assess and monitor the compliance of the third country CRA and there must be a cooperation agreement between ESMA and the relevant supervisory authority of the third country CRA.

Moreover, ratings issued by third country CRAs of entities or financial instruments issued in third countries can under certain conditions be used in the EU without endorsement by an EU-registered CRA, if the European Commission has adopted a so-called equivalence decision.[100] The legal and supervisory framework of a third country must ensure that CRAs authorized or registered in that country comply with legally binding requirements which are equivalent to the EU legal requirements and that they are subject to effective supervision and enforcement in that third country. For this purpose cooperation agreements have been concluded with the relevant supervisory authorities of third countries, as has been the case for Canada, Hong Kong, Japan, Singapore and the United States.[101]

In the case of CRAs that are established outside the EU, the requirement to comply with the Union regulatory regime has at least the potential to induce some pressure on third countries to bring their regulatory and supervisory standards in line with those applicable in

[97] Brackets added. See FSB, IMF and BIS, 'Macroprudential policy tools and frameworks. Update to G20 Finance Ministers and Central Bank Governors' (14 February 2011), available at: <http://www.financialstability-board.org/publications/r_1103.pdf> accessed 5 April 2012.

[98] See eg M Barnier, 'Restoring stability and growth: Europe is taking the right decision', Speech held at the US Chamber of Commerce, Washington DC, 23 February 2012 (SPEECH/12/121); by the same author, 'Financial regulation: how to achieve global convergence' Speech held at the Eurofi High Level Seminar, Copenhagen, 29 March 2012 (SPEECH/12/246).

[99] Reg 1060/2009 (as amended), Art 4(4).

[100] Ibid, Art 5.

[101] Commission decision of 28 September 2010 on the recognition of the legal and supervisory framework of Japan as equivalent to the requirements of Reg 1060/2009 of the European Parliament and of the Council on credit rating agencies [2010] OJ L254/46. ESMA, Press release of 15 March 2012 (ESMA/2012/158).

the EU. The EU is thus effectively encouraging the use of its own financial governance standards abroad.

In a similar vein, the new ESFS foresees the possibility of third country authorities actively cooperating with the ESAs. Participation in the work of an ESA is open to third countries that have concluded agreements with the EU whereby they have adopted and are applying Union law in the areas of competence of one or more of the three ESAs. The ESAs can moreover cooperate with third countries that apply legislation that has been recognized as equivalent in the areas of competence of the ESAs. Third countries that cooperate in such ways with the EU can have a representative, as a permanent observer, on the Board of Supervisors.[102] Beyond the unilateral adoption by a third country of the Union *acquis* in the area of financial market regulation and supervision, the ESFS thus offers the opportunity for third countries to actively participate in the development of the framework through participation in the ESAs. While currently this opening is pursued by the non-EU Member States of the European Economic Area,[103] it may also be of interest for third countries with a candidate status and other third countries with close economic ties with the EU, including for example overseas countries and territories recognized by Article 198 TFEU.

5. Conclusion

From observing the new approach to financial governance in the European Union, a mixed picture emerges with regard to the role of Europe in shaping global financial governance.

The EU arguably contributes to global financial governance by adding to the creation of global standards in the different international policy fora, either directly or through its Member States, and by transposing these standards into binding Union legislation. It is thus hardly surprising that the EU's approach in broad terms is in line with the global policy priorities and emerging new financial governance standards set mainly by the G20 and the FSB. The embracing of such governance standards by a major trading block representing some of the world's biggest economies certainly adds weight to the emerging global consensus on financial governance.

The EU seems to be conscious of this role, as it can be seen developing financial governance further and actively pursuing its policy agenda beyond its territory. The scope of the EU regulatory framework certainly takes into account such a possibility. In the absence of a global legal framework and thus, in the face of partially competing governance models, these efforts are not only geared towards creating a stable global financial system, but also at ensuring a level playing field. The frequent exchanges between the European Commission and US officials on financial market regulatory and supervisory issues are arguably a case in point.

The EU has taken the lessons from the global financial and economic crisis seriously in designing the new European System of Financial Supervision. Even if the particular character of the EU makes it difficult to consider its (institutional) approach as a blueprint for a global strategy, and despite the shortcomings of the system, its multi-level approach to financial governance nevertheless provides useful insights into how at least on a regional level financial market regulation and supervision can be integrated and how a system of micro- and macro-prudential supervision can be designed beyond the state. Specifically, the EU's approach to conflict resolution for cross-border and, moreover, cross-sectorial supervisory disputes and the designing of emergency instruments to override national authorities is noteworthy in this context in that it may also show the way forward for global governance.

[102] See respectively Art 75 Regs 1093/2010, 1094/2010 and 1095/2010.
[103] See eg Art 1(5) of the Rules of Procedures of the Board of Supervisors of EIOPA (EIOPA-BoS-11/002).

The same may also hold true for the link between financial governance and economic governance. The interaction of macro- and micro-prudential supervision with 'other types of public policy that have an impact on financial stability', while being recognized by for example the IMF and the FSB,[104] has arguably yet to be taken serious on the global level. On the one hand, the EU is an illustration of how severe shortcomings in economic governance and the resulting economic imbalances can be a clear and present danger for financial stability. On the other hand, with the new regulatory regime for the first time macroeconomic imbalances are directly addressed. The correlation between financial governance and economic governance, which is arguably not limited to a single currency area, also deserves attention at the global level. The openness of financial markets and the risks of spill-over and domino effects linked thereto arguably call for reinforced forms of transnational economic and monetary governance.

The new EU legal framework also highlights the pitfalls that come with a regulatory and supervisory system that has to accommodate the fact that the participating states are still reluctant to transfer sovereignty to the supranational level. A claim of national sovereignty in a highly integrated financial marketplace is not without risks for the ability of the financial regulatory and supervisory system to address developments in the marketplace in a timely manner and to deal effectively with any emerging crisis. Reaching consensus on the transfer of regulatory and supervisory powers to supranational/international bodies will be an even greater challenge. As such, sovereignty may very well be the big elephant in the room.

[104] FSB, IMF and BIS, n 97.

16

The EU at the G20 and the G20's Impact on the EU

Jan Wouters, Sven Van Kerckhoven, and Jed Odermatt

1. Introduction

This chapter seeks to address the relationship between the most prominent regional organization, the European Union (EU), and the most intriguing 'global club', the G20. Both entities mark, in their own very different ways, a changing world order in which states are cooperating ever more closely in order to tackle transnational challenges. Both bodies are also undergoing significant change. Since the 2008 global financial crisis, the G20 has been elevated to become the principal body in which issues such as global financial reform are discussed. The EU has also entered into a new 'post-Lisbon' era in which it seeks to play a greater role on the global stage, and to have a greater influence within international bodies. The economic crisis facing Europe has highlighted the need for coordinated, global responses. The relationship between the G20 and the EU sheds light on the changing roles of both these bodies. The present contribution discusses this ever-developing relationship, with particular attention on how the EU and G20 have responded to the global financial crisis.

The first set of questions deals with the representation of the EU at the G20 meetings. Some EU Member States had a firm place at the cradle of the G7, the predecessor of the current G20. France, Germany, the United Kingdom and Italy were original members of the group. The European Communities (later the EU) were first represented in the G7 meeting in London in 1977. In all respects (except for the hosting of a summit) the EU has been a full member of the G7/G8 and its successor the G20. The EU's membership in the G20 is a unique situation, as it is the only non-state member of the club. Interestingly, the EU's G20 membership amplifies the voices of the Member States already at the table, as they also have the strongest voice in drafting the EU's position for G20 meetings. The question arises to what extent smaller EU Member States, being excluded from direct participation in G20 meetings, have a say on the EU position at the G20. Furthermore, the 'double' representation of the four aforementioned EU Member States enables them to a certain extent to bypass the European decision-making process. In order to solve this, EU Member States increasingly coordinate before G20 summits, but have no control over the behaviour of their peers during such a summit. In contrast to this, there is no coordination in advance of G7/G8 meetings. The question arises here to what extent the EU's basic treaties, as most recently amended by the Lisbon Treaty, prescribe such coordination.

The second part of this chapter deals with the relationship between the G20 and the EU. The G20 process and its decisions have a strong influence on decisions taken at the European level. This allows the EU to move faster internally: when a regulatory issue is elevated to the G20 level and agreed there, opposition from EU Member States is often made much more difficult. The EU and the G20 thus have the potential to further each other's agendas. Coordinating the response to the crisis through the G20 and its associated bodies (eg the Financial Stability Board) has often benefited the EU, which has been able to successfully put its proposals on the G20's agenda. The EU also implements many of the commitments made at the G20, which further enhances its voice within that body. The present contribution examines both sides of this interaction.

2. EU Representation at the G20

Since the financial crisis of 2008, the G20 has emerged as the premier forum for international economic cooperation.[1] Since then, it has increasingly evolved into a key global playmaker.[2] This however has not always sat well with the traditional organizations to which the G20 delegates assignments. In relation to the OECD, for example, the G20 bypassed the OECD formal decision-making process when it drafted its grey list on tax havens.[3] The question we seek to address here is how the relationship between the G20 as a global 'club' and the EU as the most prominent regional organization has evolved. In particular, we address whether both organizations are complementary or rivals and how exactly these organizations have influenced each other.

Let us first look at the representation of the EU at the G20. European interests are represented both directly through the EU's membership of the G20 and, to a certain extent, indirectly through the membership of some of its Member States. The UK, France, Germany and Italy are full members while Spain and the Netherlands have been regularly invited to G20 meetings. The EU is the sole non-state actor which received a seat at the table of the twenty 'most significant economies'.[4] The EU is both over- and under-represented in the G20. On the one hand, it only has a total population of around 500 million[5] of a worldwide population over 7 billion, making up around 7% of worldwide population. In the G20, however, this 7% of worldwide population takes up 25% of the seats (observers not included). In terms of economic power, the inclusion of 20 significant economies does not mean that the 20 biggest economies have been included. Other than the European Union, which is the biggest worldwide economy, the other EU G20 members are ranked highly as well (Germany 6th, the UK 9th, France 10th, and Italy 11th). But Spain (13th), Iran (18th) and Taiwan (20th) are not G20 members; their places are taken by Argentina (22th), Saudi Arabia (24th) and South Africa (26th).[6] Moreover, other EU countries such as Poland (21st) and the Netherlands (23rd) closely follow. Hence, it is safe to state that in terms of economic power, the EU is probably not over-represented.[7] This stands in contrast with the G7/G8 meetings, where EU Member States have at least a 50% share of membership (or up to 57% for the G7 meetings).

The G20 meets both at the leaders level and at the level of finance ministers and central bank governors. At the leaders level, both the President of the European Commission and the President of the European Council (at the time of writing in mid-2012, Mr Barroso and Mr Van Rompuy)[8] attend the G20 Leaders meeting. For the meeting of finance ministers and central bank governors, the Commissioner for Economic and Monetary Affairs, the rotating Council presidency and the Head of the European Central Bank represent the EU

[1] G20 Leaders, *Pittsburgh Summit Declaration* (24–25 September 2009), para 50.

[2] J Wouters, S Sterckx and T Corthaut, 'The International Financial Crisis, Global Financial Governance and the European Union' in A Antoniadis, R Schuetze, E Spaventa (eds), *The European Union and Global Emergencies: Law and Policy Analysis* (Hart Publishing, 2011), 141, at 147. However, some authors already argue that the G20 has served its purpose and should be replaced, see J Vestergaard and RH Wade, 'The G20 has Served its Purpose and Should be Replaced' (2012) 2(2) *Journal of Globalization and Development* 18; JA Ocampo and JE Stiglitz, 'From the G20 to a Global Economic Coordination Council' (2012) 2(2) *Journal of Globalization and Development* 16.

[3] See J Wouters and S Van Kerckhoven, 'The OECD and the G20: an Ever Closer Relationship?' (2011) 43(2) *George Washington International Law Review* 345.

[4] G20, 'The Group of Twenty: a History' (2008). Retrieved at: <http://www.g20.utoronto.ca/docs/g20history.pdf>.

[5] Eurostat, available at: <http://epp.eurostat.ec.europa.eu/tgm/table.do?tab=table&language=en&pcode=tps00001&tableSelection=1&footnotes=yes&labeling=labels&plugin=1>. The latest number is 502,486,499.

[6] <https://www.cia.gov/library/publications/the-world-factbook/rankorder/2001rank.html> (2011 est).

[7] This is, however, less easy to state bearing in mind that both Spain and the Netherlands have been invited regularly to G20 meetings.

[8] For a more elaborate discussion on how they distribute the tasks, see P Debaere, 'The Output and Input Dimension of the European Representation in the G20' (2010) 63(2) *Studia Diplomatica* 141 at 148–149.

(at the time of writing in mid-2012, Mr Rehn, Mr Bjarne Corydon and Mr Draghi respectively).

The largest European countries, which are also the most powerful within the EU's decision-making, are the only EU Member States directly represented at the G20. This could lead to a perverse side-effect. When these countries cannot get their preferred policies within the European Council, they may try to push through their policies independently at the G20 level. The European G20 members, for example, already agreed upon lowering the number of Executive Directors at the International Monetary Fund (IMF), a decision which has caused some uproar in the smaller Member States, which are expected to lose their seats.[9] Still, it has to be noted that this generally seems less likely as the preferred policies often diverge much more at the G20 level than they do at the European level.

The inclusion of both the EU and four other European Member States in the G20 gives the EU a rather strong voice and serious leverage to push for its preferred actions at the global level. However, the EU is also challenged by the large number of Europeans around the table.[10] If the Europeans find common ground, the repetition of the same message might irritate other G20 members. And when the EU and the Member States fail to find common ground, the European voice gets lost.[11] The next section will deal with the EU's agenda-setting behaviour and coordination between the Member States in more detail.

3. The Relationship Between the EU and the G20

3.1. European agenda-setting in advance of G20 meetings

The European representation at the G20 thus consists of both EU Member States and the EU as a full member. In order to be able to push for a real European agenda, coordination between the different Member States will be necessary. From an EU point of view, the G20 is often perceived as a venue where the EU can try to persuade other countries to follow its own (internal) agenda.[12] This section deals with the coordination and the drafting of a European agenda prior to the G20 meetings.

The coordination procedure in advance of G20 meetings is not formally laid down in the EU treaties,[13] but discussion takes place in advance of the G20 meetings at Council and European Council level. Coordination efforts in advance of the G20 Leaders meetings have taken place ever since the beginning of the financial crisis. The first G20 meeting took place in Washington on 15 November 2008. In advance of this meeting, the European Council agreed on the principles for the reform of the international financial system and the approach the EU would take at the G20.[14]

The second G20 meeting in April 2009 in London was more thoroughly prepared. In February, the European members of the G20, representatives of Spain, the Netherlands and

[9] J Wouters and S Van Kerckhoven, 'Europe and the International Monetary Fund: current complexity and future directions' in KE Jorgensen and K Laatikainen (eds), *Handbook on the EU and International Institutions: Performance, Policy, Power* (Routledge, forthcoming).

[10] Other than the WTO, this is the general case for the European representation in other international organizations, such as eg the IMF: J Wouters and S Van Kerckhoven, ibid.

[11] P Debaere, n 8, at 141.

[12] J Wouters and S Van Kerckhoven, 'The EU's Internal and External Regulatory Actions after the Outbreak of the 2008 Financial Crisis' (2011) 8(5) *European Company Law* 201.

[13] However, Art 34 of the Treaty on European Union (TEU), para 1 lays down the general principle of coordination of Member States' action within international organizations and at international conferences. TEU Art 34, para 2 imposes more specific obligations for international organizations and international conferences—like the G20—where not all the Member States participate. Nonetheless, the question to what extent this Article is applicable to the G20 remains open, as it is part of the Treaty Chapter on the EU's common foreign and security policy (CFSP).

[14] European Commission, 'Economic Crisis in Europe: Causes, Consequences and Responses' (2009) 7 *European Economy* 57.

Luxembourg, representatives of the Commission and the European Central Bank, and the President of the Council (at that time Mr Topolánek) gathered informally in Berlin. They discussed aligning their positions in advance of the G20 meeting. In particular they agreed upon a stricter supervision of the IMF, more thorough regulation of the financial markets, including 'tax havens', and unification of procedures for international rating agencies.[15] Their common positions were further elaborated during the meeting of the European Council on 19/20 March 2009, resulting in the 'agreed language' with a view to the G20 summit in London. The European Council laid down that the EU and its Member States should, as general objectives, lead international action necessary to: (i) promote a swift return to sustainable economic growth; (ii) strengthen the ability to manage and prevent crises at the global level; (iii) better regulate financial markets; and (iv) support developing countries in responding to the effects of the crisis.[16] Moreover, the Council and the Commission were called upon to ensure appropriate follow-up to the Summit.[17] The major issues on which the EU was able to have its agreed language included in the G20 final declaration were: the substantial increase in IMF;[18] Multilateral Development Bank (MDB)[19] and trade finance[20] resources; fiscal stimulus and expansion;[21] credit markets;[22] IMF surveillance;[23] strengthening financial cooperation, supervision and regulation;[24] IMF reform;[25] resisting protectionism;[26] and commitment to the Millennium Development Goals.[27] In short, the agenda of the EU laid down in the agreed language, was almost perfectly reflected in the G20 declaration. Only the EU's desire to find consensus on and adopt a Global Charter for Sustainable Economic Activity was not laid out at the G20 meeting, where it was still considered as an ongoing process.[28] The biggest development of this summit was the transformation of the Financial Stability Forum into the Financial Stability Board (FSB). The FSB monitors the international and national implementation of G20 policies. The EU, which itself was working on establishing the European System of Financial Supervision (ESFS),[29] applauded this development.[30]

[15] Meeting of the European members of the G20 group in Berlin, 23 February 2009: <http://europa-eu-un.org/articles/en/article_8511_en.htm>.

[16] European Council Presidency, *Annex 1: Agreed Language with a view to the G20 Summit in London*, 19/20 March 2009 (7880/1/09) Brussels, 29 April 2009.

[17] European Council Presidency, *Conclusions 19/20 March 2009* (7880/1/09) Brussels, 29 April 2009, para 22.

[18] G20 Leaders, *London Summit Declaration*, 2/4/2009, paras 5, 17; European Council Presidency, n 16, para viii.

[19] G20 Leaders, ibid, paras 5, 17; European Council Presidency, n 17, para xxiv.

[20] G20 Leaders, n 18, paras 5, 9; European Council Presidency, n 16, para v.

[21] G20 Leaders, n 18, paras 6, 11; European Council Presidency, n 16, paras i, ii, iii.

[22] G20 Leaders, n 18, para 8; European Council Presidency, n 16, para ii.

[23] G20 Leaders, n 18, para12; European Council Presidency, n 16, para vii.

[24] G20 Leaders, n 18, paras 13, 14; European Council Presidency, n 16, paras xi and xii, xvii.

[25] G20 Leaders, n 18, para 20, European Council Presidency, n 16. The EU only talked about the IMF, while the G20 included the World Bank reform.

[26] G20 Leaders, n 18, paras 22, 23; European Council Presidency, n 16, para iv.

[27] G20 Leaders, n 18, para 25; European Council Presidency, n 16, para xxii.

[28] G20 Leaders, n 18, para 21; European Council Presidency, n 16, para x.

[29] In order to establish the ESFS, the following was agreed: The regulations and directives adopted by the European Parliament and the Council on 24 November 2010 were: Reg (EU) No 1092/2010 on European Union macro-prudential oversight of the financial system and establishing a European Systemic Risk Board [2010] OJ L331/1; Reg (EU) No 1093/2010 establishing a European Supervisory Authority (European Banking Authority) [2010] OJ L331/12; Reg (EU) No 1094/2010 establishing a European Supervisory Authority (European Insurance and Occupational Pensions Authority) [2010] OJ L331/48; Reg No 1095/2010 establishing a European Supervisory Authority (European Securities and Markets Authority) [2010] OJ L331/84; Directive 2010/78/EU amending Directives 98/26/EC, 2002/87/EC, 2003/6/EC, 2003/41/EC, 2003/71/EC, 2004/39/EC, 2004/109/EC, 2005/60/EC, 2006/48/EC, 2006/49/EC and 2009/65/EC in respect of the powers of the European Supervisory Authority (European Banking Authority), the European Supervisory Authority (European Insurance and Occupational Pensions Authority) and the European Supervisory Authority (European Securities and Markets Authority) [2010] OJ L 331/120. See also Council Regulation (EU) No 1096/2010 of 17 November 2010 conferring specific tasks upon the European Central Bank concerning the functioning of the European Systemic Risk Board [2010] OJ L331/162.

[30] G20 Leaders, n 18, para 15; European Council Presidency, n 16, paras xi, xii, xiii, xv, xvi, xvii, xviii, xix, xx.

The European Council subsequently called upon the Council and the Commission to prepare the Pittsburgh 2009 G20 meeting thoroughly[31] ahead of its informal meeting on 17 September 2009. This informal meeting resulted in 'agreed language' for the Pittsburgh G20 summit. The main objectives for the EU were: (i) achieving a sustainable recovery; (ii) prioritizing jobs; (iii) swiftly implementing the commitments for financial markets; (iv) promoting responsible remuneration practices in the financial sector; (v) strengthening international financial institutions; (vi) strengthening recovery in the world's poorest countries; (vii) sharing the effort on climate finance; and (viii) promoting energy security.[32]

At the G20 meeting in Pittsburgh (24–25 September 2009), the G20 agreed upon the following points within the agreed language of the EU: strong policy responses were maintained but exit strategies would be prepared;[33] a framework for strong, sustainable, and balanced growth was launched;[34] responsible remuneration practices had to be promoted;[35] governance of the global financial architecture;[36] energy market transparency;[37] fighting protectionism and bringing the Doha round to a conclusion;[38] an attempt to reach agreement at the Copenhagen Conference of the Parties (COP);[39] increase and harmonize accounting standards;[40] prioritizing jobs;[41] and increased regulation and supervision of financial markets.[42]

However, this time the G20 adopted broad and vague statements on most issues, particularly compared to the well-worked out European agreed language. Although the G20 decided to take necessary steps to reduce the development gap, it did not refer to Official Development Assistance (ODA) and it did not adopt the 'Everything but Arms' initiative as it was agreed upon within the EU.[43] The same holds true for climate change, for which the EU had drafted substantial objectives which were not incorporated in the G20 decision.[44] The G20 did not formally adopt the Basel II framework (as desired by the EU) but referred the matter to the meeting of finance ministers and central bank governors.[45] On the other hand, the G20 elaborated extensively on strengthening support for the most vulnerable, which had received far less attention in the EU agreed language.[46]

The conclusion from the 2009 Pittsburgh meeting is that the EU was still able to put all its agreed language on the table and managed to get agreement on the broad principles, but not always on the exact concrete objectives, as proven by the failure of officially adopting 'Everything but Arms', Basel II or concrete measures to combat climate change. The European Council afterwards still welcomed the outcome of the G20 Pittsburgh meeting and called for thorough preparation in advance of future G20 meetings.[47] Moreover, the European Council emphasized that: 'in the context of the framework for strong, sustainable and balanced growth, the IMF and the G20 will have to take fully into account the institutional economic policy set-up of the European Union and the euro area as a whole'

[31] European Council Presidency Conclusions, 18/19 June 2009, Brussels, 10 July 2009.
[32] Informal Meeting of EU Heads of State or Government, Brussels, 17 September 2009.
[33] G20 Leaders, n 1, paras 10, 14; Informal Meeting, ibid, para 2.
[34] G20 Leaders, n 1, para 3; Informal Meeting, n 32, para 3.
[35] G20 Leaders, n 1, paras 16, 17, Annex, para 13.; Informal Meeting, n 32, paras 15, 16.
[36] G20 Leaders, n 1, paras 18, 20 and 21; Informal Meeting, n 32, para 17 (US$500 billion New Arrangements to Borrow (NAB) also in G20 outcome), 18.
[37] G20 Leaders, n 1, para 26; Informal Meeting, n 32, para 29.
[38] G20 Leaders, n 1, paras 27, 28; Annex to the G20 Declaration, *A Framework for Strong, Sustainable and Balanced Growth*, paras 48–49; Informal Meeting, n 32, para 4.
[39] G20 Leaders, n 1, para 29; Annex to the G20 Declaration, n 38, para 22.
[40] G20 Leaders, n 1; Annex to the G20 Declaration, n 38, para 12.
[41] Annex to the G20 Declaration, n 38; Informal Meeting, n 32, paras 5–7.
[42] Annex to the G20 Declaration, n 38, paras 10–15; Informal Meeting, n 32.
[43] Annex to the G20 Declaration, n 38, paras 22, 23; Informal Meeting, n 32, paras 20, 21.
[44] Informal Meeting, n 32, paras 23–26.
[45] Annex to the G20 Declaration, n 38, para 13; Informal Meeting, n 32, para 11.
[46] Annex to the G20 Declaration, n 38, paras 34–42, Informal Meeting, n 32, paras 20, 21.
[47] European Council Presidency Conclusions 29/30 October 2009 (Brussels, 1 October 2009), para 32.

and again called upon 'the Council and the Commission to ensure thorough preparation by the European Union of future G20 meetings'.[48]

The next G20 meeting took place in Toronto in June 2010. In March of that year the European Council had identified as focal points for this meeting: to ensure a global level playing field regarding financial regulation and supervision,[49] and to address climate change.[50] In June, the European Council identified agreed language with a main focus on ensuring coordination and internationally consistent measures to the crisis. In particular, it insisted on introducing systems for levies and taxes on financial institutions and on exploring and developing a global financial transaction tax.[51] EU Member States generally favour a so-called Tobin tax, but fear that other major economies would take advantage of the introduction of such a tax in the EU to the detriment of the European economy. The G20 has the potential to solve this issue and align all major economies. Other than this focal point, the EU pointed to the need for coordinated exit strategies, and a reaffirmed commitment regarding the reform of the financial system and IMF governance.[52] The Toronto Summit consisted of a thorough evaluation of the progress and implementation of the measures agreed upon in earlier summits. The G20 reiterated its support for the Framework for Strong, Sustainable and Balanced Growth, continued its focus on financial sector reform and the reform of the governance of international institutions, and supported the fight against protectionism and promotion of development.[53] The EU once more was rather successful.[54] However, the global tax on financial transactions and the focus on exit strategies failed to attract agreement.

At its meeting in September 2010, the European Council stressed the importance of maintaining strong momentum in the area of financial reform. In this respect, the recent agreement between the European Parliament and the Council on the financial supervision package and the completion of the reform of the regulatory framework by the end of 2011 were expected to strengthen the EU's hand. The European Council further pointed out the need to conclude the WTO Doha negotiations and implement the Framework for Strong, Sustainable and Balanced Growth. It further stressed the need of coordinating positions.[55]

In preparation of the G20 Summit in Seoul, the European Council met on 28–29 October 2010. It decided that the G20 should send a strong signal regarding the implementation of the measures agreed in the Framework for Strong, Sustainable and Balanced Growth. Particular attention should be devoted to rebalancing world growth, confirmation of the Basel Agreement, and to inject momentum in the Doha negotiations.[56] The European Council further called for the implementation of the decision of the G20 Ministerial Meeting of 23 October 2010 on the reform of the IMF.[57] Last, it decided that further work on the levies and taxes on financial institutions was needed and coordination between different levy schemes was needed as to avoid double-charging.[58] At the Seoul Summit, the G20 decided to implement the governance reform at the IMF;[59] strengthen financial safety nets and

[48] Ibid, para 32.

[49] European Council Conclusions 25/26 March 2010 (Brussels 26 March 2010), para 6.

[50] Ibid, para 13d.

[51] European Council Conclusions 17 June 2010 (Brussels, 17 June 2010), para 17.

[52] European Council, ibid, para 18.

[53] G20 Leaders Toronto Summit Final Declaration, 27 June 2010.

[54] Statement by European Commission President Barroso and European Council President Van Rompuy following the G20 Summit in Toronto (26–27 June 2010) MEMO/10/278.

[55] European Council Conclusions 16 September 2010, para 7a; Annex 1 to the Conclusions: Internal Arrangements to improve the European Union's external policy, para D.

[56] European Council Conclusions 28/29 October 2010, (Brussels 30 November 2010), para 4.

[57] Ibid, para 5.

[58] Ibid, para 6.

[59] Ibid, para 6; G20 Leaders Seoul Summit Document 11/12 November 2010, paras 14–17.

supervision;[60] bring the Doha round to a successful conclusion;[61] tackle corruption;[62] and avoid competitive currency devaluations.[63] Special attention was devoted to developing countries, and in particular the Least Developed (LDCs) among them.[64] The G20 further made progress on the Mutual Assessment Process of the Framework for Strong Sustainable and Balanced Growth[65] and launched the Seoul Action Plan with a particular focus on: (i) monetary and exchange rate policies; (ii) trade and development policies; (iii) fiscal policies; (iv) financial reforms; and (v) structural reforms.

The EU had a less decisive influence on the agenda. The whole drafting of financial safety nets was not part of the EU deliberations beforehand, but was, together with development, the big novelty of the Seoul Summit. Significant attention was nonetheless devoted to the Basel Committee, much to the liking of the EU which had already put this point on the agenda several times.[66] Hence, many of the agenda points of the EU were once again reflected in the G20 decision. However, several non-EU issues made it to the agenda as well and the G20 once more remained silent upon the introduction of a global tax on financial institutions.

The European Council stated in its conclusions of 4 February 2011 that the EU will cooperate with third countries in order to address the volatility of energy prices and will take this work forward within the G20.[67] This was already a major talking point on the G20 agenda.[68] This commitment was reiterated at the next European Council meeting, in light of the disaster at Fukushima.[69] Presidents Van Rompuy and Barroso shared their ideas in advance of the European Council meeting. They called 'for a renewed collective G20 spirit' and considered as EU priorities: (i) restoring growth and tackling global imbalance; (ii) making progress on implementing financial market reform; (iii) making the international monetary system more resilient; (iv) boosting trade as the most effective way to support global growth; (v) ensuring food security and promoting the G20 development agenda; (vi) continuing to address corruption and energy and climate challenges; and (vii) improving global governance.[70] Moreover, they referred to the proposal for a financial transaction tax[71] and expressed their conviction that 'a similar approach among G20 partners can help us all meet global challenges. We will therefore strongly support further discussions by the G20 in this field'. The preparation and objectives for the next G20 summit were laid down during the European Council meeting of 23 October 2011. The EU once more reiterated that the G20 should work to ensure strong, sustainable and balanced growth.[72] Specific progress was needed on the reform of the international monetary system by reinforcing coordination,

[60] European Council Conclusions,, n 56, para 6; G20 Leaders, ibid, paras 19–26.

[61] G20 Leaders Seoul Summit Leaders' Declaration 12 November 2010, para 4; G20 Leaders, n 59, paras 7, 42–45.

[62] G20 Leaders, n 61, para 13; G20 Leaders, n 59, paras 39, 69–71 and Annex II: G20 Anti-Corruption Action Plan: G20 Agenda for Action on Combating Corruption, Promoting Market Integrity, and Supporting a Clean Business Environment.

[63] G20 Leaders, n 61, para 9; G20 Leaders, n 59, para 6.

[64] G20 Leaders, n 61, paras 5, 9, 15; G20 Leaders, n 59, paras 7, 44–54 and Annex 1: Seoul Development Consensus for Shared Growth, Annex II: Multi-Year Action Plan on Development.

[65] G20 Leaders, n 61, para 9; G20 Leaders, n 59, paras 1–3, 11; see Policy Commitments by G20 Members.

[66] G20 Leaders, n 59, paras 27–33.

[67] European Council Conclusions 4 February 2011 (Brussels, 8 March 2011), para 14.

[68] G20 Leaders, n 59, paras 61–63.

[69] European Council Conclusions 24–25 March 2011 (Brussels, 20 April 2011), para 31.

[70] Joint letter of President Van Rompuy and President Barroso on the G20 Summit in Cannes, EUCO 93/11, 7 October 2011.

[71] Common Rules for a Financial Transaction Tax—Frequently Asked Questions, MEMO/11/640 (Brussels, 28 September 2011), retrieved at: <http://europa.eu/rapid/pressReleasesAction.do?reference=MEMO/11/640>; Financial Transaction Tax: Making the financial sector pay its fair share, IP/11/1085, retrieved at: <http://europa.eu/rapid/pressReleasesAction.do?reference=IP/11/1085&format=HTML&aged=0&language=EN&guiLanguage=en>.

[72] European Council Conclusions, 23 October 2011 (Brussels, 30 November 2011), para 11.

supervision and crisis management, strengthening the regulation and supervision of the financial sector (implementation of Basel II, II-5, III, reform of over the counter (OTC) derivatives, and remuneration principles), tackling volatility of commodity prices, promoting sustainable and inclusive growth (implement G20 Development Agenda), resisting protectionism and providing momentum into the Doha round, and combating climate change (by mobilizing sources for climate change finance).[73]

During the G20 Cannes summit of November 2011 (the first one to take place in Europe), special attention was devoted to the Eurozone crisis.[74] The G20 agreed on an Action Plan for Growth and Jobs. The G20 decided to continue to work towards a more stable and resilient international monetary system, which was also an important point on the EU agenda.[75] The G20 further agreed to reform of the financial sector.[76] Agreement was further reached to address commodity price volatility;[77] improve energy markets;[78] combat climate change;[79] avoid protectionism;[80] address the challenges of development;[81] intensify the fight against corruption;[82] and to reform global governance for the 21st century.[83] The Cannes Summit looked very rewarding from a European viewpoint, as the issues on the European agenda were all addressed during the Summit. Even the Basel accords were explicitly called upon.[84] Still, the list of policy commitments did especially target the European Union and the Euro area in order to address the deficiencies displayed as the Eurocrisis emerged.[85] Moreover, the global financial tax once again failed to be agreed upon.[86] However, the G20 'acknowledge[s] the initiatives in some of our countries to tax the financial sector for various purposes, including a financial transaction tax, inter alia to support development'.[87] French President Sarkozy, however, pledged to continue pursuing this initiative.[88]

In summary, the EU has so far been able to influence the G20 agenda in a fairly satisfactory way. However, it has regularly failed to get specific objectives adopted (such as a global tax on financial institutions and the 'Everything but Arms' initiative) and has also witnessed some issues being included in the agenda that were not part of the European agenda, such as currency wars and global financial safety nets. The next section examines how decisions taken within the G20 impact at the EU level.

3.2. Impact of G20 decisions on EU financial legislation

One area in which the G20 has been considerably influential is the field of financial regulation. The problems flowing from a global financial system, especially the risks created by integrated financial markets, require responses at the global level, a fact which has been recognized by the EU since the outbreak of the financial crisis.[89] This need for a global response to the crisis is reflected not only in European positions within the G20, but also in

[73] Ibid, para 12.
[74] G20 Leaders, Cannes Summit Declaration, paras 2, 11.
[75] G20 Leaders, n 74, paras 9–21. Compare European Council Conclusions, n 72, paras 8–11.
[76] G20 Leaders, n 74, paras 22–39. Compare European Council Conclusions, n 72, paras 12–17.
[77] G20 Leaders, n 74, paras 40–51. Compare European Council Conclusions, n 72, paras 18–19.
[78] G20 Leaders, n 74, paras 52–57. Compare European Council Conclusions, n 72, para 20.
[79] G20 Leaders, n 74, paras 58–64. Compare European Council Conclusions, n 72, para 21.
[80] G20 Leaders, n 74, paras 65–68. Compare European Council Conclusions, n 72, paras 22–24.
[81] G20 Leaders, n 74, paras 69–84. Compare European Council Conclusions, n 72, paras 25–28.
[82] G20 Leaders, n 74, paras 85–89. Compare European Council Conclusions, n 72, para 29.
[83] G20 Leaders, n 74, paras 90–94. Compare European Council Conclusions, n 72, paras 30–32.
[84] G20 Leaders, n 74, para 23.
[85] G20 Cannes Policy Commitments as annexed to the Cannes Action Plan for Growth and Jobs, 4 November 2011, available at: <http://www.g20.utoronto.ca/2011/2011-cannes-action-111104-en.html>.
[86] Reuters, 4 November 2011: <http://www.reuters.com/article/2011/11/04/g20-tax-idUSN1E7A302520111104>.
[87] See contribution by Van Vooren in this volume; G20 Leaders, n 74, para 28.
[88] Reuters, n 86.
[89] European Commission, n 14, at 1; Communication from the Commission: From Financial Crisis to Recovery: A European Framework for Action [2010] OJ C76/28, Brussels, 29 October 2008 COM (2008) 706 final.

the EU's implementation of commitments made within the G20 framework. Additionally, by aligning itself with global rules, the EU makes its own response more effective.[90] Moreover, the EU legislature continually refers to G20 commitments in EU legislation and policy documents, demonstrating that it takes these commitments seriously. In some fields, such as banking regulation, the EU has been a forerunner. In other fields, such as regulation of OTC derivatives, the EU has lagged behind other G20 members in fulfilling its commitments.

3.2.1. *European Systemic Risk Board*

The European Systemic Risk Board (ESRB) was established[91] in 2010 to help mitigate systemic risks to financial stability by providing macro-prudential regulation and supervision at the EU level. The ESRB was a recommendation of the *de Larosière Report* which stated that the EU 'must work with [its] partners to converge towards high global standards, through the IMF, FSF, the Basel committee and G20 processes'.[92] One of the goals of the ESRB, as outlined in its preamble, is to contribute 'towards implementing the recommendations of the IMF, the FSB and the Bank for International Settlements (BIS) to the G20'.[93] The ESRB is to cooperate with the IMF and FSB, which are also tasked with mitigating systemic risks.

3.2.2. *OTC and commodity derivatives markets*

The G20 Cannes Final Declaration stated that: 'Reforming the over the counter derivatives markets is crucial to build a more resilient financial system. All standardized over-the-counter derivatives contracts should be traded on exchanges or electronic trading platforms, where appropriate, and centrally cleared, by the end of 2012'.[94] The topic of OTC derivatives has been a central concern of the G20 since 2008, especially since the lack of regulation in this field is seen as one of the key problems that caused the financial crisis.[95] The need for greater transparency and standardization in OTC derivatives was also a key recommendation of the *de Larosière Report*.[96]

On 15 September 2010, two years after the collapse of Lehman Brothers, the European Commission proposed a regulation on OTC derivatives,[97] which it said is 'fully in line with the EU's G20 commitments'[98] and has been inspired by the G20 leader's commitment to 'improve transparency and regulatory oversight of over-the-counter derivatives in an internationally consistent and non-discriminatory way'.[99] Furthermore, the Commission added:

[90] European Commission, ibid, at 78.

[91] Reg 1092/2010/EU of the European Parliament and of the Council of 24/11/2010 on European Union macro-prudential oversight of the financial system and establishing a European Systemic Risk Board [2010] OJ L331/1.

[92] Report of The High-Level Group of Financial Supervision in the EU Chaired by Jacques de Larosière (Brussels, 25 February 2009), at 3.

[93] Reg 1092/2010/EU of the European Parliament and of the Council of 24 November 2010 on European Union macro-prudential oversight of the financial system and establishing a European Systemic Risk Board [2010] OJ L331/1, Preamble, Recital 8.

[94] G20 Leaders, n 74.

[95] GF Peery, *The Post-Reform Guide to Derivatives and Futures* (Wiley Finance, 2012) at 18; JE Stiglitz, *Freefall: America, Free Markets and the Sinking of the World Economy* (Norton WW, 2010).

[96] Report of The High-Level Group of Financial Supervision in the EU Chaired by Jacques de Larosière, Brussels, 25 February 2009, Recommendation 8.

[97] European Commission, *Proposal for a Regulation of the European Parliament and of the Council on OTC derivatives, central counterparties and trade repositories* (2010).

[98] European Commission Press Release, *Making derivatives markets in Europe safer and more transparent* (Brussels, 15 September 2010).

[99] European Commission, Explanatory Memorandum, n 97, p. 2.

'The European Commission has also gained valuable information by participating in various international fora, in particular the OTC Derivatives Regulators Group and the Basel Committee's Risk Management and Modeling Group. The Commission has recently also gained observer status on the steering committee of the joint CPSS-IOSCO9 working group that is currently reviewing the recommendations for CCPs and preparing recommendations for trade repositories. In addition, the Commission has engaged in frequent dialogue with non-EU authorities, in particular US authorities (the CFTC, the SEC10, the Federal Reserve Bank of New York and the Federal Reserve Board and the US Congress) and is co-chairing a work stream of the Financial Stability Board (FSB) focusing on addressing the challenges related to the implementation of the reporting, clearing and trading obligations agreed at G20 level.'[100]

On 9 February 2012 the European Parliament and Council came to an agreement on new rules regulating OTC derivatives[101] and on 29 March 2012 the European Parliament approved the proposed regulation with amendments.[102] This proposed Regulation, which is still slowly winding its way through the EU legislative process, is seen as the EU's equivalent to the US Dodd-Frank Act, and would constitute a major step towards Europe's implementation of the G20 reform agenda.[103] On 20 October 2011 the European Commission tabled proposals to revise the Markets in Financial Instruments Directive in response to the goals set out by the G20 in Pittsburgh, including 'the need to improve the transparency and oversight of less regulated markets—including derivatives markets'[104] and the goal of ensuring that standardized OTC derivative contracts be cleared through central counterparties by the end of 2012. Technical standards are to be developed by European Supervisory Authorities (ESAs) and adopted by the Commission before 30 September 2012.[105]

3.2.3. Bank capital and liquidity standards

In their Declaration at the Pittsburgh Summit, G20 Leaders 'commit[ted] to developing by end-2010 internationally agreed rules to improve both the quantity and quality of bank capital and to discourage excessive leverage. These rules will be phased in as financial conditions improve and economic recovery is assured, with the aim of implementation by end-2012'. On 20 July 2011 the Commission adopted a proposal to strengthen the regulation of the banking sector.[106] The Commission states that this proposal 'translates in Europe international standards on bank capital agreed at the G20 level (most commonly known as the Basel III agreement). Europe will be leading on this matter, applying these rules to more than 8000 banks, amounting for 53% of global assets'.[107] So far, however, the CRD (Capital Requirements Directive), one of the most significant—and also politically sensitive—regulatory measures proposed since the financial crisis, is moving very slowly through the legislative process. On 15 May 2012 European finance ministers agreed on banking rules

[100] European Commission, n 97, Explanatory Memorandum, p 4.

[101] European Parliament Press Release, 'EP–Council deal on rules for a safe and transparent derivatives market' (9 February 2012).

[102] European Parliament legislative resolution of 29 March 2012 on the proposal for a regulation of the European Parliament and of the Council on OTC derivatives, central counterparties and trade repositories (COM (2010) 0484—C7-0265/2010–2010/0250 (COD)).

[103] 'EU agrees deal on derivatives overhaul' *Financial Times*, 9 February 2012: <http://www.ft.com/intl/cms/s/0/8f08ee20-5350-11e1-aafd-00144feabdc0.html#axzz1lybR0OXF>. Accessed 9 February 2012.

[104] European Commission Press Release, 'New rules for more efficient, resilient and transparent financial markets in Europe' (Brussels, 20 October 2011).

[105] See Press Release, 'Regulation on Over-the-Counter Derivatives and Market infrastructures—Frequently Asked Questions', 29 March 2012: <http://europa.eu/rapid/pressReleasesAction.do?reference=MEMO/12/232>.

[106] European Commission, Proposal for a Directive of the European Parliament and the Council on the access to the activity of credit institutions and the prudential supervision of credit institutions and investment firms and amending Directive 2002/87/EC of the European Parliament and of the Council on the supplementary supervision of credit institutions, insurance undertakings and investment firms in a financial conglomerate COM (2011) 453.

[107] European Commission Press Release, 'Commission wants stronger and more responsible banks in Europe' (20 July 2011).

to implement Basel III after a compromise agreement was reached that would give flexibility to national regulators.[108]

3.2.4. Systemically important financial institutions (SIFIs)

At Cannes, G20 Leaders pledged that they were 'determined to make sure that no financial firm is "too big to fail" and that taxpayers should not bear the costs of resolution'. G20 Leaders at Pittsburgh committed to act together to '... create more powerful tools to hold large global firms to account for the risks they take'[109] and to 'develop resolution tools and frameworks for the effective resolution of financial groups to help mitigate the disruption of financial institution failures and reduce moral hazard in the future'.[110] 'Too big to fail' institutions, or Systematically Important Financial Institutions (SIFIs) are seen as another area of reform necessary to adequately respond to the crisis, and one that requires coordinated reforms in different states. On 4 November 2011 the FSB delivered a set of 'Policy Measures to Address Systemically Important Financial Institutions' at the request of the G20. In response to these developments, the European Commission is developing an EU-wide crisis management framework[111] to address SIFIs. This work has been done in connection with the work on SIFIs by the Committee on Payment and Settlement Systems and IOSCO. The Commission is set to present legislative proposals and states that they 'will be accompanied by an impact assessment, and will complete the Commission's implementation of the principal G20 reforms in the area of financial regulation'.[112] As yet, the Commission has not formally adopted a legislative proposal, but has issued a consultation document[113] and discussion paper on the technical aspects for a European framework for bank recovery and resolution. According to these papers, the Commission seeks to establish a harmonized regime for the rescue of banks and financial institutions in EU Member States, rather than creating an overarching regulatory body.

3.2.5. Hedge Funds

The commitment to reform of hedge funds made at the G20's Toronto meeting was referred to in the Directive on Alternative Investment Funds Managers:[114]

> 'G20 Leaders in Toronto reaffirmed their commitment and also committed to accelerate the implementation of strong measures to improve transparency and regulatory oversight of hedge funds in an internationally consistent and non-discriminatory way.'

The Directive also incorporates principles of the IOSCO *Hedge Funds Oversight* report of 2009, which supported a globally consistent approach. Although they are not considered to have been an immediate cause of the crisis, the regulation and oversight of hedge funds has been a topic raised in G20 discussions. The European Commission President stated that:

[108] P Geitner, 'European Finance Ministers Reach Compromise' *New York Times*, 15 May 2012: <http://www.nytimes.com/2012/05/16/business/global/european-finance-ministers-reach-compromise.html?_r=1>.

[109] G20 Leaders, n 1, para 13.

[110] Ibid.

[111] Communication from the Commission to the European Parliament, The Council, The European Economic and Social Committee, the Committee of the Regions and the European Central Bank, An EU Framework for Crisis Management in the Financial Sector (Brussels, 20 November 2010): 'The Commission is helping to shape the work of the FSB and the G20, and is also closely monitoring other international developments' p 3.

[112] Ibid.

[113] European Commission, DG Internal Market and Services, Working Document, Technical Details of a Possible EU Framework for Bank Recover and Resolution, 6 January 2011.

[114] Directive 2011/61/EU of the European Parliament and the Council of 8 June 2011 on Alternative Investment Fund Managers and amending Directives 2003/41/EC and 2009/65/EC and Reg (EC) No 1060/2009 and (EU) No 1095/2010 [2010] OJ L171/1.

'[the] directive—which coincides with the G20 Summit meeting in Seoul—is another example of how the EU is leading the way in implementing our G20 commitments'.[115]

3.2.6. *Credit Rating Agencies*

The 2009 Regulation on Credit Rating Agencies[116] was influenced by international commitments to regulate credit rating agencies, also seen as one of the causes of the global financial crisis.[117] The Regulation, which oversees the registration and supervision of credit rating agencies, states that: 'Credit rating agencies should, on a voluntary basis, apply the Code of Conduct Fundamentals for credit rating agencies issued by the International Organization of Securities Commissions (IOSCO Code)' and is broadly based on the Code of Conduct.[118]

4. Conclusion

The relationship between the EU and the G20 is both symbiotic and problematic. The EU is rather well represented at the G20, and the European coordination in advance of the G20 summits has also proven to be very fruitful. Generally, the EU has been able to put its 'agreed language' on the G20 agenda. However, in some cases, such as a global tax on financial institutions, the G20 did not agree upon the practicalities as they were cast by the EU. Along with influencing the outcomes of G20 meetings, the EU has also managed to implement many of the commitments it made within the G20, especially in the field of financial regulation. The EU sees these issues as closely interlinked.[119] By being a forerunner in certain areas of financial reform, and by implementing G20 commitments, the EU's position within the G20 is strengthened, allowing it to have greater influence in future meetings. In some fields, such as creating greater oversight mechanisms, the EU has moved quickly to implement reforms. It is also noteworthy that the EU consistently refers to the G20 commitments in the preambular language of its legislation and policy documents as well as in media statements. This reflects the fact that the EU takes seriously the commitments made at G20 summits.

Nonetheless, there is also a more problematic side to the relationship. There is no policy nor legal basis regarding the European external representation at the G20, as is the case in the post-Lisbon era with many other international organizations. Consequently, EU Member States at the G20 could still deviate from the 'agreed language' and represent their national interests. Moreover, the stronger EU Member States also have a seat at the G20 table and hence could override smaller EU Member States, which are not only deprived of direct influence at the G20, but are as well less powerful in coming to the 'agreed language'. Some Member States also fear that the G20 might push the EU to move too fast in terms of financial legislation.[120] Another question relates to the role of the European Parliament. Although the Parliament has generally supported the EU's positions at the G20,

[115] European Commission statement at the occasion of the European Parliament vote on the directive on hedge funds and private equity, MEMO/10/573, 11 November 2010.

[116] Reg 1060/2009/EC of the European Parliament and the Council of 16 September 2009 on credit rating agencies [2009] OJ L302/1.

[117] See contribution by Amtenbrink to this volume.

[118] Code of Conduct Fundamentals for credit rating agencies issued by the International Organization of Securities Commissions (IOSCO Code).

[119] European Commission, Communication From the Commission to the European Parliament, The Council, The European Economic and Social Committee and the European Central Bank, Regulating Financial Services for Sustainable Growth, Brussels, COM (2010) 301, 26 June 2010.

[120] C Stoltenberg; B Crutchfield George, KA Lacey and M Cuthbert, 'The Past Decade of Regulatory Change in the US and EU Capital Market Regimes: An Evolution from National Interests toward International Harmonization with Emerging G20 Leadership' (2011) 29(2) *Berkeley Journal of International Law* 577, at 644.

particularly in areas such as pushing for a global financial tax,[121] there has been criticism that the institution has been side-lined in the debates.[122] This feeds into wider criticisms concerning the democratic representation of the G20, which is making decisions with far-reaching consequences, and the desire for the Parliament to play a greater role in global affairs.

Both the EU and G20 are interesting bodies in the international arena. The G20 is not a classical international organization like those referred to in Article 220 of the Treaty on the Functioning of the European Union[123] and the Lisbon Treaty gives little guidance on the EU's relationship with such bodies. Moreover, the EU is not a state, and this creates problems for bodies such as the G20 in which the EU sits alongside its Member States in a club which is, with the exception of the EU, solely composed of nation states. Nevertheless, the financial crisis and the need for a global response have thrust a great number of issues on the agenda of both these organizations. In many ways the relationship between the two is symbiotic: the EU relies on the G20 to push forward with its agenda on the international stage while it uses G20 commitments to push through its domestic legislative agenda. At the same time, for reasons discussed above, the relationship entails many existing and potential problems.

[121] European Parliament resolution of 8 March 2011 on innovative financing at global and European level (2010/2105(INI)) 8 March 2011. The Parliament 'calls on the G20 leaders to speed up the negotiations for an agreement on the minimum common elements of a global FTT and to provide guidance on the desired future of these various kinds of taxation'.

[122] European Parliament Press Release, 'Parliaments must be involved in G20 decision-making, says Othmar Karas' 27 February 2012.

[123] Art 220(1) TFEU: '1. The Union shall establish all appropriate forms of cooperation with the organs of the United Nations and its specialized agencies, the Council of Europe, the Organization for Security and Cooperation in Europe and the Organization for Economic Cooperation and Development'.

17

The Proposed Financial Transaction Tax Directive: The Quest to Create Momentum at the G20 Through Internal Legislation

Bart Van Vooren

1. Introduction

In the wake of the 2008 financial crisis, taxation of the financial sector has forcefully re-emerged on the European Union political agenda.[1] Since then, several EU Member States and the European Parliament have sought to stimulate this idea in the form of a financial transaction tax (FTT). What had for years existed as a political utopia in the minds of grass roots movements, reached a legal and political milestone during Commission President Barosso's State of the Union speech on 28 September 2011. There he presented a proposal for an EU Directive on a financial transaction tax installed across the 27 EU Member States, to serve as an example for potentially global implementation. In a previous paper I have outlined key features of such a global implementation.[2] I argued that the Union would have to propose a binding multilateral treaty, with as broad as possible a global membership. This multilateral Convention would establish the legal framework within which to levy, manage and disperse the proceeds of an international FTT—and, in short, would imply thorough reform of the global financial governance system as it exists at present. The Cannes G20 Meeting in early November 2011 under French chairmanship was expected to launch the global dimension of the FTT, using the momentum created by the proposed EU FTT Directive two months earlier. However, the European sovereign debt crisis was reaching the heights of the Greek Drama,[3] and with the EU teetering on the brink, momentum for a global FTT seemed utterly lost. Nonetheless, political discussions within the Union continued, and at the time of writing—Spring 2012—discussions in the Council were ongoing. Thus, the EU proposal may yet become law, if not at global, then at regional level.

The global implementation of the EU FTT Directive is a tale of divided political views between Member States of the Union, the pursuit of an elusive single voice in the G20, and the use of legal instruments for political reasons, with an as of yet unwritten (though fairly predictable) final outcome. It is therefore well-suited to explore the central theme of this book: the (lack of) influence of the EU in global governance regimes in a multi-polar world, in line with its binding, rule-of-law based mission statement of Article 21 of the Treaty on European Union (TEU). In light of this, this contribution investigates EU (im)potence to affect legal and institutional processes in global governance required for implementation of the FTT.

[1] This contribution was closed on 21 March 2012.

[2] B Van Vooren, 'The EU as a Global Robin Hood: Proposal for a Multilateral Convention on a Global Financial Transaction Tax' (2011) 2011/4 CLEER Working Papers.

[3] See the contribution by Amtenbrink to this volume.

2. The Union's Mission in Global Financial Governance

The 2001 Laeken Declaration on the future of the European Union strongly asserted a global role for the EU in its characteristically grand language:[4] 'Does Europe not, now that it is finally unified, have a leading role to play in a new world order, that of a power able both to play a stabilising role worldwide and to point the way ahead for many countries and peoples?'. The European Convention started work soon after that declaration was made, in order to draw up a Constitutional Treaty for the European Union. In an early draft produced by the Commission (called the Penelope project), that institution's proposal of December 2002 contained the following provision under the heading 'external economic relations policy':[5] 'Article III—97 External economic action by the Union shall contribute to the harmonious development of the world economy. To that end the Union shall adopt a single position in relations with non-member countries and in international organisations with responsibilities for economic and financial matters. *It shall support the effectiveness and transparency of the financial markets in order to reduce financial volatility and speculation at global level*'. This Commission proposal took the EU single voice far beyond the comparatively narrow scope of the Common Commercial Policy. However, the call for unified EU representation in global economic governance writ large was not picked up by the Convention, and it did not find its way into the draft Constitution or the Lisbon Treaty. Should this have happened, a strong case could have been made that the Union would have a legally binding obligation to implement a financial transaction tax, or a global measure with equivalent effect of reducing financial volatility and speculation.[6] Even so, the Union could still reap great benefits from the successful global implementation of the FTT:[7] First, success in this regard would be supportive of the Union's self-imposed image of the value-based international actor;[8] and second, it would do much to provide post-Lisbon legitimacy towards its own citizens through effectiveness as an international actor. An FTT would have as its purpose the financing of global public goods such as the Millennium Development Goals (MDGs) and additional funding to climate change; and therefore respond to calls for a fairer contribution of the financial sector to society writ large. Additionally, such a tax would have a significant regulatory impact towards a more stable financial system which is currently dominated by non-binding soft law.[9] In sum, the FTT would lead to—and require a sea-change to—international financial law and governance, with the European Union guiding the way in line with its constitutional objectives.[10]

Even though no mission statement for the EU in global financial governance has been included in EU primary law, the more general legal obligations to that end are nevertheless pertinent. A role for the Union whereby it 'stabilizes' the world, and 'points the way ahead' is not merely a moral imperative, but a legally binding obligation embedded in primary law.

[4] European Council, *Laeken Declaration on the Future of the European Union* (14–15 December 2001), subheading 'Expectations of Europe's citizens'.

[5] European Commission, *Feasibility Study, Contribution to a Preliminary Draft, Constitution of the European Union* (4 December 2002), available from: <http://ec.europa.eu/economy_finance/emu_history/documents/treaties/Penelope%20pdf_en.pdf> last accessed 19 March 2002. I am grateful to Joris Larik for pointing me to this provision.

[6] On such effects see n 2, 10–14.

[7] Although certainly, the hazards and pitfalls are equally great. See n 2.

[8] U Khaliq, *Ethical Dimensions of the Foreign Policy of the European Union—A Legal Appraisal* (CUP, 2008); R Petrov and P Leino, 'Between "Common Values" and Competing Universals—The Promotion of the EU's Common Values through the European Neighbourhood Policy' (2009) 15 *European Law Journal* 654–671.

[9] C Brummer, 'Why Soft Law Dominates International Finance—and not Trade' (2010) 13 *Journal of International Economic Law* 623, 627; E Baltensperger and T Cottier, 'The Role of International Law in Monetary Affairs' (2010) 13 *Journal of International Economic* Law 911, 935.

[10] See the chapter by J Larik in this volume, and B Van Vooren, 'Global Implementation of the Financial Transaction Tax: Utopia or Opportunity to Reform the International Financial Legal Order' in D Kochenov and F Amtenbrink, *European Union's Shaping of the International Legal Order* (CUP, 2013, forthcoming).

Article 3(5) TEU states that in its relations with the wider world, 'the Union *shall*... contribute to peace,... the sustainable development of the Earth, solidarity and mutual respect among peoples, free and fair trade, eradication of poverty... as well as to the strict observance and the development of international law, including respect for the principles of the United Nations Charter' (emphasis added). The language 'shall' indicates the binding nature of this mission statement, which has been confirmed by the European Court of Justice (ECJ) in a recent judgment of 22 December 2011 concerning the global reach of the Emissions Trading Scheme. Here the court affirmed that this Article imposes a substantive, legal obligation on the Union 'to contribute to the strict observance and the development of international law'.[11] Thus, the Union is not just morally, but in fact legally obliged to pursue equality amongst wealthy and poorer nations, to support their development and ensure 'fairness' between them. In doing so, the TEU not only imposes substantive requirements on EU international relations, but also a strong methodological imperative: according to Article 3 TEU and confirmed in Article 21(1) TEU, the EU 'shall be guided by the principles which have inspired its own creation and which it seeks to advance in the wider world:... respect for the principles of the United Nations Charter and international law'. In other words, the Union must pursue a just and fair global order, entrenched in multilateral solutions based on the rule of law. The global implementation of a financial transaction tax through a multilateral, binding international convention requiring unprecedented positive change to international financial governance does exactly that.

If the argument stemming from EU primary law is perhaps slightly abstract and legalistic, the connection to expectations of European citizens should be less so. Indeed, the financial transaction tax is a concrete iteration of where the Laeken Declaration in the abstract invoked of EU citizens' wishes. This is underlined by the Commission's public consultation on the FTT which ended in April 2011. That consultation clearly showed that civil society across the European Union broadly supports the financial transaction tax.[12] From the Commission's summary report,[13] it is clear that non-governmental organizations and trade unions are strongly in favour of a broad-based financial transactions tax and that individual citizens also 'generally favour' such a broad-based levy. Conversely, and unsurprisingly, financial organizations and businesses, consultancies and their relevant representative organizations generally oppose any and all types of additional tax burden on the financial sector or financial markets in general.[14] Thus, given the broad popular support amongst European citizens it is submitted that successfully working towards the FTT at global level could bring the Union *legitimacy through effectiveness*. Individual Member States will be unable to exert sufficient influence in the G20 to realize a global financial transaction tax, but should the Union manage to speak with its proverbial single voice in a sustained lobbying effort at the highest echelons, success may be within reach with commensurate effects on the EU's standing in the hearts and minds of European citizens.

In the remainder of this contribution I shall trace the EU's efforts in placing the FTT on the global political agenda, so as to draw conclusions on the EU's ability to deliver on its mission statement of pursuing a multilateral law-based governance agenda, and to deliver upon its citizens' wish have the financial sector contribute more fairly to society writ large.

[11] Case C-366/10, *Air Transport Association of America (ATAA)* (unreported) 21 December 2011, para 101.

[12] All responses to the consultation, as well as a summary by the Commission, are available at: <http://ec.europa.eu/taxation_customs/common/consultations/tax/2011_02_financial_sector_taxation_en.htm> last accessed 16 August 2011.

[13] Commission summary report, May 2011, available at: <http://ec.europa.eu/taxation_customs/resources/documents/common/consultations/tax/financial_sector/summary_results_en.pdf>.

[14] 'Banks and markets oppose financial transaction tax' *EurActiv*, 18 August 2011:<http://www.euractiv.com/en/euro-finance/banks-markets-oppose-financial-transaction-tax-news-507022>.

3. A Global FTT: Political Context at EU and International Level

At their September 2009 meeting in Pittsburgh, political momentum mid-financial crisis was such that G20 leaders agreed to pursue a number of deep changes to global economic governance. They agreed to set up 'a framework for strong, sustainable and balanced growth', 'an international regulatory system for banks and other financial firms that would reign in the excesses that led to the crisis', and 'to reform the global economic governance architecture to meet the needs of the 21st century'.[15] Through these transformations, they wished to curb excessive risk-taking and recklessness in the global financial system, which was perceived as the root cause of the financial crisis of 2008. However, the Pittsburgh communiqué did not refer to international financial taxation in any form, and focused on reforming capital requirements,[16] compensation in the financial sector, improved over-the-counter (OTC) derivatives markets,[17] and moral hazard problems related to systemically important financial institutions (SIFIs). It did, however, request that the International Monetary Fund (IMF) prepare a report 'on the range of options . . . as to how the financial sector could make a fair and substantial contribution toward paying for any burdens associated with government interventions to repair the banking system'.[18] The IMF delivered that report by the June 2010 G20 summit in Toronto.[19] In the lead-up to that event, the European Council strongly voiced its support for the FTT:

> 'The EU should lead efforts to set a global approach for introducing systems for levies and taxes on financial institutions with a view to maintaining a world-wide level playing field and will strongly defend this position with its G20 partners. The introduction of a global financial transaction tax should be explored and developed further in that context.'[20]

Upon delivery of the report the Toronto Summit merely 'thanked' the IMF, and beyond the mentioning of a few generic principles in the final summit communiqué, the EU did not succeed at having the idea discussed more substantively at that meeting.[21] What seemed a tempest in a teapot was no longer even mentioned in the Declaration of the Seoul Summit in November 2010. The communiqué from the February 2011 G20 meeting of finance ministers and central bank governors only cursorily referred to the financial transaction tax in preparation of the G20 meeting in Cannes on 4 November 2011. The intentions of the French Presidency were quite clear in this regard. On 20 September 2010, Nicolas Sarkozy addressed the General Assembly of the United Nations, where he stated that:

> '. . . *as the future president of the G20 and the G8 . . . I will strive to promote the idea of innovative financing* . . . [W]e must find new sources of financing to fight against poverty . . . We can decide here to implement innovative financing, the taxation of financial transactions. Why wait? Finance has been globalized. Why shouldn't we demand that finance contribute to stabilizing the world through a minuscule tax on each financial transaction?' (emphasis added)

Whether President Sarkozy was truly committed to the fight against poverty, or saw this as a pet project to woo voters in preparation for the French presidential elections in April 2012, is a political question beyond the purview of this contribution. Undoubtedly both factors played an important role, with the end result being that France was the most vocal EU Member State favouring the global, and if not possible, EU-level implementation of the

[15] G20 Leaders' Statement, The Pittsburgh Summit, 24–25 September 2009, 2. [16] Ibid, 8.
[17] Ibid, 9. [18] Ibid, 10.
[19] International Monetary Fund, *A Fair and Substantial Contribution by the Financial Sector*, Final Report for the G20 (June 2010).
[20] European Council Conclusions, Brussels, 17 June 2010, 6–7.
[21] K Lannoo, 'The EU's Response to the Financial Crisis: A mid-term review', CEPS Policy Brief No 241 (April 2011), 6.

financial transaction tax. However, this points to the first central obstacle to the EU pursuing the global implementation of the financial transaction tax. Indeed, in the highlighted portion of the quoted speech by Mr Sarkozy, it said that *he himself*, as president of the G20 and G8, would be promoting the idea of a financial transaction tax. This in opposition to the 27 Member States *qua* European Union, using its political capital and diplomatic resources to convince the global community of the merits of this idea. The European Council of June 2010 may have adopted conclusions that it support the exploration of a global financial transaction tax, but the Member States themselves are entirely divided as to whether this is truly a key issue on its international relations to-do list.

The United Kingdom and Sweden have been the most vocal, sceptical Member States on the merits of this idea. For example, speaking in September 2010 the UK Chancellor of the Exchequer stated that he could not see how the FTT would work in practice, and that 'while it has been discussed for many decades, it would be discussed for many more decades to come'.[22] Germany had been more receptive to the idea. This EU Member State indeed defends the FTT in principle—with its Finance Minister stating that the technical problems are not insurmountable, and that the tax provides an answer to the financial sector contributing its fair share to financing public coffers, but he stated explicitly that his country would not introduce such a tax unilaterally.[23] The first crucial obstacle to Union success on the international scene as regards the financial transaction tax therefore lies within itself. On the one hand we have France, supported by other Member States such as Austria, Belgium, the Netherlands, Italy, and Spain, in favour of the global or EU financial transaction tax. On the other hand we have the UK joined by Malta, the Czech Republic and Sweden who are far more sceptical of the idea. These countries offer legal, political and economic resistance to the notion that the FTT would provide for a fairer contribution of the financial sector; that it would stabilize financial markets, and that it would remove much of the 'useless' gambling-like financial transactions. One oft-quoted example is Sweden, which unsuccessfully adopted a tax similar to the FTT from the mid-1980s. The tax was progressively widened in scope and heightened in rate, and by 1990 more than 50% of its securities trading activity moved to London and other financial centres.[24] Because of this real risk of geographical relocation, Sweden is urging other G20 countries not to adopt the FTT, but rather to opt for alternatives to the taxation of financial transactions.[25] Whether or not the Swedish example is due to design flaws in the tax, in political minds there is an undeniable apprehension towards any risk of geographical relocation, with commensurate effects on financial centres and national economies. Given the crucial role of London in global finance, and commensurate revenues for UK public coffers, the United Kingdom is the most vocal intra-EU opponent to the EU-wide or global implementation of the financial transaction tax. The reasons for this are not merely related to the risk of relocation of 'the City' to third countries, but rather of a public financial nature. Indeed, the United Kingdom actually has a form of financial transaction taxation, from which it receives up to six billion pounds annually.[26] A global or EU FTT with funds earmarked for funding climate change or the fight against global poverty is therefore not beneficial for UK public budgets.

As regards support from the EU institutions, the European Parliament is most supportive of the FTT. In a Resolution of 8 March 2011,[27] the European Parliament stated that, in its

[22] 'Finance Ministers Fail to Agree on EU Financial Transaction Tax' *Taxation International* 7 September 2010.

[23] See n 21.

[24] European Parliament, Special Committee on the Financial, Economic and Social Crisis, 'Crisis Management, Burden Sharing and Solidarity Mechanisms in the EU: A Follow-up Study to Financial Supervision and Crisis Management in the EU' (June 2010), 42.

[25] However, the Leading Group report argues that this is a poor example due to design problems in the Swedish tax. See n 37, 17.

[26] See n 39.

[27] European Parliament, Resolution on innovative financing at global and European Level (8 March 2011).

opinion, the EU should promote the introduction of an FTT at global level, failing which the EU should implement an FTT at European level as a first step.[28] In spite of the cold reception at G20 level in June 2010, during 2011 the idea of an EU-level financial transaction tax slowly began to gain traction: in June 2011 Commission President Barroso spoke favourably of that option, and he indicated that during the autumn of 2011 the Commission would publish a proposal to that effect.[29] Similarly, at the joint Sarkozy–Merkel meeting of 16 August 2011,[30] both leaders stated that they would push towards taxing 'corporate' transactions.[31] The idea underlying the European implementation of the financial transaction tax is that the Union would 'lead by example', and that other nations would follow suit once the EU has proven that the FTT does not have the feared relocation effects on financial markets. However, at the technocratic level that enthusiasm has so far not been uniformly shared with political leadership. Politically the Tax Commissioner may support the FTT,[32] but in reality the Commission services clearly take a more sceptical stance. During the second half of 2010, the Commission published two thoroughly researched Communications which clearly disfavour the FTT idea (both at EU or global level) on the basis of technical, legal and institutional hurdles.[33] We can thus already observe that a second obstacle to the EU acting as an effective global actor is institutional: a disjunction between the technocrats'—not wholly unjustifiable—belief that the EU better spend resources on less utopian pursuits than the global FTT, and the top-down political pressure to work out a credible proposal and give it their full backing. This tension was replicated in conversations of the author with an official of the Directorate General of economic and financial affairs (ECFIN),[34] and was also put as a question of the House of Lords EU select committee to Commissioner Šemeta: 'My understanding was that your own directorate and that of ECFIN were sceptical in giving that advice to the Commission President but that Mr Barroso wanted to bring about and propose the financial transaction tax as a kind of counterweight at the time of the financial crisis. Were those the origins? Did you give advice that FTT was a difficult thing to introduce?'.[35] When the Commissioner avoided the question, the Chairman of the Committee continued: 'I understand that, but did you have reservations when you discussed it in the Commission about whether this was a viable tax and should be brought forward? Did you and DG ECFIN have those reservations?'.[36] Mr Šemeta replied that his services had initially concluded that a financial activities tax[37] was equally viable as a financial transaction tax, but that they decided to present the latter, for the FTT provided greater potential revenues. However, the scenario that it was President Barrosso who pushed the Commission services to draw up an FTT proposal is evidenced by the fact that Commissioner Šemeta in a speech of October 2010 has gone on record *against* the transaction tax.[38] Thus it happened that on 28 September 2011 in his 'State of the Union'

[28] See n 10, para 16.

[29] S Taylor, 'Barroso to push for financial transaction tax' *European Voice* (21 June 2011).

[30] A transcript of the press conference is available at: <http://www.businessinsider.com/live-coverage-the-big-merkel-sarkozy-meeting-youve-been-waiting-for-2011-8>.

[31] H Mahony, 'Merkel and Sarkozy plan "true economic government"' *EU Observer* (18 August 2011).

[32] A Šemeta, EU Commissioner for Taxation and Customs Union, Audit and Anti-Fraud, 'Taxing the Financial Sector' Press Conference, Brussels, 7 October 2010, SPEECH/10/530.

[33] Communication from the Commission to the European Parliament, the Council, the European Economic and Social Committee and the Committee of the Regions on Taxation of the Financial Sector, Brussels COM (2010) 549/5; European Commission Staff Working Document, Taxation of the Financial Sector, Brussels COM (2010) 549.

[34] Conversation with official of DG Tax, October 2011.

[35] House of Lords, Select Committee on European Union, Unrevised transcript of evidence taken on the Financial Transaction Tax, 16 February 2012, 4.

[36] Ibid.

[37] A tax on the balance sheet of a financial institution rather than the transaction itself.

[38] A Šemeta, EU Commissioner for Taxation and Customs Union, Audit and Anti-Fraud, 'Taxing the Financial Sector', Press Conference Brussels, 7 October 2010, SPEECH/10/530.

speech, Commission President Barroso presented a proposal for an EU Directive on the FTT, to be implemented by 1 January 2014 across all 27 Member States.[39] Speaking to the House of Lords EU Select Committee on 16 February 2012, Commissioner Šemeta strongly defended the EU line, and confirmed that this EU-level proposal must be seen as a stepping stone to the eventual global implementation of the FTT. He also made explicit reference to the need to have the UK on board if this was to be successful:[40]

> 'An EU financial transaction tax can help to address many of the major challenges that we are confronted with as a Union today. It will deliver significant revenues, complement our regulatory framework for a more stable and responsible financial sector and contribute to a stronger single market. Moreover, by implementing a well-designed and well-functioning FTT across Europe, we can pave the way for a global approach, an objective which, like us, the UK Government have also committed to within the G20. An EU FTT can achieve this without compromising our competitiveness, without increasing unemployment or driving business from Europe. An EU FTT can achieve this without undermining the strength of the financial services industry in the EU. It is in the overall European interest to have strong financial centres in London as well as in Paris and Frankfurt. In this context, we need the UK on board, actively engaged in the discussions on the design, fine-tuning and implementation of the financial transaction tax.'[41]

In Cannes, on 3–4 November 2011, the EU proposal for a global financial transaction tax fell—if not on stony ground—far short of the result the French Presidency had hoped for. The meeting in Cannes was entirely dominated by the European sovereign debt crisis, notably in light of the Greek Prime Minister's surprise announcement that a bail-out to his country would have to be approved by popular referendum. However, at his evening press conference on 4 November 2011, President Sarkozy stated that after Cannes, 'the financial transaction tax is still on the table, and that is an amazing achievement!'.[42] However, the language of the G20 Summit is as usual rather less enthusiastic:

> 'We agree that, over time, new sources of funding need to be found to address development needs. We discussed a set of options for innovative financing highlighted by Mr Bill Gates, such as Advance Market Commitments, Diaspora Bonds, taxation regime for bunker fuels, tobacco taxes, and a range of different financial taxes. Some of us have implemented or are prepared to explore some of these options. We acknowledge the initiatives in some of our countries to tax the financial sector for various purposes, including a financial transaction tax, inter alia to support development.'[43]

Thus, little has changed since the Toronto summit of June 2010, and it is uncertain what the G20 in Mexico will bring. In the following sub-section I examine the EU proposal for a Directive implementing the FTT at regional EU level, and assess its potential as a stepping stone for global implementation. At this juncture, we may conclude that as regards the EU position on a global FTT, both horizontal (intra-institutional) and vertical (EU—Member State) dividing lines exist. Whereas the Tax Commissioner now defends the EU line, agreement by all 27 Member States is still lacking, and it is clear that the latter schism is the most damaging to the single EU message in pursuit of the global financial transaction tax.

[39] European Commission, Proposal for a Council Directive on a common system of financial transaction tax and amending Directive 2008/7/EC, Brussels COM (2011) 594 final of 28 September 2011.

[40] House of Lords, Select Committee on European Union, Unrevised transcript of evidence taken on the Financial Transaction Tax, 16 February 2012.

[41] House of Lords, Select Committee on European Union, Unrevised transcript of evidence taken on the Financial Transaction Tax, 16 February 2012, uncorrected evidence, 2.

[42] The press conference was streamed live via a dedicated website, which is currently no longer available.

[43] Cannes summit final declaration, 'Building our common future: renewed collective action for the benefit of all', 4 November 2011, para 82.

4. Essential Features of the EU Proposal for an FTT Directive

4.1. Objectives of the EU proposal

When James Tobin proposed to levy a small percentage on all spot conversions of one currency into another, the objective was to 'throw sand in the wheels of the excessively efficient international money markets',[44] ie to deter short-term speculative currency transactions. The idea of deterring what are perceived as excessively risky activities by financial institutions is integral to the idea of the EU-wide financial transaction tax, and additionally the Union wishes 'to complement regulatory measures aimed at avoiding future crises'.[45] However, there is deep disagreement on the economic merits of the FTT, essentially reflecting different economic schools' ideologies on the desirability of regulatory intervention in markets. As a consequence, reaching consensus on the FTT proposal has been a vast hurdle towards implementing the tax at European—let alone global—level. In the previous sub-section I have already indicated that this is but one of the many obstacles to global implementation of the FTT. The Commission proposal makes clear proposals in this respect, and indicates the following chief objectives for implementing an EU-wide FTT:[46]

(i) The first objective is to ensure that financial institutions make a fair contribution to covering the costs of the recent crisis, and to ensure that financial services which are exempted from VAT are treated equally to other sectors. Related to this argument, although not mentioned as an objective for the EU–FTT per se, is that the EU foresees that the projected revenue of an EU-wide FTT (57 billion Euros) would gradually displace national contributions to the EU budget, thereby helping to relieve national budget deficits.

(ii) Second, market correction, namely to correct behaviour such as trend-chasing and short-termism out of step with the real economy, and complement ongoing regulatory initiatives to ensure systemic, macro-economic stability. The FTT does this by limiting perceived excesses across the EU's 27 Member States, and creating appropriate disincentives for transactions that endanger the stability and efficiency of financial markets.

If the EU can manage to transform these objectives into a coherent message to the world, the proposed EU Directive on an FTT is an important stepping stone for global implementation in that it provides crucial regulatory inspiration for its global implementation. From the perspective of market correction notably, the EU directive makes important regulatory choices, underlining the maturity of the proposal and its complementarity to the G20 Pittsburg Statement to reform global financial governance for the 21st century. In essence, the EU Directive sets up a harmonized system in order to limit financial transactions which are not desired for their rationale (speculative), large volume (compared to real economy) or high speed (high-speed algorithmic trading). What is rather unfortunate, however, is that the Commission proposal does not make an explicit connection to innovative financing for development or climate change. Elsewhere I have argued that this is a political mistake on the part of the Union.[47] This is because if it had done so, it could create political momentum through projecting itself as a 'Global Robin Hood', taxing the rich and giving back to the poor. By short-sightedly connecting potential revenue of the FTT Directive to the negotiations on the next multi-annual budget cycle, the Union has lost an important source of political legitimacy to its citizens, and grass roots movements across the world. Thus, it

[44] J Tobin, 'A Proposal for International Monetary Reform' (1978) 4 *Eastern Economic Journal* 153–159.

[45] European Commission, Proposal for a Council Directive on a common system of financial transaction tax and amending Directive 2008/7/EC, Brussels COM (2011) 594 final of 28 September 2011, 12 (preamble, para 1).

[46] Ibid, 2. [47] See n 2.

would be important to rectify that error in translating the EU proposal to a global message, and it would be crucial for the Union to emphasize the FTT as integral to global redistributive justice. In any case, in setting up a system of taxing financial transactions, there are three distinct concerns which need to be addressed at EU and at global level. First, a targeted FTT would have to be meticulously designed to reduce the risk of geographic relocation to non-tax jurisdictions. Second, it is necessary to ensure that the FTT does not hamper the real economy by limited access to capital. Third, it is necessary to ensure that tax incidence does not befall individual citizens.

4.2. Core legislative choices in the EU proposal

A commonly quoted statistic is that in 2007, the volume of financial transactions stood at a level 73.5 times higher than nominal world GDP, owing largely to the growth in derivatives trading.[48] In particular, trading on derivatives markets expanded significantly stronger than trading on spot markets: in 2008, the volume of derivatives trading was 66 times higher than world GDP, whereas spot trading amounted to only eight times world GDP. The argument goes that this indicates the skewed relationship between the needs of the real economy and the international financial markets. Intervention is necessary because only a small share of transactions stem from 'useful' hedging activities and the greatest part of transactions is purely speculative.[49] Of speculative trading, high speed algorithmic trading is considered particularly harmful since it is based on the trades of others, thereby amplifying fluctuations away from equilibrium based on real economic indicators.[50] The nature of the EU's FTT is such that it would correct market behaviour through rendering speculative trades more costly, in particular high frequency technical trading which is automated to chase trends in the short term. Through rendering such trades more expensive, the FTT would curb speculation and improve market efficiency, increase transparency, reduce excessive price volatility, and create incentives for longer term investments with added value for the real economy by freeing up resources for more productive uses.[51] Counter-arguments to the FTT consider that it would limit parties' ability to hedge risk,[52] thereby reducing liquidity and increasing short-term volatility of asset prices. The EU Directive clearly chooses to follow the Keynesian line of reasoning in this debate. This is distinctly illustrated by the taxable amount of the FTT on derivatives. Namely, the EU proposal takes the notional amount at the time the derivative agreement is purchased/sold, transferred, concluded or modified.[53] This implies that derivatives are taxed on the basis of the value of the underlying principal, which implies a potentially large amount of tax to be paid compared to the actual amounts changing hands between parties to the derivative contract. Even though the proposal sets the tax rate at 0.01% instead of the 0.1% for other transactions, this is clearly intended to render short-term, speculative trades in financial derivatives much more costly.

Further illustrative of the fact that the focus of the Directive is on trading which is not useful for the real economy but speculative, are the following three mitigating elements:

- First, the tax is set at a low rate to minimize impact on the cost of capital for non-financial investment purposes.

[48] S Schulmeister, 'Short-term Asset Trading, Long-Term Price Swings and the Stabilizing Potential of a Transactions Tax' (WIFO—Austrian Institute of Economic Research, October 2010), 19.

[49] Ibid, 20.

[50] Ibid.

[51] D Baker, 'The Benefits of a Financial Transactions Tax' (Centre for Economic and Policy Research, December 2008), 3.

[52] K Alexander, 'International Financial Regulatory Reform and Financial Taxes' (2010) 13 *Journal of International Economic Law* 900 (himself a proponent of the FTT, but quoting a number of counter-arguments).

[53] See n 9.

- Second, there is the exclusion from the scope of the FTT of transactions on primary markets both for securities (shares, bonds)—so as not to undermine the raising of capital by governments and companies—and for currencies.
- Third, the exclusion of financial transactions, for example with the European Central Bank (ECB) and with national central banks, from the scope of the FTT, so that the directive will not affect the refinancing possibilities of financial institutions or the instruments of monetary policy.

Further, with its market correction objective in mind, the EU Directive aims to install an FTT which is broadly defined in scope as regards products, transactions, types of trade and financial actors, as well as transactions carried out inside a financial group. For example, the definition of *financial institutions* includes investment firms, organized markets, credit institutions, insurance and reinsurance undertakings, collective investment undertakings and their managers, pension funds and their managers, holding companies, financial leasing companies, special purpose entities, and foresees in delegated powers to the Commission so that it may set targets for 'significant' activities of other entities whereby it would also be classed as a financial institution. As regards *financial transactions*, the proposal includes spot transactions (shares, bonds, currencies) and derivatives transactions (forwards, futures, options, swaps, currency derivatives, commodity derivatives),[54] and this both on organized markets and 'over-the-counter' transactions between financial institutions. This aspect illustrates the choice for a sweepingly broad financial transaction tax, but also raises an important question for global implementation. Namely, it is clear that the EU legal order is well-suited for the kind of EU-wide harmonized approach necessary to implement this tax. Indeed, Member States are obliged to implement this Directive by 2014 if it enters into force as planned, and Member States are only given discretion to impose a higher tax rate than required by the Directive if they so desire. This has important implications at a global level. It is indeed questionable whether the 'nature of governance' in the global financial system as it stands can accommodate the level of legal cooperation needed to install this tax. It is beyond the scope of this contribution to assess the legal changes needed to the global financial legal order. However, in different contributions I have argued that this would require nothing less than a revolution in global financial governance.[55]

Having pointed to the fact that the EU Directive clearly has the market-intervention objective of limiting transactions that are not considered useful, we must now point to another, and very contentious issue surrounding the FTT: that of relocation. Relocation covers two distinct phenomena, namely that financial transactions would disappear altogether, or they would be avoided through engineering or geographic relocation outside of the taxing jurisdiction. Now more than ever, financial markets operate at global level. Implementing the financial transaction tax in a regionally or nationally fragmented way exponentially increases the risk of financial engineering to avoid the tax; with financial institutions fleeing the area where it has been implemented. Furthermore, there would be the incentive to avoid taxes through integration (conducting transactions within businesses rather than between them), resulting in larger financial institutions. In the proposed EU Directive, the FTT will be levied on the basis of the *residence principle*. This implies taxation in a Member State on the basis of establishment of financial actors, independent from the location of the transaction. This aspect is meant to increase geographic distribution across its territorial field of application, ie to avoid the burden of the tax being concentrated solely in the financial centres. However, it does illustrate that the tax can only truly be effective if

[54] Impact assessment, volume I, n 64, 39.

[55] See n 2 and Bart Van Vooren, 'Global Implementation of the Financial Transaction Tax: Utopia or Opportunity to Reform the International Financial Legal Order' in D Kochenov and F Amtenbrink, *European Union's Shaping of the International Legal Order* (CUP, 2013, forthcoming).

participation is as inclusive as possible. Indeed, if the FTT is implemented only in the Eurozone, might we not see simply see massive relocation from Euro countries to the City of London? Furthermore, if the FTT is implemented at EU level, how does this impact EU financial markets? The simulations of the EU's impact assessment in implementing the tax in the EU-27 considers 'a relocation of securities markets by 10%, a relocation of spot currencies by 40% and a relocation of derivatives instruments of 70% or 90%'.[56] Relocation here implies the move of activities outside of the taxing jurisdiction, as well as their disappearance altogether. However, this is partially to be expected and even desirable, since it is one of the core objectives of the EU FTT: to the extent that algorithmic trading is considered harmful, such trading is currently about 40% of all transactions. It is these which would be rendered economically unviable, and which would be impacted the most.

A final point is that of *tax incidence*, where an important critique is that it is uncertain where the burden of the tax would fall. According to the IMF, the real burden may fall largely on final consumers rather than earnings in the financial sector in the form of reduced returns on saving, higher costs of borrowing, and/or increases in final commodity prices.[57] Commissioner Segeta ceded that point when asked about it on the day the EU Directive was launched, but argued that it is not problematic.[58] On the one hand, he argued that the Directive defines taxpayer such that financial institutions will be liable, even if the private person is involved. Hence, whether the financial institutions pay, or pass it on to the consumer, depends on the competitive environment. Taking into account that there are more than 8,800 banks in the EU, the argument goes that competition is sufficiently strong so that the possibility to pass this tax on to individual consumers is rather limited. On the other hand, he argued that such taxes as would befall individual citizens would only be relevant for high income households. According to the Commissioner, citizens at a lower level of income, or middle income, do not engage in speculation in financial instruments. Hence there is a progressivity to the tax incidence, mainly linked with those who have a higher level of income. A similar argument has been made at global level. An expert report commissioned by the Leading Group argued that there would be a trickle-down effect whereby proportional to their involvement, economic market participants who benefit from globalization would pay a small contribution equal to their involvement.[59] To avoid individual citizens being negatively affected as much as possible, the EU proposal excludes from its scope the lending and borrowing activities of private households, enterprises or financial institutions, and other day-to-day financial activities, such as insurance contracts, mortgage lending, payment transactions or credit card payments. What would be included in the scope of the tax is the subsequent trading of these via structured products (derivatives), but those are not activities engaged in by ordinary citizens. Similarly, spot currency transactions are excluded to preserve the free movement of capital,[60] but derivatives based on currency transactions are included.[61]

These being essential characteristics of the EU's proposal, in the following penultimate section I examine the FTT Directive as a stepping stone for global implementation, and the potential for the Union to shape global financial governance through this initiative.

[56] Impact assessment, volume 1, n 64,49.

[57] See n 27, 21.

[58] Q&A with the press at Algirdas Šemeta, Press Conference on the FTT, 28 September 2011, transcript on file with author.

[59] Leading Group, 'Globalizing Solidarity: The Case for Financial Levies', *Report of the Committee of Experts to the Taskforce on International Financial Transactions and Development* (June 2010), 6, available at: <www.leadingroup.org>.

[60] The Commission has gone this route so as not to violate Art 63 of the Treaty on the Functioning of the European Union.

[61] *Proposal for a Council Directive*, n 45, 8.

5. The EU FTT Directive as a Stepping Stone: Creating Alliances at the G20

As mentioned above, the June 2010 Toronto G20 Summit Declaration only cursorily mentioned financial taxation, and the level of 'consensus' reached by the Leaders was limited to say the least. However, within the limited paragraphs on financial taxation, there is room to accommodate the stated objectives of innovative financing and market correction.[62] The relevant paragraphs state as follows:

> '21. We agreed the financial sector should make a fair and substantial contribution towards paying for any burdens associated with government interventions, where they occur, to repair the financial system or fund resolution.
>
> 22. To that end, we recognized that there is a range of policy approaches. Some countries are pursuing a financial levy. Other countries are pursuing different approaches. We agreed the range of approaches would follow these principles:
> - Protect taxpayers;
> - Reduce risks from the financial system;
> - Protect the flow of credit in good times and bad times;
> - Take into account individual countries' circumstances and options; and,
> - Help promote a level playing field.
>
> 23. We thanked the IMF for its work in this area.'[63]

The above quotation from the Toronto Summit Declaration does not make a connection between a financial levy and dispensing the revenue towards innovative financing for climate change or in support of the Millennium Development Goals. The only statement on the distribution of the revenue is the 'protection of taxpayers', language which is deliberately open-ended on connecting taxation to refunding taxpayers for the bail-outs in a number of advanced economies. We have seen that the EU FTT Directive states that it is meant to serve as: (i) a new source of revenue to meet post-crisis budgetary needs; (ii) a means to recover costs from the 'bailouts' of financial institutions, and (iii) a way to cover the costs of potential future financial crisis.[64] Those being the EU's objectives, they are in rather strong contrast with the objectives for which civil society has advocated the financial transaction tax.[65] Often, using the currency-specific Tobin Tax as the most popular example, the argument has traditionally been that proceeds should be earmarked for the funding of global public goods. This includes development and support for the MDGs, initiatives focusing specifically on health care or the environment, and combating climate change. Asked about any such earmarking at a press conference, Commissioner Šemeta made clear that there was no such earmarking written into the EU proposal.[66] He pointed to the fact that the EU, together with its Member States, is the biggest donor in the world. The FTT will contribute to Member State and EU budgets at a ratio to be decided in the multi-annual financial framework, but at any rate will contribute to public coffers. Thus, according to the Commissioner, through alleviating pressures on public coffers, the FTT will contribute to financing for development and climate change.

[62] The G20 Toronto Summit Declaration, 27 June 2010, 5.

[63] Ibid, 18.

[64] Commission Staff Working Paper, Impact Assessment accompanying the document 'Proposal for a Council Directive on a common system of financial transaction tax and amending Directive 2008/7/EC'—Volume I, Brussels COM (2011) 594 final of 28 September 2011, 25–26.

[65] Such initiatives include robinhoodtax.org or financialtransactiontax.eu; underwritten by diverse grassroots social movements.

[66] Algirdas Šemeta, Press Conference, 28 September 2011, transcript on file with author.

I submit that especially the argument of replenishing public coffers post-crisis bailouts will not provide sufficient traction towards installing the FTT at global level. Furthermore, the merely indirect contribution to global public goods will not suffice to garner global support. Indeed, and this is a purely political–strategic decision, if the EU wishes to have an FTT installed at global level it must emphasize the 'fair contribution' perspective. This is so because G20 significant countries such as China, India, Australia and Canada did not engage in bail-outs, as many European countries and the US have done. This argument would therefore have less traction. Hence, in mustering political support for a global FTT, and in designing the distribution of FTT proceeds, it is best to focus on earmarking revenue for the provision of global public goods.

Aside from the final recipients of the 'fair contribution' to be made by financial institutions, the language in the Toronto Summit Declaration is deliberately vague on the national, regional or global level at which to pursue a financial levy. The reference to government interventions '*where they occur*' came at the request of countries such as India, Canada, Japan and China which did not bail out their financial sectors. These do not feel as compelled as Western nations to have the financial sector compensate them for their interventions. The quotation from the 2011 Cannes Summit Declaration earlier in this contribution replicates that schism between different nations at G20 level: 'Some of us have implemented or are prepared to explore some of these options. We acknowledge the initiatives in some of our countries to tax the financial sector for various purposes, including a financial transaction tax, inter alia to support development'.[67] Notably Canada has been a vocal opponent, with its finance minister stating that: 'We will continue leading that charge against a transactions tax and I am confident that our allies on this point, who are the emerging economies, will stay with us and join us in opposing what we view as a counter-productive tax... I am actually confident that we have enough of them in the G20 that we will be successful on that initiative'.[68] Canadian opposition explains why the Toronto Summit Declaration was so light on the topic of an FTT, and also shows the importance of the EU Directive and French presidency building momentum towards the Cannes summit. The fact that this summit was overshadowed by the European sovereign debt crisis decimated any such momentum, as it was rather clear that the European Union had—to put it colloquially—'bigger fish to fry'. In any case, the distinction between some countries pursuing the financial levy and other countries having different approaches makes clear that while a global FTT is not excluded, enthusiasm is certainly highly limited and common agreement is lacking. The key for the EU proposal to succeed is not merely to emphasize its innovative financing aspect, but to argue that it is compatible with the BRIC nations' regulatory vision. Prior to the 2008 crisis, Western nations' approaches were broadly deregulatory, whereas for India, China or Japan the opposite was true. Since the latter countries have been less averse to regulating their financial sectors,[69] they view this as being one of the key reasons for not having had to bail out their financial institutions. India could be one important BRIC nation the EU might sway to the pro-FTT camp. While currently sceptical, arguing that it might hurt its domestic banks, it did in the early 2000s argue in favour of the financial transaction tax at global level. Therefore, if the EU wishes to realize the FTT, it must emphasize the systemic market corrective function of international financial taxation, and push an FTT complementary with emerging powers' vision on regulating finance. In this sense, the EU is to actively engage

[67] Cannes summit final declaration, 'Building our common future: renewed collective action for the benefit of all', 4 November 2011, para 82.

[68] Quoted in J Greenwood, 'Clark Sings Praises of Basel Rules on Capital' *Financial Post* (5 October 2011).

[69] Special Section on International Banking, *The Economist* (15 May 2011).

the changed power structure of global economic governance as part of the process of installing the FTT.

6. Conclusion

The objective of this contribution was to examine the global potential for the EU's FTT proposal in a multi-polar world and a global economy negatively affected by the Eurozone sovereign debt crisis, in line with its binding, rule-of-law based mission statement of Article 21 TEU. What is certain is that the European Union in primary law has a strongly worded obligation to pursue multilateralism based on the rule of law: de Búrca's governance mode of foreign policy.[70] In light of this, it has been argued that the global financial transaction tax carries with it great potential for 'legitimizing' the European Union as a global actor through effective implementation of its FTT proposals—the EU as a global Robin Hood. However, this contribution has pointed to numerous internal and external obstacles to any such role for the EU on the global playing field. The first obstacle to EU global success lies within itself: strongly divided opinions between the Member States, and within the EU institutions themselves, on the merits of the global or regional financial transaction tax. Within the EU institutions, we have seen that Commissioners Barroso and Šemeta did not agree on its merits, but that the latter realigned himself in light of political pressure from his hierarchy. Thus, from the Commission perspective we have seen a 'single voice' emerge. However, the same is not true for agreement between the Member States themselves. At the time of writing, Spring 2012, discussions within the Council were ongoing on the EU-wide implementation of the FTT. Indicators for agreement among the EU-27 were not good. Early February 2012, a splinter group of EU countries led by France and Germany—joined by Austria, Belgium, Finland, Greece, Spain, Portugal and Italy—asked the Danish Presidency to fast-track plans for the FTT, possibly even through enhanced cooperation.[71] By the end of March 2012 political momentum had waned even further, with the German finance minister stating that he would back equal alternatives such as an extended stock market tax.[72] Thus, potential for an EU single voice delivering a single message on the global stage is minimal.

Assuming that the European Union does manage to pull together and political momentum is (re-) created at a later stage,[73] obstacles globally are equally, if not more, insurmountable. Elsewhere I have pointed to the fact that such would require a revolution in the way global finance is governed, and the Toronto and Cannes summits have shown that at present, the global FTT is a stillborn idea. Should the Union wish to plod onwards with a global financial transaction tax, the Union can only partially transpose its objectives to the global level. First, while the EU should certainly emphasize the market corrective and regulatory function as set out in the proposed EU Directive; it should pursue this tax towards raising extra funds for global public goods where funds are currently lacking due to significant public deficits. Indeed, (EU Member) States should not view this as an opportunity to replenish public coffers of those nations which have bailed out financial institutions. Clearly, widely different responses across the globe—especially in Asia—would hinder consensus and render the FTT even more unlikely at G20 level. Second, the market

[70] See contribution by de Búrca to this volume.

[71] V Pop, 'Nine EU countries form splinter group on financial tax' *EU Observer*, 8 February 2012.

[72] 'Germany gives up on financial transaction tax' *EU Observer*, 26 March 2012; 'EU countries explore alternatives to financial tax' *EU Observer*, 31 March 2012.

[73] In the Joint letter of the Presidents of the European Council and Commission to the EU Heads of State ahead of the G20 Summit in Los Cabos, Mexico in June 2012, the financial transaction tax was not mentioned at all, and this is unlikely to change any time soon given the failed re-election of former French President Sarkozy. See 'Joint letter of President Van Rompuy and President Barroso to the EU Heads of State or Government on the G20 Summit in Los Cabos, Mexico', Brussels, 25 May 2012, EUCO 96/12.

corrective function should be framed such to assure G20 members that geographical relocation will not pose grave risks to the major financial centres and the economies of the countries that host them. As a consequence, this section concludes that the *global option* in function of *market stabilization* and the provision of *global public goods* is the only feasible avenue towards implementing a credible financial transaction tax. This sets the stage for the legal and institutional features of a multilateral financial transaction tax convention.[74]

[74] B Van Vooren, 'Global Implementation of the Financial Transaction Tax: Utopia or Opportunity to Reform the International Financial Legal Order' in D Kochenov and F Amtenbrink, *European Union's Shaping of the International Legal Order* (CUP, 2013, forthcoming).

PART VI

THE EU AND GLOBAL SOCIAL GOVERNANCE

18

Towards International Migration Governance? The European Contribution

Daniel Thym

1. Introduction

Migration has been a defining feature throughout human history and has been reinforced by various strands of 'globalization' in recent years. Economic interdependence and societal transnationalism sustain a growing number of cross-border movements.[1] Given that cross-border migration is—as the 'human dimension' of globalization—by definition a transnational phenomenon, one would expect widespread international cooperation. However, the legal and institutional picture looks different: while numerous international organizations and conventions regulate trade, security, climate change or human rights, migration appears as a sanctuary of domestic rule-making. With the notable exceptions of the 1951 United Nations Convention relating to the Status of Refugees and the humanitarian activities of the United Nations High Commissioner for Refugees (UNHCR), few international treaties and organizations relate to the transnational movement of people.[2] Migration continues to be dominated by domestic rules and politics. This national orientation might eventually be complemented by varied forms of international migration governance—with the active support of the European Union.

Although change has been limited, the quest for international migration governance received much attention in recent years. In 2005, the Global Commission on International Migration prominently challenged the prevalent 'unwilling[ness] to commit fully to the principle of international cooperation in the area of international migration'.[3] As a result, various reports and advisory bodies highlighted the migration–development nexus and sought to establish political forums for continued debate.[4] Also, a growing body of academic literature scrutinizes the conditions, pitfalls and implications of international migration governance. Despite the dominance of political science, they all recognize the need for multidisciplinary analysis.[5] A blind spot on the global governance agenda is thus rapidly being mapped.[6] This contribution adds the perspective of EU law concentrating on (il)legal migration.[7] Its reference to international 'governance' mirrors the fragmented character

[1] cf S Castles and J Miller, *The Age of Migration* (4th edn, Palgrave Macmillan, 2009) chs 5–7.

[2] For an overview see T Aleinikoff, 'International Legal Norms on Migration' in R Cholewinski, E MacDonald and R Perruchoud (eds), *International Migration Law* (TMC Asser, 2007) 467–479.

[3] GCIM, 'Migration in an Interconnected World: New Directions for Action', Report of 5 October 2005: <http://www.gcim.org>, ch 6, para 6.

[4] See the overview by K Newland, 'The Governance of International Migration: Mechanisms, Processes, and Institutions' (2010) 16 *Global Governance* 331–343.

[5] For an early reflection see B Ghosh (ed), *Managing Migration. Time for a New International Regime?* (OUP, 2000).

[6] In 2011, four edited volumes were published in parallel: A Betts (n 8); R Hansen, J Koehler and J Money (eds), *Migration, Nation-States, and International Cooperation* (Routledge, 2011); R Kunz, S Lavenex and M Panizzon (eds), *Multilayered Migration Governance: The Promise of Partnership* (Routledge, 2011) and R Koslowski (ed), *Global Mobility Regimes* (Palgrave, 2011).

[7] For legal accounts on cooperation on asylum and refugees see A-S Millet-Devalle, 'La protection des migrants et des réfugiés dans le cadre des accords entre l'Union européenne et les Etats tiers' in A-S Millet-Devalle (ed), *L'Union européenne et la protection des migrants et des réfugiés* (Pedone, 2010) 91–132 and M den Heijer, *Europe and Extraterritorial Asylum* (Hart Publishing, 2012).

of existing initiatives which extend to different forums and degrees of cooperation and do not establish a coherent multilateral framework,[8] despite the EU's commitment to 'promote multilateral solutions to common problems'.[9]

The European Union positions itself as a key player in the pursuit of international migration governance. It actively seeks to establish cooperation with third states, whose success or failure will influence global events. Our analysis cannot predict the outcome of this venture. It can, however, shed light on the underlying normative framework. Europe's focus on international migration governance is no coincidence: primary law and European self-perception are biased in favour of international cooperation (section 2). An assessment of existing cooperation regimes, including the widely touted mobility partnerships, indicates that success is not a foregone conclusion. The objective of international migration governance is easy to declare, but difficult to achieve (section 3). Such practical trials and errors reflect underlying difficulties to accommodate countervailing migration control objectives, human rights standards and legal migration opportunities. Legal, political and conceptual reasons complicate the realization of international migration governance (section 4).

2. Legal and Institutional Framework

Pre-existing norms and institutions influence migration governance projects. The EU approach is indeed characterized by distinctive features: reflecting on its experience with integration through law, the EU Treaty and official strategy papers promote a cooperative vision of international relations (sub-section 1). We should nonetheless distinguish Europe's internal experience of transcontinental mobility from immigration policy towards third country nationals with its distinct aim of ensuring the 'efficient management of migration flows' (sub-section 2) with due respect for human rights (sub-section 3). While the substance and orientation of the various policy initiatives described later are in flux, the rules analysed in this section provide a stable bedrock for future initiatives.

2.1. Projection of European experiences

European integration perceives itself as the realization of a rule-based international order. Despite its focus on the European continent, this approach has always had a corollary international dimension. Article 21(1) of the Treaty on European Union (TEU) solemnly reaffirms the international vocation of the European project. Although 'hard' legal obligations determining specific policy outcomes cannot be deducted from this Treaty objective in regular circumstances,[10] the formulation hints at the self-characterization of the EU outlook. The Stockholm Programme, Europe's five-year plan for justice and home affairs, confirms this standpoint: invocations of 'globalization', 'partnership' and the 'external dimension' pervade the strategic guidelines.[11] On this basis, the Commission has repeatedly promoted a 'global approach'.[12] Initial setbacks, such as with mobility partnerships discussed below,

[8] See A Betts, 'Introduction' in A Betts (ed), *Global Migration Governance* (OUP, 2011) 1–33; 'governance' in this sense is not only an alternative to state-like foreign policy, as demonstrated by Gráinne de Búrca in this volume, but also an alternative to multilateral cooperation based on treaties and organization which dominate international cooperation in other policy fields.

[9] Art 21.1(2) TEU and s 2.1.

[10] See the argument by Larik in ch 2 of this volume and D Thym, 'Foreign Affairs' in A von Bogdandy and J Bast (eds), *Principles of European Constitutional Law* (2nd edn, Hart Publishing/C H Beck, 2009) 309, 314–316 and 326–330.

[11] cf The Stockholm Programme: An Open and Secure Europe Serving and Protecting the Citizens [2010] OJ C115/1, ss 6 and 7; see also The Hague Programme [2005] OJ C53/1, s III.1.6 and III.4.

[12] See in particular Commission Communication COM (2005) 390 of 1 September 2005 and Commission Communication COM (2006) 735 of 30 November 2006.

have not derailed the project. Following the 'Arab Spring', the Commission underlined its commitment to international cooperation with much fanfare.[13]

In short, both the EU Treaty and official policy declarations take the objective of international migration governance seriously. But one should not equate declarations of intent with policy substance. The normative bias of Treaty objectives and policy declarations does not necessarily translate into policy substance (below section 3).

2.2. Public Migration Management

There is nothing new in describing EU actorness in terms of normative power and export of the European model.[14] When it comes to migration, however, one important distinction needs to be drawn. Europe's domestic free movement regime is, in rather abstract terms, often portrayed as a prototype for international migration and features prominently in accounts of transnational or cosmopolitan citizenship.[15] But from a legal perspective, intra-European migration follows a distinct rationale, since it originates in constitutional free movement guarantees, which define the rights of Union citizens as a quasi-federal status.[16] Immigration law vis-à-vis third-country nationals follows a different conceptual logic. During the past twenty years it has gradually emancipated itself from the internal market logic. In its place, the area of freedom, security and justice represents an alternative framework.[17]

The Lisbon Treaty strengthens immigration as a self-sufficient policy in its own right. Its principle objective is laid down in Article 79(1) TEU: 'ensuring, at all stages, the efficient management of migration flows'.[18] This indicates that migration management is an end in itself. Immigration is not meant to occur 'outside the law'—like in the US[19] or in many developing countries[20]—but rather, as far as possible, under the control of public authorities. From the perspective of the Lisbon Treaty, it is not the economy or the society which primarily define the movement of people but the state.[21] Of course, this objective remains counter-factual; in Europe, the state is not in full control. The EU Treaty expresses the desire that public authorities should aim for regulatory leverage, reflecting Europe's wider 'social model' of active state involvement in social and economic policy.[22]

Arguably, the objective of migration management involves a paradigm shift, which has occurred during the past ten years. While European states have always played an active role in immigration,[23] they realized that domestic policies had limited impact in practice. Domestic laws often reacted 'passively' to external events instead of 'proactively' shaping migratory realities.[24] One may describe immigration policy in Western Europe as a

[13] cf Commission Communication COM (2011) 743 of 18 November 2011 and, a few months earlier, COM (2011) 292 of 24 May 2011.

[14] See M Cremona, 'The Union as a Global Actor' (2004) 41 *CML Rev* 553, 554–555.

[15] See, eg Y Soysal, *Limits of Citizenship* (University of Chicago Press, 1994) chs 7–8 and J Hollifield, *Immigrants, Markets and States* (Harvard University Press, 1992) chs 8–9.

[16] See S Kadelbach, 'Union Citizenship' in A von Bogdandy and J Bast, n 10, 435, 461–468.

[17] For further reflection see D Thym, 'Freizügigkeit in Europa als Modell? EU-Migrationspolitik zwischen Offenheit und Abschottung' (2011) *Europarecht* 486, 495–502.

[18] This overarching objective also encompasses the 'fair treatment' of third-country nationals and 'enhanced measures to combat illegal migration'.

[19] See H Motomura, 'Immigration Outside the Law' (2008) 108 *Columbia Law Review* 2037–2097.

[20] It should be noted that approximately 60% of all international migrants live outside developed countries in the northern hemisphere.

[21] Similar objectives are laid down in, among others, s 1(1) of the German Immigration Act (*Aufenthaltsgesetz*) and Art 2 bis of the 2009 Spanish Immigration Law: <http://www.gesetze-im-internet.de/englisch_aufenthg> and <http://extranjeros.mtin.es/es/NormativaJurisprudencia> accessed 8 September 2012.

[22] One might perceive migration management critically as a novel form of 'biopower' in a Foucaultian sense.

[23] Especially in comparison to the US, see S Castles, 'The Factors that Make and Unmake Migration Policies' (2004) 38 IM Rev 852, 855–856.

[24] cf also the (in)famous aspiration of 'immigration choisie, non subie' by the French President Nicolas Sarkozy in 2003 as minister of the interior.

sequence of state failures to achieve the declared policy objective with regard to 'guest workers', family reunification and asylum.[25] This is not an argument in favour of or against restrictionist policies, but an attempt to understand why states strive for regulatory leverage: Europeanization overcomes the limited impact of national migration control. This impetus has been described (and criticized) as 'securization' by many observers[26] and is now projected upon relations with third states. Cooperation is meant to facilitate the 'efficient management of migration flows' (Article 79(1) of the Treaty on the Functioning of the European Union (TFEU)).

2.3. Human rights protection

Migration management is only one side of the coin. While many national governments supported Europeanization to enhance migration control, many NGOs and influential voices within the supranational EU institutions insisted that new initiatives must be firmly embedded into Europe's human rights culture. Article 78(1) TFEU upholds this commitment: 'The Union shall develop a common policy on asylum... in accordance with the Geneva Convention... and other relevant treaties'. Respect for human rights might be stating the obvious for European lawyers,[27] but it remains noteworthy from a comparative immigration law and policy perspective. Outside Europe, the cross-border movement of people is often still treated as an arcane sphere of state sovereignty, where human rights hold little sway.[28] Most European jurisdictions and the European Court of Human Rights, by contrast, have long embraced the human rights dimension of cross-border movements.[29] EU migration law continues this route.

Within the context of Europe's international migration governance projects, human rights serve a double function. First, they are used as source of legitimacy by the supranational institutions in Brussels and Luxembourg, which often rely upon human rights to justify their policy initiatives (also compensating for weak democratic legitimacy).[30] This reflects Europe's general experience with 'inclusive', transnational law-making, in contrast to traditional state practices of excluding the immigrants' outsider perspective from policy deliberations.[31] Secondly, human rights serve as a tool of judicial interpretation and it seems that the European Court of Justice (ECJ) positions itself to take human rights seriously when interpreting migration law instruments (section 4.2 below). In both respects, human rights balance the claim to effective migration management described above. Also within the EU, the 'liberal paradox' of European democracies, which aim at managing migration, while at the same time preventing oppressive control through human rights standards, is maintained.[32] The EU's external migration policy is no exception in this respect.

[25] For various domestic and external reasons, many guest workers settled; 'zero immigration' policies did not stop family reunification; and asylum procedures functioned as de facto immigration policies (moreover, illegal immigration persists); see J Hollifield, 'The Emerging Migration State' (2006) 38 IM Rev 885, 894–899.

[26] cf V Guiraudon, 'European Integration and Migration Policy' (2000) 38 JCMS 251–271.

[27] See also the contribution by Geert De Baere to this volume.

[28] This conclusion concerns the point of entry and exit in particular, while (legally) resident foreigners usually benefit from civil, political (and social) guarantees; cf J Fitzpatrick, 'The Human Rights of Migrants' in A Aleinikoff and V Chetail (eds), *Migration and International Legal Norms* (OUP, 2003) 169–184.

[29] For an overview see P Boeles and others, *European Migration Law* (Intersentia, 2009) 141–148, 291–314.

[30] All legislative proposals emphasize their respect for human rights; most are publicly presented as an instrument of 'fair' treatment supporting human rights compliance.

[31] On the democratic benefits of transnational law-making see, recently, A Somek, 'The Argument from Transnational Effects I' (2010) 16 ELJ 315–344.

[32] For the 'liberal paradox' see Hollifield, n 15, 27–37.

3. Trials and Errors of International Cooperation

Not all foreign policy initiatives succeed. Indeed, migration is a policy field in which the outcome of EU cooperation schemes remains mixed. Despite limited practical impact it is nonetheless noticeable that migration has become a key policy concern for the Union. In contrast to earlier association agreements, the cross-border movement of people is now covered on a regular basis (sub-section 1). Considering the substance, control measures stand out (sub-section 2), whereas cooperation in the field of legal migration remains patchy (sub-section 3). The output of the EU's external migration policy is therefore much more modest than the euphoria of declarations of intent suggests. This may have to do with general problems in designing a functioning neighbourhood policy.[33] Yet, trials and errors described in this section hint at more deep-rooted structural difficulties with regard to migration, which will be discussed in the last section.

3.1. From non-issue to mobility partnerships

Only 15 years ago, migration did not feature prominently on the agenda of the EU's association policies. Most association and cooperation agreements did not include many migration-related rules. The major exceptions were agreements with neighbouring states, which associated the latter with certain or most aspects of the single market. In such cases, rules on the free movement of workers and establishment were incorporated into association agreements,[34] although privileges of migrant workers were usually limited to equal treatment without labour market access.[35] As a result of liberal ECJ case-law, which interpreted the provisions in parallel to single market rules, some of these agreements had a tangible impact, especially the Association Council Decision on the status of Turkish workers.[36] This approximation of third-country nationals and Union citizens motivated the Member States to be ever more careful, thereby pre-empting future generosity on the part of the ECJ.[37] Even agreements with potential accession candidates nowadays contain only narrow and cautiously drafted rules on migrant workers.[38]

These changes reflect a change of perspective. Rules on workers in association agreements do not any longer follow the single-market paradigm which favours extensive free movement rules with limited state control. Instead, migration-related considerations reflecting the policy objectives of the area of freedom, security and justice take centre stage. This is most visible in agreements with countries without accession perspective: in these agreements rules on workers have always been more limited.[39] They are nowadays absorbed by migration and social policy provisions. Instead of free movement, cooperation in migration and social policy is supported.[40] This shift of emphasis signals that migration shall henceforth be an independent subset of association and neighbourhood policies—including in relations

[33] cf K Smith, 'Enlargement, the Neighbourhood, and European Order' in C Hill and M Smith (eds), *International Relations and the European Union* (2nd edn, OUP, 2011), 299, 317–320.

[34] For far-reaching rules see Arts 28–45 of the EEA Agreement of 2 May 1992 [1994] OJ L1/3 and the free movement agreement with Switzerland of 21 June 1999 [2002] OJ L114/6.

[35] cf the equal treatment provisions in Art 6 of the EEC–Turkey Association Council Decision No 1/80 and the Europe Agreements (EAs) with Central and Eastern European states, eg Arts 37–54 of the EA with Poland of 16 December 1991 [1993] OJ L348/2.

[36] In 2010, 12% of all third-country nationals living in the EU were Turkish nationals; on diverse rulings see Boeles and others, n 29, 91–114.

[37] Speaking to members of the German negotiating team, I learnt that careful (and restrictive) drafting of future agreements was a direct response to generous ECJ case-law.

[38] cf the Stabilization and Association Agreements (SAAs) with the countries of the Western Balkans, eg Arts 49–58 SAA with Serbia [2008] Council doc 16005/07.

[39] See eg Arts 64–68 'first generation' Euromed Agreement with Tunisia of 17 July 1995 [1998] OJ L97/2.

[40] See among the first 'second generation' Euromed Agreements Art 64 of the agreement with Lebanon of 17 June 2002 [2006] OJ L143/2; it should be noted that these rules remain rather general.

with the 77 African, Caribbean and Pacific (ACP) countries, which comprise those African states where many (illegal) migrants come from. While the original Lomé Conventions remained largely silent on migration, the Cotonou Convention of 2000 and a Joint Declaration on the occasion of the 2010 revision illustrate the new focus.[41] Step by step the EU's commitment to global migration governance is being realized.

For the time being, cooperation with potential partner countries has resulted in few legally binding commitments, as the analysis in the following subsections suggests. Instead, migration governance is enhanced on an informal basis through political dialogue and projects on the ground. Such forums for consultation include multilateral settings, such as the migration dialogue with African states,[42] and bilateral initiatives, such as the dialogue on 'four common spaces' with Russia with its justice and home affairs component.[43] Most prominent, however, are the 'mobility partnerships' which the Commission proposed in 2007 and which have in the meantime been concluded with several third countries, including Cape Verde, Moldova and Georgia.[44] As a laboratory for cooperation, 'mobility partnerships' are deliberately loosely knit. They constitute political frameworks for cooperation and are not legally binding.[45] They lead to specific initiatives among partner countries including hard law instruments (eg visa facilitation and re-admission), technical and operational cooperation (eg border control and passport security) and the promotion of normative standards (eg human rights and refugee law).

There is widespread agreement both within the Commission in Brussels and among academic observers that mobility partnerships have so far not lived up to their promises.[46] In particular, the much-touted circular migration concept, which was meant to open new channels for legal migration, has failed to be realized in practice (sub-section 3). In a rather sobering assessment the Commission concludes that 'mobility partnerships are a long-term process of trust building and . . . need time and engagement to evolve'.[47] The most pressing problems, which the Commission identifies, are a lack of commitment on the part of the Member States, limited self-interest of the partner countries, and noticeable implementing problems.[48]

However, this modesty of the initial result need not be our final conclusion. It seems that the EU institutions are eager to develop the instrument further. In 2011, following the migration-related side-effects of the Arab Spring, the Commission proclaimed its intention to re-activate 'mobility partnerships', also taking on board the lessons learned. A new agreement with Armenia was signed[49] and negotiations with Turkey, Morocco and Egypt were put on the agenda.[50] It therefore seems that the reality check for mobility partnerships is yet to come. The countries mentioned are crucial states of origin and transit of migrants to Europe. If these agreements were successful, the EU would succeed in establishing true

[41] See the migration dialogue in Art 13 and on remittances Art 80 of the Cotonou Agreement of 23 June 2000 [2000] OJ L317/6 and the Declaration No 2 attached to the second revision of 22 June 2010 [2010] OJ L287/3 in contrast to Arts 5, 155.1 of the Lomé IV Convention of 15 December 1989 [1991] OJ L229/1.

[42] cf S Kingah, 'The European Union's New Africa Strategy' (2006) 11 *EFA Rev* 527, 536–538.

[43] cf P Van Elsuwege, 'The Four Common Spaces' in A Dashwood and M Maresceau (eds), *Law and Practice of EU External Relations* (CUP, 2008) 334–359.

[44] For more detail see R Parkes, 'EU Mobility Partnerships: A Model of Policy Coordination?' (2009) 11 EJML 327–345.

[45] Read No 17 of the joint declaration with Moldova, Council doc 9460/08; for declarations with other countries see n 74.

[46] Among the academic analyses see S Carrera and R Hernández i Sagrera, 'Mobility Partnerships' in R Kunz, S Lavenex and M Panizzon, n 6, 97, 101–109.

[47] Commission Staff Working Document SEC (2009) 1240 of 18 September 2009 (also available as Council doc 13489/09) 8.

[48] Commission Staff Working Document, ibid.

[49] See Council doc 14963/11 of 6 October 2011.

[50] Commission Communication, n 13, 2.

cornerstones for international migration governance. Our conclusions can therefore be preliminary only.

3.2. Prevalence of control measures

From the perspective of the EU Treaty, the prevalence of migration control measures does not come as a surprise. Article 79 TFEU explicitly calls upon the EU institutions to design a policy 'aimed at ensuring, at all stages, the efficient management of migration flows'. State authorities strive for regulatory leverage (see section 2.2). Since international migration stretches across borders by definition, the regulatory impact of EU policies can be improved through cooperation with third states. This concerns all aspects of the migratory cycle: admission, border control, circular movements and return policies all benefit from transnational collaboration. The example of readmission illustrates that cooperation has so far been particularly fruitful with control measures.

States are obliged, under customary international law, to readmit their own nationals in cases of (forced) return from third states.[51] In practice, this obligation fails to deliver, since people concerned often obstruct their (forced) return and states of origin do not cooperate with the state initiating the return. As a result, there is a clear discrepancy between the obligation to leave EU territory and actual returns to the country of origin. Readmission agreements are meant to improve compliance/enforcement. Germany spearheaded the conclusion of bilateral agreements with neighbouring European states in the early 1990s within the wider context of the Schengen conventions.[52] They soon became a popular instrument of the emerging EU immigration policy.[53] The Lisbon Treaty underlines their relevance with the introduction of an explicit legal basis in Article 79(3) TFEU.[54] By 2011, the EU had concluded 12 re-admission agreements with diverse third states, while negotiations with six other countries were ongoing.[55]

The underlying rationale of readmission agreements is simple. By establishing procedures for transnational cooperation, defining standards of proof, relevant documents and points of contact as well as modalities for return, readmission agreements facilitate the operation of the customary readmission obligation in practice.[56] These technicalities are the backbone of the agreements, since they support effective returns in practice (this also explains why standardized readmission clauses in bilateral agreements without implementing arrangements have been abandoned).[57] Although reliable data on implementation is notoriously sparse,[58] the Commission claims that the agreements contribute to the migration management objective by rendering return policies more effective and discouraging illegal entries.[59] Be it as it may, readmission agreements have become the most developed component of the EU's external migration policy based on hard legal rules.

It is no coincidence that readmission agreements serve as the legal backbone of bilateral migration governance. They allow EU states to confront the pervasive mismatch between policy intentions and empirical outcomes which often renders migration policies ineffective

[51] See K Hailbronner, 'Readmission Agreements and the Obligation on States under Public International Law to Readmit their Own and Foreign Nationals' (1997) 57 *Heidelberg Journal of International Law* 1, 11–15.

[52] Ibid, 6–11.

[53] For an overview see N Coleman, *European Readmission Policy* (Brill, 2008) 19–26 and C Billet, 'EC Readmission Agreements' (2010) 12 EJML 45, 47–51.

[54] For the legal situation previously see Billet, ibid, 59–63.

[55] cf the Commission Staff Working Document, SEC (2011) 209 of 23 February 2011.

[56] For an extensive analysis see N Coleman, n 53, 87–110; for a representative example see the detailed provisions in the agreement with Serbia of 18 September 2007 [2007] OJ L334/46.

[57] Such standard provision, eg in Art 13(5)(c) of the Cotonou Agreement, n 41, failed to deliver tangible outcomes on the ground.

[58] For the Maghreb countries see: <http://www.mirem.eu>.

[59] See the evaluation report in Commission Communication COM (2011) 76 of 23 February 2011, 4–5.

(it should be noted that EU law commands respect by the Member States for refugee rights including *non-refoulement* obligations).[60] But they are not the only instruments through which the EU seeks to enhance migration control. EU institutions have developed other mechanisms to motivate third states to (in)directly support migration management—as two examples illustrate:

First, visa-free access to the Schengen area is, for some third states, effectively dependent upon the conclusion of visa facilitation agreements establishing technical standards on passport security, which are meant to facilitate immigration control by EU Member States both at the point of entry and during the stay in the Schengen area.[61]

Second, the EU supports third states in enhancing border control capacities. It has earmarked specific funds for this purpose in the framework of its external assistance programmes[62] and may instruct the EU border agency, FRONTEX, to support border controls.[63] Within the framework of the mobility partnerships various projects focus on capacity-building in third states to enhance migration control.[64]

To sum up: with the active support of the EU institutions, the control component of cooperative migration governance projects is alive and kicking. Of course, migration control cooperation remains one-dimensional in so far as it does primarily serve the EU interest.[65] Such criticism is premature though. The experience of readmission illustrates that cooperation need not remain one-sided. Third states ask for concessions, calling upon the EU to live up to the promise of 'partnership' and 'cooperation'.

3.3. Routes for legal migration

During the negotiation of readmission agreements it became evident that third states would only agree to their conclusion if they received something in exchange.[66] Such need for reciprocal give-and-take does not come as a surprise from a realist perspective of international relations. Without mutually beneficial trade-offs, inter-state cooperation rarely works (see section 4.3). With regard to readmission, a suitable incentive for third states was soon established: 'visa facilitation', which simplifies or abolishes visa requirements for partner countries. Visa concessions include waivers for certain categories of persons, reduced application fees, simplified procedures through easier documentation, and multi-entry visas.[67] In the case of Ukraine, Russia, China and the Western Balkans, the link between readmission and visa facilitation was most evident.[68] For the citizens concerned (in particular from the Western Balkans) smooth travel with the Schengen area provided an attractive *quid pro quo*. Their governments therefore agreed to a deal as the result of mutual interest.

[60] cf Arts 4–6 of the 'Return' Directive (EC) 2008/115 [2008] OJ L348/98 and the 'Asylum Qualification' and 'Asylum Procedures' Directives (EU) 2011/95 [2011] OJ L337/9 and (EC) 2005/85 [2005] OJ L326/13.

[61] See, eg Art 8(4) of the short-stay visa waiver agreement with Mauritius of 28 May 2009 [2009] OJ L169/17.

[62] See, eg Art 5(2)(i) of Council Reg (EC) 1905/2006 establishing an instrument for development cooperation [2006] OJ L378/41 or Art 4(1)(a), (2)(a)(f) of the European Return Funds established by Council Decision (EC) 2007/575 [2007] OJ L144/45; for a critical assessment see Court of Auditors, Special Report No 12/2009.

[63] cf Art 14 of the 'Frontex' Reg (EC) 2007/2004 [2004] OJ L349/1 as amended by Council Reg (EU) 1168/2011 [2011] OJ L304/1.

[64] See, eg paras 9–11 of the joint declaration with Moldova, n 45.

[65] For a critical evaluation see R Cholewinski, 'The Criminalization of Migration in EU Law and Policy' in H Toner, E Guild and A Baldaccini (eds), *Whose Freedom, Security and Justice?* (Hart Publishing, 2007) 301–336.

[66] See C Phuong, 'Building a Community Return Policy With Third Countries' in H Toner, E Guild and A Baldaccini (eds), ibid, 337, 348–52 and n 59, 6–8.

[67] For a representative example see the text with Serbia of 18 September 2007 [2007] OJ L334/137.

[68] See the visa agreements signed in parallel to readmission agreements with Ukraine of 18 June 2007 [2007] OJ L332/68, Russia of 25 May 2006 [2007] OJ L129/27, China of 12 February 2004 [2004] OJ L83/14 and countries of the Western Balkans [2007] OJ L334.

For other countries, simplified visa rules are less attractive, since the agreements in question do not change immigration rules. They facilitate entry, but do not offer new routes for legal migration. Few citizens from Sub-Saharan or Northern African countries would benefit from visa facilitation agreements by visiting the EU as tourists or for similar reasons.[69] They long for economic opportunities instead, including access to work permits. Many economists and development theorists support legal migration, especially for low-skilled workers on a temporary basis, which are considered to enhance the benefits of migration for development purposes.[70] This philosophy also designates the starting-point of the Commission's original concept for mobility partnerships. They aim to stretch the cooperative approach beyond the sphere of visas and readmission by exploring the positive impact of circular and temporary labour migration.[71]

In contrast to visa and readmission agreements, the ambitious objective of mobility partnerships as a means to foster labour migration has not been realized. To date readmission and visa facilitation provide the most tangible outcome of existing mobility partnerships with Moldova and Georgia.[72] The original idea of including bilateral arrangements between individual EU Member States and partner countries on new routes for legal migration, including temporary migration programmes,[73] was not received enthusiastically by the Member States. Only very few specific commitments have been made within the context of existing mobility partnerships, for instance on mobility for students and better information about existing labour migration programmes.[74] That may be better than nothing, but still falls considerably short of initial promises—especially, if one compares these limited commitments with the Member States' efforts to support the control capacities of partner countries.[75] In short: there is little mobility in current mobility partnerships.

If we broaden our analysis beyond existing mobility partnerships, the overall picture looks slightly more promising. There are other forms and legal bases for unilateral, bilateral and multilateral activities establishing (limited) routes for legal migration to the European Union, especially for better-qualified workers. Since space precludes a thorough analysis, these initiatives are listed here without further comments:

First, unilateral EU harmonization measures include initiatives which open channels for legal migration. Reflecting the protection clause of Article 79(5) TFEU these instruments do not oblige Member States to admit a certain number of third-country nationals.[76] Nonetheless, they establish new opportunities including, amongst others, for students, researchers and (soon) seasonal employment. Some provisions of the directives concerned have been designed to facilitate circular migration.[77]

Second, resettlement programmes facilitate access of refugees from outside Europe, when EU Member States admit refugees from third countries in collaboration with

[69] See Art 4(1) of the agreement with Serbia, ibid, for the different categories of people which benefit from simplified application procedures.

[70] For an overview see H de Haas, 'Migration and Development' (2010) 44 IM Rev 227–264.

[71] See the Commission Communication COM (2007) 248 of 16 May 2007 and, before, COM (2006) 735, n 12.

[72] For Moldova see the agreements of 10 October 2007 [2007] OJ L334/149 and 169 and for Georgia of 22 November 2010 [2011] OJ L52/34 and 47; negotiations with Cape Verde were ongoing at the time of writing.

[73] See n 71, 5–6.

[74] See No 1 of the annex with Georgia, Council doc 16396/09 of 20 November 2009, No I of the annex with Armenia, Council doc 14963/11 of 6 October 2011, No 4 of the annex with Moldova, n 46 and No 2 of the annex with Cape Verde, Council doc 9560/08 of 21 May 2008.

[75] For a critical assessment see S Carrera and R Hernández i Sagrera, n 46, 101–105.

[76] For further reflection see section 4.1.a.

[77] See, eg Arts 3(3), 8(4), 14(1)(f), 16 of 'Blue Card' Directive (EC) 2009/50 [2009] OJ L155/17; other directives concern long-term residents, family members, students, and researchers; future projects consider seasonal workers and intra-corporate transfers; their potential for developing countries is explored by P Devisscher, 'Legal Migration in the Relationship between the European Union and ACP Countries' (2011) 13 EJML 53, 65–78.

UNHCR. Some European countries have long-standing resettlement schemes, which are common in North America.[78] In early 2012, the Council decided that the EU should in future support resettlement more actively.[79] The Commission has long championed the expansion of resettlement within the 'global approach' as a tool to complement enhanced protection both in Europe and regions of origin.[80]

Third, different Member States concluded bilateral migration and development agreements with selected third countries in recent years (some with controversial contents).[81] They follow the model of EU mobility partnerships, but tend to reach further—even if there are few new routes for legal migration. France and Spain are trend-setters in this respect.[82] Earlier precedents include the 'guest worker' agreements which central European states signed in the 1950s and 1960s.[83]

Fourth, trade law supports market access of international service providers, including the presence of natural persons abroad within the meaning of the General Agreement on Trade and Services (GATS)'s Mode 4. While the EU has made only limited commitments in the WTO framework,[84] agreements with some third states reach further. The Economic Partnership Agreement (EPA) with the Caribbean Forum (CARIFORUM) countries signals modest improvements, especially for quality services.[85] Other countries, such as India, ask for similar concessions.

To sum up: initial attempts to extend the cooperative approach to legal migration did not succeed. Combined readmission and visa facilitation agreements with selected third states are the only tangible output. Other routes for legal migration remain limited to certain categories of better qualified workers. Low-skilled labour migration, in particular, does not feature on the EU's agenda.

4. Structural Obstacles for International Governance

The trials and errors of Europe's quest for international migration governance present us with mixed results. Migration has been engraved into the EU's foreign policy agenda; various policy aspects are nowadays regularly discussed with third states and have started featuring in association and cooperation agreements. Yet the substantive output remains modest. While control initiatives thrive, new routes for legal migration have not been initiated widely beyond the example of visa facilitation. This humble conclusion hints at underlying structural obstacles to international cooperation, which are discussed in this section and concern legal (sub-section 1), conceptual (sub-section 2) and political (sub-section 3) impediments. While it is too early to draw definite conclusions, these challenges help us to identify the potential for future projects, thereby also designating the capacity of the EU to influence the global migration regime.

[78] cf G Goodwin-Gill and J McAdam, *The Refugee in International Law* (3rd edn, OUP, 2007) 497–500.

[79] See the press release of the 3151st Council meeting, Council doc 7308/12 of 8 March 2012.

[80] See Commission Communication COM (2009) 447 of 2 September 2009 and Millet-Devalle, n 7, 106–110.

[81] Most controversially, the agreement between Italy and the (former) Libyan regime of Colonel Muammar al-Gaddafi was not openly debated and lacked human rights guarantees; other agreements do not share these deficits.

[82] N Ward, 'Facilitating the Temporary Movement of Natural Persons' in R Kunz, S Lavenex and M Panizzon, n 6, 143, 148–51 and M Panizzon, 'Franco-African Pacts on Migration' in the same volume, 207–248.

[83] See H Knortz, *Diplomatische Tauschgeschäfte* (Böhlau Verlag, 2008).

[84] For an overview see M Solomon, 'GATS Mode 4 and the Mobility of Labour' in R Cholewinski, E MacDonald and R Perruchoud, n 2, 107–128.

[85] For analyses see T Van Criekinge, 'Integration of Migration Issues in EPAs' in G Faber and J Orbie (eds), *Beyond Market Access for Economic Development* (Routledge, 2009) 173, 181–188; P Devisscher, n 77, 91–93; and the contribution by Jeff Kenner to this volume.

4.1. Legal impediments

Three legal impediments stand out: the vertical delimitation of competences between the EU and its Member States complicates progress in the field of legal migration (a), which also explains the dominance of informal cooperation frameworks without binding obligations enshrined in international treaties (b). Informal arrangements support the criticism voiced by human rights groups which present the EU's external migration policy as an attempt to shift responsibilities onto third states which often lack the will or capacity to respect human rights and refugee law (c).

a) Division of competences

With the entry into force of the Treaty of Lisbon, the EU has acquired express powers for the conclusion of readmission agreements and projects to enhance 'partnership and cooperation with third countries for the purpose of managing inflows of people applying for [refugee] protection' (Articles 78(2)(g) and 79(3) TFEU). These rules clarify that the EU may pursue an external asylum and readmission policy as a means to its own end, ie irrespective of repercussions for the EU's domestic policies.[86] Policy initiatives which are not covered by the EU's express powers may proceed on the basis of implied external migration competences. In accordance with the general rules governing external relations, such implied external competences may be exclusive whenever the EU has adopted internal legislation (ie visa facilitation agreements affecting the EU's visa regime) or shared when no internal policy would be directly affected by international cooperation (ie support for border control in third states).[87]

On the basis of its express and implied competences the EU may pursue cooperation projects concerning most aspects of the migratory cycle—from border controls and visa issues to refugee protection, legal migration and return. The EU's capacity to act is, however, compromised by the reluctance on the side of the Member States to facilitate decision-making at EU level. This reticence concerns both political objections during the legislative process[88] and Article 79(5) TFEU, which reserves the right to regulate labour migration by quantitative means to the Member States.[89] As a result, the EU institutions lack the legal muscle and political clout to commit themselves on labour migration vis-à-vis third states. This conclusion is not trivial. On the contrary: the experience of mobility partnerships illustrates that the absence of meaningful offers on (low-skilled) labour migration to Europe explains their limited impact.[90] If cooperative migration governance is meant to succeed, the EU must be willing to make concessions on labour migration.[91] Legal and political restraints of the EU's negotiating position compromise prospects of success.

[86] Such as Regional Protection Programmes supporting African states to protect refugees irrespective of whether these activities influence asylum flows to Europe (alternatively, Arts 208–209 TFEU on development may serve as a legal basis); for further reflection on competences, including the controversial project to establish off-shore 'reception centres' for asylum seekers, see D Thym, in E Grabitz, M Hilf and M Nettesheim (eds), *Das Recht der EU* (looseleaf, 42nd edn, CH Beck, 2010); Art 78 TFEU, paras 45–47.

[87] In cases of *shared* competences the political institutions must decide whether the EU should act or leave the matter to the Member States; *exclusive* competences may only be exercised by the EU in line with Art 3(2) TFEU codifying ECJ case-law; cf P Eeckhout, *External Relations of the European Union* (2nd edn, OUP, 2011) ch 3.

[88] For labour migration see B Ryan, 'The European Union and Labour Migration' in H Toner, E Guild and A Baldaccini, n 65, 489, 496–503; when harmonization measures leave the Member States much discretion, the exclusivity of implied external competences is less advanced.

[89] The exact meaning of the provision is subject to debate (see Thym, n 86; Art 79 TFEU, paras 43–5), but it does in any case bolster political unwillingness on the side of the Member States to cede too much power in the field of economic migration.

[90] See P Devisscher, n 77, 55–57 and S Lavenex and R Nellen-Stucky, 'Partnering for Migration in EU External Relations' in R Kunz, S Lavenex and M Panizzon, n 6, 116, 136–137.

[91] cf on the position of African countries T Van Criekinge, n 85, 181–183.

Not surprisingly there is a noticeable parallelism between successful cooperation and the scope of the EU's external powers. Where the EU has express external competences (eg on readmission and visa facilitation), cooperation is more successful than in areas of fragile legal bases which fail to deliver substantial outputs (eg on legal migration). It may therefore be tempting for EU institutions to expand their sway by interpreting existing legal bases generously. The Common Commercial Policy (CCP) and development cooperation may in particular be used to advance the migration governance agenda.[92] But we should be careful not to overstate the potential of these rules. First, development policy cannot be used to harmonize rules on legal migration to the European Union.[93] Second, trade agreements may cover services, including GATS-style Mode 4 presence of natural persons abroad, but the EU lacks the capacity to implement these rules without Member State support.[94] Labour migration *senso stricto* is also not covered by CCP.[95] If the European Union wants to offer new routes for legal migration, Member State participation remains the only option.

b) Preference for soft law instruments

Mobility partnerships do not establish legal obligations enshrined in international treaties, but provide a non-binding framework for political cooperation.[96] Even if association agreements include migration-related provisions, they usually remain rather vague. They are legally binding but limit themselves to general obligations to cooperate—as the example of the (revised) Cotonou Convention on relations with 77 ACP states illustrates. Article 13 of the Convention calls for an 'in-depth dialogue' on migration and lays down a number of policy objectives, but falls short of hard legal obligations. In a similar vein, the Declaration on Migration adopted on the occasion of the 2010 revision emphasizes the commitment to 'strengthen and deepen their dialogue' in the field of legal migration without, however, subscribing to specific obligations.[97] This prevalence of informality has been criticized as a deliberate strategy by interior ministries to circumvent control mechanism at national and supranational level.[98] But a broader perspective invites a different conclusion.

During the past decade it has become a common feature of EU foreign policy that political forums for continued dialogue precede tangible outcomes, including international treaties. The Eastern Partnership and the Union for the Mediterranean are two prominent examples. Against this background, the prevailing informality of migration governance projects does not necessarily reflect the specific position of interior ministries, but mirrors and reinforces a wider trend towards soft law instruments in EU external relations.[99] This approach can have tangible benefits: soft law instruments facilitate ongoing negotiations, learning processes and trust-building, thereby paving the way for hard legal obligations.[100] Such success is certainly

[92] Whenever two or more legal bases cover one policy initiative, the substance and aim of the policy concerned designate the appropriate legal basis; cf ECJ, Opinion 2/00, *Cartagena Protocol* [2001] ECR I-9713, para 22.

[93] Art 209 TFEU may be used to support migration-related projects *in* third states, but migration *to* the EU is subject to Art 79 TFEU as *lex specialis*.

[94] See Art 207(6) TFEU; B Martenczuk, 'Visa Policy and EU External Relations' in B Martenczuk and S van Thiel (eds), *Justice, Liberty, Security: New Challenges for EU External Relations* (VUB Press, 2008) 21, 48–49 and the contribution by M Cremona to this volume.

[95] Trade in services (Art 207 TFEU) does not cover transnational migrant workers who aim to find new employment within the EU single market.

[96] See s 3.1.

[97] For references see n 41.

[98] See S Lavenex, 'Shifting Up and Out' (2006) 29 *West European Politics* 329, 331–338.

[99] See B Van Vooren, *EU External Relations Law and the European Neighbourhood Policy* (Routledge, 2011), ch 5 and M Cremona, 'The European Neighbourhood Policy: More than a Partnership?' in M Cremona (ed), *Developments in EU External Relations Law* (OUP, 2008) 244, 275–277.

[100] cf M Koskenniemi, *From Apology to Utopia* (2nd edn, CUP, 2005); specifically for migration see S Lavenex and R Nellen-Stucky, n 90, 135; and for trust-building R Hansen, 'Making Cooperation Work' in R Hansen *et al*, n 6, 14, 18–19.

no foregone conclusion, but it may work in the field of international migration governance like in other policy fields.

In so far as migration is concerned, the prevailing informality serves another purpose. As mentioned at the outset, migration policy is characterized by a widespread implementation deficit, when actual migration patterns deviate from legal–normative rules. Illegal migration and the practice of visa over-staying illustrate the compliance/enforcement deficit in cases of third country nationals who do not have a (human) right to enter or stay in the EU.[101] Contemporary migration illuminates the regulatory limits of historically constructed nation states.[102] Informal cooperation, including practical projects to improve migration control and refugee protection capacities, allow the EU, its Member States and partner countries to improve their migration management capacities and support regulatory impact. Once these capacities have been improved, they may provide the starting point for hard legal commitments to which states will not subscribe without a certain degree of compliance. Cooperation without impact is gesture politics.

c) Human rights accountability

From the perspective of the EU Treaty it is evident that external migration policy must respect human rights (section 2.3)—and it seems that the ECJ positions itself to enforce this obligation. References to the Charter of Fundamental Rights and the Geneva Convention feature prominently in recent judgments.[103] Moreover, the European Court of Human Rights (ECtHR) in Strasbourg has always served as a safety net reminding the High Contracting Parties of their obligations under the European Convention for the Protection of Human Rights and Fundamental Freedoms also in situations of external migration management, such as Italy's cooperation with Libya or diplomatic assurances for humane treatment of returnees.[104] In a similar vein, the ECJ has made clear that it will mandate compliance if the Member States violate EU human rights guarantees when implementing EU rules.[105] When EU projects violate human rights, both the ECJ and/or the ECtHR stand ready to intervene. Moreover, the EU legislator feels committed to uphold the EU's human rights culture. After years of criticism against border control practices in the Mediterranean, the 2011 amendment to the Frontex Regulation makes a noticeable effort to ensure practical respect for legal commitments through training courses for border guards, the elaboration of a human rights codex and a compliance strategy.[106]

Human rights do not stop at the EU's external borders. In its external relations the EU has always presented itself as a normative power which promotes the export of human rights.[107] Against this background, it does not come as a surprise that the EU requests partners to respect migrant and refugee rights, for instance by ratifying and implementing the Geneva Convention as an expression of 'good governance' within the framework of the European Neighbourhood Policy[108] or by supporting a Regional Protection Programme for refugees in

[101] cf the references in nn 23–25.

[102] See S Sassen, *Losing Control?* (Columbia University Press, 1996) ch 3.

[103] For asylum see ECJ, Joined Cases C-175/08 *et al*, *Abdulla* [2010] ECR I-1493, para 53 and for immigration ECJ, Case C-540/03, *Parliament v Council* [2006] ECR I-5769, paras 35–39, 104–107.

[104] For diplomatic assurances see ECtHR judgment of 28 February 2008 (GC) *Saadi v Italy* (Application No 37201/06), paras 132–148 and for cooperation with Libya the judgment of 23 February 2012 (GC), *Hirsi Jamaa et al v Italy* (Application No 27765/09).

[105] See on family reunification ECJ, Case C-578/08, *Chakroun* [2010] ECR I-1839, paras 43–44 and for asylum ECJ, Joint Cases C-411/10 and C-493/10, judgment of 21 December 2011, *NS et. al.*

[106] See Arts 1(2)(2), 2(1a), 2a, 26a of the revised 2001 'Frontex' Reg, n 63.

[107] See, generally, Art 21(1) TEU and, for a critical assessment, A Williams, *EU Human Rights Policies: A Study in Irony* (OUP, 2005).

[108] See Commission Communication, COM (2010) 207 of 12 May 2010, 2–3.

the Great Lakes Region.[109] These projects need not be window-dressing. It should be noted that the EU has a track record in setting up functioning refugee protection systems and equitable migration laws in Southern and Eastern Europe. Countries whose citizens were applying for asylum 20 years ago, are nowadays destination countries for refugees from outside Europe.[110] Such expansion of migrant and refugee rights can only be welcome. The international community should strive for universal acceptance of its values.

One would, therefore, expect widespread acclaim for the EU's quest for universal human rights compliance. But pro-migrant non-governmental organizations (NGOs) tend to differ. They point the finger at a hidden agenda in which some EU actors (in particular national governments) support changes in third states as a means to shift responsibilities onto these states.[111] The underlying rationale is simple: without functioning refugee protection systems third states will not be recognized as 'safe' countries of origin or transit to which third country nationals can be returned without violating *non-refoulement* obligations.[112] In the field of migration, some human rights NGOs therefore have the unlikely impact of not supporting international cooperation for fear of human rights violations.

4.2. Conflicting policy imperatives

The constraints of international migration governance reflect conflicting political visions. At the international level, different actors approach migratory issues from either a security/control, development/humanitarian or trade/economic perspective. Similarly, domestic debates are embroiled in disputes about whether to approach migration from an angle of fairness, legitimacy, security or social welfare (including the labour market).[113] These countervailing and sometimes contradictory imperatives explain why policy debates about migration expose deep-rooted sensitivities and are protracted. When it comes to the design of international migration governance, the overlap of fundamental interests cannot be reconciled without trade-offs and compromises which complicate and sometimes paralyse discussions. The technical language of 'migration management', the invocation of normative (human rights) standards or praise for 'partnership', and 'triple-win situations'[114] cannot disguise the political character of many decisions.[115] Two examples illustrate why conflicting imperatives matter:

First, reticence on the side of the Member States to cede more powers to Brussels to decide upon quantitative aspects of low-skilled labour migration (section 4.1.a) reflects national political sensitivities about the impact of labour migration on the welfare state and, more generally, the societal and cultural dimension of migration.[116] That is no vindication for reticence on the side of the Member States, but explains why the structure of domestic political debates complicates international migration governance. Political science shows

[109] For an overview of Regional Protection Programmes and related projects see Millet-Devalle, n 7, 99–117.

[110] See R Byrne, G Noll and J Vedsted-Hansen (eds), *New Asylum Countries?* (Kluwer, 2002) and A Geddes, *The Politics of Migration and Immigration in Europe* (Sage, 2003), chs 7 and 8.

[111] cf the contributions to S Lavenex and E Uçarer (eds), *Migration and the Externalities of European Integration* (Lexington Books, 2002).

[112] Both Art 3 of the Human Rights Convention and Art 33 of the Geneva Convention mandate that foreigners may not be sent back to 'unsafe' countries; it should be noted that Art 3 of the Human Rights Convention applies to all third-country nationals, including those who do not qualify for refugee status.

[113] See C Boswell, 'Theorizing migration policy' (2007) 41 IM Rev 75, 87–95.

[114] In terms of benefits for migrants, receiving and sending states.

[115] International actors and NGOs tend to portray their activities in technical and/or normative language; see M Geiger and A Pécoud, 'The Politics of International Migration Management' in M Geiger and A Pécoud (eds), *The Politics of International Migration Management* (Palgrave Macmillan, 2010) 1, 12 and R Kunz and others, 'Introduction' in n 6, 1, 18–19.

[116] See J Hollifield, 'Migration and the "New" International Order', in B Ghosh (ed), *Managing Migration* (OUP, 2000) 75, 92–94 and Boswell, n 113.

that domestic coalitions supporting new routes for legal migration are difficult to sustain.[117] Political, cultural and ideological arguments stand in the way of effective international migration governance.

Second, external migration policy spans across policy fields which have traditionally been assigned to different actors, both within EU institutions and at national level. These actors pursue different objectives. That is most evident when you contrast the position of national governments sitting in the Council with the similarly diverse positions of different Directorates General of the Commission.[118] To date these different positions have not been consolidated into a truly 'global approach'. The paradigmatic juxtaposition of human rights and migration control, discussed above, illustrates the practical relevance of contradictory approaches. Such absence of clear policy concepts is particularly troubling for supranational EU institutions which often justify their initiatives in output-oriented terms of expert knowledge.[119] Without consensus about policy priorities, vested interests tend to obfuscate international migration governance initiatives.

4.3. Give-and-take in the mutual interest

The experience of mobility partnerships shows that the EU has so far failed to stretch cooperative migration governance beyond the narrow field of readmission and visa facilitations agreements. In particular, new routes for low-skilled labour migration have not been established (section 3). This indicates that a very basic precondition for international cooperation is absent: mutually beneficial trade-offs which benefit both the EU and partner countries. Political science shows that states rarely engage in cooperation without the promise of mutual benefits.[120] In international migration reciprocal give-and-take has hitherto not been established. Control measures disproportionately benefit rich European states, while poorer states of transit and origin will not actively support this agenda without counter-offer. What is attractive for Europe need not be advantageous for its neighbours. Four final considerations illustrate reasons why mutually beneficial migration governance has been difficult to achieve.

First, the pursuit of reciprocal give-and-take does not negate power asymmetries. Of course, the EU has greater political, economic and financial clout than many partners, especially in Africa. But such power asymmetries do, generally speaking, not hamper reciprocal trade-offs. The outcome may not be 'fair' but does still present a realistic compromise.[121] But the EU has so far not regularly engaged in real negotiations seeking cooperative settlements, in particular by blocking any request for legal migration.[122] If mobility partnerships are to succeed, reciprocal trade-offs based on real negotiations in the shadow of power asymmetries are necessary.

Second, readmission and visa facilitation remain the only examples where genuine give-and-take has been established (and explain why cooperation works reasonably well in these fields). In other respects, the promise of 'partnership' has not been realized. When considering future projects, more attention should be paid to incentives. These may concern migration (eg labour migration, remittances, capacity building, financial assistance) or wider compromise packages, in particular within the context of association agreements (eg with regard to trade or development).[123]

[117] See G Lahav, *Immigration and Politics in the New Europe* (CUP, 2004) 204–211 and 221–225 and G Menz, *The Political Economy of Managed Migration* (OUP, 2011) 261–264.

[118] See P Devisscher, n 77, 57–64 and T Van Criekinge, n 85, 180–192.

[119] cf C Boswell, *The Political Uses of Expert Knowledge* (CUP, 2009).

[120] For migration see R Hansen, n 100, 17–20.

[121] For general considerations see R Hansen, n 100, 17–18.

[122] See s 3.3 and S Lavenex and R Nellen-Stucky, n 90, 129–130.

[123] See Commission Communication, n 59, 3–8 as well as R Hansen *et al*, 'Introduction' in R Hansen *et al*, n 6, 1, 10–11.

Third, the EU has deliberately opted for bilateral mobility partnerships. Negotiating with third countries directly increases its leverage, especially in comparison to multilateral negotiations, but is also diminishes the role of the partner country.[124] Their position tends to be sidelined; they sign up to outcomes for which they lack commitment, reflecting wider problems to design a functioning neighbourhood policy without the incentive of enlargement.[125] With its preference for bilateralism, the EU joins the US and other receiving states, which flatly reject multilateral migration initiatives.[126] Migration does not live up to the EU's self-imposed objective of enhancing multinational cooperation.

Fourth, migration may be a global phenomenon but its legal underpinning remains bilateral or regional. This outcome does not reflect power asymmetries only: migration patterns are much less inter-related than international environmental or trade policies; reciprocal give-and-take is difficult to organize in a multilateral setting without country-specific solutions.[127] Migration to and from Indonesia or Central America is largely irrelevant for Europe, but not for Australia and the US. Arguably, these differentiated migration patterns in the real world are a rational explanation for the dominance of bilateral and regional negotiations.

5. Conclusion

EU primary law and official strategy papers support international migration governance reflecting the EU's domestic experience. The success of Europe's quest for cooperative migration management would be a remarkable achievement. Migration would—as the 'human dimension' of globalization—eventually be subject to international norms and institutions, thereby spearheading global governance into a new domain. Closer inspection, however, supports a cautious conclusion. With its quest for cooperative migration governance, the EU pursues two countervailing policy objectives. Cooperation is meant to enhance state control of cross-border movements. This favours restrictionist policies, while the EU's commitment to international human rights and refugee law points in a different direction. If international migration governance is to succeed, these countervailing imperatives need to be balanced.

Reconciliation of migration management and human rights is not the only precondition for successful cooperation. International migration governance with third states requires reciprocal give-and-take which motivates the EU and its partners to engage in cooperative projects and support their implementation. Without meaningful compromises and real-life impact on cross-border movements, migration governance initiatives will remain dead projects. Indeed, the trials and errors of existing projects present us with mixed results. Readmission and visa facilitation agreements with selected third states are the only examples of successful collaboration. By contrast, the much touted 'mobility partnerships' have largely failed. In particular, they have not led to new routes for legal migration of (low-skilled) migrant workers which are a core demand of many countries of origin and transit with which the EU seeks to cooperate. Mobility partnerships have resulted in some capacity building, but not much more.

This modest conclusion need not be the final outcome. EU institutions have often shown their stamina not to be frustrated by initial setbacks. Thus, the informal policy framework of mobility partnerships may gradually lead to more meaningful cooperation, possible even

[124] For the EU see R Kunz, n 115, 17.

[125] S Lavenex and R Nellen-Stucky, n 90, 125–126 emphasize the interaction between mobility partnerships and the wider European Neighbourhood Policy context.

[126] Such as the 1990 UN Migrant Worker Convention or the UN Dialogue on Migration; cf A Betts, n 8, 8–9 and R Hansen, n 100, 20–21.

[127] See J Hollifield, n 116, 101.

within plurilateral settings, when all actors involved learn from failures and build trust. Such a gradual approach towards international migration governance may work, even if it is hindered by structural impediments. Legal, conceptual and political obstacles complicate cooperation. When it comes to legal migration, the Member States cautiously guard their prerogatives in order to control the societal and economic impacts of (labour) migration. Furthermore, any migration policy requires political decisions about trade-off between countervailing interests both domestically and in inter-state relations, which rhetorical invocations of 'partnership' cannot conceal. Cooperation is not necessarily in everyone's interest. In short: the EU aspires towards international migration governance, but existing projects have so far yielded limited results.

19

Economic Partnership Agreements: Enhancing the Labour Dimension of Global Governance?

*Jeff Kenner**

1. Introduction

Labour rights tend to rise to prominence on the global governance agenda in the wake of international crises. In 1919, the International Labour Organization (ILO) was established as an anxious response to the Bolshevik Revolution, offering a reformist route to social justice and belated recognition that the industrial revolution, or 'first globalization',[1] had spawned a vast global marketplace in which, all too often, labour was a mere commodity or factor of production.[2] The 1944 Philadelphia Declaration anticipated the principles of human dignity and equality in the UN Charter and, in proclaiming that 'poverty anywhere is a threat to prosperity everywhere', signified a shift away from non-interventionist economic policies that had led to the Great Depression.[3]

Fast forward to 2008, the collapse of the iconic and seemingly invincible Lehman Brothers symbolized the negative consequences of an extended period of inadequately regulated financial risk-taking by those who had come to regard themselves as the 'masters of the universe'.[4] The global financial crisis, which has hit the poorest countries the hardest,[5] has shaken complacent assumptions about the unalloyed benefits of the unholy trilogy of market liberalization, deregulation and privatization,[6] and coincided with fresh demands for 'fair globalization' that gives due weight to its neglected social dimension.[7] The EU, as the 'world's biggest trader' and 'foremost donor of development aid',[8] faces the challenge of living up to its commitment 'to shoulder its responsibilities in the governance of globalization' by playing the role of 'a power... seeking to set globalization within a moral framework, in other words to anchor it in solidarity and sustainable development'.[9]

This chapter assesses the EU's capacity to 'shape' globalization[10] by recalibrating the economic and social dimensions of global governance in a fashion that respects the needs of

* This chapter is based on research concluded during a period of research leave funded by the UK Arts and Humanities Research Council.

[1] F Maupain, 'New Foundation or New Facade? The ILO and the 2008 Declaration on Social Justice for a Fair Globalization' (2009) 20 EJIL 823, 825.

[2] See H Collins, *Employment Law* (OUP, 2003) 3–5.

[3] Annex of the ILO Constitution: <http://www.ilo.org/ilolex/english/constq.htm> accessed 27 August 2011.

[4] T Wolfe, *Bonfire of the Vanities* (Farrar, Straus, Giroux, 1987) and 'Greenwich Time', *New York Times*, 27 September 2008: <http://www.nytimes.com/2008/09/28/opinion/28wolfe.html> accessed 27 August 2011.

[5] The World Bank, 'Global Monitoring Report 2010—The MDGs after the crisis': <http://web.worldbank.org> accessed 16 January 2012.

[6] J Williamson, 'What Washington Means by Policy Reform' in J Williamson (ed), *Latin American Readjustment: How Much Has Happened?* (International Institute for International Economics, 1989).

[7] 'Declaration on Social Justice for a Fair Globalization' (ILO, 2008): <http://www.ilo.org/public/english/bureau/leg/declarations.htm> accessed 27 August 2011.

[8] In 2007 the EU accounted for 20% of global imports and exports and 55% of humanitarian aid (including the contributions of its Member States): Commission, *The European Union in the World*: <http://www.delago.ec.europa.eu/ao/ue_global/en.pdf> accessed 27 August 2011.

[9] 'The Laeken Declaration', Presidency Conclusions of the European Council, Annex I, 14–15 December 2001: <http://ec.europa.eu/governance/impact/background/docs/laeken_concl_en.pdf> accessed 27 August 2011.

[10] 'EU Declaration on Globalization', Presidency Conclusions of the European Council, 14 December 2007: <http://www.consilium.europa.eu/uedocs/cms_Data/docs/pressdata/en/ec/97669.pdf> accessed 27 August 2011.

people in developing countries undergoing rapid transition. Three main propositions are developed. First, promotion of the ILO's interlinked human rights and sustainable development initiatives, its Core Labour Standards (CLS)[11] and Decent Work Agenda (DWA),[12] can underpin this objective in conjunction with the UN Global Compact (UNGC)[13] and the Organization for Economic Cooperation and Development (OECD) Guidelines on Multinational Enterprises.[14] Secondly, the EU can play a pivotal role in enhancing the *labour* dimension of globalization by acting as an ally of the ILO on the global stage. The EU is uniquely equipped to facilitate the implementation of ILO policies in a fashion that is consistent with its duty to promote its own 'values',[15] including equality and human rights, through its external actions. Unilateral measures, such as the Generalized System of Preferences (GSP),[16] and bilateral agreements are useful tools, but of particular importance, is the strengthening of multilateral partnerships and deepening regional integration under the EU's longstanding relationship with the African, Caribbean and Pacific (ACP) group of countries,[17] now under the Cotonou Partnership Agreement (CPA),[18] which is regarded as a model approach to governance and development.[19] Thirdly, Economic Partnership Agreements (EPAs), adopted within the CPA framework, are among the most sophisticated regional trade and development instruments and have the potential to contribute to policy coherence and good governance by reconciling trade and labour rights with sustainable development objectives.[20] The EU–CARIFORUM EPA,[21] the first EPA with Caribbean ACP countries, is explored as a potential model for this approach.

2. Strategies for Strengthening Global Social Governance

2.1. Core Labour Standards—transcending the trade versus labour debate

From the early 19th century there has been a recurring debate about the extent to which emergent industrialized nations should have the freedom to introduce and maintain protective and life-enhancing measures for the benefit of their own citizens without being undercut by foreign competitors capable of producing goods and providing services at lower cost with little or no regulation, or what has become known as preventing 'social dumping'.[22] The need to address deregulatory pressures leading to a downward spiral of

[11] 'Declaration on Fundamental Principles and Rights at Work' (ILO, 1998): <http://www.ilo.org/public/english/bureau/leg/declarations.htm> accessed 27 August 2011.

[12] 'Decent Work' (ILO, 1999): <http://www.ilo.org/global/about-the-ilo/decent-work-agenda/lang--en/index.htm> accessed 27 August 2011.

[13] Launched in 2000 as a strategic initiative for businesses to sign up to human rights, including the CLS: <http://www.unglobalcompact.org/> accessed 27 August 2011.

[14] Launched in 1976 and most recently updated in 2011: <www.oecd.org> accessed 8 August 2011. J Murray, 'A New Phase in the Regulation of Multinational Enterprises: The Role of the OECD' (2001) 30 ILJ 255.

[15] Treaty on European Union (TEU), Arts 2(3) and 3(5).

[16] See <http://ec.europa.eu/trade/wider-agenda/development/generalised-system-of-preferences/> accessed 13 April 2012.

[17] The ACP was established under the Georgetown Agreement, 6 June 1975, 1247 UNTS 148. The ACP comprises 79 countries: 48 from Sub-Saharan Africa, 16 from the Caribbean and 15 from the Pacific: <http://www.acp.int/content/secretariat-acp> accessed 16 May 2012.

[18] 2000/483/EC [2000] OJ L317/3 as rectified [2004] OJ L385/88. The CPA has been revised twice: [2006] L209/26 (entered into force 1 July 2008); [2010] L287/3 (applicable on a provisional basis from 1 November 2010).

[19] Commission, *Governance and development* (Communication) COM (2003) 615 final of 20 October, intro, para 5.

[20] Commission, *Policy Coherence for Development—Establishing the policy framework for a whole-of-the-Union approach* (Communication) COM (2009) 458 final of 15 September.

[21] [2008] OJ L289/3, signed on 15 October 2008. CARIFORUM represents the Caribbean ACP states.

[22] B Hepple, *Labour Laws and Global Trade* (Hart Publishing, 2005); S Charnovitz, *Trade Law and Global Governance* (Cameron May, 2002) 211–232; C McCrudden and A Davies, 'A Perspective on Trade and Labour Rights' [2000] JIEL 43; C Barry and SG Reddy, *International Trade and Labor Standards: A Proposal for Linkage* (Columbia University Press, 2008).

labour standards provided the rationale for establishing the ILO but progress towards a formal trade–labour linkage foundered at the onset of the Cold War.[23]

Against this backdrop, one of the earliest challenges for the Community was to determine the optimum method of achieving 'closer integration' within a regional free trade area, permitted as an exception under the General Agreement on Tariffs and Trade (GATT),[24] whilst offering the peoples of Europe an improvement in living and working conditions.[25] The problem was avoided on the basis that the Member States were deemed to be adhering to ILO standards and, it was assumed, the common market would lead to social progress and was unlikely to hamper improvement of living standards.[26] In practice the Community had little room for manoeuvre and, while it gradually introduced a modicum of minimum standards to provide a 'social dimension' of the internal market, it remained circumspect when acting externally because, so long as labour standards were not recognized as a trade issue, it wished to avoid the taint of protectionism.

In the early 1990s, as the curtain came down on the Cold War, a new age of globalization dawned with economic liberalization ascendant. The sheer pace of market liberalization, together with rapid and diffuse technological innovation and increased volume and diversification of trade, services, and migration flows, concentrated the minds of participants in the Uruguay round of trade negotiations. Several industrialized countries, including the US, mooted the idea of a 'social clause' in the WTO Agreement to pre-empt a further widening of the social deficit in global governance. The Commission sided with this group, but was wary of any mechanism that would 'impose' on developing countries the 'higher wage levels and better working conditions which pertain in the industrialized world'.[27] Moreover, the Commission was not prepared to support action 'designed to erect new barriers to trade under cover of a social agenda'.[28] Such defensiveness highlighted the problem of perception arising from linking market access directly with labour standards. Many developing countries regarded the 'social clause' as a device to undermine their 'comparative advantage' in world trade arising from lower labour costs, especially wages, that are variable according to each country's stage of development. Indeed it was feared that such a clause might have the perverse effect of forcing some countries to lower labour standards to compete with each other for foreign investment in a 'race to the bottom'.[29]

Ultimately, attempts to make market access contingent upon adherence to ILO standards, leading potentially to trade sanctions, were destined to fail. The WTO ministerial meeting at Seattle, in 1999, became a theatre of protest for and against globalization and neo-liberalism, North versus South, and so on, at the expense of rational debate about a coherent transnational approach to advancing labour rights for their own sake.[30] Despite the immediate disappointment of advocates for a trade–labour linkage, this apparent defeat ultimately had beneficial effects by acting, first, as a spur to reforming ILO governance,[31] secondly, as a catalyst for forging closer EU–ILO relations and, thirdly, in necessitating a decoupling of

[23] See the Havana Charter for an International Trade Organization, 24 March 1948, UN Doc E/Conf 2/78, Art 7 (not in force).

[24] GATT, Art XXIV.

[25] EEC Treaty, Art 117 (now Treaty on the Functioning of the European Union (TFEU), Art 151).

[26] The 'Ohlin Report' on 'Social Aspects of European Integration' (1956) 74 Intl Lab Rev 99. See J Kenner, *EU Employment Law* (Hart Publishing, 2003) 2–5.

[27] Commission, *The Trading System and Internationally Recognized Labour Standards* (Communication) COM (96) 402 final/2 of 4 September, 3.

[28] Ibid.

[29] The 'comparative advantage' theory relates to lower labour standards that prevailed during the development of what are now 'developed' countries. It follows that to impose today's European labour standards on developing countries would put the latter at a competitive disadvantage and slow down development. See McCrudden and Davies, n 22, 49.

[30] BA Langille, 'Seeking Post-Seattle Clarity—and Inspiration' in J Conaghan, RM Fischl and K Klare (eds), *Labour Law in an Era of Globalization* (OUP, 2002).

[31] Maupain, n 1, 828.

trade and labour issues by repackaging 'core' labour standards as fundamental rights to fit with the emerging global human rights agenda.

Once global players accept that guaranteeing an agreed set of fundamental labour rights is an obligation not only for states but also for international organizations and socially responsible multinational corporations, it is possible to implement a positive rights-based approach transcending the sterile trade versus labour standards debate. Moreover, advancing fundamental labour rights is interconnected with strategies for promoting sustainable development and combating poverty, such as the UN Millennium Development Goals (MDGs).

In the late 1990s the ILO sought to revitalize itself from its somewhat moribund role as a specialized standard-setter, with monitoring and enforcement functions only over ratified conventions. States could pick and choose those conventions they wished to ratify 'cafeteria-style'.[32] Increasingly marginalized from the centre stage of global governance, there was a need for realignment to make the organization relevant to the emergent agenda of fundamental rights' promotion and sustainable development.

The 1998 ILO Declaration on Fundamental Rights and Principles at Work is at once pragmatic, in focusing on an irreducible 'core' of labour standards that can be regarded as providing efficient outcomes in world markets,[33] and visionary, in repackaging a grouping of established labour standards as 'fundamental rights' to be respected unconditionally under international law. The advantage of this method is that mere labour standards are mainstreamed into international human rights norms. The impact of mainstreaming the CLS as a technique of global governance has been threefold. First, the Declaration requires the CLS to be promoted by all ILO Member States as a condition of membership, irrespective of whether or not states have ratified the specified conventions.[34] The ILO set a target of 2015 for universal ratification of these conventions and significant progress has been made in this direction. Second, the CLS are a yardstick for measuring the social responsibility of multinationals under the UNGC and the OECD Guidelines.[35] Third, the EU, as a regional entity with a 'global vocation' to promote human rights,[36] now had an imperative to mainstream the CLS—both importing and exporting them—using the full set of its governance tools.[37]

The choice of CLS conventions required a number of compromises. The selected conventions were designed to balance 'social progress and economic growth'.[38] Conventions concerning working hours, night work, and unemployment were not included because they might be regarded, if raised to the level of human rights norms, as a threat to economic competitiveness.[39] The CLS are narrower in scope than the labour rights in the EU's Charter

[32] F Maupain, 'Revitalization Not Retreat: the Real Potential of the 1998 ILO Declaration for the Universal Protection of Workers' Rights' (2005) 16 EJIL 439, 448.

[33] See 'Trade, Employment and Labour Standards: A Study of Core Workers' Rights and International Trade' (OECD, 1996).

[34] The CLS, n 11 comprise four fundamental principles and rights at work to be observed by all ILO member countries, namely: (1) freedom of association and the effective recognition of the right to collective bargaining (87 and 98); (2) the elimination of all forms of forced or compulsory labour (29 and 195); (3) minimum age in employment and elimination of the worst forms of child labour (138 and 182); and (4) the elimination of discrimination in respect of employment (100 and 111).

[35] See nn 13–14. 6000+ businesses in 135 countries are participants in the UNGC. The labour principles are drawn directly from the CLS: <http://www.unglobalcompact.org/AboutTheGC/TheTenPrinciples/labour.html> accessed 8 October 2011.

[36] M Cremona, 'Rhetoric or Reticence: EU External Commercial Policy in a Multilateral Context' (2001) 38 *CML Rev* 359, 359.

[37] TEU, Art 21. See T Novitz, 'In search of a coherent social policy: EU import and export of ILO labour standards?' in J Orbie and L Tortell (eds), *The European Union and the Social Dimension of Globalization* (Routledge, 2009).

[38] Preamble of the ILO Declaration, n 11.

[39] Hepple, n 22, 59.

of Fundamental Rights (CFR).[40] Moreover, as McCrudden and Davies note, none of the conventions directly concern the level of wages as part of a 'clear attempt to lessen the accusation of protectionism and the erosion of comparative advantage'.[41] What remains is a selection of conventions that, from a classical labour law perspective, is incomplete, and yet there is an underlying logic to choosing those labour standards that command the widest consensus and avoid conflict with the prevailing drive for trade liberalization.[42]

Predictably, the adoption of the CLS led to a polarized debate between supporters, such as Langille,[43] who regard them as reinforcing the non-core conventions as part of a coherent framework,[44] and critics, notably Alston, who are concerned about excessive reliance on 'principles' that are 'delinked from corresponding standards and thus effectively undefined'.[45] According to Alston, the concentration on the CLS produces major flaws including 'an ethos of voluntarism in relation to implementation and enforcement, an unstructured and unacceptable decentralization of responsibility, and a willingness to accept soft "promotionalism" as the bottom line'.[46]

In response to this debate it is important to note that although the Declaration promotes rather than sets standards, inverting the ILO tradition, its aim is the bigger prize of triggering broad adherence to, and enforcement of, the specified conventions by building alliances with global institutions and regional powers. The most distinguishing characteristic of the CLS is that they have come to be regarded, through a process of meta-institutional iteration, as an élite set of higher human rights norms to be applied under international law irrespective of the traditional method of ratification or an individual country's level of development.

Whilst a close association between labour standards and human rights is hardly novel,[47] the adoption of the CLS has revived the notion that labour rights are capable of having a transformative emancipating effect on the lives of individuals and therefore should be promoted centre stage as freestanding universal and indivisible human rights. The umbilical linkage between trade and labour standards is excised in the process. In turn, the EU has been presented with both an opportunity and a challenge to promote the implementation of the CLS through its external actions rather than to seek to impose its economic and social model on other countries.[48] Harnessing globalization to serve social and economic goals, in a balanced fashion, can thus be presented as a mission for utilizing governance tools to advance fairness not protectionism.

2.2. Decent work for all—an essential component of sustainable development

The ILO's DWA was launched as a corollary of the CLS in 1999. Decent work equates to a basic aspiration to offer *all* men and women access to decent and productive work 'in conditions of freedom, equality, security and human dignity'.[49] It recognizes that while the CLS are important for those in employment, there is an urgent need to address the fact that one-third of the working age population worldwide are unemployed or under-employed

[40] Adopted in 2000. For the text, as adapted on entry into force of the Lisbon Treaty [2010] OJ C83/389. See P Alston, '"Core Labour Standards" and the Transformation of the International Labour Rights Regime' (2004) 15 EJIL 457, 487.

[41] McCrudden and Davies, n 22, 51–52.

[42] Ibid.

[43] BA Langille, 'Core Labour Rights—The True Story' (2005) 16 EJIL 409.

[44] Ibid.

[45] Alston, n 40, 457.

[46] Ibid.

[47] See CW Jenks, *Human Rights and International Labour Standards* (Stevens & Sons, 1960).

[48] Commission, *The Social Dimension of Globalisation—the EU's policy contribution on extending the benefits to all* (Communication) COM (2004) 383 final of 15 May, Exec Summary.

[49] See n 12.

with, in 2006, 1.3 billion people unable to earn enough to lift themselves and their family members out of poverty.[50] The DWA seeks to address 'the dual challenge of creating new productive jobs and improving the quality of existing ones'.[51]

The DWA has four strategic pillars: creating jobs; guaranteeing rights at work; extending social protection; and promoting social dialogue. Gender equality is cross-cutting.[52] The ILO aligned the DWA with needs and resource-based sustainable development objectives evolving from the Brundtland Report 1987,[53] to the World Summit on Social Development 1995[54] and now combining, interdependently, economic and social development with environmental protection.[55] Therefore, decent work was rapidly integrated into policies to promote sustainable development and eradicate poverty. Significantly, the MDGs, designed to halve 1990 poverty levels by 2015, include a commitment to 'achieving full and productive employment and decent work for all, including women and young people'.[56]

The ambition of the DWA is to offer pathways out of poverty through employment, decent remuneration and safe working conditions. For the EU it provides an opportunity to utilize governance mechanisms, such as development partnerships, to encourage job creation and improved labour conditions within a framework of CLS compliance. As the Commission explains:[57]

> 'The objective of *promoting decent work and sustainable development* is no longer to deal with the negative effects of opening up trade, but rather at supporting or boosting the endogenous development of labour standards resulting from the part played by trade in development.'

3. The EU–ILO Relationship—An Effective Institutional Alliance for Global Social Governance?

EU–ILO relations can be traced back to 1953 when a cooperation agreement was concluded between the ILO and the European Coal and Steel Community.[58] From that point the relationship was conducted mainly through polite exchanges of correspondence concerning arrangements to liaise over matters of mutual interest.[59] Following the 1956 Ohlin Report,[60] the ILO regarded the Community as being primarily concerned with economic matters. The Community was not formally recognized as an observer at the ILO until 1989, with full membership remaining the preserve of the Member States. Moreover, the Court of Justice held that the conferral of internal competence on the Community concerning certain labour standards, and the exercise of that competence, did not necessitate an implied exclusive role, on the part of the Commission, to negotiate ILO conventions in the same area because this would displace the role of Member States within the ILO's tripartite structure.[61]

50 'Key Indicators of the Labour Market' (5th edn, ILO, 2007).

51 UN ECOSOC Res 2008/18, preamble, recital 7.

52 <http://www.ilo.org/global/about-the-ilo/decent-work-agenda/lang–en/index.htm> accessed 8 October 2011.

53 Report of the UN World Commission on Environment and Development <http://www.un-documents.net/wced-ocf.htm> accessed 8 October 2011.

54 <http://www.un.org/esa/socdev/wssd/text-version/> accessed 16 May 2012.

55 Johannesburg Declaration on Sustainable Development, 2005: <http://www.un.org/esa/sustdev/documents/WSSD_POI_PD/English/POI_PD.htm> accessed 8 October 2011.

56 Target 1B <http://www.un.org/millenniumgoals/poverty.shtml> accessed 8 October 2011. See also, UN ECOSOC Min Decl, 'Full and Productive Employment and Decent Work' (2006) UN Doc GA, 61st Session, Supp No 3 (A/61/3/Rev1), ch III, para 50, and UN ECOSOC Res 2008/18, 24 July 2008.

57 Staff Working Document: *The EU's contribution to the promotion of decent work in the world* COM (2008) 412 final, Exec Summary 7.

58 [1953] OJ 11/167.

59 See A Johnson, 'EU–ILO relations: between regional and global governance' in Orbie and Tortell, n 37; J Murray, *Transnational Labour Regulation: The ILO and EC Compared* (Kluwer, 2001) 59–99.

60 See n 26.

61 Opinion 2/91 (re: ILO Convention No 170) [1993] ECR I-1061.

The launch of the CLS and DWA triggered a joint effort to renew cooperation and establish more systematic inter-institutional policy coordination.[62] The Commission committed itself to 'promoting core labour standards throughout its external relations policies and in its development cooperation' and 'collaborating' with the ILO 'at an operational level in the service of sustainable development'. Both sides now regarded each other as allies in promoting the social dimension of globalization through structured dialogue.[63] The development of closer ties can be explained by reference to a distinct shift in the EU's orientation concerning fundamental rights and development cooperation. It has spurred the establishment of a 'strategic partnership' in the field of development with the aim of enhancing the effectiveness of both partners in promoting the CLS and DWA.[64]

Turning first to fundamental rights, the Community adopted a non-binding Charter of the Fundamental Social Rights of Workers in 1989, partly sourced from ILO conventions, signifying a rights-based approach to social policy that transcended mere economic integration. The Social Charter was influential in framing EU legislation mirroring ILO conventions, such as the Working Time Directive,[65] and as a point of reference for the Court of Justice in upholding fundamental social rights.[66] Having internalized ILO conventions in this manner, the EU sought to construct a broader human rights foundation with the adoption of the CFR in 2000,[67] with a Solidarity Chapter containing workers' rights. The CFR became the reference point for the Union's internal and external actions to uphold human rights, including the CLS,[68] prior to its elevation to the 'same legal value' as the treaties at Lisbon.[69] In other respects the Lisbon Treaty reinforces the fundamental rights *acquis* by requiring the Union to promote 'respect for human rights' among its foundational 'values'[70] in 'its relations with the wider world'.[71] Article 21(1) TEU, containing the general provisions on external action, requires the Union to advance the 'universality and indivisibility' of human rights in its action on the international scene including 'respect for the principles of the United Nations Charter and international law', which implicitly includes an obligation on the EU's third country partners to ratify or otherwise put into practice the relevant CLS conventions.

Moreover, mainstreaming of human rights ensures that all internal and external EU actions must promote fundamental rights by reference to international law.[72] In order to put this into effect, fundamental rights clauses have been elaborated as an 'essential element' of international agreements. Under these clauses the parties commit themselves to respecting fundamental rights by reference to observance of international obligations. In some cases, reference is made to 'fundamental social rights' and it is now commonplace to find a clause referring to the parties' obligations under the CLS. Separate provisions allow for 'appropriate measures' to be taken in the event of violation of an 'essential element' including suspension

[62] [2001] OJ C165/23.

[63] The Commission contributed to the ILO's 'World Commission on the Social Dimension of Globalization' (2004): <http://www.ilo.org/public/english/wcsdg/index1.htm> accessed 9 January 2012. J Orbie and O Babarinde, 'The Social Dimension of Globalization and EU Development Policy: Promoting Core Labour Standards and Corporate Social Responsibility' (2008) 30 *J European Integration* 459, 473.

[64] Commission–ILO Memorandum of Understanding, 15–16 July 2004: <http://ec.europa.eu/europeaid/what/social-protection/documents/memorandum_of_understanding_ec_ilo_en.pdf> accessed 30 December 2011.

[65] European Parliament and Council Directive 2003/88/EC of 4 November 2003 concerning certain aspects of working time [2003] OJ L299/9.

[66] See Case C-173/99 *BECTU* [2001] ECR I-4881, para 43.

[67] Adapted text [2010] OJ C83/389.

[68] Commission, *Promoting Core Labour Standards and Improving Social Governance in the Context of Globalisation* (Communication) COM (2001) 416 final, point 3.

[69] TEU, Art 6(1).

[70] TEU, Art 2.

[71] TEU, Art 3(5).

[72] Commission, *The European Union's Role in Promoting Human Rights and Democratisation in Third Countries* (Communication) COM (2001) 252 final.

of agreements in whole or in part for a 'material breach' within the meaning of Article 60 of the Vienna Convention.[73] In practice, the EU favours an incentive-based approach rather than sanctions.[74]

The combined effect of the EU's commitment to upholding international human rights law, the elevation of the CFR to Treaty-level status, and the obligations that flow from the EU's impending accession to the European Convention for the Protection of Human Rights and Fundamanetal Freedoms,[75] is to inculcate the promotion of human rights considerations, including labour rights, in all aspects of EU external action.[76]

Second, the EU elevated its commitment to sustainable development to Treaty status from 1999.[77] Once the ILO launched the DWA within the framework of UN initiatives, the EU was obliged to ensure that promoting decent work was at the heart of its development agenda. Thus, decent work is an important component of the 'European Consensus on Development' (ECD), which is intended to coordinate the EU's and Member States' development policies and make them more coherent and effective.[78] The ECD promotes the principle of ownership of development strategies and programmes by partner countries.[79] Decent work is regarded as one of the multi-dimensional aspects of poverty reduction, essential for strengthening the social dimension of globalization.[80] Examples of implementation of the CLS and DWA in EU external actions include:

- the European Instrument for Democracy and Human Rights Regulation (EIDHR), which imposes an obligation on those submitting tenders for EU-funded contracts to respect the CLS;[81]
- the GSP+ special incentive arrangement for sustainable development and good governance, under which advantageous trade preferences are granted to countries who ratify ILO conventions and introduce measures to implement them.[82]

In pursuing 'good governance' in development, the EU is concerned with the ability of partner countries to serve their citizens by promoting social dialogue and implementation of ILO conventions.[83] The ILO's initiatives are integral to a governance-driven development strategy. Social policy is recognized as a productive factor that contributes to sustainable development.[84] It builds the capacity for autonomous institutions of employers and workers to be freely established and, in due course, empowers them to develop bespoke social

[73] E Fierro, 'Legal Basis and Scope of the Human Rights Clauses in EC Bilateral Agreements: Any Room for Positive Interpretation?' (2001) 7 ELJ 41.

[74] Orbie and Babarinde, n 63, 462.

[75] TEU, Art 6(2). Recent European Court of Human Rights (ECtHR) judgments have interpreted Art 11 of the European Convention, on freedom of assembly and association in light of ILO conventions 87, on freedom of association and protection of the right to organize, and 98, concerning the application of the principles of the right to organize and bargain collectively, where the state in question has ratified those conventions. On that basis the ECtHR has upheld the right of public sector workers in Turkey to bargain collectively and to strike: *Demir and Baykara v Turkey* (Application No 34503/97) 12 November 2008; *Enerji Yapi-Yol Sen v Turkey* (Application No 68959/01) 21 April 2009.

[76] See also 'Human Rights and Democracy at the heart of the EU External Action—Towards a more effective approach' COM (2011) 866 final of 8 December, Brussels.

[77] EC Treaty, Art 177. See now TEU, Art 21(2)(d) and TFEU, Art 208(1).

[78] [2006] OJ C46/1: Joint statement by the Council and the representatives of the governments of the Member States meeting within the Council, the European Parliament and the Commission.

[79] Ibid, paras 5 and 14.

[80] Ibid, paras 11, 38 and 99.

[81] European Parliament and Council Regulation (EC) 1889/2006 on establishing a financing instrument for the promotion of democracy and human rights worldwide [2006] OJ L386/1, Art 14(12).

[82] Council Regulation (EC) 732/2008 of 22 July applying a scheme of generalized tariff preferences (2009–2011) [2008] OJ L211/1, Arts 8–9. European Parliament and Council Regulation (EU) 512/2011 [2011] OJ L145/28 extends the scheme to 31 December 2013.

[83] Commission, *Governance in the European Consensus on Development: towards a harmonized approach within the European Union* (Staff Working Document accompanying the Communication) SEC (2006) 1020, 4–5.

[84] Commission Communication, *Governance and development*, n 19, para 13.

policies. It is in this context that we need to assess EPAs as a vehicle for the EU and its ACP partners to further the labour dimension of global governance.

4. Economic Partnership Agreements—A New Model for Enhancing the Labour Dimension of Global Governance?

4.1. The Cotonou Partnership Agreement—towards fundamental social rights?

In order to identify the rationale for EPAs we must first consider the broader framework of EU–ACP relations under the CPA, which replaced the Lomé accords in 2000 while preserving the *acquis*.[85] As the EU's most wide-ranging multilateral agreement, the CPA extends to all areas of EU international relations—trade, investment, development, environment, foreign policy and security—and has human rights and labour standards clauses. The EU, its Member States, and 78 ACP countries concluded a long-term agreement, 2000–2020, based on reciprocal rights and obligations, subject to revision every five years.

Economic integration of ACP countries into the world economy through regional EPAs is intended to go hand-in-hand with political integration and advancing shared development priorities. The fight against poverty is sustained by an enhanced political dimension, increased participation, a more strategic approach to cooperation, new regional and differentiated economic and trade partnerships, EPAs, and improved financial cooperation.[86] Governance is reinforced by the revisions of 2005 and 2010,[87] which incorporated the ECD and MDG targets, provided a facility for direct funding of non-state actors, placed greater emphasis on regional integration, and introduced performance indicators. DWA objectives feature among the indicators, including increasing the share of women in waged employment in the non-agricultural sectors and cutting youth unemployment rates.[88]

The CPA signalled a departure from the paternalistic 'donor and recipient' relationship that created a 'dependency paradigm',[89] which still persists.[90] It emphasizes 'equality of the partners' and 'ownership of the development strategies' among the 'fundamental principles'.[91] Although the central government is the main partner, participation is 'open to different kinds of other actors' to encourage the integration of non-state actors such as trade unions and employers' organizations. This, in turn, raises concerns about the independence and representativeness of such actors in a partnership based on democratic principles.[92] Ownership of development strategies and participation in the partnership is to be delivered by 'dialogue' and fulfilment of mutual obligations.[93]

The 'pivotal role' played by political dialogue is elaborated in Article 8 CPA, as revised. Political dialogue includes issues such as child labour and discrimination 'of any kind'.[94] Article 9 contains the 'essential elements' regarding human rights, democratic principles, and the rule of law, building on previous efforts to introduce a human rights dimension into

[85] See n 18.

[86] See: <http://ec.europa.eu/europeaid/where/acp/overview/cotonou-agreement/index_en.htm> accessed 16 January 2012.

[87] See n 18.

[88] Indicators 11 and 45 annexed to the revised CPA.

[89] G Forwood, 'The Road to Cotonou: Negotiating a Successor to Lomé' (2001) 39 JCMS 423, 426; J McMahon, 'Negotiating in a Time of Turbulent Transition: The Future of *Lomé*' (1999) 36 *CML Rev* 599, 622; O Babarinde and G Faber, 'From Lomé to Cotonou: Business as Usual?' (2004) 9 *EFA Rev* 27, 34–35. By 2000 over 90% of ACP exports were entering the EU duty and quota free and €30 billion of European Development Fund (EDF) assistance had been provided, and yet 39 of 63 UN-designated LDCs were ACP countries and 95% of the ACP population, concentrated in Africa, had experienced successive falls in income.

[90] M Carbone, 'The European Union, Good Governance and Aid Co-ordination' (2010) 31 TWQ 13.

[91] Art 2.

[92] McCrudden and Davies, n 22, 61.

[93] Art 2.

[94] Art 8(4).

ACP–EU relations.[95] Separately, in a weaker formulation, 'good governance' is defined as a mere 'fundamental element', reflecting the highly contested nature of this concept in both process and outcome.[96] Additional resources are available to countries that have demonstrated improved governance through the EU's unilateral 'governance incentive tranche' developed to promote 'aid effectiveness'.[97]

Article 9 CPA, as revised, contains several features linking development objectives and human rights to labour standards and social policies. First, development is 'centred on the human person', as the main protagonist and beneficiary of development, entailing 'respect for and promotion of all human rights'. Respect for human rights is regarded as integral to sustainable development. Second, the definition of human rights includes respect for 'fundamental social rights'. This term is not defined, although the preamble declares that the parties are 'anxious to respect basic labour rights taking account of the principles laid down in the relevant conventions of the [ILO]' and refers to UN texts from which labour rights can be drawn.[98] Article 9(2) refers to the parties' 'international obligations and commitments concerning respect for human rights', which are deemed 'universal, indivisible and inter-related'. The parties conclude that respect for human rights, thus defined, along with democratic principles and the rule of law, together 'underpin' the partnership and constitute the 'essential elements'. This phraseology is strikingly similar to the preamble of the CFR, serving to emphasize the language of rights when referring to labour standards. Third, procedures for political dialogue and suspension under the essential elements provisions have been refined.[99]

The process leading to suspension under the CPA is highly convoluted, except in 'special urgency' situations,[100] but it has been invoked against several states. Cited violations include failure to hold democratic elections but, in the case of Zimbabwe for example,[101] there has been no reference to violations of fundamental social rights or breaches of ILO conventions, despite the reporting of systematic denial of labour rights and acts of oppression.[102]

While essential elements clauses provide a broad human rights framework, the CPA also has a labour clause, Article 50, on 'trade and labour standards', sourced from the CLS. The first paragraph declares:

> 'The parties reaffirm their commitment to internationally recognized core labour standards, as defined by the relevant [ILO] Conventions, and in particular the freedom of association and the right to collective bargaining, the abolition of forced labour, the elimination of the worst forms of child labour and non-discrimination in respect of employment.'

This is followed by a rather loose commitment to 'enhance cooperation' in particular fields, including 'the formulation of national labour legislation and strengthening of existing

[95] The first attempt can be traced back to the 'Uganda Guidelines', Bull EC 6–1977.

[96] Art 9(3) defines 'good governance' as 'the transparent and accountable management of human, natural, economic and financial resources for the purposes of equitable and sustainable development'. The significance of the distinction between an 'essential element' and a 'fundamental element' lies with the fact that a breach of the latter, the 'good governance' provisions, cannot lead to suspension. See M Holland, '20/20 Vision? The EU's Cotonou Partnership Agreement' (2003) BJWA vol 9/2, 161, 165–167; W Hout, 'Governance and Development: changing EU policies' (2010) 31 TWQ 1; N Slocum-Bradley and A Bradley, 'Is the EU's Governance "Good"? An assessment of EU governance in its partnership with ACP states' (2010) 31 TWQ 31.

[97] Bradley and Bradley, ibid, 38; N Molenaers and L Nijs, 'From the Theory of Aid Effectiveness to the Practice: The European Commission Governance Incentive Tranche' (2009) 27 DPR 561. See Commission, *Supporting Democratic Governance through the Governance Initiative: A Review and the Way Forward* (Staff Working Paper) SEC (2009) 58 final of 19 January.

[98] Including the International Covenant on Economic, Social and Cultural Rights (1966) 993 UNTS 3.

[99] Arts 8, 9 and 96 as revised and new Annex VII.

[100] Art 96(1)(a) as revised.

[101] Council Decision 2002/148/EC [2002] OJ L50/64.

[102] eg see reports of the arrest of trade unionists, assaults against members of the Zimbabwe Congress of Trade Unions and the arrest of its Secretary General in December 2008: <http://www.ituc-csi.org/spip.php?article2605>.

legislation' and 'enforcement of adherence to national legislation and work regulation'.[103] Finally, in a reiteration of point 5 of the ILO Declaration, the parties agree that 'labour standards should not be used for protectionist trade purposes'.[104]

How important is Article 50 CPA in the overall scheme? It can be criticized as merely reaffirming 'standards' that do not, in themselves, create hard obligations and are, at best, promotional and may undermine ILO's supervision.[105] Article 50 should not, however, be viewed in isolation. The effect of this clause is to crystallize within a sophisticated trade and development regime the essentially soft commitments that the parties have endorsed in the ILO Declaration and convert them into a binding multilateral obligation to adhere to the 'relevant [ILO] conventions' as mainstreamed human rights.[106] On this interpretation, the parties have bound themselves to, where necessary, introduce laws and ensure their effective application in respect of, at least, the 'core' conventions.[107] Although the agreement to enhance cooperation appears vacuous, the CPA framework provides a basis not only for ratification of conventions, but also requires proactive monitoring of CLS compliance in practice, by expecting partners to improve the quality of labour legislation and the effectiveness of enforcement of the relevant ILO standards.

Article 50 entrenches the CLS within the partnership as recommended by the World Commission on the Social Dimension of Globalization (WCSDG).[108] The WCSDG report recognized that the ILO cannot realize its objectives by acting alone, but can more effectively pursue them aided by regional actors, such as the EU and ACP, and private stakeholders under the UNGC. The 'constitutional obligation'[109] that flows from the ILO Declaration is rendered more effective through its transposition directly into the CPA and is subject to the oversight of the parties and coordinated action under the EU–ILO strategic partnership.[110]

To what extent does Article 50 fortify the parties' agreement to uphold 'fundamental social rights'? If the CLS equate to 'fundamental social rights' within the meaning of Article 9 CPA, it follows that Article 50 may serve as a conduit for action under CPA procedures in the event of violations, especially when reported by the ILO. Moreover, promotion of these rights is additional to the parties' obligations to observe all ratified ILO conventions, including those not listed among the core. One danger arising from the presumption of a hierarchy of labour standards is that it may deter states from ratifying 'non-core' conventions, leading to an irrational prioritization. This stratification is, to a certain extent, rigidified by the DWA, which promotes soft programmatic solutions in areas such as employment and remuneration falling outside the core.[111] Nevertheless, the CLS process is designed to increase the number of ratifications in combination with action arising through mainstreaming instruments. It follows that, within the revised ACP–EU *acquis*, both 'core' and 'non-core' ILO conventions are 'relevant' and subject to political dialogue and, ultimately, the consultation procedure.

Discussion of these issues leads us a further related question. If it is accepted that violations of fundamental social rights, or ratified ILO conventions, can be pursued under the CPA, why has the EU shown such timidity on labour rights' issues? The answer, in part, is pragmatism in the choice of violations to emphasize in cases involving multiple breaches of the essential elements.[112] The EU must be satisfied that any violation is sufficiently serious to justify restrictions on market access that may run counter to its economic interests and, more importantly, the immediate needs of the population of the country in question. It also reflects the reality that the ground for any conflict over labour rights' violations has to be carefully chosen and proposed measures must be proportionate to ward off charges of

[103] Art 50(2). [104] Art 50(3). [105] Alston, n 40, 511. [106] Art 20(2).
[107] ILO Declaration, point 2, n 11. [108] See n 63.
[109] Hepple, n 22, 59. [110] See n 64. [111] Alston, n 40, 488.
[112] A Davies, 'Should the EU Have the Power to Set Minimum Standards for Collective Labour Rights in the Member States?' in P Alston (ed), *Labour Rights as Human Rights* (OUP, 2005), 186.

protectionism. Moreover, states facing allegations may be able to point to formal ratification of the relevant conventions and have sufficient support among other states to resist pressure.[113] Regionalization and differentiation under the EPA model may, inadvertently, serve to reinforce such resistance. If the EU's caution persists in cases where there is strong evidence of violations, it would be regrettable because such reticence tends to reinforce the perception that 'social rights are like paper tigers, fierce in appearance, but missing in tooth and claw'.[114]

Nevertheless, the ACP's endorsement of the CLS and DWA indicates that safeguarding labour rights is now accepted as an integral part of EU–ACP policy.[115] It enables the parties to act to enforce the CLS and ratified ILO conventions as human rights norms without breaching WTO rules. It can be argued that consultations flowing from alleged violations of labour rights must be regarded as wholly separate from trade matters on the basis that the ILO has functional autonomy over labour issues. Any actions flowing from persistent violations must, by reference to the CLS, be objective and proportionate with trade liberalization objectives and WTO norms. The EU continues to face difficulties in advancing global labour rights but, by accepting caveats concerning protectionism, the EU is able to extol rather than export its social model and pursue its 'moral' obligations in global governance.

4.2. Economic Partnership Agreements—an overview

EPAs are region-by-region agreements designed to facilitate the creation of viable regional markets and foster 'smooth and gradual' integration of ACP states into the world economy.[116] EPAs offer a differentiated reciprocal approach to trade, investment, development and capacity-building, and, potentially, a corresponding deepening of governance requirements concerning fundamental social rights.

So far, so good, but it is important to recognize that behind the consensual façade of economic *partnership*, the reality is that EPAs are forced arrangements driven by the post-Seattle necessity to establish non-preferential arrangements, or equivalent alternative trading arrangements,[117] by 2008, when the WTO waiver permitting preferential market access for ACP goods expired.

The CPA was intended to spawn an unspecified number of EPAs. ACP countries who are Least Developed Countries (LDCs)—39 of the world's 49—are entitled to maintain preferential non-reciprocal market access arrangements under the WTO-approved 'Everything But Arms' (EBA) Regulation.[118] ACP countries who are neither LDCs nor signatories of an EPA are deemed to be weaker partners entitled only to a narrow range of trade preferences and subject to strict rules of origin requirements under the EU's GSP.[119]

The process of negotiating and concluding EPAs has provided a testing ground for the EU and ACP regional groupings, both established and emergent,[120] to commence a new phase of their relationship in which the promotion of the CLS and DWA are among the mechanisms of governance. For the EU, in particular, it is necessary to address perceptions, heightened by its initial negotiating strategy, that EPAs amount to mere pseudo-

[113] Zimbabwe, eg has ratified the conventions on freedom of association and the right to organize.

[114] B Hepple, 'Enforcement: the law and politics of co-operation and compliance' in B Hepple (ed), *Social and Labour Rights in a Global Context* (CUP, 2002), 238.

[115] Hepple, n 22, 51.

[116] CPA, Art 36(2).

[117] Such arrangements are regarded as a stepping stone to full regional EPAs: Commission, *Economic Partnership Agreements* (Communication) COM (2007) 635 of 23 October, para 2.1.

[118] See: <http://ec.europa.eu/trade/wider-agenda/development/generalised-system-of-preferences/everything-but-arms/> accessed 16 January 2012.

[119] See Babarinde and Faber, n 89, 39–42.

[120] There are seven ACP regions: five in Africa, one in the Caribbean and one in the Pacific: <http://ec.europa.eu/trade/creating-opportunities/bilateral-relations/regions/africa-caribbean-pacific/> accessed 16 January 2012.

partnerships derived from asymmetrical 'North–South' power relations and neoliberal globalization and liberalization imperatives, and may prove unsuitable vehicles for promoting labour standards and effective supervision and enforcement of fundamental rights.[121]

Motivated by the need to respond to such concerns and a desire to rapidly conclude agreements, the EU made an improved offer under which it agreed to remove almost all remaining quota and tariff limitations on access to the EU market for ACP goods and offer improvements to the rules of origin. Despite this offer, only the CARIFORUM–EU EPA,[122] was concluded before the deadline. Instead, a mix of interim 'stepping stone' agreements have been reached with other ACP regional groups and individual countries while negotiations continue for full EPAs.[123] There are several reasons for the failure to make progress. First, the EU is perceived to be imposing its own agenda when negotiating as a unified actor with small, often loosely established, heterogeneous regional groups. The EU's region-by-region approach has accentuated the asymmetry in EU–ACP relations and, critics suggest, is driven by a Eurocentric and polycentric perspective that neglects the unique difficulties of ACP countries and amounts to a divide and rule strategy.[124] Secondly, LDCs and non-LDCs entered the negotiations from different starting positions, with the former granted market access without the need for EPAs, whilst the latter are divided between those eligible to apply for the GSP+,[125] considered only slightly less 'generous' than EPAs, and others falling back on the standard GSP.[126] Thirdly, many ACP countries are altering their perception of the EU. This is not only due to the EU's changing identity, as newer member states do not have colonial links, but it also reflects changing power relations, accentuated by the global financial crisis and Eurozone problems, as ACP countries increasingly look to China, which is expanding its influence, especially in Africa, without requiring conditionality in return for trade and investment.[127]

Against this backdrop, the prospects for enhancing labour standards through EPAs are not auspicious. EPAs are regarded as trade rather than development agreements responding to the ticking clock of hard WTO obligations rather than soft, indeterminate ILO declarations. EPA provisions not dealing with market access issues are referred to as 'non-trade aspects', carrying no positive requirement to include commitments to labour rights. Also, it is difficult to reach agreements on labour issues if some countries have not ratified core ILO conventions. Critics argue that any attempt to include labour provisions in EPAs is mere window dressing for coercive 'EU neoliberal governance', which may increase poverty and dependency, especially for indigenous peoples.[128]

Despite these concerns, the EU has responded in a manner that has at least the potential to convert EPAs into vehicles to enhance labour standards and social market values where this is supported in ACP regions. An influential EU European Economic and Social Committee (ECOSOC) Opinion on how to integrate social aspects into the EPA negotiations[129] referred to 'serious and growing' inequalities between the parties in trade, development and social rights, and in negotiating capacity, and resolved that these inequalities must not stand in the way of including social aspects.[130] Suggestions included: prioritizing

[121] See M Meyn, 'Economic Partnership Agreements: A "Historic Step" Towards a 'Partnership of Equals'?' (2008) 26 DPR 515; and Bradley and Bradley, n 96, 34–36.

[122] [2008] OJ L289/3 (signed 15 October 2008).

[123] State of play by region: see *Trade Negotiation Insights* July/August 2011.

[124] Bradley and Bradley, n 96, 40; Meyn, n 121, 526.

[125] See n 82.

[126] L Curran, L Nilsson and D Brew, 'The Economic Partnership Agreements: Rationale, Misconceptions and Non-Trade Aspects' (2008) 26 DPR 529, at 542.

[127] Meyn, n 121, 526.

[128] R Icaza, 'Global Europe, Guilty! Contesting EU neoliberal governance for Latin America and the Caribbean' (2010) 31 TWQ 123.

[129] [2006] OJ C65/73.

[130] Ibid, paras 2.3.2. and 4.7.

decent jobs as 'the essential tool' in combating poverty;[131] including a gender dimension, such as promoting women's entrepreneurship;[132] establishing regional social dialogue committees;[133] and promoting ratification of non-core ILO conventions.[134] Most radically, it recommended stricter requirements for enterprises that benefit from public funds to practice social responsibility.[135]

The parties were encouraged to adopt a 'development-friendly' approach to EPAs by the EU–ACP Joint Parliamentary Assembly's 'Kigali Declaration',[136] which highlighted the need to promote coherence in development and called for agreements, whether or not full EPAs, to ensure that 'no country is left worse off' after the expiry of the deadline.[137]

By 2008, therefore, the debate had subtly shifted and the parties now recognized that simply liberalizing trade between unequal partners, with sustainable development and respect for human rights as a mere gloss, is ineffective and ultimately runs counter to EU–ACP partnership goals and furtherance of the regional integration model of governance.[138] It is in this context that the CARIFORUM–EU EPA[139] needs to be evaluated as a potential model for enhancing global labour rights through regional integration and development.

4.3. The CARIFORUM–EU EPA—a model agreement?

The Caribbean states have a strong tradition of economic and political integration, predating the establishment of the ACP, where they have been represented by Caribbean Forum (CARIFORUM) since 1990. CARIFORUM operates alongside the Caribbean Community (CARICOM), which was created in 1973 for the purposes of economic integration. CARICOM has established the Caribbean Single Market and Economy (CSME).[140] Several of its smaller members have completed an economic and monetary union.[141] Caribbean states have strong political and trading relationships with their neighbours in Central America,[142] Latin America,[143] the US and Canada. There are pockets of extreme poverty in the Caribbean but, of the CARIFORUM group, only Haiti is an LDC. The EU has strong ties with the Caribbean, where several Member States retain outposts,[144] and has established a partnership with the region based on shared values and aimed at deeper regional integration, promoting good and effective governance, including capacity-building for social partners.[145] The Caribbean faces many problems, not least its dependency on markets for specific agricultural products—bananas and sugar cane—and heavy reliance on intensive

[131] Ibid, para 4.1.

[132] Ibid, para 6.5.

[133] Citing a 2003 World Bank study on the link between improving economic performance and sound labour relations, ibid, para 5.5.

[134] Ibid, para 5.6.1.

[135] EU ECOSOC Opinion, n 129, paras 4.5.5, 5.6.2 and 5.6.3.

[136] [2008] OJ C58/44. See also European Parliament resolutions of 23 March 2006 [2006] OJ C292E/121; and 23 May 2007, [2008] OJ C102E/301.

[137] Ibid, para 8.

[138] European Parliament resolution of 23 March 2006, n 136, point J.

[139] See n 21.

[140] CARIFORUM comprises all members of CARICOM except Montserrat. It includes the Dominican Republic which is not in CARICOM. Cuba is in CARICOM and CARIFORUM but is not a part of the CPA or EPA. The full list of signatories of the EPA is: Antigua and Barbuda, Bahamas, Barbados, Belize, Dominica, Dominican Republic, Grenada, Guyana, Haiti, Jamaica, St Christopher and Nevis, St Lucia, St Vincent and the Grenadines, Suriname, Trinidad and Tobago.

[141] The Organization of Eastern Caribbean States (OECS).

[142] Through the Association of Caribbean States (ACS) and the Organization of American States (OAS).

[143] Mainly through the Rio Group.

[144] France, the UK, and The Netherlands.

[145] Launched in 1999. See Commission, *An EU–Caribbean Partnership for Growth, Stability and Development* (Communication) COM (2006) 86 final of 3 May.

tourism,[146] both of which raise concerns about the fragility of the labour market. Nevertheless, it was hardly surprising that CARIFORUM, with its strong economic and political cohesiveness, and a higher relative level of development, was the first ACP group to conclude an EPA. What is most remarkable is the comprehensiveness of the EPA, as a new generation agreement concerning trade, development, investment, security and, for the purposes of this analysis, human rights, employment and labour issues, linked to capacity-building and fostering long-term growth.[147]

As an indicator of the potential of EPAs to enhance the labour dimension of global governance, and the broader strategy of development through regional integration, the substance of the EPA suggests a more confident and sophisticated approach.

First, there is specific preambular reference to respect for 'basic labour rights' in line with the parties' ILO obligations. These commitments are directly connected to the need for 'economic and social progress for their peoples in a manner consistent with sustainable development'. This indicates a degree of comfort in referring to labour rights rather than standards or principles, and referencing commitments extending beyond the CLS and including, at least, all ratified ILO conventions.

Secondly, the co-operation priorities contain a commitment to enhance the technological and research capabilities of CARIFORUM states so as to 'facilitate development of, and compliance with... internationally recognized labour and environmental standards'.[148] In this way, fulfilment of international labour standards is mainstreamed into a core development objective tied in with capacity-building and growth.

Thirdly, in perhaps the most innovative feature, consistent with the EU ECOSOC Opinion,[149] the 'behaviour of investors' is directly addressed. Investors are required to 'act in accordance with [ILO] core labour standards'.[150] More forcefully, under Article 73 on 'maintenance of standards', the parties 'shall ensure' that 'foreign direct investment is not encouraged by lowering domestic environmental, labour or occupational health and safety legislation and standards' or 'by relaxing core labour standards'. Although enforcement is left to each country, subject to ILO overview, this clause sends a clear message to potential investors to demonstrate social responsibility in practice not merely through rhetoric. Moreover, it rejects social dumping and incorporates the established EU principle that, even within differentiated agreements, states are expected to guarantee a floor of labour standards.[151]

Fourthly, mirroring Article 50 CPA, the EPA has a separate chapter on 'social aspects' of trade: Articles 191–196. This chapter encourages 'high levels' of social and labour standards 'consistent with internationally recognized rights', subject to the social development priorities of each state.[152] In addition, it contains a provision on 'upholding levels of protection'[153] that reinforces the parties' commitment to maintain and improve labour standards by agreeing 'not to encourage trade or foreign direct investment or maintain a competitive advantage' by: '(a) lowering the level of protection provided by domestic social and labour legislation'; or '(b) derogating from, or failing to apply, such legislation or standards'.[154] This is backed up by detailed consultation and monitoring procedures including a facility to appoint a Committee of Experts and seek ILO advice.[155]

Finally, it expresses unconditional support for linking trade, labour standards and 'decent work'.[156] Article 191(3) declares:

[146] See M Busse and S Lüehje, 'Should the Caribbean Countries Sign an Economic Partnership Agreement with the EU?: Challenges and Strategic Options' (2007) 22 JEI 598, 603–605.
[147] Curran *et al*, n 126, 549.
[148] Art 8(v). [149] See n 129. [150] Art 72. [151] TFEU, Art 153(4). [152] Art 192.
[153] Art 193. [154] Ibid. [155] Art 195. [156] Art 191(2).

'The Parties recognize the beneficial role that core labour standards and decent work can have on economic efficiency, innovation and productivity, and they highlight the value of greater policy coherence between trade policies, on the one hand, and social policies on the other.'

This paragraph represents, at least, a shared appreciation of what McCrudden and Davies describe as the 'positive synergies between trade liberalization and labour rights'.[157]

5. Conclusion

This chapter has traced the gradual shift towards an increasingly important and leading role for the EU in global labour governance. In turn, as the EU has assumed this role it has been mindful of the need to act within the parameters of the CLS and the DWA and to ensure that its policies promote sustainable development and are WTO-compatible. The EU has had to adapt its negotiating strategy for the EPAs to take account of genuine concerns about its use of asymmetric power. The first EPA, operating under the CPA umbrella, provides a tangible example of how the EU, working in tandem with the ILO, and aligning with UN initiatives, can exert its external influence positively in a long-term relationship to help shape global labour governance to match its strategic ambitions and those of its partners. Moreover, it provides evidence that good and effective governance is concerned not only with political structures and institution-building, but also with enhancing the quality of policies.[158]

For the first time in ACP–EU relations, fundamental labour rights have been mainstreamed in a binding multilateral regional governance instrument and combined with structured social dialogue, a commitment to socially responsible investment practices, and support for qualitative and quantitative employment initiatives and decent remuneration as a positive foundation for growth and sustainable development. The CARIFORUM–EU EPA's strongly worded philosophical objection to social dumping, as the downside of globalization, amounts to a reassertion of the foundational values of labour law and serves as an antidote to the hitherto dominant paradigm of neoliberal governance that is increasingly being questioned as the global financial crisis deepens.[159]

Labour rights are merely a singular thread among a complex web of issues that provide the dynamic of EU international relations. However, the labour-trade-development-investment-human rights nexus is immeasurably strengthened if mutually reinforcing EU–ILO strategies can be entrenched through effective regional partnerships. Finalizing long-term EPAs with other ACP regions presents a greater challenge and engenders concerns about variable geometry within regions and, in the scramble to satisfy WTO compliance, it may heighten asymmetry and lessen the emphasis on social values. The challenge now is to adapt the EPA model to further enhance the quality of governance by promoting more comprehensive regional partnerships in practice, through social dialogue and social responsibility initiatives under ILO supervision, and, as economic and social conditions improve, allow space for indigenous regional strategies to develop to respect and sustain fundamental social rights and decent work as part of a more coherent and equitable construct for the governance of globalization.

[157] McCrudden and Davies, n 22, 48.

[158] See Commission EU–Caribbean Partnership Communication, n 145, 6.

[159] eg see the debate throughout the Americas and the Caribbean over the merits of the US-backed Free Trade Area of the Americas (FTAA) and the alternative, supported by Cuba and Venezuela, of the Invictia Bolivariana para las Americas (ALBA)—see Commission EU–Caribbean Partnership Communication, n 145, 17.

CLOSING PART

20

Conclusion: The Role of the EU in the Legal Dimension of Global Governance

The Editors

1. Introduction: Cosmopolitanism versus Geopolitics

Globalization and the financial crisis that started in 2008 have deeply uprooted the well-being and security of European citizens. It has been starkly illustrated that the European Union (EU) and its Member States are highly dependent on global forces partially beyond the control of traditional, national provinces of governance. This phenomenon is captured by 'global governance', which has become the central concept coalescing research on the principles, processes, modes and institutions through which such global societal challenges are tackled. Amongst the legal and political science research which has been burgeoning in this field,[1] we have sought to adopt two starting points from which to advance the literature in this area. First of all, we have chosen not to focus on the legal–theoretical dimensions of global governance. The purpose of this volume was therefore not to examine the 'legitimacy' of global governance, or the existence and nature of a process of global 'constitutionalization'. Rather, with this book, we sought to bring together legal scholars with practitioners so as to establish a connection between the international relations and legal aspects of diverse regimes of global governance, eg law as it lives in day-to-day policy-making. Second, in this volume[2] we sought to provide a European perspective to the subject matter, and notably confront the EU's *sanguine world view* with the *daunting reality* of global governance.[3] Namely, Articles 3(5) and 21 of the Treaty on European Union (TEU) prescribe that the Union's international action shall be guided by the principles which have inspired its own creation, thus constitutionally mandating the EU to pursue its international relations in a multilateral fashion through the progressive development of international law. The legally mandated world view whereby the EU seeks to contribute to the 'sustainable development of the Earth, solidarity and mutual respect among peoples...' (Article 3(5) TEU) has been called by one of our contributors, 'cosmopolitan Romanticism'.[4] This very much captures the tension that this book explores: on the one hand there is the cosmopolitanist imagination of the world as it ought to be by the EU; and on the other hand there are the harsh

[1] A selection: G Chan, P Lee and L Chan, *China Engages Global Governance: A New World Order in the Making?* (Routledge, 2012); J Wouters, H Bruyninckx, S Basu and S Schunz (eds), *The EU and Multilateral Governance* (Palgrave, 2012); C Ku, *International Law, International Relations and Global Governance* (Routledge, 2012); C Secchi (ed), *Global Governance and the Role of the EU: Assessing the Future Balance of Power* (E Elgar, 2012); J-U Wunderlich and DJ Bailey, *The European Union and Global Governance, A Handbook* (Routledge, 2011); TG Weiss and R Thakur, *Global Governance and the UN: An Unfinished Journey* (Indiana University Press, 2010); J Whitman, *The Fundamentals of Global Governance* (Palgrave Macmillan, 2009); J L Dunoff and JP Trachtman, *Ruling the World? Constitutionalism, International Law, and Global Governance* (Cambridge University Press, 2009); L Martin (ed), *Global Governance, Essays in international relations* (Ashgate, 2008); AF Cooper, CW Hughes and P De Lombaerde, *Regionalisation and Global Governance: The Taming of Globalisation?* (Routledge, 2008); SM Rai and G Waylen, *Global Governance: Feminist Perspectives* (Palgrave, 2008); J Grugel and N Piper, *Critical Perspectives on Global Governance: Rights and regulation in governing regimes* (Routledge, 2007); K Alexander, R Dhumale, J Eatwell, Global Governance of Financial Systems: the International Regulation of Systemic Risk (OUP, 2006).

[2] Unless otherwise stated, all references in this concluding chapter are to contributions included in this edited volume.

[3] Larik.

[4] Larik, 'Shaping the international order as a Union objective and the dynamic internationalisation of constitutional law' CLEER Working Papers 2011/5, 37.

realities and global upheavals confronting the EU's ideals. As the European Council recognized in September 2010,[5] less than one year after the Treaty of Lisbon entered into force—Europe is facing a plethora of challenges in a rapidly changing world. The financial and economic crisis, followed by the Eurozone sovereign debt crisis, has uprooted the well-being of many Europeans, to the point of challenging European integration itself, and has substantially weakened the EU's position in the world. This goes hand in hand with the quickly accelerating rise and assertiveness of a number of emerging powers, in particular the BRICS countries (Brazil, Russia, India, China and South Africa) and with the partial shift by the United States of its resources away from Europe. The EU—the people, the 27 and soon 28 Member States, the supranational organization—is seeking to define itself amidst this tempestuous global reality. In abstract terms, there is thus the EU-internal and EU-external political reality in contrast to the optimistic world view embedded in the EU Treaty: to shape the world according to the principles which guided its own creation. It is from this contrasting picture that we—as lawyers—wished to examine the current and future practices of the EU in shaping global governance. The research question which all contributors to this volume were asked to address was then the following: 'How and to which extent can the EU shape the ongoing reorientation of the legal principles, processes, modes and institutions of global governance in a multi-polar world in line with its rule-of-law based mission statement?'.

2. The EU in the World: In Pursuit of Rule-of-Law Based Collective Governance

In the first part of the book, the contributors explored the rule-of-law based mission statement of the EU in global governance. Together, these chapters provide the conceptual framework through which to examine the EU's position in global governance across all subject areas. Larik observed that the world view stated in the Treaties introduces a manifest legal dimension to global governance through *constitutionally* providing substantive and methodological guidance to EU foreign policy. The author agrees with de Búrca's assessment that these external objectives in the Treaties can be usefully classified utilizing Wolfers' concepts of possession goals and milieu goals.[6] Possession goals are those which 'focus on the protection or strengthening of national possessions and resources, such as territory, trade advantages, and domestic sovereignty'.[7] In other words, these are the EU's own 'interests', which Article 3(5) TEU obliges the EU to pursue in its relations with the wider world.[8] Milieu goals, on the other hand, are those which seek to shape and stabilize the surrounding and international environment. They 'emphasize the promotion of long-term security, stability, sustainability, cooperation and peaceful international relations'.[9] The Lisbon Treaty has done much to streamline the EU's global objectives, and Larik finds that while Article 3(5) TEU has left the door open to the pursuit of 'interests' rather than values (eg possession goals), the majority of EU external objectives fall within the category of milieu goals.[10] These include objectives such as the sustainable development of the Earth, global peace and stability and free trade, but are joined by references to promoting human rights, the rule of law and the support and progressive development of international law. De

[5] See Ch 1, Introduction.

[6] A Wolfers, *Discord and Collaboration: Essays on International Politics* (Johns Hopkins University Press, 1965), 73–76.

[7] de Búrca.

[8] In our submission, it is not coincidental that Art 3(5) TEU first refers to the EU upholding and promoting its values and interests (possession goals), and only then to the milieu goals. We could read in this a prioritization of possession over milieu goals.

[9] de Búrca.

[10] Larik.

Búrca, like Larik, rejects the sharp distinction between EU values and its pursuit of interests across these different objectives. Utilizing regional (neighbourhood policy) and international examples (the International Criminal Court (ICC), efforts to combat climate change), she argues that the EU pursues what she terms 'a governance mode of foreign policy'. For her, this concept does not imply any judgment on the EU being a soft power, normative power, and so on. Rather, it implies that from the EU Treaties emanates a preference for collaborative, collective governance over its antipode—unilateralism. In other words: the EU's foreign policy lays emphasis on pursuing milieu goals in joint cooperation with others: a preference for multilateralism.[11] As we can see in all subsequent parts of the volume, de Búrca's definition of the governance mode is very much supported, and fleshed out by empirical evidence: What emerges from the different parts of the book is a seemingly hierarchical order of different options of multilateralism. On the top end stands global multilateralism, 'in particular in the framework of the United Nations', in implementation of Article 21(1), final sentence TEU; over cross-regional partnerships (such as the EPAs or relations with MERCOSUR), to bilateralism and strategic parterships on the bottom of the hierarchy. There are a number of conditions[12] which will influence the extent to which the EU 'prefers' multilateral governance; what exactly multilateralism means in that specific instance, and how to define 'governance' in terms of which methodologies, modes, processes or institutions the EU adopts or participates in.

De Búrca's second claim is that in its pursuit of multilateral governance,[13] the Union certainly takes to heart the constitutional objective of Article 21(1) TEU, ie that it shall be guided by the principles inspiring its own creation. Thus, de Búrca argues that the EU will regularly seek to replicate or externalize in its foreign policy some of the modes of governance it has developed for similar policies in its internal realm. At a more theoretical level, the contribution by Micklitz and Patterson shares that view. They examine how the Member States' nature has evolved in the context of European integration, and how this acquires a global dimension in the sphere of economic regulation. Their contribution supports the observations and submissions of Larik and de Búrca, and similarly provides a case study of the transformation processes the EU seeks to engender through its own way of doing international relations. It is noteworthy that these contributions highlight distinct, but related aspects of what may be termed the *outside-in* and *inside-out relationships* between the EU (as an international actor and legal order) and global governance (institutionally and substantively). On the one hand de Búrca argues that the governance mode implies the EU transposing internal governance processes to the external domain, whereas on the other hand Micklitz and Patterson observe a converse, although not necessarily contradictory phenomenon. In their view, 'the outer space of statecraft' (eg global governance) can serve as a means of circumventing EU-internal regulatory mechanics. Using the example of private law, they point to the phenomenon of the EU generating 'internal statecraft' through international legal means which can overcome internal tensions between

[11] De Búrca distinguishes 'collective' from 'multilateral' governance so as to define the EU's preference for collective governance in the most general terms. Since multilateralism itself is already quite broad in international relations, we shall not further make that distinction. See eg Keohane, who defines multilateralism as 'the practice of coordinating national policies in groups of three or more States' (R Keohane, 'Multilateralism: An Agenda for Research' (1990) 45 *International Journal* 731). Other authors, in defining multilateralism, have argued that it is not so much the number of parties or the number of relations that is under consideration, but rather the nature of the relations. Multilateralism not merely implies coordinating national policies in groups of three or more states; it also pre-supposes the existence of certain principles for ordering the relations among those states (JG Ruggie, 'Multilateralism: The Anatomy of an Institution' (1992) 46 *International Organization* 566–567). Ruggie describes multilateralism as a generic institutional form in international relations, adding that its 'generalized organizing principles' logically entail a socially constructed indivisibility among the members of a collectivity with respect to the range of behaviour in question (p 571).

[12] See further the contribution by De Witte and Thies.

[13] In her words, collective governance.

the Member States' (nation state) private legal orders and market state European private law. Thus, where the EU has or acquires external competence, the global regulatory realm may present opportunities for a more unified regulatory approach than is sometimes possible within the EU legal space.

This interlocks with the contribution by De Witte and Thies, who depart from the EU legal order as the more mature, and sometimes preferred venue for law-making over the international legal order. Starting from that premise, their contribution examines the factors why a particular level of governance (or venue as they call it) is chosen for law-making broadly defined. This connects strongly with de Búrca's arguments, since this contribution explores the conditions under which the EU prefers a certain kind of collective governance at a given level within the global system.

Their analysis focuses both on Member States' legal and policy considerations influencing venue choice, as well as those of the EU as an international actor itself. In the case of the Member States, they point to the EU as a logical, central framework for cooperation, but they show that other regional or international venues for cooperation remain available and may be preferred in a number of instances over the 'more obvious' EU route. In that sense, venue choice is integral to the broader process of legal agenda setting, and De Witte and Thies argue that this decision mainly depends on four factors: (1) path dependence, (2) the geographical nature of the subject, (3) ease of decision-making and (4) effectiveness. Many contributions in the area-specific book parts of this edited volume have shown these factors to implicitly or explicitly guide the final choice on which mode of governance of EU foreign policy.[14] Moving to the EU itself, De Witte and Thies argue that the same four factors remain relevant for the Union, but that the latter's constitutional specificity does add complexity to the final outcome. This means that in addition to the previous four factors, the choice for international law-making by the Union depends on (1) its own competence, but also on (2) its need to carve out an international identity for itself, as well as (3) its variable recognition as a global law maker. Given the broad range of examples on which these authors draw, their findings complete the conclusions of the other contributors' findings on the two-way relationship between the EU and global governance. They conclude that the relationship between regulatory initiatives at the international and EU level is in essence one of reciprocal processes whereby parallel law-making initiatives cross-fertilize each other. Interestingly, their findings are complementary to those of Micklitz and Patterson on utilizing the international order for the purposes of internal statecraft. De Witte and Thies elaborate this picture with their argument that in light of the co-existing international law obligations imposed on individual EU Member States, and in spite of the EU's growing ambitions to contribute to the development of international law, there is nevertheless still a clear phenomenon of import of international law into the EU domestic legal order. Like Micklitz and Patterson, De Witte and Thies point to the concepts of norm synergy and norm conflict to explain this interrelationship between legal orders. Both contributions reach a complementary and mutually supporting conclusion: Micklitz and Patterson point to the phenomena of convergence, conflict and hybridization in the EU-internal legal order, and argue that in case of incomplementarity, these processes could lead to international action providing a way to circumvent norm conflict within the EU. De Witte and Thies look at the reverse process, arguing that the prior adoption of EU legislation may either complicate or facilitate subsequent international standard-setting on the same issues. From a positive perspective, it may be useful to start from a template to see what works and what does not. More negatively, EU internal regulation may also limit negotiation space internationally since it focuses on existing legislation rather than opening novel regulatory avenues. In other

[14] Notably in the trade (examples of Anti-Counterfeiting Trade Agreement (ACTA) and rare earths), environment (biofuels and deforestation) and finance book parts (financial regulation and financial taxation).

words, the global regulatory arena, the regional (EU or otherwise) regulatory arena and the national sphere are inter-locking and there is no pre-dominant 'best choice'. Thus, the role of the EU in the legal dimension of global governance must be captured by a set of legal and political factors, which will influence: (1) the extent and under which conditions the EU 'prefers' collective governance; (2) what is understood under the 'collective' aspect of EU foreign policy; (3) and how to define 'governance' in terms of which methodologies, modes, processes or institutions the EU adopts or participates in.

If the role of the EU in global governance depends on the aforementioned factors, to what extent are those influenced by the *constitutional* objectives of the EU? Pulling together the threads of the four conceptual contributions, all agree that there is something distinct to the EU's approach to global governance stemming from its Constitution. Employing de Búrca's terminology, the EU's governance mode of foreign policy focuses on the establishment of networks of stable, institutionalized and iterative relationships with other states, entities and regions, which often entail the creation of other policy-making, norm-generating, coordinating and monitoring institutions, often created in the EU's own image. The contributors point to some of the influential factors in choosing different regulatory methodologies, but one thing they all agree upon: a preference for the collective, for the above-national, and a preference for law. As Larik submits, it is in the EU Treaties that the legal dimension of global governance finds its strongest and most vigorous expression—a constitutional obligation to cooperate towards the rule-of-law based provision of global public goods. Do these constitutional objectives raise unrealistic expectations? Larik answers in the negative, arguing that these objectives are neither excessively constraining nor entirely unrealistic. For him, they fix the basic parameters of EU foreign policy (eg de Búrca's 'governance mode'), arguing that evidently the EU is still most capable of acting within the whole range of foreign policy areas, as long as constitutional objectives are not manifestly disregarded. The consequence is that multilateralism is not necessarily the ultimate solution to all international affairs—although it is still the EU's preferred solution.

A number of questions emerge, which the subsequent contributions of the edited volume aim to answer: what does this guiding function of constitutional objectives mean for the EU's approach to organizations such as the United Nations (UN), the World Trade Organization (WTO) and the International Monetary Fund (IMF)? In the view of the EU, are they or are they not the best institutional response to questions of international trade, international security, or international finance? Or is (regional) bilateralism, or perhaps even uncut unilateralism on the part of the Union, equally acceptable in pursuit of Article 3 (5) and 21 TEU? Does the response to that question on method change depending on whether the EU pursues possession or milieu goals—or should the EU's values always prevail over its interests? Related to these issues, de Búrca queries whether the governance approach to foreign policy is more effective than the alternatives, and whether the 'collectivity' pursued by the Union is truly participatory, or rather a thin veil under which the EU still seeks to export its own substantive rules or promote its own particular interests—without regard to those of other participants? In her conclusion de Búrca points out that these questions require further empirical research, and the chapters of parts 2 through 5 of this book provide exactly that.

3. Security Governance: Willing but Unable?

Accepting rule-of-law based collective governance as the essence of the EU is the starting point of Koutrakos' contribution, though with a twist. In his contribution, this author starts out from accepting the idea that European integration has always been in essence a security policy project: avoiding future armed conflict in Europe is a central part of the DNA of the European polity. However, this introvert and self-referential aspect of the EU system has limited explanatory value, and geopolitical evolutions have impacted the Union too.

Koutrakos particularly notes the fact that third parties (the US, the UN) expect the EU to share the responsibility of monitoring and restoring international security. In other words: there is a calling for the Union to become a global player in international security from within itself, but also from the outside world. What, according to Koutrakos, does it take for the Union to respond to that call, and is the world ready to listen?

Koutrakos' response to global receptiveness of the EU as a security actor is prudently positive. Looking at the architecture of global security governance, he argues that the field is ripe and ready to provide the necessary legal and political space for the EU to become a central player. Similarly, Blockmans and De Baere point to the openness of the United Nations system itself to regional arrangements sharing the burden of the maintenance of international security. For Koutrakos, however, the EU is ill-prepared to take up that challenge, and the problem lies exactly in what the EU heralds as its core defining feature: the importance of rules, institutions and procedures as the glue of European integration itself. The principles which guided its own creation, and which it seeks to export abroad, are exactly part of the problem. To illustrate this, Koutrakos points to the fact that the Lisbon Treaty contains legal developments which suggest progress in strengthening the Common Security and Defence Policy (CSDP) machinery: the European Defence Agency's treaty-based role, a commitment to improve Member States' military capabilities for the implementation of CSDP, and so on. These were in response to the deeply held—yet for Koutrakos erroneous—belief that it is institutions and procedures which an effective CSDP was lacking pre-Lisbon. Rules, he says, do not take account of individual Member States' defence priorities in terms of spending, strategy, or political priorities; and legal rules and procedures cannot in themselves enable the Union to become an effective security and defence actor. Through a variety of examples such as the quest for policy coherence, the role of judicialized institutional turf battles, or coordination of military capabilities, he essentially argues that the rule-based approach *within the Union* is what stifles its global security ambitions. For him, it renders the CSDP into something which has little to do with defence. The antidote, argues Koutrakos, is *not* a (revision of the) grand strategy for the EU that others are calling for. To his mind, the problems facing the global calling of the EU in security governance are so deeply embedded in the EU's DNA that they cannot be addressed in the current post-financial crisis economic and political climate. A rather grim prospect indeed, and it is not immediately clear what the solution would be. Importantly, does Koutrakos' finding of a schism between the rule-based integrative approach and geopolitical reality render the external projection of rule-of-law based collective security governance invalid?

The three subsequent chapters provide answers from three different perspectives: they respectively examine the EU and the responsibility to protect (R2P—De Baere), the EU and its contribution to the peaceful settlement of international disputes (Blockmans), and who is accountable when things go awry, the EU's influence on the legal regime governing responsibility for military operations (Wessel and Sari). They provide good case studies as to whether the EU is indeed so poorly equipped to deal with global security challenges, and whether the EU in practice contributes to global security, and progressively develops the legal regime of security governance within which it operates.

As regards the responsibility to protect, De Baere points to the problematic nature of R2P itself: is it a legal and/or political obligation—if it is an obligation at all; and if so, what is its scope and substance? De Baere finds that this vagueness itself is rather evidently a problem, since it is difficult to implement a norm, the legal status of which itself is contested. The role of the EU may thus be twofold: to contribute to conceptually defining what R2P actually is; and to contribute through executing the definition it accepts and all that it entails. De Baere points to the EU certainly having rhetorically adopted the concept of R2P in its form espoused in the 2005 World Summit Outcome Document, with the EU expressing support for this UN General Assembly instrument through prominent internal political documents such as the 2005 European Consensus on Development and the 2008 report on the implementation of the European Security Strategy. To study whether the EU 'walks the walk and not just talks the talk', De Baere examines its operational implementation in the case of the Libya intervention during the 2011 Arab Spring. In UN Security Council Resolution 1970, the Security Council had referred to the Libyan authorities' responsibility to protect its population, and had permitted UN Member States to act nationally or through regional arrangements to take all necessary measures to protect civilians and civilian populated areas. If we apply Koutrakos' findings, we may expect a limited capacity for the EU to carry out R2P-related activities in this respect: all rhetoric but no substance. Initially, De Baere's findings seem to support Koutrakos' analysis, and the former points to the total absence of the EU in the Libyan intervention: the EU Force (EUFOR) Libya mission which never saw the light of day and would perhaps have been doomed from the start, the initially haphazard French, English and High Representative (HR) responses, as well as the German abstention in the Security Council voting on UN Security Resolution (UNSCR) 1970. We may thus conclude that the EU Member States' overriding national logic to which Koutrakos points reared its head in this context as well. Nonetheless, De Baere is optimistic: he argues that one should not rush to the conclusion that the EU's role in the implementation of R2P is marginal verging on the non-existent. To support his view, he enumerates the EU policies and initiatives which support the different pillars of R2P, notably its enlargement policy, but also contributing to the widest possible participation in the Rome Statute on the ICC, the protection of civilians in CSDP operations, and institution-building under the Instrument for Stability. Taking Koutrakos' more critical perspective, we may ask whether this is not a mere palliative, an exercise in compensatory self-delusion? Is the EU living up to its ambition to be or become a global security actor? For De Baere the answer is a balanced one, as he argues that the EU's most valuable contribution to R2P is the consolidation of reconciliation within Europe through its accession process, and at the same time sharing its experiences in post-conflict rebuilding with other regions in the world. Thus, the EU is—at least partially—living up to its mission statement in Article 3(5) and 21 TEU. De Baere concludes that this is where the EU could contribute most valuably to the legal dimension of global governance, namely through developing and pursuing an integrated and balanced approach to the notion of R2P, combining elements such as democracy and the rule-of-law with responsibility, prevention and possibly, intervention.

The contributions by Blockmans, and Wessel and Sari latch on well to these themes. Blockmans follows a bottom-up approach which examines the operational aspects of the EU as a global peace broker, thereby evaluating its overall contribution to global security in its aspects of peaceful dispute settlement. Wessel and Sari's contribution is rather top-down in nature. As the EU seeks to advance its interests in global security, what happens when or if it breaches international law or causes damage and injury to private parties? Does it contribute to the accountability dimension of the global security regime in this respect?

Blockmans examines the legal and institutional contribution of the EU—as an international actor, above and beyond its Member States—to the global governance of peaceful dispute settlement (PSD). His analysis follows the language of Article 33(1) of the UN Charter and focuses on the EU's diplomatic tools to peacefully settle disputes beyond its borders. In terms of the EU's vocation to act as global peace broker, Article 21(2)(c) TEU resonates the Member States' preambular resolve to implement a Common Foreign and Security Policy 'in order to promote peace, security and progress in Europe and in the world'. Blockmans argues that this particularly cosmopolitan world view expressed in EU constitutional objectives (Larik), fuelled by the ambition of the EU's external action protagonists (HR, President of the European Council, President of the Commission), and supported by a new diplomatic service vying for success, creates a danger of political overreach for the Union (similarly, see also Van Vooren in this volume on the EU financial transaction tax). Such overreach would bring back the ghosts of diplomatic failure which haunted the

EU throughout the 1990s, when it assumed leadership to stop the wars in the Balkans but ultimately had to rely on the US to put the fire out. Since the Treaty of Amsterdam endowed the Union with a 'monsieur PESC' and limited support structures, the EU has been successful in a handful of cases to peacefully resolve status disputes between third (*de jure* and de facto) states: the 2001 Ohrid Framework Agreement to keep Macedonia together; the 2002 Belgrade Agreement to peacefully and gradually disband the Federal Republic of Yugoslavia; and the implementation of the 2005 Aceh Peace Agreement are cases in point.

On the basis of a geographical quick scan, Blockmans shows that the EU's track record in involvement in third party mediation has so far been largely limited to—and has been most effective in—its immediate neighbourhoods and/or upon the express invitation of parties to a conflict. The picture that emerges from his examination of EU diplomatic involvement in PSD is one of concentric circles emanating from the Union's bureaucratic and geographic centre: as the ripple effect expands, the impact thereof weakens. In general, the alluring promises of future membership and the conclusion of an Association Agreement serve the EU's strategic interests in sustainable conflict resolution. Such prospects have helped to increase prosperity and growth opportunities in destitute countries and regions, improve links with vital transport and energy routes across borders, and to increase the EU's weight in the immediate neighbourhood, as indeed in the world. This finding is parallel to that of De Baere, who points to the EU's greatest successes in R2P in its own near-abroad. As Blockmans notes, the Cyprus issue stands out as a notable exception to the Union's success story in wielding its 'soft power' to impose durable peace on aspirant members. This is, however, not due to the EU's lack of trying. The consistent implementation of enlargement conditionality gains importance in the light of recent challenges to stability in the eastern neighbourhood of the EU, most notably the Southern Caucasus. While the 'carrot' of future EU membership is lacking in the context of the European Neighbourhood Policy (ENP), those 'European' states that could theoretically fulfil all EU membership conditions mentioned in and attached to Article 49 TEU could perhaps be swayed more easily and effectively than their non-European brethren in the ENP to resolve their internal and/or cross-border disputes. Further afield, the influence of the EU as an independent peace broker wanes. Arguably, its power of attraction is lost beyond the European periphery and really only defined in terms of development assistance and trade relations. With a history of colonial domination, the EU's diplomatic slate is not as clean as that of the Swiss and the Norwegians. However, some Member States' familiarity with previously held overseas territories may play to the Union's advantage in bringing a political *savoir faire* to the negotiation table. Yet, apart from Aceh, the jury is still out on whether the EU can and will produce success in the Middle East peace process and the non-proliferation talks with Iran. As a first conclusion of the geographical quick scan, Blockmans' argument is in parallel to that of De Baere, ie that as a vector of peace, the EU is thus very much a *regional* rather than a *global* actor.

A second conclusion of Blockmans is one that supports the rather sceptical stance of Koutrakos to the EU's own capacity to be a global security actor. Blockmans finds that while in practice fact-finding, mediation, conciliation and other instruments are already an integral part of the EU's external action toolbox, the EU has so far used these diplomatic tools in a rather ad hoc fashion. This exposes a raft of internal problems to which Koutrakos also pointed. First, nothing in the EU Treaties seems currently sufficient to enable the EU to fulfil the task of peace broker internally. The unresolved status issue of Cyprus is a stark reminder of that. The Union's policies in this area are primarily (if not exclusively) related to conflicts within or by states that are not members of the EU. This clearly distinguishes the EU from other regional arrangements and agencies, which see as their primary task the settling of disputes, threats to or breaches of the peace, among their members (cf the European Convention for the Peaceful Settlement of Disputes (Council of Europe, 1957) and a number of Organization for Security and Cooperation in Europe (OSCE) conventions and mechanisms related to early warning, conflict prevention and crisis management). The EU is thus acting *in foro externo* without having built up the capacities *in foro interno*. Second, the EU currently does not possess the proper institutional framework to engage in lengthy peaceful dispute settlement procedures: the EEAS does not (yet) pack the diplomatic punch in terms of personnel for preparing, implementing and following up on the task of peace mediation. Training EU Special representatives and drawing up a roster of expert mediators would be first steps in the right direction. When strengthening its PSD capacities, the EU will arguably make best use of the resources and expertise which are already available in the United Nations, regional organizations such as the African Union, the League of Arab States, national, local and civil society actors. In this respect it is worth noting that the EU is happy to play second fiddle to the efforts deployed by such other regional actors in PSD. The EU seems to prefer plurilateral coordination and cooperation in PSD. Thirdly, and this resonates a point made by Koutrakos and other contributors to this volume (migration—Thym), the EU famously suffers from political fragmentation in the realm of CFSP, which makes it hard to reach common positions among Member States to sign up for difficult peace processes in far-flung corners of the world. Inter-institutional turf battles only aggravate the negative impact on coalescing around a common interest and on projection the Union's values.

Against the background of all these attempts by the Union to become a global security actor—what if things go wrong and international law is violated in the context of an EU mission? Wessel and Sari examine the legal regime pertaining to accountability in the context of global security governance, and query whether the EU has contributed to the legal dimension of this aspect of global security. In their chapter, they argue that the key for the EU to contribute to the regime governing responsibility of international organizations participating in global security lies within the Union itself. They submit that the EU's contribution to global governance is largely dependent on a clarification of the complex division of responsibilities between the EU and its Member States. Examining the International Law Commission's Draft Articles on the Responsibility of International Organizations (DARIO), they argue that the draft articles do not address this question adequately. On the basis of an examination of the internal legal framework of the Union, as well as the practice of EU military operations, they ask whether EU military operations can be considered as either *de jure* or de facto organs of the Union. They find that, *de jure*, no presumption can be made to the effect that the wrongful conduct of national contingents serving in EU military operations should be attributed to the EU. De facto, however, they argue that EU military missions should be classified as organs of the EU. How does the Union contribute to global security governance? The response is in line with Koutrakos' critique of the focus on internal rules and procedures: internal structures stifle the full development of the CSDP. For Koutrakos this is the core obstacle to be overcome. A similar argument is formulated by Wessel and Sari: the EU should adopt a more unequivocal and clear position towards the legal consequences of its own internal constitutional organization. Concretely, the EU should accept that the wrongful conduct in the context of its crisis management missions are, in principle, attributable to it. In this fashion the Union would be seizing an important opportunity to contribute to the development of the law of international responsibility in the field of global security governance, since the DARIO are currently lacking in this regard.

In sum, these contributors argue that on the whole, the global system is ready to receive the EU as a global security actor. Notably the UN, but equally if not more, prominent strategic partners such as the United States are expecting the Union to do its part. As regards the EU's own global ambitions for a multilateral security order, there is no problem. Rhetorically the Union is pursuing Article 3(5) and 21 TEU, as evidenced by the commitment to the responsibility to protect, to peaceful dispute settlement and to improved global rules on accountability for crisis management missions. The proof of the pudding is in the eating, and there the contributors' findings are mixed at best. Success in the EU's role as a global peace broker is not found at the global level, but rather in its close neighbourhood through accession or post-conflict institution building (Blockmans and De Baere). At most, the EU thus can be said to be a regional security actor, with aspirations to the global level remaining exactly that. At the legal–conceptual level, things are more promising. The Union has what it takes to contribute to the progressive development of international law as regards R2P (De Baere), although as regards the accountability regime of international organizations in the security sphere it is yet to explicitly take that step (Wessel and Sari). All authors seem to agree that in the field of global security governance, the problem lies *within* the Union. As regards the legal or the political, the problem is not purely its institutions or procedures, but rather the eternal problem plaguing the Union: what it currently lacks is the unified political will to live up to its calling as a global security actor, and Koutrakos was not optimistic that such will would be mustered any time soon. While the latter author is not convinced that an update of the 2003 Security Strategy would ameliorate that problem, we do submit that a collective interpretation of the EU's interests (Article 3(5) TEU) is integral to recruiting the necessary political will for the EU to become a global security actor.

In sum, in this first part of the book the argument by De Witte and Thies is thereby certainly affirmed, namely that EU constitutional matters such as competence will crucially define what action is or is not taken in the context of the governance mode of EU foreign policy. When we examine trade, environment, finance and the social dimension of global governance, the focus of the contributions to this book changes: in these areas, the internal decision-making methodology ('community method') and nature of competences (shared or exclusive) is markedly different from the security field, and closely connected to the EU internal market. As a consequence, with internal disagreement on European integration itself reduced to more manageable levels, the EU can focus more on actual policy substance: what are the EU's interests, and what are its values; does pursuing them collectively imply multilateralism, or could the EU go about it bilaterally or unilaterally, and so on. This is clearly the case in the oldest of EU external competences, international trade.

4. Trade Governance: With Great Power Comes Great Responsibility

A global role for the EU in the sphere of international trade has been integral to European integration since the 1957 Treaty of Rome. The exclusive nature of the EU competence is such that Member States are entirely subjected to the discipline of EU law, placing it in stark contrast with the comparatively limited role for the EU in international security. The EU's internal machinery is far more advanced in this policy area, and as a consequence we can observe more time spent on shaping global trade governance in line with its identity, values and interests. The contribution by Hoffmeister takes the institutional perspective on how the EU goes about shaping global trade governance. He starts from the observation that former EU Trade Commissioner Pascal Lamy has described the WTO as a 'medieval' system, a comment which followed the collapse of the Doha Development Round in Cancun 2003. Hoffmeister examines relevant WTO procedures and the recent rise to prominence of the G20, in order to query whether under the current institutional structure of the global trading system, the EU can live up to its constitutional commitment to contribute to 'free and fair trade' as laid down in Article 3(5) TEU?

Focusing on the WTO and the G20, Hoffmeister meticulously examines the rules and procedures pertaining to what may be termed 'legislative moments' in the global trading system. In the WTO context, he looks at how the Organization adopts amendments to covered agreements (with focus on Agreement on Trade Related Aspects of Intellectual Property Rights (TRIPS)), how decisions on the accession of new members are taken (Russia), how waivers from WTO discipline are adopted (aid to Pakistan), and how negotiations in the WTO rounds are conducted (Doha). He compares the Union role in the WTO's mix of law and politics with that within the G20, clearly preferring the WTO structures in that comparison. The G20 is a relatively new form for international economic governance, a sort of intergovernmental collective which is not based on a constituent document, without a secretariat and with no formalized voting or enforcement mechanism. Hoffmeister is critical of the 'imperial glamour' the G20 imparts through grand statements, since its practical effect is limited in the absence of a proper monitoring system. For him, a (reformed) WTO should therefore remain the central institutional structure of global trade governance. The existing mechanisms of the WTO work 'perhaps not splendidly, but certainly sufficiently',[15] and the G20 as some kind of 'world economic forum' should not take its place. What is the vision and the role of the EU in that debate? Under Article 3(5) TEU the Union is to contribute to 'the strict observance and the development of international law', and the latter may impose specific requirements in any WTO reform. In terms of contributing to the development of global governance in the trade field, the EU's institutions are generally rather cautious towards both the WTO and the G20. Hoffmeister argues that rather than simply transposing the EU's own image to the international scene and trying to build strong institutions everywhere, the EU's focus is on 'effectiveness' of the multilateral system. What Larik observed in the abstract, can be seen in practice in the arguments outlined by Hoffmeister: the constitutional objectives of the TEU are general chalk lines, but are not all too constraining. In the sphere of trade, this means that the EU's political institutions tread carefully when it comes to the doxa of EU international relations, guided by the principles which guided its own creation. Hoffmeister argues that such a focus on effectiveness allows for a more tailor-made approach, 'taking duly account of the EU's commercial (self-) interests and its political (altruistic) interest in striving for a fair and free world trade order for all'. In other words, a balance must be struck between rule-of-law based collective governance and the EU's economic interests, or stated differently: between possession and milieu goals. This is entirely in line with Article 3(5) TEU which states that in relations with the wider world 'the Union shall uphold and promote its values and interests'. Relatedly, the contribution by Van Vooren on the financial transaction tax is a strong affirmation of this need for the Union to tread carefully and not overreach in working to attain its sanguine world view.

Hoffmeister argues that it is not all roses at the WTO, as since the Uruguay round geopolitical realities have changed so radically that decision-making structures of WTO institutions require change to adapt to this new circumstance. He makes several propositions in order to clear some of the largest hurdles to progress in global trade governance, which are certainly interesting in light of the conceptual framework of the edited volume. Notably, he proposes to re-examine the role of consensus-based decision-making, and explore majority voting in certain instances. Further, he also proposes that plurilateralism can be a temporary—although not a permanent—tool to overcome obstacles in decision-making on amending the WTO agreements. Very concretely, he proposes to establish a steering group of most pertinent decision-makers within the WTO structures to attain novel results and dislodge the ailing Doha round. In other words, we find de Búrca's argument expressed in Hoffmeister's contribution: the EU in principle prefers collective governance, but this does not necessarily imply multilateralism. Whether and when it does depends on many factors, in this case mainly ease of decision-making: a partial retreat from consensus and multilateralism *pur sang* may open up new avenues to advance the trading regime where it is currently failing to tackle essential questions such as the fair distribution of rights and obligations between members with different levels of development. We can superimpose De Witte and Thies' conceptual framework upon this question. They argued that aside from EU-specific peculiarities, the four essential factors as regards legislative venue choice are: (1) path dependence, (2) the geographical nature of the subject, (3) ease of decision-making and

[15] Hoffmeister.

(4) effectiveness. In Hoffmeister's contribution, all four are clearly in play: the G20 is opening a new institutional path to global economic governance, in line with the all-encompassing geographical scope of the topics it covers. However, its decision-making is rather ineffective, and therefore the WTO seems the more logical venue choice to tackle the big questions of global trade governance: trade and investment, trade and currency, trade and environment, or trade and development. However, ease of decision-making is not guaranteed, and the proposed avant-garde or plurilateral groupings may be more effective in advancing EU interests and values therein. Here, effectiveness outweighs the fact that this non-multilateral approach may be at odds with the inherent global scope of matters at hand, as well as the global calling of Articles 3(5) and 21 TEU themselves. In terms of leveraging the EU interest in global trade governance, the contributions by Cremona and Wu examine the interplay of bilateral and multilateral approaches on the part of the EU to attain its objectives. Substantively these contributions uncover the extent to which the EU tries to shape global governance in line with its own image, through diverse methodologies.

Cremona examines the notion of 'an external regulatory policy' of the Union. Whereas Article 206 of the Treaty on the Functioning of the European Union (TFEU) explicitly states international trade liberalization as an objective of the EU, it is silent on a corresponding regulatory dimension. With a brief account of the relevant Treaty provisions she concludes that the EU competence in trade indeed has such a regulatory dimension, and that the EU can thus engage in external regulatory activity affecting trade in goods and services, Intellectual Property Rights (IPR) and Foreign Direct Investment (FDI). The practical implementation of this should be viewed both in its internal and external dimension: internally, it concerns rules of the internal market which may have an important impact on the external competitiveness of EU business; externally it concerns the rules, principles and policies which the EU pursues at global level. Political institutions have explicitly emphasized the need for coherence between EU action in both dimensions, for it has a significant impact on the competitiveness of EU business both on the home market and on third country markets. In substance, EU policy has been directed at seeking to lessen regulatory barriers for EU exports, and generally supporting a rule-based approach to trade and investment and improving discipline on the enforcement of for example intellectual property and state aid rules, as well as assisting the development of and promotion of international standards.

In the context of this volume, the following questions arise: does the EU external regulatory policy simply pursue the interests of EU business overseas; and/or is attention paid to its 'values' as Articles 3(5) and 21 mandate? And in pursuing interests and/or values, where is the EU on its methodology of collective rule-of-law based governance? On the first issue, Cremona points to the fact that EU regulatory policy is not simply one of building an EU-friendly regulatory environment. The fact that the Commission does put some emphasis on the greening of trade and the social dimension supports that assertion. Parliament notably adopted resolutions requiring the envisaging trade not as an end in itself, but as a tool for the promotion of European values as well as commercial interests, and as an instrument of fair trade. Cremona focuses more on IPR than on the trade–environment or trade–social nexuses, but suffice it to state that Morgera, Marín Durán (as regards environment) and Kenner (as regards labour rights) in their respective contributions entirely affirm and deepen Cremona's findings.

On the second question, the case studies of Anti-Counterfeiting Trade Agreement (ACTA) (Cremona) and access to raw materials (Wu) provide further insight into the normative self-perception of the EU in practice, with notable impact on the 'collective' methodology. Cremona points to compatible methodologies pursued by the EU in its external regulatory policy: the bilateral approach and the multilateral approach as mutually supportive. The bilateral approach consists of deep and comprehensive Free Trade

Agreements (FTAs) such as that recently concluded with South Korea. In terms of an EU regulatory policy the EU does not pursue mutual recognition or harmonization with its own standards, but refers to the international system. Thus, it is based on the Technical Barriers to Trade (TBT) and Sanitary and Phytosanitary Measures (SPS) agreements and other relevant international conventions, pointing to the conclusion that bilateral relations do not directly export the EU's own standards, but act as a framework for cooperation on *global* standard-setting. In connection to the conceptual framework of this edited volume, the EU's bilateral approach of deep FTAs is thus supportive of collective global trade governance, which remains the final objective for the Union in line with Articles 3(5) and 21 TEU. What the EU pursues is the promotion of international standards which are substantively—at least—consistent with EU standards, and which are effectively implemented through a variety of multilateral or plurilateral instruments. In other words, the progressive development and strict observance of international law is achieved through a wide variety of instruments and methodologies, with the rule-of-law based global multilateral order as the long-term end goal. There is no doubt, however, that the EU will seek to shape that global regime substantively in line with its own regulatory approach.

For Cremona the EU's involvement in the negotiation of the ACTA is an example of such leadership in that final point. When it comes to developing global regulatory standards, the Commission argues that EU standards are well-placed as a reference point for global standards given that they are trade-friendly, set high standards, draw upon different Member States' traditions as well as international standards and best practices, and so on. In the case of ACTA, the EU was keen to ensure that the agreement on intellectual property enforcement would closely follow EU rules on this topic, although not in the sense that EU best practice had to be exactly incorporated into the ACTA. Cremona reaches conclusions which thicken the conceptual framework of this volume: the factors influencing venue choice of De Witte and Thies, but also the EU's global self-perception. Notably, the ACTA was not innovative in substance, and both the US and the EU stressed that the agreement does not require any change to their domestic laws. But why conclude this agreement at all? Cremona notes that ACTA does not advance ('ratchet up') IPR protection since in substance it is not innovative on issues such as enforcement in a digital environment. Indeed, the EU has been relatively successful in shaping the new international rules (if they ever see the light of day) so that they would fit EU rules already in existence. In this sense, the EU's contribution to global governance is shaping the global regime in its own image, even if global rules are not a carbon copy of EU rules. The observation made by De Witte and Thies was visible in the ACTA: the EU *acquis* provided a solid ground on which to base its negotiating position, but this also rendered the EU unwilling to re-open previously fought and sometimes hard-won battles within its own institutions. Whereas internal rules may give the EU a strong international negotiation position, this makes it difficult to launch really innovative regulatory approaches at the international level. The lessons for the EU's contribution to global governance are double: first, if the EU's international position is strengthened but also bound by internal regulation; the EU legislative process should ensure sufficient attention to the international dimension of the internal market from its initiation. In this sense, the internal market itself is a defining contribution to global trade governance. Second, for the EU 'advancing' international law means shaping it like itself, but *not necessarily advancing* the system *beyond* its own internal achievements. The underlying assumption is potentially significant. It seems that the EU's contribution to the progressive development of international law implies that global governance should be organized as the EU is organized, institutionally and in substance: the EU as an exemplary endpoint in advancing international law. It would go too far to say that such self-confidence permeates all that the Union does, and we certainly do not argue that this is desirable, but the underlying trend certainly exists. This is true not just in trade governance, as is shown in other contributions to this edited volume such as that by Scott and Rajamani on environmental governance. In conclusion, since EU internal regulation should not be assumed to have achieved perfection, the EU must take care not to stifle innovation and the advancement of global governance in pursuit of the principles which guided its own creation.

More must be said on the balance between values and interests, especially in the context of international trade. This tension between EU commercial interests and its professed value-based approach to global trade governance is perhaps most tangibly felt in the EU's efforts in accessing to raw materials it does not possess, and the problem of export restrictions of such products which are often vital to the EU economy. The case study by Wu examines EU efforts to secure sustainable supplies of raw materials for the EU economy, which is composed of three pillars: access to raw materials on world markets, sustainable supplies from European sources, as well as the reduction of European consumption. Wu points to the fact that the logic of the WTO focuses mainly on the liberalization of import restrictions and guaranteeing market access, and is not ideally suited to regulate export restrictions, such as, for example, limited exports of rare earths from China to world markets. The EU thus pursues regulatory discipline on export restrictions at the bilateral and multilateral level. Wu queries whether its chosen approaches are in line with Article 21(1) TEU, which instructs the EU to 'promote multilateral solutions to common problems'. In Wu's contribution, we find a stark contrast between the bilateral and the multilateral track. In the bilateral negotiations of FTAs such as the Economic Partnership Agreements (EPAs) with developing nations, as well as WTO accession negotiations, he finds that the EU has been relatively successful in securing commitments pertaining to export restrictions. However, he notes that for developing nations this quest for access to their raw materials is seen as an aggressive limitation of these countries' policy space, in particular as regards stimulating their own industrialization and infant industries. In parallel, Wu finds that the EU has had limited success in negotiating new rules on export restrictions in multilateral negotiations on market access for non-agricultural products (NAMA). Due to the WTO context, developing nations could act as a bloc to frustrate EU efforts in this regard. This is integral to the ailing Doha Development Round discussions: allowing EU access to their natural resources needs to be viewed in the broader balancing of rights and obligations between developing and developed countries of the global trading system. Overall, Wu therefore negatively assesses the EU's contribution to global governance through its Raw Materials Initiative (RMI). The proliferation of bilateral trade rules on export restrictions reduces WTO members' incentives to engage in multilateral rules, and in the long term marginalizes this framework. In relation to the trade-development nexus, Wu argues that while the EU may gain on the trade front, using its bargaining power in such a way leads to it losing goodwill and soft power in the area of development. Finally, he finds that in most cases, EU trade interests have outweighed the long-term vision on an inclusive multilateral trading order incorporating development and environmental concerns alongside that of trade liberalization.

It is rather truistic to conclude that the EU still has the tools and the weight to influence global trade governance. However, with great power comes great responsibility. First of all, the EU must take care not to axiomatically overstate or assume the significance and 'correctness' of its own internal achievements. Exporting consensus of 27 to the international stage cannot be equated to multilateralism, or collective governance as described by de Búrca. Second, in light of the ailing Doha round, the continued importance of the EU in global trade governance, and its self-declared role as a normative global actor, the EU has a greater responsibility than other global actors in reforming the WTO along the lines formulated by Hoffmeister. Finally, dare we say it: policy coherence remains crucial. In the pursuit of EU commercial interests other competing policy objectives (trade, development, labour) ought not be obscured.

5. Environmental Governance: Global Multilateralism or the Reluctant Unilateralist?

Contributing to the improvement of the quality of the environment takes a central position in the TEU and TFEU. The internal market is to ensure a high level of protection of the environment (Article 3(3) TEU), and in its external relations the Union must pursue the sustainable environmental development of developing countries (Article 21(2)(d) TEU) and generally contribute to the preservation and improvement of the environment and sustainable management of global natural resources (Article 21(2)(f) TEU). In the TFEU, we also find a general obligation to integrate environmental protection into the definition and implementation of all EU policies with a view to promoting sustainable development (Article 11 TFEU). When in 2009 the EU failed to place its stamp on the Copenhagen COP15 climate summit, the connection between this sanguine world view and the reality of global environmental governance contributed to the idea for this edited volume: what role for the EU? Morgera, Marín Durán and Scott and Rajamani examine the EU's strategy to act as a global environmental leader.

Morgera starts from the constitutional objectives of the EU in global environmental governance, pointing to the exceptionally high ambitions of the Union therein: alongside the objectives of Article 21 TEU, Article 11 TFEU requires the greening of non-environmental policies of the EU, and externally it requires 'a holistic approach' to environmental law-making in light of the fragmented nature of the international environmental regime: climate change, biodiversity and so on. The stakes for the Union's role in global environmental governance are therefore high: it is to avoid subordination of one environmental regime to another and must seek to reconcile them at the law-making level in pursuit of the emerging principle of mutual supportiveness. Morgera outlines the complex set of instruments the EU uses to live up to its mission statement: domestic regulation with extra-territorial implications (the subject of Scott and Rajamani's contribution as well), various unilateral and bilateral actions in external relations, and corresponding negotiating positions in multilateral fora. Morgera takes a positive view to these actions, stating that the EU has certainly acted as a norm generator and exporter, but an initial critique stems from the complexity of the EU toolbox itself. The number of uni-, bi-, pluri- and multi-lateral initiatives is extensive, yet lacking a systematic monitoring of its combined effectiveness. Because of this, the trade-offs between environmental, social or commercial considerations become un-transparent with internal and external consequences: within the Union there is the risk of waste and duplication of resources, and difficulty in making relevant policy choices across the complex areas. Externally, there is the risk of misunderstanding and possibly mistrust by third country counterparts and relevant stakeholders.

Utilizing the examples of biofuels and forest management, Morgera examines the EU's contribution to global environmental governance through the lens of the principle of common but differentiated responsibility. In her case studies, she queries whether the EU's professed preference for rule-of-law based collective governance is tangibly present. Biofuels and forest management are an excellent case study for the diversity of tools to global environmental governance: they combat climate change by reducing reliance on fossil fuels, but may negatively impact biodiversity, notably through deforestation. When looking at biofuels, the Renewable Energy Directive unilaterally sets standards to protect biodiversity; but these were expressly based on international standards. This regulatory approach is an expression of what Scott and Rajamani have termed 'contingent unilateralism': the EU setting certain standards within its own legal order promoting a given global objective, with penalties and disincentives for external partners if they are not respected. In terms of the external consequences of this internal stance, one sees the dynamic observed by De Witte and Thies and Cremona returning here as well: the EU systematically referred to the

Directive in its negotiation position in the Convention on Biodiversity as regards biofuels with the aim of developing international standards at least consistent with EU standards. Bilaterally too, the Directive has been used to build alliances with individual third countries in order to arrive at common or closer negotiating positions multilaterally, or to inspire domestic action in those countries. However, as noted when we dealt with the global trade governance section of this concluding chapter: EU internal regulation cannot be presumed to be perfect. Indeed, Morgera recalls that the actual environmental benefits and scientific soundness of the EU legal framework on biofuels have been subject to continued criticism. Notably, in light of common but differentiated responsibility, whereas the EU is taking the lead in the environment, it is not clear that the EU is truly taking into account the different circumstances of developing countries. In other words, what we can observe in trade governance returns in the field of environment: internal legislation provides a useful benchmark for global (negotiating) positions of the EU, but renders the EU a rigid negotiating entity and partner. In this case, the peculiar nature of the Union, together with its pre-existing acquis, implies that it may not actually possess the leeway and flexibility to ensure compliance with the principle of common but differentiated responsibility. For Morgera, this rigidity can be partially overcome through bilateral and inter-regional dialogues which must do more to take stock of individual countries' needs and concerns, so as to positively influence the substance of multilateral negotiations.

In terms of methodology, Morgera refers to the statement by AG Kokott in her opinion in the *ATAA* judgment: if the multilateral approach fails to attain a certain stated objective, the EU 'could not reasonably be required to give… [multilateral] bodies unlimited time in which to develop a multilateral solution'.[16] In his contribution, Hoffmeister made a similar point: in relation to Doha, an avant garde or plurilateral grouping may be more effective in advancing global governance than the unquestioned dogma of consensus and all-inclusive multilateralism. In Morgera's contribution too, we find the argument that recourse to unilateralism and bilateralism can be beneficial if multilateral progress is out of reach; as long as such efforts are carried out in good faith on part of the Union. She and Hoffmeister are thus on the same lines, and in practice compound the argument made by de Búrca: multilateral governance is the preferred option; but while it is the end goal—it is not a one-size-fits-all solution. Of course, stopping at that would be misrepresenting the subtlety of these authors' arguments: such non-multilateral approaches must exist in a context of good faith; against a backdrop of advance consultation through bilateral or inter-regional dialogues; and general openness on the part of the EU to the inherent diversity of global governance. In other contributions too we have seen that the EU's monolithic nature, due to internal competence, institutional or legislative realities, does not always permit such flexibility.

In their study of the EU's efforts to reduce CO2 emissions, Scott and Rajamani consider the EU to be a self-conscious leader in the efforts to counter climate change, actively working towards an ambitious, multilateral, legally binding, global climate regime. However, prospects for success have been slim, and as a consequence the Union has adopted a different approach, which Scott and Rajamani have coined 'contingent unilateralism'. In the abstract, utilizing De Witte and Thies' factors defining legislative venue choice, the central considerations for the EU have been those of effectiveness and ease of decision-making: global governance as all-encompassing multilateralism would have been preferred given the scope of the challenge in tackling climate change. In the area of civil aviation emissions, the Union invested considerable efforts to promote multilateral action in the International Civil Aviation Organization, but failing such, the EU decided to unilaterally include aviation

[16] AG Kokott Opinion, C-366/10 *Air Transport Association of America and Others*, 6 October 2011, paras 145–147.

emissions in its Emissions Trading Scheme (ETS) for all flights arriving in or departing from the EU. This thus includes emissions generated outside of EU airspace, touching a legally and politically raw nerve across the globe. The EU has nonetheless been willing to challenge its strategic partners in global environmental governance through *uncut* unilateralism. Scott and Rajamani coin this unilateralism as 'contingent' because the global extension of EU standards depends upon there being no adequate international agreement or individual third country climate action living up to EU standards. In terms of bringing to fruition the objectives of Articles 3(5) and 21 TEU and 11 TFEU, this approach is a means of incentivizing urgently needed climate action elsewhere, although it is not the EU's preferred option. In what Scott and Rajamani term the EU as 'a reluctant unilateralist', we clearly see an extension of the theme uncovered by Morgera and Hoffmeister. As Scott and Rajamani argue, the EU is 'shaping the legal structures of global governance in the multi-polar world by testing the boundaries of permissible unilateral action and by experimenting with a form of action-forcing contingent unilateralism that conceives unilateralism as a necessary policy option but one which, ultimately, is second best'.[17] Scott and Rajamani's contribution thus further deepens our understanding of the objective of 'collective' governance. In a best case scenario, they conclude that contingent unilateralism on aviation emissions will certainly alter the background conditions for national and international action on climate change and that it could indeed encourage individual states to pursue more effective climate action in the sectors concerned. Furthermore, it could help destabilize those dynamics of the multilateral negotiations on climate change that are action-suppressing. It is this destabilizing, or perhaps better 'dislodging' effect of the non-multilateral approach which Hoffmeister similarly argued might benefit the Doha Round negotiations at the WTO.

As before, the actual content of the EU standard deserves further scrutiny, and not merely EU negotiation tactics through which to influence global governance in line with its own internal rules. Scott and Rajamani thus query whether the EU's internal legislation respects the principle of common but differentiated responsibilities (CDR). The Commission argued that the decision to include aviation into the ETS was fully compliant with this principle; or alternatively and more recently, that it does not apply to private business—in this case airlines obliged to participate in the ETS. Scott and Rajamani argue that the principle certainly does apply since the EU regulation burdens on developing country businesses, and because it is a principle which is a fundamental part of the conceptual apparatus of the climate change regime. Therefore, any limiting interpretation of the EU must be rejected. In conceptual terms, we may infer that Scott and Rajamani argue that the EU is not fully living up to its constitutional obligation to 'progressively develop international law' (Article 3(5) TEU) as regards CDR. The authors make a number of suggestions whereby the Union could mitigate this concern, either by providing specific treatment to developing nations, or to earmark revenue from developing country flights to the Green Climate Fund established at the COP16 Climate Summit in Cancun 2010. In this way the EU could provide a more comprehensive positive contribution to global environmental governance.

The contribution by Marín Durán closes the circle between Parts 3 and 4 of this edited volume by studying the multilateral and regional approaches of the Union in shaping the 'mutual supportiveness' between trade and environmental governance. In this contribution one sees the dynamics observed by Wu, Hoffmeister and Scott and Rajamani echoed yet again: the EU had been the leading proponent of including environmental concerns in the 2001 Doha Development Agenda (DDA), playing an active role in the relevant WTO Committee. However, in light of the absence of progress at the multilateral level, the EU switched tack and used bilateral and regional tools to pursue the trade and environmental nexus. The question Marín Durán poses is most salient: is the substantive content of the

[17] Scott and Rajamani.

mutual supportiveness between trade and environment identical in the multilateral and bilateral/regional levels? As the case may be, is the bilateral/regional approach supportive of the global, multilateral level? In the context of aviation emissions the unilateral approach was considered supportive in that sense; and in the case of *ACTA* too (Cremona), the plurilateral approach was expected to progress the cause of IPR protection multilaterally and globally in the medium term.

In the multilateral context, Marín Durán points to the position of the EU as a player actively requesting clarification of the relationship between WTO rules and trade-related provisions in multilateral environmental agreements. They were subsequently included in the Doha negotiations, where the EU has pursued a holistic approach so as to establish general principles to govern the Multilateral Environmental Agreement (MEA)–WTO relationship within the broader system of global governance on sustainable development. For the Union, mutual supportiveness would be one core principle, implying that no WTO member is prevented from taking measures for the protection of the environment at the level it considers more appropriate. However, the most tangible outcomes in these negotiations were located in the institutional sphere, meaning the strengthening of coordination and synergies between the Committee on Trade and Environment in the WTO and relevant MEA Secretariats. Marín Durán concludes that the EU did not succeed to secure support in substance, such as requiring mandatory deference to MEA expertise in the context of trade disputes before the WTO bodies. She asserts that this ought not be viewed as a clear-cut failure, however. To be sure, the EU has had to lower its ambitions, but one should not expect anything else in a negotiation requiring consensus among over 150 WTO members. Limited success at the multilateral level is one of the reasons for the EU to pursue a more regional approach in the trade–environment nexus, but not the only one. Marín Durán points to the fact that, in addition, the EU has simply changed its policy priorities since the Doha Round was initiated in 2001. Notably the Global Europe Strategy of 2006 approaches the trade and environment nexus as part of a broader objective of using the Common Commercial Policy more actively to enhance the EU's competitiveness in a changing global economic order. As Marín Durán puts it, the regional trade agreements which the EU pursues since 2006 are focused on avoiding a race to the bottom in environmental regulation, and ensuring a level playing field between regional partners as regards environmental standards. In abstract terms, the balance between values and interests seems to have tilted somewhat since 2001 and from 2006 onwards: Marín Durán points to statements by the EU that 'there shall be no European retreat from multilateralism', and that Doha remains the first (long-term) priority; but contrasts this with the shorter term reality that the EU is placing emphasis on ensuring that the new regional trade agreements serve EU commercial interests. This shift is not merely methodological, and Marín Durán uncovers a substantive difference as well: the Doha negotiations are premised on what WTO members *are permitted* to do in terms of implementing the trade–environment nexus, whereas the regional EU approach is focused on what parties *should do* in terms of promoting a high level of environmental protection.

In sum, Marín Durán concludes that success for the EU in shaping the substance of global environmental governance is largely felt at the bilateral and interregional level; a finding which is in keeping with the other two contributions in the environmental governance part of this volume. Finally, she also queries the relationship between the multilateral and the regional/bilateral approach of the Union: here Marín Durán finds that there is no substantive connection between the two. Although the Commission argues that the regional approach is a stepping stone to the multilateral negotiations, the author finds no such relationship. Whereas trade and sustainable development chapters of relevant regional agreements certainly could serve as 'laboratories' for global regulation, there are little or no considerations to that effect. The partial abandonment of multilateralism has thus led to a substantive shift in the trade–environment nexus, although it may not be rhetorically acknowledged by the Union.

6. Financial Governance: An Ailing Unilateralist for Lack of a Better Alternative

The 2008 financial crisis nearly brought the global financial system to a grinding halt and in doing so uncovered systemic insufficiencies in the national, regional and global regulatory and supervisory systems of the financial markets. In this section, the contributors focus on three aspects of an EU role in making amends to the global system of financial governance: Amtenbrink explores the extent to which the EU contributes to global governance in this area through internal standard-setting which can be transposed globally, or through unilaterally extending their reach; Wouters, Van Kerckhoven and Odermatt look specifically in the interactions between the EU and the G20, the latter which, elevated to the level of heads of state and government since November 2008, has played a major role in addressing the financial crisis and is further broadening its agenda, thereby becoming an ever more important actor in global governance. Van Vooren examines the EU's attempt and methodologies to see the global implementation of a financial transaction tax—and how it fell on stony ground. Together, these three contributions provide a good insight into the tension underpinning the research question of this volume: the EU as the value-based international actor would wish 'to support the effectiveness and transparency of the financial markets in order to reduce financial volatility and speculation at global level'.[18] However, within the Union, there is certainly no agreement on that objective or how to attain it; and at global level, the legal, socio-economic and political diversity of interests is such that global financial governance is in essence a technocratic, 'insider-dominated' system of standards lacking binding legal force. This stands in rather glaring contrast with the legalized, enforceable and institutionalized governance which characterizes international trade in the WTO context, and provides further insight into the capacity of the EU to shape the global legal order in areas which are of great (and grave) interest to it.

Amtenbrink observes that since 2009 the EU can be seen to have taken a *hyper*-active role in the fields of financial and economic governance, fields which were long hampered by lack of political consensus on the need for—and direction of—measures at EU level. The events of 2008 have served as a wake-up call for the EU. The systemic problems to financial governance were many: the inherent risk of removing financial market restrictions without a commensurate regulatory framework; the continuing predominance of national regulatory logics; the institutionalized overreliance on credit rating agencies who themselves reject the public function they inherently serve; and consequently the realization that even sovereigns are not invulnerable to systemic instabilities in financial markets. Against his analysis of the ailments of the financial system, the question arises on the extent to which the EU has responded to addressing these old shortcomings. Amtenbrink's hypothesis is that the EU's contribution to global financial governance lies not so much in the substantive scope of its regulatory and supervisory framework as such, but rather in its methodology, namely its multilevel approach to European financial regulation and supervision which it promotes at the global level.

Examining 'the EU stamp' on global financial governance is complicated by what may be a chicken-or-egg debate: many of the EU's regulatory initiatives—such as those on Credit Rating Agencies (CRAs)—have been identified in G20 Summit statements as priority areas of action. Only an empirical research exercise into the untransparent inner workings of G20

[18] Van Vooren, quotation from an early version of the Draft Constitution (Penelope) stating that this would be one of the objectives of external economic relations policy for the Union.

agenda-setting can uncover the fashion in which these levels of governance interact (see the contribution by Wouters, Van Kerckhoven and Odermatt). What is certain, however, is that the EU is not establishing new standards in splendid isolation or independent of global discourse; and that it is not the only important economic player to reinforce financial governance: the United States too has adopted similar regulatory and supervisory initiatives in line with G20 priorities, including oversight over CRAs and increased monitoring of systemic risk. Amtenbrink uses the CRA example to point to the fact that the European legislator has (at least initially) quite heavily relied on international standards; the (obviously legally binding) regulation on CRAs of 2009 strongly resembled the non-binding code of conduct of the International Organization of Securities Commissions. More recently, however, the Commission has begun to 'push the envelope' on CRA regulation, spearheaded by the services of European Commissioner for the Internal Market Michel Barnier. Indeed, the new CRA regime should (at the time of writing it is under consideration by the European Parliament) include novel elements such as a CRA's liability for its credit ratings. Another important example studied by Amtenbrink is that of national fragmentation in supervisory functions. The EU is an excellent case study for any kind of global system of financial governance which goes beyond the mere exchange of information and best practices, into a truer centralization of supervisory power. Here Amtenbrink and Van Vooren reach parallel conclusions on the potential for any such far-reaching innovation in the global financial system: the current global governance regime simply lacks the solid institutional framework to support anything more than coordination. Even if EU Member States travelled a bumpy road towards imperfect supranational supervision, such is all the less likely at global level. Amtenbrink remains somewhat optimistic by stating that: 'In the absence of (the prospect of) such a coherent global system of financial governance, despite or rather because of the absence of a centralized system, the EU may still provide inspiration for the future design of a global structure, especially with regard to the dealing with cross-border disputes between national supervisory authorities and the cross-sectorial consistency of the regulatory and supervisory regime'.[19] This because the EU is in effect a 'laboratory'[20] for arrangements which are being debated at the global level, such as the design of macro-prudential policy tools and other related measures. Through regular bilateral dialogues with key strategic partners such as the US and Japan, the Commission is actively working towards the emergence of global best practices, and a global level playing field.

As in the fields of trade and environment, the contribution of Amtenbrink highlights the EU's 'contingent unilateralism'. Building further on the CRA example, he points to elements whereby third country ratings can be endorsed, whereby those rating agencies must comply with conditions set out in the EU regulation, and whereby the legal and supervisory framework of a third country must ensure that CRAs authorized to work in that third country must comply with legally binding requirements which are equivalent to EU legal and supervisory requirements. In order to implement this aspect of the EU CRAs Regulation, cooperation agreements have been concluded with supervisory authorities of third countries including Japan and the US. In this fashion, the EU is exerting pressure on third countries to encourage the use of its own financial governance standards abroad.

Wouters, Van Kerckhoven and Odermatt study the interactions between the EU and the G20, with financial regulation as their case study, thereby complementing the contribution by Amtenbrink. In their analysis of this two-way interconnection, they note that the EU–G20 relationship is both symbiotic and problematic. The EU is rather well represented at the G20 with four Member States and the EU itself each being a member, and European coordination in advance of G20 summits has proven to be fruitful. Generally, the EU has been able to put most of its 'agreed language' in the outcome of G20 summits. However, in

[19] Amtenbrink. [20] Cremona.

some cases, as is shown in the case study by Van Vooren on the financial transaction tax, the Union failed to convince the G20 of the viability of their policy proposals. Nonetheless, in other issue areas of global financial governance the EU did influence the outcomes of G20 meetings. Importantly, Wouters, Van Kerckhoven and Odermatt point to the fact that the EU has worked steadfastedly to implement in a timely manner the commitments it made within the G20, notably in the field of financial regulation. In terms of the EU's contribution to global financial governance, they find that the EU explicitly considers 'doing as it preaches' in its own internal legal order, integral to reforming global financial governance. According to the authors, this entails a positive feedback loop: by being a forerunner in certain areas of financial reform, and by faithfully implementing G20 commitments, the EU's position within the G20 is in turn strengthened, allowing it to have greater influence on pertinent normative processes.

However, Wouters, Van Kerckhoven and Odermatt also point to the more problematic side of the EU–G20 relationship. There is no policy or legal basis regarding the European external representation at the G20, as it is the case in the post-Lisbon era with many other international organizations. Consequently, EU Member States at the G20 may still deviate from the 'agreed language' and represent their national interests, as rather painfully demonstrated at the G20 summit in Los Cabos in June 2012. Moreover, the four largest EU Member States have a seat themselves at the G20 table and could hence override smaller EU Member States, which are not only deprived of direct influence at the G20 but are also less powerful in coming to the 'agreed language' within the EU coordination process itself. Some Member States also fear that the G20 might push the EU to move too fast in terms of financial regulation. These observations feed into wider criticisms concerning the democratic representation of the G20, which is making decisions with far-reaching consequences. Is the Union 'advancing international law' in line with its constitutional objectives when it comes to responding to the widely heard call for G20 reform? But is this even necessary? Indeed, as Hoffmeister has argued, the EU may perhaps better spend its political capital and diplomatic weight in strengthening the inner institutional workings of the WTO as the predominant international organization of global trade (and perhaps economic) governance.

The case study by Van Vooren is perhaps the most shining example of the EU's cosmopolitan—even utopian—world view: the implementation of a global financial transaction tax (FTT). This idea had for many years existed as wishful thinking in the minds of grass roots movements, and reached a legal and political milestone on 28 September 2011. In his 'State of the Union' speech, the Commission President presented a proposal for an EU Directive on a financial transaction tax installed across the 27 EU Member States. Explicit to this proposal was the fact that it should serve as an example, as a stepping-stone for the global implementation of such a tax. Substantively, the proposal was to show how markets could be stabilized through taxation, and how this could provide a great source of public revenue. Thus, the EU was to serve as a laboratory for this FTT experiment, illustrating its feasibility and added value to the world, thereby creating the necessary political momentum for a similar initiative at the global level.

The FTT case study by Van Vooren paints a bleak picture of the EU's ability to influence the global financial governance regime. First, he unfolds the tale of divided political views within the EU institutions, as well as between EU Member States. Here, much like in the findings on global security governance in this volume, the internal divisions within the EU formed the core obstacle for the EU to further its interests globally. In fact, it was not even possible to reach agreement over whether the FTT was in the EU's interest within its own legal order, let alone globally. Second, the author points out that around the Autumn of 2011 a great deal of political momentum had been created both by the European Commission and several Member States—notably France and Germany. However, this case study clearly illustrates how the EU's wings have been clipped following the 2008 financial crisis and the ongoing sovereign debt crisis in the Eurozone. The Eurozone crisis and the position of Greece entirely overshadowed the G20 Summit at Cannes, where France had hoped to launch the FTT proposal. However, not all is lost for the taxation of the financial sector. At the time of writing, the EU institutions were still considering less utopian alternatives to the full-blown taxation of all financial transactions on a pan-European or global scale. These include a stock market tax such as that which has been in place in the UK for years, or a financial activities tax such as had been proposed originally by the European Commission. Such proposals are more likely to see the legislative light of day, and it may yet be possible that the EU fulfil its role of laboratory for financial regulation.

From Van Vooren's case-study we can draw several lessons in light of the research question of this book: first of all, the cosmopolitan world view of the EU constitutional objectives (Larik) should not lead to 'politically overreaching' on the part of the Union. This is one of the few instances where the EU has pursued its lofty goals in a fairly unadulterated fashion at global level. This happened under the pressure of the highest political levels of EU institutions and Member States, yet the EU failed due to political ambitions overriding civil servants' warnings. Van Vooren does not argue for rule-by-technocracy, but in the EU's quest to be the globe's Robin Hood, its current economic and financial weakness, lack of political capital, internal dividedness, as well as the enormous legal and technical challenges to organizing a global financial transaction tax proved insurmountable. This is a stark reminder that the EU's sanguine constitutional objectives are at most long-term and aspirational; they are general chalk lines, standards of achievement for EU foreign policy. Van Vooren's contribution mirrors the argument put forward by Hoffmeister. The latter argued that EU institutions are generally cautious in simply transposing the EU's own image onto the international scene and trying to build strong institutions everywhere. This warning was certainly not heeded in the case of the FTT. Second, the case study's findings are in line with those of Koutrakos in the context of global security governance. The EU could certainly play an important part in global financial governance, but inability to reach a common position within the Union is highly constricting to that global calling. Third, applying De Witte and Thies' criteria of venue choice to the FTT example, it is rather self-evident that the Union has put the cart before the horse by choosing the 'less effective' legal venue. With a piece of untested, not yet negotiated draft legislation at EU level, the Union attempted to generate momentum in order to negotiate such a tax at global level. It thereby ignored its own laboratory function, and was as a consequence unable to override large hurdles such as path dependence or the ease of decision-making in global financial governance. The lesson is not that the EU should not be ambitious, but that it should not ignore its own internal and external realities. As regards financial taxation, the EU may actually still learn that lesson: an EU-wide implementation of a stock market tax, or similar supranational approaches to a fair contribution by the financial sector to public coffers, may over time whet the appetite of other global partners such as Brazil or India to join the EU in its efforts in global financial governance.

7. The Human Dimension: The Ugly Duckling of Global Governance?

If the financial crisis brought home one lesson, it is that globalization and (lack of) global governance (economic, financial, or otherwise) significantly affect the individual. It impacts citizens' livelihoods, (financial) security and welfare and has commensurate effects in other areas: it may generate migration flows and create social tensions with significance and impact beyond national borders. The EU's global ambitions are equally applicable in this field: the human dimension of global governance, or what Kenner coins 'global social governance'. The contribution by Thym examines its migration aspects, whereas Kenner studies the extent to which the EU seeks to enhance the labour dimension of global governance.

Thym commences from the finding that the EU's aspiration to a rule-of-law-based and cooperative international order is equally touted in the sphere of migration. Articles 3(5) and 21 TEU apply in this area as well, which is being mirrored in relevant policy documents. However, he finds that while the objective of international migration governance is easy to declare, it is difficult to achieve and EU policy has displayed some prominent failures in the recent past. In substance, EU external migration initiatives are strongly focused on measures controlling cross-border movement of persons, which is no surprise given the fact that Article 79 TFEU explicitly calls upon the EU to implement a policy which aims at the 'efficient management of migration flows'. Managing migration is arguably a euphemism for 'limiting' migration, which is vindicated by the fact that very little has happened in the sphere of stimulating legal migration. Thus, the EU's predominant contribution to international cooperation in migration is the control component with instruments such as the EU border agency FRONTEX, or its conclusion of various readmission agreements. Extending the more cooperative approach of migration did not succeed: the value of visa facilitation agreements is limited, and other routes for legal migration are either limited to highly qualified workers under overly stringent conditions; or not addressed at all in the case of low-skilled labour. The obstacles to a truly holistic contribution by the Union to what could be coined global migration governance are many: First, Thym points to the legal impediments within the EU. The vertical division of competences within the Union hampers an integrated migration policy for the Union, and there is a noticeable parallelism between successful cooperation and the scope of EU powers: express external competences correlate with success, whereas fragile legal bases fail to deliver substantial output. Second, this has as its consequence that international cooperation usually remains in the informal, non-legally binding sphere. Some argue that this is to circumvent legal control mechanisms, though Thym is of the opinion that this is merely transitional towards hard legal obligations. Third, substantively, the EU's external migration policy often shifts responsibility onto third states which often lack the will or capacity to respect EU international obligations as regards human rights or refugee law. Fourth, the EU's quest for global migration governance pursues countervailing policy objectives: cooperation is meant to enhance state control of cross-border movements, whereas the EU's legal and policy commitment as regards international human rights and refugee law points in the opposite direction. Finally, at this juncture, in its relations with international partners the EU does not sufficiently take into account the wishes of its partners as part of a reciprocal give-and-take. In sum, global migration governance and the role of the EU therein is mired in legal and political problems. Taking a macroscopic perspective, any migration policy requires political decisions about trade-offs between countervailing interests both domestically and in inter-state relations. Within the Union, in the current state of European integration, invocations of partnerships cannot conceal that no such balancing of interests has taken place. Until such a moment, the role of the EU in global governance will be limited to what the EU Member States see as the greatest utility for supranational and international cooperation: that of limiting migration flows across EU external borders. There is thus a stark contrast between the EU's role in global trade and environmental governance, and that in the field of migration. In the former field, discussion focuses on uni-, bi- and multi-lateral approaches, and the substantive balancing between EU interests and values; and interests of external partners. In migration, there is simply no global multilateral approach; and international cooperation implies unilateralism and bilateralism focused on restrictive policies.

Migration policy is—rightly or wrongly—closely associated with the essence of national identity and thus the exercise of sovereign powers. Therefore, findings on the EU role may be different in areas where such is equally true, though to a lesser extent, eg in the areas of social protection and labour rights. Kenner observes that the latter tend to rise to prominence on the global governance agenda in the wake of international crises. Thus, the recognition during the early 20th century that the industrial revolution had spawned great social injustices led to the creation of the International Labour Organization (ILO) in 1919. A similar process took place in the wake of the 2008 global financial meltdown, with a questioning of the benefits of liberalization, deregulation and privatization. With poorest nations hit the hardest by the latest crisis, Kenner looks in particular at the EU's capacity to shape the economic and social dimension of global governance in a fashion which respects the needs of people in developing countries. He does this by looking at the wide range of tools the EU can deploy to that effect: unilaterally through the generalized system of preferences, bilaterally through its free trade agreements, and through strengthening multilateral partnerships in the context of the ILO as well as support for regional integration in the context of the Cotonou agreement. For Kenner, the latter should be of particular importance for an EU role on the global stage.

Kenner's study starts with an inquiry into the trade–labour nexus at the WTO discussed during the Uruguay round negotiations, and here we may usefully draw the parallel with the contribution of Marín Durán on the trade–environment nexus in the Doha Round. In the latter case the EU was a proponent of mutual supportiveness between the WTO and multilateral environmental agreements (MEAs). However, Marín Durán noted that the EU did not succeed in securing support in substance, such as requiring mandatory deference to MEA expertise in the context of trade disputes before the WTO bodies. She concluded that this was not a clear-cut failure since there were advances in the institutional dimension of mutual supportiveness and since this triggered the promotion of similar efforts at regional level. In Kenner's chapter we see a similar development. At the end of the 1990s the US had proposed to include a 'social clause' in the WTO Agreement in order to pre-empt a further widening of the social deficit in global governance. The EU sided with this proposition but was wary of imposing on developing nations certain labour obligations, as well as of the possibility of the social agenda being used to erect new barriers to trade. Furthermore, many developing countries feared that such a clause would undermine their comparative advantage. The multilateral efforts to that effect failed. Interestingly, according to Kenner this defeat had the consequence of strengthening the ILO, injecting the social agenda into the global human rights agenda, and importantly, forging closer EU–ILO relations. This further fleshes out de Búrca's conceptualization of collective governance as the predominant mode of EU foreign policy. Namely, across the trade, social and environmental dimensions of global governance, we can observe the trend of a 'retreat' towards regionalism and plurilateralism in the wake of limited success at global, multilateral level. Across different contributions to this volume, we have seen that the EU views this as a second best and a temporary transition to be replaced by global governance at a later stage, but at times also a conscious reversal of the previous preference for the multilateral, all-encompassing approach.

In contrast to the contribution by Thym, the findings of Kenner are rather optimistic, notably on the alliance between the EU and the ILO to influence global social governance. He finds that the launch of Core Labour Standards (CLS) and the Decent Work Agenda (DWA) in the ILO, together with the EC's historic shift in the 1980s to place greater focus on fundamental rights, created a joint effort of more systematic and useful cooperation in this field. He examines the fashion in which the EU has 'injected' this social agenda in its relations with the African, Caribbean and Pacific countries. In his examination of the Cotonou Agreement he shows that—with some caveats—the EU has substantively included both CLS and DWA through proactive monitoring of compliance in practice and the general enforcement of relevant ILO standards. He also examines the region-to-region Economic Partnership Agreements (EPAs), which are essentially trade agreements rather than development agreements (such as Cotonou). Although critics viewed any inclusion of labour provisions into the EPAs as mere window-dressing, Kenner is more positive and argues that the CARIFORUM–EU EPA can serve as a model for enhancing global labour rights through regional integration. He refers to the commitment to socially responsible investment practices, as well as the strongly worded objection to social dumping, among others, to show that the hitherto dominant paradigm of neoliberal global governance is increasingly being questioned. In conclusion, he finds two challenges for the future. First, in finalizing other EPAs, the EU may find it difficult to keep that balance in the scramble to satisfy WTO compliance. In the trade–labour balance the former may thus be favoured after all. Second, the challenge will be for the EPA model to organically adapt as economic and social conditions improve, and allow space for indigenous non-EU regional strategies to develop as part of the future development of global governance in this area.

8. Conclusion: The EU Governance Mode of Foreign Policy Vindicated

In outlining the governance mode of foreign policy as characterizing the EU mode of international relations, de Búrca makes two central claims. First, the EU lays emphasis on pursuing milieu goals in joint cooperation with others, with a preference for embedding such cooperation in legal instruments (Larik). Second, the EU will regularly seek to replicate or externalize in its foreign policy some of the modes of governance it has developed for similar policies in its internal realm.

As regards the first point, de Búrca submitted that this preference for rule-of-law based collective governance does not necessarily imply 'multilateralism' such as that of the UN or the WTO. Several contributors supported that point in their case studies in various areas of governance: when multilateral solutions are out of reach, the EU may—in good faith—pursue unilateral, bilateral or plurilateral approaches which better contribute to the milieu goals it pursues. Authors were clear, however, that such methodologies ought to be either temporary or transitional, and that the multilateral foundation of global governance remains sacrosanct. Concretely however, we have seen that what Scott and Rajamani coined EU 'contingent unilateralism' applies not only in the sphere of environmental governance, but also in the fields of trade and finance. In all instances where such was observed, the multilateral level was seen by the EU as incapable—for the time being—of providing the policy objectives set forth by EU institutions. In finance, the global system is not providing the enforceable legal standards which financial markets so urgently need; in climate change, progress on a new instrument replacing the Kyoto Protocol has been scant; and in trade the Doha development round is stuck due to deep disagreement amongst the 150+ members of the WTO. This does not always mean a resort to unilateralism *pur sang* on the part of the Union; and therefore we should rather use the notion '*contingent retreat from multilateralism*'. If considered desirable, the EU is ready to move the global, multilateral solution to the long-term perspective, and opt for a blend of uni-, bi-, or plurilateral action to achieve desirable policy objectives at the international level. In terms of the framework sketched by De Witte and Thies, there is thus a shifting balance between effectiveness, ease of decision-making, and geographic scope, resulting in a different final outcome as regards the collective governance approach of the EU (de Búrca).

The export of EU internal rules to the global level has its benefits and its downsides. Across different areas of governance, we have seen that EU internal legislation can be a strength and a weakness: it provides a strong, and often high regulatory standard. However, as witnessed in the trade and environmental fields, this often renders the EU an immovable monolith in international negotiations, without the flexibility to respond to the diversity of its counterparts in global governance. The solution offered in the sphere of trade, but undoubtedly valid in other areas of governance as well, is increased utilization of bilateral and interregional dialogues in order to prepare the Union's receptiveness to individual third countries' concerns, and facilitate convergence of positions at the global level and in multilateral negotiations.

Many of the contributions to this volume have pointed to the truly multilateral being rather ineffective, not simply for the EU to attain its own interests and project its own values, but to achieve any common solution at all. At the very least, this volume shows that there is no lack of challenges of a global scope requiring commensurate solutions. However, the multi-polar world of the 21st century is clearly characterized by interests so diverse, leading most authors to suggest what they consider second-best, but more effective alternatives to all-encompassing multilateral governance. In that sense, we may find that the Union—in spite of all its flaws, political or economic—is not doing as poorly as one might be led to believe in the global context of the post-2008 financial crisis. Leading the way towards the long-term objective of a global, multilateral, rule-of-law-based order; but not forgetting its interests and alternative methodologies along the way. Where the EU possesses a significant degree of integration (trade and environment), the authors' considerations are more of a substantive (is the EU's approach legal, effective, or just?), or a tactical (how should the EU go about attaining its short-and long-term interests and objectives?) nature. Where European integration is less advanced (security, migration and finance) contributions point to the internal power and turf battles seriously and negatively impacting the projection of the EU's milieu and possession goals. This may be a rather self-evident conclusion from this volume, but there is important added-value in the benefit of comparison: in trade and environment we can see a truly significant (though 'perhaps not splendid', as Hoffmeister submitted) role for the Union in shaping global governance. In security and migration, internal divisions take the upper hand, and tie the Union's hands in shaping the relevant legal and political regimes.

Index